# ETHNICITY AND GROUP RIGHTS

## NOMOS
# XXXIX

## NOMOS

**Harvard University Press**

**The Liberal Arts Press**

**Atherton Press**

**Aldine-Atherton Press**

**Lieber-Atherton Press**

**New York University Press**

# NOMOS XXXIX

Yearbook of the American Society for Political and Legal Philosophy

# ETHNICITY AND GROUP RIGHTS

Edited by

**Ian Shapiro,** *Yale University*
and
**Will Kymlicka,** *University of Ottawa*

NEW YORK UNIVERSITY PRESS • *New York and London*

NEW YORK UNIVERSITY PRESS
New York and London

Library of Congress Cataloging-in-Publication Data
Ethnicity and group rights / edited by Ian Shapiro and Will Kymlicka.
p. cm.—(Nomos ; 39)
"Began as papers and commentaries read at the Annual Meeting of
the American Society for Political and Legal Philosophy held in
conjunction with the Association of American Law Schools, held in
New Orleans, Louisiana in January 1995"—Pref.
Includes bibliographical references and index.
Contents: Introduction / Will Kymlicka and Ian Shapiro—
Classifying cultural rights / Jacob T. Levy—Cultural toleration /
Chandran Kukathas—Response to Kukathas / Michael Walzer—Human
diversity and the limits of toleration / Adeno Addis—The idea of
nonliberal constitutionalism / Graham Walker—Group rights and
ethnicity / Thomas W. Pogge—Justifying special ethnic group
rights: comments on Pogge / S. James Anaya—Group agency and group
rights / James W. Nickel—Common-law constructions of group
autonomy: a case study / Denise G. Réaume—Tale of two villages
(or, legal realism comes to town) / Nomi Maya Stolzenberg—Deferring
group representation / Iris Marion Young—What is a balanced
committee? Democratic theory, public law, and the question of fair
representation on quasi-legislative bodies / Andrew Stark—Self
-determination: politics, philosophy, and law / Donald L. Horowitz—
Tribes, regions, and nationalism in democratic Malawi / Deborah
Kaspin—"That time was apartheid, now it's the new South Africa":
discourses of race in Ruyterwacht, 1995 / Courtney Jung and Jeremy
Seekings—From ethnic exclusion to ethnic diversity: the
Australian path to multiculturalism / John Kane—Straight gay
politics: Limits of an ethnic model of inclusion / Cathy J. Cohen.
ISBN 0-8147-8062-8 (alk. paper)
1. Ethnicity—Congresses.   2. Human rights—Congresses.
3. Toleration—Congresses.   4. Multiculturalism—Congresses.
I. Shapiro, Ian.   II. Kymlicka, Will.   III. American Society for
Political and Legal Philosophy. Meeting (1995 : New Orleans, La.)
IV. Association of American Law Schools.   V. Series.
GN495.6.E879   1996
305.8—dc20          96-35605
                    CIP

New York University Press books are printed on acid-free paper,
and their binding materials are chosen for strength and durability.

Manufactured in the United States of America
10 9 8 7 6 5 4 3 2 1

# CONTENTS

# PREFACE

The present, thirty-ninth, volume of NOMOS began as papers and commentaries read at the Annual Meeting of the American Society for Political and Legal Philosophy held in conjunction with the Association of American Law Schools, held in New Orleans, Louisiana in January 1995. The topic chosen by the membership was "Ethnicity and Group Rights," and Will Kymlicka put together an excellent program for that meeting. He also proved to be a model coeditor for this volume. His efficient intelligence is a rare commodity; it was a pleasure to collaborate with him.

Our managing editor, Kathryn McDermott, took the occasion of the present volume to bring NOMOS up to speed with the computer revolution. With the aid of Niko Pfund and Despina Papazoglou Gimbel at NYU Press, not to mention the cheerful cooperation of authors, she ensured that the entire volume could be typeset electronically from the same disk. This is no mean feat when dealing with more than a score of authors, working with different computers and software, and scattered over several continents. She and the rest of the production team are deserving of our continuing gratitude.

The paperback edition of NOMOS XXXVI, *The Rule of Law,* and NOMOS XXXVII, *Theory and Practice,* are both now available.

I. S.

# CONTRIBUTORS

**ADENO ADDIS**
*Law, Tulane University*

**S. JAMES ANAYA**
*Law, University of Iowa*

**CATHY J. COHEN**
*Political Science, Yale University*

**DONALD L. HOROWITZ**
*Law, Duke University*

**COURTNEY JUNG**
*Political Science, Yale University*

**JOHN KANE**
*Politics and Public Policy, Griffith University*

**DEBORAH KASPIN**
*Anthropology, Yale University*

**CHANDRAN KUKATHAS**
*Politics, University of New South Wales/Australian Defense
Force University*

**WILL KYMLICKA**
*Philosophy, University of Ottawa*

JACOB T. LEVY
*Politics, Princeton University*

JAMES W. NICKEL
*Philosophy, University of Colorado*

THOMAS W. POGGE
*Philosophy, Columbia University*

DENISE RÉAUME
*Law, University of Toronto*

JEREMY SEEKINGS
*Sociology, University of Cape Town*

IAN SHAPIRO
*Political Science, Yale University*

ANDREW STARK
*Management, University of Toronto*

NOMI MAYA STOLZENBERG
*Law, University of Southern California*

GRAHAM WALKER
*Politics, The Catholic University of America*

MICHAEL WALZER
*Institute for Advanced Study, Princeton University*

IRIS MARION YOUNG
*Public and International Affairs, University of Pittsburgh*

# ETHNICITY AND GROUP RIGHTS

## NOMOS
# XXXIX

# PART I

# MEANINGS OF ETHNICITY AND GROUP RIGHTS

# 1

# INTRODUCTION

## WILL KYMLICKA AND IAN SHAPIRO

When the Berlin Wall fell in 1989, liberalism appeared to many commentators as the only ideology which retained any validity or viability in the modern world. Initially, the collapse of communism seemed to many to signify the "end of history." But liberalism proved incapable of containing or defusing the ethnic conflicts which were unleashed in the former communist regimes, and what replaced communism in most of Eastern Europe and the former Soviet Union was not liberal democracy but ethnonationalism. As we approach the twenty-first century, commentators are increasingly wondering whether liberalism can contain ethnic conflict in the West. What used to be seen as stable liberal democracies are now riven by bitter disputes between ethnocultural groups over immigration and multiculturalism, and some even face the threat of secession.

The resurgence of ethnonational conflict in both the East and West has reignited interest in the issue of "group rights." However, it remains a comparatively unexplored topic within Western political philosophy. There is a long-standing literature on the idea of "group" or "collective" rights. But until recently it tended to focus on a narrow and somewhat formalistic range of questions. The major aim was to categorize rights as "individual" or "collective" along various dimensions; for instance, whether a particular right is exercised by an individual or group, or whether the beneficiary of a particular right is an individual or a group, or whether the

3

right logically entails the prior existence of a group. Using these sorts of criteria, various rights from all areas of the law (family law, corporate law, labor law, etc.) would then be categorized as either individual or collective rights.

There is an increasing recognition, however, that this familiar debate obscures as much as it reveals. In particular, it does not help us grapple with the normative issues raised by ethnocultural conflicts. For many of the claims raised by ethnocultural groups seem to fall on the "individual" side of the ledger. For example, the right to use one's mother tongue in the courts is a right exercised by individuals, as is the right to be exempted from legislative or administrative requirements which conflict with one's religious beliefs. Conversely, many of the most familiar features of a liberal-democratic order seem to fall on the "collective" side of the ledger. For example, the right of Oregon to send two representatives to the Senate, or the right of the American people to restrict entry into the United States. Even the rights to freedom of the press and assembly, or the right to a jury trial, have important "collective" elements. And in any event, many of the clearest cases of collective rights, such as the rights of unions and corporations, have nothing in particular to do with ethnic conflict.

Focusing solely on whether the rights are exercised by individuals or groups misses what is really at issue in cases of ethnocultural conflict. The important question is whether the familiar system of common citizenship rights within liberal democracies—the standard set of civil, political, and social rights which define citizenship in most democratic countries—is sufficient to accommodate the legitimate interests which people have in virtue of their ethnic identity. Are there legitimate interests which people have, emerging from their ethnocultural group membership, which are not adequately recognized or protected by the familiar set of liberal-democratic civil and political rights as reflected, say, in the American Bill of Rights, or the French Declaration of the Rights of Man?

This way of looking at the problem directs our attention away from the formal features of claims toward more substantive moral and institutional questions. To what sorts of interests do ethnic identity and cultural membership give rise? How does membership in an ethnic group differ from other groups, such as professional, lifestyle, or advocacy groups? How important is ethnicity to personal identity and self-respect, and does accommodating these interests require more than standard citizenship rights? How salient is ethnicity to political conflict, and does this require taking measures to ensure the adequate representation of ethnic groups? If so, how do we identify and individuate the relevant ethnocultural groups, and who should we accept as their legitimate spokespersons? How can we ensure that in protecting ethnic minorities from the majority, we don't allow the group to mistreat its own members? What forms of ethnocultural accommodations are consistent with democratic equality, individual freedom, and political stability?

The seventeen essays in this volume, all previously unpublished, address many of these questions. They discuss the distinctiveness of ethnicity as the basis for legal claims (Pogge, Anaya); the extent to which the expression of ethnic identities can (or should) be accommodated within traditional liberal institutions (Stolzenberg, Walker; Kukathas; Walzer; Addis); the potential for group representation (Young; Stark); and the capacity of groups to acquire legal status and exercise legal autonomy (Réaume; Nickel). Several authors also evaluate the strengths and weaknesses of various strategies for resolving ethnic conflict around the world, from secession to nation-building to multiculturalism (Horowitz, Jung and Seekings, Kaspin, Cohen, and Kane). They help illustrate the important progress which is being made in this previously neglected field, as well as identify areas where further research is needed.

## I. Meanings of Ethnicity and Group Rights

To begin with, however, the next chapter provides an overview and typology by Jacob T. Levy of the rights-claims which are at stake in recent ethnocultural conflicts. Levy argues that normative work on the rights of ethnocultural groups requires a way to identify the rights-claims which are morally and institutionally similar, and those which are not. He identifies eight clusters of rights-claims which seem to have a similar normative structure and similar institutional implications. These are (1) *exemptions* from an ostensibly neutral law which unfairly burdens a cultural minority; (2) *assistance* to overcome unfair disadvantages or burdens to engaging in the same activities as the dominant group; (3) *self-government*, whether through secession or autonomy within a larger state; (4) *external rules* limiting the freedom of nonmembers in order to protect an endangered culture or cultural practice; (5) *internal rules* which limit the freedom of members, and which must be obeyed for continued recognition as a member of group; (6) *recognition and enforcement of customary legal practices* by the dominant legal system; (7) *guaranteed representation* for minority group members within government bodies; and (8) *symbolic claims* about the nature of the polity and the representation of its constituent groups. Levy provides several examples within each category and identifies the kinds of arguments which are made for and against rights-claims in that category. He argues that this sort of typology is more useful than existing typologies, which tend to conflate different kinds of rights into two or three overly broad categories and which focus on the formal legal structure of rights-claims while neglecting their normative foundations and institutional implications.

## II. THE IDEA OF TOLERATION

Levy's chapter provides a helpful survey of the rights-claims being advanced by ethnocultural groups. But how should we evaluate these claims? For most of our authors, the primary concern is with the potential role of these rights within liberal democracies, and the next three chapters focus directly on this question.

The liberal tradition has been ambivalent towards the aspirations of ethnocultural groups. On the one hand, liberalism is an individualistic theory—indeed, it seems to be the quintessentially individualistic theory—with a marked tendency to view politics as solely about the relationship between individuals and the state, with little or no room for groups in-between, other than as transient outgrowths of the combinations of individual interests. This attitude seems antagonistic to the claims of ethnocultural groups.[1] On the other hand, liberalism is committed at a very deep level to the idea of toleration—indeed, many recent authors argue that liberalism emerged as a generalization of the principle of religious toleration.[2]

These two aspects of liberalism—its individualism and its commitment to toleration—need not come into conflict if the ethnocultural group is itself individualistic and shares the basic liberal-democratic principles of the larger society. But what if an ethnocultural group is nonindividualistic—or perhaps even anti-individualistic—cherishing group solidarity or cultural purity while repudiating ideals of individual freedom and personal autonomy? Does liberal tolerance extend to such illiberal groups?

In chapter 3, Chandran Kukathas takes up this question by exploring the idea of toleration and its role within liberal theory. He focuses in particular on the extent to which a liberal society should tolerate minority communities and their practices when those practices seem 'intolerable' or illiberal. He concludes that even illiberal communities should be tolerated, for a number of reasons. The most important reason is that the conception of public reason which underlies liberalism can only emerge—and acquire normative authority among citizens—if such cultural differences are allowed expression. Toleration, on his view, requires and justifies a principle of nonintervention in the affairs of ethnocultural groups (so long as individuals have a right of exit). He ties this argument to a broader debate about the nature of liberalism. Indeed, one of his main aims is to defend an account of liberalism which views it as a doctrine recommending compromise and the accommodation of different ways of life, rather than as a doctrine offering a comprehensive moral view grounded in already-formulated principles of justice or freedom. For this reason, the ideal which lies at the core of liberalism is toleration.

Both Michael Walzer and Adeno Addis respond to Kukathas. Walzer argues that Kukathas's vision of a regime of toleration—in which there is no "common standpoint of morality"—is simply not viable. According to Walzer, Kukathas's ideal of toleration is only viable at the international level. Indeed, the international order already has many of the characteristics Kukathas associates with a tolerant regime, such as the absence of an overarching moral consensus or of an authoritative decision-making body, constant mutual adjustment and accommodation between groups, and a general rule of nonintervention in the internal affairs of groups. Walzer argues, however, that the sorts of intergroup relations which exist *within* a state are necessarily very different from those which exist between states at the international level. The difference between national and international society, he argues, is ineradicable. International society lacks a common history and culture, but every domestic society inevitably develops a "common moral standpoint," however disputed, as a result of shared history and experience. Human beings invariably feel attached to and want to defend their society's common moral standpoint. Consequently, Walzer concludes, a society of the sort Kukathas advocates would either have to be "inhabited by beings of another sort" or else "break up in the radical way suggested by its international analogue."

Adeno Addis raises related concerns about Kukathas's project, and goes on to propose a quite different conception of toleration. He describes Kukathas's view as a form of "negative toleration"—that is, nonintervention. Defenders of negative toleration, like Kukathas, argue that not only does it minimize the risks of conflict, but it also provides the most secure protection to cultural and ethnic minorities. Addis argues, however, that negative toleration, as it is usually articulated, is not as generous to minorities as its supporters claim, nor will it provide the minimal level of solidarity among groups that liberal democratic societies need to sustain themselves over a long period of time. In place of negative toleration, Addis endorses what he calls "pluralistic solidarity," a way of imagining institutions and vocabularies that will affirm multiplicity while cultivating solidarity. His contention is that a genuine sense of pluralistic solidarity will develop only through a process where majorities and minorities are linked in institutional dialogue, rather than when they merely tolerate each other as the strange and alien Other. In particular, Addis argues that there are three institutions that are central to this discursive process—the education system, the media, and the law. He briefly discusses how each of these systems can be reformed so as to create genuine dialogue across differences.[3] According to Addis, this conception of pluralistic solidarity will not only help secure justice for ethnocultural groups but also help to protect individuals within those groups from abuse or mistreatment.

This perennial debate about the appropriate interpretation of liberal toleration shows no signs of abating. But it has become more urgent since the fall of communism. Graham Walker contends in chapter 6 that the only sort of constitutional settlement which has any hope of being realized in Eastern Europe and the former Soviet Union is one which accommodates strongly felt ethnonational identities and aspirations. The future of liberalism in these countries, therefore, may depend on the extent to which liberal theories, and liberal institutions, can be reformed so as to accommodate (some of) the claims of ethnocultural groups.

But even if liberalism can be reformed in these ways, it will still face serious obstacles in many parts of the world which lack traditions of individual liberty. This raises the question whether there is a nonliberal conception of toleration. Walker argues that there is, and that it provides the most appropriate approach for multiethnic countries in many parts of the world. Walker is strongly critical of American constitutional "Johnny Appleseeds," who have promoted the adoption of American-style liberal constitutionalism in Eastern Europe without considering the very different ethnocultural makeup and political traditions of these countries.

According to Walker, although constitutionalism has enjoyed a certain renaissance since the fall of communism, it is stymied by its conceptual conflation with liberalism. This excludes the only kind of constitutionalism likely to fit many world situations: a nonliberal kind, whose center of gravity is something other than individual liberty entitlements. Walker argues that recovering the idea of constitutionalism from its modern shrinkage of meaning is easier now that liberals have lost some of their triumphal certainty which accompanied the initial collapse of communism. Moreover, the constitutional experiences of countries like Israel, or the Native American nations, provide useful insight into forms of constitutionalism which are grounded not in individual liberty but in the promotion of certain collective ethnocultural goals. Walker argues that a nonliberal version retains constitutionalism's appeal as a superior objectivity that limits powerholders and thwarts despotism. It prevents the abuse of power and helps to protect minorities. It thereby makes the resources of constitutionalism more fully available where they are needed most—in the postcommunist region and elsewhere where conditions preclude the political embrace of individualist liberalism.

## III. The Normative Status of Ethnicity

Much of the debate about the claims of cultural groups—whether these are evaluated within a liberal or nonliberal framework—has focused on the rights of *ethnic* groups rather than lifestyle groups (e.g., gays), advocacy groups (e.g., environmentalists) or other identity groups (e.g., women, the disabled). This is understandable in one sense, insofar as ethnic groups have displayed greater potential to cause political instability, whether in the form of political violence or even secession. But the question arises whether ethnic groups differ in any principled way from other groups with which people identify. Are people's interests in their ethnic-group membership stronger, or more worthy of respect, than their interests in other forms of group membership?

Thomas W. Pogge's chapter is explicitly addressed to this question. He argues that we should oppose not only "low chauvinism," which values one ethnic or religious group over others of the same type, but also "high chauvinism," which values cultural groups of one type (ethnic, religious, linguistic, lifestyle) above those of other types. Pogge is especially concerned to challenge the privileging of ethnic groups and, more generally, the view that ethnic groups are owed greater accommodation by society than cultural groups of other types. Privileging ethnic groups is untenable, Pogge argues, for several reasons. For one thing, the distinction between ethnic and nonethnic groups is vague in several respects. But more importantly, privileging ethnic groups violates the requirement to treat citizens as equals, irrespective of the character of their deeper affiliations and identifications. To live up to this ideal, Pogge insists, we should not conduct separate debates about the rights of groups of different types but rather should consider the various types of groups together, aiming for a unified account of groups and group rights within a just society. Such an account will attach no importance to whether a cultural group is of this or that type. It will instead give weight to other, crosscutting factors, such as the role this group plays in the lives of those who are affiliated or identified with it, and the strength and state of this group within society.

Pogge is not opposed to all group rights-claims. On the contrary, he takes certain group rights as an inevitable feature of any just and democratic society. However, he insists that the legitimate grounds for such rights—in particular, respect for identity and effective political self-government—can also be claimed by non-ethnic groups.

In a brief commentary in chapter 8, S. James Anaya argues that Pogge tends to downplay—even trivialize—the extent to which the effective realization of equality requires in many instances differential treatment of ethnic minority groups in ways that are not necessary for, or even relevant to, other types of groups. In particular, Anaya argues, ethnic groups with distinctive cultural attributes are properly regarded differently from other types of groups to the extent that there is a widely shared interest in securing the integrity of diverse cultures. Furthermore, there are often good reasons to accord ethnic groups special protection or entitlements because of certain conditions related to minority status including historical or continuing patterns of discrimination. Anaya illustrates these points by reference to recent developments in international law, including recent provisions regarding the rights of indigenous peoples. [4]

## IV. GROUP RIGHTS AND GROUP AGENCY

One source of discomfort with group or collective rights is the belief that many groups, particularly ethnic groups, are deficient as rights holders. Our next three chapters focus on the conditions which hinder or promote the ability of groups to become effective rights holders. In chapter 9, James W. Nickel discusses what he calls the "deficiency thesis." According to this thesis, assigning rights to groups is generally a bad idea, since groups are often unable to play an active role in exercising, interpreting, and defending their rights. The source of this alleged inability is that groups lack effective agency and clear identity. Nickel, however, denies that the deficiency thesis is true of all or even most groups but agrees that it may be true of some ethnic minorities—particularly nonterritorial ones. He also defends the view that clear identity and effective agency are needed for groups to benefit from most of the rights that are currently put forward as group rights. Together, these two propositions imply that nonterritorial minorities should not be given legal rights as groups. But there are practical measures available to construct the clear identity and effective agency of minority groups, and Nickel concludes with some suggestions about how even dispersed minorities can become effective rights holders.

In chapter 10, Denise Réaume develops this theme about the practical measures needed to construct a group's legal autonomy. She starts with the problem of judicial intervention. When courts are asked to resolve a dispute within a minority group, does this judicial intervention undermine the group's autonomy? There are two familiar approaches to this problem. According to the "deferential approach," the courts should look for an internal decision maker to whom the court can defer, while the "interpretivist approach" engages with the substantive dispute between the parties in order to provide the court's interpretation of the rule or practice at issue. Using two famous cases involving church property disputes as a case study, Réaume argues that these two seemingly doctrinal approaches are not that different after all. If each approach is understood to rely on a prior determination of the group's constitutional structure, they constitute complementary strategies for respecting minority group autonomy. The first step in resolving a dispute within a minority group must be to articulate the "rule of recognition" for the group, which requires ascertaining whether the group is constituted solely by reference to primary rules (which specify the obligations of members) or by both primary and secondary rules (which specify the rules for changing and adjudicating primary rules). In the case of a group consisting only of primary rules or of some primary rules beyond the scope of any of the group's secondary rules, the only way a court can respect a group's autonomy is to do its best to interpret the substantive rule in issue according to the group's own understanding. However, if a group has secondary rules which give internal decision-making bodies authority over the dispute at hand, respect for the group's autonomy requires deferring to those bodies. The latter form of constitutional structure enables a group to enjoy a more robust form of autonomy, because the group is not only assured that its affairs will be regulated by its own rules but that members of the group itself will have the final say in interpreting or changing those rules. According to Réaume, this means that minority groups that have the most complete formal structure, whose internal organization most closely mimics a legal system, are in a position to ensure for themselves a greater degree of autonomy in the conduct of their affairs. This not only helps explain what measures are needed to construct group autonomy but also why some groups have had more difficulty in achieving autonomy than others. For example, religious groups seem have a greater ability to develop agreed-upon primary and secondary rules than do many ethnic groups.

Nomi Stolzenberg continues exploring this theme of the legal construction of a group's autonomy in chapter 11. Through a mix of legal analysis and political theory, Stolzenberg attempts to move beyond the familiar debate between liberals and communitarians regarding the accommodation of groups within liberal democracies. Liberals traditionally assume that ethnocultural and religious groups should remain in the private sphere, while communitarians denounce the "privatism" which liberal democracies impose on these groups. But Stolzenberg notes that this familiar debate ignores an important paradox inhering in a liberal political regime: namely, that groups, whose corporate identity has traditionally been recognized only in the private sphere, can in fact, under certain conditions, assume sovereign or quasi-sovereign authority within a given government locale. As evidence of this counterintuitive phenomenon, Stolzenberg focuses on the municipality of Kiryas Joel in upstate New York, a community of Satmar Hasidic Jews, which sought and ultimately gained state support for a public school district composed entirely of Satmar children. A telling foil to Kiryas Joel is that of Airmont, another municipality in New York state, which sought to stem the tide of Orthodox Jewish settlement by adopting zoning laws that strictly limited the creation of new synagogues and prayer halls within its boundaries. A close analysis of the litigation surrounding the two towns reveals that the boundary between private and public spheres of activity was frequently blurred to the extent that religious—or for that matter antireligious—groups could gain hold of the reins of governmental power. One important result of her analysis is to problematize a set of distinctions long deemed sacred to the American constitutional order: those between religious and secular functions, general and particularistic concerns, and intent-based and effect-based conceptions of neutrality.

## V. Group Representation

The authors in part 4 focus primarily on issues of group autonomy—on the capacity of groups to exercise meaningful forms of self-government. But many groups are most concerned, not with governing themselves in separate institutions, but rather with having greater participation and influence in the decisions of the larger polity. In particular, there is a concern among many groups about their lack of representation in legislative bodies. This has given rise to calls for some form of guaranteed representation of groups in the political process. These are taken up in part 5.

One of the most influential discussions of group representation is Iris Marion Young's book *Justice and the Politics of Difference.*[5] In that book, Young argued for a principle of special representation for oppressed and disadvantaged groups in political decision making. In her chapter for this volume, Young responds to some of the criticisms of her position. In particular, she focuses on the criticism that it is unrealistic to attribute a set of common attributes or interests to a particular group, insofar as this ignores the fact that any individual belongs simultaneously to many overlapping groups. Young agrees that treating gender or racial groups as fixed and unitary in their interests is problematic, because it "inappropriately freezes fluid relational identities into a unity," and "recreates oppressive segregations." Moreover, it implies that "the dominant group within the groups suppress or marginalize the perspective of minorities". In order to respond to these problems, while still increasing the representation of women and cultural minorities, Young argues that it is necessary to rethink the meaning and functions of political representation.

In opposition to the idea that a representative stands for the unified will of the citizens, Young interprets representation as a "deferring relationship" of authorization and accountability. On this view, constituents and representatives defer to each other's judgment, without ever assuming a unity of interests or identities. She argues that this conceptualization dissolves some of the problems that have plagued traditional theories of representation. Young then proposes that citizens should be represented along three dimensions: their interests, their opinions or principles, and their "perspective." She argues that while members of oppressed or marginalized groups are rarely unified in their interests or opinions, they often do share a certain perspective which emerges from their experiences as group members. She develops this notion of perspective as the basis for a new argument for the special representation of oppressed or disadvantaged groups.

Political theorists generally approach questions of group representation—such as what groups ought to be represented, and who should represent them—as they arise in legislative contexts. Much attention, for example, has been devoted to issues such as affirmative gerrymandering and proportional representation. But as Andrew Stark notes in chapter 13, nowhere in public discourse have issues of group representation been confronted more directly, and debated more richly, than in the realm of quasi-legislative advisory bodies, such as the President's Commission on AIDS, the White House Conference on Aging, the National Commission on the Observance of International Women's Year, and the Grace Commission on Cost Control in Government. The Federal Advisory Committee Act stipulates that such advisory groups must have "fair representation" of "affected interests." Since the inception of that Act, groups representing various interests have repeatedly gone to court seeking representation on such committees which, they claim, are not properly representative of the affected interests. In so doing, they have provoked a rich body of discourse—court decisions and briefs, legislative debate and legal commentary—over issues that centrally preoccupy theorists concerned with group representation in general: how do we determine what kinds of groups ought to be represented in different kinds of forums, and how do we identify both the membership of such groups and those who speak for them? Stark reconstructs a discourse surrounding the principle of "fair representation" on quasi-legislative bodies, and draws from its structure a framework within which to assess quasi-legislative representation.

In particular, he focuses on debates over the definition of

committee mandates (and hence who is affected by their deliberations) and over the representativeness of groups (and hence who
a group can claim to speak for). He argues that these disputes
often reflect divergent conceptions of the nature of political
power (do political bodies always seek to expand their jurisdiction
and thereby affect more interests, or do they stay within clear and
restricted mandates?) and of group behavior (do group leaders
pursue their own interest, or do they accurately reflect the interests of group members?). He points out a number of interesting
and seemingly paradoxical tendencies of these debates. For example, those people who have a benign conception of political power
(as nonexpansionary) often have a cynical conception of group
behavior (as elite-manipulated), whereas those who have a benign
conception of group behavior (as public-interested) often have a
cynical conception of political power (as inherently expansion-
ary). Stark concludes that resolving disputes over group representation will require greater research into the sociologies implicit in
the contending positions.

## VI. Dynamics of Inclusion and Exclusion

The final five chapters explore strategies for resolving problems
of intergroup relations, each of which involves its own distinctive
dynamic of inclusion and exclusion. At one end of the spectrum
are strategies which seek to reduce ethnic conflict by separating
the groups, through ethnic cleansing, racial segregation, or secession. At the other end of the spectrum are strategies which seek
to reduce ethnic conflict by integrating ethnocultural minorities
into the larger society, through various forms of cultural assimilation and "nation-building." In-between are various models of
multiculturalism and group rights, although where exactly to locate these models on the integration-separation model is of
course a matter of great debate.

One of the most common responses to ethnocultural diversity,
historically, is to create and maintain some sort of sharp separation between different racial or cultural groups. Separatist strategies often reflect a fear of the other and a desire to retain cultural
or racial purity. However, two of the more familiar forms of separatism—namely, ethnic cleansing and racial segregation—are

now almost universally denounced as illegitimate, and as a violation of basic human rights (although both continue to be practiced around the world). Secession, by contrast, is enjoying something of a renaissance, both in theory and practice.[6]

Donald L. Horowitz provides a critical assessment of the secessionist strategy for resolving ethnocultural conflicts. As he notes, this renewed interest in secession comes after a remarkable period of stability in territorial boundaries. For nearly fifty years after World War II, most irredentist movements were dormant, and most secessionist movements failed. Now, however, secessionist movements have begun to meet with greater success, and new justifications for ethnoterritorial self-determination have emerged in political philosophy and in international law. Horowitz begins by clarifying the conditions under which secessions and irredentas arise and explaining the reasons for the rarity of successful cases until recently. He also explores the historical ambivalence about ethnic self-determination within Western political thought. He goes on to suggest that new justifications for ethnic self-determination have been advanced without adequate consideration of the conditions that foster and inhibit ethnoterritorial change, and argues that the encouragement of territorial self-determination will neither reduce ethnic conflict nor enhance the treatment of minorities. Most groups will need to find ways to live together in the same territory, rather than seek illusory territorial "solutions" to their ethnic conflict.

The remaining chapters explore such strategies of "living together." In chapter 15, Deborah Kaspin explores one such strategy—namely, nation building—as it was practiced in Malawi. Thirty years of dictatorship ended in Malawi in 1994 when President Hastings Banda was voted out of office and replaced with Bakili Muluzi in the country's first multiparty election. Many commentators were dismayed to see the electorate divided on regional lines, since regionalism was understood to mean tribalism and to point to Malawi's inevitable fragmentation. However, Kaspin argues that these so-called tribal constituencies were in reality multiethnic regional constituencies which became seats of political identity as a result of President Banda's "nation-building" policies for national development. These included programs for economic growth predicated on regional favoritism and a policy of official nationalism that politicized ethnicity while purporting to meld a multiethnic population into a national citizenry. These policies favored the Chewa population and attempted to give the Chewa language and culture official status in Malawi. This was bitterly resisted by the non-Chewa groups in Malawi, a fact reflected in the 1994 elections, and the new government has reversed many of these policies. But Kaspin argues that Banda's nation-building policies were not entirely unsuccessful and have left an ambiguous legacy. On the one hand, these nation-building policies failed in their effort to subordinate minority identities to an official Chewa-based national identity. On the other hand, they did succeed in focusing the attention of all groups on the national level. Minority groups may have disagreed with the attempt to imbue Malawian identity with Chewa content, but the response of these groups has been to politicize the issue of national identity, not to retreat from the national level into regional or ethnonationalist separatism. According to Kaspin, the Malawi example illustrates the power of the state to create a nationality and its internal divisions at one and the same time, and to do so within a fairly narrow time frame.

In chapter 16, Courtney Jung and Jeremy Seekings discuss emerging forms of integration in the postapartheid South Africa. Until recently, South Africa was perhaps the paradigmatic example of the strategy of racial segregation. But the government now is committed to a "nonracial" South Africa, and to the full integration of racial minorities into the larger society. The worry remains, however, that the scars of racism run too deep to allow this integration to occur. Jung and Seekings examine discourses of race among white South Africans living in Ruyterwacht—a poor suburb of Cape Town—to see how much attitudes have changed.

According to Jung and Seekings, the predominant discourses of race in South Africa resemble the "modern" forms of racism found in contemporary America more closely than the "old-fashioned" forms of racial bigotry found in America up to the 1960s and in South Africa in the heyday of apartheid. Discourses of race in Ruyterwacht are characterized by a mix of egalitarianism and prejudice. Negative representations of black people are not explicitly based in characterizations of blacks as racially inferior but rather are linked to (1) the attribution of "unacceptable" behavior to particular (and not all) black people, or (2) the perception that black South Africans are collectively acting "unfairly" (e.g., in demanding affirmative action). The predominance of discourses of race corresponding to modern forms of racism is tentatively attributed to the uneven transformation of public discourse and power relations in the "new"—i.e., democratic and postapartheid—South Africa. While this modern form of racism is pervasive, Jung and Seekings see a greater openness to integration—especially of the Coloureds—among the whites.

Apartheid in South Africa involved a system of officially recognizing ethnic and racial groups, for the purposes of segregating them. In other countries, recognition is given to ethnocultural groups in the hope that this will aid in their integration into the larger society. This is the motivation for the "multiculturalism" policies which initially emerged in Canada and Australia in the 1970s. John Kane's chapter explores this multiculturalism strategy in the Australian context. As he notes, Australia is often cited as an exemplary success story for the political ideal known as multiculturalism. But the image this presents is radically at odds with that presented throughout most of Australia's history. The Australian polity has moved in the past thirty years from a practice of excluding ethnic minorities through a racially restrictive immigration policy to a policy of what Joseph Raz calls "affirmative multiculturalism." The latter goes beyond mere toleration, seeking instead to integrate polyethnic immigrant groups into a politically unified Australian society by positively affirming the value of their separate identities.

Kane's chapter traces the historical path that Australia has taken from a strong assertion of a common racial identity to a belief in the possibility and desirability of political unity within cultural diversity. It uses the Australian experience to explore some of the themes thrown up by multiculturalist theory, in particular that of the limits of multicultural toleration of ethnic practices. He concludes that the real value of multiculturalist theory in Australian society may lie less in the political practices that issue from it than in its symbolic rejection of its racist past, in the assurance this extends to immigrant groups of their place in society, and in the positive image it projects abroad to potential trading partners in Asia.

In our concluding chapter, Cathy J. Cohen explores the limits and consequences of an ethnic model of inclusion as it is currently being employed by many marginal groups. She uses the term *ethnic model* to refer to those political strategies used specifically by white immigrant groups in the United States to win formal inclusion, equal opportunity, and often equal results. This model promises that, in the tradition of white ethnic groups, members of any marginal group who can prove themselves "deserving" will eventually be assimilated and integrated into the dominant society. Cohen is interested in the requirements and costs of inclusion through such a model. What must marginal groups do to gain the label of "deserving" necessary for inclusion? Why do groups or classes of people who have a history of exclusion or marginalization from dominant institutions and social relations undertake more traditional political strategies, such as the ethnic model of inclusion, to win both recognition and rights?

Throughout, Cohen focuses on the power relationships found within marginal communities, exploring the specific strategies used by more privileged members of marginal groups to "police" or regulate the behavior and/or "culture" of other group members deemed nonconformist or nondeserving. For the purposes of the essay, Cohen focuses on the politics of lesbian, gay, bisexual, and transgendered communities, using the framework of marginalization to highlight the limits of an ethnic model of inclusion as it is currently being promoted within these communities. Whereas Kane and Jung and Seekings are comparatively optimistic about the potential for integrating previously excluded or segregated groups into a liberal polity, Cohen emphasizes that this inclusion has often come at a high price for many of the most vulnerable members of these groups.[7]

## NOTES

1. For an influential statement of this view, see Vernon Van Dyke, "The Individual, the State, and Ethnic Communities in Political Theory," *World Politics* 29/3 (1977): 343–69; and "Collective Rights and Moral Rights: Problems in Liberal-Democratic Thought," *Journal of Politics* 44 (1982): 21–40.

2. See, in particular, John Rawls, *Political Liberalism* (New York: Columbia University Press, 1993).

3. As Addis notes, to emphasize the importance of institutional dialogue among various groups seems to presuppose that there is a common language or languages in the polity. He briefly explores some of the ways in which pluralistic solidarity (with its emphasis on institutional dialogue) can be reconciled with linguistic pluralism. But in the end, he concludes that if linguistic pluralism is inhibiting shared deliberation, then the latter will have to take precedence. He argues that a stable and just political community requires that its ethnic and cultural communities be linguistically capable and willing to communicate with one another, a requirement which may justify the imposition of a majority language. This is an important issue which has not yet received the attention it deserves. It is remarkable, for example, how often "discourse ethics" or "deliberative democracy" is invoked as a means for addressing intergroup conflicts, without even asking in which language this discourse/deliberation will take place.

4. For a more extended statement of Anaya's views, see his *Indigenous Peoples in International Law* (Oxford: Oxford University Press, 1996).

5. Iris Marion Young, *Justice and the Politics of Difference* (Princeton: Princeton University Press, 1990); cf. "Polity and Group Difference: A Critique of the Ideal of Universal Citizenship," *Ethics* 99/2 (1989): 250–74.

6. Allen Buchanan, *Secession: The Legitimacy of Political Divorce* (Boulder, Colo.: Westview Press, 1991).

7. Indeed, it is interesting to note that the evidence from South Africa discussed by Jung and Seekings bears out some of Cohen's concerns. It seems that the integration of Coloureds in South Africa has been achieved, at least in part, precisely by distancing themselves from blacks, and by emphasizing that they are more "respectable" than blacks.

# 2

# CLASSIFYING CULTURAL RIGHTS

## JACOB T. LEVY

### I. INTRODUCTION

A vast array of extant and proposed policies seek to accommodate cultural pluralism; these do not lend themselves to being normatively analyzed as a single group. On the other hand, many of them do rise or fall by similar arguments. This chapter seeks to identify those cultural rights-claims which are morally alike and (as importantly) those which are unlike. It does not argue for or against any set of policies or rights-claims. Instead, it offers a way of sorting those policies which may facilitate and clarify such arguments.

Normative work on cultural rights is difficult to structure. One can rarely say with any precision what implications a given philosophical turn had for the sets of policies being endorsed or disparaged. Arguing by analogy from one case to another is necessary, but it is also frustrating without a framework for identifying the traits which made policies like or unlike in relevant ways.

Drawing purely philosophical distinctions sometimes provides little guidance in sorting actual institutions or policies. The discussion about individual and collective rights, for example, important as it is on a philosophical level, provides little guidance when confronting concrete policies and rights-claims, some of which seem to fit into neither category, some of which are all-too-easily redescribed as part of either one. Yael Tamir derives the right of a national group to its own (not necessarily independent) government from the individual right to practice one's culture, and argues that this derivation means national self-determination should be understood as an individual right.[1] Darlene Johnston holds that "the prevalence of collective wrongs such as apartheid and genocide demonstrates the need for collective rights."[2] This seems to redescribe the right not to be murdered by one's government, the right to vote, and other classic individual rights as group rights. Such redescriptions in one direction or the other are far from unique, and dispute over what would constitute a collective right in any event—a right to a collective good? a right which could only be exercised by members of a collective? a right which could only be exercised by a collectivity itself?—adds to the confusion. An argument that the only morally important rights are individual ones might still lead to support for a variety of cultural rights-claims (suitably redescribed); an argument that groups can have rights does not prove that any *do,* or which groups have which rights.

On the other hand, sorting rights-claims by the kind of group making the claim[3] clarifies some issues but also makes it difficult to distinguish among the various kinds of claims a group can make. It also, in my view, unnecessarily distinguishes between quite similar claims made by a variety of different groups. What follows, then, is the set of categories which I have found most useful in sorting cultural rights-claims. It seems to me that there are clusters of claims which lend themselves to similar sorts of arguments (pro and con), clusters within which one policy may be taken as precedent for another but among which such claims are much harder to sustain. I have proceeded inductively, from particular cases and arguments to categories. I therefore do not present a logically exhaustive typology; I have been unable to find or generate any such typology which captured the range of policies and rights-claims at issue.

I thus aspire to and claim usefulness, not truth, for this classification. I am aware that it has difficulties and that there are hard cases for it (several are noted in the essay); I would be happy to see a classification or typology which was *more* useful. I am also aware that the classification lacks a certain elegance (a problem related to the fact that it was constructed from the ground up) and, again, would be happy to see more elegant ways of sorting provided these did not sacrifice utility. In the meantime, I hope this classification will prove of use. Success would mean that one could construct a cultural rights theory by saying, "I argue in favor of exemption rights, against assistance rights, for this kind but not that kind of recognition right," and so on, and that others would understand what was being argued.

For each category, I provide real or proposed examples from the theoretical and empirical literature, and a sketch of the normative issues at stake in such rights-claims. Such a discussion cannot be exhaustive, and my primary concern will be to show the normative problems which set one category apart from another. I also identify important clusters within some categories, clusters which raise additional normative issues or which are clearly recognizable patterns of rights-claims actually made. Following the classification, I discuss some alternative methods of sorting cultural rights-claims, and some examples of arguments which I think would be clarified by use of a framework like the one presented here.[4]

I have by and large included only the sorts of claims which are subject to serious normative dispute. I do not, for example, try to categorize claims like "we seek to rule over another ethnic group" or "we seek to end a government policy which singles us out for special mistreatment on the grounds of our ethnicity." Genocide, ethnic exclusions from the vote, forcible conversions, bans on the private use of one's own language, prohibitions on minority-language names, and ethnic cleansing are all too real but not matters for which a serious moral argument can be made. Demands to end such openly discriminatory or oppressive treatment are, of course, vitally important in the world; but I take it that they are not subjects of serious dispute among philosophers and normative theorists.

## II. THE CLASSIFICATION

Cultural rights-claims and special policies for accommodating ethnic and linguistic pluralism include exemptions, assistance, self-government, external rules, internal rules, recognition/enforcement, representation, and symbolic claims.[5]

| CATEGORY | EXAMPLES |
|---|---|
| *Exemptions* from laws which penalize or burden cultural practices | Sikhs/motorcycle helmet laws, Indians/peyote, hunting laws |
| *Assistance* to do those things the majority can do unassisted | multilingual ballots, affirmative action, funding ethnic associations |
| *Self-government* for ethnic, cultural, or "national" minorities | secession (Slovenia), federal unit (Catalonia), other polity (Puerto Rico) |
| *External rules* restricting nonmembers' liberty to protect members' culture | Quebec/restrictions on English language, Indians/ restrictions on local whites voting |
| *Internal rules* for members' conduct enforced by ostracism, excommunication | Mennonite shunning, disowning children who marry outside the group |
| *Recognition/enforcement* of traditional legal code by the dominant legal system | Aboriginal land rights, traditional or group-specific family law |
| *Representation* of minorities in government bodies, guaranteed or facilitated | Maori voting roll for Parliament, U.S. black-majority Congressional districts |
| *Symbolic claims* to acknowledge the worth, status, or existence of various groups | disputes over name of polity, national holidays, teaching of history |

### Exemptions

Exemption rights are individually exercised negative liberties granted to members of a religious or cultural group whose practices are such that a generally and ostensibly neutral law would be a distinctive burden on them. Often this is because the law would impair a minority's religious practices, or would compel adherents to do that which they consider religiously prohibited; exemptions are thus often analogous to the status of conscientious objector which exempts, among others, Quakers and the Amish from conscription.

Examples abound. The ceremonial use of wine by Catholics and Jews was exempted from alcohol Prohibition in the United States. The religious use of peyote by American Indians is similarly exempted from laws on narcotics and hallucinogens.[6] The Amish in the United States have sought or obtained exemptions from mandatory schooling laws;[7] regulations of private schools like the requirement that schools have certified teachers;[8] participation in Social Security and some states' workers' compensation and unemployment insurance schemes;[9] a requirement that slow-moving vehicles display a standardized reflective symbol;[10] and a variety of health care and land use regulations.[11] A century ago American Mormons sought an exemption from laws against polygamy.[12] Jews and Muslims in a number of states have sought or obtained exemptions from sabbatarian laws, especially Sunday-closing laws for businesses.

Not all exemption-claims are religiously based. Aboriginal peoples in several countries have sought and obtained exemptions to various hunting and fishing regulations, arguing that the rules would unfairly burden their traditional way of life or even their ability to gain sustenance. At various times Afrikaner, Quebecois, and Irish citizens of South Africa, Canada, and the United Kingdom have sought exemptions from conscription, saying that they should not be forced to fight on behalf of England. Some exemptions are religious only in an inverse sense to those on the conscientious objection model. For instance, some Muslim states ban the use of alcohol, but exempt non-Muslims from the rule. The exemption is not granted because alcohol consumption is a *duty* of all non-Muslims; it differs from the exceptions to American Prohibition noted above. It is granted because the rule itself is there for an openly religious reason. The state is intimately involved with the majority culture and religion, and considers it appropriate to turn the sinful into the criminal; but by the same token holds that those who do not hold alcohol sinful should not be held criminally liable for it either.

A variety of exemption claims revolve around dress codes and restrictions. Sikhs in Canada have sought exemptions from mandatory helmet laws and from police dress codes, to accommodate their religiously required turbans. American Orthodox Jews requested an exemption from Air Force uniform regulations to accommodate their yarmulkes.[13] Muslim women and girls have faced similar situations with regard to the *chador* they are required to wear, though the most famous of these—the expulsion of Muslim girls from French schools because the *chador* violated rules about the display of religious symbols—is a special case. Ordinarily exemption disputes involve rules which only accidentally impinge on the minority practice; it's not that the U.S. Air Force bans yarmulkes *per se* but rather that it has a standardized uniform of which yarmulkes would be one sort of violation. But the rule in France was very specifically against anything which would allow one to identify students by religion. The *chador* is precisely the sort of thing the rule was intended to keep out.[14] One is reminded of the rule that all names must be in the state's dominant language, imposed at various times on peoples as disparate as Germanic South Tyrolians in Italy and the non-Han Chinese aboriginal inhabitants of Taiwan. Such rules are intentionally aimed at the minority group, and so it makes little sense to seek an exemption while leaving the rule intact. Again, repeal rather than an exemption is what is wanted. These cases obviously have something important in common with those in which an exemption is sought to a rule left otherwise intact; but they differ, too.

In cases where an exemption is demanded or granted, a practice which has a distinctive status and meaning in a minority culture is banned, regulated, or compelled because of the very different meaning it has for the majority culture. The exemption is justified as a recognition of that difference, as an attempt not to unduly burden the minority culture or religion *en route* to the law's legitimate goals.[15] As noted, many are defended as part of the freedom to practice and live according to one's religion and seek their defense in the broader theory of religious freedom, but all defenses of exemptions stress the distinctive meaning which the practice has for the nondominant group. The fact that exemptions are individually exercised, and that many of the laws in question are so-called victimless crime laws, makes exemptions easy to ground in liberal and libertarian theories emphasizing individual freedom from coercion. This is far from their only possible means of defense, however; Raz argues that the exemption for conscientious objectors has been a protection for religious *communities* as much as if not more than a deferral to *individual* conscience, and the argument is easily extended to other exemption rights.[16] Sandel provides a communitarian argument for (at least religious) exemptions as exercises of the right to carry out one's duties.[17]

Exemptions are criticized as a group for the distinctions they draw in the law; they grant liberties to some which others lack. This is particularly a problem for republican or liberal theories which place overwhelming importance on *equal* liberty. It is also a problem for the conception of the rule of law which emphasizes the general applicability of laws and the absence, as it were, of proper nouns from legitimate lawmaking. Exemptions are also subject to criticism because they require the state to identify individuals as members of various groups; perhaps most problematically, religious exemptions can require judicial inquiry into whether a person is a sincere and faithful member of the religion or whether the exemption is being claimed opportunistically. All exemptions, though, require an official determination of the group membership of individuals, a process some might think problematic.[18] On the other hand, exemption rights are wholly immune to the criticism that "groups cannot be rights-bearers," for while they are group-differentiated they are not "group rights" in any meaningful sense.[19]

Of course, most arguments are about specific exemptions rather than exemptions as a class; and these arguments require reference to the law from which an exemption is sought. Laws whose purpose is to protect the interests of children (say, compulsory vaccination or mandatory schooling) raise a particular set of arguments, and one could easily argue for most exemptions while arguing against exemptions from laws designed to protect children.[20] Rules which seek to protect outsiders or the environment (land use, hunting and fishing, slow moving vehicles) raise another set of issues and might also be used as limits on a general endorsement of exemptions. Those moralistic or paternalist rules which regulate the behavior of adults (alcohol or drug prohibitions, motorcycle helmet laws) are subject to yet different arguments. Under current American law, exemptions are to be granted to those whose religious practices or convictions are impaired by a law except when universal adherence to the law is necessary for advancing a compelling state interest. Those who agree that this is the correct standard could nonetheless disagree on which state interests are compelling. Still, they would have agreed on a general rule for the treatment of exemptions, a rule which would have little or no bearing on other kinds of cultural rights-claims.

*Assistance*

Where exemption rights seek to allow minorities to engage in practices different from those of the majority culture, assistance rights are claimed for help in overcoming obstacles to engaging in common practices. Special provision is sought because of culturally specific disadvantages or because the desired common activity has been designed in such a way as to keep members of nondominant groups out.

The most prominent clusters of assistance rights are language rights; funding for ethnocultural art, associations, and so on; and preferential policies (in, for example, hiring and university admission). All impose a direct cost onto at least some members of the majority or dominant culture; all seek to allow the minority or subordinated culture to do those things which the majority culture can allegedly do already.[21]

Language rights present simple examples; speakers of the minority language seek special provision to allow them to interact with the state or receive state protection and benefits. These include ballots printed in multiple languages; interpreters in court and in administrative agencies, or the appointment of bilingual judges and civil servants;[22] the provision of bilingual or minority-language public education; and offering college entrance exams in more than one language. Voting, using the courts and the schools, having access to the bureaucracy—these are common activities which speakers of the minority language are effectively prevented from engaging in. Overcoming that obstacle requires special provision which imposes a cost; interpreters are expensive, a requirement that judges or civil servants be bilingual even more so, and there is a direct cost associated with printing ballot papers in more than one language. Supporters of assistance rights maintain that these costs are less important than the injustice which would result if minority-language speakers were denied access to the activities in question. Bruno de Witte summarizes the general argument in favor of such assistance rights, which he refers to as rights of linguistic equality (as opposed to mere linguistic freedom, the right to speak one's own language):

> The freedom to use one's own language in addressing [judicial or administrative] authorities is ineffective if those authorities have no corresponding duty to understand and act upon that language; and with "negative" rights, no such duty can be imposed upon them. Indeed, in the absence of such a duty, the individual members of the administration or the judiciary could themselves invoke their own linguistic freedom against that of the citizen with whom they deal. In the context of administrative and judicial usage, the primary interest of minorities *is* the recognition of a form of linguistic equality rather than linguistic freedom.[23]

Subsidies to a variety of cultural and linguistic institutions and associations are also common. It is argued that the majority culture, simply by being in the majority, has its cultural integrity and heritage protected for free, as it were, while other cultural groups have to create, maintain, and fund institutions such as private schools, fraternal associations, museums, art galleries, theater companies, community newspapers, cultural clubs, and so on in order to preserve their cultural integrity to anything like the same degree. Special state measures to ease that burden are assistance rights. These can include direct subsidies to ethnic associations, special tax deductions for contributions to such associations, the provision of tax credits, vouchers, or direct subsidies to cultural private schools or the parents of children who go there, and so on. Kymlicka also argues for support for "ethnic associations, magazines, and festivals," seeing them as a logical extension of state funding for arts and culture generally and possibly as security against discrimination in the allocation of such funds.[24] Carrying the logic of these assistance rights farther, Yael Tamir suggests the provision of cultural vouchers which can be donated to a wide variety of cultural institutions.[25]

With the possible exceptions of the language of public education and subsidies for private education,[26] the most controversial and explosive assistance rights are preferential policies.[27] They are also extremely common worldwide. Affirmative action, preferential hiring and admissions, quotas, and set-asides are present in various places in private employment, the civil service, bank loans, the military, universities, the awarding of government contracts, and land allocation.[28] For reasons which are either systematic and permanent or at least in theory contingent and temporary, members of one group are held to be at a disadvantage in competing for the resources or positions in question, a disadvantage which these assistance rights attempt to overcome.[29]

The explosiveness of preferential policies comes in part because the costs of the policy are apparently concentrated on the marginal members of the nonpreferred group, those who are better qualified or more competitive than some members of the preferred group who nonetheless are awarded the positions or resources. In this they differ from language rights or funding for ethnic associations; those assistance rights do have costs, but they are dispersed among a society's taxpayers. They are also highly controversial because of their open departure from principles of merit and equal treatment, although Iris Marion Young argues that such principles are themselves biased and unequal.[30]

Language rights and cultural subsidies (though not preferential policies) are immune to fears about identifying individuals on the basis of group membership; such identification is not generally necessary for their exercise. Arguments for the separation of culture and state, or against the legitimacy of claims for cultural support, *do* impact on language rights and cultural subsidies.[31] Many assistance rights are integrationist and so not subject to charges of separatism; this is the case for multilingual ballots, for example, which allow all to participate in a common political system. On the other hand, funding for minority-language schools, newspapers, radio stations, and so on, while allowing the minority to do the same sorts of things as the majority, do not encourage the two groups to pursue their activities *together* and do not seem integrationist.

As ought be clear, some differences in justification necessarily surround the clusters of assistance rights; but they are importantly similar as well, in ways which make them dissimilar to other kinds of cultural rights claims. All assistance rights involve costs to members of the majority culture (though these are not costs in liberty; policies imposing such costs require different justification are discussed separately under "external rules"), and those costs must be justified. All involve the aspiration or the desire to do things which members of the majority already or easily do, and are therefore not typically subject to criticism on grounds of leading to or encouraging separatism.[32] Unlike exemptions, which are readily defended in terms of liberty and only indirectly (à la Kymlicka) in terms of equality, arguments about assistance rights are almost always arguments about equality one way or the other. They are opposed on the grounds that they single out members of specific groups for receipt of unequal benefits; they are supported on the grounds that members of the minority culture face an unfair inequality in their chances to do or participate in something.

The *unfairness* of the inequality is an important part of the argument; it is typically stated that the inequality comes from historical injustice, actions of the state or of the majority group, or from the bare status of being a minority, rather than from choices made by individual members of the group.[33] Note that this does not mean assistance rights are all thought to be *temporary*, although preferential policies are very often temporary in principle (even if not in practice). The argument for language rights, for example, would only yield temporary conclusions if the minority language group were made up of a group which was expected to assimilate entirely (and, if the group is made up of immigrants, not to be replenished by newcomers). Even if members of the minority were all rightly expected to learn the majority language, supporters of language rights could argue that it is unfair to force them to speak, read, listen, or write in a second language when (for example) defending themselves in court. Permanent assistance rights are typically sought when the disadvantage is a result of the simple status of minority, rather than a result of (for example) a history of discrimination and oppression.

### Self-government

Self-government claims are the most visible of cultural rights-claims and among the most widespread; ethnic, cultural, and national groups around the world seek a political unit in which they dominate, in which they can be ruled by members of their own group. These political units might be joined with others in a confederation, or they might be cantons, states, or provinces in a federal system, or they might be fully independent. They might instead occupy a distinctive status not quite like that of other political units; this is true for the semisovereign Indian nations of the United States. Examples range from Quebec to KwaZulu, from Eritrea to Tibet; Slovakia, Scotland, Kurdistan, Catalonia, Brittany, Kashmir, the Basque lands, and the Jura canton in Switzerland do not begin to exhaust the list of places where self-government has been demanded or obtained. The normative claims are similar in all of these cases: there ought to be a government which members of the group can think of as their own. They should not be ruled by aliens. Borders ought to be drawn, and institutions arranged, to allow the group political freedom from domination by other groups.

Self-government claims are ordinarily treated as distinct from other cultural rights-claims, and the normative issues they raise are well explored elsewhere; I shall not rehearse them at length.[34] A few points should be emphasized, though. The justification of self-government claims is unique in that it requires addressing questions of territory and borders. These claims are also more about government structure, and less about what private persons may do, than most cultural rights-claims. The incidental effects on minorities-within-minorities raise distinctive issues (distinctive even from policies *designed* to affect such local minorities, external rules); the question of whether those minorities in turn have a right to self-government is a perennial one.

The link between rights of cultural practice and self-government rights are not easy to draw, though Tamir tries to ground self-government rights in an extension of the individual right to practice one's culture; and even she recognizes the need for a separate argument showing the importance of having a public sphere of one's (culture's) own. The language of individual rights is more commonly thought irrelevant to self-government claims, except to condemn them if the self-governing group is thought likely to be illiberal or undemocratic.

Where a self-government claim or right is neither about full independence (Lithuania) nor about a general system of federalism (Switzerland) but is instead about a distinctive self-governing status within a larger state (Indian tribes, Puerto Rico) the issues raised may differ somewhat from those in the other cases; on some accounts it is thought easier to justify two separate states than it is to justify differentiated citizenship within one state.

## External Rules

In some cases, it is claimed that protecting a particular culture requires restrictions on the liberty of nearby nonmembers. One of the most prominent such external rules is the ban on English-language commercial signs in Quebec; the province has other language laws including one requiring that businesses with more than fifty employees be run in French.[35] Kymlicka argues that preserving American Indian culture requires creating areas "in which non-Indian Americans have restricted mobility, property, and voting rights."[36] The restrictions on mobility and property rights take the form of "denying non-Indians the right to purchase or reside on Indian lands";[37] the proposed restriction on voting rights would (where the property and mobility restrictions are not in effect) require a three-to-ten year residency requirement before non-Indians gained the right to vote for or hold office in regional government.[38]

There are similar examples of external rules in other contexts. Quebecois as well as Indians have sought the power to limit the settlement of immigrants in their area. Where ownership or sovereignty do not already grant such control, an aboriginal veto over mining or development on tribal land would serve as an example of an external rule,[39] as would extraordinary powers to control mining or development on nearby but nontribal land. Buchanan seems to suggest that the Amish and Mennonites be given the power to keep pornography and other "cultural influences that threaten to undermine the community's values" out of the areas near their settlements.[40] In a slightly different vein, hate-speech laws come under this heading.

External rules are often argued to be an extension of the cultural community's right of self-government; the power to limit outsiders is compared with the comparable power held by states (such as the power to pick and choose among would-be immigrants). Some critics of Kymlicka suggest that external rules can *only* be justified in such a way, that is, with reference to the specific, partially independent status of the communities in question.[41] Similarly, Buchanan seeks to promote external rules as a viable alternative to secession, letting cultural minorities have statelike powers to protect their societies without the need to become independent states.

One thus might say of the right to impose external rules that it is derivative of the right to self-government, and that only a group with the latter right has the former. (This by itself, on Kymlicka's more recent account, would take the Amish out of the running.) The question of which external rules are legitimate might then be reduced to the question of what rules states themselves can legitimately impose on nonmembers. Even on this theory, some account is required of what those rules are, and whether the rules a small, culturally endangered state may impose on nonmembers are different from those which may be laid down by a large state which is not so endangered. If no such difference is stipulated, then the justification for external rules simply reduces to the justification of self-government (and of the claimed right of all states to control, for example, immigration). If there is such a difference—if an Indian tribal government may restrict non-Indians in a way that the United States could not morally restrict, say, resident aliens, or if strenuous requirements for voting are thought legitimate near Indian lands but not in Estonia—then the appeal to self-government cannot do all of the justificatory work, and one of the arguments described below will be needed.

If external rules are not simply derivative from self-government, if some groups without valid self-government claims can nonetheless impose external rules legitimately, the supporter of an external restriction must argue for the priority of a culturally related end *over the liberty of nonmembers,* which is what makes external rules distinct in the kind of justification they require. What this entails obviously depends on the status of liberty in the general political philosophy of which the cultural-rights theory forms a part. This might be done by arguing that the liberty lost is of no very high value; this is part of the approach in defending hate-speech laws. Or it might be done by stressing the importance of cultural membership to the exercise of liberty at all, and then limiting the external rules to those necessary to protect the good of cultural membership.[42] An argument about the externalities of nonmembers' actions is also likely to play an important role. This is most evident in the case of an indigenous veto on mining or development but forms a necessary part of any argument for an external rule: your exercise of your freedom has the side-effect of damaging my culture. External rules can be argued against by reversing any of these steps; liberty (or the particular liberty at stake) might be argued to have a greater importance, the cultural good might be argued to have a lesser (moral) importance, or the existence or magnitude of the externalities might be disputed (thus denying the necessity of the external rule for the protection of the culture).[43]

### *Recognition/Enforcement*

It is fairly common for cultural communities to seek to give their traditional law a status in the law of the land, to seek to have their members bound by the traditional law of the community rather than the general law of the wider state. Very often, these claims seek to have the general law recognize a culturally specific way of establishing certain rights which are established otherwise by the general law. A simple, and fairly innocuous, example, is the authority granted to religious officials in some states to perform legally binding marriages.[44]

An extremely wide range of issues are caught up in the question of recognition for traditional law, but among the most common are land rights, family law, and criminal law. James Crawford notes that the doctrine that Australian Aborigines (whether aware of it or not) were subject to British rather than tribal law "involved the denial of land rights and the non-recognition of traditional marriages as much as the refusal to recognize Aboriginal tribal laws as a defense to crimes defined by British law."[45]

Indigenous groups in Australia and in the United States have sought legal recognition for their criminal punishment systems, which recognition would imply both that the offender should not be punished again by the state and that the tribal punisher should not be criminally liable (for example, when the tribal punishment includes a spearing).[46] Muslims in India are governed by distinctively Islamic "personal law," including most of family law and parts of property law, though the criminal law is not religiously differentiated.[47] A British court refused such recognition to traditional Indian rules about arranged marriages.[48] In some states polygamous marriages in accordance with Muslim law are recognized and given full legal status as marriages.[49] At the base of indigenous land rights claims is the notion that the legal system of the settlers ought to recognize the property systems established according to native law, and that if a particular group owned a particular piece of land under traditional law they ought to have a valid title under settlers' law as well.[50] A recognition of a property-law system need not be only or even primarily about land ownership; other issues include hunting and passage usufruct rights over land, and fishing and other marine rights. A related question is that of intellectual property. Some Australian Aborigines have sought to have the copyright law extended to protect folklore and art which Aboriginal customary law holds may only be told or reproduced by certain persons or groups.[51]

In general, legal standing might be given to a tradition's method of performing marriages; its rules about conduct within marriages; its method of obtaining a divorce; its rules about relations between ex-husband and ex-wife; its way of defining a will, or its laws about post-mortem allocation of property; its expectations about the support of the indigent; its arbitration of civil disputes or its judgments in criminal matters; its methods of establishing property rights and its rules about use of property; its hunting and fishing rules; its evidentiary rules or procedures;[52] and so on. Arguments for doing so often refer to the cultural nonneutrality of the state's general laws; to the importance of not upsetting settled expectations and plans (involving property, inheritance, norms about marriage, and so on); and to the unfairness of holding people accountable to an unfamiliar law or, worse, leaving them accountable both to the state's law and to the traditional one (which can carry sanctions like ostracism even if it is not given legal status). Too great a disjunction between the law on one hand and real practices, expectations, or shared understandings on the other is argued to be unfair; if correct, this provides strong support for recognition/enforcement claims.[53] Additionally, the more formal and less substantive the issue is from the wider society's perspective (which may not correspond with the minority's!), the easier it seems to justify recognition. On few philosophical accounts would the words spoken at a wedding ceremony be of great significance; that is not true for the question of what rights women have in the subsequent marriage.

Crawford, citing a report of the Australian Law Reform Commission, notes a variety of drawbacks to recognition and enforcement (though he ultimately endorses many such rights-claims):

> The recognition of . . . customary law has often meant its limitation or confinement. It has also been used, on occasions, as a smokescreen to avoid consideration of issues such as autonomy, including the autonomy to change or even to abandon customary ways. The spectre is that of the exhibited Aborigine, recognized as long as recognizably "traditional."[54]

Crawford also notes fears about morally unacceptable punishments (e.g., spearing); women's rights; loss of Aboriginal control over laws and traditions; and divisive and discriminatory legal pluralism. Most arguments against recognition/enforcement claims build on one or more of these fears. It is thought the very essence of discrimination to have entirely different legal codes applying to members of different cultures. The law whose recognition is sought is often religious, typically customary and traditional in some strong sense, so women's rights—or basic human rights more generally—are thought to be endangered.

Concerns about protection of basic rights are perhaps relevant to recognition of family and criminal law in a way which they are not to the recognition of claims for land rights. Land rights claims are more often argued against on grounds of distributive justice, that is, that it would be unjust if thus-and-such a small percentage of the population owned so many thousands of square miles of land.[55] Of course, such an argument might be made opportunistically, and many who make it about land would be unwilling to look too deeply into what percentage of a country's population held what portion of its liquid assets. Yet the argument can also be made sincerely.[56]

Different justificatory problems are involved if the traditional law is to have *exclusive* jurisdiction over members, or if they can choose which legal system to use. In the former case—epitomized by the millet system in Ottoman Turkey—concerns about the basic rights of members are highlighted; if the customary law is reactionary, repressive, or discriminatory, members have no opportunity to escape or work around it.[57] Where members can choose—as in the case of the Aborigine or Indian who must consent to face tribal rather than general criminal sanctions—an inequality of treatment is created which may require justification. A member of the dominant group who commits a crime must face the dominant system's legal judgment; members of the nondominant group might make an opportunistic decision, choosing the legal system expected to be more lenient. There is the further complication that not all parties to a dispute will necessarily choose the same legal system; if Muslims can choose between Muslim family law and the general family law, one spouse might seek a divorce under the *sharia* with the other seeking divorce under the general law, creating disputes as to who will be bound by which obligations.[58] Again, the more purely formal the right claimed is, the less weight these concerns hold. If a customary marriage is recognized but considered legally identical to a civil-law marriage, if native title confers rights no different from free-hold title despite its different origins, then the ability to move between legal systems is unlikely to create problems (though these situations of partial recognition may face other difficulties, political and/or theoretical).

Arguments for recognition and enforcement claims are sometimes closely linked with arguments for self-government, and it is true enough that at least some recognition/enforcement rights are likely to go along with any move to self-government; the legal system of the new unit will probably be based in part on the traditional rules and expectations of the newly self-governing group. But it is important to note the separability of the issues. Recognition/enforcement rights-claims, for one thing, involve no necessary claim to territory, and no request to govern nonmembers. They can be made even when cultural groups are thoroughly intermixed. Furthermore, granting recognition/enforcement claims does not necessarily give members of the group any special

standing in the determination of their laws; often, it is up to
courts of the general society to decide when customary law has or
has not been followed. Indeed, since these rights-claims are precisely about gaining recognition from the general legal system
(for the group's marriages, property laws, and so on) outsiders
may be given more power over the group in a very real sense,
hardly what one expects from self-government. Even enforcement
of traditional criminal law, which might be seen as a clear case of
self-government rights, seems a great deal less like self-government if the general courts must authorize it, monitor it, and
decide on its limits. On the other hand, where a group seeking
self-government is not very traditional, or is highly differentiated
internally and has no one set of rules regarded as authoritative,
or does not differ in its traditional rules from the dominant
group, self-government may include very little by way of recogni-
tion/enforcement; it may be a simple matter of seeking to control
the language of government operations and public schooling,
and bringing the capital closer to home.[59] Self-government and
autonomy claims are about the structure of government and the
identity of the governors; recognition/enforcement claims are
about the content of the law. One faces concerns about borders,
territory, and the status of nonmembers; the other faces concerns
about the justice of the treatment of members. A general system
of recognition/enforcement of minority cultural law might resemble federalism in that it creates multiple legal orders within the
state; but accepting recognition claims does not force one down a
logical or moral road to federalism, and vice versa. The *reductio*
of recognition rights might be the millet system but it is not
secession.[60]

*Internal Rules*

Many rules and norms governing a community's members are not
elevated into law. There are expectations about how a member
will behave; one who does not behave that way is subject to the
sanction of no longer being viewed as a member by other members. This sanction may take the form of shunning, excommunica-
tion, being disowned by one's family, being expelled from an
association, and so on; ostracism of one sort or another usually

stands as the ultimate punishment for violating an internal rule. The content of the rules varies enormously; one might be excommunicated for blasphemy or disowned for marrying outside one's own cultural group. Many are at least in part religious but as the (common) rule against intermarriage shows, they need not be.[61]

On most liberal or democratic accounts, these rules would be clearly unjust if they were imposed by the state. Controversy arises over how to view them when they are enforced by informal or formal but noncoercive sanctions. A state may not reserve decision-making offices for men; may the Catholic Church? The state may not punish someone for his or her choice of spouse; does the same injunction apply to parents? The state may not deprive someone of citizenship for changing religions; but should a religious group, or a religiously centered cultural group, be allowed to deprive someone of membership for such a conversion? More generally, is ostracism or expulsion to be taken as normatively different from punishment? Are associations, families, and churches subject to the same moral constraints on their actions that states are? Obviously, one's general theoretical stance about family arrangements, freedom of association and disassociation, and religious freedom will largely determine one's response to internal rules. A theory which argues that only internally democratic associations have any claim to respect from a democratic state will likely have little patience for internal rules, as will one which sees the family as a political institution and a site of unjust oppression under majority and minority culture alike.

Liberal accounts may be more sympathetic than (for example) strong democratic or feminist ones. Kymlicka, who condemns "internal restrictions"—"where the basic civil and political liberties of group members are being restricted"[62]—goes on to say:

> Obviously, groups are free to require such actions [as church attendance or adherence to traditional gender roles] as terms of membership in private, voluntary associations. A Catholic organization can insist that its members attend church. The problem arises when a group seeks to use governmental power to restrict the liberty of members. Liberals insist that whoever exercises political power within a community respect the civil and political rights of its members, and any attempt to impose internal restrictions which violate this condition is illegitimate.[63]

The strength of this qualification is unclear, though. Kymlicka later criticizes "minority cultures [which] discriminate against girls in the provision of education, and deny women the right to vote or hold office . . . [or] limit the freedom of individual members within the group to revise traditional practices," and says that "[t]hese sorts of internal restrictions cannot be justified or defended within a liberal conception of minority rights."[64] Does this mean that the right of Catholicism or Orthodox Judaism to keep women out of (some) religious offices cannot be justified or defended? That when the Amish and Mennonites limit the freedom of members to revise traditional practices (and still remain members) that they are committing rights-violations? Such would seem to be the case, based on Kymlicka's discussion of the Hutterites, a communal religious group which expelled members for apostasy and refused to divide up their communal assets in order to give a share to the ex-members. This, Kymlicka thinks, is a denial of religious freedom for it imposes a high cost on abandoning one's religion at will.[65] This high cost is characteristic of internal rules; the child disowned for intermarriage or for abandoning the faith is in a similar position to the ex-Hutterites. Similarly, we are told that liberalism "precludes a religious minority from prohibiting apostasy and proselytization."[66] If such rules constitute abridgments of the freedom to marry or freedom of conscience, then internal rules stand condemned as a class.[67]

Kukathas, on the other hand, clearly makes full use of the idea of freedom of association.[68] Indeed, he carries it beyond the range of internal rules as described here, defending the right of the Pueblo *state* to ostracize those who abandon their tribal religion. My suggestion is that, on their own terms, both Kymlicka and Kukathas have made a category mistake. Kymlicka sees internal rules as rights-violations where, based on his argument, he ought to see only associational freedom. Kukathas sees what is really a state as merely a voluntary association entitled to enact internal rules. I will return to this point in part 3.

Internal rules regarding children or childrearing may be subject to particular normative dispute, as children may not be capable of choosing to leave the group if the rule is too onerous. Rules requiring cliterodectomies or other forms of female genital mutilation stand as the obvious example.

*Representation*

In order to secure protection of their interests or rights, in order to prevent discrimination or ensure certain privileges, in order to have a say in the actions of the state, ethnic minorities often seek some form of guaranteed representation in the state's decision-making bodies, especially but not only legislatures. The mechanisms for this vary. Sometimes it takes the form of a straightforward quota; in Zimbabwe's first decade of black rule, 20 percent of parliamentary seats were reserved for whites, and three out of the nine seats on Canada's Supreme Court are reserved for Quebec. Sometimes the number of seats reserved varies with the number of people choosing to vote on the reserved electoral roll rather than the general one; Maori representation in the New Zealand parliament has some of this flexibility. An effort might be made to create "majority-minority" single-member legislative districts; this has long been the approach used in the United States to increase black representation in Congress (though its days seem to be numbered). In party-list systems, parties might have formal or informal commitments to have a certain portion of their candidates come from particular groups. Proportional representation, perhaps with a formula weighted towards smaller parties, might be adopted with the intention of letting the various parts of a plural society be represented; cumulative voting might be adopted to allow minorities to concentrate their votes.

Levine observes that "the issue central to proposals for according blacks (and perhaps other disempowered groups) special electoral rights is not quite the same as in affirmative action or 'reverse discrimination' debates. There the crucial consideration is justice. In evaluating claims for group rights to electoral power, the principal concern is democracy."[69] To put it another way, the justice and effectiveness of majoritarian democracy are called into question when its assumption of shifting and alternating majorities is violated. Each group, it is argued, should *sometimes* be in the winning coalition; and ethnic minorities often find themselves permanently locked out from decisionmaking.[70] This is thought unfair according to democratic theory's own terms, and likely to produce either ethnic conflict or oppression.

Other arguments for representation are possible. Kukathas argues that

> there may sometimes be good reason to design political institutions to take into account the ethnic or cultural composition of the society. Yet there is no reason to see this as inconsistent with liberal theory, which, at least since Montesquieu, has recognized the importance of the [sic] institutions conforming to the nature of the social order.[71]

But these are, on Kukathas's view, questions of institutional design, that is, how to design those institutions which will most effectively protect individual rights; "group rights play no part in the justification of the mechanisms that uphold the modus vivendi."[72]

Three sets of issues are involved in most arguments for representation, issues easily blurred but important to separate. One is the presence of members of the minority group; one is the chance for members of the minority group to choose representatives; and one is protection of minority group interests. These need to be argued for (or against) separately, and they imply different kinds of arrangements.

When parties in a party-list system set aside a certain number of their seats for members of a group, the group will have *members* in the legislature but not necessarily chosen *representatives*. Here the focus is on the identity of the legislators rather than the identity of the electors. The same is true if a number of seats are set aside for minority group members, but everyone votes to decide who will occupy those seats. This is a kind of affirmative action for legislators and might even be best understood as an assistance right rather than a representation right.[73] To the extent that such a system builds on the arguments for representation, it does so by assuming that *any* members of the minority group will represent the interests of that group.[74] To a large degree, though, such a system must be understood as overcoming the burdens faced by would-be legislators (e.g., a tradition of drawing candidates from professions or regions dominated by the majority). It is subject to the normal arguments (pro and con) of the affirmative action debate.

In other cases, the concern is less the disadvantage faced by members of the minority who wish to hold legislative seats than on the disadvantage faced by the minority in electing its own representatives. That is, the focus is on the identity of the electors rather than on the identity of the officials; examples include the Maori voting roll; the pre-coup Fijian constitution with voting rolls for Fijians, Indians, and others (mainly British);[75] and racially gerrymandered districts. Iris Marion Young argues that "a democratic public should provide mechanisms for the effective recognition and representation of the distinct voices and perspectives of those of its *constituent groups* that are oppressed or disadvantaged."[76]

Finally, one might worry that even with representatives of a minority group in place—even if they occupy a disproportionate number of seats—they could simply be outvoted time after time. Mechanisms to offset this danger are analyzed by the consociational school and include formal or informal requirements to have grand coalition governments; minority vetoes; Switzerland's seven-person executive council and rotating presidency; pre—civil-war Lebanon's reservation of the most important government positions according to cultural/religious status; Belgium's requirement that linguistic legislation be approved by a majority of parliamentarians from each linguistic group; and so on. Lani Guinier's recent work is focused on ways to solve this problem. Donald Horowitz suggests that this goal might be at odds with the two discussed above:

> [G]roup rights—or really, special group privileges [referring to guaranteed representation] . . . provide illusory security, easily pierced. Even if they continue to function, they consign minorities to minority status. Unless they offer a minority veto—in which case the urge to abolish them will grow—they ratify the exclusion of the minority from power. So, in the first respect, group rights provide too much—benefits that are disproportionate and are, on that account, unlikely to survive. And, in the second respect, group rights provide too little, for they do not aim at minority participation at the seat of power.[77]

Horowitz maintains that such representation undercuts the need to form multiethnic coalitions and thus increases the likelihood that the winning coalition will simply take no account of a minority group's interests. If this is so, then it becomes all the more important to separate out the various arguments involved in representation claims, for it may be that one must choose among them.[78]

Two complementary arguments are commonly deployed against representation rights-claims. One is that such claims falsely impute a unity of viewpoint based on ethnicity; that is, they assume that all members of the minority group share the same political ideas and interests. It is also argued that claims for representation assume clear *differences* of interest and viewpoint *among* groups. (It is sometimes further argued that this assumption is self-fulfilling, that is, that granting representation will encourage political cleavages along ethnic lines.)

Some representation schemes are also open to the charge that they require officially identifying voters on the basis of race, in the way that South Africa did under its 1983 (ostensibly) triracial constitution. Many plans for representation, though, have no such requirement. Changing an electoral system in a way that protects minorities—for example, adopting cumulative voting or proportional representation—might be done *in order* to protect ethnic minorities, but yield protection for any politically cohesive minority, acting through their parties and votes rather than through a separate voting roll.

### Symbolic Claims

Many ethnocultural disputes are over issues which do not directly affect anyone's ability to enjoy or live according to their culture, or the distribution of political power among groups. They concern such matters as the name of a polity, its flag, its coat of arms, its national anthem, its public holidays, the name by which a cultural group will be known, or the way a group's history is presented in schools and textbooks.[79] These symbolic disputes are about claims to recognition—recognition as a (or "the") founding people of the polity, recognition as a group which has made important contributions, recognition as a group which exists with a distinct and worthwhile identity.

While language-rights claims in courts, in schools, on ballot papers, and so on are typically claims of assistance rights, the demand to have a minority language be made one of a state's "official" languages (or the demand to eliminate or prevent the category of "official languages" altogether) is a symbolic one, albeit one that might have an important impact on the whole range of assistance language-claims. The one kind of claim is about the ability of persons to interact with the organs of the state; the other is about the very identity of the state. It is worth noting again that the more symbolic claim is not necessarily considered less important than the apparently more substantive one. From the majority culture's perspective, the cost associated with hiring interpreters or bilingual employees, or with printing documents in multiple languages, might be borne much more easily than a challenge to the official status of the *Staatvolk*. From the minority culture's perspective, the absence of interpreters at a particular government office might be viewed as an inconvenience, whereas the elevation of the majority tongue to official status, or the denial of that status to the minority language, might be viewed as an open declaration that some are not wanted as members of the state.

The symbolic nature of these claims is seen in pure form by the successful 1938 drive to have Rhaeto-Romansh declared a national language of Switzerland. Rhaeto-Romansh was *not* made a language of state business; German, French, and Italian remained the only languages with that role ("official" languages). Laws did not have to be translated; courts, legislative assemblies, and the army had no new requirement to operate even in part in Rhaeto-Romansh. Native speakers had the right to address courts and authorities in their own language, but they had had that right long before, as well. The constitutional amendment yielded almost no *practical* changes, but it meant that Rhaeto-Romansh speakers were recognized as one of the constituent peoples of Switzerland. This symbolic outcome was what was most desired by petitioners, who were indeed at pains to point out that they were *not* requesting that theirs be made a language of state business.[80]

The variety of symbolic claims and disputes is vast. Australia's Aborigines have argued for a clause in that country's constitution recognizing their prior presence; Quebec has demanded official recognition as a "distinct society." Both of these changes are sought in part because it is thought they would pave the way for other, more concrete cultural rights; but the recognition is sought

for its own sake as well. Many symbolic claims lack even that role
as a possible first step to more concrete policies. Aboriginal and
American Indian groups have argued against the symbolism of
Australia Day and Columbus Day celebrations. In 1994, the Australian government began referring to Macedonians as "Slav Macedonians" in order to placate Greek-Australians upset over the
recognition of Macedonia; this in turn outraged Macedonian-
Australians and led them to claim that they had a right not to be
renamed by the state.

Symbolic claims are impossible to commend or condemn as a
class, since they may well be contradictory; one group's request
for recognition as a founding people runs into another group's
desire for recognition as unique. Both sides in a dispute about a
polity's symbols make claims for recognition. Sometimes these
disputes can be compromised, as described by Claus Offe:

> On March 29, 1990, Slovak deputies of the Czechoslovak Federal
> Parliament entered a motion that the name of the state should
> from now on be hyphenated as "Czecho-Slovakia" (as it was written
> in the inter-war period) rather than Czechoslovakia. The Czech
> majority voted in favor of the compromise that the spelling pro-
> posed by the Slovaks should be used in Slovakia, but the unhyphen-
> ated version should be used in the Czech Lands and abroad. This
> decision was perceived by the Slovak public as deeply insulting, and
> the elimination of the hyphen was protested the next day at a mass
> rally in Bratislava by a crowd of 80,000 people. In this case, a
> compromise could be actually be found. On April 12 the parlia-
> ment changed the official state name to Czech *and* Slovak Federal
> Republic.[81]

It is not clear, however, what sort of general philosophical approach could give advice leading to such conclusions. There
might be disputes within political theory about whether political
recognition of cultures ought to be granted *at all*;[82] but once
there is a dispute about *which* cultures to recognize it may be that
the most the political theorist can say is "be fair, be statesmanlike,
avoid unnecessary offense." Even a theory dedicated to the view
that the only group membership which should be politically relevant is citizenship, that the state should not be in the business of
handing out recognition or status on the basis of culture, has not

necessarily provided an argument against all symbolic claims; for some such are arguments that one culture has *already* taken such status and so implicitly insults those which lack it.

### III. DISCUSSION

Gurr sorts cultural rights-claims into demands for exit, autonomy, access, and control, with various further subdivisions.[83] Exit is full secession, that is, the attempt to gain a fully independent state. There are obvious reasons to treat such secessions separately from internal self-government or federalist arrangements. I have lumped secession and internal self-government together under "self-government," because they have much in common with each other which they do not have with other cultural rights-claims, but I do not deny that they must be considered separately for a variety of purposes. This does not mean that internal self-government ought to be lumped in with other rights-claims, and this is what Gurr does. His category of "autonomy" includes rights from every category in my classification.[84] What seems to mark autonomy off as a separate category is that it includes the demands which might be made by a group which might otherwise secede, or by indigenous groups. All the demands which Gurr considers autonomy claims are anti-assimilationist; but that is the extent of what they have in common. Something of the same is true for access, "recognition and protection of [certain kinds of cultural groups'] interests within the political framework of a plural society."[85] Assistance, representation, and exemptions are all clearly included, and they lack even a common orientation towards integration or separation. What they do have in common is that they are claimed by those groups which are not candidates for secession, are not indigenous, and do not seek to gain control over other groups.[86]

Kymlicka sorts cultural rights-claims into self-government, polyethnic rights, and representation, with a crosscutting distinction between external protections and internal restrictions.

The self-government/polyethnic distinction, I think, largely matches Gurr's autonomy/access distinction. Both focus on the kind of group making the claim. Kymlicka's category of national groups includes Gurr's ethnonational and indigenous groups; Kymlicka's ethnic groups would seem to include at least Gurr's disadvantaged contenders and ethnoclasses. Both distinctions stress the separatist nature of one kind of claim and the integrationist or cooperative nature of the other.

Kymlicka wishes to emphasize that the legitimate claims of immigrant ethnic groups do not create a slippery slope to self-government while defending self-government for groups such as the Quebecois and Indian tribes. Similarly, Gurr wants to identify the clusters of claims which seem to march together in the world. This approach has its uses but also has limits, especially as a framework for normative work. It divides like rights-claims, and it lumps together claims which might be *made* together but which must be *justified* separately. Is the Native American Church's peyote exemption really more like tribal self-government than it is like the right of Jews and Catholics to ceremonial wine during Prohibition? In one sense, yes; the peyote and self-government claims are both made by Indians. This paper has tried to show that this is not the kind of similarity which is most important for normative political work, and that the affinity between the peyote and alcohol cases make it much more plausible to argue for or against them together than to separate them and argue peyote along with self-government. Similarly, recognition claims are scattered through several of Kymlicka's categories, depending on who makes them and on whether the law being recognized restricts group members. There may be good reason to grant legal recognition to the customary laws of indigenous peoples but not to the customary laws of immigrants, but I submit there is also good reason to treat that outcome as the answer to a single question, "What should be the legal status of cultural customary law?" If not, there is at least something useful in being able to identify the kinds of rights to which national minorities are entitled but ethnic groups are not without referring to categories defined as "the rights of national minorities" and "the rights of ethnic groups." In empirical work, too, clarity may be gained by being able to specify (for example) the kinds of rights-claims immigrant ethnic groups tend make without reference to a category defined as the claims made by nonnational, nonindigenous ethnic groups. Common terms for the kinds of policies at stake would allow us to *then* identify the kinds of claims which will be made (or should be recognized) for this or that kind of group.

Kymlicka's internal/external distinction seems to me insufficiently precise, as the (often-argued) case of the Pueblo exclusion of Protestants from communal resources and functions makes clear.[87] Here, what I have identified as self-government, recognition, and internal rights stack on top of one another. The Pueblo are a self-governing, semisovereign nation. They are also a cultural community bound together by custom, including religious customs which allocate common duties and benefits. Someone who converts out of the traditional religion and withdraws from religious obligations is ostracized and denied access to collective resources; this is a common form of internal rule. Abandoning religious beliefs and customs may well lead to an American Jew being excluded from functions of her former community and might even lead to ostracism on an informal basis.

American Jews, however, do not form a state. On a theory like Kymlicka's, in which exclusion from one's cultural membership is a serious harm, Pueblo converts are in danger in a way that Jewish ones are not, for nonbelieving Jews have long since adapted Jewish tradition into a different but still distinctively Jewish cultural tradition, and the Jewish apostate still has access to that cultural community. Given current institutions, though, Pueblo identity means to be a member of a tribe (a citizen of a particular kind of self-governing polity), to keep a set of customs (abide by a set of internal rules), *and* to follow customary law (recognized as the law of the polity). It is this stacking of cultural rights, this vesting of different kinds of powers in the same body, which complicates the matter. One could argue in favor of internal rules, self-government, and recognition separately and still condemn this stacking of them; but a simple differentiation into "internal" and "external" does not allow for that.

Kymlicka and Kukathas take the Pueblo as a clear example of their disagreement, but I am not sure that their arguments (as opposed to their stated opinions on this case) bear them out. Kymlicka has, it seems to me, provided an argument against internal rules *linked with* either recognition/enforcement rights or self-government; the stricter the cultural rules, the more space there must be between them and state enforcement. He has also (briefly) argued for the legitimacy of internal rules *simpliciter.*[88] Kukathas has argued for the legitimacy of internal rules, and briefly argued against internal rules linked with recognition/enforcement.[89] If I am right, then their arguments on this point have failed to meet each other; what one condemns, the other has not actually defended.[90] But this cannot be made clear without disaggregating the idea of cultural autonomy or self-government in something like the way done here.

## IV. CONCLUSION

An essay such as this is subject to criticism from two directions: that it has multiplied categories unnecessarily and that it has created categories which are too broad to be useful. Existing sorting devices—Gurr's, Kymlicka's, the individual/collective distinction—mostly seem to me to commit the second error, which I suppose means that I am most likely to have committed the first. In fact, I fear that some of my categories may be too broad as they stand, that perhaps exemptions must be disaggregated into religious and nonreligious, or that preferential policies need to be separated from other assistance claims. I have tried to note such distinctions without increasing the number of basic categories so much as to make the classification unwieldy, but such a balancing act is likely to be imperfect.

To the charge that this classification is already unwieldy or inelegant, I reply that we confront policies which are different in kind. We have little reason to think that, for example, representation, exemptions, and symbolic claims can be argued for or against as a group; their common ethnic or cultural referent is not enough to warrant treating them together. Even if one wishes to endorse every rights-claim discussed in this paper, it is not enough to argue for the importance of ethnocultural groups and the injustice or oppression faced by some such groups; that is only the first step. Subsequent steps require different kinds of arguments for different kinds of policies. The same holds true if one wants to condemn all of these claims; no single argument will do the job. Some policies require identifying individual citizens by ethnic group, but many do not. Some may be precedent for secession or balkanization, but others are not. Some infringe on members of other groups, but others need not. Some might be described as collective rights and thus shown to be incoherent on an individualist morality, but others cannot.

This essay has tried to provide a common language in which the cultural rights debate might be conducted. It has also tried to show the need for *some* such language, for some general differentiation of cultural rights-claims which might be used by theorists of different orientations, even if *this* classification cannot do the necessary work.


## NOTES

For comments and suggestions I am grateful to Shelley Clark, Amy Gutmann, Chandran Kukathas, Will Kymlicka, Roderick Long, Bill Maley, Tom Palmer, Nancy Rosenblum, Jeff Spinner-Halev, Yael Tamir, Roy Tsao, and Daryl Wiesen. Earlier versions of this essay were presented at the Political Theory Luncheon, Princeton University, October 1994; the Mellon Dissertation Workshop, Princeton University, May 1995; and the Annual Meeting of the American Political Science Association, Chicago, September 1995. I benefited from discussion at each of these sessions.

1. Yael Tamir, *Liberal Nationalism* (Princeton: Princeton University Press, 1993).

2. Darlene Johnston, "Native Rights as Collective Rights: A Question of Self-Preservation," *Canadian Journal of Law and Jurisprudence* 2 (1989): 19–34.

3. As in Ted Robert Gurr, *Minorities at Risk: A Global View of Ethnopolitical Conflict* (Washington, D.C.: United States Institute of Peace Press, 1993), and Will Kymlicka, *Multicultural Citizenship: A Liberal Theory of Minority Rights* (Oxford: Oxford University Press, 1995). These approaches are discussed in part 3.

4. To the extent that is possible I avoid terminological disputes, important as many of those are to the debate at hand. Ethnic, linguistic, and cultural groups will not be clearly differentiated (though I use the words *nation* and *national* sparingly and generally in reference to the work of others). I identify as rights-claims many proposed policies which, according to various philosophical rules on such matters, could not possibly be *rights* no matter how wise or prudent they might be. I do not

disparage terminological points, and plead only that I must use some terms in controversial ways because there are no uncontroversial words in some of these matters.

5. It has been suggested to me that this classification might also incorporate rights-claims made by or on behalf of, for example, women, the disabled, or gays and lesbians. It has also been suggested to me that if the classification does not prove able to incorporate such claims, it should be adjusted to do so, because of the links between cultural rights and assistance for other oppressed groups. For discussion of those links, see Iris Marion Young, *Justice and the Politics of Difference* (Princeton: Princeton University Press, 1990). If the classification can incorporate such claims, so much the better, but I am not in a position to say whether it can. If it cannot, I am open to the idea that a better ("better" here being equivalent to "more useful") one could. I am not, however, equipped to provide such an improvement.

6. The exemption for Indian religious use of peyote is explicitly granted in the laws of some states. The U.S. Supreme Court in *Employment Division, Department of Human Resources of Oregon vs. Smith* 494 US 872 (1990) held that the Free Exercise Clause of the First Amendment did not provide constitutional protection for the practice. The Religious Freedom Restoration Act, passed in response to *Smith,* has presumably entrenched the exemption for religious use of peyote in federal law.

7. This was granted in *Wisconsin vs. Yoder* 406 US 205 (1972); Ontario has informally granted a similar exemption. See Dennis Thompson, "Canadian Government Relations," in Donald Kraybill, ed., *The Amish and the State* (Baltimore: Johns Hopkins University Press, 1993), 239.

8. See Thompson, "Canadian Government Relations," and Thomas Meyers, "Education and Schooling," in Donald Kraybill, ed., *The Amish and the State* (Baltimore: Johns Hopkins University Press, 1993).

9. The Amish have a religious prohibition on reliance on or participation in organized insurance. The Social Security exemption was granted to self-employed Amish (a large majority) by legislation in 1965; denied to Amish working for wages by *United States vs. Lee* 455 US 252 (1982); extended to Amish employed by other Amish by federal legislation in 1988. Some states have granted analogous statutory exemptions from participation in their unemployment insurance and worker's compensation plans. See Peter Ferrara, "Social Security and Taxes," in Donald Kraybill, ed., *The Amish and the State* (Baltimore: Johns Hopkins University Press, 1993). A similar exemption from the Canadian Pension Plan was granted in 1974 to self-employed Amish, Old Order Mennonites, and Hutterites. See Thompson, "Canadian Government Relations," 239–40.

10. Some Amish objected to the emblem on the grounds of a consci-

entious objection to displaying worldly symbols and to putting bright colors on their carriages. They sought to use reflective tape and a lantern in lieu of the standard red triangle. They were refused federal protection in *Minnesota vs. Hershberger,* 110 US 1918 (1990), granted protection under the Minnesota constitution in *State vs. Hershberger (II),* 462 NW2d 393 (Minn. 1990). The federal case was decided in light of *Smith;* I am unaware of any reconsideration in light of the Religious Freedom Restoration Act.

11. See Gertrude Huntington, "Health Care," and Elizabeth Place, "Land Use," both in Donald Kraybill, ed., *The Amish and the State* (Baltimore: Johns Hopkins University Press, 1993). Other religious groups, notably including Jehovah's Witnesses and Christian Scientists, have also sought and sometimes obtained exemptions from health care regulations.

12. Their claim was denied in *Reynolds vs. United States,* 98 US 145 (1878). Muslims in some countries are allowed to have marriages involving one husband and up to four wives, the limit imposed by the Koran; but their case differs somewhat from that of the Mormons. In the United States, polygamy is a criminal offense; what was sought in *Reynolds* was immunity from prosecution, an exemption. Where it is more a question of the difference between unrecognized relationships and officially state-endorsed or privileged ones, because of the general law on marriages, I would argue that what has been sought or granted is a recognition right which requires more arguments to support than would a simple exemption from prosecution. I will discuss the claimed right to live under the family law of one's own religion below under "recognition and enforcement"; for now it should only be noted that an exemption from the criminal law against polygamy requires less, or perhaps different, justification than a request for full legal privileges for plural marriages.

13. The claim was denied in *Goldman vs. Weinberger* 475 US 503 (1986). Kymlicka discusses these cases at some length. He stresses their integrative capacity (because joining the Air Force or the Royal Canadian Mounted Police are acts of belonging rather than of separation), but one could easily find closely analogous examples which lacked the symbolism of belonging; consider dress codes in prisons. Nor are all of Kymlicka's examples of polyethnic exemptions so obviously integrative; exemptions from motorcycle helmet laws or Sunday closing laws don't seem analogous in this respect to the Sikh trying to join the Mounties. Kymlicka, *Multicultural Citizenship,* 114–15. See also the discussion of *Goldman* in Tamir, *Liberal Nationalism,* 38–40.

14. See Françoise Gaspard and Farhad Khorokhavar, *Le foulard et la République* (Paris: Éditions La Découverte, 1995), 163–212.

15. Kymlicka, *Multicultural Citizenship,* 108–15, offers an "equality argument" which uses reasoning like this.

16. Joseph Raz, *The Morality of Freedom* (Oxford: Oxford University Press, 1986), 252.

17. Michael Sandel, unpublished paper cited in Tamir, *Liberal Nationalism,* 38–39.

18. For instance, Arend Lijphart cites as an advantage of his proposed consociational scheme for South Africa—and Donald Horowitz agrees that it is an advantage—that it does not require such identification of individuals. South Africans, of course, have a more acute awareness than most of the dangers of identifying persons in this way. It will become clear that *not* all cultural rights-claims require this sort of identification. See discussion in Donald Horowitz, *A Democratic South Africa? Constitutional Engineering in a Divided Society* (Berkeley: University of California Press, 1991).

19. See Jan Narveson, "Collective Rights?" *Canadian Journal of Law and Jurisprudence* 4 (1991): 329–45 and Michael Hartney, "Some Confusions concerning Collective Rights," *Canadian Journal of Law and Jurisprudence* 4 (1991): 293–314, for the claim that groups cannot bear rights.

20. Some liberals who endorse exemption rights generally, including Kymlicka, reject *Wisconsin vs. Yoder* because of the additional issues raised when an exemption is sought from a law which seeks to protect children. On the other hand, Kukathas both endorses *Yoder* and suggests a similar exemption for Roma (gypsies) in Britain. Chandran Kukathas, "Are There Any Cultural Rights?" *Political Theory* 20 (1992): 105–39 at 126.

21. The language of "minorities" and "majorities," always problematic in the cultural rights debate, becomes especially so when dealing with assistance rights. In a given society different groups may feel excluded from different kinds of activities, and numbers may not be the determining factor. Malaysia has practiced various preferential policies for ethnic Malays vis-à-vis ethnic Chinese, a minority which is predominant in business and education. South Africa is of course beginning affirmative action policies for its black majority. For a similar reason, "dominant" and "nondominant" are unsatisfactory; often a group which is predominant is business is disadvantaged in politics (this has been true of Indian, Chinese, and Jewish populations around the world). On the other hand, "dominant/nondominant in the relevant sphere" and "unfairly disadvantaged/unfairly advantaged in the relevant sphere" are unwieldy, and I shall continue to use the imprecise language of majorities and minorities.

22. See Sergij Vilfan, "Introduction," and Lode Wils, "Belgium on the Path to Equal Language Rights up to 1939," in Vilfan et al., eds., *Ethnic*

*Groups and Language Rights,* Comparative Studies on Governments and Non-Dominant Ethnic Groups in Europe, 1850–1940, vol. 3 (New York: New York University Press, European Science Foundation, 1993) on the wide variety of ways in which minority-language speakers can seek to be accommodated in courts and administrative procedures. Issues include not only the right to speak one's own language in court but the language of the overall proceedings; not only the right to speak to a civil servant in one's own language but the right to have correspondence from the state in that language; not only the right to be a member of the civil service but to the language in which intracivil service communication is to be conducted. Vilfan and Wils do not address issues past 1940, but that range has only multiplied since then. The rights granted to citizens under "sunshine laws" or freedom of information laws make the language of intracivil service correspondence all the more important, and raise the question of whether minority-language speakers should be given government-funded translation of the documents they seek. Similarly, the idea of correspondence from administrators takes on new significance when it expands from answers to individual letters to the instructions for calculation of the income tax mailed to all Americans in December of each year.

23. Bruno de Witte, "Conclusion: A Legal Perspective," in Vilfan et al., eds., *Ethnic Groups and Language Rights,* Comparative Studies on Governments and Non-Dominant Ethnic Groups in Europe, 1850–1940, vol. 3 (New York: New York University Press, European Science Foundation, 1993), 303.

24. Kymlicka, *Multicultural Citizenship,* 31, 123, 223–24 n. 15.

25. Tamir, *Liberal Nationalism,* 54–55.

26. On the centrality of the question of education to ethnic and nationalist disputes worldwide, see Ernest Gellner, *Nations and Nationalism* (Oxford: Basil Blackwell, 1983); Janusz Tomiak and Andreas Kazarnias, "Introduction,"and Knut Eriksen et al., "Governments and the Education of Non-Dominant Ethnic Groups in Comparative Perspective," in Tomiak et al., eds., *Schooling, Educational Policy, and Ethnic Identity,* Comparative Studies on Governments and Non-Dominant Ethnic Groups in Europe, 1850–1940, vol. 1 (New York: New York University Press, European Science Foundation, 1991).

27. In addition to the preferential policies described in this paragraph, I think one of the available methods of group representation in legislatures actually amounts to a preferential policy rather than a genuine representation right. I return to this point in my discussion of representation below.

28. See Donald Horowitz, *Ethnic Groups in Conflict* (Berkeley: Univer-

sity of California Press, 1985), 653–80. Preferential treatment in land purchases are not analogous to indigenous land rights; the latter are discussed under "recognition/enforcement." Under preferential policies there is no need to establish any traditional ownership or any past dispossession, and no importance attached to particular pieces of land. Kymlicka, I should note, thinks that either indigenous land rights claims really are assistance claims of a sort, or that they should be. *Multicultural Citizenship*, 219–21 n. 5

29. Of course, a crucial part of the defense of such programs is showing that the stipulated disadvantage is real and that the policy is not simply a way for a politically powerful group to extend its influence into other spheres.

30. Young, *Justice and the Politics of Difference*, 192–225.

31. See, for example, Narveson, "Collective Rights," 344–45, Kymlicka, *Multicultural Citizenship*, 108–15, and Tamir, *Liberal Nationalism*, 145–50, arguing for (among other cultural rights) assistance rights, maintain that arguments for a separation of culture and state are untenable.

32. The provision of bilingual education, or state support for minority-cultural schools, are an important exception to this; this may suggest that such policies are better understood as part of another category, though it is unclear which that would be. If the cultural community can tax its own members and provide its own schools, a form of self-government would seem to exist. Perhaps bilingual education provided by the state should be understood as an assistance claim while schools provided or assisted by the state which intend to keep students in the minority culture (for instance, through minority monolingual education) should be understood as part of self-government; but that, too, would seem strange as a description of a policy which provided tax deductions for contributions to private minority-language schools or which provided vouchers to attend them.

33. On the fairness or unfairness of various advantages and disadvantages accruing to cultural and ethnic groups, see Robert Simon, "Pluralism and Equality: The Status of Minority Values in a Democracy," and Joseph Carens, "Difference and Domination: Reflections on the Relations between Pluralism and Equality," in Chapman and Wertheimer, eds., *NOMOS XXXII: Majorities and Minorities* (New York: New York University Press, 1990).

34. Secessionist claims for full independence are dealt with most thoroughly in Allen Buchanan, *Secession: The Legitimacy of Political Divorce* (Boulder, Colo.: Westview Press, 1991), but also in Harry Beran, "A Liberal Theory of Secession," *Political Studies* 32 (1984): 21–31; Anthony Birch, "Another Liberal Theory of Secession," *Political Studies* 32 (1984):

596–602; Avishai Margalit and Joseph Raz, "National Self-Determination," *Journal of Philosophy* 87 (1990): 439–61; and Cass Sunstein, "Constitutionalism and Secession," *University of Chicago Law Review* 58 (1991): 633–70. See also Crawford Young, *The Politics of Cultural Pluralism* (Madison: University of Wisconsin Press, 1976), 460–504. Federalism, confederalism, and regional autonomy as specific responses to ethnic pluralism are less well explored in the normative literature, though several of those works address the matter briefly and Kymlicka, *Multicultural Citizenship,* does so at length. The comparative literature on self-government short of secession is much larger; see Horowitz, *Ethnic Groups in Conflict,* 601–28, for an overview.

35. See Charles Taylor, *Multiculturalism and the Politics of Recognition* (Princeton: Princeton University Press, 1993), 52–55. The overruled Toubon law in France might have provided a similar example, and would have illustrated that in a global society it is not only minorities within a state which can feel culturally endangered. On the other hand, unlike in Quebec, the English threat (if that's what it is) in France comes not primarily from anglophones but from francophones adopting anglicisms, and the Toubon law was seen as focused on members rather than nonmembers, so it is probably disanalogous to the Quebec case and better understood outside the framework of external rules.

36. Will Kymlicka, *Liberalism, Community, and Culture* (Oxford: Oxford University Press, 1989), 136.

37. Kymlicka, *Liberalism, Community, and Culture,* 146. The inalienability of native land (or, more precisely, its alienability only to the Crown/Commonwealth/federation/federal government) has been a recurrent rule in the Anglo-settler colonies, and, as Kymlicka notes, it is both a restriction on nonmembers and a restriction on members. The degree to which it is one or the other depends in part on whether the rule is that native lands cannot be bought and sold *at all* or that they cannot be sold to or bought by *non-indigenes.* There is also variation in whether the rule simply prevents individual sales or whether even the tribe as a whole is incapable of selling even part of its land, again, with slightly different implications.

38. Kymlicka, *Liberalism, Community, and Culture,* 147.

39. This is the state of the law in Australia. Aborigines there do not have self-government or sovereignty; and ordinary landowners in Australia do not have either ownership of subsurface minerals or the right to refuse access to mining interests. Legislation recognizing Aboriginal land rights (in the Northern Territory in 1976, nationwide in 1993) granted special rights and powers to native titleholders to control or veto mining; this is an external rule, a limitation on the rights miners would have

elsewhere in Australia. If all landowners had such rights, no special provision for Aborigines would be needed; that is, the ordinary common-law rule governing relations between landowner and miner need not be thought of as a cultural right. I argue against the Australian situation, in favor of the common-law rule granting all landowners mineral ownership and veto rights. Jacob Levy, "Reconciliation and Resources: Mineral Rights and Aboriginal Land Rights as Property Rights," *Policy* 10:1 (1994): 11–15; and "The Value of Property Rights: Rejoinder to Brennan and Ewing," *Policy* 10:2 (1994): 44–46.

40. Buchanan, *Secession*, 59. It is worth noting that the Amish themselves have never sought such a power; to do so would violate their own norms. They believe that Christians should have nothing to do with the violence and the power of the state, which is "worldly." Indeed, they ordinarily refuse to act as plaintiffs in court; seeking to control and direct the power of the criminal law would be unthinkable. Buchanan refers to the "government of a territorially concentrated religious community such as the Amish or Mennonites" as analogous to Indian tribal governments, which is ambiguous at best and mistaken at worst; the relevant religious authorities would be extremely resistant to seeing themselves as force-wielding governments.

41. John Tomasi, "Kymlicka, Liberalism, and Respect for Aboriginal Cultures," *Ethics* 105 (1995); John Danley, "Liberalism, Aboriginal Rights and Cultural Minorities," *Philosophy and Public Affairs* 20 (1991): 168–85. Kymlicka himself seems to have come around to this view; he now argues for external rules only on behalf of national minorities (all of which, on his view, have a right to self-government) and using the analogy between the powers of such groups and the powers of states.

42. This, or something close to it, was Kymlicka's original approach, and seems to still carry that part of the justification for external rules which cannot be borne by the appeal to self-government.

43. Narveson, "Collective Rights?" clearly embraces both of the first two arguments: liberty is extremely important, and the preservation of a culture, while perhaps valuable, is not morally important enough to give rise to a right. Kukathas, "Are There Any Cultural Rights?" seems to use both as well. Tamir, *Liberal Nationalism*, 38–42, stresses that, since cultural membership is partially chosen, it should not be "entirely isolated from 'the market of preferences.'" For Rawlsian liberals, identifying culture as chosen deprives it of the sort of moral status which could trump liberty claims, which is why Kymlicka, *Liberalism, Community, and Culture*, takes pains to identify a culture as a "context of choice" rather than the result of choices.

44. In other states—France and Germany, for example—the religious ceremony lacks legal standing, and must be supplemented with a civil ceremony before a secular civil official.

45. James Crawford, "Legal Pluralism and the Indigenous Peoples of Australia," in Oliver Mendelsohn and Upendra Baxi, eds., *The Rights of Subordinated Peoples* (Oxford: Oxford University Press, 1994), 181–82, footnotes omitted.

46. See K. E. Mulqueeny, "Folk-Law or Folklore: When a Law Is Not a Law. Or Is It?" in Stephenson and Ratnapala, eds., *Mabo: A Judicial Revolution* (Brisbane: University of Queensland Press, 1993).

47. See Veena Das, "Cultural Rights and the Definition of Community," in Oliver Mendelsohn and Upendra Baxi, eds., *The Rights of Subordinated Peoples* (Oxford: Oxford University Press, 1994); also Rajeev Dhavan, "Religious Freedom in India," *American Journal of Comparative Law* 35 (1987): 209–54, at 241–50.

48. Kukathas, "Are There Any Cultural Rights?" 133.

49. As noted above at note 12, this differs from a simple exemption from criminal laws against bigamy, and one could easily support the exemption claim while opposing the recognition claim. Granting the recognition claim has implications for the whole array of legal privileges which adhere to marriage in most states. Those privileges (among many others they include preferential tax treatment, extension of health insurance, default rules about power of attorney, child custody, and property allocation after a death *in testate*) are often shaped and supported on grounds of public-policy rather than justice. Those public-policy arguments, formulated in the context of two-person marriages, might or might not make any sense in the context of plural marriages. Of course, a claim in justice might then be made saying that unequal treatment of different family arrangements was unjustified; but this is a different kind of argument from that saying that one ought to be free to have religiously-but-not-legally binding plural marriages without facing criminal penalties.

50. See *Mabo vs. Queensland (no. 2)* (Austr. 1992) 175 CLR 1, which put this question in stark form: Could Australian law recognize and incorporate the property law of the Mer people of the Torres Strait Islands, or must it be bound by the doctrine of *terra nullius* which held Australia to be legally unowned? Many land rights cases in Canada and the United States are one step removed from this question, and seek to undo seizures of land which were either illegal according to *settler* law or which violated treaties which recognized native title; but the root issue is the same, although the British in North America recognized native own-

ership much earlier than they did in Australia. Still, many Indian nations in North America did not sign treaties with the settler governments, and their land-rights claims are straightforward recognition claims. Tully explicitly argues for indigenous land rights as part of an argument for the recognition of indigenous legal systems. James Tully, "Aboriginal Property and Western Theory: Recovering a Middle Ground," *Social Philosophy and Policy* 11 (1994): 153–80. Shepherd provides an interesting discussion of the Han Chinese settlement of Taiwan and conflicts over the recognition of the land tenure system of the island's indigenous inhabitants; *module* the difference between English and Chinese law, the history and issues are remarkably like those in North America, Australia, and New Zealand. John Shepherd, *Statecraft and Political Economy on the Taiwan Frontier 1600–1800* (Stanford: Stanford University Press, 1993), 241–56 and *passim*. Where land rights claims are based on the illegality of the seizures under instruments of the dominant legal system (the Proclamation of 1763, Indian treaties) it seems to me that no special issues related to culture or ethnicity are raised. Any problems raised are problems in the theory of restitution, as is also the case in the current return of seized property to dispossessed blacks in South Africa and dispossessed Asians in Uganda.

51. See Kamal Puri, "Copyright Protection for Australian Aborigines in the Light of *Mabo,*" in Stephenson and Ratnapala, eds., *Mabo: A Judicial Revolution* (Brisbane: University of Queensland Press, 1993). If there should be intellectual property in such works, standard copyright law is poorly suited to accommodate it because of, *inter alia,* its restriction to work with one or a small and identifiable group of authors and its exclusion of purely oral works. These rules have good reasons, and are thought important to preserving freedom of speech and intellectual and artistic freedom; but, Puri argues, those reasons and those categories reflect particular understandings about what it means to be the creator of a work of art, understandings not shared by Aboriginal customs.

52. As, for example, when testimony which takes the form "I know this is my land because my father told me so, and he told me that his father told him, and . . ." is accepted from members of a group which relies on oral tradition rather than written evidence, instead of being rejected as hearsay. This is true in Canada, Australia, New Zealand, Papua New Guinea, and several of the formerly British states in Africa; I do not know the state of the law on this matter in the United States. See B. A. Keon-Cohen, "Some Problems of Proof: The Admissibility of Traditional Evidence," in Stephenson and Ratnapala, eds., *Mabo: A Judicial Revolution* (Brisbane: University of Queensland Press, 1993). See also *Baker Lake vs. Minister of Indian Affairs* (1979 Canada) 107 DLR (3rd) 513; *Simon vs. R*

(1985 Canada) 24 DLR (4th) 390; *Milirrpum vs. Nabalco* (1971 Australia) 17 FLR 141.

53. This argument is obviously compatible with certain communitarian visions (for example, Walzer's theories about the importance of shared understandings). The argument is not limited to communitarian philosophies, though. In another context, Tamir warns that a government and a legal code disconnected from the culture of the ruled creates the risk of "alienation and irrelevance," "the enfeeblement of formal law and the marginalisation of government activities." Tamir, *Liberal Nationalism,* 149.

54. Crawford, "Legal Pluralism," 179.

55. They are also sometimes argued against on the grounds that recognition raises the question of what other aspects of the minority legal system must be incorporated into the dominant legal system; as Crawford notes in the passage quoted above, the legal rationale for excluding Aboriginal criminal law from Australian law was the same doctrine as that used to exclude recognition of Aboriginal land rights. Tully's argument would also seem to suggest that once land rights are conceded there is a live question about the legal status of other parts of minority customary law.

56. As it is in Kymlicka, *Multicultural Citizenship,* 219–21, and Tamir, *Liberal Nationalism,* 40–41. Kymlicka, I think, understates how much a distributive egalitarianism argues against land-rights claims and how much real land-rights claims are based on recognition rather than distribution. The question ranges beyond the current paper but I pursue it in a separate unpublished paper on the implications of land-rights claims.

57. The concern for the protection of the basic rights of members animates Kukathas's rejection of exclusive recognition/enforcement of customary family or civil codes as well as Kymlicka's. Kukathas, "Are There Any Cultural Rights?" 128–29 and 133; Kymlicka, *Multicultural Citizenship,* 39–42. On neither account, I think, is it clear whether recognition without exclusive jurisdiction is being condemned as well.

58. On the other hand, these disputes might not be any more complicated than those arising because of competing jurisdictions in a federal system.

59. The secession of the Czech Republic and Slovakia from each other would seem a polar case. So far as I know, no claim was made that the Czechs were disrupting traditional Slovak law, or that independence would allow Slovaks to live according to their own traditional rules.

60. Special treatment is probably required for nonterritorial, noncustomary cultural self-government, sometimes called nonterritorial federalism. Bauer and Renner proposed such a system for Austria-Hungary;

Lijphart describes it in the case of the Netherlands. This resembles self-government claims in some respects, recognition claims in others. With further research into the mechanisms of such systems and their normative implications I hope to be able to say more about them; but it may simply be the case that they are importantly normatively different from standard claims in either category.

61. So far as I can tell, the old American taboo against "miscegenation" between blacks and whites differs dramatically from more common forms of the rule against intermarriage, in that it was motivated entirely by racism, a vision of superior and inferior groups, and a fear of "pollution." On the other hand, many cultural groups in plural societies are concerned about the continuation and strength of their culture across generations; intermarriage is frowned upon not so much because outsiders are dirty or inferior as because of a responsibility to make sure that the next generation grows up in the culture and a fear that mixed marriages do not provide such cultural integrity. Even if the outsiders are thought well of, they are thought unlikely parents of future members.

62. Kymlicka, *Multicultural Citizenship,* 36.

63. Ibid., 202 n. 1.

64. Ibid., 153.

65. Ibid, 161.

66. Ibid.

67. As should be clear, I find Kymlicka's arguments here puzzling, not because they condemn internal rules but because of the way in which that condemnation occurs. I'm not sure what it *means* to tell a religious group that it cannot prohibit apostasy. Must the person who openly rejects the faith continue to be welcomed as a member of it? It is simple enough to say that the *state* cannot prohibit apostasy, that the millet system was unjust; but Kymlicka says more than that. The rule may be that a religion cannot be so central or dominant a part of a person's life that abandoning it imposes high costs; that is clearly a rule for which one could articulate a defense, though it would require a standard for measuring the size of the costs. But it would hardly be a *liberal* standard.

68. Kukathas, "Are There Any Cultural Rights?" and Kukathas, "Cultural Rights Again: A Rejoinder to Kymlicka," *Political Theory* 20 (1992): 674–80.

69. Andrew Levine, "Electoral Power, Group Power, and Democracy," in Chapman and Wertheimer, eds., *NOMOS XXXII: Majorities and Minorities,* 215–52.

70. See Lani Guinier, *The Tyranny of the Majority: Fundamental Fairness in Representative Democracy* (New York: Free Press/Macmillan, 1994), 3–6,

41–156; Arend Lijphart, *Democracy in Plural Societies* (New Haven: Yale University Press, 1977), 25–41; Kymlicka, *Multicultural Citizenship*, 131–51.

71. Kukathas, "Are There Any Cultural Rights?" 131.

72. Ibid., 132.

73. Kymlicka makes related points; *Multicultural Citizenship*, 141–42, 148–49. He seems to consider elector-centered institutions as affirmative action, too. He is, however, using "affirmative action" to refer to policies should be seen as overcoming past disadvantage and therefore temporary. I am using "affirmative action" in the narrower sense of policies designed to speed the entry of members of certain groups into certain positions.

74. If the argument for guaranteeing seats in the legislature rested on the idea that deliberation is improved and more ideas heard when there is greater diversity among the deliberators, then this would be a democracy-based representation claim rather than one about affirmative action. Of course, often both arguments are made simultaneously. The strength of the deliberation argument depends in part on the structure of the legislature; if it is based on strict party discipline, with decisions made by party leaders rather than by caucus, the argument would be difficult to sustain.

75. See Vernon Van Dyke, "The Individual, the State, and Ethnic Communities in Political Theory," *World Politics* 29 (1977): 353.

76. Young, *Justice and the Politics of Difference*, 185; emphasis added.

77. Horowitz, *A Democratic South Africa?* 136.

78. Horowitz thus suggests, e.g., single transferable vote systems, which he thinks encourage alliances across ethnic boundaries at voting time. Consociationalists disagree, and argue for proportionality at election time and transethnic alliances at the elite level. If their argument is correct, then allowing direct minority-group representation is compatible with, indeed is a crucial part of, ensuring protection for minority group interests.

79. See Horowitz, *Ethnic Groups in Conflict*, 127, for examples in addition to those discussed below.

80. Bernard Cathamos, "Rhaeto-Romansh in Switzerland up to 1940," in Vilfan et al., eds., *Ethnic Groups and Language Rights*, Comparative Studies on Governments and Non-Dominant Ethnic Groups in Europe, 1850–1940, vol. 3 (New York: New York University Press, European Science Foundation, 1993), 98–105.

81. Claus Offe, *Ethnic Politics in European Transitions*, Papers on East European Constitution Building no. 1 (Bremen: Center for European Law and Policy, 1993), 7 n. 5.

82. Taylor, *Multiculturalism*, argues for the importance of such recog-

nition. I think Taylor's essay and the comments on it are directed more towards what I identify as symbolic claims than towards other cultural rights-claims.

83. Gurr, *Minorities at Risk,* 294–312.

84. Ibid., 299.

85. Ibid., 306.

86. Gurr's "control" lies, I think, outside the framework of this paper; it is defined as the aim to establish or maintain hegemony. Groups seeking control seek to preserve or obtain power over other groups, unequal economic privilege, a state which imposes a particular religious view, and so on; the category is constructed so as to only include claims which are clearly illegitimate on almost any general normative account. Gurr seeks to describe the possible aims of real groups in the world, not just those aims which raise interesting moral issues; hence the difference.

87. See, among others, Frances Svensson, "Liberal Democracy and Group Rights: The Legacy of Individualism and Its Impact on American Indian Tribes," *Political Studies* 27 (1979): 421–39; Kymlicka, *Liberalism, Community, and Culture,* 195–99, and *Multicultural Citizenship,* 152–70; Kukathas, "Are There Any Cultural Rights?" 121–23, and "Cultural Rights Again."

88. Kymlicka, *Multicultural Citizenship,* 202 n. 1.

89. On the second point, see Kukathas, "Are There Any Cultural Rights?" 133. As was noted above under "Internal Rules," this means I think Kukathas got the particular case of the Pueblo wrong on his own terms; he has argued for the legitimacy of internal rules but has not met the additional hurdle of linking internal rules with self-government to allow for a state-imposed religion. That is, he has seen an association where there is really a state.

90. The same is not true of their disagreement about external rules and assistance claims.

# PART II

# THE IDEA
# OF TOLERATION

# 3

# CULTURAL TOLERATION

## CHANDRAN KUKATHAS

Toleration an attack upon Christianity! What, then! are we come
to this pass, to suppose that nothing can support Christianity but
the principles of persecution? Is that, then, the idea of establishment? Is it, then, the idea of Christianity itself, that it ought to have
establishments, that it ought to have laws against Dissenters, but
the breach of which laws is to be connived at? What a picture of
toleration! . . . I am persuaded that toleration, so far from being an
attack on Christianity, becomes the best and surest support that
possibly can be given to it. The Christian religion itself arose without establishment,—it arose even without toleration; and whilst its
own principles were not tolerated, it conquered all the powers of
the world. The moment it began to depart from these principles, it
converted the establishment into tyranny; it subverted its foundations from that very hour.

—Edmund Burke, *Speech on the Relief of Protestant Dissenters*

## I. Introduction

Many of us think that we should be tolerant of cultures or ways of
life other than our own, even—or perhaps, especially—when we
find them settled in our midst. Some would go further to argue
that these cultures are owed more than mere toleration: they are
owed a form of "recognition" which concedes that their ways are
deserving of at least a "presumption of equal worth."[1] Yet while
this may all be very well as an attitude of mind, there is a practical
problem which remains: how should we respond to cultural practices which we regard as intolerable? After all, we must surely not
let cultural tolerance become, as Sebastian Poulter puts it, "a
cloak for oppression and injustice."[2] So how do we deal with

69

cultural variety; or, to put the question a little differently, what forms should cultural tolerance take, and what are the limits of cultural tolerance?

The scope of the question might be made clearer by noting at the outset, at least in general terms, what could count as intolerable practices. Some such practices would include group or community customs which restrict the opportunities of women (say, by denying them the right to hold property; or limiting their access to education, or "forcing" them into unequal marriages). Another kind of practice would include customs of childrearing which restrict the opportunities of the child to prepare for life outside the original community. A third example would be practices which reject conventional medical treatments (such as blood transfusions), even when the lives of children are at risk. A fourth example would be practices which mandate operations (performed with or without the fully informed consent of the subject) which are physically harmful: clitoridectomy and ritual scarring are two such operations. A fifth example would be practices which exposed members of the community to exceptionally high risks: some initiation rites might come into this category. A sixth example would be practices which involve the use or treatment of animals—in sport, in science, or for food—in ways which could be regarded as cruel or distasteful. A final example would be practices of punishment which might be regarded as cruel and inhumane, or as disproportionately severe for the offences in question.

In all of these cases, the practices in question are objected to not because they directly harm the interests of the wider community but because they are regarded as morally unacceptable. The reasons why they are so regarded vary, but to the extent that harm is a consideration, it is the harm to the members of the relevant group or community that is at issue. More generally, the concern is with "injustice" within the group. There is, of course, another way of looking at the matter, which is to consider it indirectly harmful to the wider society to ignore injustices within groups, since tolerating such "injustices" serves to undermine the wider community's own principles of justice. But a distinction can nonetheless be drawn between practices which are objectionable because they are morally intolerable in themselves or because they harm individuals in the groups which carry them out, and practices which are objectionable because they harm the wider society more directly.[3]

The issue considered in this essay is how we deal with practices which do not directly harm the wider society but which nonetheless seem intolerable. Yet while the problem of intolerable practices is the immediate concern of this essay, it is not the only concern. In touching upon the topic of toleration it is not possible to avoid more fundamental questions of political theory. And indeed, many approaches to issues of toleration see no need for separate principles of toleration, arguing that the moral principles which circumscribe political relations within a society themselves supply the necessary guidance to the problem of toleration. Among liberal theories, for example, it has been argued by some that the scope of toleration is to be settled by looking at the fundamental ideas of the good that underlie liberal principles, while others have argued that an appropriate understanding of neutrality will supply the answers to the problem. In both cases, the suggestion is that we begin by settling the fundamental question of the terms of political association and then ask what can justifiably be tolerated. We establish the limits of tolerance in principle and then whether or not particular practices are consistent with them, and thus determine whether or not to intervene in traditional societies or minority groups by providing state subsidies, disincentives, or penalties for particular practices.

I want to suggest, however, that the problem should be approached differently—in a way which does not presuppose the existence or the authority of the state. That is to say, I want to begin without presuming that it is already established that there is a "we" who are faced with the problem of determining how far to tolerate particular groups in "our" midst. This is not to say that there is no such problem. That is, indeed, the problem with which I opened this discussion. It is, rather, to emphasize that how one approaches the problem has a significant bearing on the conclusions reached. And since some of the conclusions I want to reach are about the nature of the state, I do not want to begin by assuming that certain things about it—in particular, about its authority—are settled or uncontroversial.

This chapter begins in section 2 by examining a number of

modern liberal answers to the question of toleration, looking at particular arguments advanced by John Rawls, Will Kymlicka, and Deborah Fitzmaurice. In section 3, I argue that these theories are not tolerant enough. From here I attempt to develop a different view of how public or general moral standards should be arrived at. Finally, in section 4, I consider and try to respond to objections to this way of addressing questions of injustice within minority communities. The chapter concludes with an assessment of its implications for the nature of political society.

## II. SOME CONTEMPORARY LIBERAL VIEWS OF TOLERATION

Let us begin by looking at how some liberal theories treat the question of toleration. This is an appropriate starting point because these liberal theories tend to advocate toleration and, even when arguing against its extension, generally adopt a presumption in its favor.

The most comprehensive contemporary philosophical statement of liberal principles is to be found in the work of John Rawls. Having begun with the assertion that justice is the first virtue of social institutions, Rawls tried to show—in *A Theory of Justice*—that a just society is best understood as one in which liberty and equality were honored. In such a society, liberty could be violated only for the sake of liberty, and inequalities had to be justified before the worst-off members of society. Justification for the two principles, however, had to proceed without resort to claims that one way of life or one particular conception of the good life was superior to others. This, in effect, mandated institutions which accommodated many different ways of life or forms of "social union," all of them sheltered under the umbrella of the two principles of justice. The plausibility of the two principles as principles of justice rests on the claim that they are the principles we would converge upon if asked to choose in a setting (or original position) in which our tendency to partiality was suitably constrained.

The case for toleration, in this political philosophy, is based solely on the principles of justice. "Moral and religious freedom follows from the principle of equal liberty; and assuming the priority of this principle, the only ground for denying the equal liberties is to avoid an even greater injustice, an even greater loss of liberty."[4] Breaches of liberty are only allowable if it could be shown, by generally accepted forms of argument, that there is a case for intervention in the name of public order. Liberty, Rawls goes on to explain, "is governed by the necessary conditions for liberty itself."[5] And an implication of this, he argues, is that many grounds of intolerance accepted in past ages are mistaken. Thus, Aquinas's justification of the death penalty for heretics (on the grounds that corruption of the faith, which is the life of the soul, was far worse a crime than the capital offence of counterfeiting money) is unacceptable because its premises "cannot be estab-lished by modes of reasoning commonly recognized."[6]

Arguments for limited toleration are similarly ruled out. For example, Rousseau's view that we cannot tolerate sects which claim that there is no salvation outside the church (because mem-bers of such sects will not be able to live peacefully with those they see as damned) is unacceptable because Rousseau's conjecture is not borne out by experience. Justice, according to Rawls, requires that claims about the disturbance to public order and to liberty be "established by common experience."[7]

The importance of justice in Rawls's approach to toleration cannot be emphasized too strongly. He rejects claims for tolera-tion which suggest, for example, that the law must always respect the dictates of conscience. On the contrary, "the legal order must regulate men's pursuit of their religious interests so as to realize the principle of equal liberty."[8] Whether and how far any practice will be tolerated must always be determined, ultimately, by its compatibility with the conception of justice: thus a "theory of justice must work out from its own point of view how to treat those who dissent from it."[9] What is also made clear in this context is the importance of preserving or perpetuating the order in which the true principles of justice prevail; toleration of differing ways is permissible only to the extent that it serves this end. Thus Rawls writes:

> The aim of a well-ordered society, or one in a state of near justice, is to preserve and strengthen the institutions of justice. If a religion is denied its full expression, it is presumably because it is in viola-

tion of the equal liberties of others. In general, the degree of tolerance accorded opposing moral conceptions depends upon the extent to which they can be allowed an equal place within a just system of liberty.[10]

What is important about this argument is that toleration is upheld or endorsed on the basis of another substantive foundational moral principle—justice—which is taken to form the common standpoint of the society as a whole. There is, of course, a deeper commitment involved here, since the conception of justice in question is one which upholds *autonomy* as the fundamental value.[11] But what this means is that when the issue of toleration of any practice arises, the question that has to be asked is whether or not toleration is consistent with the commitment to autonomy which is at the heart of society's common moral standpoint.

It is in recognition of this that Rawls has, in his more recent writings, sought to modify or reinterpret his theory. Fearing that a conception of justice with a commitment to a substantive value like autonomy could not gain the support of some groups in society, he presents his principles of justice as principles which would command the allegiance of an "overlapping consensus" of diverse groups within society, and so help to preserve stability and social unity. They would command this allegiance, he argues, because they represent a *political* liberalism which does not endorse any substantive or comprehensive *moral* conception of the good life. The principles are undemanding because they do not rest on the value of autonomy but look to build up a consensus through their acceptability to a diversity of substantive moral views.

The problem with this "political liberalism," however, is that it does not quite relinquish its dependence on the comprehensive moral ideals which may be at odds with the values of some, or even many, groups in society. And when Rawls's political liberalism comes into conflict with these, his comprehensive moral position has simply to be asserted and enforced. This is made clear in Rawls's discussion of the problem of education of the children of religious minorities who are opposed to the modern world and wish to lead their common life apart from it. While political liberalism will not, unlike the liberalisms of Kant and Mill, impose requirements designed to foster the values of autonomy and individuality, it will nonetheless require some public education.

> It will ask that children's education include such things as knowledge of their constitutional and civic rights, so that, for example, they know that liberty of conscience exists in their society and that apostasy is not a legal crime, all this to ensure that their continued membership in a religious sect when they become of age is not based simply on ignorance of their basic rights or fear of punishment for offenses that do not exist. Moreover, their education should also prepare them to be fully cooperating members of society and enable them to be self-supporting; it should also encourage the political virtues so that they want to honour the fair terms of social cooperation in their relations with the rest of society.[12]

Rawls, of course, recognizes that requiring children to be schooled in these ways may "in effect, though not in intention," educate them into a comprehensive liberal conception; but the "unavoidable consequences of reasonable requirements for children's education may have to be accepted, often with regret."[13] But he also thinks this is not demanding too much, since his conception of justice "honors, as far as it can, the claims of those who wish to withdraw from the modern world" and asks only that they "acknowledge the principles of the political conception of justice and appreciate its political ideals of person and society."[14] Thus the state's concern with children's education "lies in their roles as future citizens, and so in such essential things as their acquiring the capacity to understand the public culture and to participate in its institutions."[15]

Yet, particularly from the point of view of the minorities in question, the limits of tolerance are significant. This is brought out very clearly by Deborah Fitzmaurice, who argues that, in spite of his best efforts, Rawls is not able rationally to ground his two principles while remaining agnostic about the good for man. And since the derivation of the two principles presupposes the goodness of autonomy, "it is to be expected that the institutions which they ground will be hostile to non-autonomy supporting ways of life, *and* not justifiable to the non-autonomy valuing adherents of such modes."[16] Her argument is convincing, and is further borne out by Rawls's remarks about the education of children. In arguing that the "state's concern with their education lies in their role as future citizens, and so in such essential things as their acquiring the capacity to understand the public culture and to participate in its institutions," he is placing great weight on the importance of our involvements in particular ways of life being, in some way, the product of reflection and choice. It is important that all people become aware of the wider society, of their place in it, and of the fact that their way of life may be at odds with it.

While Rawls hesitates over the commitments to autonomy implicit in his work, however, Fitzmaurice argues that liberals should accept autonomy as a good fundamental to the liberal conception. But the implications of this, she maintains, should be recognized: "once liberal principles are seen to depend on the claim that autonomy is a good, it is clear that the liberal state is bound to be to some extent inhospitable to traditional ways of life. For the principle of autonomy implies that we, as liberals, have an obligation to sustain a public sphere, accessible to all, which is supportive of autonomy."[17] Liberal theories like that of Rawls (which is wary of autonomy), no less than liberal theories like that of Joseph Raz (which embraces autonomy),[18] must treat non-autonomy-supporting modes of life as morally inferior. "It is wrong to tolerate them because they harm their adherents."[19] According to Fitzmaurice this means, among other things, that we should sustain an education system which "nurtures habits of critical reflection," refuse permission to schools which would fail to encourage such habits, and support "members of non-autonomy-supporting communities seeking either voice or exit."[20]

A similar stand is taken by Will Kymlicka in developing an account of liberalism which considers the claims of cultural minorities. The conclusion he reaches is that liberalism requires that minority cultures be granted recognition and group rights so that they might enjoy some cultural protection. Nonetheless, he argues that such groups still need to respect certain liberal norms; and indeed he suggests that the problem of liberalizing such communities poses a challenge which liberals should try to meet.[21] Once again, autonomy is of central importance. The appeal to autonomy:

identifies an essential aspect of a *liberal* conception of minority rights. A liberal theory can accept special rights for a minority culture against the larger community so as to ensure equality of circumstances between them. But it will not justify (except under extreme circumstances) special rights for a culture against its own members. The former protect the autonomy of the member of minority cultures; the latter restrict it. Liberals are committed to supporting the right of individuals to decide for themselves which aspects of their cultural heritage are worth passing on. Liberalism is committed to (perhaps even defined by) the view that individuals should have the freedom and capacity to question and possibly revise the traditional practices of their community should they come to see them as no longer worthy of their allegiance. Restricting religious freedom or denying education to girls is inconsistent with these liberal principles and indeed violates one of the reasons liberals have for wanting to protect cultural membership — namely, that membership in a culture is what enables informed choice about how to lead one's life. Hence a liberal conception of minority rights will condemn certain traditional practices of minority cultures just as it has historically condemned the traditional practices of majority cultures and will support reform.[22]

None of these liberal writers is hostile, or even insensitive, to the concerns of minority cultures. For Rawls, interceding in the schooling of minority schoolchildren is something to be done "with regret." Kymlicka is concerned to preserve liberal autonomy but is equally anxious to grant minority communities "group rights" to afford them protection from the wider community. Even Fitzmaurice, who is the most forthright in her recognition that liberalism mandates intolerance of minority ways of life which harm their adherents, insists that her conclusions do not license "Jacobin invasions of the personal sphere."[23] For one thing, she notes, the autonomous life cannot be achieved through directly coercive measures; and for another, wrenching members of such societies out of their social forms may deny them any sort of life at all: "We should therefore interfere with traditional societies only in order to prevent powerful members directly coercing or harming co-members in order to sustain traditional ways of life."[24]

Yet there is something else shared by these liberals, besides their commitment to autonomy, which accounts for the way in which they define the boundaries or limits of toleration. All pre-suppose the existence of a liberal political order: that is, an order in which the value of autonomy, embodied in principles of justice, is authoritatively upheld in the public sphere. To put it slightly differently, all presuppose the existence of a common standpoint of morality which is established. Toleration is something which arises as an issue, then, because of the possibility of dissent—whether by word or by practice—from the values implicit in that common standpoint. However, toleration is not possible when minority practice goes against the values implicit in the public sphere: values which have already been established.[25] Minority practice is tolerated only for so long as it abides by the fundamen-tal moral principles of the wider society; otherwise minority com-munities will be restructured (so far as is practicable) to be brought into accord with majority practice.

I want to suggest, however, that this approach offers insufficient toleration to minority communities. What it evinces, ultimately, is a greater concern with the perpetuation or reproduction of a liberal social order, but at the risk of intolerance and moral dogmatism.

### III. An Alternative View

The approach taken by the authors discussed above does not give sufficient toleration to minority communities, I want to argue, because it does not give any independent weight to toleration at all. This is so because all dealings with illiberal communities are conducted on the basis of settled principles of liberal justice. This point is accepted explicitly by Fitzmaurice, who concludes her own reflections on the issue by stating that the "requirement to sustain individual autonomy becomes the moral basis of our politi-cal relations with non-liberal minorities," and that *"No independent principle of toleration is required."*[26] At this point two questions arise: first, why should we be concerned if there is no independent value attached to toleration; and second, can there be a defense of toleration which does not subordinate it to some other value and, thereby, undermine it?

Let me approach these questions, first by arguing why tolera-tion ought to be valued independently, then by showing how there can be defence of toleration as an independent value, and finally by indicating why other attempts to grapple with this question have foundered on a misplaced concern with social unity.

Toleration is important, in part, because it checks or counters moral certitude. If we are convinced beyond doubt of the correctness of our beliefs or about the immorality of the practices of others, there is less reason to tolerate those whose beliefs or practices differ from our own.[27] Yet if there is any possibility of doubt or uncertainty about the correctness or reliability of our judgment, then there is some reason to tolerate. It is in recognition of our own fallibility that we are inclined to tolerate what we think is mistaken. Now, at first blush, this seems to give toleration a purely instrumental value: toleration is a means to some other end: perhaps it is valuable because it enables true beliefs to prevail over false ones—given sufficient time. But this is not the case; or at least, there is more to it than that. Toleration is also valuable because it is the condition which gives judgments worth.

This requires some elaboration. Whatever the strength of our convictions, whether they be about matters of fact or of value, there must always be some element of doubt about them because there is no method or mechanism by which to establish their correctness (beyond anything more than "reasonable" doubt). And there is no authority with any independent access to the truth of the matter. To what or whom, then, can we appeal when asserting or defending our judgments and convictions? The liberal answer has always been that we appeal to a universal audience through an appeal to reason. The appeal to reason means invoking a range of cognitive procedures, strategies, and standards— though none of these procedures or standards are fixed or beyond criticism and revision. This last point is of crucial importance because it indicates that our warrant for paying attention to the determinations of reason has nothing to do with settled standards or procedures: reason's "authority," such as it is, rests on its being implicated in a structure of openness and criticism. Reason has "authority" only in public, and to secure this position toleration is vitally important.

This account of reason is developed most carefully, according to Onora O'Neill's persuasive interpretation, by Kant.[28] Towards the end of the *Critique of Pure Reason* Kant writes:

> Reason must in all its undertakings subject itself to criticism; should it limit freedom of criticism by any prohibitions, it must harm itself, drawing upon itself a damaging suspicion. Nothing is so important through its usefulness, nothing so sacred, that it may be exempted from this searching examination, which knows no respect for persons. Reason depends on this freedom for its very existence. For reason has no dictatorial authority; its verdict is always simply the agreement of free citizens, of whom each one must be permitted to express, without let or hindrance, his objections or even his veto.[29]

What this passage captures is Kant's emphasis on reason's dependence upon a public realm of freedom for its existence. This public realm is, essentially, one in which tolerance reigns, for restrictions of the public use of reason, besides harming those who seek to reason publicly, also undermine the authority of reason itself.[30] Toleration, then, is fundamental to Kant's thought, for it is the "precondition for the emergence of any reasoning mode of life."[31] It is not simply that toleration and free discussion will lead to the discovery of truth or reduce false beliefs or make us hold truths less smugly; nor is it that toleration will be effective in restraining tyrants: "Such instrumental justifications of toleration all *presuppose* that we have independent standards of rationality and methods of reaching truth. Kant's thought is rather that a degree of toleration must characterize ways of life in which presumed standards of reason and truth can be challenged, and so acquire the only sort of vindication of which they are susceptible. The development of reason and of toleration is interdependent . . . Practices of toleration help constitute reason's authority."[32]

Now if we take this argument of Kant's seriously, as I propose we should, then toleration becomes a something we should value independently. Liberals in particular should hold toleration in high esteem because it turns out to be implicated in the very foundations of liberalism—insofar as liberalism is committed to the use of free public reason.[33] But the question now is, why should regarding toleration as the key to the liberal commitment to free discussion and criticism of all standards and judgments, lead to toleration being accorded any independent value in circumscribing relations with nonliberal minorities? Why not think, instead, that free public reason helps to establish the principles of justice, which then become the basis of those relations?

The answer has, I think, to do with the fact that relations with nonliberal minorities involve disputes in the realm of public reason itself. To put it differently, the public sphere of liberal society is one in which many fundamental disputes have not been resolved. Indeed, it is a defining characteristic of liberalism that it conceives of that public sphere as one in which the existence of disagreement cannot be denied, wished away, or suppressed. My criticism of the arguments of Rawls, Kymlicka, and Fitzmaurice is that they want to begin by assuming that there is a common established standpoint. From that point onwards, differing views are treated as dissenting from the received view, and tolerance is not possible since relations with dissenters are conducted on the basis of the principles implicit in the established standpoint.

This claim that relations with nonliberal minorities involve disputes in the realm of public reason itself is an important one for the argument offered here, and needs to be accounted for more fully. How can these relations be seen as involving disputes in the realm of reason—especially when many of the minorities in society are not at all interested in taking part in the public discourse of liberal political society? The Amish or (better still) the Hutterites, for example, are interested not so much in participating in as in withdrawing from modern society. My contention, however, is that they are still a part of the realm of public reason. To the extent that others are aware of their existence and of their ways, the Amish and the Hutterites offer accounts of different ways of living and different understandings of what has value. The fact that this is not articulated does not alter the fact that some alternative views are in the public realm. The worth of the alternatives are in dispute to the extent that others do not join or imitate these groups—though, from the perspective of such minorities, the fact that the majority's ways are not universally accepted suggests that that alternative is no less a matter of dispute.

The absence of a *dialogue* does not alter the fact that there is a dispute and that it exists in the realm of reason. Consider the case of the three little pigs: Peter, Paul, and Mary. They went their separate ways, Peter quickly building himself a house of straw,

Paul—less quickly—a house of sticks, and Mary—very slowly—a house of bricks. (Peter wanted instant gratification, while Mary looked furthest into the future; Paul was a middle-of-the-roader.) When no danger threatened, Peter's course looked the most sensible, for he was enjoying a sheltered existence, living the good life while the others were still laboring in preparation. Had his house been able to withstand the wolf's huffs and puffs, Peter's conjecture about the best way to go would have proven right. He would have been secure and the others would probably have been eaten in their unfinished houses. But he and Paul were wrong and Mary was right. Happily, however, the brothers were able to exit their wolf-destroyed dwellings and join Mary in her more substantial accommodations. Mary had the good grace never to mention her brothers' foolishness, but everyone knew what lesson had been learnt in this episode.[34]

There was a dispute here not because the pigs argued with one another but simply because their lives exemplified different possibilities. Each possibility was capable of being assessed rationally at a number of levels. Peter's ends were leisure and comfort; his judgment was that they could be satisfied quickly by the cheapest means at his disposal. But Mary reasoned that safety was so important that it was worth sacrificing leisure and risking the short-term perils of shelterlessness to be properly prepared for the dangers that would always return. Her thoughts were of trouble and hers were steady, so she was ready when trouble came. (Though, of course, if there had been no wolves—or if wolves had had weaker lungs—the others may really have chosen more wisely.) The point, however, is that ends, and the means of pursuing them, could be compared and evaluated; trade-offs could be identified; and risks could be assessed. The absence of dialogue does not change this. Example can speak—and reason—as eloquently as words.

In the world of human settlements, relations between liberal majorities and illiberal minorities amount to a dispute about the nature of the good life to the extent that none is prepared to forsake its own ways and embrace one of the alternatives. For as long as toleration prevails, and no one tries to compel or manipulate the other to live differently, reason also prevails.[35]

Now, contrary to this view, it has been argued that a distinction must be made between the kind of toleration that leads to reason and the kind that does not.[36] Tolerating some kinds of groups will not promote reason; and some groups will not be able to contribute to the promotion of reason unless they are provided with the right resources (and so, the objection goes, it is necessary to explain what kinds of resources these are). But this is to misunderstand the point being made here. Toleration is not important because it *promotes* reason (or leads to there being more reason in the world); the point is not to maximize reason—to have more of it in the world. The argument advanced here is, rather, that toleration is important because if toleration is forsaken then so is reason. A stance of toleration *upholds* or *honors* reason since it forswears the use of force in favor of persuasion (whether by argument or by example). Whether or not it promotes reason is a contingent and highly disputed matter.[37] What is important, from the liberal point of view, however, is not that reason be promoted but that it be honored.

For this reason it is a mistake to argue, for example, that the need to challenge dominant modes of reasoning would seem only to justify selective toleration. On this argument, if there are two hundred Hare Krishna groups in the country, it might be sufficient to tolerate only ten, from whom enough could be learnt for us not to need the others. Similarly, continuing with this argument, the need to challenge dominant modes of reasoning might be better met by promoting some (relatively scarce) illiberal groups and discouraging other (more numerous) ones. The mistake here, in part, is to think that the way to challenge the dominant modes of reasoning is by allowing the dominant group to tolerate selectively. More importantly, however, it is a mistake to assume that reason is honored or upheld by giving anyone the authority to maximize it—or even to uphold it.

All this said, however, the problem which arises here for my argument is that, if there is no common standpoint from which our deliberations begin, how is any kind of moral engagement possible between different groups? Surely there must be some kind of stable public realm defined by particular normative commitments which make for social unity? The resolution of these problems depends on the plausibility of a different kind of account of the liberal public realm—which I shall now offer.

Rather than conceive of the public realm as embodying an established standpoint of morality which reflects a desirable level of stability and social unity, we should think of the public realm as an area of convergence of different moral practices. All societies, to varying degrees, harbor a variety of religions, languages, ethnicities, and cultural practices and, so, a variety of moral ideals.[38] The public realm is the product of interaction among these various ways. Indeed, it is a kind of settlement reflecting the need of people of different ways to develop some common standards by which to regulate their interaction—given that interaction is unavoidable.

This settlement might be thought to amount to something like what Rawls calls a *modus vivendi,* but this would be a mistake. A *modus vivendi* is an arrangement which is the product of political bargaining: it is a kind of consensus founded on a balancing of the power of different group interests.[39] The settlement I have in view is not a balance of power. It describes something much more like the rules of the commons which have arisen and developed over time to deal with interaction between communities in areas where property rights do not exist and there may be conflicts over the use of common resources. In practice, "tragedies of the commons" are often averted by networks of agreements establishing rights of use.[40] The reason this amounts to more than a balance of power is that the agreements reached are not *merely* compromises made by groups (or their representatives) with one another. Agreements or understandings reached between individuals and groups come to be accepted (or internalized) as more basic norms governing social relations. The product over time is a commons which acquires the character of a public space without a sovereign power—unowned but governed by norms which circumscribe behaviour within it.

My suggestion is that the same process can account for how a public sphere emerges out of the interaction among groups or communities whose differences lie less in their conflicting interest in land-use than in their differing moral beliefs. The commons they share an interest in preserving is not land or some other natural "common pool resource" (to use Elinor Ostrom's terminology) but civility and civil life. This moral commons has always been important because isolationism has seldom been an easy or attractive option for communities. Interaction has been made necessary by a range of circumstances from the need for trade, to the desire to marry outsiders—members of other communities. This has required the development of standards to regulate inter-communal conduct; but it has also produced changes within communities which have had to develop norms or laws regulating relations with welcome intruders—be they merchants or sons-in-law. Communities have thus to strike a balance between retaining their own practices and moral ideals and compromising them in order to enter the public realm of civil life.

In the end, a public realm is created even if some groups consider isolation a viable option (though "isolation," it ought to be noted, is here a matter of degree).[41] But what has to be recognized about this public realm is that it is the product of a convergence which produces a stability and social unity that falls short of the permanence or durability many thinkers seek. What we have here is a form of social order whose underlying characteristic is toleration, even though it is not the result of any attempt to produce such an order. But it lacks the social unity that would come only with an attempt to articulate and institutionalise (or entrench) the values thought to be dominant in the public realm.

Political philosophers such as Rawls have thought it important to articulate and institutionalize these values to secure social unity because they look to treat these values as the basis of the legitimacy of the state: "What is needed is a regulative political conception of justice that can articulate and order in a principled way the political ideals and values of a democratic regime, thereby specifying the aims the constitution is to achieve and the limits it must respect."[42] This conception, in Rawls's view, not only provides a shared public basis for the justification of political and social institutions but also helps ensure stability from one generation to the next.[43]

My point is that stability and social unity in this sense can only be bought at the cost of toleration. This is because articulating a political conception of justice, and presenting it as the first principle governing conduct the public realm, subordinates toleration, entrenches a particular comprehensive moral conception, and excludes certain moral ideals as unacceptable. Given this choice between social unity and greater toleration, I would argue that we should opt for greater toleration. The question, of course, is why?

## IV. OBJECTIONS AND SOME REPLIES

It might be worth indicating at the outset what kind of argument it is that I am advancing for toleration, before going on to detail what toleration might amount to in practice, and why such forms of toleration should be thought defensible against a number of objections.

Although the skeptical temper will be evident in much of what I have said and will have to say, the argument offered does not rest on skepticism.[44] Nor does it rest on the kind of epistemic abstinence advocated by Thomas Nagel in his discussion of the problem of "Moral Conflict and Political Legitimacy."[45] Nagel suggests that, in the defense of the political legitimacy of a set of institutions, we seek agreement based on "a kind of epistemological restraint," captured by the distinction that must be recognized between what one believes to be true and what is true.[46] Out of this Nagel seeks to derive institutions which uphold a certain level of toleration. My argument, however, is that a commitment to discovering what is true about the good life or about proper moral practice requires a social order whose fundamental disposition is to toleration. Toleration is the condition of rational inquiry and therefore of moral inquiry.

What, then, will toleration amount to in practice? The answer to this question is shaped not only by my claim about the fundamental importance of toleration but also by the understanding of the public realm I have put forward—one which sees the public realm as the result of a *convergence* of moral practices. On my understanding, the public sphere is, firstly, not stable because the interaction of different ways of life may shift the points of convergence and, secondly, not coextensive with the state. To put it differently, the public sphere of civil society does not end at the boundaries of the state. Indeed, there are, in a sense, many (overlapping) public realms representing settlements where different practices have converged on particular standards to govern social interaction. The state does not subsume civil society.

In practice, then, there would be a very considerable measure of toleration in such a society because groups with "intolerable" practices would have the option of withdrawing from the wider moral community. Of course, the price of maintaining such practices may be very high, since withdrawal is neither costless nor easy. Moreover, the pressures to enter the moral community would be considerable given the possibility not only of moral criticism from other communities but also of inducements for members to defect from communities whose practices they find harmful or obnoxious. (The evidence of interaction between cultural communities and the wider society bears this out. The Amish, for example, experience varying rates of defection across the country and also have integrated into local society to varying degrees.)

Nevertheless, there would in such a society be (the possibility of) communities which bring up children unschooled and illiterate; which enforce arranged marriages; which deny conventional medical care to their members (including children); and which inflict cruel and "unusual" punishment. All of this is possible in the name of toleration. Yet, if this is what toleration might lead to, is it defensible?

There are at least four initial objections that need to be considered. First, this level of toleration in effect condones the oppression of internal minorities (minorities within minority communities), and of the weakest members of such communities in particular. It risks turning society into a "mosaic of tyrannies."[47] Moreover, the fact that individuals may take the option of exit from the oppressive minority community is insufficient to ensure any kind of freedom from oppression since it is precisely the most vulnerable members of such communities who would find exit most difficult and costly.

Second, even if toleration is regarded as the basis of rational inquiry and, therefore, of moral inquiry, this does not establish any more than a requirement for a minimal level of toleration. Indeed, it could be argued that moral inquiry would be better served if institutions recognized certain rights of internal minorities which would enable all individuals to take part in the moral discourse of society.

Third, what of individuals who choose to reject the authority of the wider society or the state and withdraw into communities as small as a single family (or individual)? Are they not licensed, under the present defence of toleration, to reject the authority of the law and to do entirely as they please?

Fourth, this understanding of toleration does not allow us to recognize political society as a kind of moral community. It does not admit that a society as a whole (encompassing many different communities) may have certain important shared moral standards which help to define it, and which may legitimately be imposed on those who deviate from them. The understanding of toleration here, it might be argued, weakens political society.

Let me consider these objections in turn, beginning with the objection that this kind of toleration condones the oppression of internal minorities. The objection is a serious one because significant harms can be inflicted (by the dominant powers in the group) on the most vulnerable members of a minority community—usually, women, children, and dissenters. In some cultural groups, girls are forced to suffer clitoridectomy—an operation which, as Amy Gutmann has rightly observed, may in typical practice qualify as a form of torture.[48] In others, children may be denied blood transfusions in life-threatening circumstances; and religious dissenters may be forced to adopt the community religion on pain of expulsion into an outside world they cannot easily enter. These are clearly cases of oppression.[49]

Yet if the concern is oppression, there is just as much reason to hold (more) firmly to the principles of toleration—since the threat of oppression is as likely to come from outside the minority community as it is from within.[50] Consider, for example, the brutal suppression of the Baha'i in postrevolutionary Iran; or the taking of children from Aboriginal families by the Australian state—not to mention the horrific crimes of persecution against the Jewish people in this century in particular. Indeed, the history of oppression is to a large extent the story of the pursuit of the heretic through the ages by established authorities.[51]

Furthermore, we should be wary of conceding to established authorities the right to intervene in the "intolerable" practices of minorities because there is little assurance that the power will not be abused. For one thing, minorities have often been demonized, with horrible practices attributed to them in order to justify persecution. Other peoples have constantly been accused of a variety of barbarous vices, from cannibalism to incest, on the flimsiest evidence. Thus the ancient inhabitants of Ireland were described as cannibals; and in medieval Europe Jews were accused of devouring Christian children.[52]

Even in cases where there is clear evidence of terrible practices, however, there is good reason not to give established authority the right to intervene. First, persuasion is always preferable to force, morally speaking, so it would be better to allow the effects of interaction between peoples and communities of different moral outlook to work towards the elimination of dubious customs.[53] Just as missionaries sought to convert other peoples to Christianity, there is no reason why individuals should not seek to convert people away from customs they regard as barbarous. This would be preferable to imposing the moral principles of the dominant society—even if those principles are the product of sustained reflection on one's considered judgments.[54]

Second, conversion through persuasion is often more effective since it seeks to have people internalize new moral notions rather than simply comply with them. Force, on the other hand, can lead to greater resistance on the part of the group as a whole against the impositions of outsiders. Elites within the group can assert that the practice under threat is central to the group's identity or way of life (even if it's not); and the victims of the practice may even rally behind the leadership in solidarity. Thus, we find support among Kenyan and Sudanese village women for clitoridectomy in defiance of central governments and urban elites.[55]

And thirdly, conversion through persuasion is not as damaging to or dislocating of group life as invasion by an external power. Now this may well leave within the wider society a number of cohesive but oppressive communities: islands of tyranny in a sea of indifference. Against this, however, I would maintain that the decentralization of tryanny is to be preferred. One reason to prefer it is that while all power tends to corrupt, absolute power corrupts absolutely.

Yet while it may be granted that there is a strong case for toleration, there is still the second objection that this does not establish more than a need for a minimal level of toleration. And moral inquiry might be better served by the according to all, including internal minorities, of certain minimal civil rights—

such as, say, freedom of worship and liberty of conscience, as well as basic entitlements to education—whose violation would not be tolerated by the dominant society. The first reply to this objection is that it still presupposes that some ultimate moral authority is both desirable and feasible. This presupposition is not defensible for reasons already discussed. For one thing, we have no assurance that the dominant authority will not abuse its moral authority to persecute dissenters. In morality, as in politics, there should be a separation of powers. For another, a unitary system of morality is not appropriate in a society of conflicting moral standards.

A second reply to this objection is that if liberty of conscience is taken to be of fundamental importance, then it demands not only that dissenters be respected but also that those who wish to remain loyal to their traditions or practices equally be respected. Just as dissenters should be free to dissociate themselves from beliefs and practices (and so, communities) they cannot in good conscience embrace, so should communities be able to dissociate themselves from those who do not wish to conform to their ways, and whom they cannot, in good conscience, tolerate.

A third reply to this objection is that a more extensive list of basic civil rights (including rights to education, for example) does not in itself necessarily serve to open up moral dialogue and further moral inquiry. On the contrary, it places significant limitations on this process by denying to some the right to practice what they can now only preach. For example, if the Pueblo Indians were required to tolerate (Christian) dissenters this could mean not so much opening up dialogue between Pueblo and Christian traditions as closing down the Pueblo voice.

Against this, however, it may be argued that groups like the Pueblo do not need to practice what they preach in order to enter into a moral dialogue. Illiberal groups can question liberal norms without having actually to act in illiberal ways—say, by engaging in debate. In the Pueblo case, requiring them to tolerate Christian converts need not lead to the closing down of the Pueblo voice (which is, here, the voice of traditional religion Pueblo) since the majority would still dominate. And if this means that more of the traditional Pueblo might be converted to Christianity, this surely is to the good since it would amount to no more than the victory (through proselytization) of reason.

Here, a number of things need to be said. The first is that, important though debate may be, it is not always an adequate substitute for demonstration through practice. This is all the more so when the subject of dispute is how one should live. Not all people are capable of articulating their reasons for thinking their way of life is better—or even just better for some. (Nor, for that matter, are all capable of articulating their reasons for regarding some influences as malign or corrupting.) Indeed, they may not be aware of many of the advantages (though also, of course, disadvantages) of their practices simply because these are side-effects which have not much to do with why they prefer to stick to their ways.[56] Nonetheless, in being able to live a particular way of life they may be quite capable of demonstrating (intentionally or not) its merits. Some need to practice in order to preach.

The second thing is that, if one is to demonstrate through example the worth of a particular way of living, it matters enormously whether or not one can live in that way or only live (what one regards as) some compromised version. The Pueblo, in this regard, may feel that accepting Christian dissenters in their midst requires that they change their way of life and live a compromised version. How can they demonstrate the virtue of their ways (particularly to their children) if they cannot live it—especially if they are required to associate with dissenters who repudiate important aspects of Pueblo life? This would be like requiring Christians to offer adherents of the Jewish faith not just the freedom to practice and proselytize elsewhere but the right of reply in church. To be sure, such a debate within the church may serve to enlighten, but it would surely not be unreasonable for the church to say their concern is not debate but worship, and that those who find their forms of worship wanting (or are curious about alternatives) should look elsewhere? (People could then also compare unlike with unlike.) The Pueblo would, equally, be quite reasonable if they left their members free to seek out alternative ideas and ways but refused to to allow proselytizers to enter and preach within their communities.

A third point that must also be made here, however, is that none of this implies that some groups such as the Pueblo may not do better—for their culture or for their present members or for both—by being more liberal or tolerant of internal dissent. The argument put forward here is not that isolation and intolerance of internal dissent necessarily promote the triumph of superior ways of living. The claim is, instead, the weaker one that requiring internal tolerance does not necessarily make it more likely either. More than this, however, it is also to say that, while it is surely right that the solution to a problem is more likely to be found if different answers compete openly, we do not improve our chances of finding that solution by decreeing that every answer must have a particular structure or be reached using a particular methodology. This stricture holds even against the demand that every answer or methodology at least be the product of open debate and criticism. In science, openness and criticism is important, but science would be the poorer if theories arrived by unconventional—indeed, unscientific—methods could not be heard until modified to conform to the dominant view of what constitutes science. In science there are many authorities; and there must be authorities if scientific investigtion can proceed without endless debate. If there is an ultimate authority, however, that determines what is acceptable or what is true, science is lost.

In a liberal society, similarly, there are many authorities governing a multitude of practices or ways of life—many of them competing alternatives. Such authorities are needed if those ways are to be lived without endless debate. If there is an ultimate authority, however, that determines what ways are morally acceptable, liberalism is lost.[57]

Yet if we tolerate communities of people who reject the authority of the wider society, runs the third objection, what is to prevent individuals from unilaterally rejecting all authority and withdrawing into communities of one—or perhaps, communities comprising only a single family? In reply to this concern, I would concede that this is, in principle, quite possible. The cost of such a move, however, would make this extremely unlikely since the individuals or families "seceding" in this way would, in effect, sentence themselves to the status of "outlaw." In repudiating the authority, they would deny themselves the protection of any legal community. That outlawry has, historically, served as a particularly severe form of punishment indicates that this is not a very likely outcome of strong principles of toleration.[58]

This objection is worth considering, however, because the reply to it helps to bring out an important point. This is that there is already a substantial pressure toward conformity exerted by the fact of human interdependence. Short of the use of force, dissociation is the most powerful threat a community can make against an individual. Those who wish to "go it alone" will not survive unless they can persuade others to join them (or not to defect). The fewer people they can attract to their community, the less likely they are to survive. The more they can attract, the less reason there is not to tolerate them. This holds not only at the individual level but also at the group level. The likelihood of particular communities seceding or withdrawing from the larger political society and rejecting its authority is small because, usually, the costs are too high and the gains insufficient.[59]

This brings us to the final objection: that such an understanding of toleration weakens political society. It is all very well to tolerate minorities, but unless certain minimal moral standards are enforced, there cannot exist a single polity. There will be only a patchwork of interdependent communities rather than a unified political order. This objection is well founded. The greater the diversity of cultural groups with independent moral traditions within a polity, the less the extent of social unity within that political society. If the moral coherence of a political society is to be preserved, greater social conformity will be required.

This objection may take the form of the following challenge, which deserves to be addressed.[60] If it is legitimate for illiberal subgroups to prevent their own members from forming liberal subgroups within that minority, why is it not legitimate for liberals to prevent illiberal subgroups from forming in their midst? It would, after all, "seem inconsistent to prohibit liberals from doing what you allow illiberal groups to do." For example, if the tribal council of the Pueblo Indians has the authority to demand of its members (including those who have converted to Christianity) that they adhere to the tribal religion as a condition of membership, why should not the liberal state be able to say to the Pueblo (or to the Amish, or to any other such group) that they should abide by liberal norms (which allow freedom of religion) as a condition of membership in liberal society. In essence, why should liberals not be able to impose liberal norms on their own members just as illiberal subgroups may?

The first part of the answer to this objection is to acknowledge that what is sauce for the goose must indeed be sauce for the gander. If illiberal subgroups should be free to require conformity (or face expulsion) the same should hold for liberal subgroups. But the rest of the answer requires a closer look at what is the liberal group in question. If the liberal group is another association such as the Pueblo or the Amish they would be as entitled to require conformity to their liberal strictures as the latter two would be to require conformity to their illiberal ones. But when the group in question is the state or the larger society of which these subgroups are a part, matters are importantly different. For, as I have said at the outset, there is no reason to begin by assuming that there is an established "we" in the form of the state which possesses the authority to determine how far to tolerate dissenting groups within its midst. That is the model of toleration which is being rejected here.

Moreover, the state is not a community in the same way that the Pueblo or the Amish societies are. It is much more of an association of associations. More importantly still, it is not an association of *like* associations but of *diverse* associations. It is not for the state to determine what forms—or form—the associations which comprise it will take. The state is a political settlement which encompasses these diverse associations; but it is not their creator or their shaper. This holds all the more strongly if the state is claimed to be a liberal state. The liberal state does not take as its concern the way of life of its members but accepts that there is in society a diversity of ends—and of ways in which people pursue them. It does not make judgments about whether those ways are good or bad, liberal or illiberal.

Yet what if the dissenting groups are not groups like the Pueblo, who were already settled in the land when the state's sovereignty was asserted? Suppose that the groups in question are immigrants to the society, or members of the settler society which formed the state in the first place. These groups are not "involuntarily incorporated minorities" but members of the liberal society. Why can a liberal group like the state not impose liberal norms on its *own* members or on voluntary migrants?[61] Why should the liberal state not prohibit its voluntarily incorporated members from forming illiberal subgroups?

There are two answers to this set of questions since two kinds of dissenting groups are being identified. With regard to dissenters who have not withdrawn from mainstream society but are dissatisfied with the decrees of the liberal state to which they belong, Kymlicka has suggested that the state must have the authority to enforce liberal norms. In the case of *Mozert v. Hawkins,* for example, in which parents sued Tennessee schools for teaching children about matters which ran contrary to their own Christian beliefs, should the state not be able to uphold the inculcation of liberal standards? In this instance liberals are trying to impose their views on their own members, who have converted to an illiberal brand of fundamentalism. There is no reason to think that such individuals should be treated as a separate group with whom a separate settlement should be sought, since they have not sought to exit from the mainstream of society. And to regard them as separate on the basis of their declaring themselves to be born-again Christians who no longer are a part of that group called liberal society would be unwarranted. (After all, the tribal council of Pueblo society are not required to regard the Pueblo dissenters as a separate group with whom some accommodation must be made.) Surely liberals should be able to say to these Christian dissenters: "adhere to our beliefs or leave?"

In reply to this argument I would say, first, that once again a great deal turns on whether the membership the dissenters are invited to leave is a liberal subgroup or the state. If the subgroup wishes to remain constituted as a group upholding liberal values and to dissociate from those who reject such values, there is no reason there should not be a parting of the ways with Christian dissenters. If we are talking about the liberal state, however, it is not for the state to determine what values its members must accept. Second, from the standpoint of the state, the members of the Pueblo community are no less members of the society—indeed, as much so as are the Christian parents in the case of *Mozert v. Hawkins.* (Which is, again, why it does not make sense to think of the state as another liberal group like the Amish or the Pueblo—who are all American subjects.) Third, in the case of *Mozert v. Hawkins* itself the dispute arose because the parents in question wished both to accept schooling provided by the state and to reject (a part of) the content. More significantly still, the parents wanted to raise their children to live in mainstream society and yet shield them from its corrupting influences. If they had wanted to achieve this by withdrawing from the state's influence (and, perhaps, reconstituted themselves in communities with other like-minded people) there is no reason to think that they have any less claim to do so than the Pueblo have to living separately. The fact, however, is that—as is always the case with the exit option—doing so is costly and the likelihood of people thus withdrawing is small. The parents, in this particular case, did not seek to pay the price of withdrawal from the community but, rather, hoped to change the community's rules in their favor.[62] Nonetheless, if they had wished to withdraw and form an illiberal subgroup they should, in principle, be as entitled to do so as the Pueblo. While they may have no claim to be subsidized by the state or wider society, there is no reason why that withdrawal should be refused toleration because the group is illiberal.

This brings us, however, to the argument that a distinction needs to be made between the Tennessee Christians and the Pueblo since the first are members of the settler society which formed the society in the first place, while the Pueblo were involuntarily incorporated. Those who—like immigrants—are voluntary members are under a greater obligation to abide by society's norms; it is thus more legitimate to impose liberal norms on original settlers and immigrants than it is to impose them on indigenous peoples. The problem with this view is that it is vulnerable to the standard objections raised by David Hume against the argument that we have obligations founded on consent. While consent, or voluntary entry into an ongoing practice, may indeed generate obligations, this does not establish what is consented to. Nor does it establish the obligations of descendants who did not voluntarily enter into any agreement or arrangements. Children are clearly *involuntary* immigrants.

Even if we were to leave aside the moral effects of generational transition, however, it is difficult to argue that first generation immigrants are necessarily voluntary joiners in their new societies. Some may be refugees who are simply relocated; others, in more extreme cases, may be slaves (as were a large percentage of the early American settlers) or transported convicts (as were a large percentage of the original Australian settlers). If *voluntary* membership is to be made the basis of the legitimacy of the authority of the state over members then a sizable proportion of the citizens of the United States, for example, have no reason to recognize the authority of the government.[63]

The immediate point of all this is to say that there is no justification for distinguishing between involuntarily incorporated groups and original settlers or voluntary immigrants in an attempt to establish the scope of the authority of the state. If the state possesses authority, it has it over all its members. The larger point, however, is that the state should not be viewed as a group in the way that other associations are. To be sure, the state is a community of sorts, but as a community of communities its concern is with the terms of association among the different groups and not its own claims as a group. Thus to assert that a liberal state should have as much right to impose liberal norms on its members as groups within in have to impose illiberal norms on theirs is a mistake. It would be like saying that an association of households (say, in a neighborhood association) must have the same right to impose particular requirements on its members as each household has of imposing particular demands on its inhabitants.

The image of the state as a settlement among different groups living under an arrangement of mutual toleration appears, however, to present political society as a kind of international society. International society, Michael Walzer has suggested, is essentially a maximally tolerant regime; and the doctrine of sovereignty is essentially a doctrine of toleration. The question is, he asks, do we want to make domestic society more like international society?[64] In that kind of society, all groups are (ideally) of equal standing and every negotiated settlement is a point along the way in the practice of society; and we celebrate key moments of the settlement—building monuments if necessary to mark these moments in a society's history. There is a settlement because there is a society—which is something much thicker than international society. In this circumstance, when newcomers arrive, the question "should 'we' tolerate 'them'?" is not an avoidable question.

In response, I would argue that, if the image of a society of mutual toleration presents domestic society as a kind of international society, this is because that is indeed what domestic society is like. It is much more like international society than has, perhaps, been conceded. My concern is to argue that it should be recognized and accepted as such and that demands to view it as something "thicker" should be resisted. This means resisting demands that the central authority take an active interest in shaping or constructing society to ensure that the communities which comprise it conform to particular substantive values. It also means taking a more skeptical attitude towards established political authority, regarding it as (at best) not much more than the outcome of compromise among different peoples, with different ways, who have to find terms under which to coexist.

When such settlements have been especially enduring, people have often been inclined to attach greater significance to them—and to look for some deeper basis on which social unity rests. (Sometimes such a basis is identified in an effort to construct a social unity that will endure.) The appropriate attitude towards all this, I suggest, is one of Humean skepticism: an attitude which sees that particular political arrangements are typically the outcome of usurpation or conquest; and that arguments setting out to establish them on some loftier basis are to be viewed with suspicion, since they usually reflect some partisan interest—although we should be no less suspicious of "violent innovations" which threaten the stability of government and, thus, the peace and stability of society.[65] Hume rightly noted that, "as human society is in perpetual flux, one man every hour going out of the world, another coming into it, it is necessary, in order to preserve stability in government, that the new brood should conform themselves to the established constitution, and nearly follow the path which their fathers, treading in the footsteps of theirs, had marked out to them."[66] To the extent that this is so, there is an issue of whether "we" should tolerate newcomers if the peace and stability are in danger. But this has not much to do with the "thickness" of domestic society. While we may not be able to avoid the question of whether we should tolerate newcomers, we can certainly answer it in the affirmative. Unless they threaten "violent innovation," there is no reason not to let them go their own way.

My general response, then, to the concern that the understanding of toleration advanced here (in forswearing the establishment of liberalism as a comprehensive ideal regulating group life) weakens or reduces social unity is to say that we should be less concerned about social unity in the polity.[67] If the choice is one between toleration and establishment, so much the worse for establishment. In this regard, my approach to the whole question of the foundations of a multicultural society differs from that of theorists such as Will Kymlicka, for whom social unity is a pressing problem for liberal political theory. Kymlicka's response to the problem has been to develop a comprehensive liberal philosophy of multicultural citizenship, dealing with illiberal minorities who dissent from the established standards with a considerable measure of toleration since he is reluctant to impose liberalism on minority cultures.[68]

My approach to the question differs from this inasmuch as I wish to return toleration to a more central place in liberal theory. For Kymlicka, "if two cultures do not share basic principles and cannot be persuaded to adpt the other's principles, they will have to rely on some other basis of agreement, such as a *modus vivendi.*" In cases where the minority culture is illiberal, this may mean an arrangement similar to the sort that I propose; but this, he argues, "would be a compromise of, not the instantiation of, liberal principles."[69] My contention, however, is that it is an instantiation of liberal principles, for at the core of liberalism is the idea of toleration. In a liberal settlement among groups with different ways of life, the illiberal groups which are tolerated are illiberal precisely because they are intolerant. In some respects, we do not have any trouble accepting this: although we think there should be toleration of different religions, we do not expect each religion to be itself tolerant. Thus, while Christians should allow Muslims to worship God as they see fit, this does not mean that they should tolerate Muslim worship in their churches. What is contended here is that this understanding should be generalized to cover cultural communities more broadly.

My hope, then, has been to show that, however much liberalism may turn out to recommend compromise among different ways of life, that recommendation is not in itself a compromise of liberalism. It is a recommendation rooted in the ideal of toleration; and that toleration, as Burke might have put it, is not a "connivance" but a principle which lies at the very heart of liberalism.

## NOTES

Earlier versions of this chapter were presented at the Institute for Humane Studies Summer Fellows' Seminar; to the Department of Philosophy at Bowling Green State University; and at the 1995 meeting of the American Society for Political and Legal Philosophy. I am grateful to these audiences for discussion and criticism, and in particular to my commentators at the NOMOS meetings, Michael Walzer and Adeno Addis. I wish also to thank for their helpful advice Brian Beddie, Hans Eicholz, Jacob Levy, David Miller, Don Morrison, Emilio Pacheco, and Ian Shapiro. I am especially grateful to Will Kymlicka for his detailed comments and criticisms, many of which deserve a fuller and better response than I have been able to offer here.

1. Charles Taylor, *Multiculturalism and "The Politics of Recognition"* (Princeton: Princeton University Press, 1992), 72.

2. Poulter, "Ethnic Minority Customs, English Law and Human Rights," *International and Comparative Law Quarterly* 36 (1987): 589–615, at 593.

3. An example of such practice might be the polluting of rivers running through the community's land into other public or private property.

4. John Rawls, *A Theory of Justice* (Oxford: Oxford University Press, 1971), 214.

5. Ibid., 215.

6. Ibid., 215.

7. Ibid., 215.

8. Ibid., 370.

9. Ibid., 370.

10. Ibid., 370.

11. Rawls's interpretation in *A Theory of Justice* of his theory as an expression of a Kantian view of autonomy is to be found in ch. 40, pp. 251–57.

12. John Rawls, "The Priority of Right and Ideas of the Good," *Philosophy and Public Affairs* 17:4 (1988): 251–76 at 267.

13. Ibid., 268.

14. Ibid.

15. Ibid.

16. Deborah Fitzmaurice, "Autonomy as a Good: Liberalism, Autonomy and Toleration," *Journal of Political Philosophy* 1:1 (1993): 1–16 at 13.

17. Ibid., 14.

18. See Joseph Raz, *The Morality of Freedom* (Oxford: Clarendon Press, 1988).

19. Fitzmaurice, "Autonomy as a Good," 14. She is here identifying a point made by Raz, *Morality of Freedom*, 423.

20. Fitzmaurice, "Autonomy as a Good," 14. She adds quite sharply, "To entertain the notion that principles of neutrality, or of toleration, require the liberal to, for example, support the establishment of separate secondary schools for Muslim girls is to mistake the foundations of our own political principles."

21. Kymlicka's argument is developed most fully in *Liberalism, Community, and Culture* (Oxford: Clarendon Press, 1989). I have taken issue with him in my "Are There Any Cultural Rights?" *Political Theory* 20:1 (1992): 105–39. See also, in the same volume, Kymlicka, "The Rights of Minority Cultures: Reply to Kukathas," 140–46; and my response, "Cultural Rights Again: A Rejoinder to Kymlicka," *Political Theory* 20:4 (1992): 674–80.

22. Kymlicka, "The Rights of Minority Cultures: Reply to Kukathas," 142.

23. Fitzmaurice, "Autonomy as a Good," 14.

24. Ibid.

25. By "established" I do not mean necessarily politically established, but at least philosophically established. This assumption might thus be made by theorists writing about how a future state ought to deal with "dissenting" minorities.

26. Fitzmaurice, "Autonomy as a Good," 16 (emphasis added).

27. In this I assume that toleration is something we extend to those we are capable of suppressing; there may be a case for "tolerating" those whom we cannot suppress, but that is another matter.

28. Onora O'Neill, *Constructions of Reason: Explorations in Kant's Practical Philosophy* (Cambridge: Cambridge University Press, 1989), 28–50. There are some obvious affinities with the arguments of philosophers as diverse as Popper and Habermas.

29. Immanuel Kant, *The Critique of Pure Reason*, trans. N. Kemp Smith (London: St Martin's), A738/B766.

30. See O'Neill, *Constructions of Reason*, 37.

31. Ibid., 38–39. In the interests of brevity, I have contracted O'Neill's much more subtle and careful argument. I can only refer the reader to her discussion on pp. 34–39 and recommend fuller reading of her interpretation of the developmental framework of Kant's account of the grounds of reason on pp. 37–38.

32. Ibid., 39.

33. I do not, by this, mean to suggest that liberalism has Kantian foundations; even though this particular argument offered by Kant is

important, accepting it does not require acceptance the rest of Kant's moral theory.

34. Or, at least, each thought he knew.

35. What counts as manipulation is obviously important here; since the boundaries between compulsion, manipulation, and persuasion are not self-evident, this will itself be subject to dispute. More needs to be said than can be covered here.

36. This was put to me by Adeno Addis in his comment at the NOMOS meeting; Will Kymlicka also formulated a version of the same concern in written comments and I address that in the passage that follows.

37. Tolerating Nazi groups and their publications, for example, seems to me to be unlikely to do much for the amount—or for the quality—of reason in society.

38. I have argued that diversity is common within societies throughout history in "The Idea of a Multicultural Society," in my *Multicultural Citizens: The Philosophy and Politics of Identity* (St. Leonards: Centre for Independent Studies, 1993), 19–30.

39. See Rawls, "The Idea of an Overlapping Consensus," *Oxford Journal of Legal Studies* 7:1 (1987): 1–25 at 10–11.

40. An important game theoretical account (with historical case studies) is offered by Elinor Ostrom, *Governing the Commons. The Evolution of Institutions of Collective Action* (Cambridge: Cambridge University Press, 1990).

41. Even the Amish have difficulty isolating themselves from the ways of the outside world. For a discussion, see Donald B. Kraybill, *The Puzzles of Amish Life* (Intercourse, Pa.: Good Books, 1990).

42. Rawls, "Idea of an Overlapping Consensus," 1.

43. Ibid.

44. I have argued that cultural diversity does not demand scepticism about the possibility of moral knowledge in my "Explaining Moral Variety," *Social Philosophy and Policy* 11:1 (1994): 1–21.

45. "Moral Conflict and Political Legitimacy," *Philosophy and Public Affairs* 16:3 (1987): 215–40. See the powerful criticism of this position by Joseph Raz, "Facing Diversity: the Case of Epistemic Abstinence," *Philosophy and Public Affairs* 19:1 (1990): 3–46.

46. Nagel, "Moral Conflict," 229.

47. Leslie Green, "Internal Minorities and Their Rights," in Judith Baker, ed., *Group Rights,* 101–17, at 116.

48. Gutmann, "The Challenge of Multiculturalism in Political Ethics," *Philosophy and Public Affairs* (1993): 171–206 at 195.

49. For a fuller analysis of the notion of oppression, see Iris Marion

Young, *Justice and the Politics of Difference* (Princeton: Princeton University Press, 1990), ch. 1.

50. This point is recognized by Kymlicka, "Rights of Minority Cultures," 145 and 146 n. 8.

51. On this, see George H. Smith, *Atheism, Ayn Rand and Other Heresies* (New York: Prometheus Books, 1992), especially the essay "Philosophies of Toleration."

52. On this, see Urs Bitterli, *Cultures in Conflict: Encounters between European and Non-European Cultures, 1492–1800,* trans. Ritchie Robertson (Stanford, Calif.: Stanford University Press, 1989).

53. I have tried to provide an account of how this might happen in my "Explaining Moral Variety."

54. The missionary position is preferred to the original position.

55. Though, arguably, the matter is more complicated still since it is not unambiguously the case that such practices are kept in place by traditionalist communities against the wishes of the "oppressed." See, for example, Vicki Kirby's analysis of clitoridectomy in Sudan, which maintains that generally it is a practice which is supported by women—to the extent that a significant proportion of such operations are performed despite the opposition of fathers (let alone governments, and international agencies). See Kirby, "On the Cutting Edge: Feminism and Clitoridectomy," *Australian Feminist Studies* 5 (1987): 35–55.

56. For example, practicing Christian Scientists, who forswear many conventional medical treatments such as immunizations (for themselves and their children), tend to do better on the standard health indicators: longevity, rates of illness, incidence of heart disease and cancers, and others. I am grateful to Tris Englehardt for pointing this out to me.

57. I should emphasize that this sentence is not intended to suggest that liberalism is incompatible with the existence of any kind of higher authority—such as that of the government of the state. It is only to say that, in the liberal state, government is not authoritative with respect to the question of what is an acceptable way for people to live. It is, however, authoritative in a range of matters having to do with the interests of the liberal state.

58. On this, see Harold J. Berman, *Law and Revolution: The Formation of the Western Legal Tradition* (Cambridge: Harvard University Press, 1983), passim.

59. Jeff Spinner also takes this view in *The Boundaries of Citizenship: Race, Ethnicity, and Nationality in the Liberal State* (Baltimore: Johns Hopkins University Press, 1994).

60. The following argument was put to me in some detail by Will Kymlicka in written comments from which I quote.

61. See, on this, Kymlicka, "Rights of Cultural Minorities" and *Multicultural Citizenship* (Oxford: Oxford University Press, 1995).

62. Here I leave to one side the question of whether the rules should have been changed to accommodate parents such as these Christians. Clearly, taxation for education places an unfair burden on those looking to take the exit option (since they must relinquish claims they have paid for). Equally, I leave aside the question of whether it is appropriate for the state to be involved in the business of education in the first place.

63. In the long list of reasons why "voluntary membership" does not describe the status of citizens of the United States, one would have to include, at least, the unwillingness of loyalists to break away from Britain in the American Revolution; the involuntary incorporation of Texas and much of Mexico in the mid-nineteenth century; and the forcible incorporation of the Confederacy into the Union in 1865.

64. This analysis and question were presented by Professor Walzer in his comments during the NOMOS meeting when this essay was first presented.

65. See, in particular, "Of the Original Contract," in Hume's *Essays Moral, Political, and Literary* (Indianapolis: Liberty Fund, 1987), 465–87; for a brief account of Hume's politics, see Knud Haakonssen, "Introduction" to David Hume, *Political Essays,* ed. Knud Haakonssen (Cambridge: Cambridge University Press, 1994), xi-xxx.

66. Hume, "Of the Original Contract," 476–77.

67. I have addressed this question more fully in "Liberalism, Communitarianism and Political Community," *Social Philosophy and Policy* 13:1 (1996): 80–104.

68. See his "Rights of Minority Cultures," 144.

69. Ibid.

# 4

# RESPONSE TO KUKATHAS

## MICHAEL WALZER

There are many different actual and imaginable regimes of tolera-tion. Professor Kukathas invites us to consider the possible virtues of a regime in which there is no "common standpoint of morality" that governs the political decision to extend or deny toleration. There is, then, no individual or institutional agent occupying such a standpoint and making such decisions. And so there are no decisions at all, or no authoritative decisions, only a process of mutual adjustment and accomodation among the groups or com-munities that constitute the larger society (if that's what it is). No sovereign One tolerates the Others; they all tolerate one another. The different communities coexist, constantly negotiating and renegotiating the terms of their coexistence. These negotiations produce not one but a series of practical moral convergences, a series of "settlements," each of which, in its time, determines everyday practices in this or that area of social life. Commerce is the most obvious example.

We might say that the communities discover their "overlapping consensus," but this consensus is always unstable, since new com-munities join the negotiations (immigration to the country where all this is taking place is unrestricted) and old communities change, revising their views, reforming their own practices, with-out reference to the previous "settlement." The settlements can only be enforced within limits; coercion must stop as soon as the deviant community opts for withdrawal from the larger society and from whatever advantages the most recent negotiations had produced. This does not require a geographic removal; any community, like any household, that makes itself self-sufficient, can, as it were, secede in place, freeing itself from the rules to which everyone else is still committed. Its members can exit, for example, from the common markets. They would then exchange goods and services among themselves in any way they pleased—or in any way that the dominant members pleased.

Kukathas writes about this regime of toleration as if it doesn't yet exist, as if he is making a radical proposal. But it seems to me (and now, in the revised version of his paper, to him as well) that the regime he describes with conditional verbs already exists. International society is a regime of that sort, a maximally tolerant regime, where all the presumably intolerable practices that Kukathas lists are in fact tolerated.[1] Indeed, in international society, the radical innovators are not people like Kukathas who want to extend toleration: for it is hard to imagine that it could be extended much further than it already is. The innovators are people who want to restrict it, to establish and enforce a set of rules that derive from a "common moral standpoint." The standard argument against any such establishment and enforcement is exactly Kukathas' argument: that the existence of oppressive communities, "islands of tyranny in a sea of indifference," is preferable to the centralized tyranny (of a world state) that would be necessary to end the oppression.

Sovereignty is a doctrine of toleration—an especially effective doctrine since it doesn't depend on individual forbearance or respect for difference. In the society of sovereign states, toleration is institutionalized, and the costs of intolerance (as a policy, since it remains costless as an idea or a feeling) are raised very high indeed. Now moral crusaders have to be prepared to muster armies, cross borders, and shed blood. They are disconcertingly ready to do this but not often capable of doing it. The dominant rule in international society is therefore nonintervention, which can be interpreted as practical toleration.

But toleration is not absolute even in international society. There are limits, at least in principle, that reflect, I suppose, a certain moral convergence or settlement. Hence the practice, ragged and incoherent as it is, of *humanitarian intervention,* whose standing in the lawbooks suggests that massacre and "ethnic cleansing," while they may in fact be permitted, are not strictly speaking tolerated. Actions that "shock the conscience of humankind" should be stopped. The use of military force against their perpetrators by any member state (the international equivalent of citizen's arrest) is morally and legally allowed, perhaps even required. But the requirement is an imperfect duty, which is to say, no one's duty in particular, so in fact the brutalities and oppressions of international society are more often denounced than interdicted. I think that Kukathas is prepared to accept a similar outcome in his own regime of toleration (though even his state would probably intervene in communal life to stop a massacre).

And yet the limits putatively maintained by humanitarian intervention are modest indeed; they are minimalist limits. Advocates of an international Bill of Rights have a considerably more restrictive set in mind. They would make international society into something very close to the liberal domestic society that Kukathas criticizes. The question that his criticism poses, then, is best stated like this: do we want instead to make domestic society into something much more like the already existing international society?

My own inclination is to defend the difference between the two societies or, perhaps better, to argue that it isn't an eradicable difference; it arises out of and is manifest in a profound asymmetry between the two. There is one international society (in the contemporary world) and many domestic societies. The oneness has to do with the virtual absence of a common history and culture: member states participate equally in international society because none of them has to adapt to someone else's rules and practices. The manyness has to do with what we might think of as the absolute presence of particular histories and cultures, which necessarily have differentiating effects. And yet none of the many different domestic societies comes close to Kukathas's ideal, none even among those (a growing number) with populations made up of diverse groups. Why not?

Kukathas's ideal is a domestic society all of whose constituent groups have exactly equal standing in a very special sense, which no theory of equality has yet described: it is as if they had all arrived on the ground, in the country, simultaneously, and then participated actively and equally in the negotiated settlement of common rules and social practices. Or, since they didn't in fact arrive simultaneously, it is as if every negotiated settlement is purely provisional, subject to immediate renegotiation whenever a new group arrives. But the second "as if" is no more plausible than the first, and the whole picture mistakes what it means to "settle" on a set of rules and practices.

In reality, every settlement is or is on its way to becoming a way of life. Important things are at stake here; the negotiations take place over a very long period of time; they represent the gradual shaping of a common life—at least, a common political life. Their participants come to value the rules and practices that they slowly settle on; they want the settlement to endure; they want to pass on their ways of doing things (soon: their customs and traditions) to their children and grandchildren. So they celebrate the key moments of the settlement process; they mark off holidays and design ceremonial reenactments of crucial events (the moment when everyone took the sacred oath, say, or signed the covenant, or accepted the constitution); they write histories, build monuments, require the study of foundational texts, give to their practices and institutions the qualification of goodness. The result of all this is that every domestic society develops a "common moral standpoint," a set of shared understandings that is much thicker than that of international society, even if it is (as it always is) internally disputed, uncertain in its extent and coverage, allowing room at the margins for deviant or simply diverse practices. Religious difference and cultural pluralism are entirely compatible with this kind of commonality: indeed, they are likely to make for social conflict and civil war without it.

Then, when a new group arrives from abroad or rises to visibility from within, the question that Kukathas wants to exclude is necessarily posed (one might say: it poses itself): "Should *we* tolerate *them*?" This question, quite rightly, gets answered in different ways. The answers depend on what the way of life that *we* have constructed is like and on what *their* social practices are like. Some minimalist version of toleration probably ought to be required of all regimes and, similarly, a minimalist set of constraints on toleration. But considerable room is sure to remain, however these minimums are described, for maneuver and negotiation: here *we* can decide how much of *our* way of life *they* will have to accept and how much of *their* way *we* will respect and allow. (The pronouns are important; I have italicized them so as to highlight their unavoidability.) I suspect that liberal democracies, which naturalize newcomers with relative ease and recognize their children as citizens from birth, will be less tolerant of practices that oppress or injure these future fellow citizens than illiberal regimes would be. The Ottoman empire, for example, would have had no problems with Mormon polygamy—and wouldn't have had problems whatever its own standard family arrangements.

Imagine a society that has overthrown this or that form of imperial or authoritarian rule and created a liberal democratic regime (and a version of toleration)—over a long period of time, through difficult, perhaps even violent, political struggles. It has established the principle of equal citizenship, provided for the free education of all its children, vindicated the right of political opposition, separated church and state, barred discrimination on grounds of race, religion, and gender . . . and so on. (We have come, perhaps, to take the list too much for granted.) Then along comes a new group—not immigrants, let's say, but a group "gathered" by a political or religious prophet. Its members want to "bring up children unschooled and illiterate . . . enforce arranged marriages . . . deny conventional medical care [to themselves and their children] . . . and inflict cruel and 'unusual' punishment." These are Kukathas's examples (we can imagine the likely extensions of the list), and they demonstrate his seriousness; he is not interested in trivia. But how can he believe that in such a case the question, "Should we tolerate . . . " can be avoided? One would have to believe a lot more: that the people who had lived through the struggles for a liberal democratic politics, or heard about them from their parents, would have so little investment in their outcome that they would be prepared to welcome without qualification, to admit as fellow citizens, and to join in political decision making with, these others who reject both liberalism and democracy, who find themselves at odds with every aspect of liberal culture, not only in theory but in practice too. But, of course, Kukathas does not really expect toleration to prevail in such a case; he is only recommending it in theory. I would find the theory easier to understand if he could tell a plausible story about how a society might come into existence whose members would find this kind of toleration morally acceptable. Of course, the liberal democracy that I have been imagining didn't "come into existence." Like most political regimes, it was in part, at least, a creation, the project of committed men and women—and in such cases there will certainly be questions about whether to tolerate people with radically different projects.

Still, there is a plausible story that can be told, which is suggested by my Ottoman example. If a great warrior, or a warrior tribe, conquered a large number of communities and was content to rule them indirectly, collecting tribute or taxes, leaving the local notables in place and allowing them to work out patterns of coexistence with their immediate neighbors, this would be a regime of toleration close to, though not identical with, Kukathas's ideal. Unlike international society, which just happens, this would, again, be a creation, someone's project. But now the project would not necessarily make for intolerance. The conquering warriors could celebrate their triumphs, build monuments, write histories, and so on, without giving rise to a culture that was common to all their subjects. They would probably have contempt for their subjects—and no interest in commonality—but contempt of this sort is entirely consistent with toleration. The subject communities could still organize their own lives, maintaining among their members practices that a liberal democracy would not tolerate.

If Kukathas is committed to communal equality, however, this won't do. What imperialism produces, at best, is a conjunction of domination and tolerance, while what Kukathas wants is tolerance without domination. But in the absence of domination, the various "settlements" will have to be worked out by the people directly involved, and these people will then develop the kind of attachment to the settlements that I have already described; with whatever qualifications, they will come to share a moral standpoint. Human beings cannot be philosophically detached about their own way of life or morally indifferent to the history and content of the practical arrangements they collectively accept. The domestic society that Kukathas wants us all to live in would, therefore, have to be inhabited by beings of some other sort. Or, it would simply break up in the radical way suggested by its international analogue. The analogy would become an identity.

## NOTE

1. This volume, 70.

# 5

# ON HUMAN DIVERSITY AND THE LIMITS OF TOLERATION

## ADENO ADDIS

Out of the crooked timber of humanity no straight thing was ever made.
> —Immanuel Kant, "Idea for a Universal History with a Cosmopolitan Intent"

Civil tolerance . . . *merely* requires a recognition that in a pluralistic society we must "live and let live."
> —Chief Judge Lively, *Mozert v. Hawkins County Board of Education*

True generosity consists precisely in fighting to destroy the causes which nourish false charity.
> —Paulo Freire, *Pedagogy of the Oppressed*

There are about 8,000 distinct cultural groups inhabiting the more than 180 independent countries that are currently members of the United Nations.[1] Most nations are multiethnic and multicultural. For some countries, such as many in the developing world, such diversity is most often the result of political boundaries arbitrarily drawn by the former colonial powers. For others, such as the former colonial powers of Europe, multiethnicity is, to a large extent, a consequence of the presence of citizens from the former colonies. In France, for example, the issue of diversity is raised more intensely in relation to cultural activities of citizens from France's former colonies in North Africa.[2] The debate about diversity and multiculturalism in England is again a debate about how inclusive the country ought to be in relation to its citizens that have come from Britain's former colonial possessions such as

112

South Asia and the Caribbean or trace their ancestry to those places.[3] Still for others, such as the United States and Australia, which consider themselves immigrant nations, diversity is the defining feature of the nation rather than an "unintended" consequence of certain activities and structures.[4] Whether the multiplicity is the "unintended" consequence of colonialism or the organizing principle, the defining feature, of the particular nation-state, the uncontroverted fact is that most nations are indeed multiethnic and multicultural.

Given this fact, the question many cultural and ethnic groups in many nation-states have been asking is whether they can "all get along" as members of the same nation-state and what should be the institutional responses to tensions and skirmishes that result from such diversity. Of course, the question of "getting along" invites more questions: What does "getting along" mean? What are the institutional conditions for "getting along?"

There is, of course, an alternative to the attempt to get along. Married couples sometimes make that choice. They separate. Political separation, formally known as secession, is an alternative to attempting to make the political marriage work. Some groups have made that choice. As a general response to diversity in political units, however, separation seems as impractical as it is dangerous. It is impractical partly because not all groups that believe themselves to be marginalized and excluded from the social and political life of the polity live in a defined territorial unit. In such circumstances, secession will not be a viable answer to the problem of exclusion and discrimination. Indeed, the notion of separation under these conditions is likely to lead to a process of ethnic cleansing.[5] It is also true that not all groups that have grievances against a dominant majority want to secede, even if that were practically possible. They simply wish to participate equally and fully in the life of the political community.

Political separation as a general response to discrimination and exclusion of groups is also, in my view, dangerous. First, in many cases there are likely to be subunits in the new nation-state that are likely to invoke the same principle, the right of self-determination, that was relied upon by the new nation-state to separate itself from the larger political unit. Perhaps the most prominent current examples of this possibility are the destructive conflicts that have ravaged some of the countries that have been formed out of the former Yugoslavia, particularly Bosnia-Herzegovina and Croatia. Ethnic Serbs who live in those two countries invoked the same principle of self-determination to justify their desire for political separation that the two countries invoked when they separated from the former Yugoslavia. But the problem is not confined to the Balkans. It is a potential problem of every region. Thus, for example, some members of the English speaking population of Quebec, estimated to be about 18 percent of Quebec's population, are apparently insisting "that if Canada is divisible then Quebec is also divisible,"[6] and that they will fight for a separate entity in the event that Quebec separates from the rest of Canada.

The consequence of political divorce as a solution to multiplicity would be the proliferation of new mini-states that could be only barely economically viable and would be politically vulnerable. This can hardly be conducive to either political peace or economic progress, especially when the world is inhabited by as many distinct ethnic groups and cultures as it is. The impact of secession will be more pronounced in many developing countries, especially in Africa, where borders were arbitrarily drawn by colonial powers. To attempt to redraw the map through the process of political divorce is to plunge virtually every African country into an endless chaos. In addition, even if groups do not ultimately decide that political divorce is the answer to their unfavorable social and political conditions, if secession is enshrined either in the basic laws of the country, as is the case in relation to Ethiopia,[7] or is in some other ways recognized as an option, it is likely that the normal process of political bargaining will be seriously undermined. Some groups might use the threat of secession as a first resort to extract concessions from the central government, concessions that on the whole might be inefficient and bad for the nation.[8] Even if these groups do not succeed to extract the concession they sought, the energy and resources that the nation has to expend to persuade them not to make such damaging demands under the threat of secession are resources and energy that could fruitfully be devoted somewhere else.

It is also the case, as Allen Buchanan has argued, that secession is an inherently conservative remedy to the facts of diversity and the problems of oppression and exclusion.[9] Conservative, in the sense that the remedy is about multiplying states and not about challenging the nature and structure of state authority which quite often is the primary cause of the oppression and exclusion that make the notion of political divorce attractive. Here, the argument is that given the fact that the long-term solution to the problem of exclusion and oppression is going to be the rethinking of the nature of state authority and the notion of sovereignty, political theorists and legal scholars ought to spend a great deal of their time and energy exploring the features of self-determination that can be attained internally, as a result of the transformation of state authority, than to continually believe that "[l]et[ting] the people go who want to go"[10] will solve the problem that forced or prompted them to want to go. Secession quite often simply conserves and reproduces the very institutions that turned diversity into destructive conflict.

So, given the impracticality, unsatisfactory nature, and, at times, dangers of secession as a general response to the exclusion and marginalization of ethnic and cultural groups, it appears that there are no real alternatives to the process of "getting along." But, of course, as indicated earlier, the crucial questions are: What constitutes getting along in a multiethnic and multicultural polity? And what are the conditions of getting along?

The issue of how to deal with the facts of value diversity and social diversity (pluralism) is not new and has been with us for a long time, certainly since the end of the dominance of natural law cosmologies in the sixteenth and seventeenth centuries and the eventual separation of church and state.[11] Indeed, in many ways the major subject for political theorists and political philosophers seems always to have been one of defining and defending institutional structures that would deal with the facts of diversity, to be precise, defining and defending an acceptable relationship between majorities and minorities. But the issue has recently assumed a degree of urgency and has become a prominent subject of discourse among political and legal theorists and among philosophers. The renewed popularity of the subject is tied to a number of relatively recent political and social developments. The first is the disintegration of the Soviet Union and of communism as practiced by the Soviet Union and Eastern European countries.

The collapse of communism, the ideology of universality and unity, and the subsequent fragmentation of the Soviet Union and some of the Eastern European countries, brought with them the old ethnic rivalries and strife. These were conditions that were suppressed during the authoritarian era, though the self-serving proclamation was that those ethnic and cultural differences had been transcended.

Second, the demise of the Soviet Union transformed the bipolar world of international politics with a significant impact on ethnic conflicts in various parts of the world. The rivalry between the two superpowers had virtually led to the division of the world into two spheres of influence, each superpower helping materially and politically those regimes that it perceived to be sympathetic to its geopolitical and security interests. This meant that, in many cases, internal dissent, ethnic resentments, and resistance were successfully suppressed with the help of the particular superpower as long as the regime in power was seen to be sympathetic to the interests of the superpower, or perhaps more correctly, if it was seen to be sufficiently anti-the-rival-superpower. The end of the cold war meant that many repressive regimes could no longer count on superpower help to put down dissent and suppress ethnic consciousness and aspirations, and this allowed many groups that had felt excluded and marginalized to start challenging the status quo. Thus, it can be argued, the collapse of communism has led not only to the emergence, or reemergence, of ethnic conflicts in those countries that had defined themselves as communist, but also to the intensification of ethnic rivalries in countries that did not officially denominate themselves as communist.

Third, the debate in this country in the last decade or so about the various institutions of the country, especially the education and legal processes, has raised the issue of what constitutes "getting along," mainly among the races, and has placed it on the conversational agenda. Although the relationship between majorities and minorities has always been an important subject of deliberation in this country, in the last decade or so the issue has received renewed emphasis. The reason seems to be clear. Given the facts that, even after the efforts of the 1960s and 1970s, all aspects of life—schools, housing, houses of worship, even work—

remain segregated[12] and that the relationship among the races does not appear to be improving (and in some ways might be getting worse), the questions of what constitutes "getting along" and what institutional structures are conducive to "getting along" are being raised again and done so with vigor. The banner under which the issue is often debated is "multiculturalism."[13]

So, whether it is because of the collapse of communism, or the end of the bipolar world, or the multiculturalist challenge in this country, the issue of what constitutes getting along and what institutional structures are conducive to such end have become central aspects of political and legal discourse.[14]

One and very familiar response to the fact of social and value diversity has been to rely on the notion of toleration.[15] The argument from toleration goes as follows: given the possibility, even the likelihood, that diversity will be a permanent feature of many societies, the only way to respond to that fact of pluralism in a liberal democratic society will be to practice toleration. Toleration is seen as the bridge that links liberalism and pluralism.[16] But, of course, a polity cannot cultivate toleration in all aspects of its life and remain a political community. There must be principles, common bonds and institutions that must have the allegiance of all members of the political community. As a result, those that offer toleration as a virtue tend to define toleration as an attitude to be displayed and practiced in civil society. While public life is to be regulated by common standards, constituted through law, toleration is to prevail in what is denominated as the private realm.[17] Thus, what seems central to the notion of toleration is that there are two spheres—public and private—and that whatever is denominated as being part of the private realm is not amenable to state regulation, and is thus an area properly left as the realm of toleration. On the other hand, what is denominated as the public realm is one which is the proper area of state intervention and regulation. Toleration, therefore, seems to be both a virtue and a marker.

What is to be put in the private domain and what is to be a subject for collective reflection and deliberation has of course not been made clear. Indeed, part of the problem with the notion of toleration is that it is not always clear as to why a particular area is to be seen as private, and hence immune from collective deliberation (state intervention and regulation), while another area is viewed as a proper subject for collective reflection and judgment. Are religious convictions or cultural practices[18] better left to the private realm or are they proper subjects for collective judgment? All religious convictions? All cultural practices? It might be important to note here as a preliminary point that many currently prominent liberal theorists who make toleration central to their enterprise seem to determine what goes into the public or the private basket (and therefore what is a proper subject for toleration and what is not) on the ground of how controversial an issue is.[19] What this tends to do is to narrow, to limit, the political field (the public realm) as the variety of controversial issues grow and appear to be enduring and reasonable. I shall say something later about the consequence of attempting to cope with increasing diversity by a corresponding restriction of the political field, the public realm. Suffice it to mention here that what you would have under those circumstances is a dialogue among people who have been emptied of what seems to matter to them—public deliberation among people whose social selves have been drained of their depth.

While there might even be a measure of agreement as to what values are to be immune from state regulation, the reasons for such exclusion vary. Thus, for example, although there is some measure of agreement about the desirability of not making religious convictions subjects of collective deliberation, the reasons given on behalf of such a separation between the secular and the sacred vary greatly. For some, the reason for bracketing religious commitments from collective deliberation is that religious outlooks are underdetermined by reason and thus are not amenable to a common measure or ranking. Still for others, the bracketing is simply a pragmatic judgment: religious differences have, throughout history, been sources of destructive conflicts and the best way to avoid such conflicts is to ensure that no religious outlook dominates public institutions or public deliberation. And for others still, religious outlooks and cultural commitments are best defended as belonging to the private realm on (individual) autonomy grounds.[20] Regardless of the reasons offered for leaving cultural and religious commitments to the private realm and thus the realm where toleration governs, each one of these arguments claims that such course of action will be the most generous to cultural and religious minorities. The ultimate beneficiaries of the process of toleration are seen to be minorities. As an initial matter, this seems to be the case. Majorities, at least in liberal democracies,[21] do not need the space that toleration is seen to provide. So, it appears that toleration is actually the price majorities pay in the form of allowing certain practices and convictions from a minority that offend, or might be incommensurate with, strongly held principles of the majority. At first blush, therefore, the cost of toleration seems to be paid by the majority, in the form of either moral or economic injury. But toleration as currently understood and frequently practiced imposes hidden costs on the minority, costs that, as I shall argue, often far exceed the benefits that toleration is supposed to provide for those minorities. To paraphrase Paulo Freire's comment in another context, toleration is often a kind of false charity.[22] Note, my intent is not to argue that toleration is not a virtue but simply to recount what I see as the costs that those who advocate toleration do not but should reflect on.

Advocates of toleration appear to embrace positive and negative aspects of the concept.[23] In the context of the relationship among groups, the negative dimension of toleration restrains the majority from trampling on the views, beliefs, and commitments of minorities. Quite often, it is in this negative sense that the concept of toleration is appropriated. And it is this dimension of toleration that is viewed as most generous to minorities. But there is a positive dimension to toleration as well that some defenders of the concept articulate. One such view holds that the development of reason is strongly tied to the development of toleration in a given society. This view is held by Chandran Kukathas who defends the position in a chapter of this collection,[24] and to some extent by Lee Bollinger who defines and defends First Amendment jurisprudence on the grounds that free speech is an exemplar process through which the body-politic progressively develops forms of rational interaction among individuals and among groups.[25]

But first to the negative version of toleration. As I argued in the last section, one of the reasons that advocates of toleration offer in their defense of the concept is that in a democracy toleration will provide better protection for minority cultures.[26] It, of course, is better for a minority to be left alone to practice its religion and culture than to be coerced with the power of the state to abandon those cultural and religious commitments. Even more, it appears as if the cost of toleration is born by the majority, in the form of injury to its moral outlook and perhaps even to its economic interests.[27] But in fact there is an enormous hidden cost that is born by the "tolerated" minority communities, a cost that might be very high, and one we need to reflect on.

First, to tolerate is not necessarily to respect. Indeed, quite often toleration in the negative sense is simply the kinder and gentler side of nonrespect, the less kinder side being suppression (conquest) or annihilation. We might want to refer to this type of toleration as paternalistic toleration. Here, the toleration by the majority is either based on indifference or is accompanied by nonrespect. A majority, for example, might be prepared to tolerate a minority culture in the sense that it will not use the coercive power of the state to prohibit the practice, but the majority might continue to believe that the cultural practices are uncivilized and strange with no merit either to be taken seriously or to be engaged in a dialogue. I call this aspect of negative toleration paternalistic, because the toleration is one *extended* by the majority as an act of self-restraint by the majority (as an act of social generosity) to share a social space with a culture that the majority believes does not merit to share such social space. For minorities, paternalistic toleration is often purchased at the heavy price of not being recognized as equal participants in the polity, ironically the very thing that toleration is meant to cure.

Some might argue that even if the toleration is informed by paternalism, the important thing is that multiplicity is recognized through the process of toleration. The result not the intention is what is important, the argument might go. But that misconceives the nature of the problem and the injury. To be tolerated as the strange Other is to be simultaneously defined as one whose legitimacy in the polity is not fully secure. The paradox of paternalistic toleration is, therefore, that it appears to affirm the right of the Other to be part of the polity while simultaneously announcing the Other's marginality. This ambiguous position is what many minorities experience, with substantial psychic cost to members of the minority. By psychic cost, I mean to suggest that members of minority groups are forced to deal, perhaps on daily basis, with the seemingly irreconcilable "two-ness,"[28] that members of the majority are not subjected to. But the cost is not simply psychic. Insofar as the majority culture forms the background framework within which sense is made of public deliberations about the terms and conditions of political life and institutional arrangements, to be simply tolerated as the strange Other is not to have one's culture and "horizons of significance"[29] inform the constitution of public institutions and the development of public values. Thus, while what is important for members of the majority implicitly or explicitly constitutes the public identity of the polity, what seems central to the lives of members of a minority becomes, to use a phrase employed by Stephen Carter to describe the role that important religious commitments of individuals play under current Supreme Court jurisprudence of the separation of church and state, a "kind of hobby."[30]

To treat individuals with "equal respect" entails, at least partly, respecting their traditions and cultures, the forms of life which give depth and coherence to their identities. And to treat those forms of life with respect means to engage them, not simply to tolerate them as strange and alien.

Second, insofar as paternalistic toleration does not provide for, and is in fact hostile to, the notion of the tolerator taking the tolerated group seriously and engaging it in a dialogue, the polity cannot cultivate an important virtue, what Benjamin Barber has referred to as "civility (reciprocal empathy and respect)."[31] One can hardly develop empathy for those that one only knows as the alien and strange. To have reciprocal empathy is to first attempt to understand the Other, but there cannot be understanding the Other if one is not prepared to engage the Other in a dialogue. And here I am not simply, even primarily, talking about individual dialogues[32] but rather institutional dialogues. I shall elaborate on this point later, but for the moment it suffices to say that I have in mind three institutions—the legal, education, and the communication processes—that can play a role in this institutional dialogue. Dialogue is not only necessary to understand the Other, but it is also essential for self-discovery on the part of the majority insofar as the majority defines itself in reaction to the minority. In the process of engaging the Other, rather than through practicing the simple toleration of "live and let live," the majority might discover that the Other is in fact sedimented within it. In addition, multiethnic and multicultural societies, if they are to sustain themselves over a long period of time (while remaining democratic), have to cultivate and reconcile pluralism and solidarity (in the form of what I call later pluralistic solidarity). Toleration might affirm a notion of pluralism, but it is too thin to cultivate and sustain any sense of solidarity.

Also, there is the pragmatic issue of decisionmaking in a democratic society. Given the fact that legislative and administrative decisions, and to some extent judicial decisions as well, are influenced by the preferences of the majority, a society where the majority tolerates the minority as the strange Other may find it difficult to develop policies and programs that would correct current and historic injustices against the minority. This could happen in one of a number of ways. The majority might put pressure on its elected officials not to adopt (or to dismantle) remedial policies designed to give more opportunity to historically disadvantaged groups that are viewed as the strange Other. It is arguable, for example, that the current movement in this country to dismantle affirmative action is partly informed by the majority's view of African Americans as the undeserving and strange Other. Recent surveys show that when the question is affirmative action for women, as opposed to for minorities, there is an 11 percent increase in the support for affirmative action.[33] At other times the tradition of tolerating the minority as strange and alien might even lead to a situation where general principles of nondiscrimination are not extended to members of that minority. A good example is the resistance in this country to extending the protection of nondiscrimination to gay Americans, even though many, and perhaps most, Americans think that they tolerate homosexuality. And lastly, the tolerated Other might be excluded in the guise of a neutral application of laws that clearly were not devised with the tolerated minority in mind, such as a school code that required students not to wear headgear.[34] To develop reciprocal empathy that would inform inclusive politics as well as prepare the ground for what I have called pluralistic solidarity, what is required is not simple toleration but dialogic engagement. Of course, if there is to be genuine dialogue between majorities and minorities, the process has to be mindful of the fact that the economic market is as partial to the majority, as is the political market of whose capacity to be neutral among groups we are rightly suspicious. The policy implication of this observation is that affirmative steps are necessary to ensure that minorities have equal access to the means of communication. That is, in the communication process, as in other areas, we should not treat the market status quo as neutral.

Third, in the guise of generosity to minorities, the paternalistic tolerator treats ethnic and cultural minorities as no different than private associations, such as, for example, the American Association of University Professors (AAUP). Take Chandran Kukathas, who argues, in an earlier work as well as in the essay included in this volume,[35] that most prominent liberal theories that seek to protect cultural minorities are neither sufficiently protective of cultural minorities nor sufficiently liberal. Here he is mainly referring to the works of Will Kymlicka and John Rawls. They are not sufficiently protective of cultural minorities, he argues, because they demand that those cultural minorities adhere to some important (substantive) liberal values such as respecting the autonomy of the individual members in those communities. Respecting the autonomy of the individual means that those communities cannot coerce or harm individual members so as to force allegiance and commitment to the tradition, even if such coercive measure is deemed important to sustain the tradition. Kukathas argues that recognizing the right of cultural communities only when they comply with certain liberal values is not generous or tolerant enough, especially when the very liberal value according to which they are to organize and regulate themselves, as a minimum condition for being tolerated, seriously undermines central aspects of the culture. On the other hand, argues Kukathas, those same liberal theories are not liberal enough. Even though they require that minority cultural groups adhere to certain liberal principles (such as individual autonomy) as a condition of toleration, they still recognize the notion of group right (the rights of cultural groups). Recognizing group right, even in this restricted way, the argument goes, violates two important precepts of liberalism: one normative and the other empirical. The normative principle is that individuals are the only sources of moral concern and hence the only bearers of rights. The notion of cultural right is therefore seen as a metaphysical absurdity. The empirical argument holds that group identity (such as the formation of cultural communities) is informed by historical and political factors and that it changes when those specific contexts change.[36] One ought not, therefore, talk of cultural rights as if cultures were stable and prepolitical.

The way to cure these twin defects of prominent liberal theories, Kukathas argues, is to embrace a notion of toleration that would allow groups, including illiberal groups, to organize and govern themselves without the requirement that they adhere to any liberal principle except that they allow members to exit to the wider community when those members no longer wish to adhere to the organizing principle of the group.[37] Notice, the model Kukathas seems to be following is that of voluntary associations (or what one might call nonorganic groups). Cultural or ethnic groups are tolerated only insofar as the majority liberal order gets a chance to redescribe them in terms of organizations that are familiar to the liberal order. Members of cultural and ethnic minorities have the right to freedom of association in the same way that university professors can join the American Association of University Professors (AAUP), or gun enthusiasts and hunters can join the National Rifle Association (NRA).

But that redescription has enormous cost for minorities. Kukathas might be more tolerant than other liberal theorists but only after he has reduced cultural and ethnic minorities into the status of private organizations with no more social significance than those private associations. The reality is of course quite different. While those private associations are usually organized around one particular issue, one's affiliation to ethnic and cultural groups will tend to affect one's entire set of choices and options. In this sense, one could say that even though one's membership in various voluntary organizations contributes to one's identity, one's membership in a cultural or ethnic group provides the primary factor. I will call the first set of factors as second-order factors and the second set as first-order factors. That being the case, our concern for the survival and flourishing of social groups from which first-order factors of identity are derived, such as cultural and ethnic groups, must be qualitatively different than our concern for those voluntary groups which supply us with the second-order factors of our identities. Not only because the dislocation to the individual identity resulting from the misrecognition or disappearance of the first is more serious than is the case with the disappearance of the second,[38] but also because the false symmetry[39] utterly misdescribes the nature of the disputes among ethnic and cultural groups in multicultural and multiethnic societies. The complaints many cultural and ethnic minorities have against majorities is not that they are forbidden to affirm privately their convictions and commitments and the capacity to plead as special interests in the political and economic markets, but rather that they ought not be seen as special, narrow, and private interests while the culture and the ethnic affiliation of the majority is viewed implicitly or explicitly as representing the general interest. To view cultural and ethnic groups as similar to voluntary and one-issue associations is in my view already to stack the deck against those minorities in the dispute between majorities and minorities. Thus, Kukathas's seemingly generous toleration of cultural and ethnic minorities actually comes with a heavy price. Toleration comes in abundance only after the tolerated group has been redescribed so as to rob it both of its significance and the nature of its complaints.

Also, the sort of toleration that is modeled after the right of free association of voluntary organizations does not help us to deal with most of the significant questions that arise between majorities and minorities in multicultural and multiethnic societies. Those questions include whether minorities can, for example, rightly insist that their cultures and beliefs be part of the agenda for public discourse about public institutions and priorities within the polity, whether their cultures and sense of history should be part of the curriculum interrogating the majorities' sense of history and culture.[40] It is at the moment when minorities seek to engage majorities in some sort of institutional dialogue, not when they withdraw into private associations, that conflicts arise between majorities and minorities.[41] Thus, even the most generous notion of toleration does not appear to provide for the institutional possibility of the minority interrogating the majority both to show that the majority is as contingent as the minority, whose contingency and contexuality the majority likes to point out, as well as to develop a sense of solidarity between majorities and minorities, something that liberal democratic political communities need to develop if they are to sustain themselves over a period of time.

In place of what I see to be the limits of negative toleration, I shall, in the next section briefly sketch what can be referred to as pluralistic solidarity. Pluralistic solidarity, unlike negative toleration, will, I believe, allow us to cultivate and to reconcile two important principles that must define every multiethnic and multicultural nation-state: pluralism and solidarity. I shall then make a brief attempt to puzzle out the implication of pluralistic solidarity to an important concern of those that advocate a second, positive, dimension of toleration—the development of reason in a multiethnic and multicultural society.

The task of political and legal theory in the late twentieth century must be one of imagining institutions and vocabularies that will affirm multiplicity while cultivating solidarity, a task that seems to demand reconciling seemingly irreconcilable commitments. A society that acknowledges the fact of pluralism (and its normative desirability) without providing the institutional means through which the ethic of reciprocal empathy, respect, and inclusiveness are cultivated is a society which at best allows minorities to be tolerated as the marginal Other or, at worst, lays the ground for an endless and destructive conflict, where in most cases the minority will probably shoulder the greater cost. Emphasis on solidarity without providing the mechanism through which the fact of pluralism (and difference) can be recognized and normatively affirmed is to commit the error of the communitarian, who simply asserts solidarity, with the consequence that minorities will be either forcibly assimilated or forcibly removed. Either option is not, and ought not to be, attractive to minorities.

Before I explore the issue of how these two commitments could be cultivated, let me make one important point. Some defenders as well as critics of multiculturalism and ethnic revival misunderstand the nature of the claim of cultural and ethnic minorities. They read these tendencies as rejections of solidarity and commonality. While critics are alarmed by the prospect[42] and defenders tend to be more positive about it, both seem to read ethnic and cultural revivals as signs that community and solidarity are being rejected. But the fact is that it is not solidarity and reciprocal empathy that ethnic and cultural minorities have come to challenge. Rather, it is the terms of the social union, the patterns of connection, which do not give them much role in the constitution of the national identity, that they challenge under the banner of multiculturalism. The call is not for the destruction of commonality but for a vision of commonality *through* diversity where the connections and commonalties embody our actual experiences.

What is the nature of the solidarity, "shared identity," that I want to defend here, and how is it different from the sort of solidarity communitarians defend and that I think is hostile to multiplicity? By "shared identity" I mean to refer to an identity that bonds together, partially and contingently, minorities and majorities, such that different cultural and ethnic groups are seen, and see themselves, as networks of communication where each group comes to understand its distinctiveness as well as the fact that that distinctiveness is to a large degree defined in terms of its relationship with the Other. Viewed in this way, the notion of shared identity is not a final state of harmony, as communitarians would claim. It is rather a process that would allow diverse groups to link each other in a continuous dialogue with the possibility that the life of each group will illuminate the condition of others such that in the process the groups might develop, however provisionally and contingently, "common vocabularies of emancipation,"[43] and of justice. I think Seyla Benhabib is right when she observed that "[t]he feelings of friendship and solidarity result . . . through the extension of our moral and political imagination . . . through the actual confrontation in public life with the point of view of those who are otherwise strangers to us but who become known to us through their public presence as voices and perspectives we have to take into account."[44]

As I have argued earlier, toleration is simply too thin to lead to such an environment. Indeed, the surest way to destroy what is important to an opponent is to ignore it, if one has the power to so ignore. And under the tolerant regime majorities get to do that. They neither have to take seriously nor engage some important aspects of the cultures of the minority, an important aspect of the identity of the minority. A genuine sense of shared identity, social integration, in multicultural and multiethnic societies will develop only through a process where minorities and majorities are linked in institutional dialogue. Shared identity, like justice itself, is defined discursively. I believe there are three institutions that are central in this discursive process. I have in mind the education system, the media and, of course, the law. I have explored elsewhere the importance of the media and the law in the cultivation of the virtue of pluralistic solidarity, shared identity,[45] and I am currently exploring the role of education as constitutive narrative. Here, I want to briefly set out why I think the communication process is important in the development of that shared identity. But first let me give a brief sketch of why I think that the three institutions are central in the development of the identity of a polity, that "social union of social unions" to use Rawls's imagery.[46] It is through the media, the legal, and education processes that we "tell stories about where we have been, what is important to us, how we relate to one another, and what and who the problems are, as well as possible solutions to those problems."[47] It is through these institutions that we develop an elaborate image of "us." All three cultural institutions define what is acceptable, relevant and credible evidence in determining what experiences define the shared identity of the political community.

Quite often, however, these institutions narrate the story of the political community as if the minorities (and their past) do not form part of the story, or, even worse, that they are seen as the negation of the majority, as an overflow of the identity of the majority. Minorities are either invisible or are resurrected as The Problem Other, as the negation of the moral and normal order. This normal and moral order is one that closely describes and represents the social world that roughly accords with the world view of the majority. To take solidarity seriously is to take these cultural institutions seriously and to open them up to minorities so that the story of the political community will develop in the process of the various communities in the polity interrogating each other.

Take the communication process, for example. As far back as 1968, the United States Supreme Court observed that the media, especially the electronic media, is "demonstrably a principal source of information . . . for a great part of the Nation's population."[48] That observation is even more true now (given the revolution in communication technologies) and applies to a greater part of the world.[49] And indications are the media, especially the electronic media, will play an increasingly important role in defining what the common bonds are that tie the various communities in a political community. The role will be more decisive in political communities such as those in the developing countries where the notion of nationhood is still fragile and physical isolation still a factor. But the role of the media will also be as important in many developed countries, such as the United States, where certain minorities still live a segregated existence. In the United States, for example, black Americans, as a general matter, are isolated from the majority. Neighborhoods and schools are still highly segregated. So are churches. The most sustained contact blacks and whites have is through the media. It is through the media, not through individual contacts and conversations, that they construct each others' images. As I have argued elsewhere, the image of the minority that is constructed by the media is one that views minorities as the transgressing Other, the negation of the normal and moral order which is inhabited by the majority.

The prevalent image of blacks as problems is facilitated by two facts. First, quite often, blacks become of interest to the mainstream media primarily in relation to unusual or exceptional events, when there is crime, rioting, or a controversial statement by a member of the black community. In a segregated world, those exceptional events often become the dominant context in which the majority encounters the minority. The life of the minority gets reduced to that of the community being, or having, a problem. The complaint here is not that the media reports bad news about minorities, especially African Americans, or that the media tends to focus on the unusual and exceptional as news items.[50] Rather, it is that topics which are routinely part of the coverage of the majority—social, economic, and cultural life—do not play a large part in the media coverage of the African American community, and consequently, in a segregated world, the negative exceptional event becomes the dominant context through which the majority constructs the identity of the minority. This, of course, has enormous consequences for how the majority structures its responses toward the minority.

Second, the image is developed in the context of a professional environment that had, until recently, excluded blacks as communicators. There are still very few blacks in the communication process, either as owners of the media or as employees in management positions where decisions are made as to what to communicate and how it ought to be communicated. As a general matter, blacks have been objects of deliberation rather than deliberating subjects, their stories told by others and consequently their identities constructed in their absence.

I think it is fair to assume that given the increasingly important role that the media is playing in various polities the position and image of marginalized minorities in other countries won't be different. If they do not have access to the media, they will continue to be viewed either as a group with a problem or as the problem, and that the identity of the political community will be constructed as being exhausted by the story of the majority. Worse, the majority will define its identity with the unfavorable image of the minority as the background opposition.

If we want to cultivate a more defensible and more inclusive identity for a political community defined by plural communities, that is a society where pluralistic solidarity reigns, then we have to pay a great deal of attention to institutions, such as the communication process, through which communities continually and explicitly produce their identities and what they deem to be the negation of those identities. And only when we cultivate pluralistic solidarity will we avoid destructive conflicts among various groups.

Not only do I argue that pluralistic solidarity will be far superior than simple toleration, especially that defended by Kukathas, from the point of view of peaceful coexistence in a multicultural and multiethnic political community, but I also contend that pluralistic solidarity will lead to the development of more defensible forms of reason(s) in a pluralistic world than that offered in the seemingly generous toleration model embraced by those such as Kukathas.

Some of those who advance toleration as central to a liberal democratic social and political order argue that toleration is important not only because it might allow us to live in the same political entity (political "community") with different outlooks and horizons of significance, but because it is the process through which reason, normalcy, itself develops. In a pluralist age where the notion of a universal reason is under serious, and some would say effective, challenge, many liberal theorists have turned to what they consider to be a more defensible notion of reason, which is localized and historicized. Reason is no longer perceived as universal, unitary, and abstract but local, plural, and practical. After all, if the social world is defined by plural values (plural traditions) and moral universes (and traditions) that may often be incommensurate[51] with one another, then it would be logical to assume that there are correspondingly plural reasons.[52] But exactly how does reason, in this new, modest incarnation, develop and how will we be able to tell that a particular interaction or decision is informed by reason rather than something else, such as the subtle exercise of power over others or simple manipulation. Here, different theorists supply different answers. My interest here is how those who see toleration as the bridge that connects liberalism and pluralism view the development of reason.

In a chapter included in this volume, Chandran Kukathas defends toleration, following Kant, as an independent value (as opposed to the Millian notion that views toleration as simply being instrumental to achieving other values, such as truth) partly because "[t]oleration . . . is the condition which gives judgments worth." By this, Kukathas means that the extent to which judgments are authoritative depends on the degree to which they are based on reason and that reason is not so much a matter of settled standards but rather one that is practical and develops in the process of public conversations and debates. It is this belief that leads Kukathas to quote Kant approvingly: "The development of reason and of toleration is interdependent. . . . Practices of toleration help constitute reason's authority."[53]

To the extent that Kukathas believes that reason is local, historical, and practical, I am in complete agreement with him. But unlike him I do not see a necessary connection between reason and toleration. Indeed, in many cases toleration without more reason might lead exactly to the opposite, to unreason. As I have argued earlier, toleration does not necessarily require that various communities be linked in continuous dialogue. Given that, a majority might simply tolerate a minority as the strange, or the problem, Other. Under those circumstances, it would be difficult to contend that whatever judgment flows from that state of affairs leads to the development of reason in terms of the relationship of majority and minority communities. Stereotypes and prejudices, not reason, would prevail in such a context.

Furthermore, even if one grants that there are times where toleration leads to dialogue between majorities and minorities, those who advance the thesis that reason and toleration are inter-dependent do not supply us with the criteria by which we might be able to identify which practices and actions that emerge from the apparent interaction among majorities and minorities are properly viewed as reasonable and which are not. Simply to as-sume that whatever emerges out of a way of life that appears to be characterized by toleration, even when there appears to be some dialogue between majorities and minorities, is the vindication of reason is in my view dangerous, and especially so for minorities. I say that, because even when it appears that there is a consensus on a "common standard," the consensus might be more a function of power and unequal cultural capital than the authority of reason in display. No amount of disclaimer that this is not a *modus vivendi* would change the fact that it looks very much like one.[54]

Of course, one way to avoid this pitfall is to do what Jürgen Habermas does. Habermas also holds the view that reason emerges in the process of communication. For Habermas a norm is correct and therefore valid if it is the result of rational practical discourse.[55] Reason is defined not in terms of transcendental subjectivity but in terms of communication. Habermas's attempt to reconstruct reason in terms of practical discourse is accompa-nied by a counterfactual—what Habermas calls the ideal speech situation—so as to enable us to decide as to when the force of the better argument has won.[56] The toleration model, at least in Kukathas's version, simply asks us to *assume* that toleration would lead to the convergence of various ways giving rise to the establishment of a common (and authoritative) standard by which interactions among groups would be regulated.

Habermas's notion of the development of reason is superior to that of the toleration model. First, unlike the toleration model Habermas's communication model views dialogue as a condition for the development of reason. Indeed, Habermas refers to reason as "communicative rationality." Second, Habermas, through his notion of the ideal speech situation, gives us a counterfactual through which we can determine as to what sort of communication can lead to rational norms and what cannot. Also, in some of his more recent work, [57] Habermas has recognized that dialogue cannot be viewed in strictly individual terms. An adequate theory of individual rights and capacities to communicate must be sensitive to the importance of collectivities (such as cultural and ethnic groups) in the lives of individuals and to the possibility that members of cultural and ethnic communities might be continually outbid and outvoted in the communication market.[58] However, Habermas seems to be ambiguous as to the strategy by which cultural and ethnic minorities could be institutionally included in the dialogic process.

What I have termed *pluralistic solidarity* sees the development of public reason as one that emerges out of the dialogue among various communities and traditions where these communities and traditions have the necessary resources to engage each other in a dialogue. This would often require that there be affirmative steps to provide cultural and ethnic minorities, which are often outbid and outvoted in the market, with the necessary resources. In relation to the communication process, as I have argued earlier, there are two specific ways to admit minorities into the communication process: as owners of the media of communication and as employees in management positions where decisions about what is to be communicated and in what form it is communicated are made.

Why do I think that dialogue among the various communities is essential to develop a rational standard by which the life of the multicultural society would be regulated? There are at least three factors that make a principle or a standard rational. It is fully informed, relatively neutral, and integrative. First, to be rational a principle must be derived from the fullest information available. No one particular community (or tradition) can possess all the necessary information through which matters of political and ethical life could be viewed and analyzed.[59] It is true that it is individuals who must confront, and make judgments on, issues of political and ethical life. But individuals make sense of those ethical and political questions not as abstract individuals, but as members of a particular culture, race, religion, and so forth. It is within certain cultural frameworks that judgments about such issues avail themselves and are made sense of. Thus, a principle or a standard developed without the involvement of some traditions (or histories) is unlikely to be based on the fullest information available and cannot therefore be considered rational.

My notion of full information requires not only that all relevant traditions engage in the process but also that we abandon the sharp distinction between public and private insofar as the distinction is employed to screen certain information (information that is an important aspect of the identity of a group) out of the public conversation on the account of it being private and not public concern, especially when the very notion of what constitutes private is defined in terms of how controversial (reasonably or otherwise) the issue is. If issues are taken off the public conversational table (the deliberative process) on the grounds that those issues are controversial, it is likely that it is those issues that matter for minorities and marginal groups that, in the main, will end up being pushed out. Insofar as it is unfamiliarity in part that leads to viewing a position or a practice as strange and controversial, it will be practices of minorities which have not achieved hegemonic status that will be prime candidates for such exclusion.

Second, the principle by which common life is to be regulated among the various traditions must be as impartial as practicable. One view holds that impartiality will be developed through the "*decoupling* [of] the majority culture from the political culture with which [the political culture] was originally fused, and in most instances still is."[60] The notion of decoupling is also the story of the law. The law is said to be impartial to the extent that it is decoupled from the culture, gender, and color of the majority. But I believe decoupling is impossible and illusory, for in most instances the political culture and the majority culture (gender and color) are intertwined to such an extent that each assumes the other unreflexively. In these circumstances color-, gender-, and culture-blindness will merely be blindness to the minority and to the marginalized. I think the best course might be to broaden the pool (to expand the sources, the heterogeneous publics) from which the political culture can draw rather than to attempt to decouple the majority culture form the political culture. When majorities have to engage minorities in a dialogue, the resulting principle is likely to be more impartial, and hence more rational, partly because of what Jon Elster calls "the civilizing effects of hypocrisy." [61] The belief that one has to justify to another tradition a particular act or interest is likely to affect the way the interest is cast, for the interest has to appear reasonable to those to whom it is presented. The interest will appear reasonable only to the extent that it is viewed as attending to the differences and interests that define the Other. Cumulatively, the effect might be not only that rhetorical devices that attend to differences develop but also through the communication process the dialogue partners might come to understand, transcend, and transform their initial understanding of their interests.

Third, a principle or a standard is rational to the extent that it is integrative. By "integrative," I do not mean that it leads to a harmonious union. Rather, I mean two things. First, that it encourages critical reflection and conceptual clarity about the common interest. Second, it ensures not only more awareness about the nature and intensity of the differences and conflicts, when such conflicts and differences exist, but it will likely lead to a coherent ordering of those interests. Dialogue among the various groups is likely to be integrative in both senses. In the first sense, such a dialogue is likely to make the various groups aware of the things that are common to them. In the second sense, the integrative function is much more complex. In the course of dialogue, not only might various traditions discover commonality, but the dialogue partners might also be forced to engage in a coherent ordering of the various issues and interests over which there are conflicts. This conceptual clarity about the intensity and order of the interests might make agreements on certain matters easier. I think it is also reasonable to assume that in the course of engaging the minority in a dialogue the tendency for majorities to view and define minorities as the (strange) different Other, as the negation of the normal and moral order, is likely to be reduced.

In sum, the presence of minorities in the media or in the education and legal processes, and the dialogue between majorities and minorities that that is likely to foster, will lead to the development of practical rationality by supplying the three ingredients I suggested are constitutive of reason: fuller information, a degree of impartiality, and critical reflection on and conceptual clarity about the nature and order of the interests that are both common to and divide the various communities.

Let me now address a possible objection to the process I have outlined as a way of developing practical rationality. The objection might go this way: While dialogue might be a desirable, even necessary, means of developing practical rationality in multicultural and multiethnic societies, in the real world (in the world we inhabit) it is impossible to institutionalize dialogue among the various communities in a political entity. The challenge here is not to the normative desirability of dialogue as I have outlined it but to its institutional feasibility. To this objection I have three responses.

First, I simply deny the truth of the assertion. My suggestion that we diversify the education, legal, and communication processes as to allow the various traditions and cultures to interrogate one another is in fact institutionally specific and feasible. I have indicated in this essay how the communication industry could be diversified. Diversifying the educational and legal institutions will not be any less feasible. So, when critics allege that dialogue is institutionally unfeasible they must mean that it is not normatively desirable or defensible. But that is a different issue, which I hope I have addressed adequately in this essay.

My second response, is the answer Alexander Meiklejohn gave to (anticipated) critics of his notion of "self-government" as a primary justificatory principle for the First Amendment (for freedom of expression). He wrote: "However far our practice falls short of the intention expressed by the words ['we govern the U.S.'], they provide the standard by which our practices must be justified or condemned."[62] Thus, even if it is accepted that the institutional structures we currently inhabit are such that we might not be able to fully capture the dialogic process that I am advocating, the notion of dialogue, like Meiklejohn's "self-government" and Habermas's "ideal speech situation," will act as a standard by which we will be able to measure the democratic and rational nature of the interactive process, and toward which we can reform our political structures and institutions.

My third response is to argue that in fact we have institutionalized the concept of dialogue in many areas and we have done so because we believe that such dialogue will lead to rational principles and rational decisions. Take, for example, the adjudicative process. We have an adversarial system which is based partly on the belief that a decision would be more rational and just if the narratives of the two opposing sides are admitted and engage each other as well as if the judge has the opportunity to engage in dialogue the lawyer-advocate for each party to the dispute. And in the appellate context, not only do judges engage the lawyer-advocate in a dialogue, but often they also engage each other in a dialogue, deliberation in a judicial conference, before they announce a decision or perhaps a new norm with the decision. Thus, in the adjudicative process the notion of dialogue as a prerequisite for rational decision making seems to be central, though not fully or well articulated. Even in other areas, such as the communication process, the notion of dialogue as a means of developing rational principles or arriving at rational decisions seems to be institutionally affirmed. Take, for example, the notion of the "right of reply," the "right of correction," talk-back TV, and so on. All are, if fairly rudimentary and tentative, attempts to give substantive content to the notion of dialogic exchange being an important aspect of developing rational principles and arriving at rational decisions.

So the issue, it seems to me, is no longer whether dialogue is necessary for the cultivation of practical rationality or whether we are capable of institutionalizing dialogue. It appears that many of our institutions assume that it is through dialogue that we develop practical rationality and that there are attempts to institutionalize some version of dialogue in the various spheres. Rather, the issue is whether cultural and ethnic identities should be seen as relevant factors that should publicly matter in the dialogic process and if so how should they be factored in that process? I have argued in this essay that ethnic and cultural membership should be institutionally included in the dialogic process if we are to cultivate pluralistic solidarity as well as to develop practical rationality. I have also suggested that three institutions are good candidates for such inclusive process: the legal, educational, and communication processes.

There is now one more issue to address which I shall address relatively briefly. The issue is this: how does the notion of pluralistic solidarity, which emphasizes dialogue among groups and among traditions and which views multiethnic and multicultural societies as networks of communication, deal with the question of linguistic plurality? That is, if the demand for pluralism by groups include the demand to cultivate and use their own language in schools, courts, and the media, how would dialogue (and shared deliberation) be possible without the dominant group coercively imposing a single language (more likely its language) on all citizens?[63] This is perhaps the most difficult question that a multicultural and multiethnic society has to address. The dilemma is this: on the one hand, a genuine concern for the survival and flourishing of a group's culture will have to show concern for the survival of the group's language as well. This is because, as I have argued elsewhere,[64] the survival of a group's culture is, to some extent, dependent on the vitality of its language. Language is not a mere medium of reality. It is partly constitutive of that reality. It affects how we think and how we view and perform the rituals that are central to the particular culture. Thus, to destroy a group's language might contribute to the destruction of that group's culture. There is also a pragmatic reason that argues against coercive linguistic assimilation. The point is vividly illustrated by what has been happening in Sri Lanka for the past few years: a bloody civil war, between the Tamil minority and the Sinhalese majority, has brought enormous destruction to that island nation. Some have argued that the beginning of the tension that ultimately led to the civil war can partly be traced back to 1956. During that year the Parliament of then Ceylon, by a simple majority, passed a law that made Sinhala, the language of the majority, the only official language of the island. The Tamil minority viewed this as an assault on the very existence of its culture.[65] Thus, it is not only the centrality of language to cultures and cultural developments that counsels against coercive linguistic assimilation, but also the political fact that undermining the language of minorities might, as the Sri Lankan example suggests, lead to conflict and destruction rather than to stability and harmonious union as assimilationists probably desire and believe.[66]

On the other hand, if democratic political communities are to sustain themselves over a long period of time the various cultural and ethnic communities have to engage each other in continuous and institutional dialogue rather than seeing each other as alien and strange. There cannot be such dialogue unless there is a common language or common languages. So, the question becomes whether one can be committed to linguistic pluralism and pluralistic solidarity simultaneously or whether my commitment to pluralistic solidarity necessarily excludes any commitment to linguistic plurality. The short answer is "not necessarily," but it makes it harder. Let me now give the complicated answer. One can be committed to linguistic pluralism and shared deliberation under certain conditions. A political community may, for example, recognize all languages in the polity as official or national languages. Switzerland has taken that route.[67] But in my view in most instances this will be plausible only if there were two or three spoken languages in the political community. However, many countries, especially developing countries, are faced not with two or three but dozens of languages.[68] Under those circumstances, it is likely to be financially prohibitive and administratively chaotic to attempt to give equal status to all languages that are spoken in the polity.

Alternatively, a polity may give official status to selected minority languages.[69] Such an approach affirms some degree of linguistic plurality and is still committed to shared deliberation. But then the question arises as to what would happen to those minority languages which are not selected as official languages and by what criteria would and should a polity decide as to which languages are good candidates for official or national status. If the consequence of elevating some languages to official status entails (or is the bargain that leads to) the destruction or total neglect of other minority languages, then it appears to me to be troublesome. This is so for two reasons. First, it is likely that the languages that get selected as official are going to be languages of communities that are viewed as "significant" either in terms of their number or the power they possess, more than likely the latter. Thus, the very groups, small and marginal groups, which are likely to be, to use a phrase popularized by Will Kymlicka, "outbid and outvoted"[70] in the market in relation to the resources they need for the survival and flourishing of their language and hence might need state intervention and official affirmation, end up shouldering the cost of selective recognition, the cost of the bargain. Second, selective recognition might foster ethnic tension rather than resolving it. Those whose languages are excluded from this process of official affirmation might feel the exclusion more intensely than they would if only one language was selected as the official or national language, for to be excluded in the name of one national language and hence national unity might be more tolerable for some than to be excluded as not being "significant" or important enough to be included as one of several.

Where does this leave us? If a political community is unable, either for financial or administrative reasons, to accord official status for all the languages spoken in the polity, as it is likely to be the case in relation to most multicultural societies, perhaps one alternative way would be to adopt one national language, but to allow linguistic minorities to preserve their language in one of two ways. The most generous would be to allow them to use their language as the medium of educational instruction at the elementary level. But that, of course, would require that they teach the national language as a subject at that level since postelementary education will be conducted in the national language. The second option, what I consider as the minimalist position, will allow linguistic minorities to teach their language as a subject at the elementary, and perhaps secondary, level while maintaining the national language as the medium of instruction at all levels.

The advantage of the first option is that it is likely to be more conducive to the flourishing of the particular language. The survival and flourishing of a language will be considerably enhanced if it is used as a medium of instruction. The disadvantage is that those minorities might find themselves at a competitive disadvantage as they proceed up the educational ladder and ultimately enter the job market. And given these disadvantages, minority language groups might in fact choose the second option as a sensible compromise. But the important thing is to give these groups the chance to make the choices for themselves. There are two reasons for this. First, a choice, a trade-off, made by the relevant language group is likely to have more legitimacy in the eyes of members of the language minority and hence likely to reduce the chances of conflict among language groups. Second, it seems plausible to assume that the relevant language group will make the better substantive choice, the better compromise, given that it is the group that would be affected by whatever choice it makes and how much weight it puts on one concern (i.e., survival and development of the language) as opposed to another (i.e. the disadvantage that members of the group will face as they go up the ladder in the event that they do not have mastery of the national language).

There could probably be numerous other ways to accommodate the commitment to shared deliberation and linguistic pluralism.[71] It is beyond the scope of this essay to explore all the alternatives or to canvas what the political, administrative, or financial consequences of choosing one or another alternative are likely to be. But in my view if linguistic pluralism and shared deliberation cannot be reconciled then the latter will have to take precedent. At a minimum, a political community requires that ethnic and cultural communities be linguistically capable of communicating with each other.

As the epigraph from Immanuel Kant alerts us, and as Isaiah Berlin, who used a variation of the statement as the title of his book,[72] has continually insisted, we should accept the fact that the social world is defined by multiple, and often incommensurate, values and traditions. We embrace multiplicity, not only because living with multiplicity is normatively desirable but also because attempts to cure us of diversity have led to cruelty—cruelty to individuals as well as to forms of life and traditions associated with minority groups.

But what would living with diversity entail? This essay has argued that the toleration model of "live and let live" is an insufficient way of dealing with multiplicity. The toleration model in large measure does not accomplish what its defenders claim it does accomplish: that it is generous to minorities and that it facilitates the development of reason. Indeed, to paraphrase Paulo Freire in another context, the toleration model, at least in its Kukathasian version, "nourish[es] false charity" towards minorities.

What we need is to explore institutional structures and processes that would simultaneously allow us to affirm and respect plurality while also cultivating some notion of solidarity. Without some sense of solidarity among the various communities in a polity, it will be difficult for a political community to sustain itself over a period of time while remaining democratic. What I have termed *pluralistic solidarity* is meant to respond to that issue. Whether or not there is pluralistic solidarity, I have argued, will depend on the existence of institutions that encourage, and are conducive to, fair moral compromises. Such compromises are possible if two conditions exist. First, there is a dialogic process that will link all groups and traditions in a continuous network of communication. Second, the communicative process recognizes and takes into account the existence of political and social inequalities among groups (participants in the communication process). Not only would such a process generate fair compromises but, so I have argued in this essay, it will also provide the condition for the development of practical rationality, making further moral (and other) compromises possible and perhaps easier. Put simply, a fair and inclusive communicative (dialogic) process is the condition for rational and hence moral inquiries, and for cultivating legitimacy for public institutions and decisions in a multicultural and multiethnic political community.

## NOTES

This essay grew out of my comments on Chandran Kukatha's "Cultural Toleration," chapter 3 in this volume, at the 1995 Annual Meeting of the American Society for Political and Legal Philosophy. I benefited from the comments of a number of people on an earlier draft of this chapter. I would especially like to thank Kathryn Abrams, Donald Horowitz, Will Kymlicka, Edward Rubin, and John Stick.

1. Karin von Hipple, "The Resurgence of Nationalism and Its International Implications," *Washington Quarterly* 17 (Autumn 1994): 18.

2. See, for example, Ann Elisabetta Galeotti, " Citizenship and Equality: The Place of Toleration," *Political Theory* 21 (1993): 585.

3. See the collected essays in John Horton, ed., *Liberalism, Multiculturalism and Toleration* (New York: St. Martin's Press, 1993), especially Jagdish S. Gundara, "Multiculturalism and the British Nation-State," 18–31.

4. There is a need for some qualification here. The stories of Native Americans and African Americans in the United States and that of the Aborigines in Australia, of course, challenge the official (dominant) narrative that suggests that the stories of these countries can be accurately told as stories of immigrant countries. I think this challenge to the self-image of the two countries is a powerful challenge, for the consequence of viewing themselves as immigrant countries has been to underemphasize, or totally ignore, that part of their history which points to the fact that some groups are part of the polity not as a result of their free choice, as the image of an immigrant country seems to suggest, but as a consequence of either brutal conquest or the practice of slavery. For purposes of my classification here, however, I shall take the self-image as the point of departure.

In this essay, I shall use "African Americans" and "blacks" interchangeably.

5. "The generic idea of ethnic cleansing is that of *attempting to eliminate or greatly reduce [either through mass killing or forced relocation] the size of an ethnic or national group in order to achieve greater homogeneity within a territory.* It is usually governments, or military groups, that attempt to do this" (emphasis in original). James W. Nickel, "What's Wrong with Ethnic Cleansing?" *Journal of Social Philosophy* 26 (1995): 6.

6. Clyde Farnsworth, "Now Quebec's Anglos Talk of Separation," *New York Times,* 25 March 1995, 4.

7. Article 39(1) of the new Ethiopian Constitution provides: "Every nation, nationality or people in Ethiopia shall have the unrestricted right to self-determination up to secession."

8. See Amitai Etzioni, "The Evils of Self-Determination," *Foreign Policy* 89 (Winter 1992–93): 21–35.

9. Allen Buchanan, "Federalism, Secession, and the Morality of Inclusion," *Arizona Law Review* 37 (1995): 54.

10. The phrase is taken from Michael Walzer, "Notes on the New Tribalism," in *Political Restructuring in Europe,* ed. Chris Brown (New York: Routledge, 1994), 197. To put Professor Walzer's comment in the context of his argument let me quote a portion of the paragraph in which the phrase appears: "Rather than supporting the existing unions, I would be inclined to support separation whenever separation is demanded by a political movement that, so far as we can tell, represents the popular will. Let the people go who want to go."

I am in complete agreement with Walzer that there are circumstances when political divorce might be the only sensible solution. But I must disagree that whenever there is a popular majority for political divorce at a given time we should allow that as of right. I believe, as I have argued in the text, that would lead to dangerous and destructive fragmentation. Also, as an empirical matter, I am not quite persuaded that if a group, the majority of whose members desire separation, is allowed to secede, ultimately, if there is political or economic disadvantage in that departure, that group "will find a way to re-establish connections . . . [in] some sort of union" with the entity from which it has seceded. I think Walzer's optimism neglects the fact that separation has its own dynamics and even the existence of objective needs may not be sufficient to bring the entities back together. First, there might be other neighbors that perceive their security and economic interest in terms of keeping these entities divided. They will certainly do their best to ensure that the division remains, either by using front groups in those countries or by employing economic and military intimidation. Second, we should also not forget that a new country means a new bureaucracy which will develop its own interest, an interest that might not always converge with the interest of the political entity, and is likely to view its existence in terms of the existence of the political entity and hence might fight for that separate existence. The point is that we ought not deceive ourselves by thinking that even after political divorce reassociation is simply a matter of the groups realizing that there are economic and political imperatives that compel the union. It might not be that easy. We might in fact end up making the people whose right for self-determination compelled us to support political divorce prisoners of a new bureaucracy and the imperatives of regional (and perhaps global) power and security arrangements.

11. Charles Larmore, *Patterns of Moral Complexity* (Cambridge: Cambridge University Press, 1987).

12. See Adeno Addis, "'Hell Man, They Did Invent Us': The Mass Media, Law and African Americans," *Buffalo Law Review* 41 (1993): 530–31.

13. The literature on multiculturalism in this country is extensive both in terms of number and reach. Just to cite two examples, see Charles Taylor, *Multiculturalism: Examining the Politics of Recognition*, ed. Amy Gutmann (Princeton: Princeton University Press, 1994) and "Symposium: Race and Remedy in a Multicultural Society," *Stanford Law Review* 47 (1995): 819–1096.

14. Applauding John Rawls's recent work (*Political Liberalism*) as raising and grappling with the right question, the question of which institutional structures are defensible and appropriate to keep diverse commu-

nities together as a political entity, Bruce Ackerman observes that if the right answers are not found, America "is finished as a nation." Bruce Ackerman, "Political Liberalism," *Journal of Philosophy* 91 (1994): 365.

15. In his recent work, for example, John Rawls has attempted to extend the doctrine of toleration that emerged to accommodate religious diversity to other areas such as cultural, moral, and philosophical differences. John Rawls, *Political Liberalism* (New York: Columbia University Press, 1993), 10.

16. For the argument that historically toleration played a role to link liberalism and pluralism, see Steven Lukes, *Moral Conflicts and Politics* (Oxford: Oxford University Press, 1991), 17. Lukes observes: "Liberalism was born out of religious conflict and the attempt to tame it by accommodating it within the framework of the nation-state. The case for religious toleration was central to its development." Some even argue that the fact of pluralism tends to support the normative claims of liberalism and what is seen to be liberalism's central feature—toleration. George Crowder reads the works of Isaiah Berlin and Bernard Williams as implying this. See George Crowder, "Pluralism and Liberalism," *Political Studies* 42 (1994): 293–305.

17. By private realm I mean to refer to all areas that are immune from state intervention. Under this definition a private realm could be individual- or group-specific.

18. The question of what constitutes culture is of course a difficult one given that culture is a concept that has been used to cover a wide range of things. In its widest sense, culture of course includes religious convictions and practices and in this essay I shall at times use culture to include religious commitments and practices. Rather than offer a general description of what constitutes culture which might be misleading, and in any case might not be possible to do, I shall simply offer examples that I have in mind when I refer to the notion of culture. The kind of examples that I have in mind are distinctive cultural dress, rituals, language, etc.

19. See John Rawls, *Political Liberalism* (New York: Columbia University Press, 1993); Bruce Ackerman, *Social Justice in the Liberal State* (New Haven: Yale University Press, 1980); Bruce Ackerman, "Why Dialogue?" *The Journal of Philosophy* 86 (1989): 5–22. For Rawls, it is how reasonable the differences are on the issue that compels that the issue should not be a subject for public deliberation, while for Ackerman it might be sufficient that the differences on the subject are strong.

20. See, for example, Joseph Raz, *The Morality of Freedom* (Oxford: Clarendon Press, 1986).

21. I leave aside the situation in nonliberal societies where power is

held by a minority which is not accountable to the wishes and preferences of the majority.

22. The quotation in the epigraph of this chapter comes from Freire, *Pedagogy of the Oppressed,* trans. Myra Bergman Ramos (New York: Seabury Press, 1970), 29.

23. The distinction between negative and positive toleration is drawn by Peter Nicholson. See Peter P. Nicholson, "Toleration as a Moral Ideal," in *Aspects of Toleration: Philosophical Studies,* eds. John Horton and Susan Mendus (New York: Methuen, 1985), 158–59. However, I appropriate the distinction to describe a slightly different set of categories than those suggested by Nicholson.

24. Chandran Kukathas, "Cultural Toleration," this volume, pp. 69–104.

25. See Lee Bollinger, *The Tolerant Society: Freedom of Speech and Extremist Speech in America* (New York: Oxford University Press, 1986). Bollinger argues that the extraordinary tolerance that freedom of expression, and the First Amendment, require of citizens, even in relation to extremist speech which is often itself intolerant and unworthy of protection, can best be defended not on the ground that free speech is unique and merits special protection but rather we are using the free speech area as an exemplar to develop "a social capacity to control feelings evoked by a host of social encounters" (10).

26. Chandran Kukathas invokes and develops what seems to him to be the most generous notion of negative toleration in relation to minority cultures. To the question of how a liberal society should deal with minority cultural practices which do not directly harm but are intolerable to the wider society, his answer is that liberal societies should tolerate such minority practices as long as those minorities allow their members to leave for the wider society when those members conclude that they no longer can adhere to the requirements of membership. Kukathas, "Cultural Toleration," this volume. The version of negative toleration to which I am responding in the following pages is, primarily, the seemingly generous version adopted by Kukathas.

27. I shall put aside the issue of direct physical harm, either against the person or property. Even in its most generous moment, toleration seems to be constrained by the principle that physical harm is beyond what a polity should allow as a permissible aspect of sustained diverse lives and practices.

28. W. E. B. DuBois captured this sense of unreconciled "two-ness" in his description of the experience of African Americans in the United States. As DuBois put it: "One ever feels his two-ness,—an American, a Negro; two souls, two thoughts, two unreconciled strivings; two warring

ideals in one dark body, whose dogged strength alone keeps it from being torn asunder." W. E. B. DuBois, "The Souls of Black Folk" (1903); reprinted in *Three Negro Classics,* with an introduction by John Hope Franklin (New York: Avon Books, 1965), 215.

29. The phrase is Charles Taylor's: "Things take on importance against a background of intelligibility. Let us call this a horizon. It follows that one of the things we can't do, if we are to define ourselves significantly, is suppress or deny the horizon against which things take on significance for us." Charles Taylor, *The Ethics of Authenticity* (Cambridge: Harvard University Press, 1992), 37.

30. Stephen Carter, "Evolutionism, Creationism, and Treating Religion as a Hobby," *Duke Law Journal* (1987): 978.

31. Benjamin Barber, *Strong Democracy: Participatory Politics for a New Age* (Berkeley: University of California Press, 1984), 219. Reciprocity and mutual respect is also a theme in John Rawls's work. Rawls, *Political Liberalism,* 16–17. Rawls writes: "[T]he idea of reciprocity lies between the idea of impartiality, which is altruistic . . . and the idea of mutual advantage understood as everyone's being advantaged with respect to each person's present or expected future situation as things are."

32. This, of course, is not to imply that interpersonal dialogues among members of different cultural or ethnic groups are not important but to recognize that there are limits to the transformative potential of interpersonal dialogues in a world where people's "experiences" and views are constantly, and to a considerable degree, shaped (mediated) by large institutions, such as the media. To alter institutionally entrenched images (entrenched through law, the media, and education) will require institutional interventions. The limits of interpersonal dialogue to cultivate reciprocal empathy becomes even clearer in polities where ethnic and cultural groups lead either segregated (such as blacks in the United States) or geographically isolated (such as many groups in developing countries) existences. Under these circumstances institutional dialogue might in fact improve the possibilities of interpersonal engagements among members of various groups.

33. See *Los Angles Times,* 30 March 1995, A1; *Atlanta Constitution,* 6 August 1995, 1B.

To put the figures I cited in the text in a fuller context, this is what the surveys show: when people were asked if they supported affirmative action for minorities 52 percent of all polled answered affirmatively, but only 45 percent of whites (and 35 percent of white men) said yes. When the question was support for affirmative action for women, 61 percent of all polled said yes, and 56 percent of whites (and 45 percent of white men) were supportive.

34. An enforcement of such a regulation in a school where there are Sikhs would certainly not have equally neutral impact on all students. It will strike at the heart of what it means to be a Sikh. See *Mandla v. Dowell Lee* [1983] All E. R. 1062 (H.L.). A similar point was made by Justice Brennan in a dissent in *Goldman v. Weinberger*, 475 U.S. 503, 521–524 (1985). The case involved an Orthodox Jew, a commissioned officer in the U.S. Air Force, who sought to wear a yarmulke while on duty and in uniform, though Air Force regulation prohibited the wearing of headgear except under limited circumstances. A closely divided U.S. Supreme Court (5:4) upheld the constitutionality of the regulation. Justice Brennan, in his dissent, thought that the regulation was unconstitutional and observed that the seemingly "neutral" standard resulted in the disparate treatment of Christian members (the majority) and members of minority religious groups, such as Orthodox Jews and Sikhs.

35. See Chandran Kukathas, "Are There Any Cultural Rights?" *Political Theory* 20 (1992): 105–39; Kukathas, "Cultural Toleration". See also William A. Galston, "Two Concepts of Liberalism," *Ethics* 105 (1995): 516–34. Galston defends what he calls the diversity model, which he contrasts with what he refers to as the autonomy model, which he argues stands for the proposition that there should be toleration to all sorts of groups, even those that "may be illiberal in their internal structure and practices as long as freedom of entrance and exit is zealously safeguarded by the state" (533).

36. "The primary reason for rejecting the idea of group claims as the basis of moral and political settlements is that groups are not fixed and unchanging entities in the moral and political universe." Kukathas, "Cultural Rights," 110. See also Harold R. Isaacs, *Idols of the Tribe: Group Identity and Political Change* (New York: Harper and Row, 1975; reprint, Cambridge: Harvard University Press, 1989), 205 (page citations are to the reprint edition). Donald Horowitz, whose work on ethnic minorities is perhaps the best and the most comprehensive, has made that point repeatedly. See, for example, Donald L. Horowitz, *Ethnic Groups in Conflict* (Berkeley: University of California Press, 1985), 66–68, 589.

Let me make a point here about the moral and political implications of viewing something as a "social construction." The fact that something is a social construction and thus amenable to change as conditions change does not mean that it is not worthy of our moral and political concerns.

37. Kukathas, "Cultural Rights," 117, 128. I might note in passing that it is not quite clear to me why Kukathas thinks that the right to "emigrate" (the right to exit to the wider liberal community) is any less a liberal

good than is autonomy. Recall, Kukathas's critique of liberal theorists who insist that minority cultures respect the autonomy of their members, as a condition of toleration, was because such a demand is unreasonable (certainly not generous enough) insofar as it conditions toleration on minorities becoming more like liberal communities. The complaint is that minorities are forced to embrace a central liberal good before they are tolerated. If that is the complaint, then why is it not also true that the requirement that those groups allow their members to choose to leave (the right to exit) for the wider community is also forcing those groups to embrace a liberal good as a condition of toleration? Put simply, why is the right to choose to leave any less a liberal good (or any more a neutral framework) than is respecting the autonomy of the person?

38. A relatively recent newspaper article reported about a lawsuit by a group of Australian Aborigines against the Australian government. The plaintiffs were kidnapped and taken away form their parents at an early age, with government sanction, and raised either by white families or church-run orphanages. The purpose: "to assimilate the Aborigines into Australia's white culture." The practice lasted well into the 1960s.

One of those who was a victim of forced removal is quoted as saying: "I lost my family, my language, my culture, and I am still isolated today." The dislocation has apparently had enormous social consequences. "Alcoholism, the most serious health problem faced by Australia's Aborigines, is pronounced among members of the Stolen Generation." Philip Shenon, "Bitter Aborigines Are Suing for Stolen Childhoods," *New York Times,* 20 July 1995, sec. A4.

For a very interesting exploration of the varying level of impact on the integrity and health of the individual self that the loss of different kinds of affiliations may pose, see Meir Dan-Cohen, "Between Selves and Collectivities: Toward a Jurisprudence of Identity," *University of Chicago Law Review* 61 (1994): 1213–43.

39. False symmetry is prominent in current political and legal discourse. Not only are cultural and ethnic groups seen to be similar to various private and voluntary groups, but the significance (or force) of their complaints, claims, and institutional concerns are often diminished by seeing those concerns and complaints as analogous to complaints, claims, and institutional concerns of the dominant majorities. Thus, for example, in the United States, current legal and political discourse views affirmative action that is designed to remedy the effects of past and current discrimination as similar to government enforced discrimination against minorities. *Plessy v. Ferguson* (163 U.S. 537 [1896]) is seen as morally indistinguishable from *Metro Broadcasting v. FCC* (497

U.S. 547 [1990]). I am exploring the notion of false symmetries in a paper I am writing that carries the same title. Part of that argument is also developed in Adeno Addis, "Role Models and the Politics of Recognition," *University of Pennsylvania Law Review* 144 (1996): 1377–1468.

40. Jürgen Habermas put the issue correctly: "Should citizens' identities as members of ethnic, cultural, or religious groups *publicly* matter, and if so, how can collective identities make a difference within the framework of constitutional democracy? Are collective identities and cultural membership politically relevant, and if so, how can they legitimately affect the distribution of rights and the recognition of legal claims?" (emphasis in original). Jürgen Habermas, "Multiculturalism and the Liberal State," *Stanford Law Review* 47 (1995): 849.

41. Contrary to what the legal and political literature might indicate, the paradigmatic case for a multiethnic and multicultural society is not *Wisconsin v. Yoder* (406 U.S. 205 [1972]) (where the Amish desired and were allowed to keep their children from getting a mandatory high school education) or even *Mozert v. Hawkins County Board of Education* (827 F.2d 1058) (where the plaintiffs wanted certain materials excluded from the school's basic reading for their children). The major issue is *not* total withdrawal or the displacement of contrary views from the conversational agenda. Rather, it is whether what matters for cultural, ethnic and religious minorities should be part of the public agenda and thus politically relevant. The quotation from *Mozert* in the epigraph of this chapter is from the majority opinion, page 1069.

42. "Rather than following the integrative path of our predecessors, the United States now may be traveling down the strife-torn road of countries in which the manifestations of separatism predominate." J. Harvie Wilkinson III, "The Law of Civil Rights and the Dangers of Separatism in Multicultural America," *Stanford Law Review* 47 (1995): 1000. Harvie Wilkinson III is a federal judge on the Court of Appeals for the Fourth Circuit.

43. Brian Walker, "John Rawls, Mikhail Bakhtin, and the Praxis of Toleration," *Political Theory* 23 (1995): 114.

44. Seyla Benhabib, *Situating the Self: Gender, Community, and Postmodernism in Contemporary Ethics* (New York: Routledge, 1992), 140.

45. See Addis, "Hell Man," 523–626.

46. John Rawls, *A Theory of Justice* (Cambridge: Harvard University Press, 1971), 527.

47. See Adeno Addis, "Recycling in Hell," *Tulane Law Review,* 67 (1993): 2259.

48. *United States v. Southwestern Cable Co.,* 392 U.S. 157, 177 (1968); see also, *Shurberg Broadcasting of Hartford, Inc. v. FCC,* 876 F.2d 902, 943 (D.C. Cir. 1989) (Wald, C. J., dissenting). ("For good or ill, a large portion of the American polity relies upon the broadcast media as a principal source of information about the world in which they live.")

49. I give a detailed account of the information and communication revolutions in their international contexts in a forthcoming book, Adeno Addis, "The New World Information and Communication Order: The Attempt to Restructure the International Communication Process" (unpublished manuscript with the author).

50. The argument in this section is fully developed in Addis, "Recycling in Hell," 2265–66.

51. I mean to use the term incommensurate in the same way that Joseph Raz has used it. Two things are incommensurate when there is no common standard by which they can be meaningfully evaluated. See Raz, *Morality of Freedom,* 322: "A and B are incommensurate if it is neither true that one is better than the other nor true they are of equal value."

52. As Alasdair MacIntyre put it: "since there are a diversity of traditions ... there are ... rationalities rather than rationality." Alasdair MacIntyre, *Whose Justice? Which Rationality?* (Notre Dame, Ind.: University of Notre Dame Press, 1988), 9.

53. Kukathas, "Cultural Toleration," this volume, 80.

54. Kukathas, for example, makes this disclaimer. Ibid., 84.

55. "[T]he only regulations and ways of acting that may claim legitimacy are those to which all who are possibly affected could assent as participants in rational discourse." Jürgen Habermas, "Postscript to *Faktizität und Geltung,*" *Philosophy and Social Criticism* 20 (1994): 144.

56. Habermas proposes an "ideal speech situation" of unencumbered communication from which program of social development might be reverse-engineered. See Jürgen Habermas, *Communication and the Evolution of Society,* trans. and introduction Thomas McCarthy (Boston: Beacon Press, 1979), 1–68. My purpose here is not to defend the ideal speech situation but simply to make the point that whatever one thinks of the ideal speech situation as a normative and descriptive construct, Habermas at least gives us a standard by which we can appraise the validity and the correctness of what appears to be common (and reasonable) standard by which interaction among groups are to be regulated.

57. See Jürgen Habermas, "Struggles for Recognition in the Democratic Constitutional State," trans. Shierry Weber Nicholsen, in *Multiculturalism: Examining the Politics of Recognition,* ed. Amy Gutmann

(Princeton: Princeton University Press, 1994), 107; Habermas, "Struggles for Recognition in Constitutional States," *European Journal of Philosophy* 1 (1993): 128–55.

58. Will Kymlicka, *Liberalism, Community, and Culture* (Oxford: Clarendon Press, 1991), 182–83.

59. Bernard Manin makes the same point, but only in regard to deliberation among individuals. Bernard Manin, "On Legitimacy and Political Deliberation," *Political Theory* 15 (1987): 338.

60. Habermas, "Multiculturalism and the Liberal State," 852 (emphasis in original). See also Jürgen Habermas, *Faktizität and Geltung* (Frankfurt/Main: Suhrkamp, 1992), 636, quoted in Veit Bader, "Citizenship and Exclusion," *Political Theory* 23 (1995): 223.

61. Quoted in Melissa Williams, "Justice Toward Groups," *Political Theory* 23 (1995): 87.

62. Alexander Meiklejohn, "The First Amendment Is an Absolute," *Supreme Court Review* (1961): 258.

63. This was put to me by Will Kymlicka in a written comment on an earlier draft of this chapter.

64. See Adeno Addis, "Individualism, Communitarianism, and the Rights of Ethnic Minorities," *Notre Dame Law Review* 67 (1992): 666–69.

65. M. L. Marasinghe, "Ethnic Politics and Constitutional Reform: The Indo-Sri Lankan Accord," *International and Comparative Law Quarterly* 37 (1988): 560–61.

66. Donald Horowitz makes another and very important point as to why conflict over language might be very intense and "not readily amenable to compromise." The language issue quite often has a symbolic dimension. To see one's language affirmed is to see oneself and one's sense of dignity affirmed. And to see another language affirmed over one's language is to see oneself devalued in relation to the group whose language has earned official or national recognition. Horowitz, *Ethnic Groups in Conflict,* 219–24; Marasinghe, "Ethnic Politics and Constitutional Reform," 561. Marasinghe quotes a member of the Ceylon Parliament as having said during the Parliamentary debate in 1956 to make Sinhala the only official language: "They [the Tamils] do not want to feel that their language and through their language, themselves are looked down upon as an inferior section of the people of this country," at 561.

67. Switzerland has four national languages, the languages of the four ethnic groups—French, German, Italian, and Romansh. See Francesco Capotorti, *Study on the Rights of Persons Belonging to Ethnic, Religious, and Linguistic Minorities.* UN Doc. E/CN. 4/Sub.2/384 Rev. 1 (New York, United Nations, 1991), 76.

68. Ethiopia is a good example here. See Addis, "Individualism," 667.

See also Robert L. Hess, *Ethiopia: The Modernization of Autocracy* (1970), 14. Hess estimates that there are "seventy languages and two hundred dialects spoken in Ethiopia."

69. Finland, for example, gives official status to the language of the Swedish minority, which is about 6 percent of the population, while not according official status to the language of the Lapps who are said to number around four thousand. Capotorti, *Rights of Persons,* 76. Finland has a population of "4.9 million, of whom 6.1 per cent are Swedish speaking . . . [and] a Lapp minority of around 4,000." "Finland-Facts," *Reuters,* 15 March 1987. See also "Population and Society Overview: Demographic and Societal Indicators," *Business International,* 30 July 1991. And Canada is a bilingual nation, both English and French recognized as national languages, though no language of the indigenous peoples is given official or national status.

70. Kymlicka, *Liberalism, Community, and Culture,* 180–81.

71. As I noted in the text, the issue of linguistic pluralism and its relationship to my notion of pluralistic solidarity needs a full length treatment and that I will be unable to do in this short essay. The purpose of the comment on linguistic pluralism is simply to indicate how it might be possible to reconcile the commitments to pluralistic solidarity and linguistic pluralism. There are probably a number of other ways to reconcile these two commitments not only in the area of education but also in the other two areas—media and the legal system—that I have argued are important for the development of pluralistic solidarity. For the exploration of other alternatives see Capotorti, *Rights of Persons,* 75–89.

72. The quotation used in the epigraph appears in Isaiah Berlin, *The Crooked Timber of Humanity: Chapters in the History of Ideas,* ed. Henry Hardy (New York: Alfred A. Knopf, 1991), 19.

# 6

# THE IDEA OF NONLIBERAL CONSTITUTIONALISM

## GRAHAM WALKER

Constitutionalism is often praised as the antidote to tyranny. Not surprisingly, the momentous political transitions now underway in various parts of the world—most of them exiting tyranny of one sort or another—have sparked a revival of interest in constitutionalism. Especially in the postcommunist region, constitutional government has a huge appeal after several generations of unconfined rule by one party in the pursuit of a grandiose ideal. As the mechanism of the vaguer hope called democracy, constitutionalism seems as opposite to Stalinism as the rule of law is opposite to the rule of men. Still, in postcommunist lands as elsewhere, there is sometimes less than full enthusiasm for the liberal, individual rights-oriented approach to constitutions urged by American legal scholars. How could there be, in the presence of long-standing communal identities—ethnic, religious, and moral—that are often at variance with Western liberal ideals?

But it is hard for these lawyers. As I will show, they usually conceive of constitutionalism as a system whose ultimate purpose is securing the rights and liberties of individuals. And who can blame them? America's constitutionalism is liberal, or at least it is now. In twentieth-century America, the word "constitutional" has rarely been spoken in one breath without "rights" being uttered in the next. So when American legal experts shuttling across the Atlantic encounter misgivings about draft constitutions devoted to liberal norms, they can only be puzzled or vexed: Why would anyone resist such a manifestly good thing as constitutionalism?

The lawyers' predicament suggests the need to conceptualize a constitutionalism that is not defined by its liberal elements. I propose that the modern absorption of constitutionalism by liberalism need not be permanent. It is now possible, and maybe necessary, to realize a constitutionalism which retains the primary appealing qualities of constitutionalist government while demoting or at least qualifying the central values of Western liberalism, such as individual autonomy and the neutral state. I do not write this as an enemy of liberal constitutionalism; I simply do not consider the adjective superfluous. The distinct character of liberal constitutionalism is only obscured by the conflation of liberal and constitutionalist principles.

Some liberals might wish for a world in which they could admonish founders and reformers to "take liberal constitutionalism whole or not at all." If liberalism inevitably triumphs at the end of history, perhaps this advice is supposed to hasten benevolent fate.[1] In any event, many liberals imagine that holding out for unadulterated liberalism will induce reforming nations to embrace liberalism wholesale. Such a stance may instead induce them to refuse constitutionalism altogether, leaving the public order of new states at the mercy of many fearful impulses, without benefit of constitutionalist impediments to those impulses. In those places—notably in the third world—where the cultural consequences of liberalism ("Westernization") are unwelcome, but where autocracy is equally troubling, reformers will find little wisdom in such counsel. Nor will it be of much help in liberal societies when problems like the environment, property and education start to seem intractable within the confines of a dominantly liberal constitution.[2] An immobilized liberal society might be uniquely vulnerable to populist autocrats.

Most of all, wherever people value some aspects of communal identity more than the autonomy of individual choice, such values need to be crafted into a constitutionalist structure which can simultaneously give them public status and impede their more worrisome expressions. In the many places around the world where profound political transitions have been underway since the close of the Cold War, this basic issue is arising over and over again: how to constitute a nontyrannical politics with a decent rule of law, while at the same time affirming in a public, institutionalized way a particular ethos—whether of nationality, moral solidarity, religious tradition, or some more or less alarming combination of all three. Liberals have criticized the Baltic states, for example, for their use of an ethnic franchise that excludes Russians. But can these newly free countries find any constitutionalist means to counter Stalin's ruthless Russification of their territories and cultures? Can the Hungarian state offer its patronage to Magyar identity without fatally undermining its progress toward the rule of law? Can the very raison d'être of the new Slovak Republic—the first-ever independent state for Slovaks—be reconciled with constitutionalist government and the needs of the Hungarian and Romany minorities? Can Russia constitutionally affirm the historical and cultural centrality of Orthodoxy without inviting a slide to fascism? Can the massively Roman Catholic character of Polish society be enacted in its public institutions in a way that is consistent with constitutionalist aspirations? Can the Islamic character of Tajikistan be similarly enacted without making a sham of its new constitution? Can the new Palestinian sovereignty be Islamic in a way parallel to the Jewish state out of which it is emerging, without putting itself on the road to eventual despotism? Can a postapartheid rule of law in South Africa legitimately stop short of "race-blind" political individualism? Can Canadian constitutionalism survive the multicultural grant of group rights to native peoples and to the distinct society of Québec?

If the answer in every such case is no, as an unflinching liberalism requires, then much of the world seems consigned to multiform tyranny. For the illiberal impulses in question are not withering away. But a constitutionalism conceived independent of liberal criteria may allow a different but equally principled set of answers. Refusing nonliberal constitutionalism will not have the effect of securing liberal constitutionalism. It will have the effect of making tyranny more likely.

## LIBERAL DOUBTS, CONSTITUTIONALIST PROSPECTS

If the idea of nonliberal constitutionalism has recently become more urgent, it has also become more accessible. For just when many countries are poised to embark on constitutionalist experiments, faith in liberal principles is eroding. Of course liberal societies indulged a brief splurge of self-congratulation at winning the Cold War. But they harbor a growing undercurrent of self-doubt. Liberalism has for some time been accused of a reductive approach to knowledge and the human self.[3] More recently, non-Western intellectuals have joined Western feminists, postmodernists and even traditionalists to indict the notion of individual autonomy rights as a form of naive and homogenizing universalism, and to unmask the ethnic and moral "neutrality" of the liberal state as a covert form of coercion.[4] Whether valid or not, such criticism receives serious attention. Its presence shows that liberal principles are becoming casualties of the larger disintegration of the self-confidence of modern Western rationalism: they no longer enjoy the status of self-evident verities.

These developments obviously threaten the standard categories of Western constitutional law. Stanley Fish illustrates the threat most acutely. Duke Law School's postmodernist, postliberal extraordinaire, Fish is skeptical about individual rights of all kinds. According to Fish, for example, "There's no such thing as free speech, and it's a good thing, too."[5] This is because all discourse is embedded in some scheme of understandings and values. Embeddedness constrains speech; it also makes it possible in the first place; "restriction . . . is constitutive of expression." And what holds existentially also holds politically. Every political regime— including every regime that claims to value freedom—necessarily exists within the parameters of a dominant value scheme which inescapably circumscribes the freedom that will be tolerated. Fish upends the liberal distinction between freedom of speech and freedom of action—the former supposedly absolute to liberals and the latter qualified. Speech *is* action, Fish points out. There is no "weightless verbal exchange," since all speech is *about* something. Speech is "always doing work," always impinging on the world "in ways indistinguishable from the effects of physical action" (except for unstructured vocalization, which is hardly what liberals think they are championing). The American Supreme Court's doctrine distinguishing speech that incites to action from speech *per se* plays into Fish's hand. The "fighting words" test, he points out, does not insulate speech from public prejudice; it effectively leaves it at the mercy of public prejudice. The incitable sensibilities of the dominant public finally determine the bounds of speech "freedom." Fish is not complaining. He is revealing the incongruity of liberal free speech orthodoxy. Fish also argues that formulas like "free speech" are semantic prizes that, when successfully appropriated, covertly impose the substantive values of the successful group.

The same holds for other liberal rights principles. Fish mentions religion as a parallel case.[6] He is not alone in noticing how the liberal principle of religious freedom, when combined with the principle of public religious neutrality, inadvertently imposes religious individualism, privatism and indifferentism on all but the hardiest religious dissenters.[7]

Fish explains this sort of thing—and much else—by asserting that there simply are no *principles* which can be counted upon to guide public law. Moreover, he says, humans possess no neutral, nonpartisan reasoning power for finding and using such principles, even if they did exist. Everything, therefore, is "politics," a power struggle as much over the meaning of words as over the allocation of resources. Because liberalism conceives its rational principles precisely as suprapolitical and nonpartisan, "one can only conclude, and conclude nonparadoxically, that liberalism doesn't exist."[8] This does not render Fish indifferent among alternative laws and forms of public order. He has emphatic preferences, but they do not rest on rational principles, only on contingent consequentialist judgments. In late-twentieth-century America, for example, hate speech codes do more good than harm, especially in combating "flat-out lies" like holocaust denial.[9]

I cannot offer here the response that Fish's views demand.[10] I will only observe that Fish's argument does not establish all of its claims. Successfully undermining the naive, rationalist view of "rights" does not preclude less naive, more universal standards of political morality that do not depend on liberalism. Nor does it void an architectonically political—or, put more simply, a constitutionalist—rationale for free speech and other liberal rights. Even if Fish is right, it might still be wise on other grounds to treat "rights" politically as if they were just the sort of thing that naive liberalism once considered them to be as a matter of metaphysical truth. However that may be, the arguments of Fish and like-minded doubters increasingly dissolve the liberal conception of freedom of speech.

Do Fish's observations dissolve the notion of constitutionalism, of which freedom of speech has seemed to most people to be an integral element? I don't think so. If we concede his persuasive deconstruction of liberalism but not his assertive deconstruction of rationality, Fish's observations can instead help open up a nonliberal vantage point on constitutionalism. For the demise of liberal certitude makes it easier, even for those with liberal sympathies, to conceive of a nonliberal form of constitutionalism, and to notice constitutionalist or potentially constitutionalist experiences in unexpected places. After all, there have occasionally been political outcomes besides liberal constitutionalism and illiberal despotism. It may help to glance at a couple of members of this rather large set of oddities.

The modern state of Israel embodies an equivocal mix of constitutive principles that cannot be resolved in favor of either its liberal or illiberal elements.[11] The 1948 Declaration of Independence that proclaimed Israel a Jewish state also announced protection for the rights of all, regardless of religion or ethnicity. Jewish values, symbols, and the Hebrew language are paramount, and Jews (returning from diaspora) have entitlements under the Law of Return that are available to them by accident of birth and are *not* available to Christians, Muslims, Buddhists, or Gaians. Yet non-Jewish citizens of Israel enjoy legal protection for their voting, speech, and religious rights. Indeed, Israel bends over backwards, in a way that more consistently liberal polities do not, to accommodate its minority religious sub-communities: the Jewish state funds their schools and allows them exclusive authority (for their members) over laws of personal status (e.g., there is no civil marriage). One can hardly deny that the Jewish state fails its *noncitizen* residents in many regrettable ways; nevertheless, it supports a relatively decent public order that inhibits the arbitrary use of power, and gives non-Jewish citizens protections that are far from trivial. And it does this in considerable defiance of liberal norms.

Native American nations are an even more striking case. Based on early treaties and their claim to primeval nationhood, the tribes enjoy unique constitutional status in both the United States

and Canada. Internally, the public order of tribal life is almost
wholly at odds with liberal norms. Membership is primarily ascriptive rather than voluntary. The choice prerogatives of individuals
are systematically subordinated to holistic conceptions of tribal
solidarity. Many political and social roles are allocated by decision
of elders or by accident of birth; public functions are often prede-
fined by gender, for example. Yet powerholders are highly constrained by written and unwritten rules, and the use of power is
rarely arbitrary or tyrannical.[12] When American liberals promoted
the "Indian Civil Rights Act" of 1968, it was hardly surprising that
they encountered Native American opposition. The Act looked
like an assimilationist instrument whose exaltation of individual
rights would erode tribal cohesion, undermining the authority of
communities over their individual members.[13] The final version of
the Act pointedly omitted any no-establishment-of-religion clause;
such a provision was unthinkable where the integration of spirituality and public order constituted tribal identity, and where that
spirituality itself constrained the use and abuse of power.

I will touch on other examples below (including, perhaps to
Stanley Fish's relish, the evolving multiculturalist/tolerationist
American university campus, possibly an embryonic version of
nonliberal constitutionalism writ small). All such cases seem to
resemble in principle the arrangements toward which others are
groping, in the postcommunist region and elsewhere. Unless we
dismiss them as flukes, we might interpret the Israeli and Native
American experiences under the terms of a nonliberal conception
of constitutionalism, which, when fully developed, could also
apply elsewhere. But doing this requires us first to recover the idea
of constitutionalism from the modern narrowing of its meaning.

## CONSTITUTIONALISM'S MODERN CONSTRICTION

Constitutionalism predates the enlightenment. Liberalism does
not. Aristotle placed the term "constitution" (Greek *politeia*) at
the center of his political inquiry. His deliberate focus on constitution—on the configuration of public order in terms of norms,
jurisdiction, and accountability—led him to praise on prudential
grounds a mixed constitution that splices rival moralities and

social groups.[14] Polybius followed his lead, as did Cicero and other constitutional theorists of Republican Rome. Medieval arguments about power within the Church, and between the Church and temporal authority, expressed a complex and highly self-conscious notion of constitutionalism. The Reformation spawned its own characteristic set of constitutional arguments. And of course the social contract philosophers of the early liberal tradition deployed the notion of constitutionalism most famously and successfully against royal absolutism.

Charles Howard McIlwain authoritatively recorded the premodern use of the term in his eminent little 1940 book on *Constitutionalism, Ancient and Modern*. Rather than further narrating his account, it suffices to take McIlwain himself as my starting point. For having painstakingly traced varying usages, he concludes that "in all its successive phases, constitutionalism has one essential quality: it is a legal limitation on government; it is the antithesis of arbitrary rule; its opposite is despotic government, the government of will instead of law. . . . [T]he most ancient, the most persistent, and the most lasting of the essentials of true constitutionalism still remains what it has been almost from the beginning, the limitation of government by law."[15] Intriguingly, McIlwain's 1940 definition is not a liberal one, at least not necessarily. That is, it does not centralize the liberty claims (rights) of individuals, nor does it require public authority to be a neutral arbiter among competing value systems. McIlwain's definition lost favor, however, and it wasn't long before constitutionalism acquired a more narrowly liberal meaning.

Carl J. Friedrich was probably one of the most influential narrowers. His famous text on *Constitutional Government and Democracy,* republished eight times for several generations of college students, records the evolution. In what he later called the "prewar form" of his text, Friedrich depicts the "essence of constitutionalism" as "effective restraints upon governmental action," of which there are two: a division of power and a rule of law.[16] These restraints in turn depend, he says, upon on a sufficiently widespread common agreement on fundamental values.[17] By the time he attached a new preface in mid-1941, however, his liberal convictions—understandably enhanced by the war against European fascism—had already begun to eclipse the definition contained inside. Centralizing what his text actually made subsidiary, his preface announced breathlessly that recent events in Europe had compelled even cynics to rediscover "the essential of constitutionalism: a vivid appreciation of the rights of free men." And in a deliberate reversal sure to please postwar liberals, his preface announced further that constitutionalism is really the "only system of government which seems able to get along *without* . . . agreement on fundamentals."[18] In successive editions, Friedrich progressively rewrote the text in the image of that hurried preface until, by the final editions in the mid-1960s, he explicitly fused constitutionalism and liberal individualism. Restraints on government, divided powers and law—all these he now subordinated to the single "function" of constitutionalism: safeguarding each person in the exercise of "individual rights."[19] A companion volume is even more explicit: The "core objective of constitutionalism" is to guarantee "a sphere of genuine autonomy. The constitution is meant to protect the *self.*"[20]

Friedrich's equation of constitutionalism and liberalism was a congenial habit for Americans. It fit the dominant interpretation of their own experience and the universal tendency of American constitutional law courses to treat individual liberties jurisprudence as the rosetta stone of American constitutionalism. The recent triad of American bicentennials—of the Declaration of Independence, the Constitution, and the Bill of Rights—focused largely on the values of the third, and thus on the second sentence of the first. *A March of Liberty*[21] seems to me a characteristic title among the many books on constitutional subjects published in this period. In an important 1986 casebook promoted for use in undergraduate law courses, Walter Murphy recapitulated Friedrich. Like Friedrich, Murphy and his coauthors begin broadly, noting that "Constitutionalism is . . . constantly concerned with the human penchant to act selfishly and abuse power." But also like Friedrich, they end narrowly: "For the constitutionalist, political morality [can only be weighed] against the moral criteria of individual rights." Rigorously distinguishing democratic from constitutionalist theory, they explain how constitutionalism regards democratic processes as a means toward "the ultimate civic purpose of protecting individual liberty," or better yet, "individual autonomy."[22] Murphy has ably reiterated this conception of constitutionalism for the benefit of constitutionmakers in eastern Europe and elsewhere.[23]

Indeed this outlook characterizes most of the "constitutional Johnny Appleseeds"[24] who have advised a host of reforming countries since 1989. The American Committee on the Czechoslovak Constitution, for example, began instructing Czechs and Slovaks before the dust of the Velvet Revolution had settled. Its advisory papers urged them to focus on "constitutionally protected freedom of the individual,"[25] taught them (unsuccessfully, it now seems) that drawing "distinctions based on ethnicity or national origin is . . . illegitimate" for a constitutionalist regime,[26] and warned them fervently against adopting any "limitations clause" that could qualify the paramount values of individual autonomy, privacy, and choice.[27] Even those most anxious to be culturally sensitive nevertheless convey a predominantly liberal notion of constitutionalism.[28] A. E. Dick Howard, who has consulted self-effacingly with constitution drafters in almost a dozen countries, measures "whether constitutionalism is a reality" by the degree to which it serves "the sanctity of the individual . . . personal privacy and autonomy." Howard does mention constitutionalism's classic concern with preventing concentrations of power; he subsumes this concern under a greater concern—that of preventing "a threat to individual liberty."[29]

In the American context, Howard's explanation is unobjectionable. Largely constituted by their public liberalism, Americans do not detect any narrowing of values in such statements. Exhibiting the success and power of their own constitutionalism, they take it for granted that liberty is the good that public authority ought to serve. What other kind of danger does concentrated power pose besides a threat to individual liberty? What greater positive purpose could there be for governmental authority besides preserving our liberties? Yet to admit the predominantly liberal character of American constitutionalism does not require us to deny the possibility of authentically constitutionalist experiences unlike the American one. From the perspective of other places and other histories, there may well be other harms to avoid, and other goods to pursue publicly, besides individual freedom. (As I have suggested above, some people might locate a harm precisely in the cultural consequences of publicly established liberalism.)

To a remarkable degree, constitutionalism has become an American synonym for *liberal* constitutionalism; the adjective is understood even when omitted. The conflation was usually unconscious, always innocent. Where it was deliberate, the motivation was good. Walter Murphy, for example, has clearly hoped to prevent the assets of a constitutionalist approach to politics from being lost inside the increasingly amorphous category of "democracy." But conflation has impoverished the idea of constitutionalism, and made it almost impossible to conceive of constitutionalist arrangements that do not pivot on liberal values.

## Toward Clarity: Constitutionalism, Liberal and Otherwise

Even if they developed it too narrowly, Friedrich and Murphy were right about the impulse behind constitutionalism: dread of unfettered power. The appeal of constitutionalism, now and in previous eras, seems precisely to lie in its capacity to ward off tyranny by structuring public life and institutions in a way that keeps them accountable to general public standards. More simply, constitutionalism appeals to people because it secures the political conditions necessary to a relatively decent human life. Let me propose an understanding of constitutionalism that accounts for the qualities that give it its appeal—the appeal it now has in postcommunist Europe and elsewhere—and that permits a nonliberal variety apt to be serviceable where liberalism is not. My proposal is in continuity with the history of usage, but requires going back to where the road branched off at liberalism, ignoring definitional barricades erected at the mouths of other branches.

Constitutionalism in its essence is not individual rights but fettered power. This formulation invites a fuller account of both constitution and constitutionalism. A *constitution* is a polity's normative architecture; it is that ensemble of standards, aspirations and practices that form and are authoritative for a people's common life. Every polity, in so far as it is a functioning polity, has a constitution, whether written or not. But obviously not every polity practices constitutionalism. *Constitutionalism* requires a certain kind of constitution: one that is self-limiting in character, as I shall try to explain. Furthermore, the self-limiting schema of such a constitution must be consciously articulated, for this is the pivotal underpinning of its limited and limiting quality. Constitutionalism so constructed quells the fear that inspires it: that is, it obstructs despotism, whether of absolute rulers or absolutized principles.

Let me consider articulation first. In a constitutionalist polity, the constitution is made self-conscious so that its authority can be explicit when necessary. Written constitutional texts are an attempt to lay down in words the actual constitution, or important aspects of it. And it is probably safe to say that a written constitution usually indicates what the members of a polity currently regard as the most important aspects of their actual constitution, or as the aspects most in need in of mention. But the defining quality of constitutionalism is not having definite texts; it is the public articulation of (at least some of) a polity's normative architecture, that is, of those conventions and practices, principles and understandings that, when not simply taken for granted, are invoked to control more particular disputes. These things can be articulated via all forms of influential public discourse. Articulating a constitution has certain logical, possibly psychological, and certainly political, consequences. Most importantly, to articulate a polity's normative architecture is to objectify it. It is to confer upon it a kind of separate existence—separate, especially, from the immediate holders of power, even if those holders of power are the ones doing the articulating. Public articulation means that the shape and purposes of the polity are no longer hostage to the vagaries of their subjectivity.[30] Whether purposely or inadvertently, and whether to a greater or lesser degree, constitutionalism pries the polity away from the holders of power and makes the constitution itself an object to be reckoned with. In this light, those who insist on written texts as the hallmark of constitutionalism are literally wrong but intuitively right; their appetite for objectified standards fastens itself on too narrow an object.

Small polities constituted by unquestioned, organic relationships—especially in premodern times—may never have felt the need to articulate consciously their normative architecture. They simply lived together and always had; what was there to talk about? Such traditional orders are not, properly speaking, constitutionalist. If they are constituted in a self-limiting way, they might be called protoconstitutionalist. In pre-Columbian times, Native American nations relied on myth, poetry, and narrative to fill a function analogous to constitutional articulation. Subsequently, contact with potent, alien alternatives made self-consciousness a necessity and triggered efforts among many tribes to articulate (sometimes in writing) their normative architecture. By such a process protoconstitutionalist orders can become effectively constitutionalist, making it possible to identify some Native American nations with a nonliberal form of constitutionalism (as I have done above).

There is, of course, one constitution whose articulation does nothing to foster constitutionalism: the kind organized around the whim of one man or one group, whatever it should happen to be. This is a bleak and lamentable constitution, and no less so if the whim in question happens to be majority whim. The public articulation of this constitution does not make for constitutionalism because it does not even attempt to constitute the polity objectively. Such a scheme simply puts power fully and formlessly at the disposal of its wielders. It is anticonstitutionalism, for it operates by the rule of *ipse dixit.* Europe's communist constitutions were of this character, since they had one effective provision: the "leading role" of the Party, which could have been more simply restated, "Obey us!" Like many modern tyrants, however, the Stalinist parties couldn't resist the temptation to mimic constitutionalism, surrounding their simple constitution with a bunch of excess verbiage. Such mimicry may or may not be dangerous to tyrants. It depends on the fate of the excess verbiage.[31]

As the anticonstitutionalist case makes plain, the content of the thing articulated matters very much indeed. A constitution of limitation is the heart of the matter. In all of its incarnations, constitutionalism has somehow always signified "limited government." Articulation provides the beginnings of limitation because of the objectifying effect I have described: a constitution that is somehow an articulate matter of public record makes it hard for power to be anything and everything at any time. But constitutionalism embraces limitation in two other, more substantive re-

FIGURE 1  CONSTITUTIONALISM AND THE MEANING OF
"LIMITED GOVERNMENT"

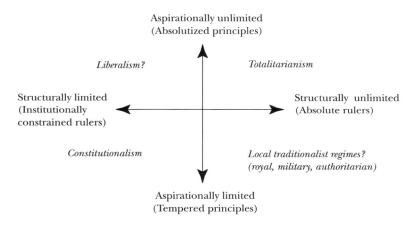

spects: in its structures and in its normative aspirations. This produces an array of constitutive possibilities like that attempted in figure 1, in which each axis can be a continuum (and in which regimes are identified speculatively as pure types).

Structural limits are the easy part. Any number of institutional devices can thwart concentrations of power and keep power holders accountable, including bicameralism, enumerated powers, separated and/or overlapping powers (as in the French mixture of presidential and parliamentary government, or the American "checks and balances" system), judicial review, concordats among various social bodies, federalism, and mechanisms of popular participation, notably voting. A combination of some such devices is necessary to constitutionalism. None by itself is privileged—although some are more dangerous to omit than others, especially some form of popular participation. Indeed, since each structural device has its own inner logic, healthy constitutionalism would seem to require a complementing array of devices (and norms), lest the unlimited logic of one device domineer to the detriment of the whole—as in recent laments over "gridlock" caused by the American separation of powers system.

Normative or aspirational limits are subtler. At bottom, of

course, no polity constitutes itself by reference to a wholly un-
bounded aspiration to justice or truth (except the most fleeting
utopian experiments). Any effective political constitution stipulates, at least implicitly, some variety of political morality. After all,
one couldn't enact, wholesale and simultaneously, socialist, Islamic, tribal, and liberal conceptions of justice. In other words, a
successful constitution brings *political* closure to many big normative questions; it forms a normative frame of reference within
which intrapolity disputes are typically enacted.

As I have discussed at greater length elsewhere, a constitutionalist system capitalizes on this narrowing effect.[32] It embraces as a
virtue the necessity of a stipulated and therefore lowered normative horizon. For even within the constraints imposed by logic
and effectiveness, it is possible to have more and less ambitious
aspirations, more and less expansive norms. The more profoundly
constitutionalist a regime, the more qualified its aspirations. The
Leninist polities achieved a result about as far removed from
constitutionalism as possible because they aimed at the transformation of human nature: the New Socialist Man, who would be
liberated from all distortions (allegedly induced by the mindset of
private property). This nearly boundless aspiration, unhindered
by meaningful structural limits on Party power, made it easy to
call the resulting system totalitarian. Localized regimes rooted
in local social traditions have seldom embraced such sweeping
aspirations, even when they have had a similarly low regard for
structural limitations on their power holders.

Aspirational and structural characteristics obviously interact.
The more exalted or limitless the constitutive aspirations, the
more vulnerable are institutionalized, structural limits on power.
Or again, constitutional structures (as means) can serve constitutional norms (as ends); the American esteem for individual liberty, for example, produced a written Bill of (individual) Rights
and shaped the development of judicial power. But structures
(like federalism) can also obstruct the attainment of norms. A
constitutionalist, always concerned with limitation, will sometimes
welcome such obstruction.

The question of aspirations or norms leads directly to the
distinction between liberal and nonliberal constitutionalism: the
one centralizes liberal norms, the other does not. Both lodge

their animating norms in institutional structures that limit the discretion of power holders—even their discretion to pursue the system's constitutive aspirations. Moreover, in both cases (if they remain constitutionalist) the animating norms themselves are somehow tempered.

Liberal constitutionalism gives its heart to liberalism: to the rights or liberty entitlements of individuals, to the ideals of private choice and free contract. It restricts the state to make possible the unrestricted individual. Such a scheme is arguably constituted by no normative orientation; normative orientations are the business of individuals who choose them. Looked at this way, political authority operates as a neutral arbiter among competing value systems, and forswears any concern with the character of the citizenry. Seen another way, and especially from the perspective of alternative systems, such a system simply pivots on liberal norms. To the degree consistent with constitutionalist limitations, it fosters a liberal disposition in its citizens.[33]

Nonliberal constitutionalism (as I propose the term) is defined by contrast to its rival: the gravitational field of liberal values does not regulate its normative orbit. This leaves open a lot of possibilities. At least it means that nonliberal constitutionalist systems are overt about what Stanley Fish might call their embeddedness in given systems of meaning—which typically derive from culture, ethnicity, religion, and the like. Their animating norms are substantive, and their institutions feature some means to promote favored patterns of life or attitude—at least to the degree consistent with constitutionalist limitations. While liberal visions of good character are cosmopolitan, autonomist and choice-loving, nonliberal visions of character more often view the individual not as the source of value but as a participant in a given system of meaning to which allegiance is naturally owed. Nonliberal values are typically more local than universalistic in character, except insofar as they are rooted in religions with universal pretensions. We may be tempted to think of these as traditionalist regimes but, as I will suggest below, progressivist versions of it are equally feasible.

Either variety of constitutionalism may emerge from, or corrode into, nonconstitutionalist illiberalism on the one hand or nonconstitutionalist liberalism on the other. Call the alternatives fascism and hyperliberalism. Regimes committed to illiberal norms pose obvious dangers when they slip the leash of constitutionalism. It is hardly necessary to enumerate the horrors committed by undiluted ethnic, religious or ideologically moralistic regimes when they set out to fulfill their principles with unfettered political power. Probably the most important task of a nonliberal constitution is to impose adequate limitations—both conceptual and structural—upon its own constitutive norms.

But liberal regimes, too, can slip the leash of constitutionalism. Although life in a liberal society makes it harder to recognize this danger, the contemporary critiques of liberalism that I cited above—feminist, postmodern, non-Western, and traditional—amount to just such a complaint. According to this criticism, unfettered liberalism does not respect the plurality it organizes. Instead, it trivializes pluralism by transforming substantive differences—in such matters as religion, morality, and ethnic culture—into differences of private choice and personal taste. Neutrality, or privatism, effectively operates as the substantive commitment that displaces rather than tolerates its predecessors. For untempered liberal norms—especially when reinforced by a commercial marketplace organized around choice and contract—have a diffuse but identifiable social consequence. They foster a society dominated by individualists who venerate personal autonomy, who regard their own identities as largely self-created, and who come to view their experience of other social communities (guild, religion, family) as hanging contingently on their private choices. They most emphatically do not believe in the divine right of kings; they believe in something rather like the divine right of individuals. Among such people, subcommunities with nonliberal orientations find themselves legally privatized and socially on the defensive. If this analysis is near the mark, then some liberal regimes, especially in North America, may be in the process of losing their constitutionalist character, gradually giving way to a stark liberalism tempered only by democratic procedures (themselves wielded by a mass public increasingly liberal-individualist in temper).

In liberal constitutionalism, liberal values naturally have the upper hand. But the liberalism of a constitutionalist regime must somehow be what Rawls calls a merely political liberalism, which imposes no metaphysical doctrine and does not inexorably purge social life of its nonliberal qualities and institutions.[34] Whether this is possible remains a matter of debate. Assuming it is possible, the arrangement might perhaps more clearly be termed constitutionalist liberalism than liberal constitutionalism.

Authentic constitutionalism is difficult to maintain for many reasons, but not least because of the political psychology of morality—that is, because of the drive of any single normative system to the consummation of its principles. The perfect justice principle, of course, would pose no threat, since it would have no unexpected, harmful consequences. Constitutionalism copes with the absence of any such principle by tempering both principles and power structures. It might lead some newly organizing political societies deliberately to mix aspects of different normative systems, structuring tensions to forestall the supreme ascendancy of any one. A society with a strong illiberal orientation, for example, might do well to incorporate some liberal values into a larger nonliberal constitution. As I have argued elsewhere, such a mixed constitution is probably the best form of nonliberal constitutionalism.[35]

In any event, nonliberal constitutionalism must have both the generic qualities of constitutionalism and the particular qualities that make it a nonliberal species of the genus. This requires distinguishing the generically defining objectives of constitutionalism from the various means deployed towards them. The strictly liberal account confuses things by mixing up means and ends. The constitutional elevation of individual rights, for example, is a constitutionalist means, not a constitutionalist end. Nonliberal constitutionalism deploys other means to the same ends—the ends of warding off arbitrary power, of fostering nonabsolute organs of power, and of articulating general norms to which everyone in the polity is accountable.

Applying the concept of nonliberal constitutionalism in particular times and places makes for largely uncharted territory. Was nonliberal constitutionalism anticipated in some features of Republican Rome or of medieval Europe?[36] Or in the *millet* system of the Ottoman Empire?[37] And what about contemporary regimes? I have already described modern Israel and Native American nations as rough prototypes of a nonliberal constitutionalism. If I were to go further I might consider Canada in the period before the 1982 Charter of Rights and Freedoms, when the country's "Red Tory" character was more pronounced. I might speculate about Ireland's constitutional reconciliation of a very public Roman Catholicism with a very equitable rule of law. I might examine how the constitutional jurisprudence of the Federal Republic of Germany eschews the idea of the neutral state, making it possible to protect individual rights while also authorizing a "social market economy" and tax support for religious institutions.[38] I might speculate on postcommunist Poland, which seems likely to configure itself eventually around both its Catholic and liberal elements.[39]

Such speculations must be judged by historians and area specialists. Since my task here is conceptual rather than applied, I will conclude with a series of clarifications that they may appreciate.

## FEDERAL, DEMOCRATIC, COMMUNITARIAN, CONSERVATIVE?

Federalism (or its consociational variant) is a mechanism that can graft together liberal and nonliberal orders into a constitutionalist whole that tempers both. For example, federal-level norms and institutions can be liberal while substantive illiberalism operates at subfederal levels, so that the difference in level matches the difference in constitutive norms.[40] Something like this was arguably the original version of American constitutionalism.[41] It was most visible in the Tenth Amendment, by which the states retained powers not delegated, traditionally understood as including the "police powers" to regulate the health, safety, welfare *and morals* of their citizens. The reverse arrangement, where a superior illiberal sphere constitutionally guarantees a subordinate liberal sphere, is in principle equally possible, though never yet seen.

To a constitutionalist concerned with multidimensional limitation, federalism poses challenges along with its benefits. Either pole in a federalist graft may end up subverting or escaping the other. More likely, the principles of the top jurisdiction will tend to overwhelm those of the bottom. Unless federal-level norms are articulated in proximate and functional, rather than ultimate and principled, terms, the gravitational pull of the positionally superior federal norms will eventually prevail over local norms. Moreover, the American experience suggests that a mixture of principles needs to be established at both levels of a federalist structure, for otherwise the absolutizing tendency of each set of principles finds no check within its own sphere. For example, the toleration of slavery at the level of state jurisdiction was a fatal, deplorable weakness in the original American scheme. On the other hand, the correction of that error—the Fourteenth Amendment and its judicial incorporation of the First Amendment against the states—has resulted in the trivialization of the states as meaningful political subcommunities; they are no longer able to dissent in any vital way from the norms of the liberal nation. Perhaps the error here was that the nonliberal prerogatives of the subordinate parts—the states—were from the start tacit rather than explicit (with the sole exception of slavery, that is), whereas the liberal norms of the federal union were announced explicitly and majestically in the Declaration of Independence and the Bill of Rights (and the subsequently influential *Federalist Papers*). But whether explicit or tacit, scant attention was paid to the juxtaposition of liberal and nonliberal considerations *within* each jurisdictional level.

Is nonliberal constitutionalism consistent with democracy? It is common to posit an opposition or at least a tension between constitutionalism and democracy.[42] The idea of nonliberal constitutionalism retains this tension. Liberals call it a conflict between the power of the democratic majority on the one hand and the rights of individuals on the other—rights the majority may not abrogate however much it wants to. In fact, of course, this is simply the opposition between liberalism and democracy. The idea of nonliberal constitutionalism obliges us to see the tension with democracy at a prior and more elemental level. To make this clear, we must take democracy in its pure or technical sense as a system in which the mass public gets what it wants, a system in which the will of the mass public is the most authoritative public norm.[43] Understood in this undiluted form, democracy negates constitutionalism because it is not objectively constituted; for the logic of pure democracy is precisely to enshrine the subjectivity of its power holder, the mass public.

The irreducible theoretical tension between democracy and

constitutionalism does not make them incompatible. After all, popular participation can be politically meaningful even if it is structured in ways that qualify pure democracy. Constitutionalism qualifies democracy just as it qualifies other powers and principles. Liberal constitutionalism tempers democracy primarily by entrenching individual liberties. Nonliberal constitutionalism tempers democracy by instituting a *variety* of crosscutting institutions and norms (sometimes including individual liberties in some subordinate capacity). Keeping our actual democracies adulterated is close to the heart of constitutionalist wisdom. Keeping our *notion* of democracy unadulterated helps us to see more clearly the nature of its tension with constitutionalism.

Does nonliberal constitutionalism entail what is now known as "communitarianism"?[44] The two share common traits but are distinct in principle. Opposition from liberals confirms that communitarianism is not liberal.[45] But communitarianism can easily sanction a nonconstitutionalist illiberalism, with little effective regard for constituted constraints on a community's power to reinforce its values.[46] Indeed, nonliberal constitutionalism has precisely what communitarianism, by itself, lacks: effective, objectified limits on community norms and institutions.

In the same vein we may ask: is nonliberal constitutionalism conservative? Even leaving aside the American newspaper usage that confuses "conservative" with "nonliberal," we may still understand the suspicion that constitutive norms are apt to derive from a community's longstanding traditions. Yet nonliberal constitutionalism differs in principle from conservatism, and may differ hugely in practice. This is because a nonliberal constitutionalist order might well embody and foster orientations that are anything but conservative.

Consider current efforts in a few American cities, and on many American university campuses, to institutionalize a community-wide ethic of multiculturalist tolerationism. Although they are on a microscale, such efforts could be a version of nonliberal constitutionalism, insofar as certain orientations—in this case traditionalist ones—are overtly discouraged, and others—notably progressivist, feminist and sexually inclusivist ones—are overtly sanctioned. "Politically correct" thinkers who now promote such policies are often unapologetically hostile to notions of "individual rights" because they see that rubric—with some reason—as a mask for the dominance of Anglo masculine values. If it didn't go against the grain of newspaper usage, one might say that nonliberal constitutionalism is the best candidate for an underlying *political* theory for political correctness. The movement to constitute politically correct communities has made itself vulnerable to criticism from liberal constitutionalists, however, because it has not always been clear whether the movement is constitutionalist in character. Does it aim to meaningfully constitute—and so also limit—its intended illiberal campus or public power? Or does it intend arbitrary rule by anointed P.C. authorities, unconstrained by anything other than their own ideological predilections? Ambiguity on this point makes the protagonists of the movement a great deal more suspect than necessary.

### EVALUATING NONLIBERAL CONSTITUTIONS

How can we evaluate political orders—existing or proposed—that are constitutionalist but not liberal? Some liberals think that outside of liberalism all is normative chaos; nevertheless, being open to varieties of nonliberal constitutionalism does not require abandoning all standards of evaluation. First, one may measure constitutionalist claimants against constitutionalist criteria. Second, one may measure them against broader, more authoritative criteria surpassing constitutionalism (and liberalism) altogether.

On the first score, any system claiming the title of nonliberal constitutionalism must frame public life in a way that implements self-limitation across multiple dimensions simultaneously. In other words, nonliberal constitutions must make their positive moral purposes systematically nontotalist, and they must frame structures for the exercise of governmental power that are systematically nontyrannical.

On the second score, there may yet exist (despite Stanley Fish's assertions) higher and broader norms than liberalism can provide, more minimal but more sovereign human goods to which liberal or even constitutionalist values are but means, and in whose light any regime can be judged.[47] Constitutionalism doggedly imposes constraints on the *political* sway of all normative principles. But nothing about constitutionalism requires a dogged

moral or metaphysical skepticism. Indeed, nonliberal constitutionalism is made for peoples who feel rather sure that some ways
of life are better than others—but who feel sure also that there
are good reasons to put some limits on the political promotion of
even the best way of life.

I have mentioned Native American tribes as examples of nonliberal but constitutionalist nations. As such, their membership
practices, which I passed over above, highlight a central evaluative
issue. In a word, they are unabashedly exclusivistic. Tribes determine who belongs, based typically on residency, blood quantum
or descendance (birth to an enrolled mother or father, similar to
criteria under the Israeli Law of Return). Moreover, many Native
American constitutional documents, like that of the Cheyenne
River Sioux, specifically authorize the exclusion of "non-members
whose presence may be injurious to the members of the tribe
morally or criminally."[48] In other words (to speak in liberal terminology) the ascriptive quality of membership lets tribal governments treat people unequally who are otherwise alike except in
accident of birth. In this sense the unequal protection of the laws
is an established part of Indian tribal polity. (It has been sanctioned through a series of Supreme Court decisions, notably *Santa
Clara Pueblo v. Martinez*).[49] Nearly all actual or aspiring nonliberal
constitutionalist regimes feature some such exclusivism—if not
always among different people, certainly among alternative sets of
values. In effect, the problem of exclusivity simply poses the problem of nonliberal constitutionalism itself. Can such a system-de-
fining exclusivity be justified? If so, how can we distinguish better
and worse forms of it?

Exclusivity can be justified because it is inescapable. No polity
constitutes itself as mankind writ large; every polity excludes and
includes, favors and disfavors. Liberal polities are no exception.
Even so ardent a liberal as Stephen Holmes confirms that liberalism is stumped by the exclusionary start-up questions that founders everywhere must ask—questions of territorial borders, of who
shall be citizens, of who shall receive first property rights.[50] Liberal
principles condemn *any* answers those questions receive, except
in the case of the founding of a worldwide regime of cosmopolitan
individualism. Absent that liberal eschaton, every actually existing

liberal regime implements exclusion. Of course, some people will condemn nonliberal polity—even nonliberal constitutionalism—in favor of liberal polity because, they say, liberal regimes acquiesce only reluctantly to the reality of finitude; they exclude minimally and with a guilty conscience.

As I have outlined above, recent criticisms of liberalism make it hard to accept such a claim.[51] The regime of liberal freedom, although allowing individuals whatever they want, has an inadvertent tendency to make them all want the same thing, as Tocqueville already foresaw.[52] A predominantly liberal order may formally enfranchise all its residents. But it effectively favors those who sequester in private their given identities and substantive commitments and who subscribe, in public, to the "neutral" values of liberal discourse. Those unwilling to engage in this transaction are marginalized; or else they (or their children) eventually conform. Not surprisingly, liberal societies seem increasingly to be dominated by people who have internalized a privatist approach to meaning in life.

If exclusivity is inescapable, then it makes little sense simply to praise those constitutions that practice "less" exclusion and blame those that practice "more." Evaluators must instead assess the relative merits of different forms of exclusion—whether deliberate or unreflective, overt or covert, whether based on culture, descent, language or history—as part of a multidimensional estimate of a constitutionalist system as a whole. The forms of exclusion practiced by Native American tribal governments, for example, are part of a larger political and social configuration whose ability to thwart tyranny at least equals that of modern liberal states.

## DANGERS OF NONLIBERAL CONSTITUTIONALISM?

I am acutely aware that merely to state the idea of nonliberal constitutionalism is to risk becoming the darling of fascists, who may find it a convenient pretext for the assertion of unfettered power. This risk arises not from the inner logic of the idea but from the various cultural contexts in which it would be spoken—contexts sometimes burdened with a past where nonliberal impulses relentlessly escaped sublimating limitations (like constitutionalism). I have tried hard to present the idea in a way that will hinder its rhetorical appropriation by aspiring tyrants.

Unfortunately, rejecting the idea of nonliberal constitutionalism poses equal or greater dangers. An unprecedented number of political societies are currently in the process of reconstructing themselves after revolution or rupture. From Bosnia to the Baltics and from Cape Town to Kazakhstan, newly organizing peoples seek a way to incarnate their cultural, religious or moral identities. And where the salutary effects of constitutionalist government are needed most, agreement on an essentially liberal regime is the least likely outcome of all. If they perceive no constitutionalist option other than a liberal one, many peoples are far more likely to reject constitutionalism than to embrace liberalism. What they embrace will be ominous.

## NOTES

For their suport of the larger project of which this essay is a part, I gratefully acknowledge the University of Pennsylvania, Earhart Foundation, and the Pew Charitable Trusts (Evangelical Scholars Program). I am also indebted to Will Harris, Sotirios Barber, Jack Nagel, and Will Kymlicka for helpful criticism.

1. I am thinking, naturally, of Francis Fukuyama, *The End of History and the Last Man* (New York: Free Press, 1992).

2. Christopher D. Stone, *The Gnat Is Older Than Man: Global Environment and Human Agenda* (Princeton: Princeton University Press, 1993); Jennifer Nedelsky, *Private Property and the Limits of American Constitutionalism: The Madisonian Framework and Its Legacy* (Chicago: University of Chicago Press, 1990); Shelley Burtt, "Religious Parents, Secular Schools: A Liberal Defense of an Illiberal Education," *The Review of Politics* 56 (1994): 51–70.

3. Roberto Unger, *Knowledge and Politics* (New York: Free Press, 1975); Alasdair MacIntyre, *After Virtue* (Notre Dame, Ind.: University of Notre Dame Press, 1981); MacIntyre, *Whose Justice? Which Rationality?* (Notre Dame, IN: University of Notre Dame Press, 1988); Michael J. Sandel, *Liberalism and the Limits of Justice* (New York: Cambridge University Press, 1982); Michael Walzer, *Spheres of Justice* (New York: Basic Books, 1983); Charles Taylor, *Philosophy and the Human Sciences* (New York: Cam-

bridge University Press, 1985); Taylor, *Sources of the Self: The Making of the Modern Identity* (Cambridge, MA: Harvard University Press, 1989).

4. Uday S. Mehta, "Liberal Strategies of Exclusion," *Politics and Society* 18 (1990): 427–54; Tomislav Sunic, "Historical Dynamics of Liberalism: From Total Market to Total State?" *The Journal of Social, Political and Economic Studies* 13 (1988): 455–71; Edward W. Said, *Culture and Imperialism* (New York: Knopf, 1993); Iris Marion Young, "Polity and Group Difference: A Critique of the Ideal of Universal Citizenship," *Ethics* 99 (1989): 250–74; Young, *Justice and the Politics of Difference* (Princeton: Princeton University Press, 1990); Cornel West, "The New Cultural Politics of Difference," in *Out There: Marginalization and Contemporary Cultures*, ed. Russell Ferguson, Martha Gever, Trinh T. Minhha, and Cornel West (New York and Cambridge, Mass.: New Museum of Contemporary Art and the Massachusetts Institute of Technology Press, 1990); J. Budziszewski, "The Illusion of Moral Neutrality," *First Things*, no. 35 (1993): 32–37; Alain de Benoist, *Démocratie: Le problème* (Paris: Le Labyrinthe, 1985); Benoist, *Europe, Tiers monde, même combat* (Paris: R. Laffont, 1986); Mark C. Henrie, "Rethinking American Conservatism in the 1990s: The Struggle against Homogenization," *Intercollegiate Review* 28:2 (1993): 8–16.

5. Stanley Fish, "There's No Such Thing as Free Speech and It's a Good Thing, Too," *Boston Review* 17 :1 (1992): 3–26; Fish, *There's No Such Thing as Free Speech* (New York: Oxford University Press, 1994).

6. Fish, "There's No Such Thing as Free Speech," 3, 23.

7. Robert C. Bartlett, "Aristotle's Science of the Best Regime," *American Political Science Review* 88 (1994): 152; Stephen L. Carter, *The Culture of Disbelief: How American Law and Politics Trivialize Religious Devotion* (New York: Basic Books, 1993); Shelly Burtt, "Religious Parents, Secular Schools: A Liberal Defense of an Illiberal Education," *The Review of Politics* 56 (1994): 51–70; Stephen M. Feldman, "Power, Religion, and the First Amendment: On the Separation of Church and State (and Other Christian Dogma); Or, Don't Wish Me a Merry Christmas," presented at fourth biennial Georgetown Law Center Discussion Group on Constitutional Law (Washington, December 1993); Mark Juergensmeyer, *The New Cold War? Religious Nationalism Confronts the Secular State* (Berkeley: University of California Press, 1993).

While it has obvious (and historical) affinities with Protestant Christianity, an individualist and privatist conception of religion is anathema to many other religions; in those cases, submitting to it would negate one's faith.

8. Stanley Fish, "Liberalism Doesn't Exist," *Duke Law Journal* 1987 (December 1987): 1001.

9. Fish, "There's No Such Thing as Free Speech," 26.

10. But see Sotirios A. Barber, "Stanley Fish and the Future of Pragmatism in Legal Theory," *University of Chicago Law Review* 58 (1991): 1033–43; also Cass R. Sunstein, review of Stanley Fish, "There's No Such Thing as Free Speech," in *The New Republic* 209 (1993): 42–46.

11. Joav Peled, "Ethnic Democracy and the Legal Construction of Citizenship: Arab Citizens of the Jewish State," *American Political Science Review,* 86 (1992): 432–43; Gary J. Jacobsohn, *Apple of Gold: Israeli and American Constitutionalism* (Princeton: Princeton University Press, 1993).

12. Ernest L. Schusky, ed., *Political Organization of Native North Americans* (Lanham, Md.: University Press of America, 1980); Sharon O'Brien, *American Indian Tribal Governments* (Norman: University of Oklahoma Press, 1989); Augie Fleras and Jean Leonard Elliott, *The "Nations Within": Aboriginal-State Relations in Canada, the United States, and New Zealand* (Toronto: Oxford University Press, 1992).

13. Vine Deloria, Jr., and Clifford M. Lytle, *American Indians, American Justice* (Austin: University of Texas Press, 1983); Jacobsohn, *Apple of Gold,* chap. 2.

14. Aristotle, *Politics* III-VI.

15. Charles Howard McIlwain, *Constitutionalism Ancient and Modern* (Ithaca: Cornell University Press, 1940), 21–22.

16. According to Friedrich, this project has two roots: medieval natural law (supplying rules and standards to which government might be held accountable) and individualism (which he traces to the Christian doctrine of the "transcendental importance of each man's soul"). He developed at greater length the Christian sources of individualist constitutionalism in his *Transcendent Justice: The Religious Dimension of Constitutionalism,* 1964.

17. Carl J. Friedrich, *Constitutional Government and Politics: Nature and Development* (New York: Harper and Brothers, 1937), 35, 111, 136; Friedrich, *Constitutional Government and Democracy: Theory and Practice in Europe and America* (Boston: Little, Brown, 1941), 20–22.

18. Friedrich, *Constitutional Government and Democracy,* ix, italics added.

19. Carl J. Friedrich, *Constitutional Government and Democracy: Theory and Practice in Europe and America,* 4th ed. (Waltham, Mass.: Blaisdell Publishing Co., 1968), 24, 7.

20. Carl J. Friedrich, *Transcendent Justice: The Religous Dimension of Constitutionalism* (Durham, NC: Duke University Press, 1964), 16; italics original.

21. Melvin I. Urofsky, *A March of Liberty: A Constitutional History of the United States* (New York: Alfred A. Knopf, 1988).

22. Walter F. Murphy, James E. Fleming, and William F. Harris II,

*American Constitutional Interpretation* (Mineola, N.Y.: Foundation Press, 1986), 27–29. Not surprisingly, Murphy explicitly invokes Friedrich's definition of constitutionalism in a later work: Murphy, "Civil Law, Common Law, and Constitutional Democracy," *Louisiana Law Review* 52 (1991): 105.

23. Walter F. Murphy, "Constitutional Democracy in Eastern Europe," working paper prepared for the American Council of Learned Societies Conference on Constitutionalism and the Transition to Democracy in Eastern Europe, held in collaboration with Eötvös Loránd University (Pécs, Hungary, June, 1990); Murphy, "Constitutions, Constitutionalism, and Democracy," in *Constitutionalism and Democracy: Transitions in the Contemporary World,* ed. Douglas Greenberg, Stanley N. Katz, Melanie Beth Oliviero, and Steven D. Wheatley (New York: Oxford University Press, 1993).

24. Barbara A. Perry, "'Constitutional Johnny Appleseeds': American Consultants and the Drafting of Foreign Constitutions," presented at the annual meeting of the American Political Science Association (Washington, D.C., 1991).

25. Lloyd Cutler, "A Note on How the Constitution Should Be Adopted and Amended," advice paper prepared for Committee on Revision of the Czechoslovak Constitution (under the auspices of the American Committee on the Czechoslovak Constitution and the Charter 77 Foundation, 1990), 2; see also Roslyn A. Mazer, "Constitutional Protection of Freedom of Speech, Freedom of the Press, and Freedom of Association and Assembly," advice paper, prepared for Committee on Revision of the Czechoslovak Constitution (under the auspices of the American Committee on the Czechoslovak Constitution and the Charter 77 Foundation, April 2, 1990).

26. Daniel E. Troy, "Draft Paper on Issues and Options Respecting Minority Rights," advice paper prepared for Committee on Revision of the Czechoslovak Constitution (under the auspices of the American Committee on the Czechoslovak Constitution and the Charter 77 Foundation, 1990), 15.

27. Laurence H. Tribe, "Draft Paper on Issues and Options for Dealing with Limitations on Rights, and with Privacy and Religion," advice paper prepared for Committee on Revision of the Czechoslovak Constitution (under the auspices of the American Committee on the Czechoslovak Constitution and the Charter 77 Foundation, March 15, 1990).

28. Many examples could be cited. Beyond A. E. Dick Howard, I offer two. The American Bar Association's Central and Eastern European Law Initiative (CEELI), which sends armadas of American lawyers to advise, pro-bono, on postcommunist legal systems, circumspectly states that U.S.

legal traditions "offer but one approach" ("Central and East European Law Initiative. A Project of the American Bar Association," photocopy of organizational statement of purpose provided to the author in June 1994). Yet CEELI promotes itself as bringing "new rights" to "old countries" (Janet Key, "Old Countries, New Rights," *ABA Journal* [May 1994]: 68–73; article distributed regularly in publicity packets by Central and Eastern European Law Initiative). And CEELI deliberately caters to foreign interest in individual rights and the free-market system. Another example is prominent international law expert Louis Henkin, who in describing "the elements of constitutionalism" for postcommunist reformers in Hungary, gave overwhelming prominence to his discussion of only one element: individual rights (Louis Henkin, "Constitutions and the Elements of Constitutionalism," working paper prepared for the American Council of Learned Societies Conference on Constitutionalism and the Transition to Democracy in Eastern Europe, held in collaboration with Eötvös Loránd University, Pécs, Hungary, June, 1990); see also Louis Henkin and Albert J. Rosenthal, eds., *Constitutionalism and Rights: The Influence of the U.S. Constitution Abroad* (New York: Columbia University Press, 1990).

29. A. E. Dick Howard, *Democracy's Dawn: A Directory of American Initiatives on Constitutionalism, Democracy, and the Rule of Law in Central and Eastern Europe* (Charlottesville: University Press of Virginia, 1991), 2–3.

30. This means, of course, that constitutionalism is liable to all the problems that attend any attempt to pry meaning away from subjectivity and render it objective. All the really interesting problems of constitutionalism probably have their roots here. We might grant that complete objectivity is neither attainable nor desirable. Still, to disdain the attempt at its approximation is obviously problematic for constitutionalism.

31. There are two possible outcomes: either its superfluity becomes obvious to everyone or else it acquires some degree of real constitutional significance in spite of itself. In the communist cases, the provision declaring the Party's leading role obviously trumped everything else in the text, revealing the true anticonstitutionalist constitution with ugly clarity. Of course excess verbiage may enjoy the other outcome as well. For example, when the Warsaw Pact countries formally embraced the Helsinki Accords, it was supposed to have the effect of legitimizing and making permanent the Soviet Union's postwar hold over eastern Europe. But since the document included the so-called third basket of human rights guarantees, it gave a foothold to opponents of the regime who now had a quasi-constitutional place to stand while pressing their demands for reform. In the end, what the tyrant may have tolerated as excess verbiage became an incipient counterconstitution.

32. Graham Walker, "The Constitutional Good: Constitutionalism's Equivocal Moral Imperative," *Polity* 26 (1993): 91–111.

33. Stephen Macedo, *Liberal Virtues: Citizenship, Virtue, and Community in Liberal Constitutionalism* (Oxford: Clarendon Press, 1990); William Galston, *Liberal Purposes: Goods, Virtues, and Diversity in the Liberal State* (New York: Cambridge University Press, 1991).

34. John Rawls, "Justice as Fairness: Political Not Metaphysical," *Philosophy and Public Affairs* 14 (1985): 223–51; Rawls, *Political Liberalism* (New York: Columbia University Press, 1993).

35. Graham Walker, "The New Mixed Constitution: A Response to Liberal Debility and Constitutional Deadlock in Eastern Europe," *Polity* 26 (1994): 503–15.

36. McIlwain, chaps. 2–4; Julian H. Franklin, ed., *Constitutionalism and Resistance in the Sixteenth Century: Three Treatises by Hotman, Beza, and Mornay* (New York: Pegasus, 1969); Brian Tierney, *Religion, Law, and the Growth of Constitutional Thought: 1150–1650* (Cambridge: Cambridge University Press, 1982).

37. Jacobsohn, *Apple of Gold,* chap. 2; Benjamin Braude and Bernard Lewis, eds., *Christians and Jews in the Ottoman Empire: The Functioning of a Plural Society* (New York: Holmes and Meier, 1982).

38. Donald P. Kommers, *The Constitutional Jurisprudence of the Federal Republic of Germany* (Durham, N.C.: Duke University Press, 1989).

39. Maciej Zieba, "The Liberalism That We Need," *First Things,* no. 40 (1994): 23–27.

40. Paul Piccone, "The Crisis of Liberalism and the Emergence of Federal Populism," *Telos,* no. 89 (1991): 7–44.

41. Jean Yarbrough, "The Constitution and Character: The Missing Critical Principle," in *To Form a More Perfect Union* (Charlottesville: University Press of Virginia, 1992).

42. E.g., Friedrich, *Constitutional Government and Democracy*; Murphy, "Constitutions, Constitutionalism and Democracy."

43. This can be made much more subtle, of course, by elaborating the various decision procedures and inclusion rules that the mass public would seem to have to follow if it is to be true to itself. Some theorists insist on such qualifications to the notion of democracy. But if they pose them as obligations, or rational self-obligations, of the mass public, instead of making them contingent on the actual wishes of an actual mass public, then their maneuver really introduces a competing authoritative principle which vies for supremacy with an actual democratic will. This competing authority is called reason. I personally welcome the vitiation of democracy by recourse to this alternative authority. But it is a vitiation, and little is gained *conceptually* by imagining it otherwise.

44. Sandel, *Liberalism and the Limits of Justice*; MacIntyre, *Whose Justice?*; Amitai Etzioni, *The Spirit of Community: Rights, Responsibilities and the Communitarian Agenda* (New York: Crown Publishers, 1993).

45. Amy Gutmann, "Communitarian Critics of Liberalism," *Philosophy and Public Affairs* 14 (1985): 308–22; Robert Thigpen and Lyle Downing, "Liberalism and the Communitarian Critique," *American Journal of Political Science* 31 (1987): 637–55.

46. William B. Breslin, "The Constitutionalist Challenge to Communitarianism" (Ph.D. diss., University of Pennsylvania, 1995).

47. Michael Walzer spoke recently of a "minimalist universalism" that condemns practices like ethnic cleansing and genocide but that does not enjoin the more culturally specific standards of Western rights-liberalism or even of the Universal Declaration of Human Rights (Michael Walzer, et al., "Nationalism and Ethinic Particularism: A Roundtable," *Tikkun* 7:6 [1992]: 49–56). The idea of a decent minimalism could be expanded in a positive direction as well, recognizing such generic virtues as humaneness, sexual responsibility, the sustenance of marriage and family, and a manageable material basis of human life. Are such values mere parochialisms because they do not necessarily derive from liberalism?

48. O'Brien, *American Indian Tribal Governments*, 200, 219.

49. *Santa Clara Pueblo v. Martinez*, 1978; 436 U.S. 49.

50. Stephen Holmes, "Back to the Drawing Board: An Argument for Constitutional Postponement in Eastern Europe," *East European Constitutional Review* 2 (Winter 1993): 2–25.

51. Cf. Mehta, "Liberal Strategies of Exclusion"; Said, *Culture and Imperialism*; Sunic, "Historical Dynamics of Liberalism"; Young, "Polity and Group Difference."

52. Alexis de Tocqueville, *Democracy in America*, vol. 2 (New York: Alfred A. Knopf, 1945 [1835]), 9–13.

# PART III

# THE NORMATIVE STATUS OF ETHNICITY

# 7

# GROUP RIGHTS AND ETHNICITY

## THOMAS W. POGGE

In political philosophy, the topic of group rights raises moral questions of the form: May/should a just society grant legal group right(s) $R$ to group(s) $G$ on moral ground(s) $M$? I address only one aspect of this complex: Should ethnic groups, as such, be favored in the distribution of legal group rights? My negative answer exemplifies the broader view that different types of groups should be considered together and on a par. Here "group" stands for any set of persons who are identified with this set: viewed as belonging together. And the relevant types of groups are, in the first instance, ethnic, religious, linguistic, and lifestyle groups.[1] My main thesis is then that, in deciding what group rights we, as a society, may or should grant to various groups, we ought not to favor groups of one type, as such, over groups of another.

This principle is the generalized analogue to one now widely accepted, namely the principle that we ought not to favor some religious (or ethnic, or lifestyle) groups over others. This latter principle does not preclude us from treating groups of the same type differentially, from conceding more extensive group rights to the Amish than to the Anglicans, for example. But such special treatment must not be based on the mere fact that they are the Amish. It must be based on relevant differences, on grounds that bring out that, though they are treated differently, these groups and their members are nonetheless treated with equal respect and concern. In the example at hand, one might say, for instance,

187

that the Amish religion is much smaller and more remote from the American mainstream (hence stands in greater need of special protections) and also tends to play a much deeper role in the lives of its adherents. My principle is proposed in the same spirit. It precludes differential treatment of types of groups, not differential treatment of groups of different types. This means that differential treatment of groups must never be based on their difference in type.

We might confront ethnic or religious chauvinism with a version of the Golden Rule: Base any claims you make for your own ethnic (religious) group on principles that you would be prepared to extend to any other ethnic (religious) group. I support a generalized Golden Rule: Base any claims you make for some group(s) on principles by which you would be prepared to judge the claims of any other group as well. Here is one neat way to "enforce" this rule: Whenever someone claims group rights for some group, or for groups of some type, we take her to hold that these rights should be granted to any other claimant group as well. If she believes that the rights should be extended only to some or to none of these other groups, then the burden is on her to show that the groups she proposes to exclude are dissimilar to hers in a way that renders them ineligible for the rights in question.

One reason for an evenhanded treatment of groups of different types is that the distinctions between types of cultural groups cannot, in the end, be given the clarity and sharpness they would need to support significant normative political differentiations. While the classification of many groups is straightforward, others involve overwhelming empirical complexities. In the case of the North American Jews, for instance, ethnic, religious, linguistic, and lifestyle elements are all intertwined and, moreover, their relative importance in the mix has changed significantly over time and also varies widely from one Jew to the next. How can we let the group rights of Jews depend on their unavoidably arbitrary classification?

A stronger reason for evenhandedness derives from the ideal of treating all citizens as equals, regardless of their identifications and affiliations. This ideal claims authority not in our private lives, but only where we, as citizens, participate in the design of policies, laws, and social institutions. It does not demand that all persons and groups should be equally important to me, that I should value them equally. It demands only that, in the political domain, I should recognize them as of equal intrinsic importance or value, as having an equal claim to respect and support from society a large. It thereby opposes high chauvinism, which holds some type(s) of groups to be more valuable than others, just as it opposes low chauvinism, which holds some ethnic (or religious or language or lifestyle) group(s) to be more valuable than others. In either case, discounting the value of groups is tantamount to discounting the value and equality of their members and is therefore unacceptable in a just society.

High chauvinism is sometimes explicit, even entrenched in the law, as when only religious objectors may apply for exemption from military service, when religious groups are favored by the tax laws, or when only ethnic groups are deemed eligible for limited self-rule.[2] More often, however, it takes a different form: Authors and public figures consider groups of a particular type and make sweeping claims in behalf of such groups without considering whether what they claim can reasonably be granted to relevantly similar groups of other types as well.[3] In this case, there is no explicit claim that (identifications with) groups of the chosen type are more valuable than others—only a suggestion to this effect. I want to challenge this trend as well: We should not conduct separate debates about the rights of groups of different types but should consider the various types of groups together, aiming for common standards by which to assess the validity of their claims. Only through a unified account of groups and group rights within a just society can we live up to our democratic ideals by explaining to all citizens how our institutions and laws are treating them as equals, irrespective, in particular, of (the type of) their identifications and affiliations. Such an account will attach no importance to whether a group is of this or that type. It will instead give weight to other factors, such as: how deep and structuring a role being affiliated or identified with this group plays in the lives of its members, what status the group has within the wider society (e.g., whether it is strong or weak, revered or despised), and, to some extent, what its history has been (e.g., what its members were led to rely upon regarding the group's future rights).

As these examples show, the factors that should be given weight cut across the (vague) divisions between types of groups. So the unified account I envision—once the relevant factors have been fully identified, specified, and brought to bear—will not only oppose high chauvinism but will also avoid reaching high chauvinist conclusions by another route: It will not yield the result that groups of some type(s), though of no greater intrinsic value, should nevertheless be favored over the rest. We may find, of course, that in our world ethnic groups have more frequently than others the special characteristics that strengthen their claim to legal group rights. We may also find societies in which only ethnic groups (though hardly all of them) qualify for a particular legal group right. But such rough and contingent correlations would not show that the account favors ethnic groups as such— let alone that it favors them (in an ethnic high chauvinist way) as being of greater intrinsic value.[4]

While the dangers of religious high chauvinism are receding in North America, those of ethnic high chauvinism seem to be in ascendancy, as ethnicity is acquiring a certain moral prestige and mystique. By seeking to undermine this prestige, I am not opposing group rights for ethnic groups. I believe that rather extensive group rights can be based on the classic individual rights to freedom of association and full political participation, and on classic liberal concerns for equal protection and for fair adjustments to legal change. Being rather liberal about group rights in general, I can concede to the proponents of ethnic group rights much of what they want—though I would concede analogous rights to many other claimant groups. What I wish for, then, is a certain cultural pluralism (or multiculturalism, if you like) which understands "cultural" very broadly as covering, equally, the whole range of citizens' affiliations and identifications. But my main concern here is to argue not for the extensiveness of group rights but for their fair distribution among groups of different types. I want to challenge the ethnic high chauvinists and their political allies to overcome by argument the straightforward null-hypothesis:

(N0) It is irrelevant to the moral assessment of a claim to legal group rights whether the group for which the rights are claimed is or is not (part of) an ethnic group.

## I. Some Clarifications Concerning Legal
## Group Rights

Begin with a distinction between active and passive rights. An active right is a right to do something if one so chooses; it is violated when its possessor, while trying to exercise it, is prevented from doing so in certain specified ways. A passive right is a right not to have certain things done to oneself; it can be violated even while its possessor is not doing or trying to do anything.

This distinction can be complicated. Some standard rights contain active and passive components. The right to vote, for instance, contains the passive right that elections be held, as well as the active right that one's attempt to vote at an appropriate place during the scheduled time be successful. Also, some standard rights can be construed as active or passive. A right to some benefit, construed actively, is violated only when an eligible person's attempt to take the benefit in the appropriate way is improperly blocked. Construed passively, it is violated when an eligible person is not given or offered the benefit even though this person has made no effort to obtain it.

The expression "group rights," which I have thus far used in a broad and crude sense, may cover at least three different kinds of legal rights:

1. Group rights proper, or simply (henceforth) group rights: These are rights that a group has as a group (and, if active, exercises as a group through its group-specific decision mechanism)—for example, Oregonians may have an active right, collectively, to delegate two appropriate persons to the U.S. Senate or a passive right to be consulted before construction of a nuclear power plant on Oregon soil.

2. Group-specific rights: These are rights had only by members of a certain group rather than by all—for example, Oregonians (but not all others) have the active right to vote in Oregon elections, Sikhs (but not all others) have the active right to ride a bike without a helmet, blacks (but not all others) have the active right to receive favorable consideration in university admissions, and those neither officially accused nor convicted of a crime (but not all others) have the passive right not to be imprisoned.

3. Group-statistical rights: These are rights that protect or en-

hance the aggregate status of the members of a group—for example, blacks may have the passive right that no more than 50 percent of any age cohort be conscripted or the active right to have 80 percent of their credit applications approved. Many group-statistical rights protect or enhance the representation of the group in certain segments of the population—as when some parliamentary seats are set aside for members of a national minority, or when a certain minimum representation is guaranteed for persons of a certain color or gender in university admissions, say, or in the awarding of government contracts. Such rights, too, may be active or passive: In the first case, the right is violated only when group members seeking entry do not get entry on favorable terms; in the second case, it can be violated even when insufficiently many group members are motivated to seek entry in the first place. Rights of this third kind are funny rights: Not really the rights of groups, because it is individuals who take sole possession of the objects of the right (seats in parliament, university educations). And not really individual rights either, because no individual is entitled to anything (so long as the objects of the right go to sufficiently many of her fellow group members).

Rights of all three kinds may also be defined in relative terms, that is, in relation to other groups: The people of Oregon may have a group right to send as many delegates to the Senate as the people of any other state. Sikhs may have a group-specific right that their donations to their religious organizations receive the same tax treatment as donations by Christians to Christian churches. And blacks may have a group-statistical right that—correcting for income, perhaps—the rejection rate for their credit applications to any bank should not run more than 25 percent above that for its entire applicant pool.

I shall concentrate my normative discussion on group rights and group-specific rights because this is the domain in which I expect my position to be most controversial. At least in our part of the world, it is rarely argued that ethnic groups should be favored over nonethnic groups in the granting of group-statistical rights. In the United States, for example, affirmative action programs have targeted women and the disabled, along with African Americans, Hispanics, and Native Americans.[5]

In thinking normatively about group(-specific) rights,[6] we should appreciate that such rights are at the very heart of our international order. This order assigns two group rights to the citizenry of each state: the right collectively to own and control a certain delimited territory (with its resources, airspace, etc.) and the right collectively to determine how the interactions among the persons living on this territory will be structured (through a shared political system, laws, economic institutions, and so on).[7] These group rights ordinarily involve group-specific rights such as the right of adult U.S. citizens (not convicted of a felony) to participate in the U.S. political process. The eligibility criteria for these group-specific rights are sometimes (though rarely) defined in ethnic terms—or rather: in terms of descent (*lex sanguinis*)— as when ethnic Germans from Russia who speak no German are eligible to become citizens of Germany while ethnic Turks who have lived there all their lives are not.

Though the question of whether and how these two group rights, and the associated group-specific rights, can be justified is of the utmost importance, I here discuss legal group(-specific) rights within one state. To simplify, I also stipulate away the existence of noncitizens on the state's territory. So we begin with the ideal case of a state that exists on a determinate territory and within which all persons are full citizens. And we ask what legal group(-specific) rights are morally required, optional, or impermissible in various sorts of circumstances. In thus asking what rights of these kinds may or should be granted, we leave aside the further important question how and by whom the various decisions about granting and rescinding such rights are to be made. For now, we worry only about the correctness of such decisions.

## II. Some Clarifications Concerning Ethnicity

To constitute an ethnic group, a set of persons must satisfy three conditions: commonality of descent, commonality of continuous culture, and closure. The members of the set must understand themselves as descendants of members of an historical society (in a broad sense, including tribes, principalities and the like, as well as systems of interacting tribes or principalities).[8] They must share a common culture, or partial culture, which they take to be connected, through a continuous history, with the culture of their ancestors (however different from the latter it may have become in the process). And the group must contain all, or nearly all, of the persons who, within the relevant state, are taken to share the descent and culture definitive of the group.[9]

The first condition is necessary to distinguish ethnic groups from mainly religious and from mainly linguistic groups, such as the Mormons or Hispanics. The second is necessary to distinguish ethnic from mainly racial groups, such as African Americans or U.S. residents of Hungarian descent. And the third is necessary to distinguish ethnic groups from subgroups, such as the Organization of Chinese American Women (which excludes men and children, and contains only a fraction even of all Chinese American women).

This definition clearly includes various national majorities (such as the English in Britain and the Han in China) and minorities (such as the Québecois, the Welsh, and the Italo-Swiss). But it is also quite vague in two respects: vague about which groups should count as ethnic groups and vague also about which persons should count as members of such a group. This vagueness should arouse suspicion, because, as I have said, it helps my argument insofar as we have reasons against attaching normative political significance to a fuzzy term. My defense is that this vagueness is not of my own making, that the term has no more precise meaning in either common or academic English, and that any attempt to legislate greater precision would, without compelling need, end up drawing arbitrary boundaries within a dense and multidimensional continuum.

To eliminate vagueness, one would need to specify how broad or narrow the commonalities required by the first two conditions must be and also how far they must extend backwards in time. Depending on how we fine-tune these parameters, we might either view Native Americans, Asian Americans, and perhaps even Hispanics and African Americans, as ethnic groups or regard the first three as containing several ethnic groups (including Navajos and Sioux, Chinese Americans and Korean Americans, Mexican Americans and Puerto Ricans). One may think that progress can be made here by examining how the members of candidate ethnic groups identify themselves, how they think, feel, and behave in respect to their purported ethnicity. I endorse this strategy. But I see little promise in it, because, in problematic cases, these persons are often themselves conflicted (e.g., about whether they are primarily Asian or primarily Japanese American) and, if some are clear, others of the same group are clear the other way.

One would also need to specify how deep and important the commonalities must be felt to be. Do Arab Americans share enough in common to constitute an ethnic group? When did Italo Americans or German Americans lose this status? And how much must one have in common with the core members of an ethnic group to belong to this group? How important is it for qualifying as a Navajo, for example, what fraction of one's ancestry is Navajo, whether one checks off the "Native American" category on affirmative action questionaires, how much one knows about Navajo history, culture, and affairs, how one is regarded by other Navajos (and how good *their* Navajo credentials are)?

Stipulative definitions have their uses, of course, but when they are imported into politics and the law, when tangible advantages and disadvantages are made to depend on them, the arbitrary discriminations they involve are bound to lead to resentment. Moreover, the more legal and political significance we attach to whether some group is or is not an ethnic group, and to whether some person does or does not belong to such a group, the greater is the danger that persons' professed identifications will be, and be suspected of being, guided by self-interest—a further source of resentment and discord.

Let me forestall another sort of lexislative maneuver which involves not a sharpening but a revision of ordinary meanings. If religious groups are defined as all those groups that share deeply and conscientiously held commitments, then it does indeed seem plausible that they should be favored over other groups in regard to, say, eligibility for conscientious objector status. And if ethnic groups are defined as all disadvantaged minorities, then they and only they should perhaps be granted certain compensatory group rights. These "definitions" may be too bizarre to be taken seriously. But the point is nevertheless worth making in preparation for section V, where I discuss the objections that ethnic groups should be favored over others, because only they involve an inherited cultural identity, and that ethnic groups should be *dis*favored, because only they involve unacquirable membership. In responding to these objections, I will take them to invoke not (far-fetched) definitions but empirical generalizations subject to rebuttal. I will assume throughout that my definition, rough and vague as it is, limits how the expression *ethnic group* may be used.

## III. IDEAL THEORY: CONVENTIONAL GROUP (-SPECIFIC) RIGHTS

It is occasionally held to be impossible, or very difficult, to "make room" for group rights within the context of our standard Western or liberal values, centering around the ideal of a democratic society of free and equal citizens. But this is false, as each of the following two considerations will show.

First, our Western societies are very strongly committed to freedom of association and freedom of contract. This commitment requires and justifies legal group rights, such as the rights of the set of owners of a corporation, the rights of the set of members of a political party or club, and so forth. Marriage, too, involves various group rights (the two spouses have an active right to make various decisions together about their assets and the upbringing of their children) and group-specific rights (each of the two spouses, but no one else, is entitled to spend from the family finances, to incur liabilities for both, and officially to represent the interests of their children).

Second, every democratic society assigns to the group of its active citizens (excluding children and also, perhaps, felons and the insane) group-specific rights to political participation. These citizens (but not all others) may run for various political offices and may also participate in the exercise of their group right to determine the national government through nationwide elections. Moreover, every democratic society contains political subunits (provinces or states, counties, municipalities, voting districts, etc.) in which significant local decisions are made by a bounded local electorate and its representatives. Such decentralized political decision making involves additional group rights (e.g., of the people of Oregon) and group-specific rights (e.g., of those eligible to vote in Oregon). These additional group(-specific) rights also have a clearcut democratic rationale: The point of democratic procedures is to enable persons to participate in shaping the social context that shapes their lives. This value is far better promoted when we all have rather more influence upon the social context in our own locale than if we all had rather little influence equally spread throughout the country (so that every mayor, say, would be chosen by the entire citizenry). This thought supports decentralization in the making of political decisions that can vary locally (about local officials, schools, public transportation, city services, zoning, parking, and so on).

When we ask, as the title of this volume suggests, how the legal device of group rights may or should accommodate the concerns of ethnic groups within an ethnically heterogeneous society, the question therefore cannot be whether we should depart from our ordinary practice of recognizing only equal rights of individuals by granting group(-specific) rights to ethnic groups and their members. There is no such ordinary practice. Group rights and group-specific rights are staples of standard Western liberal thought.

The debate about group rights and ethnicity must then be about whether ethnic groups and their members should be favored in the shaping and/or distribution of group(-specific) rights. I will answer this question in two parts, arguing, in the remainder of this section, that the standard justifications for conventional group(-specific) rights do not support favoring ethnic groups over groups of other types, and then, in the next section, that other ways of justifying group(-specific) rights, which appeal to special circumstances, do not support favoring ethnic groups either.

Should ethnic groups and their members enjoy a more extensive freedom of association (so that associations they form would have more extensive group rights, say, than other associations) or should their interests receive special consideration in the shaping of electoral districts and political subunits? The next two subsections will explore the contention that ethnic groups and their members should be so favored over groups of other types in regard to group rights connected with freedom of association (III.1) and/or full political participation (III.2). The contention is that whether these conventional group rights ought to be granted or not will sometimes depend on whether the group demanding them is (part of) an ethnic group or (part of) some other type of group; this factor has a certain weight and can therefore be decisive even when all other things are equal. This contention must be sharply distinguished from a different one, according to which ethnicity has a certain derivative prominence—the view, namely, that, within some specific spatiotemporal region, claims for such conventional group rights by ethnic groups are more often justified, by standards that do not themselves involve reference to ethnicity, than claims for them by nonethnic groups. I have no quarrel with this latter view, but I do want to examine critically the first. I do this by confronting it with the null-hypothesis stated in the introduction. To evaluate this dispute, we must provide some account of how, according to (N0), claims to conventional group rights are to be assessed. If a group's being an ethnic one cannot contribute to the justification of such rights, what can? Following my earlier remarks about freedom of association and the right to full political participation, let me add some further content to my null-hypothesis as follows:

(N1) Legal group(-specific) rights may be justified on account of the free associative choices of individuals and they may also be justified insofar as they maximize and equalize citizens' ability to shape the social context in which they live (regardless of whether the group in question is or is not an ethnic group).

This principle is not meant to indicate the only ways in which group(-specific) rights may be justified (see section IV). But it is meant to apply equally to claims put forward by ethnic and nonethnic groups. It will support some such claims by ethnic groups, but it may also, and in the same way, support some claims by groups of other types. Subsections III.1 and III.2 will discuss, respectively, the two parts of (N1).

### III.1 Freedom of Association

Under the first part of (N1), members of ethnic groups would be free to organize ethnic associations, such as firms, churches, hospitals, political parties or lobbying groups, and private educational institutions. Since such associations have legal rights, their formation as ethnic associations would create group rights and also (since some of the rights of such associations are active rights) group-specific rights limited to a particular ethnic group:

Only members of the ethnic group would be eligible for these group-specific rights—though only those participating in the ethnic association would actually have them.

Four interdependent questions arise about the scope of this freedom to form ethnic associations: What sorts of associations may be formed in a way that ties them exclusively to a particular ethnic group? What constraints may, and should, society place on their internal structure and content (i.e., the curriculum, in the case of schools and universities, or the treatment methods, in the case of hospitals)?[10] How exclusive should ethnic associations be allowed to be—how free should they be not to employ, offer their services to, and/or do business with, citizens outside their own ethnic group? And what special benefits and burdens may or should society assign to ethnic associations—may or should ethnic private schools, for instance, be tax exempt or be entitled to the same public support (per pupil, say) as public schools receive? In order to answer these questions, one may have to ask, on the next higher level, how deep a role their ethnic affiliation plays in the lives of those who would participate in the relevant associations and how important the group(-specific) rights they claim are for their prospects of leading lives that they can appreciate as successful and worthwhile. One may further have to ask whether the ethnic group in question is strong (numerous, wealthy, well organized) or weak, in absolute terms and also relative to other groups with whom it competes or whose members would be especially affected by being excluded: What costs would the rights they claim, and the causes they pursue, impose on other persons, other groups, and society at large? And there are surely further relevant factors as well.

I have no space to discuss the balancing of these considerations in any detail. All I want to maintain is that there is no reason why this balancing should proceed differently when the (prospective) association for which group rights and group-specific rights are claimed is defined in ethnic terms. Why should two otherwise similar associations be treated differently merely because one defines itself in ethnic and the other in religious terms? A society should find a principled way, supervised by the courts, to decide about particular claimed associative freedoms on the basis of criteria that do not include, or take account of, the type of associative identity at issue.[11] Departing from this impartial approach would inevitably suggest that some identifications are more valuable, more worthy of respect and protection, than others. And this is incompatible with recognizing all citizens—irrespective of the character of their deepest identifications—as equals.

### III.2 Full Political Participation

Under the second part of (N1), ethnic groups may be entitled to accommodation in the design of the political process and in the shaping of political subunits. Let's begin with the former. In many existing democratic societies it has long been impossible for ethnic minorities to gain anything like proportional representation in the legislature. This impossibility is now widely understood to reflect an injustice—an understanding confirmed by the demand that societies should maximize and equalize citizens' ability to shape the social context in which they live. On a plausible interpretation of this demand, it implies that an ethnic group that constitutes $n$ percent of a society's adult population should be able to determine the composition of $n$ percent of the legislature.[12] Of course, it is up to the members of the group whether they, or some of them, choose to form a coalition for the purpose of filling a proportionate number of parliamentary seats. But the political process should be so designed that, if (some or all) members of an ethnic group choose to form such a coalition, they should be able to send a proportionate number of representatives to the legislature (who, according to their choice, may or may not be members of their ethnic group).[13]

While I accept this institutional imperative, my thesis here is a different one: Whatever we demand from a just and fair political process for ethnic minorities, we should also demand for any other minorities: If enough citizens share a certain identification and are willing to form a coalition for the sake of securing representation for themselves in the legislature, then they should be able to gain such representation, irrespective of the type of their identification (and of whether they are geographically concentrated or dispersed). In this case, it may even be plausible to go well beyond our standard group types (ethnic, religious, linguistic, lifestyle) to include also dentists, dog-lovers, stamp collectors, war widows, socialists, and Porsche drivers.[14] Of course, many of these imagined coalitions will never actually emerge. A just political process may well produce representatives of ethnic and religious groups, though hardly of Porsche drivers and stamp collectors. But this outcome should occur because of the distribution of deep identifications among the citizenry and not because the structure of the political process advantages citizens with some types of deep identifications over citizens with other types of such identifications.

In the case of political subunits, matters are more difficult, because the reasons for territoriality as well as geographical closure and compactness—which themselves derive from the goal of maximizing citizens' ability to shape the social context in which they live—are here much stronger. A geographically highly dispersed dentist county is not workable, to put it mildly. I have said above that political decentralization (through the creation of political subunits) increases political participation by enhancing the power of citizens to shape the conditions that shape their lives. There are always many ways of decentralizing political decision making: We can institute more or fewer levels of subunits, for example, we can define subunits territorially or nonterritorially, we can set them up to be nested or overlapping, and we can draw the boundaries of subunits in diverse ways. In wondering how to decentralize, we can invoke the ideal of full political participation. This gives us two values for comparing alternative decentralization schemes: Political decision making should be decentralized so as to *maximize* and *equalize* citizens' ability to shape the social context in which they live. Since these are two competing goals, we may in practice have to engage in trade-offs between the two; but we need not worry about this complication yet.

Subject to the compactness constraint, citizens can and should be free to shape political subunits in whatever ways they like. To make this idea more precise, let me propose, as a first approximation, the following two procedural principles for territorial subunits:

1. The inhabitants of any contiguous territory may decide— through some majoritarian or supermajoritarian procedure—to join an existing political unit whose territory is adjacent to theirs and whose population is willing—as assessed through some ma-

joritarian or supermajoritarian procedure—to accept them as members. This liberty is conditional upon the political unit or units that are truncated through such a move either remaining viable (with a contiguous territory of reasonable shape and sufficient population) or being willingly incorporated, pursuant to (1), into another political unit or other political units. The liberty is also conditional upon the proposed enlarged unit being of reasonable shape: Its area should not have extremely long borders, for example, or borders that divide towns, integrated networks of economic activity, or the like.[15]

2. The inhabitants of any contiguous territory of reasonable shape, if sufficiently numerous, may decide—through some majoritarian or supermajoritarian procedure—to form themselves into a political unit of a level commensurate with their number. This liberty is subject to three constraints: There may be subgroups whose members, pursuant to their liberty under (1), are free to reject membership in the unit to be formed in favor of membership in another political unit. There may be subgroups whose members, pursuant to their liberty under (2), are free to reject membership in the unit to be formed in favor of forming their own political unit on the same level. And the political unit or units truncated through the requested move must either remain viable (with a contiguous territory of reasonable shape and sufficient population) or be willingly incorporated, pursuant to (1), into another political unit or other political units.[16] According to these or similar procedural principles, ethnic as well as nonethnic groups could map out an appropriate territory in which they form a majority and make it into a political subunit.

It isn't crucial for present purposes whether these principles are part of the best specification of the ideal of full political participation. What matters, rather, is that there is no principled reason to prefer citizens whose deeper identifications or affiliations happen to be ethnic by favoring ethnic groups in the shaping of political subunits. And there is no pragmatic reason either: As my proposal shows, we can be quite permissive in accommodating ethnic groups without thereby losing the ability to be equally accommodating to nonethnic groups as well.[17]

This leaves the question what political subunits should be free to do within their territory. I will not discuss this issue, because my challenge thesis, here again, is that this freedom must be the same for political subunits that define themselves in ethnic terms as it is for all others. If we allow political subunits whose citizens define themselves in ethnic terms to control land sales to outsiders, then we should grant the same liberty to other such subunits whose citizens define themselves in terms of some religion or lifestyle.[18]

In the two justifications discussed in subsections III.1 and III.2, group-specific rights were justified *via* group rights. I have argued that citizens ought to have the freedom to form groups with certain sorts of group rights, namely, in particular: to form various associations with rights to control participation, to form voting coalitions that can win proportional representation in the legislature, to form territorially based political subunits that democratically govern their own internal affairs, and to form territorially based groups that may reshape internal political boundaries. Some of the group rights of these four sorts are active rights, whose exercise must be determined by some or all of the group members who then have corresponding group-specific rights to participate: in the decisions of their associations and voting coalitions, in elections and referenda within their political subunit(s), and in determining the shape of political subunits in their part of the country. I have argued that, though the groups referenced by group (-specific) rights of these sorts may be ethnic groups, they may also be groups of various other types. Citizens should be free (within certain limits) to form and maintain whatever groups they choose; and citizens who want to form or maintain ethnically defined groups should be no more, and no less, free in this regard than citizens who want to form or maintain groups defined in other ways.

## IV. REAL-WORLD THEORY: CONTESTED GROUP (-SPECIFIC) RIGHTS

Having discussed two justifications for group(-specific) rights which are widely accepted, at least in general, let us now consider two further justifications of such rights which are contested, i.e., rejected wholesale by significant segments of Western societies. In these cases, group(-specific) rights are claimed as due compensa-

tion for disadvantages suffered or as required to honor legitimate
expectations on the part of their claimants. I endorse these justifications here, at least in principle, partly because I believe them
to be valid in some cases. More relevant, however, is another
reason. Only if these justifications are valid sometimes, can they
undermine the principle I defend in this essay. Only then can
what I deny be true, namely: whether a group is or is not an
ethnic one affects how plausibly it can invoke these justifications
in support of a claim to group(-specific) rights. Let me then offer
this further extension of my null-hypothesis:

(N2) Legal group(-specific) rights can be justified as compensation for unfair disadvantages that groups and their members suffer in comparison to others, and they can also be justified by
appeal to legitimate expectations arising perhaps from promises
made to a group and honored since (regardless of whether the
group in question is or is not an ethnic group).

Both of these justifications have been used in arguments about
the conventional group(-specific) rights of the preceding section
(where I have mentioned the first as a potentially relevant factor).
But they have also been used to support claims to other group-
specific rights, e.g., to various subsidies, preferences, exemptions
and immunities. I maintain that, insofar as such justifications are
valid at all, they do not favor ethnic over nonethnic groups.

Some ethnic groups claim group(-specific) rights as compensation for disadvantages they suffer in comparison with members of
the dominant culture.[19] Justifications for such claims come in two
main variations. Variation one goes like this: Society at large
cannot be organized so as to be neutral between all ethnicities.
Its social institutions, its official language(s), its public holidays,
its official symbols (flag, money, etc.), its public buildings and
museums, the curriculum of its public schools—all these things
will be more closely associated with the history, culture, and tradition of a dominant ethnic group than with those of smaller and
weaker ones. Such a dominant ethnic group therefore receives
considerable official support, which provides much of what it
needs to ensure the continued flourishing of its community and
culture. A small and weak ethnic group is not only cut off from
such official support. It is also disadvantaged by its lesser size,
which increases even further what its individual members must

contribute to sustain their community and culture. Because it is so much harder and more expensive for members of ethnic minorities to maintain their shared culture and to lead a life they deem worthwhile, fairness demands that they be granted compensating legal group(-specific) rights.[20]

My response to such claims is, once again, that they are not at all specific to groups defined in terms of ethnicity. One can use the same sort of argument to claim group(-specific) rights for groups defined in religious or ethical or linguistic terms and even for groups defined by age, gender, or sexual orientation, by handicap or obesity, by hobby, consumer preferences, or way of life. Let me give some examples: The members of a religion can point out that English is closer to Anglicanism than to their own religion (which would favor Hebrew, perhaps, or Sanskrit) and can seek compensation for being disadvantaged through the choice of English as a public language and through the choice of public holidays and the numbering of calendar years as well. Atheists can object to the "In God We Trust" on dollar bills and to the deductibility of donations to religious associations. Rock-and-roll fans can object to the fact that opera is subsidized with tax monies, while their favorite music is not. Native speakers of Spanish can demand compensation for being disadvantaged by the fact that administrative and legal regulations are written, and legal procedures conducted, in English. Fat persons can ask to be compensated for the use of tax monies for public seats that are for them too small. Homosexual couples can demand compensation for being denied the advantages of marriage. Persons who are handicapped or claustrophobic can argue that they should be compensated for tax monies spent on subway systems which they cannot use. Persons who cherish certain unpopular sports or hobbies can claim that they should be compensated for the fact that their pursuit would be cheaper (through economies of scale) if it were more popular. Others, who cherish certain popular sports or hobbies, can claim that they, too, should be compensated when great demand drives up the price of their pursuit. Childless persons can demand exemption from property taxes targeted for day care centers and public schools. The old and the sick can demand compensation for publicly supported sports events (like a marathon). The list of possible claims is much longer than I can make it here, so let me conclude by pointing out that the examples I have given are not purely academic: Many of the claims here listed have actually been made by members of the groups in question, and some have even been litigated in the United States.

Seeing that, in this domain as well, the claims that can be made for ethnic groups are continuous with claims that can be made for other groups, it seems, once again, sensible to work out a principled response to all such claims, and a response that does not make reference to the type of group in question. Such a response might sort claims into three (not necessarily mutually exclusive) categories:

1. Some claims can be deflected by reorganizing society in a way that is more neutral. Public holidays can be replaced, or citizens be allowed to pick any seven from a list of twenty, say. Divisive references or allusions can be removed from money and public buildings. Some narrow seats can be replaced by wider ones or benches. Subways and public buildings can be made wheelchair accessible. Museums can be funded which balance the stories of dominant groups (e.g., "how the West was won") with those of others (e.g., about North America before Columbus, about the destruction of Indian societies, or about the lived reality of slavery). Public funding can be withdrawn entirely from various domains (such as the arts).

2. Some claims can be dismissed. Differential treatment of age groups does not seem unfair so long as the special benefits and burdens can be expected roughly to balance out over a lifetime. And where differences are unfair even over a whole life, compensation need not be called for: A society cannot make official every language, or celebrate every public holiday, any of its citizens prefer. And where some preference(s) must and not all can be satisfied, it is better to satisfy those shared by more citizens rather than those shared by fewer. This means that some preferences will remain unfulfilled while others are honored. But it does not follow that those whose preferences remain unfulfilled should be entitled to compensation. Society can simply let stand the good/bad luck of those who find their linguistic or holiday preferences in the majority/minority—just as, clearly, it should let stand the economic consequences of the preference distribution: Society

need not compensate me for the higher price I must pay for beachfront property as a consequence of my compatriots' love of beaches, or for the higher price I must pay for a guided tour of Goodland as a consequence of my being the only would-be customer.[21]

3. Some claims, finally, should be accepted. A translator can be supplied at public expense to help citizens in their necessary dealings with courts and the bureaucracy. Public funding can be made available to private schools that offer alternative curricula designed for the members of various minorites. Persons who want no part in our car culture can be given a special tax break.

Once we determine that the members of some group suffer disadvantages for which they ought to be compensated through legal group(-specific) rights, we still have to determine which such rights would be appropriate and how extensive they should be. For these questions, as well, we ought to seek general answers. We should never be reduced to saying, in response to the members of a disadvantaged nonethnic group seeking parity with a disadvantaged ethnic group, that they will not be granted equivalent group(-specific) rights just because theirs is not an ethnic group.

Variation two (on which, to save time, I will not elaborate) seeks to justify group(-specific) rights for members of ethnic groups as compensation for the effects of past crimes and/or for present disrespect and discrimination.[22]

In regard to both variations, it is not important to my null-hypothesis by what criteria exactly claims to group(-specific) rights as compensation should be assessed. What is important is that these criteria should not make reference to whether the group at issue is an ethnic or a nonethnic group. It is true—*re* variation one—that some ethnic groups (various Indian tribes in the United States and Canada; the Inuit in Canada; Sami in Norway, Finland, and Russia) have a culture of their own, one that differs markedly from the society's mainstream culture which, directly and indirectly, receives a great deal of offical funding, recognition, and support. Such ethnic groups have a very good claim to compensatory group(-specific) rights. But the same could be said about some religious and linguistic groups as well, such as the Amish (Quakers, Mormons) or Hispanics in the U.S. It is also true—*re* variation two—that some ethnic groups (the Indian tribes of North America, Gypsies in Eastern Europe, Arabs in France, Koreans in Japan) are suffering the effects of historical crimes and/or present discrimination. Such ethnic groups, too, have a very good claim to compensatory group(-specific) rights. But, once again, the same could be said about various nonethnic groups as well, such as African Americans, Muslims in India, the Bahai in Iran, Christians in China, and women almost everywhere. All these groups have plausible claims to group(-specific) rights, which should be decided upon by criteria that contain no essential reference to ethnicity—criteria by which some ethnic and some nonethnic groups will qualify.

Sometimes ethnic groups claim group(-specific) rights not on the basis of present disadvantages (including present effects of past crimes) but on the basis of past historical facts such as treaties in which such rights were specifically promised. These cases pose no challenge to my main thesis: If and insofar as such treaties with ethnic groups ought to be honored, similar contracts with nonethnic groups ought to be honored as well.[23] Whether such treaties or contracts ought to be honored depends not on what type of group they were made with but mainly on the moral and economic costs compliance would impose on the society's citizens and on whether they have been honored in the more recent past thereby giving rise to legitimate expectations on the part of the present members of the relevant group.[24]

These considerations can be extended to "grandfathering" more generally. We may find that there exist in our society certain group(-specific) rights that we should not or need not grant to all other relevantly similar groups and yet also should not simply rescind because of the legitimate expectations that would thereby be disappointed. Many very different groups may have plausible claims to such grandfathering. We are all familiar with claims by men, native tribes, continuing immigrant communities, religious orders and denominations, entrenched "elites," trade unions, chartered universities and foundations, aristocratic families, as well as linguistic, lifestyle, and professional groups to the effect that the rights and privileges they and/or their members have enjoyed up to now must be maintained.[25] In assessing such claims, we will, once again, have to weigh their moral and economic cost against the morally significant value of honoring legitimate expectations. I would think that, in cases where extraordinary group(-specific) rights are associated with morally significant costs,[26] they should be rescinded or appropriately modified. This can be done in a gradual, phased manner, determined and publicized well in advance so as to minimize the disappointment of legitimate expectations. Consider, for example, some Indian tribe that has thus far enjoyed an extraordinary degree of regional autonomy that allowed it to perpetuate anachronistic punishments and an inferior status for women. I see strong reasons against outlawing its practices from one day to the next, as this might cause a major shock to a (perhaps already fragile) cultural group with disappointment and disorientation of its members. But these reasons become much weaker when we imagine the offending practices to be phased out gradually over the span of years or decades: It is much harder to adjust to an immediate and dramatic change in gender relations, say, than to a slow change that will mainly affect one's children. In any case, whatever may be the right way to handle extraordinary group(-specific) rights backed by legitimate expectations, there seems to be no reason for being more accommodating to ethnic groups in this regard than to nonethnic ones.

Or is there? Kymlicka argues at length for the moral significance of historical consent. He holds that national minorities have a better claim to grandfathering than other groups because the latter have consented to the institutions of their society, typically through immigration.[27] In response, we should first note that this distinction, once again, cuts across the ethnic-nonethnic divide: There may be linguistic and religious groups whose continuous existence on the present state's territory predates the formation of this state (see note 9, above), and there certainly are, as Kymlicka himself points out, ethnic as well as nonethnic immigrant groups. Moreover, it is questionable whether so general a claim is sustainable: National minorities may have consented in ways other than immigration. Immigrant groups and indeed other nonnational groups may not have been in a position to give their free and informed consent or may have consented to an earlier set of institutions (e.g., with the understanding that the inferior status of women, or blacks, would continue forever). Finally, it is not clear why the plausibility of present claims to group(-specific) rights should be affected by what much earlier group members may or may not have consented to. Suppose we find out that some Indian tribe now enjoying extraordinary group(-specific) rights had once, two hundred years ago, waived any claims to special treatment, or that some immigrant group came here at that time on the explicit understanding that they would be allowed to practice infanticide (though they have not wanted to do so until now). Would these newly discovered facts really make it (more) permissible to strip the Indians of their special rights, or give us reason to allow infanticide? As I see it, historical consent does not have much independent moral weight,[28] but matters, if at all, only insofar as it inaugurates a continuous history of legitimate expectations.

## V. Two Objections

In response to an earlier version of this essay, Will Kymlicka has objected that the plausibility of groups' claims to special treatment depends importantly on whether or not the group is defined in terms of an inherited identity. Insofar as memberships in groups are chosen, rather than inherited, society may plausibly hold citizens responsible for choosing their memberships so that they are consonant with its institutions and culture. Some inherited memberships (e.g., gender, disability) typically do not involve deep identifications with the group. But the remaining groups, which define themselves in terms of a shared inherited cultural identity, deserve the utmost accommodation in the assignment of group(-specific) rights, because their members share a deep identification that they were not free not to choose. The groups defined through this conceptual intersection, however, are precisely ethnic groups. Therefore, contrary to the thrust of my argument, we ought to favor ethnic groups over nonethnic groups in the granting of group(-specific) rights. So there are, after all, claims to such rights which only ethnic groups can plausibly make.[29]

In response, let me first press upon the chosen-versus-inherited distinction. One has not chosen, of course, whether or not to have Hopi blood in one's veins. But blood alone is not an identity, let alone a cultural identity. Even a pure-blooded Hopi is free to go to work for IBM or New York University. She may not find such a choice appealing or even conceivable. But, if so, it is not her blood, but her upbringing that stands in the way: She was raised as a Hopi and therefore finds modern city life a nightmare of barrenness and isolation. She has not chosen this upringing, and Kymlicka is therefore right to insist that there is such a thing as a shared inherited cultural identity.

But two qualifications must nevertheless be made. First, the distinction between chosen and inherited identities is vague: a matter of degree. It is probably impossible to raise minimally intelligent human beings so that it is not possible for them to shed their cultural identification. There is always some element of choice and responsibility. To accommodate this fact, we should then have to say that the plausibility of claims to group(-specific) rights depends in part on the degree to which the identity in terms of which the relevant group is defined is an inherited rather than a chosen one. Yet this refinement would introduce not only problems of measurement but also problems of averaging: Group members differ in the degree to which their identifications with the group are inherited rather than chosen, but they and their group must nevertheless be assigned a single legal status in the public realm. With coveted rights at stake, there will be disagreement about both measurement and aggregation, which would probably make the special accommodation Kymlicka proposes for groups with an inherited cultural identity socially divisive and impractical.[30] The second qualification is that the distinction between chosen and inherited cultural identities does not track that between ethnic and nonethnic groups: Many members of ethnic groups do not identify with their ethnicity; and it seems quite doubtful that all those who do identify in this way do so without choice.[31] We could interpret "shared inherited cultural identity" broadly, perhaps, so that it nevertheless covers all ethnic groups. But it will then also include many religious, linguistic, and lifestyle groups in which children also come to have unchosen values, knowledge, and concerns. To be sure, there is no genetic component in being a Mormon, a native speaker of Spanish, or a nudist, while there is a genetic component in being a Hopi. But if, as I have argued, a genetic component is neither necessary nor sufficient for inherited cultural identity, then this difference is irrelevant to the distinction Kymlicka deems morally significant.

We have seen that the predicate "being a group with a shared inherited cultural identity" is quite vague and also cuts across the ethnic-nonethnic divide; and no more, it seems, needs to be said in response to the objection. But the moral significance of the distinction also seems dubious. Why should the accommodation we owe to citizens distinguished by some shared cultural identity vary with whether this identity is chosen or inherited? If a group of like-minded parents arrives at certain new ideas about schooling and wants to found an appropriate new school for their children, why should their proposal be held up to a higher standard than that of Catholic or Navajo parents who want their children to be schooled in accordance with their own inherited cultural identity? Or do persons discriminated against on the basis of inherited memberships really have a better claim to compensation than others discriminated against on the basis of chosen memberships? (We want to preclude that citizens are penalized for having been raised as, and being, Navajos or Catholics, to be sure. But do we not also want to preclude, and just as strongly, that citizens are penalized for being communists, or members of a subculture with Cherokee hairstyles and nose rings?) Why should cultural contents that citizens choose on their own be any less deserving of respect and accommodation than ones they have internalized before they reached the age of reason?

In sum, I believe there are strong reasons against following Kymlicka's proposal to make politically significant a distinction between inherited and chosen cultural identities. And, even if we did give it such significance, it would not track the (similarly vague) distinction between ethnic and nonethnic groups: There are not only ethnic, but also religious, linguistic, and lifestyle groups at the "inherited" end of the chosen-inherited spectrum.

The other objection I will briefly discuss comes from the other side of my null-hypothesis. It is inspired by the polar opposite of the pro-ethnic positions I have been challenging thus far, by the contention namely that ethnic groups should be *dis*favored in the distribution of group rights.[32] It opposes group rights for ethnic

groups in particular, because such rights are especially exclusionary: In the case of other groups, all citizens have open to them
some reasonably viable paths for becoming members of the relevant group and thereby joining those who benefit from and control these rights. One can convert to Catholicism, learn Spanish,
join the New Agers, or move to Oregon. But, try as one may, one
cannot become a member of an ethnic group. While the first
objection relies on the claim that members of ethnic groups are
especially unfree to choose to be nonmembers, the second protests that nonmembers of ethnic groups are especially unfree to
become members.

My response to this objection involves moves matching those
made in response to its predecessor. To begin with, the distinction
between acquirable and unacquirable memberships is not clear-
cut. Ethnic groups differ in the extent to which they accept new
members and are willing to let them become beneficiaries of any
of their group(-specific) rights—for example, after marriage to
one of their own. And there are variations in the extent to which
new members are accepted even by the same ethnic group
(whether an outside spouse will be accepted into an Indian tribe
will often importantly depend on this person's gender or race).
Like the chosen-inherited pair, the notion of acquirability does
not, then, reference a simple binary distinction but a multidimensional continuum, so that normative political lines drawn on the
basis of it are bound to be arbitrary to some extent, and therefore
controversial and divisive.

Moreover, the distinction between acquirable and unacquirable memberships does not track that between ethnic and
nonethnic groups. In the case of many ethnic groups, full membership is, I admit, typically difficult to attain for outsiders. But,
if this suffices for the predicate "unacquirable," then this same
predicate must be extended to many groups of other types as
well: Some religious denominations are very reluctant to welcome
converts and never accept them as full participants or potential
leaders. Similar phenomena occur in some linguistic and lifestyle
groups. And membership in racial and gender groups is, for
biological reasons, virtually impossible to acquire at all, at least at
the present stage of medical technology. The distinction between

acquirable and unacquirable memberships is thus not merely vague, a matter of degree, but also cuts across the ethnic-no-nethnic divide.

Once again, these considerations suffice to defeat the objection. But let us briefly look at the analogue to the last point as well, which challenges the moral significance of the distinction. Here I find the second objection to be in better shape than the first: In some cases, at least, a group's claim to legal group (-specific) rights does seem to be weakened by the fact that membership in this group is hard to acquire. For example, we generally allow group(-specific) rights associated with collective ownership of firms or residential properties only when every citizen (really: every citizen with money) can buy into them and we therefore require that every present stakeholder be free to sell to anyone (without being encumbered, e.g., by restrictive covenants). The unacquirability of group(-specific) rights granted as compensation or to honor legitimate expectations, by contrast, often seems far more acceptable. Here it matters less that other citizens cannot acquire these rights, because the excluded are already as well off without these rights as the rights' beneficiaries are with them: They do not have to suffer the disadvantages that are meant to be compensated or, respectively, the disappointment of expectations that would result if the rights were rescinded.[33]

The distinction invoked by the second objection is then morally more significant than that invoked by the first. But the objections nevertheless both fail, and for the same basic reason: The distinctions they invoke do not track that between ethnic and nonethnic groups.

## VI. Conclusion

My main thesis in this paper has been that our political decisions about what group(-specific) rights may or should be granted to particular groups ought to be made in terms of a principled account that does not favor any particular type(s) of groups as such and, in particular, not ethnic groups. I have not developed such an account. But I have sketched some of the main values it might plausibly incorporate—freedom of association, full political participation, equalizing protection of the disadvantaged, and fair adjustment to legal change—arguing that each of these values could be as plausibly invoked by nonethnic groups as by ethnic ones. In this way, I have made a preliminary case for a more sweeping null-hypothesis: It is irrelevant to the moral assessment of a claim to legal group rights whether the group for which the rights are claimed is or is not (part of) an ethnic group. According to this hypothesis, there ought to be no group rights for which, as a matter of principle, only ethnic groups can qualify (though there may, of course, be such rights for which, as a matter of contingent circumstance, only ethnic groups happen to qualify in some particular region and period). I am confident that it is a matter of some importance, in the current debates about pluralism and multiculturalism and in the present climate of proliferating claims to disadvantaged-minority status, to determine whether my null-hypothesis fails and, if so, how.

## NOTES

Many thanks to my commentators James Anaya and Donald Horowitz as well as to Marko Ahtisaari, Christian Barry, Jim Nickel, Brian Orend, Ian Shapiro, and especially Will Kymlicka for their insightful and constructive criticisms of earlier versions of this essay.

1. Groups of these four types will be loosely referred to as cultural groups. In some societies, other types of cultural groups may exist as well, groups whose members are identified with a particular vocation, world view, ethics, vision of the future, past experience (e.g. veterans), or biological characteristic (e.g., race, gender). I will focus here on the more familiar cases without worrying about exactly how far my main thesis can be extended beyond them.

2. Why cannot groups identified with a particular ethics or world view have as strong and conscientious objections to military service, and as solid reasons to hold meetings to deepen and clarify their commitments, as any religious denomination? And why cannot linguistic, religious, and racial groups have as good reasons as ethnic groups can have to seek limited autonomy in an area in which they constitute a majority?

3. Limits on what can reasonably be granted arise from the morally significant costs involved: Legal group rights restrict the freedom of persons and groups within and/or outside the possessor group and of governments at all levels. Because they impose such restrictions (opportu-

nity costs) and because they have to be fulfilled (publicized, adjudicated, policed, enforced), legal group rights can absorb considerable wealth which could be used for other morally significant purposes.

4. That such an account does not favor any particular type of groups as such is obviously only a necessary condition for its acceptability. The account may still give weight to implausible factors—for example as a consequence of being rigged in favor of some (type of) groups.

5. Even the last three groups are by no means clearcut ethnic groups, as we shall see in section II.

6. I use *group(-specific) rights* to cover both group rights proper and group-specific rights.

7. These two rights correspond very roughly to what are often called external and internal sovereignty.

8. The condition that membership must be based on descent is to be understood loosely. It leaves open what lineage qualifications count as sufficient. Ethnic groups, and their members, differ on how they regard persons of mixed descent and on whether and how they differentiate between male and female, maternal and paternal ancestors. Virtually no ethnic group requires purity of descent. Moreover, most ethnic groups accept as members persons who have no lineage qualifications at all, for example when these are adopted by or married to a member. For a group to be an ethnic group, it suffices, then, that descent be far and away the most common qualification for membership.

9. I am using *ethnic group* in a broader sense than Kymlicka, as including both (what he calls) national minorities, distinct and potentially self-governing societies whose continuous existence on the present state's territory predates the formation of this state, and ethnic groups, which formed on the present state's territory as a result of immigration. See Will Kymlicka, *Multicultural Citizenship: A Liberal Theory of Minority Rights* (Oxford: Oxford University Press, 1995), ch. 2, § 1.

10. For example, may or should society leave schools free to teach in any language, so long as students are trained to be reasonably fluent in (one of) its official language(s)?

11. Jim Nickel has objected that "ethnocide" is worse than "religiocide" because the former but not the latter involves the physical death of members and destroys the group beyond the possiblity of restoration. I don't think this point damages my position. First, an ethnicity can be destroyed by being scattered or diluted, as well as through the murder of its members (Stalin practiced all these methods); and a religion can be destroyed through murder as well as though suppression. Second, while a religion cannot, perhaps, be destroyed beyond the possiblity of restoration, it surely can be destroyed for good; and this would seem to me to

be no better a fate. Third, I need not deny that, in general, ethnocide is worse than religiocide: By advocating that, other things equal, cultural groups of different types should have equivalent rights furthering their continuation, I am not committed to the claim that violating or depriving them of these rights is equally damaging in all cases. Compare: One can advocate the same liberty of conscience for Jews, Christians, and atheists without believing that being deprived of this freedom would be equally damaging to each group.

12. It may be thought that this specification still fails to do justice to permanent minorities who, even with a proportionate number of seats in parliament, may still lose on all contested issues. Often, political decentralization, fairmindedness of the majority, or legislative bargaining (where the majority is sometimes divided) can solve this problem. But I see no plausible institutional solution for cases in which these remedies fail.

13. This ideal can be approximated through various plausible institutional designs involving, for instance, proportional representation or multidelegate constituencies. It is much harder to approximate the ideal in a system with winner-takes-all territorial electoral districts—as exemplified in the United States and Great Britain—because one must then engage in a highly deliberate, and thus often divisive ("gerrymandering"), shaping and reshaping of electoral districts. Forming a legislature through random sampling is likewise a bad way of implementing the ideal, because most persons do not want to be legislators and would not be good at it anyway (though random sampling might work better than the status quo in many so-called democracies, where legislative corruption is endemic). These matters have been understood and debated for quite a long time—e.g., by Thomas Wright Hill (1821), Thomas Gilpin (1844), and Thomas Hare (1873), all discussed in Charles Beitz, *Political Equality* (Princeton: Princeton University Press, 1989), ch. 6. Unrepresentative systems can nevertheless survive, of course, if those who stand to lose from reform can use the existing system to block reform.

14. Yes, we must keep in mind here the need for a functioning legislature. If parliament is often dysfunctional because it contains too many odd-ball parties and groupings (late Weimar Republic, present-day Poland), then it will not maximize citizens' ability to shape the social context in which they live. This is why, in many societies, the ideal will not be fully attainable, even with the help of fancy(ful) computer systems. But this problem does not require discriminations among types of groups, because there are neutral ways of reducing the number of represented groups. A society could, for instance, require a minimum number of votes (as exemplified by the German 5 percent hurdle) for parliamen-

tary representation, with the threshold set only as high as necessary to ensure its objective.

15. Perhaps we need the further condition that the number of "switchers" must not be too small; but I think the threshold could be quite low. If a tiny border village wants to belong to Maine rather than New Hampshire, why should it not be allowed to switch? Also, the contiguity condition may need some relaxing to allow territories consisting of a small number of internally contiguous areas whose access to one another is not controlled by other political units. The United States of America are not contiguous; and it does not seem absolutely necessary that each of its states and counties should be.

16. This account is continuous with my proposal in "Cosmopolitanism and Sovereignty," *Ethics* 103 (1992): 69–73. It also coheres well, I think, with the account developed in Daniel Philpott, "In Defense of Self-Determination," *Ethics* 105 (1995): 352–85, though Philpott concentrates on the redrawing of international boundaries.

17. One may think that the principles I have sketched are too permissive: that they would lead to economic injustice, as richer areas could (threaten to) sever themselves from poorer ones. To avoid this objection, economic justice should be taken care of on the highest political level which, in our model, is that of the (sovereign) state. Political subunits are to be unburdened from this function (e.g., they may decide how to structure schools, but need not worry about how to finance them—there will be the same funding per pupil everywhere in the country). It may also be thought that the principles I have sketched are too permissive because they would trigger an avalanche of applications. It may well be true that many existing groups are unhappy with their current membership status, that there is a significant backlog, so to speak, that might pose a serious short-term problem. Once this backlog will have been worked down, however, there may not be much redrawing activity as people will then be content with their political memberships, and most borders will be supported by stable majorities.

18. We might not grant such a liberty across the board and nevertheless conclude that special circumstances justify granting it to some particular Indian province, say. But then similar circumstances could justify granting analogous extraordinary group rights to a Mormon province or even to Oregon (whose citizens may have a comparable determination and concern to protect their way of life, e.g., against an overwhelming influx of Californians). Claims to extraordinary group(-specific) rights are discussed in the next section—the present one focuses on the standard justifications for conventional group(-specific) rights.

19. Such disadvantages are often used to justify group-statistical rights

as well, but this is not my topic here. For a general discussion of group rights (in the broad sense) justified as compensation, see Iris Marion Young, *Justice and the Politics of Difference* (Princeton: Princeton University Press, 1990).

20. These points are eloquently made, with respect to aboriginal groups in Canada, in Will Kymlicka, *Liberalism, Community and Culture* (Oxford: Clarendon Press 1989), ch. 9.

21. We will consider the issue of chosen versus unchosen preferences in section V.

22. A brief reply to the claim that discrimination against ethnic groups is especially invidious because members of such groups are easier to spot than members of other groups. This is not true across the board: Koreans are hard to distinguish from Japanese, for example (which is why Koreans in Japan were not allowed to adopt Japanese names). And members of linguistic and religous groups are often easy to spot because of, respectively, their accent and religiously motivated components of their dress. The same is true of gender groups. Once again, the proffered distinction cuts across the ethnic-nonethnic divide. So I need not dispute the moral significance of the distinction: In assessing claims to compensation on account of disrespect and discrimination, we may of course take obviousness of membership into account. If one of two equally despised religious sects prescribes a distinctive dress code while the other does not, then members of the former will tend to suffer greater discrimination and disrespect and may then also, other things equal, have a greater claim to compensation.

23. The Canadian government signed such an agreement guaranteeing various group rights with the Hutterites, an immigrating religious group. See William Janzen, *The Limits of Liberty: The Experiences of Mennonite, Hutterite, and Doukhobour Communities in Canada* (Toronto: Toronto University Press, 1990).

24. I use "legitimate expectations" in the sociological sense popularized by Max Weber for normative expectations that are reasonably based upon the values and practices that have been dominant in the relevant society heretofore. Thus, normative expectations (e.g., that the legal advantages husbands enjoy over their wives shall not be abolished for already existing marriages) can be legitimate and yet unjustified. What follows is based on the assumption that there is always some reason, which may of course be outweighed, against disappointing legitimate expectations. This reason may then support extraordinary accommodations for some groups and their members.

25. Some examples for the last three categories: The Rhaetians (Romansch) in Switzerland have a plausible claim that their language retain

its official status even while claims to parity by larger linguistic groups (e.g., speakers of Serbo-Croatian) are rejected. Family farmers and fishermen have a plausible claim that their way of life receive continued public support even while other groups of self-employed professionals are left to fend for themselves. Smokers and drinkers have a plausible claim to be allowed to continue their habit even while others who would like to consume other, no more harmful drugs (such as cannabis) are not allowed to do so.

26. This generally includes economic costs, which divert resources from other uses.

27. See Kymlicka, *Multicultural Citizenship*, ch. 4, § 4.

28. This conclusion is supported by Jeremy Waldron's reflections in "Superseding Historical Injustice," *Ethics* 103 (1992): 4–28.

29. In Kymlicka, *Liberalism*, 186, this chosen-versus-inherited distinction is prefigured as that between differential choices and unequal circumstances. Kymlicka there adduces Rawls and Dworkin in support of the moral significance of this distinction.

30. In the same vein: Making Kymlicka's distinction politically significant might generate perverse incentives, as those identified with a particular cultural group would have reason to ensure that as many of its members as possible will have an inherited rather than a chosen identification with it. For example, by bringing up their children so that they cannot understand and appreciate religions other than their own, parents can over time extend and strengthen their denomination's claim to group(-specific) rights. Surely, this incentive toward a narrowly controlled upbringing of children is not one that a liberal democratic society should provide. (The force of this argument is weakened when the inheritedness of a cultural identity really does have a significant genetic component. The only possible case I can think of is that of homosexuality. To the extent that homosexuality is genetic, parents could not manipulate the extent to which their childrens' identity as homosexuals is inherited rather than chosen. However, being genetically predisposed toward homosexuality is at best a necessary, not a sufficient condition for sharing an inherited cultural identity. Moreover, this group—roughly: the gay subculture—is not, of course, an ethnic group.)

31. Suppose I am wrong on this point, so that all those who identify with their ethnicity have not chosen to do so. Do ethnic groups deserve special accommodation if all those who can freely choose to keep or shed their ethnic identification choose to shed it?

32. Regrettably, I must neglect this other side here for reasons of space, even though several critics of my thesis have in fact advanced this contention. Donald Horowitz did so on the grounds that ethnic identities

tend to be especially subject to elite manipulation and ethnic groups especially prone to violence. For his argument to succeed, it must, first, be the case that at least one of his two claims is true. It must further be the case that granting lesser group rights will tend to reduce tendencies to violence or elite manipulation. Finally, it must also be true that the ethnic character of groups is the best available proxy for picking out the groups that are subject to elite manipulation or prone to violence. I find it hard to believe that, at least in today's developed Western societies, all three of these empirical presuppositions hold true. And even if they were all true, we would still have to attend to the cost of disfavoring ethnic groups: the official suggestion, namely, that identifications with ethnic groups, though intrinsically no less valuable perhaps, are socially less desirable than identifications with groups of the other types.

33. Still, even this point may not hold strictly and across the board: A claim by traditional family farmers to special subsidies would seem to be rendered morally less plausible by an additional provision that would make it virtually impossible for other families to take up farming and thereby to become eligible for the same subsidy.

# 8

## ON JUSTIFYING SPECIAL ETHNIC GROUP RIGHTS: COMMENTS ON POGGE

### S. JAMES ANAYA

I fundamentally agree with an approach that advocates evaluating claims of group rights on the basis of neutral criteria that apply across the board and not just to a certain set of groups. Professor Pogge is correct to raise concerns about chauvinistic tendencies among certain groups that claim special entitlements on the basis of ethnicity (or something like or related to ethnicity). I need not describe here the myriad problems that have arisen in the world of late in association with this brand of chauvinism. The tragic dimensions of such problems are well known.

On the other hand, I do not believe that we can fairly brand as chauvinistic all claims that are linked to a strong sense of ethnic or cultural solidarity on the part of claimant groups. And while ethnic or cultural groups may not be intrinsically superior to other types of groups (such as associations of skiers or Porsche drivers), they may in some sense be more important; and, further, there are frequently good reasons to treat ethnic groups differentially or to accord them special entitlements, as Pogge himself appears to admit. My problem with Pogge's paper is not with his important reminder of the value of inherent human equality. Rather, my concern is that Pogge tends to downplay—perhaps even trivialize—the extent to which the effective realization of equality requires in many instances differential treatment of ethnic groups in ways not necessary for, or even relevant to, other types of groups.

## CULTURAL INTEGRITY

Among the important values that are embraced by enlightened societies and now featured in international human rights law is the value attached to the integrity of diverse cultures. Of course, this value is conditioned by other interests such that certain cultural practices may be limited or altogether prohibited. (Ceremonial female genital mutilation is an often-cited example of an unacceptable cultural practice that should be prohibited.) Otherwise, there seems to be strong interest in maintaining not just the survival but also the flourishment of diverse cultures.

Attention to cultural integrity necessarily leads us to have regard for certain types of groups in ways that we do not for others. Taos Indian Pueblo, a culturally distinctive community of longstanding and continuing profound significance to its members, is clearly valued within the larger society differently from the Taos ski club. Indeed, one can easily observe that, on grounds of cultural integrity, we tend to attach greater importance to groups that comprise or generate distinctive cultures more than to other types of groups. Taos Indian Pueblo is understandably considered a more important nucleus of human interaction than the ski club. This does not necessarily place members of noncultural groups such as skiers in an intrinsically inferior position. Each member of the skier group is presumably also a member of a cultural group—even if it is the majority cultural group—and members of one cultural group can be considered equal to members of other such groups to the extent all cultures are valued equally. In any case, to the extent we value cultural integrity, we will especially value ethnic and other groups that are defined substantially by distinctive cultural attributes.

A related consequence of the attention to cultural integrity is that cultural groups are accorded a certain set of rights that other types of groups are not. Hence the International Covenant on Civil and Political Rights, one the world's major human rights treaties, which has been widely ratified, provides in its article 27:

> In those States in which ethnic, religious or linguistic minorities
> exist, persons belonging to such minorities shall not be denied the
> right, in community with the other members of their group, to
> enjoy their own culture, to profess and practise their own religion,
> or to use their own language.[1]

By its own terms, this provision is limited in its scope to certain
types of groups, i.e., "ethnic, religious [and] linguistic" groups.
The rights of cultural integrity expressed here are for the most
part simply irrelevant to other types of groups.

Article 27 of the Covenant focuses on *minority* cultural groups,
as do a number of other international human rights instruments.[2]
This emphasis is not to deny the majority the same rights of
cultural integrity. Such rights clearly are understood to apply to
majority and minority groups alike.[3] The focus on minorities,
however, is based on recognition of the typically vulnerable position that a numerical minority or otherwise nondominant group
is likely to be in with regard to the enjoyment of its culture when
there is some significant difference between its cultural attributes
and those of the larger or dominant population.

## SPECIAL PROTECTION FOR PARTICULAR GROUPS

Special protection for minority cultural or ethnic groups is justified to the extent of offsetting the vulnerabilities that typically go
along with minority status. This notion was a feature of treaties
among European powers negotiated at the close of World War I.[4]
In its advisory opinion on *Minority Schools in Albania,*[5] the Permanent Court of International Justice explained the minority rights
provisions of the European treaties as derivative of equality precepts:

> The idea underlying the treaties for the protection of minorities is
> to secure for certain elements incorporated in a State, the popula-
> tion of which differs from them in race, language or religion, the
> possibility of living peacefully alongside that population and co-
> operating amicably with it, while at the same time preserving the
> characteristics which distinguish them from the majority, and satis-
> fying the ensuing special needs.
> In order to attain this object, two things were regarded as partic-

ularly necessary, and have formed the subject of provisions in these treaties.

The first is to ensure that nationals belonging to racial, religious or linguistic minorities shall be placed in every respect on a footing of perfect equality with the other nationals of the State.

The second is to ensure for the minority elements suitable means for the preservation of racial peculiarities, their traditions and their national characteristics.

These two requirements are indeed closely interlocked, for there would be no true equality between a majority and a minority if the latter were deprived of its own institutions, and were consequently compelled to renounce that which constitutes the very essence of its being as a minority.[6]

The degree and nature of cultural differences among groups vary, and hence the degree and kinds of protection provided diverse minority groups will not in all instances be the same. The religious practices of many indigenous peoples of the United States, for example, differ radically from those of other minority groups as well as from those of the majority population. Indigenous religious belief systems are typically linked to the natural world and hence require access to and preservation of elements of nature that may have little or no religious significance to the larger population, including other minority groups. Native Americans thus have made a persuasive case that, in order for them to be able to freely exercise their religion on the basis of equality with other segments of society, they require special accommodations within the governing legal system.

This position was to a significant extent validated by the U.S. Congress when it passed the American Indian Religious Freedom Act (AIRFA).[7] The Act mandates that the federal government's administration of public lands and other federally controlled resources take into account and seek to accommodate Native American religious interests. Although the courts have declined to enforce AIRFA against the government, the Act nonetheless stands as an important policy directive by Congress and an acknowledgment of the protection to which Native Americans as a particular class are entitled for the free exercise of religion.

It should also be understood that for many groups cultural differences may extend into the political and economic realms, well beyond religious, linguistic, or aesthetic considerations. Again, the context of indigenous peoples provides an instructive example. In a case involving the Lubicon Lake Band of Cree Indians, the United Nations Human Rights Committee construed the cultural rights guarantees of article 27 of the Covenant on Civil and Political Rights as extending to the "economic and social activities" upon which the Lubicon Lake Band relied as a group.[8] The Committee, which is charged with overseeing compliance with the Covenant, acknowledged that the Band's survival as a distinct cultural community was bound up with the sustenance that it derived from the land. Thus, the Committee found that Canada, a signatory to the Covenant, had violated its obligation under article 27 by allowing the provincial government of Alberta to grant leases for oil and gas exploration and for timber development within the ancestral lands of the Band.

Also important to many indigenous cultures are autonomous institutions of governance that may be rooted in historical patterns of social and political interaction and control. These systems often include customary or written laws as well as dispute resolution and adjudicative mechanisms that have developed over centuries and that remain integral parts of community life.[9] Further, independently of the extent to which indigenous communities have retained historically rooted governance systems, they may be entitled to develop autonomous governance on grounds of securing cultural survival. Increasingly, autonomous governance for indigenous communities is acknowledged to be instrumental to their capacities of control over the development of the multifaceted aspects of their distinctive cultures, including those aspects related to land and resource use.

Thus, on grounds of securing the cultural integrity of the indigenous groups of Nicaragua's Atlantic Coast region, the Inter-American Commission on Human Rights recommended a new institutional order that would devolve authority to the indigenous groups.[10] Not long afterwards, the Nicaraguan government entered negotiations with Indian leaders and eventually developed a constitutional and legislative regime of political and administrative autonomy for the Indian-populated Atlantic Coast. Although the autonomy regime is widely acknowledged to be faulty, and its implementation has been difficult, it nonetheless is by most accounts a step in the right direction. More significantly for the present purposes, it represents the kind of context-specific extraordinary measures to which certain types of groups may be entitled on grounds of securing the integrity of diverse cultures.

## REMEDYING PAST AND CONTINUING WRONGS

In many cases, special or extraordinary measures for particular groups may be justified on the related grounds of remedying historical or continuing wrongs. Precisely because of their distinctive cultural or racial attributes, certain minority ethnic groups historically have suffered patterns of discrimination, and in many instances these patterns, even when abated, have had continuing crippling effects. This very real, nonhypothetical phenomenon of discrimination which blemishes our social cosmography clearly has affected a certain type of group—i.e., groups with distinctive cultural or racial characteristics—and not other types of groups— such as associations of skiers and Porsche drivers.

Two strains of discrimination that give rise to remedial measures are identifiable. A first strain has sought to exclude groups from full participation in the political and social life of the state by impeding their interaction with the dominant population and limiting their enjoyment of the benefits and privileges ordinarily available to citizens. This strain of discrimination, which I will call *exclusionary discrimination,* is manifested prominently in the experience of black Americans, who initially found themselves within the U.S. polity as slaves and who, even after emancipation, were denied rights of citizenship and access to social benefits on an equal basis with the dominant white population.[11] Other ethnic minority groups within the United States that have suffered from exclusionary discrimination, although without similar histories of slavery, include Mexican Americans (or Chicanos), Native Americans, Asian Americans, and others with (usually visually perceptible) racial characteristics that set them apart from the dominant population. Additionally, women, including those of the majority, constitute a group that has suffered exclusionary discrimination on the basis of gender.

The civil rights legislation of the 1960s was aimed fundamentally at remedying the historical and continuing patterns of exclusionary discrimination experienced by discrete and identifiable segments of the American populace. In addition to legislation strengthening constitutional prohibitions against discrimination, affirmative action programs emerged with the objective of breaking down the more subtle barriers to opportunity and enhancing the participation of historically excluded minorities and women in American life. In recent years affirmative action programs have come under attack, but the criticisms are mostly aimed at the methodology of affirmative action and not its core underlying objectives.[12] Affirmative action programs, as they have developed thus far, have been perceived to unfairly disadvantage members of the white majority in ways disproportionate to their remedial impact on the groups they are intended to benefit. Largely absent from the debate over affirmative action, however, is serious questioning of the need to roll back patterns of discrimination where they exist and to do something to redress historical discrimination where its effects still manifest themselves in the lives of people.

A second strain of discrimination, which I will call *cultural discrimination,* seeks actively to suppress the cultural bonds and expressions of nondominant or minority groups, upon the premise that the dominant culture is superior. This strain of discrimination has occurred even (or in many cases especially) at the same time efforts have been made to enhance participation of minorities in the larger society. Not all efforts at acculturation or assimilation amount to cultural discrimination. In particular, the assimilation of immigrant groups into the dominant culture would not be cultural discrimination to the extent it could fairly be said that such groups have in some way consented to subordinate their cultural expressions to those predominating in the receiving society. In many cases, however, groups have found themselves subjected to forces that would cause them to lose their own cultural attributes in favor of those of the dominant society, without ever having consented, even tacitly, to such an abandonment of their group cultural identity.

In the United States, Native Americans stand out as victims of pervasive patterns of cultural discrimination. From the earliest periods of European exploration in the Western hemisphere, through at least the middle part of this century, dominant societal and governmental forces attempted to extinguish the cultural attributes of indigenous peoples and displace them with those of the European or European-derived society.[13] Indigenous religious practices were actively suppressed, as were indigenous governance and land tenure systems, without the indigenous groups concerned ever having sought or freely consented to such cultural transformation. Native Americans, who by definition are not immigrants, found themselves engulfed by a settler society and corresponding political system that regarded their cultures as "backward" or "uncivilized" and that hence systematically discriminated against indigenous cultural expressions.[14]

The cultural suffocation historically experienced by Native Americans and other indigenous peoples around the world, along with other multiple effects of colonialism, have left indigenous peoples with deep wounds which manifest themselves in social, political, economic, as well as cultural spheres.[15] As indigenous peoples now seek to rebuild their communities and cultures and to recapture their destinies, usually within the framework of the states in which they live, their claim for remedial measures is strong. The current heightened international concern for indigenous peoples, symbolized by the United Nations-sponsored "International Decade of the World's Indigenous People,"[16] attests to the strength of this claim.[17] Indigenous peoples are not alone among groups with strong claims to redress for historical or continuing wrongs, but certainly not *all* groups, nor all types of groups, can make such a claim.

## Conclusion

In sum, groups with distinctive cultural attributes, whether branded ethnic or other, are properly regarded differently from other types of groups to the extent there is a widely shared interest in securing the integrity of diverse cultures. The value of cultural integrity is mostly irrelevant to innumerable other types of groups that can be imagined. Furthermore, among the world's many cultural and ethnic groups, some require extraordinary protection because of certain conditions often related to minority status, or are entitled to remedies for historical or continuing patterns of discrimination. Not all groups, or types of groups, are the same.

## NOTES

1. International Covenant on Civil and Political Rights, adopted by the U.N. General Assembly Dec. 16, 1966, art. 27, 999. U.N.T.S. 171 (entered into force March 23, 1976).

2. E.g., Declaration on the Rights of Persons Belonging to National, Ethnic, Religious and Linguistic Minorities, adopted by the U.N. General Assembly Dec. 18, 1992, G.A. Res. 47/135 (1992); Charter of Paris for a New Europe (Conference on Security and Cooperation in Europe), signed Nov. 21, 1991, part 7 (human dimension), 30 I.L.M. 193 (1991).

3. See Declaration of the Principles of International Cultural Co-operation (United Nations Educational, Scientific and Cultural Organization), proclaimed by the UNESCO General Conference at its fourteenth session, Nov. 4, 1966, art. 1 (affirming that [e]ach culture has a dignity and value which must be respected and preserved" and that "[e]very people has a right and duty to develop its culture").

4. See Natan Lerner, *Group Rights and Discrimination in International Law* (Boston: Martinus Nijhoff, 1991), 7 (listing European treaties with provisions protecting the rights of religious and ethnic minorities).

5. Minority Schools in Albania, 1935 P.C.I.J. (Ser. A/B/) No. 64.

6. Id. at 17. See also European Convention for the Protection of Human Rights and Fundamental Freedoms, November 4, 1950, art. 14, Europ. T. S. No. 5, 213 U.N.T.S. 221 (entered into force, Sept. 3, 1953) (prohibiting discrimination on grounds, *inter alia*, of "language, religion, . . . [and] association with a national minority").

7. American Indian Religious Freedom Act of 1978, 42 U.S.C. Sec. 1996.

8. Ominayak, Chief of the Lubicon Lake Band v. Canada, Communication No. 267/1984, U.N. Doc. A/45/40, Annex 9(A) (1990) (views adopted March 26, 1990).

9. See Instituto Indigenista Interamericano and Instituto Interamericano de Derechos Humanos, *Entre ley y la costumbre: El derecho consuetudinario indígena en Ameríca Latina* (Mexico City, 1990) (a compilation of studies on indigenous customary laws and institutions in Latin America).

10. Inter-American Commission on Human Rights, *Report on the Situation of Human Rights of a Segment of the Nicaraguan Population of Miskito Origin,* OEA/Ser.L/V/II.62, Doc. 10 rev. 3 (1983), at 78–82. The Inter-American Commission on Human Rights is a organ of the Organization of American States, an intergovernmental body.

11. For an insightful commentary on historical, officially sanctioned racial discrimination against black Americans and its continuing negative manifestations, see Derrick Bell, "Racial Realism—After We're Gone:

Prudent Speculation on America in a Post-Racial Epoch," *St. Louis University Law Journal* 34 (1990): 393.

12. See generally Nicolaus Mills, ed., *Debating Affirmative Action: Race, Gender, Ethnicity, and the Politics of Inclusion* (New York: Dell Publishing, 1994).

13. For materials on some of the major U.S. government programs and legal mechanisms to disassemble indigenous cultures, see David H. Getches et al., *Federal Indian Law: Cases and Materials*, 3d ed. (St. Paul: West Publishing Co., 1993), 41–82, 167–248.

14. A comprehensive explanation of the theoretical grounding of this strain of discrimination as executed against Native Americans is in Robert A. Williams, Jr., *The American Indian in Western Legal Thought: The Discourses of Conquest* (New York: Oxford University Press, 1990).

15. See Julian Burger, *Report from the Frontier: The State of the World's Indigenous Peoples* (London: Zed Books, 1987), 17–31 (describing "life at the bottom" for indigenous peoples worldwide in terms of health, employment, and social marginalization).

16. G.A. Res. 48/163 (Dec. 1993) (United Nations General Assembly resolution proclaiming the "International Decade of the World's Indigenous People" commencing December 10, 1994).

17. For a discussion of new and emerging international norms and procedures concerning indigenous peoples, see S. James Anaya, *Indigenous Peoples in International Law* (New York: Oxford University Press, 1996).

# PART IV

# GROUP RIGHTS AND GROUP AGENCY

# 9

## GROUP AGENCY AND
## GROUP RIGHTS

### JAMES W. NICKEL

One source of discomfort with group or collective rights is the belief that many groups, and particularly ethnic groups, are deficient as rightholders. (I'll call this the "Deficiency Thesis" and abbreviate it as "DT"). An extreme version of DT concludes that groups are so lacking in the characteristics required of competent rightholders that it never makes sense to attribute rights to groups.[1] In this chapter, I explore and evaluate a more modest version of DT. It doesn't deny that groups can have agency and rights, but suggests that assigning rights to groups is generally a bad idea because groups are often unable to play an active role in exercising, interpreting, and defending their rights. The source of this inability is that groups often lack *effective agency* and *clear identity*. Effective agency is a matter of being able to form goals, deliberate, choose, intend, act, and carry out evaluations of actions taken. Agency requires specific capacities such as finding information, monitoring conditions, setting and formulating goals, evaluating options, recognizing and following norms, planning, acting, and evaluating outcomes. Clear identity is a matter of having reasonably clear boundaries so that it is possible to say which persons belong to the group, share in its responsibilities, should have a say in the group's affairs, and are entitled to some share of benefits the group receives. We will see that agency and identity are closely related.

Ultimately I deny that DT is true of all or even most groups, but I suggest that it may be true of some ethnic minorities— particularly those without territories. Further, I defend the view that clear identity and effective agency are needed for groups to benefit from most of the rights that are currently put forward as group rights. Together, these two propositions suggest that it will often be unwise to give group rights to nonterritorial minorities. But there are practical measures available to construct the clear identity and effective agency that will enable nonterritorial minorities to be capable rightholders. The costs of constructing these characteristics may be high and in addition will turn the group into an entity that is less fuzzy, more durable, and more active. The social and political consequences of giving a minority ethnic group these characteristics may be profound.

My concern is with group rights that have or are intended for political and legal implementation. The sorts of rights that groups claim are extremely varied. They include rights against genocide,[2] forced assimilation,[3] and ethnic cleansing,[4] to secession,[5] self-determination,[6] semi-autonomous status, territory, control over resources,[7] recognition as distinctive and/or oppressed,[8] recognition of a group's language as one of the official languages of the country,[9] subsidies to help keep a culture alive,[10] a fair share of public funding,[11] expanded educational and economic opportunities, political participation as groups,[12] and full citizenship and nondiscrimination for their members. This list suggests that group rights are so varied that it is hard to have a single attitude towards them.

My arguments do not rely on any particular conception of what a group right is. I emphasize that many group rights require exercise, administration, and defense but view this fact as contingent rather than necessary. There are at least three reasons why a right might be considered a group right. First, a right might be considered a group right because it is a right that only some ethnic, national, or minority groups and not all citizens have. Kymlicka calls these "group-differentiated rights," and notes that some of these rights can be held and exercised by individuals.[13] Second, a right might be considered a group right because it is the group, acting through its leadership, that has the legal power to invoke or waive the right. For example, a group's right to its land may be considered a group right because only the group acting through its leadership has the power to make decisions about the disposition of that land. Third, a right may be considered a group right because the interests it protects are collective or shared rather than individual.[14] None of these conceptions of the nature of a group right enjoys universal or near-universal acceptance, so instead of relying on one of these conceptions I will work with a list of rights that almost everyone takes to be examples of group rights.

## I. Are Groups Deficient as Rightholders?

### A. The Unrestricted Deficiency Thesis (UDT)

UDT asserts that groups almost never have clear identity and effective agency. In this section, I elaborate and evaluate this thesis, ultimately concluding that UDT is not generally true. In the next section, I suggest that a more restricted version of DT probably is true.

Groups, unlike normal individuals, are often internally divided, unorganized, unclear in their boundaries, and are therefore unable to engage in actions as groups. For example, families are routinely given rights to decide on the medical care of one of their members who is temporarily or permanently unable to make decisions, but they often have difficulties in knowing which members should be allowed to participate in the decision (Is it only the spouse—if any—and children? Does it include the spouses of the children? Does it include siblings or cousins of the patient? Does it include grandchildren?). Further, their discussions and attempts to organize themselves often fail to produce a member who can legitimately speak for the family as a whole. As a result, "the family" often speaks with several inconsistent voices.

As this example suggests, identity and agency are closely related. Fractiousness and lack of clear identity often make it hard for groups to have authorized leadership that can genuinely speak and decide on behalf of the group. The most assertive or politically engaged members may attempt to speak and decide on behalf of the group, but this assumption of leadership is unauthorized and may lead to protests and schisms. In order to authorize leaders through an election, or even through acquiescence in their leadership role, it is necessary to know who the members are. Otherwise one does not know who is qualified to vote or acquiesce. Yet it is often difficult to know exactly who the members are. For example, does the group of Hispanics or Latinos in the United States include Haitian Americans, Brazilian Americans, or Italian Americans? These people come from countries with languages derived from Latin that are nevertheless not "Hispanic."

UDT can be used as part of an argument against group rights:

Premise 1: Good rightholders must have reasonably clear identity and effective agency.

Premise 2 (UDT): Groups almost never have clear identity and effective agency.

Subconclusion: Groups are almost never good rightholders.

Premise 3: If groups are almost never good rightholders, then rights should almost never be assigned to groups or recognized as belonging to groups.

Conclusion: Rights should almost never be assigned to or recognized as belonging to groups.

### B. The Implausibility of the Unrestricted Deficiency Thesis

UDT is not plausible. There are numerous examples of groups that have clear identity and effective agency. Examples of such groups include Boulder County Government, Amnesty International USA, the Mennonite Central Committee, the University of Colorado at Boulder Philosophy Department, the Boulder Medical Center, Storage Technology Corporation, and Ideal Market. These are groups with reasonably clear membership requirements and well-developed procedures for creating and maintaining leadership bodies with effective capacities to act. These groups are typical of millions of other groups. It just isn't true that groups almost never have clear identity and effective agency.

Indeed, the agency of groups is often *more* effective than that of individuals. This is true not just in the sense that large organizations can do more things and bigger things, but also in the sense that organizations sometimes have better resources for decision making and action than individuals do. Their capacities for gathering information, developing alternative options for choice, deliberating, planning, deciding, and executing are often superior to those of individuals. One reason for this is that they can select talented persons or teams and assign decision-related tasks and specific actions to them.[15]

Another way of understanding why groups sometimes have clear identity and effective agency turns on the fact that there are available effective procedures and institutions for defining the membership of a group and for creating and maintaining an authorized leadership that is able to act. If an informal group needs clear identity, it can create a constitution and bylaws that define who the members are, or what a person must do to become and remain a member. If such a group needs effective agency, it can identify some leadership roles, with definite powers and responsibilities, elect members to those roles, and hold them accountable for effective action through regular evaluations and elections. Consider the following steps that a group might take to gain a clearer identity and more effective and democratically accountable agency:

1. *Create or clarify identity.* This requires deciding who are the members of the group. There may seem to be a chicken-and-egg problem here: which comes first, identity or agency? If a group doesn't have clear identity, how can it choose a process for selecting leaders? And if it doesn't have agency, how can it define the parties eligible to vote? There are probably a number of ways to get out of this difficulty, but here is one—which I'll call "bootstrapping." It requires that a very large majority of an informal group be in favor of a constitutional scheme that defines a set of leadership roles and a procedure for electing people to those roles. This means that the constitution can be ratified and leaders chosen in an election using a broad definition of who the members are. Alternatively, it means that under any reasonable definition of the boundaries of the group, a majority will exist. Once the leaders are elected through this process, they can use their powers to define the membership, or to create a democratic process for ratifying a membership scheme.

2. *Agree on a constitutional process.* This involves having or developing some idea of how a constitution can be created. As Profes-

sor Réaume emphasizes, a key part of creating a constitution is the creation of what Hart called a "rule of recognition," a principle that allows one to determine whether a norm or decision is a valid rule or decision of the group.[16] The legal system of the country is likely to provide a legal process of incorporation— or, more likely, different sorts of processes for different sorts of organizations such as business corporations, partnerships, and nonprofit organizations. More broadly, democratic models of constitution-making are widely available and used in the contemporary world. According to these models, a legitimate constitution can come into existence if a large majority of those to be governed by it consent to it, or if a large majority of the elected representatives of those people consent to it.

3. *Use this process to create a leadership structure and election procedures.* A key part of a constitution for a group is the formulation of a decision-making structure that defines leadership positions, assigns powers and responsibilities to them, and specifies how these positions are to be filled.[17]

4. *Follow the election procedures to fill the leadership positions.* The next step is to create agency by filling the leadership positions and implementing the decision-making structure.

5. *Revisit the identity problem if necessary.* If the identity of the group remains a problem, it can be addressed formally at this point. The leaders can establish or propose for democratic approval membership criteria. These criteria may specify procedures that one must have gone through to apply for and receive membership, substantive characteristics such as ancestry, residence, culture, beliefs, loyalties, or self-perception, or some mixture of these. An appeals process for those excluded by these criteria can also be created.

6. *Set goals for the group.* The leaders of the group can now establish, or propose for approval, collective goals. This may require meetings, debate, and opinion polls of the members. Once group goals are established, it will be unproblematic to speak of the group's interests (conditions that promote those goals). It will also make sense at this point to speak of the group acting for a certain reason (e.g., to pursue one of its goals).

7. *Devise plans and strategies for achieving those goals.* Once the group has a leadership and goals, efforts can be made to deter-

mine what will be required to realize those goals and to plan for their realization. When a group is able to do these things it effectively has the capacity for deliberation.

8. *Take actions in accordance with these plans and strategies.* The next step is for the group, acting through its leadership, to take actions that pursue its goals by following its plans. The group now displays agency in action.

9. *Evaluate actions and reformulate plans and strategies.* Not all plans and efforts to realize the group's goals will be successful. To deal with this, the group's leadership will need to engage in monitoring, evaluation, and reformulation of goals and plans.

There are dozens of ways in which these steps can fail, but in fact they often succeed. It may be thought that these mechanisms work for small organizations but not for large ones. But many countries and territorial ethnic groups have used exactly these sorts of mechanisms for defining their members (citizens) and selecting their leaders.

## C. The Restricted Deficiency Thesis (RDT)

Although it is untrue that all—or even most—groups are deficient as rightholders, an advocate of DT might wish to restrict the thesis so that it only applies to ethnic minorities, or some subset of ethnic minorities.

Nonterritorial ethnic minorities[18] often lack clear identity and effective agency. Ethnic minorities in the United States such as African Americans, Hispanics, and Jewish Americans typically have no formal criteria for who their members are and rely on self-definition or broad, vague social understandings of what makes one a member. Further, such groups are not tightly organized under a single leadership that can unproblematically speak for all of the members of the group. They are nonterritorial in the sense that they do not have established territories within the country. Thus the country in which the group lives is either not territorially and governmentally differentiated along group lines, or the territorial and governmental differentiations that do exist refer only to other groups (e.g., to the Navaho, but not to African Americans).

This qualification results in a new version of DT: Restricted

Deficiency Thesis (RDT): Nonterritorial ethnic minorities almost never have clear identity and effective agency. When the argument against group rights given in section I is adapted to fit RDT, its conclusion is: Rights should almost never be assigned to or recognized as belonging to nonterritorial ethnic minorities.

But is RDT true? This is an empirical question, but the plausibility of RDT can be supported by listing some of the factors that make it difficult for nonterritorial ethnic minorities to have clear identity and effective agency. Clear identity is hard to create because many members will have mixed localities (and some will have mixed ancestry). Some will resent having to choose formally to be in or out, and they lose little if they refuse to choose. A formal and comprehensive system of membership is costly to maintain, and may have little pay-off as long as the group lives within a larger society of which its members are full-fledged citizens. The fact that the group is nonterritorial means that the easiest kind of membership system, one which equates membership with permanent residence in a territory, is unavailable. Effective agency is also hard to create because the group is likely to be large, politically and economically diverse, geographically dispersed, partially mixed with other groups, divided by factions, schisms, and competing political visions, and lacking in a comprehensive system of formal membership.

These factors make it difficult for legitimate leaders to be chosen and authorized by the group. To be authorized to speak and choose for the group, leaders must have been elected by a majority, or selected in something closely analogous to an election. But conducting an election or poll is difficult when the group has fuzzy membership criteria. If self-selection is the basis for participation in polling, outsiders may seek to influence the outcome. And if one only polls people who are clear-cut members, one may disenfranchise the dissenting views of marginal members. Notice that this argument goes from lack of clear identity to lack of effective and authorized agency. Notice also that the "bootstrapping" process described earlier may make it possible to get around this problem.

I find RDT plausible, but the percentage of cases (of nonterritorial ethnic minorities) in which it is true is far from clear. Nevertheless, no general proposition such as RDT about the agency of nonterritorial ethnic minorities needs to be true for the argument to work when its conclusion is restricted to a particular group. If the Deficiency Thesis is true of a particular group, then the argument against group rights given above can be used against group rights for that group.

## II. GROUP RIGHTS REQUIRE EXERCISE AND TENDING

The fact that a group lacks agency would not make it deficient as a rightholder unless agency is necessary to having and benefiting from rights. In this section, I defend the claim that in order for a group to benefit from politically implemented rights it generally needs to have effective agency. I do this by identifying six kinds of activities that rightholders often need to perform in order to benefit from their rights and showing that these activities are required as well for the enjoyment of most group rights. Second, I show that the circumstances that sometimes make possible the passive enjoyment of legal rights by many rightholders are not present, or are present to a lesser degree, in the case of legally implemented group rights. Finally, I show the limited usefulness in the area of group rights of schemes that empower parties other than the rightholder to exercise the rights of a group.

In mounting this argument, I will not rely on the general thesis, asserted by advocates of the "will" or "agency" theory of rights such as H. L. A. Hart, Wayne Sumner, and Carl Wellman,[19] that because genuine rights always confer powers and liberties on their holders one cannot be a rightholder unless one possesses the ability to exercise such powers and liberties. I reject this general thesis but believe that in the area of legally implemented group rights it is generally true that for rightholders to fully enjoy these rights they must have effective agency. I will try to show that this claim is contingently true of legally implemented group rights by looking at some representative examples of such rights.

### A. Group Rights Generally Require Rightholder Agency

It will be helpful in thinking about agency and group rights to have a general list of activities that rightholders often perform in relation to their legal rights. In illustrating these six kinds of activities, I will use examples of legislative and constitutional rights because these are the kinds of rights that group rights are likely to be. These activities pertain to:

*Waiver, invocation, and use.* To *waive* one's right *(R)* to *A* in a weak sense one can simply decline to do or receive *A* in a particular situation in which *R* applies. For example, one (weakly) waives one's right to emigrate if one never even considers emigrating. Waiving a right in a stronger sense involves referring to the right and rendering it inoperable in the particular situation. For example, a person charged with a crime may formally waive the right to a trial as part of a plea bargain.

We can make a similar distinction between strong and weak senses of exercising (or using) a right. To exercise one's right *(R)* to *A* in a weak sense is simply to do or receive *A* in an environment in which *R* helps to increase the availability of *A*. Using *R* in this sense doesn't require thinking about *R,* or even knowing of its existence. For example, a person may (weakly) exercise his right to freedom of speech by making a political speech in an environment in which the right to free speech helps make it safe to make political speeches. To use *R* in a stronger sense is to try to do or receive *A* while invoking *R*. To strongly invoke a right *R* to *A* is not merely to do or receive *A,* but to do or receive *A* in a particular situation while claiming *R* or reminding others of *R*. For example, a person stopped by police may decline to permit them to search her car by reminding them of her right against warrantless searches.

*Responsibilities.* Responsibilities often accompany the possession of legal rights. For example, if parents have and exercise the right to home-school their children, they incur accompanying responsibilities to actually provide their children with instruction, reading materials, and other educational opportunities. I use the word "responsibilities" here to suggest something vaguer and less formal than duties. For example, even if one doesn't have a legal duty to vote, one may have moral and civic responsibilities to exercise one's right to vote in a conscientious and informed way.

*Alienation.* To alienate a right is to get rid of it permanently. Forms of alienation include giving, selling, trading, forfeiting, and repudiating. For example, one can alienate one's citizenship by becoming a citizen of another country and repudiating one's original citizenship.

*Interpretation.* Rightholders are often required to decide whether a right applies to the circumstances they are in. Sometimes it will be obvious that a right applies, but in other cases this will be far from clear. For instance, one may be unsure whether the right to freedom of expression covers exotic haircuts for persons in prison. Since people's interpretations of constitutional and legislative rights are often rejected by officials and judges, litigation may be necessary to attempt to establish an interpretation of a right.

*Monitoring compliance and preventing violations.* The activities in this category can be done by persons other than the rightholder, but in many circumstances they cannot be done effectively without rightholder participation. To *monitor compliance* with a right to do or receive A is to regularly observe whether the addressees of that right are providing the rightholders with the liberties, protections, or benefits that the right prescribes. For example, a likely victim of employment discrimination may watch carefully for signs that discrimination is occurring. *Fending off threatened violations* of one's right, or of someone else's right, involves trying to prevent those violations before they occur. One may try to do this by reminding the potential violators of the right, or by taking steps that make it harder to carry out the violation. For example, a political dissident who fears being arrested and tortured may fend off this violation of her rights by making herself hard to find, or by seeking safety in the embassy of another country. *Stopping violations* of a right as they occur is similar, except that a series of violations has already begun. For example, a woman being subjected to sexual harassment may seek legal assistance in getting the harasser to stop.

*Remedies and compensation.* When rights that protect things of value are violated it is common for people to seek compensation or remedies for the losses they suffered. For example, a person who was convicted and imprisoned on the basis of evidence gained through an illegal search may seek release from prison, or compensation for the time spent in prison. The rightholder need not perform these activities alone. They may be done together with other people who had the same right violated, with the assistance of legal counsel, and with the assistance of political and civil rights organizations.

The sense in which these six kinds of activities are necessary to the enjoyment of a right needs clarification.[20] I do not deny that one may gain some benefit from a right even if one is unable to operate it (see below). The claim is rather that one's capacity to benefit from a right over time is likely to be greatly reduced if one is unable to operate it. As an analogy, one might benefit from having a car even though one was unable to drive (one could sleep in it, treasure it as a work of art, or get others to drive it), but to most people the benefits received from having the car would be greatly reduced.

Let's now apply these six categories to some representative group rights. The question I want to ask is whether there are likely circumstances in which a group would be significantly less able to enjoy the right if it were unable to take one of these six sorts of actions. For example, consider the group right against genocide. It is not likely that a group would wish to promote its interests by waiving or alienating this right. But a group would be significantly less able to benefit from this right if lacked the capacity to interpret the right, monitor compliance, fend off potential violations, stop violations that are beginning to occur, and seek remedies for violations.

For another example, consider a constitutional right that grants certain groups the right to secede. It is quite possible that some groups will best promote their goals by waiving or alienating this right. Further, a group will be significantly less able to enjoy this right if it lacks the capacity to engage in strong exercise of the right, fulfill its responsibilities under the process required for secession, propose interpretations of this right, monitor compliance, fend off potential violations, stop violations that are beginning to occur, and seek remedies for violations.

For a third example, consider a legislatively enacted right held by specified ethnic and indigenous groups to subsidies to assist those groups in keeping their distinctive cultures alive. It is quite possible that some of these groups will seek to promote their goals by waiving or alienating this right (for example, they may believe that dependence on the central government creates weakness).

Further, these groups will be significantly less able to enjoy this right if they lack the capacity to engage in strong exercise of the right, fulfill the responsibilities it implies to use these funds for activities that strengthen their culture, propose interpretations of this right, monitor compliance, fend off potential violations, stop violations that are beginning to occur (e.g., when the central government in a particular year severely cuts these subsidies), and seek remedies for violations.

I have attempted to show, by reference to a representative set of legally implemented group rights, that rightholder action to exercise, administer, and support these rights is likely to be required for their full enjoyment. I now turn to objections that (1) deny that these activities are always required for enjoyment, and (2) deny that the rightholder—rather than some other party—must be the one to engage in these activities.

### B. Why the Passive Enjoyment of Group Rights Is Generally Impossible

In response to my claim that rightholders regularly need to perform these six kinds of activities, it might be objected that many Americans enjoy constitutional rights such as the right to freedom from unreasonable searches and seizures and the right to a trial by jury yet never engage personally in any of the listed activities in regard to these rights. With the exception of using and waiving their rights in the weak senses defined above, many rightholders don't do anything in relation to their rights. I recognize that this is true, but will try to show how the factors that make this possible are unlikely to apply to most group rights. I'll begin by explaining, with reference to the six activities identified above, how people can sometimes enjoy rights while doing almost nothing to exercise or manage them.

*Waiver, invocation, and use.* People can use and waive rights in the weak senses above without referring to or even knowing about those rights. In these senses one uses one's right to free speech when one decides to speak, and one waives it when one decides not to speak. Second, people can enjoy a right without ever using it if the situation in which this right applies does not actually arise in their lives. For example, most people are never charged with a crime, and hence never have the opportunity to invoke or waive their rights of criminal due process. Further, even if a situation arises that brings the right into play, compliance may be automatic (e.g., everyone knows and accepts that certain sorts of searches are impermissible, or that a jury trial is required), so the right doesn't need to be invoked or claimed.

*Responsibilities.* Many rights don't impose participatory or administrative responsibilities on their holders. The right to freedom from torture, unlike the right to vote, doesn't have any associated responsibilities.

*Alienation.* One can enjoy rights without ever alienating them if they are not the sorts of rights one can sell or trade and if one has no desire to repudiate them. Property rights are frequently alienated, but constitutional and human rights are ones that people seldom alienate—and in some cases are impossible to alienate.

*Interpretation.* One can enjoy rights without ever interpreting them if one enjoys the protections created by a general system of rights without ever learning what those rights are. Also, one can let others—particularly those who are actually in the situation in which the rights come into play—do the work of raising and litigating issues about their meaning.

*Monitoring compliance and preventing violations.* One can enjoy rights without being vigilant against noncompliance if one lives in a country in which rights are generally respected, and lives in a way that is unlikely to put one in situations in which one's rights need to be invoked. Low levels of vigilance may also be reasonable if one knows that there are many watchdog organizations engaged in monitoring compliance with people's rights.

*Compensation.* If most people are never in the situation where these rights come into play, and if there is a high degree of compliance with them when they do come into play, then few people will be in a position to seek compensation for violations.

Although it is possible to have and benefit from rights that one almost never exercises and tends, the circumstances in which it is possible are unlikely to apply to group rights. I'll try to show this by once more enumerating the six kinds of activities.

*Group waiver, invocation, and use.* With the exception of rights against genocide and ethnocide and the right to secession, group rights are likely to be rights that come into play in circumstances that arise frequently or continuously. For example, if a group wants a right to political representation as a group, it is because it believes that it is in a situation in which it is inadequately represented politically and because it expects to be able to use this right, and the political representation it guarantees, on a regular basis to ensure the fair treatment and other interests of its members.

*Group responsibilities.* Group rights often confer duties and responsibilities on their holders. Hence the holders of group rights should be able to discharge these rights and responsibilities. For example, if a group acquires a right to educate its own children, along with the resources to do so, it also acquires thereby the responsibility to make educational opportunities available to those children. If a group is granted a right to subsidies for cultural support, it will have to either accept and arrange to use this money or waive the right. If a group is granted a right to semisovereign status within a territory, it will have to arrange to govern or to waive its right to do so. The responsibilities that go with many group rights cannot be discharged without active and effective attention to those rights and the associated interests of the group.

*Groups alienating their rights.* Most individual constitutional rights are not the sorts of rights one can sell or trade, and very few people wish to repudiate them. But it is easy to imagine circumstances in which a group might wish to repudiate or trade one of its rights. If a number of cultural groups including the Amish were granted subsidies for cultural support, the Amish would probably refuse to accept such subsidies on the grounds that they do not wish to be dependent on government (the Amish do this in other areas such as Social Security benefits).

*Groups interpreting their rights.* Group rights are likely to be more like contractual rights between a few parties and less like long-standing constitutional rights that apply to all residents of a country. Often, there will be few other groups holding the same rights, and the ones that do have the same rights may have significantly different interests and perspectives. Hence a group without much capacity for agency will be unable to rely on other groups to defend and litigate advantageous interpretations.

*Groups monitoring compliance and preventing violations.* The conditions that make it reasonable for persons to leave to others the monitoring of compliance with their constitutional rights are unlikely to apply to group rights. First, group rights are likely to be new rights, and hence habitual compliance with them cannot be assumed. Second, we saw earlier that most group rights apply to circumstances in which groups will regularly find themselves. And third, watchdog organizations that monitor violations of group rights are far fewer than those that monitor violations of individual rights. Groups such as the ACLU or Amnesty International are unlikely to monitor compliance with group rights. Further, minority ethnic groups are unlikely to want their rights to be mainly monitored by mainstream organizations with which they have few ties.

*Groups seeking remedies and compensation.* Since group rights are likely to be ones that most groups actually exercise and invoke, and since these rights are also likely to be new rights that the addressees must learn to accept and comply with, violations are likely to occur. Thus the desire to seek compensation is likely to arise.

### C. Can Someone Other Than the Rightholder Exercise Group Rights?

Let's now turn to an objection that says that although group rights require agents who will use and tend them for the benefit of the holders, the agents do not have to be the groups themselves. I accept this possibility since I believe that young children have both moral and legal rights even though they lack much capacity for agency. For children, we make enjoyment of rights possible by assigning other parties the responsibility of deciding issues that arise about the exercise and tending of a child's rights. The parties are typically a child's parents or guardians but sometimes are state agencies. Surely, the objection continues, it is possible to do something similar for groups so that they do not need to exercise and tend their own rights.

I have two responses to this objection. One is to continue to insist that lack of agency is a deficiency in a rightholder, even though I allow that it is a deficiency that we can sometimes get around. The other response is to suggest that for good moral and political reasons the use of outside agents to exercise and tend rights has very limited prospects in the area of *group* rights.

Before elaborating the second response, I want to allow that exercise of group rights by trustees is an important option, particularly in dealing with indigenous groups that have only recently come into contact with modern technological civilization and that have limited ability to understand their legal rights, much less to exercise and tend them. I have in mind a group such as the Yanomami of Brazil and Venezuela. The only way in which such a group can be protected by a scheme of rights that includes rights against genocide and ethnocide, and to retain and use their historic territory, is for some outside agency—perhaps a department of indigenous affairs such as FUNAI in Brazil—to exercise and tend these rights. To make the paternalism and potential for corruption involved in such a scheme more palatable, we might advocate the creation of nongovernmental organizations to monitor the decisions made by this agency to make sure that they promote the interests of the protected group.

Although this option is valuable in some cases, its general appeal is limited. It works best for rights that serve mainly to protect the survival and territory of a group (e.g., rights against genocide, forced assimilation, and to a territory). It works poorly for rights that mainly serve to promote a protect a group's ability to decide for itself how it wishes to live and interact with other groups (e.g., rights to self-determination, control over resources, political participation as a group, and subsidies for cultural support). It is the latter kind of rights that is most prominent in contemporary discussions of group rights. There is often hypocrisy or even contradiction involved when a national government tells a minority group that it has rights to decide key issues for itself but then turns around and says that agents of the national government are going to do most of the actual decisionmaking. This hypocrisy has frequently been seen in the dealings of the U.S. government with Indian tribes.

A related option is for the national government to rely on the leaders of a minority group's existing religious, cultural, and political organizations to make decisions about the exercise and maintenance of the group's rights. Instead of trying to create new, comprehensive institutions that provide leaders authorized to speak for the entire group it is often easier to rely on the leadership of existing group organizations. If subsidies were given to groups for cultural support, for example, the responsibilities for using and administering these funds might be given to existing group organizations. There are two main problems with this option. One is that the leaders of these organizations are not authorized to represent or make decisions for the entire group, and they are at best accountable to only part of the group (namely those that belong to the organization). The other problem is that this option has limited scope. It is not likely to work for the stronger forms of group rights. This sort of agency would be inadequate for the right to control resources, to secede, to limited self-government, and to political participation as a group.

## III. Creating Group Agency and Identity

If an ethnic minority lacks the effective agency needed to exercise and tend its group rights, and if the options just discussed are not widely applicable, then there are two main options. One is to avoid granting or recognizing group rights for groups that lack effective agency. Sometimes, part of the work that group rights would have done can be accomplished by giving individual rights to the members of the group (we might call this the "privatization" of group rights).

The other main option is for nonterritorial ethnic minorities to try to create the clear identity, effective agency, and legitimated leaders that are needed for the effective exercise and management of their rights. We saw earlier that there are processes or steps whereby groups can create clear identities and effective and legitimate leadership bodies, and it is possible—if not easy—for nonterritorial ethnic groups to use these procedures. It is easiest to imagine this happening if the ethnic minority is assisted by the national government that will be the main addressee of the group's rights.

In order to construct clear identity and effective agency, a group will probably need to have means of encouraging its members to participate and contribute. This is easier if a group's members mostly live on a territory that it controls. Doing it through the mail, as it were, is harder. It may be possible to do this entirely on a voluntary basis, but it seems more likely that the group will have to become something like a nonterritorial government. For this to happen, the national government will have to grant the group access to resources or the coercive power to tax its members. Further, the group will probably have to assume responsibility for providing services in areas such as education, law, and health.

The process of creating clear identity and effective agency is likely to transform a non territorial minority group into something that is less fuzzy, more active, and more durable.[21] If a group acquires a sharper identity this is likely to reinforce its members' perceptions of their distinctiveness and make them less willing to accept the gradual merger of their group into a larger ensemble of minorities or into society at large. If a group acquires both a clearer identity and more effective ability to act as a group, this may produce stronger and more politically plausible demands for recognition, support, fair treatment, or even separation. These changes may be good or bad depending on the circumstances—and I do wish to emphasize that such changes are sometimes all to the good. But the consequences of these changes are likely to be sufficiently large and enduring to warrant careful evaluation of steps intended to create clearer identity and more effective agency for minority groups. Indeed, the consequences of making minority groups into capable rightholders may be as large as the consequences of recognizing, implementing, and respecting their rights.

## NOTES

This chapter began as a commentary on Denise Réaume's essay, "Common-Law Constructions of Group Autonomy: A Case Study," but evolved into a more freestanding discussion dealing with group autonomy. I am indebted to Professor Réaume for stimulating me to take up this topic. I am also indebted for comments and suggestions to Will Kymlicka, Ian Shapiro, Peter French, Steve Munzer, Yael Tamir, and Carl Wellman.

1. See, for example, Carl Wellman, *Real Rights* (Oxford: Oxford University Press, 1995), 105–77. Wellman holds that even the best organized and most "active" groups lack agency and therefore are not possible rightholders. There isn't much practical bite to this claim, however, since he thinks that we can translate statements about the actions of groups into statements "about the actions of individual human beings acting as officials in corporate groups" (p. 165).

2. See Patrick Thornberry, "Is There a Phoenix in the Ashes?—International Law and Minority Rights," *Texas International Law Journal* 15 (1990): 421 at 444.

3. See James W. Nickel, "Ethnocide and Indigenous Peoples," *Journal of Social Philosophy* 24 (1994): 84–98.

4. See James W. Nickel, "What's Wrong with Ethnic Cleansing?" *Journal of Social Philosophy* 25 (1995): 5–15. See also Alfred M. DeZayas, "International Law and Mass Population Transfers," *Harvard International Law Review* 16 (1975): 207.

5. See Allen E. Buchanan, *Secession: The Morality of Political Divorce from Fort Sumter to Lithuania and Quebec* (Boulder, Colo.: Westview Press, 1991).

6. See Allen Buchanan, "The Right to Self-Determination: Analytical and Moral Foundations," *Arizona Journal of International and Comparative Law* 8 (1991): 41. See also Yoram Dinstein, "Collective Human Rights of Peoples and Minorities," *International and Comparative Law* 8 (1991): 102 at 106; and Thornberry, "Is There a Phoenix in the Ashes?" 451.

7. See Dinstein, "Collective Human Rights of Peoples and Minorities," 110.

8. See Charles Taylor, *Multiculturalism and "The Politics of Recognition"* (Princeton: Princeton University Press, 1992), 25–73.

9. See Will Kymlicka, *Multicultural Citizenship* (Oxford: Oxford University Press, 1995), 34, 45–46.

10. See Will Kymlicka, *Liberalism, Community, and Culture* (Oxford: Oxford University Press, 1989), 182–205.

11. See Thornberry, "Is There a Phoenix in the Ashes?" 432.

12. See Anne Philips, *Democracy and Difference* (Philadelphia: Pennsylvania State University Press, 1993). See also Kymlicka, *Multicultural Citizenship*, 131–51.

13. Kymlicka, *Multicultural Citizenship*, 7, 34–35, 45.

14. See Leslie Green, "Two Views of Collective Rights," *Canadian Journal of Law and Jurisprudence* 4 (1991): 315–27; and Michael Hartney,

"Some Confusions concerning Collective Rights," *Canadian Journal of Law and Jurisprudence* 4 (1991): 393–414.

15. For a survey of philosophical attempts to make sense of group agency, see Wellman, *Real Rights,* 157–65.

16. Denise G. Réaume, "Common-Law Constructions of Group Autonomy: A Case Study," this volume. See also H. L. A. Hart, *The Concept of Law* (Oxford: Oxford University Press, 1961), 92–93.

17. See the discussion of Corporate Internal Decision Structures in Peter French, *Collective and Corporate Responsibility* (New York: Columbia University Press, 1984), 48–66.

18. For attempts to define the concept of an ethnic minority, see Dinstein, 104; Thomas Pogge, "Group Rights and Ethnicity," this volume, 187–221; Frances Svensson, "Liberal Democracy and Group Rights: The Legacy of Individualism and Its Impact on American Indian Tribes," *Political Studies* 27 (1979): 421 at 434; Thornberry, "Is There a Phoenix in the Ashes?" 422; and Vernon Van Dyke, "The Individual, the State, and Ethnic Communities in Political Theory," *World Politics* 29 (1977): 343 at 344.

19. H. L. A. Hart, "Are There Any Natural Rights?" *Philosophical Review* 64 (1955): 175–91; Wayne Sumner, *The Moral Foundations of Rights* (Oxford: Oxford University Press, 1987); Carl Wellman, *Real Rights* (Oxford University Press, 1995).

20. For a discussion of the conditions for the enjoyment of rights see James W. Nickel, *Making Sense of Human Rights* (Berkeley: University of California Press, 1987), 100–105, 135–36. See also Henry Shue, *Basic Rights* (Princeton: Princeton University Press, 1980).

21. Will Kymlicka seeks to reassure those who worry that the leaders of ethnic groups will sometimes use the power given them by group rights to violate the individual rights of their members by drawing a distinction between group rights that make claims on a group's own members and ones that make claims against the larger society (*Multicultural Citizenship,* p. 35). The former seek to "protect the group from the destabilizing impact of *internal dissent* . . . "while the latter seek to "protect the group from the impact of *external decisions.*" Kymlicka does not wish to defend "internal restrictions," but thinks that these can be distinguished from group rights against the larger society.

There are two reasons to think that Kymlicka's strategy will fail in some cases. First, in order to protect the group from the impact of external decisions it may be necessary to give its leaders powers that they can use, de facto, to oppress internal political dissent. If the group is made into a more durable entity with more effective agency it is likely to have more effective power to oppress its members. Political powers can be used for many purposes other than those that justify them. This is one reason for insisting that when group agency is created to make possible the exercise of group rights it should be democratically accountable agency. Second, if there are truly compelling reasons for granting rights to a group, those reasons are likely to generate obligations not just for outsiders but for insiders as well. For example, if the very survival of an indigenous group is at stake, this is likely to generate claims not just on outsiders to take steps to protect the group (e.g., by granting it a secure, demarcated territory, with powers of limited self-government), but also on insiders to not abandon the group by leaving to join the mainstream society. These claims on insiders may come close to restricting "basic civil and political liberties of group members." For a discussion of a (hypothetical) Brazilian Indian's claim to freedom of association versus his duties of loyalties to his group, see Nickel, "Ethnocide and Indigenous Peoples," 96.

# 10

# COMMON-LAW CONSTRUCTIONS
# OF GROUP AUTONOMY:
# A CASE STUDY

## DENISE G. RÉAUME

In 1843, a minority of the Church of Scotland seceded and formed the Free Church of Scotland. So traumatic was this schism, that it is referred to in Presbyterian lore as "The Disruption." The new Church put out a call to its supporters to raise funds to build new churches for congregations and new manses for ministers who had been turned out of their old properties. By the end of the nineteenth century, the Free Church comprised eight hundred churches and owned three universities and had investments worth over one million pounds. Toward the close of the century, discussions were entered into on the subject of union with the United Presbyterian Church, another dissenting Church, and in due course, the two bodies were joined to form the United Free Church. This precipitated the Free Church's own version of The Disruption.[1] A very small minority of Free Church members took the view that the union with the United Presbyterian Church violated fundamental doctrinal tenets on the basis of which the Free Church had been formed, indeed had been its reasons for seceding from the Church of Scotland. Two such tenets were at issue: adherence to the Establishment principle, that is, the view that the Church is entitled to state endowment and that the state has a duty to promote the true faith; and acceptance of the

Calvinistic doctrine of predestination. In *General Assembly of the Free Church of Scotland v. Overtoun,*[2] the House of Lords decided in favor of the rump Free Church, a group comprising roughly thirty ministers and their congregations, declaring them to be the exclusive beneficiaries of all Free Church property.[3]

Earlier, in 1864, a similar dispute had arisen over control of the Walnut Street Presbyterian Church in Louisville, Kentucky. In the midst of the Civil War, the General Assembly of the Presbyterian Church of the United States issued various declarations and resolutions obliging the members to support the federal government and denounce slavery. The Presbytery of Louisville, the governing body immediately above the individual congregations in the Louisville area, took issue with this position and issued a counter declaration that the General Assembly's pronouncements were "erroneous and heretical."[4] This segment of the Church took the view that "the system of negro slavery in the South is a divine institution, and that it is the peculiar mission of the Southern church to conserve that institution."[5] A majority of the elders and trustees of the Walnut Street Church sided with the proslavery forces in this dispute; the majority of the congregation took the antislavery side. Thus began the struggle for control of the Walnut Street Church. The dispute was ultimately resolved by the United States Supreme Court in *Watson v. Jones*[6] in favour of the antislavery group, the majority in the local congregation.

In these cases, a dispute *within* a religious community over religious matters has led one side to appeal to the secular authorities—an adjudicative body outside the community—for a resolution of that dispute. The civil courts are appealed to because the dispute has secular consequences—beneficial ownership of church property. But for the litigants, the meaning of the dispute goes far beyond these secular consequences. These disputes are typically grounded in competing interpretations of articles of faith, of important principles of religious doctrine or church governance.[7] At stake is the identity of the religious community itself—what it stands for.

The resolution of these sorts of internal disputes can be examined as an exercise in the definition of the group's autonomy. A conception of group autonomy seems to me to be integral to the idea of a group right. A claim to a group right is, at least in part, a claim to autonomy: that the group be allowed to pursue and develop its own practices, norms, ways of doing things even when these do not conform to those of the mainstream or the majority. Some minority group claims are dealt with through various forms of institutional separation between two communities coexisting in the same state: federal systems of government, or more locally, separate institutional structures to operate schools organized along denominational or linguistic lines are just two examples of this strategy. These solutions are constructed legislatively, with the larger political unit, the state, creating institutions and defining powers through which particular communities within that state can exercise some degree of autonomy.

The church property dispute cases illustrate another occasion for the legal recognition or definition of the autonomy of a minority group, but since the state has not created the group in issue or set up its institutional structures the courts must turn to common law techniques in order to resolve these disputes.[8] Churches come into being without help or input from the state. Indeed they often prize their independence from the state. They initially define themselves; groups of people come together around a certain set of beliefs, sometimes forming their own institutions to regulate the conduct of communal affairs. Religious communities are by no means unique in this respect, and I use them here as an example of social groups that are self-defining and wish to maintain their autonomy. When a dispute erupts within such a community and ends up before the civil courts, the judges are confronted with a normative framework they may not share or even initially understand. Unlike the situation of a dispute over group powers which are themselves the creation of the state, in resolving a dispute within a religious community the court is an outsider.

There are many contexts in which common-law decision making effectively determines the scope of a minority group's autonomy to live according to its own norms. It happens any time conduct which is alleged to be acceptable according to the standards of the minority community is scrutinized according to common-law standards which, in effect, are those of the wider society. If the minority community's practice is judged to be unlawful, it becomes more difficult at best, impossible at worst, for the community to carry on according to its own lights. Rarely are these cases analyzed as implicating minority group autonomy, and a full analysis of all these contexts is beyond the scope of this chapter. In cases involving church property disputes, however, the group autonomy issue is harder to avoid because these cases frequently confront the courts with questions about the core identity of the group. This often prompts judges to acknowledge their status as outsiders to the religious context of the dispute and to confront the implications of that status.

If group autonomy is a value,[9] it would seem to follow that, in principle, internal disputes should be resolved internally. But what does this mean when one party within a minority group has appealed for outside help? One might think the most obvious posture to adopt in such cases would be the Pontius Pilate approach[10]—to decline to get involved at all and therefore to treat the dispute as nonjusticiable. Although courts do occasionally respond this way and it may sometimes be appropriate to do so, the Pontius Pilate approach is unsatisfactory as a comprehensive solution to disputes within minority groups. If a dispute is entirely theological and has no secular consequences,[11] the courts may safely and perhaps wisely refuse to get involved. However, when the ownership of property is at issue, or the religious community has made use of a legal instrument such as trust[12] or contract[13] to organize its affairs, for the courts to wash their hands of the dispute would be to abdicate their responsibility to administer the law. A hands-off approach would therefore deny to these groups the ability to use various legal tools with the same facility that others do, able to rely on the adjudicative mechanism provided by the state. Furthermore, to refuse to intervene in all cases would sometimes have the effect of ratifying the exercise of raw power within the group rather than protecting an autonomous normative system. The faction that happened to have the upper hand—for example, *de facto* control over church property—would have its position reinforced whether or not its behavior conformed to the norms of the group. There may be arguments in favor of a generalized Pontius Pilate approach, but they are unlikely to rely primarily on a desire to promote minority group autonomy. At least they are unlikely to do so unless one holds the view that the group's norms simply are whatever the most powerful party within the group says they are.

Without deciding whether and under what circumstances the Pontius Pilate approach should be adopted, I am more interested, for present purposes, in exploring the alternatives and their implications if courts do decide to get involved. I use these two church property disputes to begin exploring these possible legal responses to group autonomy claims in a common-law context. To anyone attracted to the Pontius Pilate approach it might seem counterintuitive to attempt to analyze any judicial intervention in these cases as autonomy protecting. However, I hope to articulate a conception of group autonomy which is consistent with certain forms of intervention. This exercise will reveal the conditions under which a church can enjoy the maximum amount of autonomy consistent with existence within a larger political entity. Although my example involves religious groups, my conclusions have implications for all the different kinds of minority groups existing within any culturally and religiously diverse society.

## THE LEGAL FRAMEWORK: ALTERNATIVE CONCEPTUALIZATIONS OF TRUST LAW DOCTRINE

Both the *Free Church* case and *Watson* are grounded in trust law: church property is almost always donated to a church in trust. But the courts' interpretations of the respective trusts in issue differ markedly, and out of this arise two different doctrinal approaches to church property disputes. With these differing interpretations go different attitudes about judicial involvement in the substantive religious dispute. It is the implications of these doctrinal and attitudinal differences for minority group autonomy that I want to explore. In the process, I shall argue that the doctrinal differences between these two cases have been exaggerated. The two cases can be read to differ not on the law but on the facts of the respective disputes before the courts.

### A. *The Interpretivist Approach—The* Free Church *Case*

In the *Free Church* case, all members of the House of Lords were united in the view that trust property must be used in conformity with the intentions of the original donors. Hence, if one faction remains true to the founding principles of the Church for whose purposes the donation was made while the other has deviated from those principles, the former is the beneficial owner and properly represents the Church.[14] This required the Court to determine what were the founding principles of the Free Church.

Their Lordships used the device of the original donors' intentions to frame their interpretive endeavor. This should not be understood as a matter of simply reading the founders' views off from an unambiguous historical record. The donations in issue came from many thousands of individuals over the fifty-year history of the Church before the dispute broke out. To think that all of these donors were of one mind in their understanding of the character of the Church is clearly implausible. The idea of the donors' intentions, then, becomes a metaphor for the enterprise of interpreting this Church from the Church's own point of view. This is clearest in the speech of Lord Robertson who attributed to the donors the intention to give property "to the Free Church, an existing Church, complete within itself as an ecclesiastical organism."[15] It is the determination of the character of that ecclesiastical organism that is doing all the work in this analysis. Thus the House of Lords approach is an interpretivist one, since their Lordships understood their task to be to interpret the norms of the Free Church on their own terms.

Appealing to historical evidence the majority concluded that the Establishment principle was of foundational importance to the key figures who led the secession from the Church of Scotland, such as Thomas Chalmers. They also denied that there was any explicit or implicit power in the Church, as understood by its founders, to change such fundamental principles. Thus, in the hands of the majority judges, the donor intention approach had the effect of freezing Free Church theological and church governance doctrine as of the time of the split from the Church of Scotland.[16] Thereafter, a member was free to change her mind about the meaning or importance of basic tenets, but necessarily relinquished membership in the group in doing so. In ceasing to be a member one also ceased to be a beneficiary of trust property set aside for the purposes of the Church. Their Lordships therefore held that, in joining with the United Presbyterian Church the majority group had converted the church property, over which it had actual control, to the use of the United Free Church, a body that was not committed to the Establishment principle. This constituted a breach of the trust.

## B. *The Deferential Approach*—Watson v. Jones

While also using the umbrella of trust law, Miller J. in *Watson* was very critical of the approach of the English courts as the sole, or even the main, framework for dealing with church property disputes.[17] He held that the interpretivist approach should be confined very narrowly to cases in which a donation had been made expressly for the propagation of "*some specific form* of religious doctrine or belief."[18] In all other cases, he held that the trust should be regarded as one for the general purposes of the religious congregation. This allows the use of the law of voluntary associations to determine whether a particular course of action falls within the general purposes of the church. On this approach, the courts need only ascertain the decision-making body within the Church properly charged with responsibility over the matter in dispute and defer to its decision. Any decision by such a body is deemed to be consistent with the general purposes of the church. In the case of a Church organized on hierarchical lines, the court should defer to the decision of the highest of the Church judicatories to have considered the issue. In the case of a Church in which individual congregations are independent of one another and owe no fealty to any higher Church authorities, the courts should follow the usual decision-making procedures of the congregation—majority vote of the congregation or elected elders, for example.

Individual congregations in the Presbyterian Church are run by elected elders. The original dispute in *Watson* arose out of the fact that a majority of the elected elders of the Walnut Street Church was proslavery while a majority of the congregation was antislavery. The congregation asked the elders not to "call" a particular proslavery minister to serve the congregation, but their wishes were ignored by majority vote of the elders. The congregation appealed to higher authorities who purported to hold an election of additional elders. The antislavery side was the majority of this enlarged body of elders. The original (proslavery) majority refused to acknowledge the authority of the additional elders. In return, the General Assembly ultimately expelled the proslavery factions in the Presbytery and Synod. Miller J.'s resolution of the dispute consisted of deferring to the decision to appoint new antislavery elders to the Walnut Street congregation and ultimately to expel the proslavery elders. This led to the conclusion that the respondents, the antislavery group, were the sole beneficiaries of the Walnut Street Church property. Miller J.'s approach avoids the static interpretation of the trust seen in the *Free Church* case; instead the trust is interpreted in line with decisions made from time to time by church authorities.

## C. Church Identity and Trust Doctrine

The interpretivist and deferential approaches in these cases are in turn tied to different understandings of the identity of the respective churches. By bringing this to the surface we get closer to the crux of the differences between the two approaches.

The House of Lords clearly framed the *Free Church* case as a dispute over the criteria identifying the Free Church of Scotland. Both sides were claiming to be *the* Free Church, properly understood. As the Lord Chancellor put it, "[the new body's] identity with the Free Church . . . is disputed; and it accordingly becomes necessary to consider *in what consists the identity* of the body designated by the donors of the fund as the Free Church of Scotland."[19] According to their Lordships, the Free Church was to be identified by reference to some body of beliefs. In Lord James's words, "the Church is not a positive, defined entity, as would be the case if it were a corporation created by law. It is a body of men united only by the possession of common opinions, and if this community of opinion ceases to exist, the foundations of the Church give way."[20] The Court took the view that it had to determine what "opinions" were constitutive of the Free Church in order to determine which side was rightfully entitled to be called the Free Church. This in turn determined which group was entitled to the use of property set aside for the use of the Free Church.

By contrast, Miller J.'s approach avoids having to identify the Presbyterian Church by reference to substantive beliefs. In deciding that trusts for "the general purposes of the congregation" require the courts to defer to an internal decision-making body to determine what the group's purposes are, Miller J., in effect, identified the church by reference to the formal rules that constitute its decision-making structure. Somewhat obliquely, he remarked,

> Here is no case of property devoted forever by the instrument which conveyed it . . . to the support of any special religious dogmas, . . . but of property purchased for the use of a religious congregation, and so long as any existing religious congregation can be ascertained to be that congregation, or its regular and legitimate successor, it is entitled to the use of the property.[21]

Identifying the congregation "admits of no inquiry into the existing religious opinions of those who comprise the legal or regular organization."[22] Therefore, who represents the Walnut Street congregation or its regular and legitimate successor must be determined by reference to the power of higher church authorities to appoint elders and expel members. Taken to the level of the Presbyterian Church as a whole, this view implicitly holds that the Church consists of that group of persons who adhere to the rules and pronouncements of the General Assembly, whatever they may be from time to time. Therefore, by their very act of disobedience, the appellants had, in effect, renounced their membership.[23]

Both courts see the issue as that of the criteria by which to identify the group. In other words, each church's basic constitution was in issue,[24] for a constitution is simply that collection of rules which define an organization. But each court fastens upon different identity criteria. The House of Lords, in deciding that the Free Church *is* those who subscribe to certain beliefs, including the Establishment principle, defined the Free Church by reference to substantive church governance or theological principles. The U.S. Supreme Court, in deciding that the Walnut Street Church *is* those so recognized by the General Assembly, defined the Presbyterian Church by reference to its formal decision-making structures.

This difference makes sense of the central doctrinal difference between the two cases. If the Free Church is constituted, inter alia, by an unalterable belief in the Establishment principle, the House of Lords had no choice but to make its own judgment about which side remained true to that principle. This is the only way to make sense of the outcome in light of the extensive and lengthy debates within the Free Church on the question of union with the United Presbyterians. Extensive preparations for union had been undertaken, each step approved by overwhelming majorities in the General Assembly. The final vote in favor of union was equally strong.[25] The will of the vast majority of Free Church members could only be so blithely ignored on the view that the Establishment principle is a substantive principle having ultimate constitutional force and therefore immune to majority vote. Conversely, it is only because Miller J. saw the Presbyterian Church as constituted by its formal decision-making rules that it was possible for him to defer to an internal decision-making body. To say that the church is the policies and rules prescribed by the General Assembly is to say that only the General Assembly can decide who controls a particular local congregation.

The key difference between the *Free Church* case and *Watson,* the difference between substantive and formal identity criteria, comes into sharper relief by looking more closely at the losing side of the argument within each case. The juxtaposition of the alternative conceptualizations of these disputes offered by the losing sides with the majority judgments in these cases reveals more clearly that the different views really hinge on the view taken of the constitution of the church in question.

In the *Free Church* case, the dissenting judges accepted the interpretive technique of discerning the original donors' intentions, but interpreted those intentions so as to incorporate dynamic processes for the evolution and reinterpretation of Church practices. Lord MacNaghten, for example, took issue with the majority's treatment as a kind of prospectus of a speech by Dr. Chalmers in support of the secession. Donors gave to the Church, he said, not as a

> Sect or a Persuasion or a Connection, *with peculiar tenets cut and dried and defined in the precise language of a conveyancer.* . . . [T]hey supported the character of the National Church of Scotland. And supporting that character, . . . they must be taken . . . to have all the powers of a National Church.[26]

This status entails that the church have the power to revise and amend its doctrine. In addition, he argued that the Free Church must have the power to change any of the articles of the Confession of Faith (the "Westminster Confession") that it finds to be unscriptural because any other rule would make the Confession and not the Bible the ultimate authority. Lord Lindley, taking up a similar line of argument,[27] ended up with a comparatively formal and dynamic interpretation of the original trust:

> A trust for the Free Church is ... a trust for such persons as shall hold the doctrines and submit in ecclesiastical matters to the government and discipline adopted by the founders of the Free Church, with such modifications as may be made from time to time by the General Assembly of that Church, provided the conditions required by the Barrier Act are observed, and provided the Church is preserved as a Reformed Church with Presbyterian government.[28]

Thus the dissenting judges' interpretation of the donors' intentions led them to an interpretation of Church practice that permits change of doctrine, such power lying in the General Assembly. It follows on this analysis that the General Assembly's decision in favor of the union is determinative of the issue whether use of the trust property for the benefit of the United Free Church is within the terms of the trust. Even though using the approach Miller J. disparaged, the dissenting judges in the *Free Church* case interpreted the trust as being for an organization that includes extensive legislative powers to change its own rules. While their doctrinal starting point differs from Miller J.'s in *Watson,* their substantive conclusion is the same.

Similarly, the appellants' argument in *Watson* resonates strongly with the interpretation of the majority judges in the *Free Church* case. The appellants interpreted the trust as dedicating church property for the use of the Church *subject to* the entire body of doctrines, rules, or principles recognized by the Church at the time of the conveyance. On this analysis, every breach of a Church rule is a violation of the trust because the terms of the trust are identical with the entire constitution of the Church. Thus, expelling the appellants for reasons that violate Church principles constituted denying access to trust property to those who are properly beneficiaries. And since it is the civil courts' obligation to enforce the terms of a trust, the court would have no choice but to engage in the process of interpreting the Church's constitution to decide whether the church authorities had acted in accordance with their own rules.

More importantly, it is clear from the appellants' argument on the merits of the religious controversy in issue that they saw the principles they thought had been violated as substantive principles that operated in a fashion similar to that of provisions in a Bill of Rights. Although they acknowledged the existence of legislative and adjudicative mechanisms for Church governance, these powers were regarded as subordinate to the Church's overarching substantive principles, the "fundamental laws of the organization."[29] The proslavery faction argued that it was contrary to the most fundamental principles of the Presbyterian Church to "pledg[e] herself, in her ecclesiastical capacity, to an unabated loyalty to the civil government."[30] This view was said to derive from "those sacred standards [of the Church] which declare that the 'visible church, which is also catholic or universal (and *not confined to one nation* as before, under the law), consists of all those throughout the world that profess the true religion' whereof 'there is no other head but the Lord Jesus Christ.' "[31] On the appellants' view, the conflict in this case raised the second branch of the debate over the relationship between church and state that occupied various churches throughout the nineteenth century. If the *Free Church* case was about the centrality of the state's duty to support the church, the controversy which gave rise to the litigation in *Watson* was about the church's duty to maintain its independence from state interference. The appellants thought that the General Assembly's pronouncements regarding slavery constituted a subjection of the Church to federal government policy.

Thus, like the majority of the House of Lords in the *Free Church* case, the appellants in *Watson* argued that at least some of the church's rules took the form of substantive rules directly prescribing certain beliefs and consequent behavior and that these were beyond the power of any authority within the church to change, even beyond any church authority's power to render final decisions about their correct interpretation. Indeed, the appellants argued that failure to recognize the fundamental place of some substantive rules would "sweep . . . away all limitations imposed upon church courts by their fundamental laws and render . . .

it impossible that churches can be organized under rules and limitations which shall bind the judicatories of their own creation."[32] On this interpretation, a court would have to determine the status and meaning of the substantive principle alleged to have such fundamental importance in order to decide whether the General Assembly's actions were consistent with the general purposes of the Presbyterian Church.

### IDENTITY CRITERIA OF GROUPS: TWO MODELS OF AUTONOMY PROTECTION

Miller J. explicitly adopted a deferential approach in order to avoid involvement in the substantive religious dispute, and justified this by reference to protecting the Church's autonomy. He appealed to autonomy both directly and indirectly. First, he argued,

> if the civil courts are to inquire into all these matters, the whole subject of the doctrinal theology, the usages and customs, the written laws, and fundamental organization of every religious denomination may, and must, be examined into with minuteness and care, for they would become, in almost every case, the *criteria* by which the validity of the ecclesiastical decree would be determined in the civil court. This principle would deprive these bodies of the right of construing their own church laws.[33]

More indirectly, he argued that the complexity of the substantive issues makes internal authorities more competent than the civil courts to settle them.

> Each of these large and influential bodies . . . has a body of constitutional and ecclesiastical law of its own, to be found in their written organic laws, their books of discipline, in their collections of precedents, in their usage and customs, which as to each constitute a system of ecclesiastical law and religious faith that tasks the ablest minds to become familiar with. It is not to be supposed that the judges of the civil courts can be as competent in the ecclesiastical law and religious faith of all these bodies as the ablest men in each are in reference to their own.[34]

On the assumption that it is more consistent with the group's autonomy that disputes about its rules and practices be resolved correctly, if the courts have a choice between letting a more and a less expert body decide, the desirability of fostering the group's autonomy dictates the former course.

The House of Lords exhibited no particular qualms about passing judgment on the substantive importance of the Establishment principle in the Free Church's self-understanding. Indeed, each of the seven separate judgments—the total running to 112 pages—carefully sifted through the mass of Church history and legislation put before the court to discern their implications for the validity of the union with the United Presbyterian Church. This included detailed discussion of the meaning of the Westminster Confession of Faith in respect of its statement of the duties owed by the civil magistrate to the Church. Two of their Lordships went on to consider more generally whether the centrality of the Confession had been compromised by certain terms of the union.[35] The Lord Chancellor extended his analysis even further to interpret the doctrine of predestination[36] contained in the Confession in order to respond to the argument that the union represented a departure from the Calvinistic doctrine of predestination and in this respect too violated fundamental Church principles. The intricacies of the argument resembled nothing so much as a complex conventional constitutional dispute.

Miller J. thought it would be the inevitable result of the adoption of the interpretivist approach that courts would be drawn into substantive religious disputes with negative consequences for church autonomy.[37] He saw the choice of the deferential model as the only means available to prevent this. Likewise, prominent commentators critical of the House of Lords' decision accused the court of infringing upon church autonomy.[38] The members of the majority in the House of Lords certainly did unabashedly get involved in interpreting the fundamental principles of the Free Church. However, I think it is too quick to see this as detrimental to church autonomy. Conversely, Miller J. too quickly assumes that deference is necessarily autonomy supporting.

Although no explicit mention was made of the Church's autonomy as a value to be fostered or as possibly threatened by the House of Lords' approach, I would argue that evidence of their Lordships' commitment to religious autonomy is found in their repeated assertions that it is not the place of the courts to pass judgment on the soundness or desirability of the contested principles,[39] but to decide according to their best understanding of the norms and practices of the Free Church. Typical is the following statement of Lord Davey:

> I disclaim altogether any right in this or any other Civil Court of this realm to discuss the truth or reasonableness of any of the doctrines of this or any other religious association, or to say whether any of them are or are not based on a just interpretation of the language of Scripture, or whether the contradictions or antinomies between different statements of doctrine are or are not real or apparent only, or whether such contradictions do or do not proceed only from an imperfect and finite conception of a perfect and infinite Being, or any similar question. The more humble, but not useless, function of the civil Court is to determine whether the trusts imposed upon property by the founders of the trust are being duly observed . . .
>
> The question in each case is, What were the religious tenets and principles which formed the bond of union of the association for whose benefit the trust was created? I do not think that the Court has any test or touchstone by which it can pronounce that any tenet forming part of the body of doctrine professed by the association is not vital, essential, or fundamental, unless the parties have themselves declared it not to be so.[40]

Understanding how the interpretivist approach can be seen as a means of protecting group autonomy rather than as an attack on it requires a deeper analysis of the idea of the identity criteria or constitution of a body such as a church. Interpreting the constitution of a church or uncovering its identity criteria can be analyzed as an attempt to articulate what H. L. A. Hart called the "rule of recognition" of each organization.[41] Hart used this idea to analyze a legal system, but I want to argue that it provides a useful framework for thinking about organizations and their normative structure more generally, whether or not they should be attributed with the status of a legal system. The rule of recognition is the main ingredient of the church's constitution, since it is the means by which the primary rules of obligation are identified as rules *of this group*. As Hart argued, the rule of recognition of a group may also contain or be intimately linked with secondary rules of change and adjudication. These secondary rules would specify the procedures for changing or authoritatively interpreting existing rules. Where there are such rules they become part of the criteria for identifying primary rules of obligation.

An organization, including a religious group, can be constituted either by reference exclusively to primary rules or by reference to both primary and secondary rules. Even in a system that consists of both types of rules, most, if not all, religions look upon some of their rules, whether primary or secondary, as having constitutional force that puts them beyond change. In the case of a religious group that is constituted exclusively by reference to primary rules, every dispute is over a foundational, substantive principle. The successful side in the Free Church litigation attributed this status to the Establishment principle interpreted as a primary rule of obligation: to be a member in good standing in the Free Church, one had to believe that it was the duty of the state to endow the Church. But even Lord Lindley, who would have decided the case the other way, thought the Free Church could change everything *except* its character as a Reformed church and its presbyterian form of government, and Lord MacNaghten argued that the Westminster Confession was amenable to change, but only because it was the Bible that was truly foundational.

In *Watson,* by deferring to the General Assembly as the appropriate ecclesiastical authority, and refusing to consider the appellants' argument that the General Assembly's pronouncements violated fundamental church principles, Miller J. effectively recognized the General Assembly as having the power to interpret its own fundamental principles. That is, he interpreted the church's constitution to have a secondary rule of adjudication conferring power on the General Assembly authoritatively to interpret the most fundamental primary rules of the church.

This analysis of the church property dispute cases differs from Lon Fuller's, and puts us in a better position to understand the autonomy implications of these decisions. Fuller distinguished between two different "principles of association" according to (some combination of) which a group can be organized: association on the basis of shared commitment, and on the basis of legal principle.[42] He argued that the approach to church property disputes represented by the *Free Church* case is grounded in an understanding of the church as an association based on shared commitment, while the *Watson* approach treats the church as an association based on legal principle. The distinction between these two principles of association is less than clear. By shared commitment Fuller seems to have in mind the substantive beliefs, values, or purposes to which the group is committed; while association according to legal principle "refers to the situation where an association is held together and enabled to function by formal rules of duty and entitlement."[43] The distinction seems to be between commitments conceived of in aspirational terms ("one fully lives up to one's status as a member if . . . "), and rules prescribing behaviour ("members must . . . ").

The distinction seems to me a false one. An organization that is committed to certain beliefs or purposes will necessarily have at least implicit rules flowing from those commitments that regulate the conduct of its members by imposing duties and establishing entitlements.[44] These substantive commitments and the rules flowing from them are two sides of the same coin. All churches are, indeed, associations based on shared commitment, but this does not mean they have no rules of duty and entitlement. Nor does a basis in shared commitment in itself dictate that the courts must adopt an approach like that in the *Free Church* case. Shared commitment might include commitment to internal procedures for changing and interpreting the group's rules. It was the absence of *this kind* of commitment and the attendant rules of change and adjudication that led the majority of the House of Lords to resolve the dispute by direct reference to which side was more faithful to substantive principles like the Establishment clause.

Perhaps Fuller's distinction was meant, instead, to draw attention to the importance of the difference between having a *formal* rule structure and not. However, this does not describe the difference between the Free Church and the Presbyterian Church of the United States either. It was not the fact that the Presbyterian Church has formal rules of duty and entitlement that enabled the court in *Watson* to defer to internal bodies, but the fact that it was understood to have formal secondary rules conferring power to change or interpret the church's primary rules establishing duties and entitlements. Nor can it be argued that the Free Church had no formal rules of duty and entitlement; it was merely thought to have no applicable formal secondary rule. Both churches had substantive commitments and formal rules of duty and entitlement; only one was thought to have applicable secondary rules of change and adjudication.

We can see now that the distinction between an interpretivist approach and a deferential one is somewhat misleading. On my reading of these two cases, there is no real difference in doctrinal approach; only in the constitutional structure of the two churches. In both cases, the court is interpreting the constitution of the church on its own terms. The House of Lords' interpretation of the Free Church's constitution led it to undertake a substantive interpretation of certain principles of church governance having theological overtones; the American Supreme Court's interpretation of the Presbyterian Church's constitution led it to discover an internal decision maker to whom it could defer.

## THE RELATIVE AUTONOMY OF MINORITY GROUPS

The question of whether the deferential or interpretive approach to resolving these disputes is more protective of the autonomy of the group takes on a new cast in light of this analysis. I argue that these two approaches represent complementary strategies for respecting minority group autonomy rather than contradictory valuations of that autonomy.

If a group's constitution consists only of primary rules of obligation, or includes at least some primary rules that have constitutional force putting them beyond change, respect for the group's own normative structure means regulating the dispute according to these rules rather than some external body of wisdom. A dispute over the application or meaning of one of these primary rules requires a court that values the group's autonomy to undertake an interpretation of this substantive rule. If the group has no secondary rules of change and adjudication at all, there will be no internal decision-making body to defer to, and the impropriety of the deferential approach will be obvious. Even if the group's constitution does include secondary rules of change and adjudication, to defer to internal bodies without ascertaining whether the substantive rule or principle in issue is beyond the reach of these internal bodies merely begs the central question in the dispute. It is hard to see how that could be regarded as protective of the group's autonomy.

Sometimes, therefore, autonomy can only be respected through the judges' efforts to interpret the Church's practices and beliefs according to its own substantive norms. This requires the judge to imaginatively enter into the group's internal religious point of view, and puts the adjudicator in a position comparable to that of an Ontario judge who, in order to decide a dispute governed by New York law, must decide as though she were a New York judge, treating the foreign law as a matter of fact. There is plenty of evidence from the judgments in the *Free Church* case that all the judges saw their task in something like this light. The device of the original donor's intention is the vehicle for that imaginative enterprise, just as the legislative intent of a foreign legislator might be in a civil suit that crosses jurisdictional boundaries. Similarly, some of the judges were at pains to point out that it was not their job to pass judgment on the theological soundness of a disputed religious practice, but merely to determine as a matter of fact what the community's practice was, just as judges deciding cases according to foreign law need not consider the wisdom of the law of a foreign jurisdiction but merely determine what that law is as a matter of fact.

But there is one very important difference between the invocation of this model of reasoning in the context of resolving an intragroup dispute within the court's civil jurisdiction, and in the context of a dispute having an international dimension. When an Ontario judge puts herself in the shoes of a New York judge to decide a case according to New York law, the decision will bind the two private parties to the dispute, but not the law makers— judicial or legislative—of New York. If the Ontario judge should get it wrong, from the point of view of the New York judge who decides the next similar case, her interpretation will simply be ignored.

By contrast, when the House of Lords decided, according to its understanding of Free Church principles, what the fundamental beliefs of the Free Church were, its decision affected for the future the constitution, and therefore the character, of the Free Church. The majority of the House of Lords, in interpreting the Free Church's practices as it did, cemented the Church's character as a fundamentalist institution. Had the dissenting opinions prevailed, the impact on the future of the Free Church would have been just as profound in the opposite direction. There is no point of view from which the civil courts' decisions can be authoritatively determined to be wrong—there are only squabbling internal factions whose points of view contradict one another. Once the courts have pronounced upon a fundamental feature of a particular Church, any departure from that principle in future is likely to be challenged by some internal group who thinks that departure unjustified. From the point of view of the judge who is not even a member of the religious group in crisis, the decision can be thought of as a matter of determining the facts about the community's practices; but from the point of view of the community, the civil courts have become its judicial system. Their decisions become the church's laws. In other words, the very fact of deciding an intragroup dispute creates a secondary rule of adjudication for the group, a rule that makes the civil courts the ultimate interpretive authority over the group's rules and practices.

On the other hand, if a minority group's constitution is such as to include secondary rules of change and adjudication which create internal bodies or processes with the authority to change preexisting rules and resolve disputes about the rules, it is possible to recognize the group's autonomy by recognizing its ability, through these internal decision-making bodies, to interpret its own norms for itself. This represents the greatest degree of autonomy. Not only is the group assured that its norms will be applied within its sphere of activity, but the interpretation and application of those norms will be controlled internally. Insofar as the group's belief system and institutional structures are complex enough to give rise to indeterminacy and the possibility of competing interpretations of the norms, the power to decide for itself the meaning of its own norms will make it more self-governing.

However, even the deferential approach still requires the courts to make an authoritative determination about whether the group's internal decision-making structures have jurisdiction over the substantive issue in dispute. Thus, even on this approach, the group's autonomy is not unlimited. Furthermore, while acknowledging internal authority over "ecclesiastical matters," the civil courts must also police the boundary between ecclesiastical and nonecclesiastical matters.[45] What counts as an ecclesiastical matter cannot be determined from the point of view of the Church without making it totally sovereign and thus opening up the possibility of irreconcilable conflict between one religious organization and another or between a religious group and the state itself.

In light of this analysis, the decisions in both the *Free Church* case and *Watson* are open to challenge. In interpreting the donors' intentions along essentially static lines, the majority judges in the *Free Church* case are insufficiently clear about whether they are interpreting "Religion," in the abstract, or the Free Church, in particular. The Lord Chancellor and Lords James and Alverstone can easily be read as laying down a generally fundamentalist conception of religion, at least with respect to what are found to be the religion's "fundamental" or "essential" principles. Lords Davey and Robertson seemed more willing to recognize that it is possible for a religion to include powers of fundamental revision, but thought that the Free Church was not such an organization. The ambiguity is unfortunate because at stake is the autonomy of religious groups. For the courts to assume that religion must be fundamentalist in nature denies religious communities the power to define for themselves the nature of their spiritual enterprise. Thus, in the final analysis it is unclear whether the majority members of the House of Lords' really had the autonomy interests of the Church at heart, or whether they were imposing their own conception of religion. Respect for autonomy requires making a determination about the character of each particular religious group on its own terms.

Ironically, the same argument can be directed against many of the critics of the House of Lords' decision who claimed that the decision impinged upon the autonomy of the Church. The focus of criticism tended to be on the static nature of the court's interpretation. For F. W. Maitland, with the decision "the dead hand fell with a resounding slap upon the living body."[46] Laski[47] and Figgis[48] took an equally dim view of the decision but went one step further in conflating criticism of the court's static interpretation with the charge that the autonomy of the church was violated. I am inclined to think that these critics were right to say that churches must be allowed to develop and grow, but it is too quick to assume that every religious organization must be founded on a fluid understanding of its basic doctrine and principles. Instead, this must be a question of fact to be determined on a case by case basis if the objective in resolving these disputes within minority groups includes respecting the autonomy of the group. The House of Lords may have wrongly treated religion as though it were necessarily a fundamentalist enterprise, but it is no advance from the perspective of autonomy to assume that there are no fundamentalist religions.[49]

Miller J., too, can be accused of a mistake equal and opposite to that of assuming that religion is necessarily fundamentalist. One interpretation of the appellants' argument in *Watson* is that the General Assembly violated a primary rule of ultimate constitutional status in prescribing a communal view on slavery. On the argument that membership in the Presbyterian Church is ultimately determined by reference to the acceptance of certain beliefs, including the contested one, those who supported the General Assembly's antislavery resolutions effectively renounced their membership and therefore their beneficial interest in the church property. Rather than meeting this challenge head on, Miller J. skirted it and redescribed the dispute in a way amenable to resolution by deferring to an appropriate internal decision-maker. In doing so, Miller J. seems too quickly to assume that all religions will have secondary rules of change and adjudication that will deal with all disputes concerning "ecclesiastical matters." A Church may have secondary rules without their scope extending to give internal institutions power to change or interpret some fundamental rules. Miller J. assumed that if a Church has any secondary rules, it must have ones that claim competence with respect to all ecclesiastical matters, just as a legal system's legislative and adjudicative rules claim competence over all matters within a particular territorial jurisdiction. If I am right that the courts cannot evade decision-making responsibility when a fundamental primary rule of obligation is in dispute, Miller J.'s approach is no more autonomy respecting than the assumption that all religions are fundamentalist and understand themselves to have no powers to change or reinterpret their practices. Applied to a church that has a different self-understanding, the deferential approach simply ratifies the *de facto* control of the faction within the Church that has the most power at the time of the litigation.

Thus, just as in the *Free Church* case, we cannot conclusively say whether the decision in *Watson* actually respected the autonomy of the Presbyterian Church of the United States. Miller J. did not go into the terms of the Presbyterian Church constitution in sufficient detail to permit us to decide whether *its* primary rules (or some of them) are subordinate to its secondary rules (or some of them) or vice versa.

Miller J. claimed to ground the deferential approach in the importance of recognizing the group's autonomy to determine its own practices.[50] More recently his approach has been given a constitutional gloss in *Presbyterian Church in the United States v. Mary Elizabeth Blue Hull Memorial Presbyterian Church,* in which the U.S. Supreme Court held that the disestablishment clause "leaves the civil courts *no* role in determining ecclesiastical questions in the process of resolving property disputes."[51] The court held that it was therefore improper to resolve a property dispute by means of assessing whether one side or the other had deviated from preexisting doctrine. It is beyond the scope of this chapter to make a full assessment of whether this conclusion is required by the First Amendment. My central concern here is which approach is most consistent with the autonomy of minority groups. It has been the burden of my argument that deference to internal decision makers is not always autonomy respecting; indeed, when a fundamental substantive principle of the church's constitution is in issue, protection of group autonomy requires an interpretation of that principle to resolve the dispute. If, then, there is a First Amendment justification for the deferential approach as the sole method of resolving church property disputes, it must rely on a value other than autonomy.

I do not wish to minimize the difficulty or delicacy of the task of interpreting another group's rules, whether primary or secondary. We have already had a taste of this in our exploration of the arguments in the Free Church litigation. The pitfalls for a judge who does not share the belief system in issue are considerable. For example, Ross notes that the Lord Chancellor came in for a considerable amount of criticism in the aftermath of the *Free Church* case for having misunderstood the Calvinistic doctrine of predestination. Ross himself extends the criticism to the lawyers who argued the point.[52] The possibility also exists, as materialized in *Craigie v. Marshall*,[53] that the court will be unable to discern any doctrinal difference between the two sides. Nevertheless, if the courts wish to respect the autonomy of minority groups they have no choice but to endeavour to enter into the group's world view to the best of their ability. The difficulties of this enterprise do mean, however, that the autonomy of minority groups risks being impaired if a judge is ill-prepared or ill-disposed to undertake her task with empathy.

In any event, a minority group existing within a larger political entity can only be partially autonomous. Whether the courts are interpreting the secondary rules of the group or are required to extend their interpretive authority to the group's primary rules, the group loses some measure of control over its own affairs. This loss of autonomy is exacerbated by the existence of vague and indeterminate rules. The more indeterminate the group's rules are, the more discretion the adjudicator has to shape them in applying them. Even a Dworkinian judge fully dedicated to discerning the gravitational force of the group's own rules and principles will face choices in deciding what interpretation will make the system the best it can be. These choices open up the group's normative system to some degree of influence from a different normative sensibility. Thus a group with no internal decision-making structures and ambiguous primary rules necessarily has very porous normative boundaries. Every dispute is an occasion for external influence over the group's practices. Autonomy is a matter of degree. There is a sense in which a group that has chosen or affirmed a porous normative structure has the degree of autonomy it wants. For those groups who want a greater degree of autonomy, the answer is to lay down a reasonably clear set of secondary rules defining the powers of internal decision makers. The prounion side in the Free Church controversy learned this lesson well. At the 1905 General Assembly of United Free Church, resolutions were passed emphatically claiming "the power of legislating in all matters of doctrine, worship, discipline, and government of the Church, including therein the right from time to time to alter, change, add to, or modify her constitution and laws, subordinate standards, and Church formula, and to determine what these are."[54]

## CONCLUSION

I have suggested that a group's autonomy can be respected by adjudicating disputes according to what the outside adjudicator takes to be the best interpretation of the group's norms or by recognizing the group's internal authority to make, change and interpret its own norms, and that the correct approach in any given case depends upon the constitutional structure of the group. Since deference to an internal authority, where possible, gives the group a greater degree of autonomy, those organizations, religious or otherwise, having the most complete formal structure—in other words, their own legal system—will be best able to preserve their autonomy vis-à-vis the outside world when internal disputes erupt and some disgruntled internal minority turns to the civil courts for help. The more clear it is that the group is constituted by reference to secondary rules as well as primary rules and the more clearly defined the decision-making powers of internal bodies are, the easier it will be for courts to adopt the deferential approach of Miller J. The groups who will have the least control over their own destiny are those amounting to a customary social order, consisting only of primary rules. Disputes within such groups are necessarily struggles over fundamental, substantive characteristics of the group. Unless the civil courts adopt the Pontius Pilate approach to such groups, every rule or practice will ultimately be subject to the interpretive authority of outsiders.[55]

If we analogize the task of the outsider interpreting fundamental substantive characteristics of a group to that of the judge having to interpret foreign law, I think we can anticipate that judges will be most comfortable with this task if there is something "fact-like" about the group's practices and commitments. The more vague and ill-defined the principles in dispute are, the more it appears that the dispute cannot be resolved without the decision maker taking a normative stand on the truth or wisdom of the group's vision for itself, the less likely that judges will be willing to embark upon such a dangerous task. We have already seen Miller J.'s reservations about having to decide obscure theological points. There was also obvious relief amongst several of the judges in the *Free Church* case who were able to conclude that it was unnecessary to go into the question of whether the union violated the Church's commitment to a particular doctrine of predestination.[56] However difficult disputed questions of church governance such as the meaning of the Establishment Principle might be, and even though rooted in theological controversy, they are more like the kind of legal issue that courts are used to handling than pure theological debates.

While I have developed this argument in the context of struggles over church autonomy, these conclusions have implications for extending the idea of group autonomy to some of the wide array of groups contending for the commitment and loyalty of individual members of society. Most churches, at least most Christian churches, have an internal structure that renders disputes reasonably amenable to outside adjudication. By contrast, suppose a dispute over who properly represents an ethnic organization dedicated to the greater glory of the *volk* (whichever *volk* it might be). Faced with such a grossly indeterminate fundamental principle, a judge might be forgiven for prescinding from the substantive controversy and resorting to other criteria for its adjudication. This, however, would be to give up any effort to decide in a way most consistent with the group's autonomy. Insofar as ethnic organizations tend not to have well-defined normative structures, including internal decision-making authorities,[57] they will be least able to enjoy a robust form of autonomy. Their controversies will be settled either according to legal norms that may be quite foreign to the group's ethos, or, if judges refuse to get involved at all, according to the free play of internal power politics. Either way, the idea of a semiautonomous normative structure regulating the relations of members *inter se* will suffer.

## NOTES

I am grateful to Elizabeth Kiss and James Nickel for their comments on an earlier version of this chapter, as well as to Michael Pratt and Kathryn Turner for their patient and diligent research assistance.

1. For a detailed account of the history of the union debate within the Free Church, see Kenneth R. Ross, *Church and Creed in Scotland: The*

*Free Church Case 1900–1904 and Its Origins,* (Edinburgh: Rutherford House Books, 1988).

2. [1904] A.C. 515 (H.L. Sc.).

3. This outcome was ultimately overturned by legislation dividing the property between the two sides. Churches (Scotland) Act, 1905 (U.K.) 5 Edw. VII, c. 12.

4. *Watson v. Jones* 80 U.S. (13 Wall.) 679 (1871) (U.S.S.C.), at 691.

5. Ibid.

6. Ibid.

7. See Ross, supra, note 1, at 7–10.

8. These cases make an interesting starting point because they deal with a kind of conflict that has been with us consistently for some time and about which, therefore, the courts have developed some expertise. It will come as no surprise that the context that seems most productive of intragroup disputes is religion, and a considerable body of law has developed here. A note in the *Harvard Law Review* remarks that at the time of its writing there were roughly twenty-five reported church property dispute cases annually in the United States. "Judicial Intervention in Disputes over the Use of Church Property," *Harv. L. Rev.* 75 (1962), 1142 at 1142 n. 3.

9. I have argued for according some value to group autonomy in "Justice between Cultures: Autonomy and the Protection of Cultural Affiliation," *University of British Columbia Law Journal* 29 (1995): 117–41. Here I am less interested in the substantive arguments for group autonomy and more in the conceptual preconditions for it and the common-law techniques available to structure its boundaries. For this reason, I make no attempt to resolve the substantive moral conflicts that may arise when a group claim conflicts with individual rights of either group members or outsiders. I think there is something to learn about common-law means of defining autonomy by looking first to those cases in which no competing individual rights are at stake.

10. I am grateful to Elizabeth Kiss for suggesting this label.

11. An example would be the dispute in *Carter v. Papineau* 111 N.E. 358 (1916) in which a parishioner brought an action because her priest refused to administer communion to her.

12. This was the situation in the *Free Church* case.

13. An example of a dispute within a minority community that was played out on the legal terrain of contract law is *Hofer et al v. Hofer et al.* (1970), 13 D.L.R. (3d) 1 (S.C.C.). See also *Dill v. Watson,* referred to infra, note 16.

14. This approach was adopted from the leading British case of *Attorney-General v. Pearson* 3 Mer. 353 (1817) at 400, in which Lord Eldon said,

> [I]f . . . the institution was established for the express purpose of
> such form of religious worship, or the teaching of such particular
> doctrines as the founder has thought most conformable to the
> principles of the Christian religion, I do not apprehend that it is in
> the power of individuals having the management of that institution
> at any time to alter the purpose for which it was founded, or to say
> to the remaining members, "We have changed our opinions—and
> you, who assemble in this place for the purpose of hearing the
> doctrines, and joining in the worship prescribed by the founder,
> shall no longer enjoy the benefit he intended for you, unless you
> conform to the alteration which has taken place in our opinions."
> In such a case, therefore, I apprehend . . . that where a congrega-
> tion become dissentient among themselves, the nature of the origi-
> nal institution must alone be looked at as the guide for the decision
> of the Court, and that to refer to any other criterion, as to the
> sense of the existing majority, would be to make a new institution,
> which is altogether beyond the reach, and inconsistent with the
> duties and character, of this Court.

Quoted in the *Free Church* case, supra, note 2, at 644 per Lord Davey.

15. The *Free Church* case, supra, note 2, at 671.

16. The same result is supported by an appeal to a contractual rubric
in the Lord Chancellor's speech, in which approving reference is made
to the judgment of Smith B. in *Dill v. Watson,* in which the following
analysis of membership in a religious community is offered:

> I do not conceive that I appeal from the Word of God to that of
> man, by proclaiming or attesting by my signature, that I concur in
> the interpretation given by a numerous body of my fellow Chris-
> tians to certain passages of Scripture. They agree with me, I agree
> with them in construction and consequent creed; but neither take
> their belief upon the authority of those others. Both draw their
> faith from the Bible as its common source; both consider the Bible
> as containing the only rule of, and furnishing the only unerring
> guide to a true faith; each, with God's assistance and the subordi-
> nate and pious aid of human instruction, interprets as well as
> man's infirmity will permit; both coincide in the same interpreta-
> tion; that interpretation regulates their faith; and all who thus
> coincide become members of the same religion. . . . [W]e do not
> coerce our neighbour by calling for his signature to our profession
> or articles of faith. . . . We but say to him, If you agree with us
> affix your signature to certain articles, or in some way notify your
> recognition of their truth; or if you disagree, withhold such signa-

ture or declaration. And we say of him in the former case, that he *is,* and in the latter case that he *is not* of our religion. We do not compel him to hold our faith; we but ask him to inform us, by certain acts, whether he does hold it or does not; and we ask this, only if he claim to be enrolled as one of our body, and to be in religious communion with us. In the absence of such a test, our Establishment would not be a rock, cemented into solidity by harmonious uniformity of opinion, it would be a mere incongruous heap of, as it were, grains of sand, thrown together without being united, each of these intellectual and isolated grains differing from every other, and the whole forming a but nominally united while really unconnected mass; fraught with nothing but internal dissimilitude, and mutual and reciprocal contradiction and dissension.

*Free Church* case, supra, note 2, at 616.

17. Although the *Free Church* case was decided after Watson, its approach is typical of many other English decisions with which Miller J. was familiar. Miller J. labeled the English approach the "implied trust" approach.

18. Watson, supra, note 4, at 722 (emphasis added).

19. The *Free Church* case, supra, note 2, at 612 (emphasis added). Lord James put the point similarly: "The Church may unite [with another body], . . . but if property is sought to be transferred to the new body the identity of that new body—that is the Free Church—after the union must be maintained; and nothing in the deed gives a power to unite so as to bring into existence a Church incapable of identity with the Free Church." At 665. Lord Robertson agreed that "the change of name and the fact of fusion put it on the respondents to *prove their identity* with the original benefactors." At 667 (emphasis added).

20. Ibid., at 656. Along the same lines, the Earl of Halsbury said, "the identity of a religious community . . . must consist in the unity of its doctrines." At 612. Lord Davey refers to "the religious tenets and principles which formed the bond of union of the association" (at 645), and later asks, "what . . . is the Church but an organized association of Christians holding certain doctrines and principles in common?" At 651.

21. *Watson,* supra, note 4, at 726.

22. Ibid., at 725.

23. As Miller J. concluded,

[T]he appellants . . . have separated themselves wholly from the church organization to which they belonged when this controversy commenced. They now deny its authority, denounce its action, and refuse to abide by its judgements. They have first erected themselves into a new organization, and have since joined themselves to another totally different, if not hostile, to the one to which they belonged when the difficulty first began.

Ibid., at 734.

24. Indeed, three of their Lordships explicitly treated the case as one of constitutional significance for the Free Church. The *Free Church* case, supra, note 2, at 631 per Lord MacNaghten; at 699 per Lord Lindley; at 705 per Lord Alverstone. See also Ross, supra, note 1, p. 6.

25. See Ross, supra, note 1, chapter 1.

26. The *Free Church* case, supra, note 2, at 635–36 (emphasis added).

27. He too claims that Scripture is the foundation of church doctrine, which Synods or Councils have the power of interpreting. Since such bodies do not claim infallibility, any particular interpretation cannot be treated as binding for all time "but may be modified, or even rejected and be replaced, by another interpretation adopted by a later Synod or Council, and declared by it to be in its judgment the true meaning of the Scriptures or Confession upon the matter in controversy." Ibid., at 695.

28. Ibid., at 701–2. Of course, the stipulations that the Free Church, as such, must remain a Reformed Church—precluding union with the Catholic Church—and retain a Presbyterian form of government are substantive.

29. *Watson,* supra, note 4, Argument for the appellants, at 706.

30. Ibid., at 713.

31. Ibid., Argument for the appellants, at 713 (emphasis in original).

32. Ibid., at 708.

33. Ibid., at 733 (emphasis in the original). Earlier, at 729, he says,

The right to organize voluntary religious associations to assist in the expression and dissemination of any religious doctrine, and to create tribunals for the decision of controverted questions of faith within the association, and for the ecclesiastical government of all the individual members, congregations, and officers within the general association, is unquestioned. All who unite themselves to such a body do so with an implied consent to this government, and are bound to submit to it. But it would be a vain consent and would lead to the total subversion of such religious bodies, if any one aggrieved by one of their decisions could appeal to the secular courts and have them reversed. It is of the essence of these religious unions, and of their right to establish tribunals for the decision of questions arising among themselves, that those decisions should be binding in all cases of ecclesiastical cognizance, subject only to such appeals as the organism itself provides for.

34. Ibid., at 729.

35. The *Free Church* case, supra, note 2, at 653 per Lord Davey; at 691 per Lord Robertson.

36. Ibid., at 621–26, per Lord Halsbury.

37. *Watson,* supra, note 4, at 727. He also explained and dismissed the implied trust doctrine relied upon by the appellants as the product of English political culture in which Church and State were not separate, and Churches were not truly free. Ibid., at 728.

38. According to Ross, supra, note 1, p. 93, this was the standard reproach of those who were in favour of the union with the United Presbyterians. See also J. N. Figgis, *Churches in the Modern State* (London: Longmans, Green and Co., 1914), 22: "Thus on the one hand the judgment denies to a Free Church the power of defining and developing in its own doctrine; on the other, while disclaiming interference in theological matters, it practically exercises it under the plea of considering the question whether or no the trust had been violated."

39. The *Free Church* case, supra, note 2 at 613, per Halsbury L.C.; at 645, per Lord Davey; at 674–75, per Lord Robertson.

40. Ibid., at 644–45. Similarly, Lord Robertson argued at 674–75, "the intrinsic importance of any particular doctrine in relation to the general body of Christian teaching is no criterion of whether it is or is not an essential or fundamental doctrine in a particular Church. . . . It is not its own importance, but the place assigned to it in the foundation of the new Church that has got to be ascertained."

41. H. L. A. Hart, *The Concept of Law* (Oxford: Clarendon Press, 1961), 92–93.

42. Lon L. Fuller, "Two Principles of Human Association," in Kenneth I. Winston, ed. *The Principles of Social Order: Selected Essays of Lon L. Fuller* (Durham, N.C.: Duke University Press, 1981), 68.

43. Ibid., 71.

44. Note that the converse is not necessarily true. It is possible to have a system of formal rules not grounded in shared acceptance of certain substantive beliefs or values.

45. Miller J. recognizes this. *Watson,* supra, note 4, at 733.

46. Maitland, "Moral Personality and Legal Personality" in his *Collected Papers,* Vol. III (Cambridge: Cambridge University Press, 1911), 319. Most commentators have read the majority approach in the *Free Church* case as requiring a static interpretation of Church doctrine and implicitly as therefore prescribing a fundamentalist conception of religion. See, for example, Dallin H. Oakes, "Trust Doctrines in Church Controversies," *Brigham Young University Law Review* (1981): 826–29, and M. H. Ogilvie, "Church Property Disputes: Some Organizing Principles," *University of*

*Toronto Law Journal* 42 (1992): 377, for analyses of the modern case law along the same lines. Ogilvie argues that the fundamentalist interpretation has predominated in the Canadian case law. Hence, my claim that the majority judgments can be interpreted as based merely on an understanding of the character of the Free Church in particular may be unorthodox. However, I would argue that the dissenting opinions in the *Free Church* case demonstrate that there is nothing inherently fundamentalist about the "implied trust" approach. Furthermore, Ogilvie notes several exceptions to this trend, which can only be treated as aberrations if the fundamentalist interpretation of the "implied trust" doctrine is accepted. My interpretation allows for these apparent exceptions to be brought within the implied trust rubric as cases in which the constitutional structure of the Church in question allowed for fundamental doctrinal change. In any event, I am less concerned, for present purposes, with whether my interpretation of this leading case has been adopted by later courts than with the normative question of whether it represents a viable judicial means of fostering the autonomy of minority groups.

47. Harold J. Laski, "Notes on the Strict Interpretation of Ecclesiastical Trusts" *Can. L. Times* 36 (1916): 190; Laski, "The Personality of Associations" *Harv. L. Rev* 29 (1915–16), 404 at 419.

48. J. N. Figgis, *Churches in the Modern State,* supra, note 38, 18–22.

49. Leicester C. Webb makes a similar point in "Corporate Personality and Political Pluralism," in L. C. Webb, ed., *Legal Personality and Political Pluralism,* (London: Cambridge University Press, 1958), 52–53.

50. Supra, 16–17.

51. 393 U.S. 440 (1968), at 447. For an argument that this approach is inappropriate in the Canadian (and U.K.) constitutional context, see Ogilvie, supra, note 46, at 393.

52. Ross, supra, note 1, at 75–76. The 1962 *Harvard Law Review* note, supra, note 8 at 1172, makes reference to the case of *Canterbury v. Canterbury,* 143 W.Va. 165, 100 S.E. 2d 656 (1957), in which the complainants alleged that another group of worshippers had departed from the church's fundamental tenets in advocating "That the birth of the spirit is not necessary except to see the church here in time; that there is not hell beyond this life; and that goats are sheep in disobedience."

53. (1850) 12 D. 523, at 560, discussed in the *Free Church* case, supra, note 2, at 614–15 per the Earl of Halsbury.

54. Quoted in Ross, supra, note 1, at 94. The unionists continued to maintain that these were powers the Free Church had always had. It is consistent with this position, that the House of Lords' decision was routinely criticized within these circles for having interfered with the Church's spiritual independence. Ross, at 93. The unionists believed that

the Church had had the power to alter its commitment to the Establishment Principle and had exercised this power over the course of the union debate. On this reading of the Church's constitution, the House of Lords' decision could not be seen otherwise than as secular interference in Church affairs. For a discussion of other attempts (in the Canadian context) to plan around the *Free Church* case decision, see Ogilvie, supra, note 46, at 384. Ogilvie's illustration of some of the pitfalls in this endeavor suggests that it is difficult if not impossible to eliminate entirely the prospect of judicial interpretation of substantive religious tenets.

55. There is an irony in this conclusion, especially in the context of religious autonomy. The more fundamentalist a faction's conception of its own religious commitments is—that is, the more people define their religious enterprise exclusively by reference to primary rules of ultimate constitutional authority—the more they subject their religious community to the ultimate authority of the civil courts whenever a dispute arises.

56. The *Free Church* case, supra, note 2, at 666 per Lord James; at 691 per Lord Robertson; at 719–20 per Lord Alverstone.

57. An exception is some Aboriginal communities which have more or less complete normative structures more or less traceable back to precontact times when Aboriginal peoples enjoyed full sovereignty.

# 11

# A TALE OF TWO VILLAGES
# (OR, LEGAL REALISM
# COMES TO TOWN)

## NOMI MAYA STOLZENBERG

### INTRODUCTION

The debate between liberals and communitarians seems to be at an impasse. The communitarian charge that liberalism atomizes community has become a commonplace, so much so that our most prominent defenders of the liberal tradition openly concede that a liberal state will adversely affect the ability of some belief systems to survive. Thus, John Rawls, in expounding his theory of "political liberalism" has acknowledged that

> it is surely impossible for the basic structure of a just constitutional regime not to have important effects and influences as to which comprehensive doctrines endure and gain adherents over time; and it is futile to try to counteract these effects and influences, or even to ascertain for political purposes how deep and pervasive they are. We must accept the facts of commonsense political sociology.[1]

Rawls's tone here is that of a rueful but resolute realist, a Darwinist with a heart, who "regrets" but stoically accepts the disappearance of certain belief systems as an inevitable fact, like death and taxes.[2] (It is more difficult to adopt this attitude if you adhere to one of the threatened belief systems. Rawls never explains why those in the suppressed position "must accept the facts.")[3] Others are less apologetic. Joseph Raz unabashedly defends a "perfectionist" ideal of a liberal state that promotes individual autonomy, pluralism, and toleration at the expense of nonliberal cultures by enforcing a code of morality (albeit a "morality which regards personal autonomy as an essential ingredient of the good life, and regards the principle of autonomy . . . as one of the most important moral principles.")[4] Though "[a]utonomy requires that many morally acceptable options be available to a person," Raz states that "[t]he ideal of autonomy requires only the availability of morally acceptable options." Perhaps more important, Raz acknowledges that this ideal is "inconsistent with various alternative forms of *valuable* lives," and not just with morally unacceptable ones. This is because attaining an autonomous life "depends on the general character of one's environment and culture." Therefore, "[f]or those who live in an autonomy-supporting environment there is no choice but to be autonomous."[5]

Rawls aims to present an alternative to the perfectionist ideal of promoting a liberal morality through political means. But, like Raz, he recognizes that a liberal state will necessarily be incompatible both with morally impermissible *and* some morally permissible (or "reasonable") ways of life.[6] In sum, Raz and Rawls agree with the communitarians that a liberal state will exclude certain belief systems.

Remarkably, liberals concede the negative effects of liberalism on some communities. Indeed, they join with communitarians in extolling the positive value of community.[7] Rawls and Raz both call for community values to be expressed and protected at levels that correspond to the conventional division between "private" and "public" realms. As pluralists, both insist that a liberal political order must allow "nonpublic" space for a sufficiently wide variety of rival belief systems to exist (notwithstanding the exclusion of some). Furthermore, both recognize that the liberal state itself embodies the values of a particular group of people. It is precisely because the liberal state reflects and enforces certain cultural values that it excludes some subcultures while sustaining others.

Illiberal and antiliberal cultures, and more generally, cultures that do not abide by the division between public and private realms, would seem to be particularly vulnerable to the inevitable demands of the liberal state. So it is not surprising that recent critics of liberalism have focused on the tensions between liberal principles and religious subgroups, especially "fundamentalist" ones, which actively oppose some of the tenets of liberalism, and seek to establish "group rights" to collective self-government and control over the transmission of beliefs. These critics lament what liberals concede: that the state enforcement of liberal principles has a "disproportionate impact" on the pursuit of such interests.

Largely unnoticed in this debate is a curious fact. Yes, the implementation of liberal principles has a disproportionate effect on such subgroups, but sometimes that effect is positive. That is, sometimes liberal principles *enable* groups that appear to be most directly in conflict with them. It has long been recognized that principles of liberal government justify the protection of some private forms of collective power that result from the coordinated exercise of individual rights. But critics of liberalism condemn the conventional divide between private and public realms, con- tending that it denies groups sufficient powers of collective regula- tion and autonomy. It is the very privatization of groups under liberalism that the defenders of community bemoan. Against this communitarian critique — or rather, as a modification of it — I will argue that critics and defenders of liberalism alike have overstated the extent to which religious and other groups are deprived of the means of collective self-regulation and self-perpetuation in a liberal political order. There are in fact two sources of power that enable such groups to survive and flourish under a liberal regime, both of which have been minimized or overlooked by both sides in the liberal-communitarian debate. First, the limits of private power have been exaggerated; individual rights sometimes con- geal to produce highly effective forms of group control. Second, the ability of a group to assume the form and command the levers of an official governmental body has been virtually ignored. Sometimes the principles of liberal government work to justify the delegation of a portion of the powers of government (i.e., local government) to precisely the sort of exclusive, particularistic, ho- listic, and even separatist subgroup that seems to be most jeopard- ized in liberal society.

This possibility is illustrated by the recent case of *Kiryas Joel*. In a well-publicized opinion, the United States Supreme Court struck down legislation that authorized the creation of a religiously homogeneous—Hasidic Jewish—public school district.[8] It held that the formation of the school district violates the constitutional prohibition against the "establishment" of religion by the state. It seemed obvious to many observers that the principle of separation of church and state, which has long informed the interpretation of the antiestablishment clause, requires such a ruling. But the Supreme Court's grounds for striking down the New York state legislation were actually quite narrow and technical. Unbeknownst to most casual observers, the reasoning offered by the Supreme Court permitted the very same public school district to be newly authorized by subsequent state legislation that took a different form from the original authorizing statute. The state of New York seized the opportunity to pass new legislation that enables every village meeting minimal procedural requirements to form its own public school district. The application of this new statute to support the continued existence of the Kiryas Joel school district has been upheld in state court,[9] underscoring the fact that, far from condemning the delegation of state power to a religious group in general, the Supreme Court in *Kiryas Joel* specifically affirmed that "we do not disable a religiously homogeneous group from exercising political power."[10]

*Kiryas Joel* reveals the employment by the current judiciary of a formalistic conception of religious neutrality that can, depending on the circumstances, work either to the advantage or disadvantage of a religiously exclusive community. That this is so, and how this is so—and how this formalistic jurisprudence fits with contemporary liberal theories—are the three main subjects of this article. Whether this is a good thing is another matter. But before we can even begin to assess the desirability of supporting insular holistic communities, we need to obtain a clearer picture of the extent to which the liberal state does support, as well as thwart, their survival.

The aim of this chapter is to present such a picture by analyzing the case of Kiryas Joel and an interesting contrast case, *United States v. Village of Airmont,* in which, in a similar milieu, a group of townspeople seceded in order to exclude their orthodox Jewish neighbors from their local government.[11] Together, these cases exhibit the staples of legal reasoning, including formalistic interpretations of the establishment clause and of religious discrimination, which justify conferring governmental power on exclusive religious, or antireligious, groups. The essay proceeds in three steps. First, I will provide the factual background to the two cases. Second, I will elucidate the principles of legal reasoning which allow for the empowerment of exclusive, illiberal groups. Finally, I will consider whether this legal reasoning is consistent with the principles of liberalism, articulated in the theories of Rawls and Raz. Before proceeding, however, it may be helpful to alert the reader to some of the surprises and counterintuitive propositions that she will encounter along the way.

First, the very assertion that liberalism supports holistic communities may seem counterintuitive, given the joint assumption of liberals and communitarians that liberalism has an atomizing effect on community. From the standpoint of this common assumption, the continued existence of holistic, illiberal communities is a puzzle. On the other hand, the real puzzle may be why their obvious persistence has been ignored in the liberal-communitarian debates. A legal realist perspective on community, which I elaborate in this article, renders obvious the private and public sources of power that liberals and communitarians have ignored. The joint stake that liberals and communitarians have in denying or understating the resources available for group survival in a liberal state is one of the mysteries to be unraveled in this essay.

Another counterintuitive proposition is that the jurisprudence exhibited in *Kiryas Joel* is a formalistic one, since the judicial opinions of the majority in that case bear the surface emblems of an *antiformalistic* style of reasoning; and since much of the reigning establishment clause jurisprudence, applied in other cases, appears to be imbued with a nonformalistic conception of state neutrality.[12] Nonetheless, I will argue that *Kiryas Joel,* like the trial court's opinion in *Village of Airmont,* is at bottom based on a formalistic conception of state neutrality, which allows exclusive religious and antireligious groups to be incorporated as local governments.

The fact that liberal principles operate in some ways to empower communitarian groups does not contradict the fact that in other ways the principles of a liberal state disable them. The point is not that liberalism has no negative effect on subcommunities, but that the negative effect is not the whole story. The whole story is far more complicated and interesting.

## I. A Tale of Two Villages

Rockland and Orange are neighboring counties in the suburbs of New York City.[13] Here, the homogeneous subdivisions, long the habitat for upwardly mobile, assimilated, second and third generation Irish, Italian, and Jewish Americans, have become home to a suprisingly diverse array of tenaciously communal, culturally distinctive ethnic, religious, and racial subgroups.[14] For example, in one town, Spring Valley, thousands of Haitian immigrants have clustered to form one of the larger Haitian exile communities in the country. Its Main Street is now festooned with signs in Creole and French. Immigrants from Jamaica, Guatemala and El Salvador also have been attracted to Spring Valley's high proportion of relatively cheap rental units, unusual in the midst of this still predominantly white and affluent suburban county.

In this dynamic environment, no group has stood out more than the various Hasidic Jewish communities which have been settling in Rockland and Orange Counties for decades. Emblematic of the settlement patterns is the new religious broadcasting station in Rockland County. WLIR-AM advertises itself as "all Jewish all the time," but from Friday night through Saturday, in observance of the Jewish sabbath, it plays only Latin and Haitian music.

While the diverse subcommunities of Spring Valley have more or less hung together, the neighboring town of Ramapo has fractured. Twelve communities in Ramapo have seceded to form their own villages, spawning numerous litigations in the process. As federal trial judge Gerard Goettel observed in 1993 *Airmont* decision, "the last two villages to be formed were the Village of Kaser, an exclusively Orthodox/Hasidic village, and the Village of Airmont,"[15] which, the plaintiffs argued, is anti-Semitic. The exclusively Jewish village of Kaser is reminiscent of the better-known Hasidic village of Kiryas Joel, located in adjacent Orange County. The Village of Airmont, on the other hand, is the very opposite of Kaser and Kiryas Joel, having been formed so that residents could escape the mounting pressure to accommodate the different kinds of land use favored by the orthodox and Hasidic inhabitants of the town of Ramapo.

Two land-use controversies in particular have fueled the village incorporation movement in Rockland and Orange Counties. First, many orthodox and Hasidic Jews object to the single-family zoning requirements typical of affluent suburbs and prevalent in many of the Rockland and Orange communities. Orthodox real estate developers, who in some cases bought land and advertised "Torah Community" subdivisions with apartment buildings before any variances from single-family housing zoning were obtained, spearheaded the demand for zoning laws to be changed to permit multiple family housing. In addition, the use of *"shtiblich,"* or informal worship congregations in basements and living areas of residential homes, as well as plans to build new free-standing synagogues, have posed conflicts with town zoning laws that strictly regulate the location and size of houses of worship.

The Village of Kiryas Joel, which is entirely composed of members of the ultraorthodox Satmar sect of Hasidic Judaism, makes a neat contrast with the Village of Airmont, which has sought to retain or recapture the typical suburban lifestyle of the American dream, replete with large lots, and well-separated single-family homes; safe, predominantly white and secular public schools; and churches and synagogues as carefully spaced out and separated from the secular realms as commercial uses have traditionally been separated from residential ones. The Satmar Hasidim of Kiryas Joel form the very picture of the tight-knit, pervasively regulated, holistic community. In contrast, the founders of Airmont were a shifting assortment of individuals. The trial judge in *Airmont* noted that "[m]any of the original core group were Jewish or had Jewish spouses albeit they were not Orthodox."[16] But the Airmont Civic Association, which was formed to promote the incorporation of a new village, was subject to internal disputes and changes in leadership, as the "old guard," whose main concern was simply to enforce the old zoning policies, came to be replaced by more vociferous (and apparently exclusively non-Jewish) opponents of the Orthodox community.

Like the Village's founders, the inhabitants of Airmont represent a loose association of individuals, united neither by religion nor by any common secular code of values, save for their joint opposition to deviating from the low-density zoning regulations.[17] Kiryas Joel is a religious community; Airmont is secular. Kiryas Joel is homogeneous—fully 100 percent of its inhabitants are members of the Satmar sect; Airmont is heterogeneous. The community of Kiryas Joel is extremely cohesive, organized around the central, charismatic figure of its "rebbe," the hereditary rabbinic leader whose religious authority extends to all aspects of his followers' lives. The residents of Airmont, by contrast, have no unifying organization apart from their sporadic involvement in the democratic procedures that state law prescribes for forming and governing local municipalities. They are not hierarchically organized; indeed, they are hardly "organized" at all.

To continue the contrast, Kiryas Joel is antiassimilationist and opposed to modern innovations. The Supreme Court observed that its inhabitants "interpret the Torah strictly; segregate the sexes outside the home; speak Yiddish as their primary language; eschew television, radio, and English-language publications; and dress in distinctive ways that include headcoverings and special garments for boys and modest dresses for girls."[18] Adult men grow long beards and sidelocks, and wear the dark frockcoats and hats of late-nineteenth-century Hungary.[19] Adult women also dress modestly and distinctively, covering their shorn heads with scarves and wigs. In short, they act and look different from most Americans, while Airmont residents conform to the cultural norm.

Yet both communities are alike in being exclusionary. The Satmars consciously resist the penetration of the outside culture; Airmont's inhabitants resist the inclusion of the traditional Jewish way of life, which conflicts with its prescribed low-density land uses. Moreover, both communities use the coercive power of collective regulation to secure and conserve their respectively favored ways of life. Perhaps the most striking fact that characterizes both villages is that they exist at all, in seeming defiance of the principle of separation of church and state. One might have thought that that principle would prohibit "a religious homogeneous group from exercising political power," yet, as we have seen, the U.S. Supreme Court insists that this is not the case. Similarly, the settled interpretation of the establishment clause as requiring that government should favor neither religion nor "irreligion" might seem to preclude the formation of a local government that is specifically designed to exclude a certain religious way of life. Yet the Village of Airmont's existence is apparently secure under current understandings of the constitution, as is the Village of Kiryas Joel's.

In the case of *Kiryas Joel*, the constitutionality of the Village, as opposed to the school district, not only went unchallenged but was repeatedly affirmed, though, as the Court noted, the boundaries of the Village were deliberately "drawn to include just the 320 acres owned and inhabited entirely by Satmars."[20] The constitutionality of delegating the power of local government to religiously homogeneous groups may seem surprising, in light of the Supreme Court's holding that the formation of the exclusively Hasidic public school district violated the constitutional principle of separating church and state. But what the tale of our two villages tells us is that a liberal legal order allows for (perhaps, even depends on) legal mechanisms that facilitate the acquisition of governmental power by self-contained nonvoluntaristic groups. I now turn to the task of analyzing the precise legal mechanisms that enable this result.

## II. Four Formalisms that Justify the Political Empowerment of Religiously Exclusive Groups

Special legislation specifically designed to enable the Village of Kiryas Joel to form its own public school district is unconstitutional. But general legislation enabling any village in the state of New York (that meets certain size and financial requirements) to form its own school district is constitutionally valid. Hence, the Kiryas Joel school district, newly authorized under such general legislation, is legally valid. So, too, is the Village of Kiryas Joel itself, though its boundaries were carefully drawn to include only members of the Satmar religion. Similarly, the Village of Airmont was exonerated at the trial level of charges of anti-Semitism, even though it was formed in order to escape the pressure to accommodate the Orthodox and Hasidic lifestyle.

What explains these results is a formalistic understanding of what official neutrality, or nondiscrimination, vis-à-vis religious groups consists in. Four different formalistic views feed into this conception of governmental neutrality and justify the results noted above. An analysis of the judicial reasoning presented in *Kiryas Joel* and *Village of Airmont* elucidates each of these "formalisms."

## A. The Neutrality of Intent—Neutrality of Effect Distinction

Neutrality is an essentially contested concept. A formalistic conception of neutrality competes with a "functionalist" conception. Like functionalist legal analyses generally, this one grows out of the first direct assault on "legal formalism" launched by the legal realists and their progressive forebears in the early part of this century. Legal realism characteristically pierces through legal formalities to look at the actual effects of actions under judicial scrutiny, and searches for functional equivalents or analogues to the types of action that the law explicitly condemns. A functionalist definition of neutrality requires the relevant action to have an "equal" effect on all of the relevant parties. According to this test, if an action helps one party, it should help the others to the same extent. Likewise, if it hinders one. Otherwise it should help or hinder none.

Though this functionalist view appeals to deap-seated notions of fairness and evenhandedness, and though it has its adherents, others reject it on the grounds that it is practically impossible to achieve. Still others reject it on the grounds that is undesirable to prevent the state from promoting values and discouraging vices, at least by noncoercive means. Neutrality itself, after all, is a value whose pursuit by the government necessarily affects different belief systems in differing degrees.

Those who reject an "effect test" for neutrality usually say that they are defining neutrality strictly in terms of "intent," "purpose," "intentions," or "motivation." These words are taken to refer to the *reasons* for a given action rather than the action itself. According to this line of thinking, the same action may be undertaken for different reasons and therefore may or may not be neutral, depending on the circumstances. If it is "intended" to favor or disfavor one party relative to others, then it is not neutral.

But if the same action merely has the "unintended" effect of favoring (or disfavoring) that party, then it satisfies the intent test for neutrality.

Devotion to such a test is one important aspect of the formalistic conception of religious neutrality responsible for the *Kiryas Joel* and original *Airmont* results. *Kiryas Joel* said in essence that the requisite position of neutrality is met if a state law confers powers of local government on an area that just "happens" to contain only "coreligionists."[21] It follows, as Justice O'Connor spelled out in her concurring opinion, that if the legislature were to replace the special act that singled out the Village of Kiryas Joel with "generally applicable legislation . . . allow[ing] all villages to operate their own school districts," then the constitutional defect would evaporate.[22]

The same distinction between neutrality of effect and neutrality of legislative purpose served to justify "the constitutionality of the Kiryas Joel Village itself."[23] According to the Court, the difference between the Village and the school district, as it was originally authorized, was that in the first case, "the religious community of Kiryas Joel . . . receive[d] its new governmental authority simply as one of many communities eligible for equal treatment under a general law," whereas in the second case it did not. "The fact that Chapter 748 [the original act authorizing the school district] facilitates the practice of religion is not what renders it an unconstitutional establishment." What does render it unconstitutional, in the eyes of the Court, is the fact that "the reference line chosen for the Kiryas Joel Village School District was one *purposely* drawn to separate Satmars from non-Satmars."[24]

Similar reasoning supported the trial judge's conclusion that Airmont was not discriminating against Orthodox and Hasidic Jews. The complaint against Airmont, based on allegations that the Village was violating constitutional protections of religion as well as federal laws against religious discrimination in zoning, also required the court to determine the content of a position of nondiscrimination vis-à-vis religious groups.[25] After toying with some alternative definitions, Judge Goettel ended up focusing on the government's "objectives." He concluded that the Village of Airmont had not engaged in anti-Semitic discrimination, because even if its regulations had the effect of burdening Jewish practices and customs, they were adopted for independent reasons of public health and safety.[26]

Though essential to their holdings, the courts' reliance on the intent-based definition of neutrality is not easy to discern. This is because they also flirt with different, contradictory tests. Indeed, on the surface, both courts seem at times to reject the formalistic intent-based standard, and to employ the competing functionalist effect test, instead.

This is especially evident in Justice Souter's opinion for the Supreme Court in *Kiryas Joel*. He uses typically functionalist rhetoric to invalidate the special act by which the school district was originally created. At the level of the explicit holding, all of the classic buzz words associated with antiformalism or functionalism in legal reasoning are present from the very first paragraph: "this unusual act is *tantamount to* an allocation of political power on a religious criterion";[27] "our analysis does not end with the text of the statute at issue"[28] (which did not refer to a religious criterion but rather to the "territory" of the village of Kiryas Joel); "the context here persuades us that Chapter 748 *effectively* identifies these recipients of governmental authority by reference to doctrinal adherence, even though it does not do so expressly."[29] In the end, the Court could not find any evidence that the government had defined the boundaries of the district in explicitly religious terms. Instead it rested its conclusion on finding "the legislature's Act to be *substantially equivalent* to defining a political subdivision and hence the qualification for its franchise by a religious test, resulting in a purposeful and forbidden 'fusion of governmental and religious functions.' "[30]

How can these expressions of antiformalism be reconciled with my contention that the underlying view of official neutrality (in these cases) is based on the intent, as opposed to the effect, test? The last quotation from the Supreme Court's opinion in *Kiryas Joel* provides a starting point. The Court is using a functionalist methodology of *interpretation* to pierce through the outer shell of a religion-neutral statute to discover what it takes to be its real content: "a *purposeful* and forbidden 'fusion of governmental and religious functions.' " The Court is not uninterested in whether the fusion is "purposeful." Its antiformalism simply applies to the question of how to interpret a statutory text—whether to confine oneself to its surface, explicit meaning, or to go "behind" the text to glean its "real" meaning from the context. It is a matter of figuring out what the meaning of the statute is, not a matter of defining the standard of constitutional validity to which that meaning will be subjected. On the contrary, Justice Souter clearly describes the standard of evaluation in terms of the formalist intent test. Thus, he states:

> Where "fusion" is an issue, the difference lies in the distinction between a government's purposeful delegation on the basis of religion and a delegation on principles neutral to religion, to individuals whose religious identities are incidental to their receipt of civic authority.[31]

There are, to be sure, other gestures that obscure the Court's commitment to an intent-based definition of governmental neutrality. For one thing, the controversial "*Lemon* test," which has governed establishment clause controversies since 1971, identifies the "effect" as well as the "intent" of advancing religion as two independent bases for finding an impermissible establishment of religion.[32] To the surprise of many, the Supreme Court in *Kiryas Joel* did not rely on *Lemon,* but it did not overturn it either. Though the Court did not explain why it found the *Lemon* test to be inapplicable, it is likely that it wanted to avoid subjecting local governmental bodies, which represent religiously homogeneous communities, to the effect test contained in *Lemon.*

The Court's repeated use of the language of "equal treatment" is a further clue to its commitment to the intent standard. Though this language might be interpreted to require equal effects regardless of intent, David Strauss has shown that in common usage, the notion of unequal treatment is "essentially equivalent" to the notion of discriminatory intent. Strauss finds that the most "plausible definition of discriminatory intent" is one that requires that the proscribed criterion (race for Strauss, religion for us) "play no role in government *decisions*." The relevant question in applying the discriminatory intent standard is whether "the government would have made the same decision even if the [identities] of those affected had been reversed."[33] In other words, have the relevant groups been treated equally or have they been differentially preferred?

Though Strauss's concern is with the career of the intent-effect distinction in equal protection jurisprudence, particularly as it applies to race discrimination, his understanding of the original function of the intent test conforms to the analysis of Justice Souter's crypto-functionalism offered above. As Strauss sees it, the intent test was developed in the context of equal protection doctrine to cover "cases in which the government was using a racial classification but, in contrast to the classic Jim Crow laws of *Strauder* or *Plessy*, was trying to conceal the fact that it was doing so." In other words, the intent test is first and foremost a device for going "beyond fully explicit racial classifications to measures that, although neutral on their face, were obviously based on surrogates for race."[34] If we substitute "religious" for "racial," this seems to be exactly the reasoning that led to the condemnation of the special act challenged in *Kiryas Joel*.

As Strauss notes, "the discriminatory intent standard works reasonably well" as an interpretive heuristic in the category of cases, like *Kiryas Joel*, in which the government has disguised actual impermissible preferences in language that is neutral on its face.[35] But there are two problems with defining neutrality or nondiscrimination *exclusively* in terms of the government's intent. First, it remains unclear why unintended effects, either positive or negative, on religious and other subgroups should be acceptable, especially when they are consequential. If a state action has the *effect* of making a religious group into a governing agency, or creating a governmental body that only represents the interests of one religious group, why should that be a matter of constitutional indifference? Second, as Strauss notes, it is far from clear that the intent standard is coherent if taken seriously, rather than supplying an excuse for reining in judicial review. Many have noted the obvious evidentiary difficulties, and the fantasy involved in imputing a unified "intent" to a collective, political body, like a legislature. Beyond this, there often simply is no answer to the question, whether the "same" state action would have been undertaken if the identity of the groups affected were different. As Strauss notes, the question is usually meaningless.[36]

Furthermore, as every first year student of criminal law learns, there are many different levels of *mens rea*, ranging from deliberate intention, through knowingness of the consequences of one's action, to reckless disregard or negligent indifference. Similarly, there are an infinite number of levels of generality at which the purpose or reason for an action can be articulated. For example, the Supreme Court justices characterized the goal of the separate school district variously as:

1. " 'A good faith effort to solve th[e] unique problem' associated with providing special education services to handicapped children in the village" (Justice Souter, quoting Governor Mario Cuomo).[37]
2. "An adjustment to the Satmars' religiously grounded preferences" (Justice Souter).[38]
3. "Providing bilingual and bicultural special education to Satmar children" (Justice Souter).[39]
4. "To separate Satmars from non-Satmars" (Justice Souter).[40]
5. To respond "to parental concern that children suffered 'panic, fear and trauma' when 'leaving their own community and being with people whose ways were different.'" (Justice Stevens, concurring).[41]
6. To "isolat[e]" and "shield children from contact with others who have 'different ways' " (Justice Stevens).[42]
7. "To cement the attachment of young adherents to a particular faith" (Justice Stevens).[43]
8. "Religious toleration" and "accommodation of the religious practices (or more precisely, cultural peculiarities) of a tiny minority sect" (Justice Scalia, dissenting).[44]
9. "Family values" (Justice Scalia).[45]

Which of these appropriately characterizes the facts of the particular case, and which count as the kind of intention that stands condemned (or excused) under the intent test? Surely, all are plausible and valid descriptions of the goal.

Certainly, as Justice Kennedy and Justice Souter both explicitly acknowledged, "the New York legislature *knew* that everyone within the village was Satmar when it drew the school district along the village lines."[46] And it would not suddenly forget this fact when it came to applying the new general statute. Nor did it lack this knowledge when it approved the formation of the Village under a general incorporation statute. Furthermore, as O'Connor notes, the Village was "consciously created by the voters as an enclave for their religious group." [47] Yet it is absolutely clear that none of the members of the Supreme Court expects such forms of consciousness to flunk the formalistic requirement of neutrality of intent. The irrelevance of the intent of the voters, on the brink of transforming themselves into a local government, goes unexplained, as does the newly formed government's own raison d'être.

Had the Court eschewed the intent standard, and instead defined state "establishments" of religion according to the functionalist test of neutrality of effect, the irrelevance of these factors would be understandable. But under a functionalist analysis, a court might be compelled to strike down general, as well as special, legislation that "effectively guarantees a religious community's control and operation of a unit of government." [48] The intent test in *Kiryas Joel* functioned simultaneously (1) to allow the Court to condemn the special act exclusively benefiting the Satmar community (despite the absence of an explicit religious classification), and (2) to leave the way open for the state to permit all subgroups meeting certain technical requirements to form their own local governments and public schools, even if this would have the effect of creating as much of an actual "fusion" of religious and political authority as in the first case.

However, the neutrality of intent test alone does not suffice to create the situation in which religious and antireligious groups can actually govern themselves in furtherance of their aims. Even if the formation of a governmental entity in a particular area is approved, its actions are still subject to the requirements of constitutional and statutory law, including the establishment clause, the free exercise clause, various antidiscrimination provisions, and state laws that require democratic procedures to be followed in local governance. Furthermore, a homogeneous population, sufficient to meet the technical size requirements for incorporation and to continue to control local democratic politics, cannot be secured in the absence of other legal mechanisms.

These other mechanisms are the subject of the remainder of part II.

## B. *The Religious-Secular Distinction*

Even if an effect standard were followed, it would still be open to question whether allowing the formation of a school district (or a village), which is "coterminous with the boundaries of an insular religious community and ... controlled by members of that sect,"[49] has the effect of delegating the authority to operate an agency of government to a *religious* group. By the same token, under an intent standard, even if the state's intent to delegate authority to the Satmar community is established, the question remains whether the resulting government is a religious one. Both of these questions hinge not on the intentions of the state (in authorizing the establishment of a local government) but rather, on the intentions—or better, the *functions*—of the governmental entity that is created. In particular, the answers to these questions hinge on whether the functions of the school district or village are deemed to be religious or secular.

The courts have employed the distinction between religious and secular functions in a variety of contexts. For example, a religious group's activities do not merit protection from governmental interference under the free exercise clause unless they are actually religious activities. (Presumptively, not all of a religious group's activities are religious activities.) On the other hand, governmental actions, like the sponsorship of public Christmas displays, are not deemed to violate the establishment clause unless their content is actually religious, as opposed to merely "cultural."

The chief problem with the distinction between the secular and the religious is knowing where draw to the line. In part, this results from the fact that different religious worldviews contain different conceptions of the content of the sacred and the secular, and of the boundary line between them. At the extreme, some religions draw no such distinction at all. According to such holistic religions, religion is not confined to activities such as prayer and church attendance; nor does it consist primarily in the conscience of the believer. Rather, it suffuses an entire way of life (thus obliterating the distinction between religion and culture.)[50]

Differing conceptions of the religious and the secular give rise to various problems. First, there is the risk of religious bias on the part of a judge whose job it is to apply the distinction. Domains that one party sincerely believes to be invested with religious meaning may go unprotected, as a result of either outright animosity or simple obtuseness toward particular religious beliefs or parties.

Another problem is that even judges who are not prejudiced may nevertheless fail to properly discern the character of particular practices or beliefs. In part, this turns on issues of credibility. Religious parties have an incentive to be tactical, to characterize either their own practices or those of the government in a way that conduces to the desired legal result. Judges must therefore make determinations about the parties' personal sincerity, while simultaneously trying to make sense of the belief system which they represent.

But differing characterizations of the secular as opposed to religious nature of an activity or domain do not always (or even usually) reflect insincerity. They may instead reflect the inherent subjectivity and consequent malleability of those characterizations. For the question of whether something is religious or secular is not an objective matter but is itself entirely a matter of subjective belief—and beliefs will inevitably differ.[51] (Thus, a creche, for example, really "is" nothing more than a secular, cultural display to one person, and really "is" a religious spectacle to another). Furthermore, the same activity may serve *both* religious and secular functions simultaneously, or (what is the same thing) may come to be (sincerely) seen as doing so. Finally, the beliefs of individuals and groups regarding these matters are never static. Beliefs evolve, with the result that certain kinds of activities formerly regarded as secular become invested, by tradition, with religious significance. Conversely, activities that used to form part of a seamless web of religious life become separated from their religious significance (as has happened, for many people, with the institution of Saturdays or Sundays as work-free days). Changes occur not only in views about the character of a particular thing (i.e., whether *it* is religious or secular), but also in general views about the nature of the sacred and secular realms (i.e., what *is* religious and secular?). At any given point in time, the terms secular and religious are likely to bear more than one meaning even within a single conceptual or cultural framework. Consequently, sincere differences in views about whether a given thing is secular or religious will obtain between different groups, between different members of the same group, and even within the mind of one individual.

The inherently subjective nature of the religious-secular characterization, and the difficulties of judgment that this creates, are well illustrated in the case of *Kiryas Joel.* The proponents of the Hasidic school district were at pains to characterize the school's functions as cultural and secular, rather than religious. Accordingly, they emphasized facts such as the following:

> The school under scrutiny is a public school specifically designed to provide a public secular education to handicapped students. The superintendent, who is not Hasidic, is a 20–year veteran of the New York City public school system, with expertise in the area of bilingual, bicultural, special education. The teachers and therapists at the school all live outside the village of Kiryas Joel. While the village's private schools are profoundly religious and strictly segregated by sex, classes at the public school are co-ed and the curriculum secular. The school building has the bland appearance of a public school, unadorned by religious symbols or markings; and the school complies with the laws and regulations governing all other New York State public schools.[52]

In the same vein, proponents argued that the school was established to accommodate the cultural and psychological, not the religious needs, of members of the Hasidic community. They asserted that the goal was to spare disabled Satmar children the "emotional trauma" they suffered in the regional public schools from the "additional handicap of cultural distinctiveness."[53] In this view, Yiddish, the spoken language of the Satmar community, serves the psychological, cultural, and basic educational goals generally associated with bilingual education rather than religious ends. So, too, being in the exclusive company of Hasidic children serves the end of creating a comfortable psychological and cultural learning environment, as opposed to a religious one.

Of course, there are counterarguments. Consider the character of Yiddish as a medium of instruction within the framework of the Hasidic worldview. In the world of Eastern European Jewry, whence the Satmars emanated, Yiddish was historically used, and consciously regarded, as a religiously suffused language. Although (and in part, because) Hebrew was always recognized as the sacred language, Yiddish is the language in which discourse *about* the fundamental sacred texts is characteristically conducted. Not knowing Yiddish implies being cut off from this religious discourse. Accordingly, Yiddish instruction might well be regarded as religious rather than—or at least in addition to—secular in character.

A more sweeping refutation of the Satmar's characterization of their "secular" school stems from the holistic conception of religion embraced by Hasidic Judaism from its inception in the radical antielitist and antitextualist ideas of its nineteenth-century founder, the "Baal Shem Tov." Hasidism is a prime example of the holistic type of religion, which subscribes to the doctrine that religion pervades all of life. It was based on a rejection of the idea that religion consists exclusively, or even primarily, in the study of the sacred texts, an activity which was inevitably confined to a small rabbinic elite. Instead, Hasidism was born proclaiming that religion was everywhere, even—or especially—in the most mundane activities. According to this view, it makes no sense to refer to anything as "religious *rather than* secular." The conventional distinction between the religious and the secular realms is not a part of the Hasidic conceptual vocabulary.[54]

The Satmars' willingness to describe their public school in secular terms therefore creates a puzzle, to which several solutions may be offered. One possibility is that their description of the functions of their public institutions is strategic and insincere. According to the most cynical take on the Satmars of Kiryas Joel, they molded the curriculum of the school to omit the most obviously "religious" aspects of instruction in order to obtain legal certification, and they will covertly supply religious instruction to the fullest extent possible. Even if they adhere to the stated curriculum and announced structure of the school, these things are themselves suffused with religious meaning (for them) because, according to their religious doctrine, everything is. To deny this is merely a cynical move on the Satmars' part.

This understanding is not implausible, but it poses several difficulties and, in any event, is hardly the only plausible view. The most fundamental issue posed by this understanding is whether the religious party's view of the secular-religious characterization (supposing we know what it is) should be entirely controlling of the analysis of legal controversies. To recognize that the characterization (secular versus religious) is intrinsically subjective does not determine *whose* characterization should control. The religious party's perceptions are surely relevant, but it is far from clear that its perspective should be dispositive of legal questions. Consider the consequences of settling all free exercise and establishment clause cases on the basis of the holistic religious view, which denies the existence of a secular realm, separate and apart from the religious. According to such a view, *no* government benefit—no public education, no social security payment, no tax subsidy, no access to a public park—could ever be granted to an adherent of such a religious doctrine without implicating the establishment clause. No government action could even occur without being laden with religious significance (in the eyes of adherents of such views). But it seems outlandish for the state to regard all of its activities as "religious" just because a religious subgroup does.[55] This suggests the need for some "objective" test of secular versus religious content—objective in the sense of being independent of any particular religious party's view (but not in the sense of being independent of *anybody's* view).

The dominant political *and* religious traditions in this country deny the holistic view, and assert a clear distinction between the religious and secular. If members of a subgroup, such as the Hasidim, adopt the dominant position, it need not be regarded as feigned. They may have come to absorb the dominant view.[56] And even if the Satmars continue to view all of life, or all of their own activities, as religious in some sense, that does not imply that the conventional distinction between the secular and the religious holds no sensible meaning for them. If they conform to the convention—if they play by the ordinary rules of the game and shear off the conventionally religious content from their public institutions—why should they be denied the legal protections and licenses that ordinarily accompany it?

Many questions have been raised here regarding the sincerity of the claims of religious believers, the nature of the beliefs of different religious subcultures, and the moral and political relevance of competing beliefs about the religious-secular distinction, none of which seem very well suited to judicial resolution. But courts are called on to supply answers to these kinds of questions all the time. This may explain their attraction to another kind of formalism—a formalistic view of the religious-secular distinction itself. A consistent judicially applied division between secular and religious functions is not so much "objective" (except in the limited sense described above) as it is formalistic. It is formalistic in at least three senses. First, it does not necessarily match or get at the "real" religious meaning of the particular action that is being typed, if we understand that real meaning (in the manner of an anthropologist— or a realist) as consisting in the belief system of the religious party involved. This is particularly true since the content of the formalistic view employed by the courts is the polar opposite of the holistic view of religion. The view favored by the courts tends to restrict the category of the "religious" to things that touch directly on religious doctrines, theology, and the conscience of the individual believer, and to exclude such things as the "national" or "ethnic" feelings of a religious group, or its social customs and political traditions. Such a formalistic view denies the religious significance of, say, the Christian traditions summoned up by Santa Claus or, in some circumstances, even a creche. Likewise, it exempts the pursuit of self-perpetuation by a religious group from the category of religious activities (in the absence of an identifiable religious law commanding that pursuit), and it permits viewing mundane activities (e.g., zoning) that result in excluding nonmembers as something other than strictly religious.

Justifying religious exclusion as a secular activity also depends on a second formalistic aspect of the prevailing religious-secular distinction: the acceptance of *post hoc* rationalizations as reasons for state actions. So long as plausible reasons for a particular government action can be supplied, including the generic sort of reasons, such as "public health, safety, and welfare," that Judge Goettel invoked in *Airmont,* courts rarely insist on establishing that these reasons were actually what motivated the local government involved. Longstanding principles of judicial deference to local government permit their actions to be justified retroactively— which casts the pious references to government "intent" in an interesting light.

It was precisely this sort of *post hoc* reasoning that enabled Judge Goettel to deny that the Village of Airmont was anti-Semitic, even though it was undeniably formed in order to minimize the presence and influence of Orthodox Jews. Judge Goettel noted that, despite palpable tensions between the Orthodox inhabitants and the Village leaders, Orthodox families and developments were included within the village boundaries. Furthermore, the Village had not yet taken any specific "actions against residential synagogues or [done] anything else which has an adverse effect on the availability of housing for Orthodox or Hasidic Jews"[57]— although leaders had early on announced their intention not to permit deviations from the old zoning code. In the absence of any specific projects being derailed, Judge Goettel found that the argument against the village boiled down to the complaint "that it was conceived in sin and cannot escape the taint of its illegitimate birth."[58] In other words, the problem was precisely the intent, or animating spirit, behind the formation of the village. But this the court clearly separated from actual official actions and discarded as legally irrelevant. Judge Goettel expressly stated that whether future village actions adverse to the interests of its Orthodox inhabitants would be deemed to be discriminatory "does not depend on 'motivation'; it depends on the nature of defendants' [village officials'] conduct."[59]

The willingness to accept *post hoc* general rationalizations for offical action, and the indifference to the "real" meaning of a challenged action within the framework of a particular belief system are two marks of the judiciary's formalistic approach to the religious-secular distinction. The prevailing distinction between secular and religious functions is also formalistic in a third way. Simply by virtue of its being a bright-line, categorical distinction, it supplies the formal qualities of an easily applicable, predictable, formally realizable rule, as opposed to a fuzzy standard.[60] This, rather than its intrinsic cultural and religious bias, may be the chief attraction of the distinction. After all, the cases of *Airmont* and *Kiryas Joel* bear out the possibility that the distinction can be biased in *favor* of a religiously exclusive subcommunity in so far as it helps it to escape having its institutions characterized as religious or antireligious, and hence in violation of the law.

The question remains how such a community assembles itself and acquires the political power, which requires legitimation, in the first place. How did the villages of Airmont and Kiryas Joel come to be, and what role did state action play in their formation? More pointedly, does the state bear responsibility for the exclusionary forms that both villages assumed?[61] If so, what legal principles excuse that role from judicial condemnation under statutory or constitutional antidiscrimination and antiestablishment laws? To understand the answers to these questions, we must turn to our next distinction, the third legal formalism responsible for the *Airmont* and *Kiryas Joel* results.

## C. The Public-Private Distinction

Villages, like all local governments, are territorially defined units. According to New York state law, any territorially defined population can incorporate itself as a separate political jurisdiction so long as it meets certain minimal population and procedural requirements.[62] Therefore, some form of territorial control over contiguous plots of land had to be exercised by the Satmars in order for them to assume the position of a homogeneous population that could then secede and establish its own local government. That preceding form of territorial control was, of course, private property.

Had the Satmars been scattered, they never could have established the Village of Kiryas Joel in the first place. The prerequisite of residing in a contiguous set of lots could have been gradually assembled though the piecemeal acquisition of numerous separate properties; or though the development of subdivisions, bound by restrictive covenants, like Ramapo's "Torah Community" real estate developments, sold exclusively to members of the group; or even through the establishment of communally or jointly owned property.[63] But somehow or other a Satmar presence had to be established through the customary forms of buying and renting private property before the Satmars could stand in the position of residents of a territorially defined area, eligible to petition for village incorporation.

What prevents non-Satmars from living in Kiryas Joel and attending its public school? Not—or not formally—the exercise of formal village or district regulatory powers. There is no explicit "zoning out" of non-Satmars, and any such attempt would most surely be struck down by the courts as illegal discriminatory state action.[64] Likewise, the school district's mandate is to serve all of the children within its boundaries, without reference to religion as a criterion of eligibility. The school district and the Village are both regarded as subdivisions of the state and cannot deliberately exclude non-Satmars if they want to. True, the zoning power could be, and arguably is, used to exclude non-Satmars indirectly, by virtue of permitting types of housing to which Satmars are attracted and others are averse. Similarly, the school district's use of Yiddish as the official language of instruction, and admission of other Hasidic children from outside the Village is hardly a lure to most non-Hasidic families. But the *uniform* filtering out of non-Satmars, some of whom might be attracted to the area's less costly, multifamily housing, could be achieved only at the level of nongovernmental actions regarding the disposition of each piece of property.

The existence of Kiryas Joel as a homogeneous, exclusive, religious community depends crucially on the exercise of private rights, on the rights of private property and contract, by which real estate is obtained and controlled, and also on the rights of "family privacy" and private education, broadly construed to encompass the informal processes of enculturation as well as the formal education that is conducted by private educational and religious institutions. In the realm demarcated as private, families and educational institutions play a pivotal role in shaping the development of beliefs, preferences, and values. Such private forces are deeply embedded in, and strongly protected by, our system of law. Little controversy attends the reigning view that the constitution implicitly protects a "right of family privacy," which confers upon parents the authority to direct the upbringing of the children "under their control," including the authority to send their children to private and parochial schools, and more generally, to submit their children to a religious (or nonreligious) upbringing of their choosing.[65] It practically goes without saying that the Satmars' collective "choice" to live together, to form a community of shared practices, customs, and language, to worship and congregate in a particular manner, and to lead their distinctive way of life, was largely a product of their upbringing. Likewise, the continuation of this way of life and system of belief will depend, crucially, on their children's education and upbringing. For most of their children, this is to be achieved by sending them to private, religious schools. But for the disabled children in the Satmar community, the cost of special needs education is prohibitive in the absence of governmental subsidies—hence, the importance of their own public schools.

The centrality of the three pillars of private power enumerated above—property, family, and education (broadly construed)—is highlighted in the treatment of the few members of the Satmar community who dared to object to the leadership's stand on various issues, including the establishment of a separate public school. The community disciplined the dissenters with social shunning, and by denying them access to the village cemetery and private places of worship.[66] Though these sanctions were not enforced at law, they were powerful nonetheless. But their efficacy depends jointly on the disciplined members' ongoing desire to participate in the community's prescribed cultural practices (a desire shaped by their acquired beliefs), and on the property rights in the cemetery and houses of worship, which gave the communal leaders (in their private capacity) the power of exclusion. Communal leaders may have even greater punitive powers at their disposal if the members' real estate is in fact subjected to the sorts of restrictive covenants and servitudes that commonly bind private property associations, which exercise significant control over the membership and the members' behavior.

The binding nature of these controls may explain why, though the Satmar community has been fractious, internal dissent was not expressed in the courts of law. The question is whether these controls are coercive, or invasive of individual autonomy, even though they result from the exercise of private individual rights. If so, the proposition that nonvoluntaristic communities are destroyed by the legal bifurcation between public and private realms would seem to be undermined. Beyond that, the public-private distinction would seem effectively to undo itself by justifying the creation and control of (public) local government institutions by a (private) "autonomy-rejecting" subcommunity.[67]

The questions raised here are precisely those upon which the original legal realist attack on legal formalism first focused. According to the familiar realist critique, the exercise of private rights involves the exercise of power, and not always the exercise of free choice. Progressives and legal realists focused in particular on relations of unequal wealth and property, which, they held, transformed contractual relations, such as those between employer and employee, into coercive ones. More generally, they insisted that the reality of private power relations can negate the voluntariness of nominally consensual arrangements. To deny this—to accept the exercise of private rights at face value as a voluntary act—is, in the realist view, the hollowest formalism, or as Felix Cohen put it, "transcendental nonsense."[68]

Though always controversial, this realist critique of the conventional distinction between private and state action was incorporated into several important legal decisions. In *Marsh v. Alabama,* the Supreme Court subjected a company town to the government's first amendment obligation to allow religious proselytizers access to its "public" spaces, despite the technicality that the entire town was privately owned.[69] And in *Shelley v. Kraemer,* the Supreme Court held that the judicial enforcement of a neighborhood scheme of racially restrictive covenants violates the state's obligation to provide equal protection of the law to all citizens regardless of race, notwithstanding that covenants arise out of the exercise of individual property-owners' rights.[70] In both cases, the underlying rationale was that the private entities and actions involved were "functionally equivalent" to public ones.

In contrast to a formalist style of analysis, this version of functionalism focuses on the actual effects on people of an action, regardless of its formal status as private or public. In this respect, it is similar to the functionalist effect test, which vies with the intent test as a standard for evaluating the constitutionality of state action. But unlike the effect test considered above, this version of functionalism is not concerned with the question whether action attributed to the state comports with constitutional standards of neutrality, but rather, with the prior question of establishing what counts as "state action." With regard to this question, legal realism assimilates private rights to public authority both by recognizing that regulative or coercive effects can occur in the private realm, and by revealing that in some cases, public action may actually be involved in, or responsible for, private action, and vice versa.

As is well known, the realist critique of the public-private distinction has, since its inception, occupied a curious position in the law: simultaneously affirmed as the most banal truism and subject to unrelenting attack. The Supreme Court has refused to apply the reasoning of *Shelley* and *Marsh v. Alabama* in numerous cases, insisting instead that the line between "state action" and private rights must be defended.[71] Yet it also refuses to overturn these holdings. So there they remain, along with other accepted doctrines based on the premises of legal realism. In the absence of a willingness to completely disgorge them, these lumps of realist reasoning continue to inform analysis of private rights, as can be seen seen in the arguments of the parties opposing the Kiryas Joel school district, and, more dimly, in Justice Souter's crypto-functionalist rhetoric. The repeated assertions that the statute creating the district "was tantamount to" delegating public authority to a religious community in fact bear two different meanings. The first, considered in section A, amounts to the claim that the state *intended* to bestow its authority upon the religious community but disguised its intentions in nonexplicit language. Such an intention in and of itself violates the requirement of the establishment clause that the state be impartial vis-à-vis religious and nonreligious groups. But, as we have seen, this defect is easily remedied by the passage of general legislation that enables all communities to form school districts, regardless of their religious character.

Such general legislation fails to cure the defect posited in the second understanding of the allegation that the statute "effectively" empowers a religious community to rule. This is the essentially realist charge that the legislation has the effect of empowering a religious community, as such.[72] Since the realist concern is with the effect, regardless of legislative intention, it is just as applicable to the general as to the special legislation. The fact that the Satmar community is not singled out for special treatment is irrelevant to the question of whether the community comes in fact to exercise official, regulatory powers. What *is* relevant to that charge is the underlying arrangement of private power within the community. Were it not the case that the public and private leadership were virtually interchangeable; that all property was held by members of the Satmar community; that the members were subject to very powerful forces of socialization and regulation within the community—then drawing local government boundaries around the community would not necessarily have the practical effect of empowering the religious community as such. Yet, given these factual conditions, that is precisely the effect of the general legislation under which the Village and school district of Kiryas Joel are now incorporated, no less than of the special legislation struck down by the Supreme Court.

The fact that the Supreme Court favored the first meaning of the functionalist allegation over the second is a sign of the ascendance of formalist over realist reasoning. The Court ultimately ignored the realist concern about practical effects and instead focused on what I earlier called a "crypto-functionalist" concern with non-express intent on the part of the legislature. In rejecting the effect standard of neutrality for purposes of evaluating the legitimacy of local governments under the establishment clause, the Supreme Court signaled its ongoing commitment to the formalist distinction between private and public action. From this perspective, the fact that only Satmars live in Kiryas Joel is an artifact, not of coercion or state action, but of the private preferences of Satmars and non-Satmars, respectively, to live with their own kind.

The case for the constitutional relevance of the underlying private preferences and arrangements would have been stronger if attention were paid to the existence of mechanisms of collective control within (and without) the Satmar community—in other words, if the realist critique of economic relations (and the realist effect standard of neutrality) were applied to the relations of cultural community. Conversely, the most powerful case for the autonomy of subcommunities would be one that directly defends their internal power structure and regulatory mechanisms. Yet, strangely, both sides of the liberal-communitarian debate have shied away from the realist critique that exposes the internal political structure and power relations within private groups. Reflecting the widening gap between the politics of class and the politics of identity, communitarians typically eschew the realist critique of liberalism's actual coercive effects in favor of the view that liberalism achieves what it purports to: namely, the enforcement of voluntary relations and individual choice in the private realm. That, after all, is the favorite target of the communitarian critique, which vanishes if the realist critique of private power is accepted. On the other hand, defenders of liberalism also tend to refrain from staking their case on the (for them) normatively unattractive proposition that liberalism actually countenances involuntary relations and collective coercion in the private realm.[73] Yet, though both liberals and communitarians shy away from it, the realist understanding of the power of private property and other nominally voluntary relations is, as we have seen, highly germane to the case of *Kiryas Joel*. Private property, the family, and private educational institutions were the three pillars of legally protected private power that enabled Kiryas Joel to found and sustain itself as a strong, nonvoluntaristic community.

*Airmont* is a less clear-cut case. Judge Goettel expressly found that the Village was not exercising its formal, regulatory powers against the Jewish community, and that members of the Orthodox and Hasidic communities were (so far) able to own and develop property in the area, and to establish and attend synagogues. He drew no inferences from these private arrangements other than that official acts of discrimination were absent, thereby displaying his affinity for the formalist style of analysis. He also exhibited the formalist's disinterest in the actions and motivations of private citizens in his peremptory dismissal of the relevance of the argument that the village was "conceived in sin." What would *Airmont* have looked like in a realist framework of analysis? Unlike the Village of Kiryas Joel, in which property-ownership, residence, and consequently, political influence are entirely Satmar-dominated, and in which the community is holistic, pervasively regulated and strongly prescriptive, the situation in Airmont is less sharply defined. Orthodox and Hasidic Jews were deliberately made a minority, but they do own some property, and it remains hazy *how much* property-ownership (from a realist perspective) is enough to rebut a charge that their options are unacceptably restricted. The remaining property is held by a loose collection of individual families, among whom the resistance to letting it into the hands of Orthodox Jews varies. How strong (and how organized) must the collective resistance be to support a *Shelley v. Kraemer*-style charge of exclusion? The non-Orthodox residents are not a tight-knit community—do they share enough of a bond to support the characterization of an exclusive group? The realist alternative to formalist reasoning supplies no certain answers to these questions; it only points to their relevance.

What is certain is that the majority of Airmont residents' aversion to the traditional Jewish way of life is as much a product of their upbringing as the Satmars' way of life is a product of theirs. The difference is only that one upbringing reflects the values of a tight-knit, insular, prescriptive group, the other, the values of a diffuse, atomized, modern, "liberal" society. In the end, a realist analysis may simply reveal that a strong community imposes stronger private controls on individuals than a weak one does. This may seem the sheerest tautology. But if so, it is a tautology that contradicts the truism that strong, nonvoluntaristic communities dissolve under the legally enforced division between public and private realms. The realist critique breaks through that truism; the formalist distinction between public and private action reinstalls it. The courts' preference for the latter is indispensable to their justification of general enabling laws, under which religiously exclusive local governments, like Airmont and Kiryas Joel, can be formed. The public-private distinction underwrites the very idea that these governments "just happen" to contain particular groups, and that they therefore bear no responsibility for the exclusion of outsiders from their borders.

## D. The General-Particular Distinction

The three preceding formalisms aggressively defend bright-line distinctions from erosion by their corresponding antiformalist (realist) critiques. Together, they create and legitimate the legal resources by which strong communities, including non-voluntaristic ones like the community of Kiryas Joel, can arise in the private realm and in turn capture (or create) local public institutions. Under a formalist analysis, this phenemonon is legitimate when (1) the mechanisms of exclusion are formally private (the public-private distinction); (2) the mechanisms of government serve secular, not religious ends (the religious-secular distinction); and (3) the mechanisms of government are available on a "general" as opposed to a "special" basis (which is determined in part on the basis of the intent-effect distinction). Even when (1) and (2) obtain, the law will regard the delegation of governmental authority to a religiously exclusive group as illegitimate if it has been authorized on a "special," i.e., group-specific basis (as in the case of *Kiryas Joel*).

Proposition (3) entails a fourth formalism, which pertains to the distinction between the general and the specific itself. This formalism differs from the others in two respects. First, the quality of generality versus specificity is not necessarily social in content, whereas the other qualities (intentionality versus effect, regardless of intent; religion versus secularism; public versus private) are. Generality and specificity are inherently formal characteristics. Consequently, the antiformalistic view of the distinction between generality and particularism does not dissolve the contrast, but rather, reconceives it. The realist critique blurs the distinction between public and private actions; it deconstructs the idea of the secular *as opposed to* the religious; it substitutes the functionalist test of neutrality of effect for the standard of neutrality of intent. But a realist view of generality and particularity preserves the distinction between them, even while it rejects a formalistic conception of what that distinction consists in.

These statements are themselves thus far utterly formal and in need of substantive content. Fortunately, an indication of the content of the formalistic view is at hand in an essay by the constitutional scholar Michael W. McConnell. More fortunately still, McConnell developed this conception as part of a vision of "multicultural" public education. In this vision:

> each school could teach from a coherent moral-cultural perspective—one that is *chosen* by its student body. Of course, educational choice is risky. It runs the risk that some will choose a moral education that is pernicious, and that many will choose ethnically and religiously particularistic alternatives that might exacerbate already-dangerous divisions. I suspect these fears are overblown, however, just as the similar fears of religious pluralism were overblown in the eighteenth century. With parents making the decisions, how likely is it that many will choose alternatives that are demonstrably worse than the results of the present system?[74]

This passage adumbrates the view implicitly adopted by the Supreme Court in *Kiryas Joel*. As McConnell notes, there are two different ways of understanding and implementing the call for multiculturalism in public education. In one, multiculturalism is opposed to particularism or cultural bias, and consists in incorporating all subcultures in one common (general) culture and curriculum, which is then made available to all. The other version, endorsed by McConnell, "comes from those who deny the very desirability of a common curriculum and advocate a pluralistic system of schools dedicated to particular, and *particularistic,* traditions."[75] In this "more radical" view, the nondiscriminatory treatment of different cultural group consists not in *overcoming* particularism, but rather, in giving each group an equal right to *be* particularistic. Generality (nondiscrimination) and particularism thus ironically converge.

This definition of generality is formalistic from the standpoint of the competing view,[76] according to which particularism consists in the advancement of the values and objectives of one particular group to the exclusion of others. Members of a particularistic culture or political system have loyalties and obligations to one another, and to the shared heritage and projected future of their group. A political system is particularistic precisely in so far as it represents a culturally specific belief system, including its conception of morality, its social and political norms, and its criteria of membership. Often, such a political system will make symbolic references to the "imagined history" of the nation or cultural group which it represents. Particularistic groups also tend to impose more far-reaching restrictions and obligations on individual members than the merely "negative" duty to leave other individuals alone. By enforcing such obligations, by promoting its own values and culture, a particularistic group excludes (or is at least biased against) competing cultural value systems.

By contrast, a political system is nonparticularistic in so far as it refrains from exclusion and bias against competing values, cultures, and beliefs. Such a system is inclusive rather than exclusive, internally pluralistic rather than one of a number of diverse (but internally homogeneous) separatist islands of cultural autonomy. From the standpoint of this conception of particularism, McConnell's "radical" vision is formalistic because it allows exclusionary, particularistic politics to proceed unchecked, within each group's separate sphere, so long as each group has an equal opportunity to establish a particularistic political sphere of its own.

The formalistic distinction between particularistic and nonparticularistic political regimes functions similarly to the public-private distinction. Both serve to shift responsibility for exclusionary regulation away from judicially cognizable "state actors." Both thus deny the reality that the observable pheonomenon of social exclusion is a function of state-backed coercive regulations. The public-private distinction locates the mechanism for excluding outsiders from local government boundaries in a multitude of private, voluntary acts and preferences, for which the state bears no responsibility. The formalistic version of the general-particularistic distinction shifts responsibility away from the state to a multitude of local political communities. Though such local communities are formally *public* entities, the formalistic distinction acts, as it were, as a moral solvent, dissolving each local government's responsibility for enacting particularistic regulation into a larger political universe. Such is the salt-water alchemy of the formalistic view of general and particular.[77]

The contrast between formalistic and substantive views of the general-particular distinction is familiar to us from another context—the doctrine of "separate but equal" racial spheres. Like the controversy over the competing intent and effect tests of governmental neutrality, the conflict over the compatibility of separatism with equality developed in the context of race relations and the jurisprudence of the equal protection clause. In this setting, the doctrine of separate but equal was denounced as a specious formalism in a line of cases that culminated in the 1954 school desegregation decision *Brown v. Board of Education.* The unanimous Supreme Court decision, holding that racially segregated public schools are unconstitutional, was firmly (or unfirmly, as critics would have it) based on antiformalistic reasoning, the hallmark of which, as we have seen, is a concern with actual effects. According to the *Brown* analysis, racially segreated education is "inherently" unequal because of its inevitably stigmatizing "effect" upon "Negro" children.[78] The Court rejected the proposition that separatism could be reconciled with equality—that particularism could be reconciled with generality or neutrality—as a hollow formalism that ignores, masks, and ultimately justifies the real, pernicious psychological and social *effects* of segregation.[79]

Since *Brown v. Board* was decided, there has been a steady

stream of criticism against the integrationist philosophy upon which it is based. Black nationalists, resurgent white supremacists, and, increasingly, the moderate middle (white and black) have questioned the wisdom of rejecting the doctrine of separate but equal. Thus, McConnell has good reason to refer to the espousal of a version of this doctrine as a "radical" position, but could also, with equal accuracy, call it a conservative position. The interesting question, for our purposes, is in what sense we might regard it (as McConnell does) as a *liberal* position.

This is the matter to be considered in the final part of this essay. But before proceeding, it may be useful to take stock and review the role played by all four of our formalist doctrines in justifying the results of *Airmont* and *Kiryas Joel.*

The formalistic version of the general-particular distinction completes that justification in the following fashion. Religiously exclusive communities (i.e., communities that exclude a certain religion or religions or communities that include only one religion) can legally create or control their own local public institutions, such as villages and school districts, when (1) the mechanisms whereby the exclusivity of the community is maintained are formally private (the public-private distinction); (2) the public regulations serve secular, not religious ends (the religious-secular distinction); (3) the group is effectively, but not "intentionally," empowered to rule (the intent-effect distinction) — a condition which is interpreted in terms of (4): the authority to govern has been delegated to the group on a "general" rather than a "special" or group-specific basis (the formalistic general-particular distinction.) In other words, the state's effective political empowerment of a particular, religiously exclusive group is deemed to be unintentional — even if the state is perfectly aware of the effect of its action, and even if the state in some sense "desires" that effect — so long as the same opportunity is afforded to every group in the "same" situation (i.e., a sufficiently concentrated and sizable population, which votes democratically to form its own political institutions).

The formalistic distinction between specificity and generality functions as gloss on the meaning of the intent-effect distinction, and in doing so, explains two of our earlier puzzles. First, it explains the judges' lack of interest in the actual motives of the local voters, of the founders of the local government, and of the local government itself, despite their professed interest in the state's intent. Notwithstanding the settled doctrine that local governments are units of the state, the formalistic general-particular distinction holds in effect that the (self-)promotion of a local community is not an intention attributable to the state so long as every local community is given an equal opportunity to promote itself. In short, generalize the group right to self-rule, and it no longer counts as the sort of particularism which violates the legal constraints placed on "state action."

Second, the formalistic distinction between general and particular gives content to the term "intent," which explains its deviation in judicial usage from more commonsense notions of the term. Coupled with the formalistic general-particular distinction, as it was in *Kiryas Joel*, "intent" is revealed to be a term of art. We recall that in *Airmont*, Judge Goettel insisted that the discriminatory nature of local government action "does not depend on 'motivation'; it depends on the nature of defendants' conduct." Yet at the same time he hewed to an intent standard of discrimination, focusing on the government's "objectives." The apparent contradiction between following the intent test and rejecting the relevance of motivation is resolved when we realize that, for Goettel, government "objectives" and government "conduct" are one and the same: to wit, actions, which are subject to *post hoc* rationalizations based on their perceived effects. If Airmont's actions are consistent with advancing the *general* health and welfare of the local community, they will not be deemed to be discriminatory (regardless of the actual "motivations" of the founders or leaders of the new village). Similarly, according to the reasoning of *Kiryas Joel*, the state will not be deemed to have intended to promote the welfare of the Satmar community (in particular) so long as it can be seen to be advancing the welfare of the general (statewide) community. The fact that it only enacted general legislation after the Supreme Court invalidated the original special legislation, and that it did so specifically in order to enable the Satmar school district to continue to exist, is simply irrelevant to this formalistic definition of intent.

The four formalisms listed above explain why general legislation empowering particularistic local communities is considered constitutional, and why special legislation is not. They thereby explain the persistence of prescriptive-regulative communities in our legal order—a phenomenon whose existence contradicts the dire prognosis for non-voluntaristic communities posited by liberals and communitarians alike. But do they explain features of a *liberal* legal order? In order to answer this question, we must consider the relationship of each of our formalistic doctrines to the theory and principles of liberalism, a project which deserves far more expansive treatment than I can offer here. A brief consideration, however, may provide some tentative support for the thesis that these four formalistic doctrines are compatible with and expressive of contemporary liberal political thought.

## III. The Liberalism in Formalism (Or Formalism in Liberalism)

The relationship of liberalism to the four formalist doctrines analyzed above is of course a matter of interpretation. John Rawls and Joseph Raz are liberal theorists whose commonalities and differences, taken together, seem representative of contemporary liberal thought. Accordingly, an analysis of the place our four formalisms have in the work of Rawls and Raz may shed light on their more general place in liberalism.

### A. The Intent-Effect Distinction

Rawls, in his latest book, expressly endorses the intent test and, in the quotation with which this essay began, rejects the effect test on the grounds of "impossibility" and "the facts of commonsense political sociology." Rawls summarizes his position:

> As a political conception for the basic structure justice as fairness [Rawls's proposed interpretation of liberalism] as a whole tries to provide common ground as the focus of an overlapping consensus. It also hopes to satisfy neutrality of aim in the sense that basic institutions and public policy are not to be designed to favor any particular comprehensive doctrine. Neutrality of effect or influence political liberalism abandons as impracticable, and since this idea is strongly suggested by the term itself, this is a reason for avoiding it.[80]

This epitaph for the effect test is followed by Rawls's observation, tucked in a footnote, that abandoning it may well allow us to justify a political environment that is hostile—*in effect*—to "religious sects that oppose the culture of the modern world."[81] He calls particular attention to the potential effects of liberalism on children's education and the possibility that "reasonable requirements for children's education" in a liberal regime may have "unavoidable" (negative) consequences for some groups. Rawls defines "reasonable" political requirements in terms of the contrast he asserts between "political" and "comprehensive" liberalism. A "comprehensive liberal" education would actively "foster the values of autonomy and individuality as ideals to govern much if not all of life," an activity which obviously—and unacceptably, to Rawls—implies driving out competing value-systems. Rawls favors "political liberalism," which is ostensibly more modest because it is pluralistic and seeks to govern only the political realm, and not "all of life." Unlike a comprehensively liberal education, a "politically liberal" education requires only the knowledge that constitutional and civic rights, such as liberty of conscience, exist. But even a politically liberal education, Rawls concedes, may end up promoting values that touch on all of life—in effect. Thus, he grants that "requiring children to understand the political conception . . . is in effect, though not in intention, to educate them to a comprehensive liberal conception," at least "in the case of some." From his earlier forswearing of the effect test, it follows that this "unintended" effect is legitimate.[82]

Rawls's discussion of neutrality is notable in one further respect. While he rejects the principle of neutrality of effect, he accepts another definition of neutrality in addition to neutrality of intent. The second definition he endorses is a version of the equal opportunity principle for competing belief systems that we referred to above as the formalistic view of nonparticularism or generality. Rawls qualifies the principle to allow citizens an "equal opportunity" to advance only each "permissible" belief system,[83] but it remains a recognizable version of the principle that there should be equal opportunity for citizens to promote their varying particularistic beliefs.

In *Kiryas Joel* and *Airmont,* the formalist standard of generality (equal-opportunity-for-particularism) combines with the intent standard of neutrality to exonerate government of nonneutral intentions, and thus to legitimate its promotion of the objectives of particularistic, exclusive groups (so long as the opportunity for particularistic local government is apparently generalized). By contrast, for Rawls, the combination of the formalistic conception of nonparticularism with the intent standard serves to qualify the principle of equal opportunity for particularistic groups so as to permit the government to impose "unintended" obstacles to a group's effective implementation of its right to advance its conception of the good. This difference reflects the fact that Rawls considers only the negative effects visited by liberal government on subgroups. But the cases of our two villages show that the effect of implementing *these* principles of liberal government can be *advantageous* for groups in some situations, as it was for the Satmar community in Kiryas Joel and the anti-Orthodox community in Airmont, the consequences of which Rawls does not consider.

Joseph Raz rejects the intent test—but he does not adopt the competing effect test. Instead, Raz rejects all three of the conceptions of neutrality delineated above, making mincemeat of them by a series of *reductios.*[84] In his view, neutrality is a chimera best abandoned in favor of a principle of "pluralism," under which "it is the goal of all political action to enable individuals to pursue valid conceptions of the good and to discourage evil or empty ones."[85] As a perfectionist principle, Raz's pluralism permits—nay, calls for—governmental action that will affect the viability of different belief systems differentially. The rationale for this is that to do otherwise "in practice would lead not merely to a political stand-off from support for valuable conceptions of the good. It would undermine the chances of survival of many cherished aspects of culture."[86] In other words, some belief systems must be sacrificed in order to enable other (autonomy-promoting) ones to survive. Neutrality of effect be damned!

In sum, both Rawls and Raz emphatically reject the principle of neutrality of effect as a measure of legitimate government action, though only Rawls endorses the formalistic intent test. As for Raz, it is as if he unearthed the value-laden content lurking behind the intent test's value-neutral shell, and turned it into a substantive, nonformalistic virtue. In doing so, he underscores contemporary liberalism's antipathy to the antiformalist principle of neutrality of effect.

## B. *The Religious-Secular Distinction*

Neither Rawls nor Raz specifically addresses the secular-religious distinction. Yet each treats the problem of religious "sects" in a way that reflects an implicit belief in that distinction, and in the fundamental assumption that the political realm should be a secular one.

For example, Rawls's notion of "comprehensive conceptions of the good" that are ruled out of bounds in the political sphere comprehends both nonreligious and religious philosophies of life, but it is religion that is his constant foil.[87] He repeatedly takes up the plight of "religious sects that oppose the culture of the modern world," a plight that he views as a consequence of the necessarily secular character of politics in a liberal regime.

But to hold that politics should be secular presumes a definition of what religion is (or at least what it is not). The holistic conception of religion, for example, is not available to Rawls because it denies the very possibility of a secular realm. Rawls's conception of religion resembles that of the courts. He invariably equates religion with theological doctrines of religious obligation, which bind the conscience of the individual believer. This doctrinal view of religion contrasts with a wider (more anthropological or realist) view of religion that sees it as a web of social practices that includes bonds of cultural or political solidarity, that may or may not be expressed in a theology of divinely prescribed individual obligations, and that may or may not require the individual to affirm a particular creed. Implicitly, Christianity (more specifically, Protestantism as it developed in the seventeenth century) serves as Rawls's paradigm or "model case" of religion.[88] Insisting upon the necessity of liberty of conscience, he makes it clear that his conception accommodates only "religious doctrines with an account of free faith." He defends this restriction on the ground that he supposes "perhaps too optimistically—that, except for certain kinds of fundamentalism, all the main historical religions admit of such an account."[89] Despite acknowledging the social dimension of religion, Rawls assumes a bifurcation between the "nonpolitical" or private sphere of the individual conscience and the secular sphere of politics, and confines religion to the former.

Raz also addresses the problem of "religious sects" along with "immigrant communities" and "indigenous peoples" as part of a brief consideration of the "troubling problem" of "the treatment of communities whose culture does not support autonomy." Unlike Rawls, Raz adopts the wider anthropological/realist view of religion as a "culture," as opposed to the narrower, doctrinal conception of religion. This leads him to differ with Rawls over the treatment of autonomy-rejecting cultures and the problem of children's education. On the premise that some such cultures "enable members . . . to have an adequate and satisfying life," Raz counsels tolerance for their "continued existence," and the protection of their "separate schools" from coercive interference by the state.[90] Rawls's attitude is less forgiving. In his view, society owes no special treatment to people whose "preferences and tastes" are so different that they fail to be satisfied by the official arrangements of society. Instead, he suggests rather ominously, such deviations should be regarded as "a medical or psychiatric" condition and "treated accordingly." Reflecting his general reluctance to conceptualize religion as a culture worthy of protection in its own right, he admonishes the reader that "we don't say that because the preferences arose from upbringing and not from choice that society owes us compensation. Rather, it is a normal part of being human to cope with the preferences our upbringing leaves us with."[91]

The differing attitudes toward culturally conditioned beliefs exhibited here by Raz and Rawls echo the sharp exchange of views between Justice Stevens and Justice Scalia in *Kiryas Joel.* For Stevens, who condemned the special legislation forming the Hasidic school district on broader grounds than the majority, the problem is that separate schooling "isolates" the children from exposure to diverse ways of life, and serves to "cement" their attachment to their parents' faith—terms that hint at the kind of pathology which Rawls seems to have in mind. As Scalia tartly responded, "so much for family values."[92]

But, as with their disagreement over the intent standard, Raz's apparent disagreement with Rawls over the nature and value of religion is deceptive. In the end, both are profoundly ambivalent about the merits of the claims of illiberal religious groups to control the education of "their" children, and to govern themselves. Rawls in fact vacillates between the doctrinal and the cultural conceptions of religion, and both Raz and Rawls vacillate over the fundamental issue of whether illiberal religious cultures deserve to be protected against the cultural influence of the liberal state. Like Stevens, Raz recognizes that "[s]ince they insist on bringing up their children in their own ways they are, in the eyes of liberals like myself, harming them." Therefore, "people are justified in taking action to assimilate the minority group, at the cost of letting its culture die or at least be considerably changed by absorption."[93] On the other hand, Rawls is anxious to limit state incursions on religious autonomy—a value which, he recognizes, protects associations and groups as well as individuals "all from one another."[94] Precisely because he does allow himself to recognize the cultural dimension of religion, he is content (in most cases) to wait out the gradual "adjustment or revision of comprehensive doctrines." He assumes that this is bound to occur because of the "looseness" and "slippage" he observes in our comprehensive views, and their adaptability to "shifting circumstances of time and place."[95] In short, like Raz, Rawls expects most religions (save for the obstinate "fundamentalist" ones) to assimilate the culture and political values of liberalism.

Neither Raz nor Rawls exactly endorses a formalistic conception of the secular and religious realms and hence neither supplies definitive proof that liberalism requires one. But their work is certainly redolent of such a distinction. The very notion, common to Raz and Rawls, that religious beliefs evolve as a result of mundane changes in external social and political circumstances bespeaks a fundamentally secular perspective from which the truth of any particular religious view, and the reality of its conception of divinity, are not denied—nor affirmed—but rather "bracketed." This mental operation of bracketing itself implies a bifurcation between secular and religious realms.

This bifurcation is formalistic in the sense that it does not fully comprehend the experience of religions that extend beyond the doctrinal model of a system of beliefs (in divinely commanded duties) adopted by the freely confessing individual. It is less clear whether it is formalistic in the sense, posited in our earlier discussion, of making *post hoc* rationalizations of the secular character of governmental action; or in the third sense, also discussed above, of positing an impenetrable barrier or "bright line" between secular and religious realms. Perhaps the law requires more simplistic, air-tight categorical distinctions, and inclines more toward *post hoc* characterizations, than does the pure theory of liberalism itself, because of the practical demands of application. Even so, some version of the formal distinction between the secular and religious appears to be assumed by contemporary liberal political thought.

### C. The Public-Private Distinction

The distinction between religious and secular realms implies a more fundamental distinction between the private and public spheres. Both Raz and Rawls consign religion to some version of the private or "nonpublic" realm, though each resists the simplistic conception of that realm as a domain of free-floating individual will, choice, and agency. Conversely, the political realm is, in both their views, implicitly secular (though suffused with moral content).

Enough ink has been spilled on the centrality of the public-private distinction to liberal thought.[96] Suffice it to say that some such distinction is clearly essential to liberalism, though not the naive variety which serves as strawman in many critiques. Raz's *Morality of Freedom* is one of the most serious attempts to wean liberalism from its dependency upon such a simple-minded distinction. Rawls, too, attempts to throw off the historical baggage associated with the distinction by replacing it with a distinction between the "political" and the "nonpolitical."[97] Despite these efforts, both continue to rely on (different) notions of a division between the affairs of government and those of the nonpolitical realm. Such notions are necessitated by the basic commitment to pluralism, which both posit as the essence of liberalism. No matter how much particular moral content each allows to be expressed in the political order, no matter how culturally-specific they recognize the liberal polity to be, the fundamental political objective upheld by both Rawls and Raz is to allow "space" for a plurality of subcultures and value systems to exist. And that "space" *is* the private domain.

Does this mean that liberalism, as interpreted by Raz and Rawls, rejects the realist critique of the public-private distinction? On the contrary, they both qualify their respective conceptions of the nature of "choice," "autonomy" and individual "freedom" in the private realm in ways that recall realist critiques and undermine any simple opposition between voluntary action (or belief), on one hand, and coercion and constraint, on the other. For example, according to Rawls, "freedom" of conscience means only that our beliefs are freely accepted "politically speaking," not that we actually accept them "by an act of free choice, as it were, apart from all prior loyalites and commitments, attachments, and affections." [98] Rawls provides no further explication of this rather enigmatic distinction, but it seems to imply that he accepts the basic realist proposition that power abounds in the private realm, as well as the "communitarian" tenet that beliefs are conditioned by culture and collective entities.

Raz offers a fuller elaboration of the concepts of individual freedom, autonomy, and choice, which likewise expresses the basic insights of the realist critique. He echoes the realist position that a person whose options are severely restricted, such as a person who is constantly fighting for survival, is not free because "a choice between survival and death is no choice." [99] Insisting that "the autonomous life . . . depends on the general character of one's environment and culture," and recognizing that "an autonomy-supporting culture . . . lacks most of the opportunities" available in a traditional society, Raz concludes paradoxically that "the value of autonomy does not depend on choice." [100]

Rawls and Raz's evident inclination to qualify the public-private distinction to the point of undermining it, combined with their various attempts to dissociate liberalism from individualism and their suggestions of grounds of liberal support for social welfare programs, indicate a basic receptivity to the realist critique. Indeed, legal realism is properly regarded as an outgrowth of the liberal tradition. Nonetheless, it remains the case that both Rawls and Raz, representing the general trend of that tradition, continually return to and resurrect versions of the public-private distinction. For all that Rawls acknowledges the collective regulatory dimension of the "nonpublic" realm, he still reverts to asserting a "contrast" with "the government's authority" because the latter (presumably unlike the former) "cannot be evaded."[101] And for all that Raz denies that autonomy is a matter of individual choice, he still defines "an autonomous person's well-being" in terms of "self-*chosen* goals and relationships."[102]

The resolution of these contradictions remains obscure. Liberalism, interpreted by Raz and Rawls, displays profound ambivalence toward the public-private distinction. With one hand, the liberal deconstructs that formalistic distinction; with the other, she resurrects it. In the end, though the matter is complex, it seems proper to regard the courts' commitment to the formalistic distinction between public and private realms as an expression of (part of) contemporary liberal thought, and not as something foreign to it, even as the formalistic public-private distinction is challenged by a competing view within both liberal theory and judicial doctrine.

### D. The General-Particular Distinction

Little systematic thought has been devoted to the general-particular distinction. The virtues of the doctrine of separate but equal have been subject to extensive discussion, especially in the context of race relations in the United States. In this context, some have floated a distinction between voluntary and self-imposed segregation (building on the public-private distinction) as a possible way of reconciling the separate but equal doctrine with the basic tenets of liberalism. Questions have been raised concerning the similarity, or lack thereof, between religion and race, which might support a revived doctrine of separate but equal self-government for religious groups, but not for racially defined ones. But the answers to these questions remain undeveloped.

More generally, the very definition of particularism has received little systematic discussion. Analyses of the meaning of "equality" and "neutrality" have been undertaken.[103] But even these fail to provide an adequate analysis of the meaning of the basic distinction between the specific and the general, or of the particular question of the legitimacy of group-specific government within a liberal state. Further rounds of the liberal-communitarian debate are bound to be fruitless until we gain a better understanding of what particularism *is*—and what its opposite is. Is particularism fulfilled, or is it negated if every group is guaranteed equal opportunity to establish its own local political institutions? Does such a guarantee demonstrate or cancel out a particularistic (i.e., biased) state "intent"? What are the conditions of "voluntary" or "self-imposed" political separatism, and can they be coherently distinguished from forced segregation—especially when children are involved? (Remember Justice Steven's view.) Should the answers to these questions differ if religion, as opposed to race is involved? Why? What is the basis of *this* distinction?

Despite a tradition of liberal condemnation of the formalistic separate but equal doctrine, we have seen that both Raz and Rawls exhibit some sympathy for a version of the equal right to be separate and particularistic. It remains unclear how far this liberal right—this "equal opportunity"—goes, in particular, whether it goes so far as to support the right of a group to create its own particularistic *public* institutions, as was implicitly approved by the *Kiryas Joel* court and by Judge Goettel in *Airmont*.

### POSTSCRIPT: GETTING REAL

On September 21, 1995, the United States Court of Appeals for the Second Circuit overturned Judge Goettel's decision in *Airmont*. Writing for the court, and joined by Judges Jose Cabranes and McLaughlin, Judge Amalya Kearse reinstated the jury's verdict against the Village that Judge Goettel had set aside, and further held that "the evidence was sufficient to establish that Airmont violated the private plaintiffs' rights under the Fair Housing Act and the First Amendment." [104]

The evidence cited by Judge Kearse consisted largely of statements by members of the Airmont Civic Association, the citizen's organization that had promoted the incorporation of Airmont as a separate village. For example: "I am not prejudice [sic] in any way, shape or form but i [sic] will not have a hasidic community in my backyard"; "what would be better, for us to loose [sic] our homes for a religious sect or for us to live as we have lived for the past 25 years"; "lets face it, the only reason we formed this village is to keep those Jews from Williamsburg out of here." [105] Judge Goettel, we recall, had determined such statements to be irrelevant to the question of the Village's discriminatory motives because the Civic Association was an organization of private citizens. Judge Kearse's opinion jettisoned this formalistic distinction between private and public actions in favor of a more realist approach. From this standpoint, less important than the fact that these statements were made before the Village was even incorporated is the fact that they were made in order to *get* the Village incorporated; less important than the fact that the authors of these statements spoke as private citizens is the fact that they were leaders of the Village incorporation movement, and would eventually assume official positions as the Village's mayor, trustees, and planning board members.

Just as the second circuit opinion rejects the formalistic view of state action, it also adopts a more functionalist approach to the question of intent. It does not eschew the requirement of establishing discriminatory intent altogether, but it displays a basic affinity for the realist approach in holding that such intent "may be inferred from the totality of the circumstances, including the fact, if it is true, that the law bears more heavily on one [group] than another." [106] In other words, discriminatory effects, like the prejudiced statements of "private" leaders of the incorporation movement, are evidence of the antireligious animus necessary to show a legal violation—a position which significantly blurs the distinction between neutrality of effect and neutrality of intent.

From the standpoint of this analysis, the idea that the same people who "forecast 'a grim picture of a Hasidic Belt from Rockland through Orange & Sullivan counties'" are not now inspired by anti-Hasidic sentiment is a hollow conceit. But if the exclusionary functions of the Village of Airmont stand condemned under the antiformalist approach, how could the Village of Kiryas Joel, and its public school system, survive under that same approach? The boundaries between public and private leadership in Kiryas Joel are at least as blurred, the exclusionary impact of their policies at least as strong as in Airmont; its official policies have at least as much of a religious function as do Airmont's zoning policies exhibit an antireligious function.

The antiformalist or realist analysis calls into question the legitimacy of any group separating itself from the larger community and establishing itself as a self-governing polity. Advocates for Hasidic and Orthodox Jews, along with other defenders of the rights of religious communities, have yet to confront the conflict between their own desire for political autonomy, which depends, as shown in our analysis, on a formalistic jurisprudence, and their opposition to religious discrimination, of the sort exhibited and eventually condemned under the realist jurisprudence of the Second Circuit in *Airmont.*

As calls for "community" proliferate, and as more and more groups actually separate themselves from the larger, more diverse political jurisdictions of which they have historically been a part, it behooves us all to be realists about the exclusion that secession entails. In my own view, *Airmont* teaches us that the implicit formalism embodied in the trial court's opinion and in *Kiryas Joel,* the formalism that underwrites the establishment and the legitimacy of the Village of Airmont, the Village of Kiryas Joel and its newly authorized school system, is wrong. Not necessarily wrong legally, nor even from the standpoint of the principles of liberal political philosophy, but wrong in terms of human consequences—in terms of its effects. One cannot take refuge in this statement of opposition to exclusionary effects, since we have seen that such opposition itself inevitably crowds out competing ways of life. But even if we cannot escape the paradox of liberalism and community, we have nothing to gain, and much to lose, by pretending that it doesn't exist, as a formalistic analysis would have it.

## NOTES

Nina Pillard, Barbara Black, Judith Levine, and the Levy family, formerly of Monsey, New York, provided various sources of inspiration for this chapter. Karen Edwards, Eugene Sheppard, Katie Waitman, and Laura Cadra provided helpful research assistance. I also received helpful comments from David Cole, Greg Keating, and participants at the Columbia Law School Faculty Workshop and at the University of Scranton conference From Ghetto to Emancipation? Historical and Contemporary Reconsiderations of the Jewish Community. I am especially grateful to two people: David Myers and Gabriel Stolzenberg, for their close readings and ever-sympathetic critiques of this essay.

1. John Rawls, *Political Liberalism* (New York: Columbia University Press, 1993), 193.

2. Rawls expresses regret in several passages. See ibid., 197, 200.

3. Perhaps he doesn't consider them to be part of the "we."

4. Joseph Raz, *The Morality of Freedom* (Oxford: Oxford University Press, 1986), 415.

5. Ibid., 378, 381, 395, 391.

6. Note the asymmetry here. For both Rawls and Raz, it is clear that only some, not all, permissible ways of life can (and must) be excluded, whereas all impermissible ways of life must be excluded.

7. This raises the question of what precisely communitarian critics of liberalism want. Is it to divest the liberal state of its (no longer) hidden value-laden content, the better to protect subcommunities with rival values? Or is it to promote values and community at the state level?

8. Hasidism is a branch of Orthodox Judaism that arose in rebellion against the aridity of traditional Eastern European rabbinic culture. Since its inception in the eighteenth century, it has developed into a number of discrete "courts" which are characterized by extreme piety, distinct dress and language, and devotion to a hereditary charismatic leader. Israel Rubin, *Satmar: An Island in the City* (Chicago: Quadrangle Books, 1972), 18–20; Robert Mark Kelman, *Growing up Hasidic: Education and Socialization in the Bobover Hasidic Community* (New York: AMS Press, 1985), 2; Jerome R. Mintz, *Hasidic People: A Place in the New World* (Cambridge: Harvard University Press, 1992), 3–10.

9. *Grumet v. Cuomo and the Board of Education of Kiryas Joel Village*, 625 N.Y.S. 2d 1000 (N.Y., March, 1995).

10. *Board of Education of Kiryas Joel v. Grumet*, 114 S.Ct. 2481, 2493 (1994).

11. *United States v. Village of Airmont*, 839 F.Supp. 1054 (Second Circuit, 1993). After this chapter was written, the trial court's judgment in *Airmont* was overturned by the second circuit court of appeals in 67 F.3d. 412 (Second Circuit, 1995). The appellate court's opinion is discussed at the end of this chapter.

12. Examples of aspects of prevailing establishment clause doctrines that seem to eschew the formalistic view of neutrality, identified in this chapter, in favor of an inquiry into substantive effects include (1) the second and third prongs of the "*Lemon* test" (so-called after the case of *Lemon v. Kurtzman*, 411 U.S. 192 [1973]), which ask whether government action either has a nonneutral "effect" on religion or is "excessively entangled" in religion; (2) Justice Kennedy's alternative "coercion" test,

used in his plurality decision in *Lee v. Weisman,* 112 S.Ct. 2649 (1992) (insofar as it looks beyond the formal character of legal coercion to ask whether, in the particular context, and taking into account the relationships of private individuals, the government's action had a coercive effect); and the "endorsement" test, expounded by Justice O'Connor and relied upon in *Lee V. Weisman, Capital Square Review and Advisory Board v. Pinette,* 114 S.Ct. 626 (1993) and *Rosenberger v. Rector and Visitors of University of Virginia,* 115 S.Ct. 2510 (1995). The argument of this chapter is not that reigning establishment clause jurisprudence, as a totality, is unequivocally or even primarily dedicated to the formalistic conception of neutrality elaborated here. On the contrary, establishment clause doctrines are clearly animated by the tension between the formalistic and the more substantive conceptions. By contrast, contemporary free exercise jurisprudence, at least since *Employment Division v. Smith,* 494 U.S. 872 (1990), has come to rely much more exclusively upon the formalistic approach discussed here. The extent of the ascendance of the formalistic approach in religion clause jurisprudence, generally, and the relationship between religion clause jurisprudence and the jurisprudence of the free speech and equal protection clauses, with regard to the contest between substantive and formal conceptions of neutrality, are interesting questions, which are beyond the scope of this chapter. (I am indebted to David Cole for his help in clarifying these points.)

13. The information in the following four paragraphs is drawn from these newspaper articles: Elizabeth Llorente, "Haitians in Rockland Back Intervention," *The Bergen Record,* September 15, 1994, A20; Raymond Hernandez, "Storm-Tossed on a Sea of Emotions, New York's Haitians Feel Betrayed, Angry and Confused by New Policy on Refugees," *New York Times,* July 8, 1994, B1, col. 2; Raymond Hernandez, "Once a Resort, Village Struggles with Urban Problems," *New York Times,* June 15, 1994, late edition, B6, col. 1; Ari L. Goldman, "Religion Notes," *New York Times,* Late Edition, October 9, 1993, Section 1, p. 11, col. 1.

14. In calling this development "surprising," I am betraying my own personal perspective, that of a second generation Jew of European origins, who took for granted the equation of suburbia with assimilated, barely ethnic, white, relatively affluent Americans. To a teenager from Cambridge, Massachusetts, making visits to Rockland County in the 1970s, the suburbs seemed exotic indeed, the "American dream" come to life. But even then, the existence of "other" communities was penetrating the fringes of suburban consciousness. The Hasidim were already a noticeable, though peripheral presence. More striking changes were indicated when a friend's sister reported that a little Haitian girl had appeared in her elementary school, only to cry every day during the

recitation of the "pledge of allegiance." Investigation revealed that the girl wept in the belief that all the children were making fun, on a daily basis, of "the one Haitian under God." More recently, I learned that the house of the assimilated Jewish family I used to visit, which had been sold to a Hasidic family, had "accidentally" burned down when a pot of *shmaltz* (chicken fat) was left bubbling on the stove. A synagogue now stands in its place.

15. *Airmont* at 1056.

16. *Airmont* at 1061.

17. Whether they were also united by anti-Semitism is the question raised in the litigation.

18. *Kiryas Joel,* 114 S.Ct. at 2585.

19. Mintz, *Hasidic People,* 51.

20. Non-Satmar "[n]eighbors who did not wish to secede with the Satmars objected strenuously" to being included, "and after arduous negotiations the proposed boundaries of the Village of Kiryas Joel were drawn to include just the 320 acres, owned and inhabited entirely by Satmars." *Kiryas Joel,* 114 S.Ct. at 2485.

21. *Kiryas Joel,* 114 S.Ct. at 2505 (Kennedy, J., concurring). Justice Kennedy here makes explicit what is implicit in Souter's opinion for the Court and in O'Connor's concurrence.

22. *Kiryas Joel,* 114 S.Ct. at 2498 (O'Connor, J., concurring).

23. *Kiryas Joel,* 114 S.Ct. at 2504 (Kennedy, J., concurring).

24. *Kiryas Joel,* 114 S.Ct. at 2492, 2494.

25. Private plaintiffs claimed that individual defendants who incorporated the Village and served as its officers, and the Village itself, violated rights protected under the Fair Housing Act, 42 U.S.C. section 3604(a), and the First Amendment's guarantee of the Free Exercise of Religion. The federal government brought claims against the Village based exclusively on the Fair Housing Act. Though the complaint challenged the legal validity of the incorporation of the village, the litigation focused on the requests (1) to enjoin the village from denying the constitutional and legal rights of persons on account of their religion; (2) to enjoin the village to change its zoning code in ways that would accommodate the land uses favored by observant Jews; and (3) for "other affirmative relief ... designed to ensure the responsiveness of village government to its observant Jewish residents. The plaintiffs also sought damages for alleged and anticipated anti-Semitic actions on the part of the village in areas such as zoning.

26. *Airmont* at 1068.

27. *Kiryas Joel,* 114 S.Ct. at 2484.

28. *Kiryas Joel,* 114 S.Ct. at 2489.

29. *Kiryas Joel,* 114 S.Ct. at 2489.

30. *Kiryas Joel,* 114 S.Ct. at 2490 (citing *Larkin v. Grendel's Den,* 459 U.S. at 126).

31. *Kiryas Joel,* 114 S.Ct. at 2489.

32. *Lemon v. Kurtzman,* 411 U.S. 192 (1973).

33. David A. Strauss, "Discriminatory Intent and the Taming of *Brown,*" *The University of Chicago Law Review* 56 (1989): 956–57.

34. Ibid., 953, 947.

35. Ibid., 953.

36. The question becomes less meaningless if we alter our notion of intent to factor in such considerations as "unconscious intent," as Charles Lawrence has advised. See Charles R. Lawrence III, "The Id, The Ego, and Equal Protection: Reckoning with Unconscious Racism," *Stanford Law Review* 39 (1987): 317–88. But to do so is to alter our "commonsense" notion of intent so considerably as to blur the very contrast between intended and unintended effects.

37. Memorandum filed with Assembly Bill Number 8747 (July 24, 1989), quoted in *Kiryas Joel,* 114 S.Ct. at 2486.

38. *Kiryas Joel,* 114 S.Ct. at 2492

39. *Kiryas Joel,* 114 S.Ct. at 2493.

40. *Kiryas Joel,* 114 S.Ct. at 2494.

41. Kiryas Joel, 114 S.Ct. at 2495 (quoting from *Board of Ed. of Monroe-Woodbury Central School Dist. v. Wieder,* 72 N.Y.2d 174, 180–81 (1988).

42. *Kiryas Joel,* 114 S.Ct. at 2495.

43. *Kiryas Joel,* 114 S.Ct. at 2495.

44. *Kiryas Joel,* 114 S.Ct. at 2506.

45. *Kiryas Joel,* 114 S.Ct. at 2514.

46. *Kiryas Joel,* 114 S.Ct. at 2504 (Kennedy, J., concurring); also see *Kiryas Joel,* 114 S.Ct. at 2489.

47. *Kiryas Joel,* 114 S.Ct. at 2498 (O'Connor, J., concurring).

48. Brief Amicus Curiae of Americans United for Separation of Church and State, American Jewish Committee, Anti-Defamation League, American Civil Liberties Union, National Council of Jewish Women, and the Unitarian Universalist Association, in Support of Respondents.

49. Ibid.

50. The courts have recognized the holistic conception of religion in a few cases, e.g., *Wisconsin v. Yoder,* 406 U.S. 205 (1972) (protecting the Amish religion) and *Wilder v. Bernstein,* 49 F.3d 69 (1995) (recognizing the claims of Orthodox and Hasidic Jews), but they have failed to do so in others.

51. From some points of view, of course, the domain of the sacred is

emphatically *not* a matter of subjective opinion—but notice how this sentence began. A liberal state cannot adopt any such point of view because there are conflicting versions. The most it can do is to respect them *as* points of view. It is precisely in this respect that liberalism may fairly be seen as undermining certain belief systems (in "effect," if not by "intention.") But this argument will not be pursued in this essay.

52. *Kiryas Joel*, 114 S.Ct. at 2506 (Scalia, J., dissenting).

53. *Kiryas Joel*, 114 S.Ct. at 2509 (Scalia, J., dissenting).

54. This does not mean that there is no distinction drawn between the sacred and the profane, nor that the Hasidic conceptual system lacks the ability to comprehend the conventional distinction between religious and secular affairs. The latter, however, is typically described by Satmars (in Yiddish) as a distinction between *yiddishkeit* (Jewishness) and *mentschlichkeit* (humanness). Rubin, *Satmar*, 103. The distinction between *yiddishkeit* and *mentschlichkeit* refers less to a difference between religious or sacred, and nonreligious or profane affairs, than to the separation between Jewish and non-Jewish realms.

As for the Hasidic conception of the sacred and the profane within the domain of *yiddishkeit*, it has more of the character of a dialectical relationship than that of a sharp distinction between two separate realms. For example, a central theological concept of Hasidism is that of *avodah be-Gashmiyut* (worship through corporeality), which "call[s] for man's worship of God by means of his physical acts," such as "eating, drinking, and sexual relations." *Encyclopedia Judaica*, vol. 7 (Jerusalem: 1972), 1407. According to this doctrine, matter is transformed into spirit, the profane is transformed into the holy, through communal worship centered around the figure of the rebbe or "*zaddik*," as the charismatic leader is also called. But—and this is a critical point in refuting the translation of Hasidic concepts into the English terms of "secular" and "religious"— "[t]hose who surround the *zaddik* are incapable of individually discerning the moment in which the transformation of secular into the holy occurs." Id. at 1408. As a result, it is impossible to assign any particular human activity or experience into one domain or another, or even to separate the two domains, either practically or conceptually.

55. And in fact the Supreme Court has refused to do so in cases like *Bowen v. Roy*, 476 U.S. 693 (1986) (denying that religious belief that a Social Security number "robs the spirit" of the person whose number it is renders the practice of using Social Security numbers a religious one for the purposes of constitutional analysis), and *Lyng v. Northwestern Indian Cemetery Protective Association*, 485 U.S. 439 (1988) (upholding the federal government's right to use property in ways that Native Americans believe will destroy the efficacy of important rituals and cause spiritual damage.)

56. There is a long tradition of traditionalist Jews adopting a position of acceptance of the dominant political order in a given society.

57. *Airmont* at 1064.

58. *Airmont* at 1064.

59. *Airmont* at 1066.

60. Much discussion has been devoted to the difference between rules and standards. See, for example, Duncan Kennedy, "Form and Substance in Private Law Adjudication," *Harvard Law Review* 89 (1976): 1685–1778.

61. Louis Henkin has pointed out that the constitutionally relevant question may be not whether the state has acted but, rather, whether the state bears responsibility for the situation under legal challenge. Louis Henkin, "*Shelley v. Kraemer:* Notes for a Revised Opinion," *U. Penn. Law Review* 110 (1962): 473.

62. New York Village Law, Article 2.

63. The latter device was used by the religious community in the Oregon state case of Rajneeshpurham, which raised similar issues, but in which the court used an antiformalistic method of analysis to reach the conclusion that the incorporation of a religious commune into a local government created an unconstitutional state establishment of religion. *Oregon v. City of Rajneeshpurham,* 598 F.Supp. 1217 (1984). Kiryas Joel is not organized as a commune. However, according to an article in *The New Republic,* the community has established restrictive housing policies, including (1) the requirement that "anyone who wants to build within its borders pay a tithe of $10,000 to Congregation Yetev Lev"; (2) a prohibition against selling or renting to a new resident without receiving written permission in advance; and (3) a requirement that new residents "sign a contract promising 'to be guided by the laws and ways of the Grand Rabbi' [and] 'only to go to the synagogues under the control of our congregation'; and to send their children 'only to the school of Torah Veyreh, and Bais Rachel, that was founded and built by the Grand Rabbi (Joel) and is under the control of the present Rabbi (Moses).'" Jeffrey Rosen, "Village People," *The New Republic,* April 11, 1994, at 11. The writer does not specify if the agency enforcing these requirements is public or private. If such requirements were actually codified in public law, they would surely be illegal. The question, which goes to the heart of the debate about the public-private distinction, is whether they should be any more tolerable if they are enforced by formally private functionaries of the community as private covenants, conditions, and restrictions.

64. Fair Housing Laws would be the probable basis for a challenge against explicit religious discrimination in zoning. Alternatively, discrimination could be challenged on constitutional grounds as a violation of the establishment, free exercise, free speech, or equal protection clauses.

65. *Pierce v. Society of Sisters,* 268 U.S. 510 (1925). Among the few voices disssenting from the approval of parental authority-family privacy are that of Justice Holmes, in his dissenting opinion in *Bartels v. Iowa,* 262 U.S. 404 (1922) (rejecting the Supreme Court's view that state laws prohibiting foreign language instruction are unconstitutional) and feminist critiques of the family privacy doctrine, such as Anne C. Dailey's "Constitutional Privacy and the Just Family," *Tulane Law Review* 67 (1993): 955.

66. Charges of harrassment of members were described in Rosen, "Village People."

67. The term belongs to Raz. It is an interesting question, given the paradoxical nature of autonomy in Raz, *what* precisely defines a community as autonomy-rejecting and, hence, whether Kiryas Joel qualifies as one. On the one hand, the community is hierarchically organized, and strongly committed to insulating its members to exposure to alternatives and apparently discourages internal critical scrutiny of the belief-system. On the other hand, the Satmar religion has been identified with the belief that "God wanted man to do good always, but He wanted him to do so on a completely voluntary basis." Rubin, *Satmar,* 50.

68. See Felix S. Cohen, "Transcendental Nonsense and the Functionalist Approach," *Columbia Law Review* 35 (1935): 809–49. The phrase echoes Jeremy Bentham's famous mockery of the concept of natural rights as "nonsense on stilts." "Anarchical Fallacies," *The Works of Jeremy Bentham* (John Bowring, ed., New York: Russell and Russell, 1962), vol. II, p. 501.

69. *Marsh v. Alabama,* 326 U.S. 501 (1946).

70. *Shelley v. Kraemer,* 334 U.S. 1 (1948).

71. For example, see *Lloyd v. Tanner,* 407 U.S. 551 (1972).

72. This was precisely the argument advanced and accepted by the court in the Rajneeshpuram case.

73. Legal scholars have begun to develop realist-style claims in a burgeoning contemporary literature on the increasingly popular (and controversial) planned community developments, condominium associations, private homeowners associations and the like. See, e.g., Gregory Alexander, "Dilemmas of Group Autonomy: Residential Associations and Community," *Cornell Law Review* 75 (1989): 1; Gerald Korngold, "Resolving the Flaws of Residential Servitudes and Owners Associations: For Reformation Not Termination," *Wisconsin Law Review* (1990): 513.

74. Michael W. McConnell, "Multiculturalism, Majoritarianism, and Educational Choice: What Does Our Constitutional Tradition Have to Say?" *The University of Chicago Legal Forum* 123 (1991): 150–51. Notice the

unexplained shift in this passage from the "student body" to the "parents making the decisions."

75. Id. at 125.

76. On the other hand, from the perspective of McConnell's "radical" view, *it* is the nonformalistic one, and the competing view, which disallows particularistic government, is the formalistic one.

77. This legal move is astutely analyzed by Gerald Neuman under the rubric of "The Single Decisionmaker Fallacy," in "Territorial Discrimination, Equal Protection, and Self-Determination," *University of Pennsylvania Law Review* 135 (1987): 261, 296–300.

78. *Brown v. Board of Education*, 347 U.S. 483 (1954).

79. Note that Herbert Wechsler's influential criticism of *Brown* was based precisely on resurrecting the formalistic equation of particularism, in the form of racially segregated public spheres, with the generality of "neutral principles." Herbert Wechsler, "Toward Neutral Principles of Constitutional Law," *Harvard Law Review* 73 (1959): 9.

80. Rawls, *Political Liberalism*, 193–94.

81. Ibid., 194 n. 28.

82. Ibid., 199–200.

83. Rawls borrows the unqualified formulation from Raz. See Rawls, *Political Liberalism*, 192–93.

84. To be fair, it should be noted that Rawls also disfavors and generally eschews relying on the concept of neutrality (*Political Liberalism,* 191). Nonetheless, he does introduce and employ the concept, in the manner delineated above, albeit "with due precautions" and "using it only as a stage piece as it were." My thanks to Greg Keating for reminding me of Rawls's stated reluctance to invoke the concept.

85. Raz, *The Morality of Freedom,* 133.

86. Raz, *The Morality of Freedom,* 162.

87. Rawls's precise formulation is that "equal liberty of conscience takes the truths of religion off the political agenda." Rawls, *Political Liberalism,* 151. He elaborates two important (and potentially capacious) exceptions to this prescription, but these are not our concern here.

88. Ibid., 145–49.

89. Ibid., 170. It is worth noting here that Judaism has been described by friend and foe as lacking any doctrine or dogma. More specifically germane to our analysis, it is maintained that "[n]o formal theology exists among the Satmarer—no systematically compiled set of dogmas which would be available to someone who might wish to learn exactly what a Satmarer Hasid is required to believe. Theology, as a distinct subject, is not offered at any level of the school system, nor do adults

study it directly. In fact, the Satmarer decidedly shun discussion or inquiry in matters of belief. . . . The reluctance to probe into the logic of religious belief stems from the fear that, in the process, one may contaminate his pure belief. Furthermore, the act of inquiring or debating is in itself viewed as a testimony of doubt, for the sincere believer should feel no need for analysis or discussion." Rubin, *Satmar,* 46.

90. Raz, *The Morality of Freedom,* 423.

91. Rawls, *Political Liberalism,* 185 and n. 15.

92. *Kiryas Joel,* 114 S.Ct. at 2514 (Scalia, J., dissenting).

93. Raz, *The Morality of Freedom* , 423–24.

94. Rawls, *Political Liberalism,* 221 n. 8.

95. Ibid., 159–60.

96. See, for example, "A Symposium: The Public/Private Distinction," *U. Penn. Law Review* 126 (1982): 1289.

97. Rawls, *Political Liberalism,* 220 n. 7.

98. Ibid., 221–22.

99. Raz, *The Morality of Freedom,* 376.

100. Ibid., 391–94.

101. Rawls, *Political Liberalism,* 222.

102. Raz, *The Morality of Freedom,* 370 (emphasis added).

103. For example, see the chapters "Neutral Political Concern" and "Equality" in Raz, *The Morality of Freedom,* 110–33, 217–44; Ronald Dworkin, *A Matter of Principle,* part 3 (Cambridge: Harvard University Press, 1984); Rawls's *A Theory of Justice* (Cambridge: Belknap Press, 1973).

104. *Le Blanc-Sternberg v. Fletcher,* 67 F.3d. 412, at 424. The appellate court reinstated portions of the original jury verdict, in favor of the plaintiffs, that Judge Goettel had set aside on the ground that they were inconsistent with other jury findings against the plaintiffs.

105. *Le Blanc-Sternberg* at 418.

106. 1995 U.S. App. LEXIS 27174, at 425.

# PART V

# GROUP
# REPRESENTATION

# 12

# DEFERRING GROUP REPRESENTATION

## IRIS MARION YOUNG

Women's movement activists and feminist scholars in many parts of the world have suggested that legislatures peopled almost entirely by men cannot be said properly to represent women. In response to such claims, some countries, such as Argentina, have enacted legislation requiring that party lists include a certain portion of women.[1] Even where there are no laws that require it, many parties around the world have decided that their lists are not properly representative without certain numbers of women, and they maintain quotas in their lists.

In the United States, similar discussions take place about the specific representation of racial or ethnic minorities. Some districts have been drawn or voting processes adjusted to make the election of African Americans or Hispanics more likely. Both the idea and practice of promoting specific representation of minorities are controversial, but the issue will not fade from the American public agenda. Many other countries of the world have schemes for specific social group representation, either in the form of reserved seats, party list rules, or voting schemes.

In earlier work, I argued for a principle of special representation for oppressed and disadvantaged groups in processes of political decision making.[2] Special representation is necessary only for oppressed and disadvantaged groups, I argued, because the dominant groups are already represented. Explicit processes for ensuring the representation of oppressed or disadvantaged groups allows the expression of otherwise unheard interests and perspectives. Group representation, furthermore, relativizes the expression and perspectives of the dominant groups so that they are less able to assume that their ideas and policies are impartial and universal.

Policies, proposals, and arguments for group representation, however, face many objections. One of these I find particularly compelling because it comes from a commitment to attend to rather than to submerge social difference, in order to undermine domination and oppression. The idea of group representation, this objection claims, presumes that a group of women, or African Americans, or Maori, has some set of common attributes or interests which can be represented. But this is usually false. Differences of race and class cut across gender, differences of gender and ethnicity cut across religion, and so on. Individual members of a gender or racial group have life histories that often make them very different people with very different interests and outlooks. The unifying process required by group representation inappropriately freezes fluid relational identities into a unity, and can recreate oppressive segregations.[3] Group representation further implies that in expressing interests and taking public positions on issues, the dominant groups within the groups suppress or marginalize the perspectives of minorities. If Latinos were to be specially represented in American politics, for example, a heterosexual perspective would be likely to dominant their discourse and policy preferences, thus marginalizing gay and lesbian Latinos.[4]

In this essay, I consider these problems with the idea of group representation. I argue that the problem of how one person can speak for many, and the tendency to freeze those represented into a unity, is not an issue only for group representation but for all representation. Thus in order to respond to the intuition that there is something wrong with decision-making bodies from which women or cultural minorities are absent, but also to avoid essentializing and marginalizing consequences for a solution to this problem, it is necessary to think about the meaning and functions of political representation altogether.

I suggest that the objection that group representation freezes the group into a unity assumes that the representative is or should be in a relation of identity with the constituents. Accounts of democracy which find direct democracy as the most authentic also tend to assume the representation relation as one of identity. I theorize representation as a differentiated relation whose most important moments are authorization and accountability, and show that this conceptualization dissolves some of the problems and paradoxes that sometimes appear in thinking about representation.

This chapter takes seriously, moreover, the claim that members of social groups usually vary greatly in their interests and opinions. I introduce and elaborate on a concept of social-group perspective, as distinct from interest or opinion, to give articulate meaning to the widely held intuition that social groups can and should be represented in some respect. I conclude by rearticulating the argument for special representation of oppressed or disadvantaged groups.

## I. Paradoxes of Representation

Problems with group representation seem particularly stark when discussing the inclusion of women in politics. On the one hand, women as a group have been and continue to be largely excluded from decision-making power, and at the same time women continue to suffer serious social and economic disadvantages. Thus, it would seem that women and their interests ought to be represented in public decision making. On the other hand, women are everywhere, and differ so vastly along so many dimensions that it seems absurd to suggest that women who might attain positions as representatives can legitimately speak for other women.

This problem appears, however, with all forms of political representation. The legitimacy of a person elected in a district speaking and acting on behalf of the members of the district might appear even more questionable than a woman speaking for women. Congressional districts in the United States contain more than 500,000 people. How can one person possibly claim to speak in place of all those people, with their huge diversity of interests, experience, and needs? The legitimacy of a particular African American acting as a spokesman for other African Americans is

often properly contested, again because there are so many different opinions and experiences among members of this group.
Even interest-group representation can be challenged in this way.
How can a handful of lobbyists and office staff be said to represent
the diverse experience and perspectives of the members of, say,
the Sierra Club?

Some theorists of democracy conclude that political representation is incompatible with strong democracy because, they claim,
representatives are necessarily distant from constituents. Political
inclusion must consist in people speaking and acting for themselves.[5] Direct democracy, where each citizen is himself present to
and directly participates in the decisionmaking process, is real
democracy. Representative democracy is at best a grudging concession to size or efficiency, and at worst simply not democracy at
all.

I believe that this elevation of direct democracy to the apex, as
the only "real" democracy, is mistaken, and that political representation is both necessary and desirable. Representative democracy
in itself is not less democratic than direct democracy but is a
specific structure of democracy that has its own degrees of more
and less. Full argument for this claim deserves an essay of its own,
so here I will only sketch some reasons.

Representation is necessary because the web of modern social
life often ties the actions of some people and institutions in one
place to consequences in many other places and institutions. No
person can be present at all the decisions or in all the decision-
making bodies whose actions affect her life, because there are so
many and they are so dispersed. Though her aspirations are often
disappointed, she hopes that others will think about her situation
and represent it to the issue forum.[6]

One might object that this argument presupposes a large-scale
society and polity which a preference for direct democracy rejects.
A democracy without representation must consist of small, decentralized, self-sufficient units. Robert Dahl gives a compelling set of
arguments, however, for how even this vision of decentralized
direct democracy cannot avoid representation. The equal participation of everyone in political deliberation, he argues, can occur
only in small committees. Even in assemblies of a few hundred
people, most people will be more passive participants who listen

to a few people speak for a few positions, then think and vote. Beyond the small committee, that is, features of time and interaction produce de facto representation. But such de facto representation is arbitrary; in fact direct democracy often cedes political power to arrogant loud mouths whom no one chose to represent them. It is fairer and probably wiser to institute formal rules of representation. Dahl also argues, I think plausibly, that the ugly tendencies of power and competition that haunt human life imply that small decentralized political units are likely to grow larger either by means of conquest or coalition. As soon as scale returns, then, representation also returns.[7]

Not only is political representation inevitable in these ways, it is also positively desirable as a means to facilitate deliberation. I assume that a democratic process guided by public discussions which aim to arrive at the most just and wise solutions to political problems is better than a process that merely aggregates the private preferences of citizens.[8] Representation facilitates such discussions by reducing the number of discussants. More important for the deliberative model, a carefully and fairly designed system of representation can better ensure that unpopular, or minority, or weak participants have a voice in the discussion than could a free-for-all direct democracy. Representative bodies can enable people from diverse groups or across large geographical areas to communicate, indirectly to show one another their circumstances and needs, thus enlarging their understanding of social policies and their effects.

These arguments seem to leave us with the following paradox. The problem of the one and the many is impossible to solve. It is not possible for one person to stand for many people, to speak and act as they would. It is impossible to find the essential attributes of constituents, the single common interest that overrides the diversity of their other interests, experiences, and opinions. Representation understood in this way is impossible. Yet representation is both necessary and desirable. I suggest that this is a false paradox generated by an implicit assumption of the representative as in some sense identical with those represented. In the next section, I will expose this assumption and argue that representation should be understood in terms of *differance* rather than identity.

## II. Representation as Differance

The conundrums about representation that I discussed above appear partly because the representative relation is often implicitly thought of as a relation of identity. Some of those who criticize representative systems because they lack women, blacks, or Muslims in significant proportions, for example, often assume a concept of "mirror" representation. They assume, that is, that a representative body should resemble the attributes of the social body. Mirror representation also seems to assume that a representative's sharing specific attributes with constituents—gender, class, race, religion, and so on—is sufficient to ensure that those constituents are properly represented.

A number of writers properly criticize this assumption that a person or group is legitimately represented when the representative identifies with specific group attributes. Having such a relation of identity or similarity with constituents says nothing about what the representative does.[9] The idea of mirror representation is also subject to the objection to group representation which I articulated earlier, namely that people with similar attributes of structural social position or cultural group nevertheless usually have very different interests and opinions.[10] Simply having certain group attributes that constituents can be said to share is not a ground for saying that the constituents are legitimately represented.

Those who object to the idea of group representation, however, also assume that representation entails a relation of identity. They object to group representation on the grounds that the social group cannot be reduced to a unity of will or condition for which the representative can speak and act. The objection seems to presuppose that in the absence of such a self-consciously unified group or interest or mandate, legitimate representation cannot occur.

I argued in the previous section, moreover, that few if any representative relations exhibit that sort of unity of the many constituents into a common will or interest for which the representative speaks and acts. Recognizing this problem that the constituency is rarely identical with itself, thus making it impossible to represent that identity, many conclude that representation is illegitimate. Direct democracy is the only real democracy, because no person can stand for another in the specificity of her experience and interests. Thus, this purism of direct democracy also assumes that representation is properly a relation of identity between the representative and constituents.

This identity assumption, I will now argue, misrepresents the meaning and function of political representation. I suggest that we adopt Jacques Derrida's critique of a metaphysics of presence, and conceptualize representation by means of his concept of *differance.*

The classical problem of the one and the many is produced by a metaphysics of presence, or a logic of identity. This metaphysics aims to capture the flowing temporality of movement and change in stable elements. It conceptualizes material processes in terms of self-identical substances, which underlie and remain the same through change, and which can be captured in a definition of their essential attributes. Individuals within a substantial category always vary in their particular attributes, but they belong to the same group because they share a common set of attributes.

This substance metaphysics of presence and identity sets up hierarchical dichotomies. One term is the substantial origin, underlying change in time, the other is the derivative supplement. Thus the hierarchical dichotomies of substance-accident, cause-effect, presence-absence polarize and freeze experienced differences. The aim is then to reduce the second pole to the first.

Derrida directs his critique of the metaphysics of presence also at a classical understanding of language and the relation of subjects to the world. This classical view of language privileges voice, the spoken word, as the origin of linguistic meaning. This philosophy implicitly takes the subject to be immediately and authentically present to listeners in speech. Writing, on this classical view, is a secondary, alienated form of language. Material marks aim to represent the authentic meaning of speech, but on this view writing is always a poor substitute, absent, ambiguous, and derivative.[11]

Derrida offers the term *differance* as the alternative for expressing experience and the operation of language. Differance has the double meaning of "to differ" and "to defer." Where the metaphysics of presence generates polarities because it aims to reduce the many to one identity, thinking of entities in terms of *differance* leaves them in their plurality without requiring their collection into a common identity. Things take their being and signs take their meaning from their place in a process of differentiated relationships. Things are similar without being identical, and different without being contrary, depending on the point of reference and the moment in a process.

Thus according to the second aspect of the meaning of *differance*, reality and meaning are best thought of as playing over intervals of space and time. Oppositions such as substance-accident, cause-effect, presence-absence, or reality-sign, locate authentic being in an origin, an always earlier time for which the present process is a derivative copy. Derrida proposes to rethink such oppositions in terms of the idea of the "trace," a movement of temporalization that carries past and future with it. This moment in the conversation, this moment in the being of the mountain, carries traces of the history of relationships that produced it, and its current tendencies anticipate future relationships.[12]

Derrida himself relates his critique of the classical account of the relation of substance and accident, sign and referent, to the context of political representation. The sign would thus be a deferred presence. Whether it is a question of verbal or written signs, monetary signs, electoral delegates, or political representatives, the movement of signs defers the moment of encountering the thing itself, the moment at which we could lay hold of it, consume or expand it, touch it, see it, have a present intuition of it.[13]

I suggest that many discussions of political representation assume a metaphysics of presence or a logic of identity through the following sort of image of the representative function. The representative is supposed to grasp and stand for "the will of the people." Ideally, "the people" meet in an original moment of presence, where they express their will, and choose a person to represent that will. In this original moment, the many become one. Representative bodies are necessary because the polity is large and requires decisions to be made by a manageable body of deliberators, in a central place from which most of the people are absent. The representative's responsibility is to be present in their place, to speak as they would speak, in their absence. His words and deeds are effects only, with their cause in the original will of the people. On this model, representation is always derivative, secondary, distanced, ambiguous, and suspect. "Real" democracy consists in "the people" meeting face to face and in one another's presence making decisions for themselves. The legitimate representative tries to re-present this original moment of decision.

Of course I am constructing an image of political representation which I believe underlies rejection of representation as democratic grounds complaints that the representative cannot bring the many into one. There is a myth of authentic democratic moment when the people are present to themselves, and this myth impedes normative thinking about political representation. Instead of conceptualizing representation as some kind of relation of identity, in which the representative stands for a unified will of the constituents, I suggest that we conceptualize representation as a *differentiated relationship*.

This means, first, affirming that there is a difference, a separation, between the representative and the constituents. Of course no person can stand for and speak as a plurality of other persons. The representative function of *speaking for* should not be confused with an identifying requirement that the representative *speak as* the constituents would, to try to be present for them in their absence. It is no criticism of the representative that he is separate and distinct from the constituents, but the two aspects in their difference must be in a determinate relation to maintain legitimately the representative function.

Second, representation as differentiated relationship implies that there is no original "will of the people" to which the representative should give voice as mere effect. Because the constituency is internally differentiated from itself, the representative does not stand for or refer to a substance or essence of opinion or interest which it is his job to describe and for which he advocates.

Conceiving representation as differentiated relationship, finally, encourages a shift in thought from substance to process. What matters about representation is neither the attributes of the representatives nor the attributes of the constituency. Nor does it matter whether the representative properly depicts an originary will or essence. Representation, instead, is a *process* involving both the constituency and the representative, and normative political theory can evaluate the democratic character of this process along lines I will develop in the next section. In her classic work about representation, Hanna Pitkin argues against a tendency to conceive representation in terms of the identity of the representative rather than in terms of the actions of representation. Thinking of representation as process rather than substances agrees with this analysis.[14]

Pitkin also discusses the debate about whether the representative should only express a mandate from the constituents or instead should be autonomous from them and act according to his reasoned view of the common good. She argues that neither the view of the representative as delegate nor the view as trustee is adequate, but rather that the representative function involves both. Conceiving representation as differentiated relation helps fill out how and why the representative is both delegate and trustee. The representative is separate from the constituents, in a different place, in a setting of discussion and decision making with other representatives from which the constituents are absent. Even if the constituents could agree on a mandate, in the setting away from them there may be new issues that arise that make the mandate irrelevant, and the representative has no choice but to act as he thinks best. If the representative thinks of himself or is thought of as pure trustee, then the relationships between him and the constituency is severed, and the representative function dissolves. Representation as differentiated relationship entails a moving dialectic between a delegate and trustee function.

## III. THE REPRESENTATIONAL RELATIONSHIP: AUTHORIZATION AND ACCOUNTABILITY

Much political theory and practice, I have suggested, implicitly brings representation under a metaphysics of presence. It mistakenly conceives the function of representation as making the voice of the absent present, speaking and deciding as they would. Thinking of representation in terms of *differance* emphasizes temporality, that representation is a process rather than a condition of substitution.[15] Representation is a deferring relationship between constituents and representative, moving between three moments of authorization, representation, and accountability. I will now elaborate on each of these three moments in the process of representation, focusing on where each moment in the process bears traces of the others.

The processes of authorization, representation, and accountability, moreover, enact differance in three senses. They consist in a flow between the representative, who differs from the constituents, and also among the constituents, who differ from one another. Second, in the process the deciding mandate is always temporally deferred. The relationship of authorization and accountability, finally, implies a dialectic in which constituents and representative each defer to the judgment of the other.

The ideal of representing the "will of the people" presumes, that "the people" exist prior to and independently of the process of representation, as the original cause of the representative's act. It also presumes that this people can form a common will that they delegate to the representative. But this image defies the plurality of the constituency, which does not exist as a unity, and is not present to itself. In most situations calling for representative bodies, the constituency is too large, or the varying activities of its members are too dispersed, or its definition and borders too vague, to expect any process where the constituency in one moment arrives at a collective will.

Nevertheless, democratic representation requires a process of *authorization* which establishes a relationship between the constituency and the representative. In the process of authorization, the people anticipate the moment of representation that will take place, and this anticipation brings the dispersed constituency into a relationship with itself. There is no constituency prior to the process of representation, no people who form an original unity they then delegate onto the derivative representative. Without the motive of a political decision deferred onto another who is accountable to them through public procedures, "the people" might not go looking for each other in order to form a base of public opinion and account.[16]

In the process of authorization the constituency forms itself in light of the issues the people believe or desire will face a representative body. Ideally, this process consists in broad and inclusive public discussion of issues, and public criticism and contestation of the constituency with itself about the content of a decision-making agenda, the actions representatives should take, and who they should be. This discussion occurs over time, and thus the precise moment of authorization is always deferred. The process aims at agreement but is always open to further contest, and so agreement is always deferred. Democratic norms of authorization should include fair and public rules of election that constitute the relationship between constituency and representative. But just as important, the ideal of democratic representation should also include structured processes of issue discussion that allow constituents to listen and be heard. Systems are more or less democratic to the degree that they allow and even encourage inclusive participatory discussion. In representative democracy, however, decision making about these policies is deferred onto the representative.

In this process, the activity of representing ideally recollects and anticipates. The representative should maintain a connection between her speech and action and the constituency. But the representative cannot be a mere effect of a prior cause in the people's will. Instead, the representative process carries, or ought to carry, the *traces* of authorizing processes of discussion and decision making. At the same time, the representative ought to act with a view to a future moment when she will be called to account by the constituency, and will have to answer for her speech and actions.

The representative's action refers backward, to the process of authorization, and forward, to the moment of accountability. The representative is authorized to act, but his judgment is always in question. Whether he acted on authority is a question deferred to a later time, when he will be held accountable. Should the constituency find his action or judgment wrong, he must defer to their evaluation.

Thus the third moment, accountability, is as important as the other two. In the process of calling to account, the constituency can meet itself anew, reform itself, and engage in new debate and conflict. Such renewed opinion formation may bear the traces of the process of authorization, but it also has new elements because then the constituents did not know just how issues would be formulated in the representative body and what arguments would be offered there. The anticipation of holding accountable and of being called to account can condition the actions of both constituents and representatives, to maintain a connection between them.

In most democracies today, the moment of accountability is weaker than the moment of authorization. Even more disturbingly, for many representatives, the only form of being held to account is reelection. Strong democracy requires some processes and procedures of constituencies calling representatives to account in addition to the processes that defer onto them representative authority. Without strong processes of accounting, the representative can effectively operate on her own, and the constituency need no longer be active after the process of authorization. This process of accountability should have the traces of authorization, but authorization itself should be conditioned by anticipation of the process of accounting. In this way there is no origin, no decisive moment when the judgment is made. Institutional means of accountability distinct from election campaigns can include citizen review boards, implementation studies, and periodic official participatory hearings that follow the process of policy making.

I describe the function of representation as a process that flows between constituents and representatives in a circle of authorization and accountability. This description has a normative dimension by indicating some criteria for evaluating degrees of democracy. Democracy is not an all or nothing affair; the idea of a pure and authentic democracy, in comparison to which everything else is a sham, is a dream. Instead, as Frank Cunningham argues, democracy is a matter of degree.[17] Representative processes can be more or less democratic. They should be normatively evaluated according to the degree to which they enable inclusive discussion among constituents, institute fair voting procedures that aim to promote political equality in influence and not merely number, and have independent mechanisms of accountability.

## IV. MODES OF REPRESENTATION

The representative should not be thought of as a substitute for those he or she represents, I have suggested, nor should we assume that the representative can or should express and enact some unified will of the constituency. The representative can stand for neither the identity of any other person nor the collective identity of a constituency. There is an inevitable difference and separation between the representative and constituents, which always puts in question the manner and degree to which constituents participate in the process that produces policy outcomes. Yet representation is both necessary and desirable in modern politics. Rather than devaluing representation as such, participatory and radical democrats should evaluate the degree to which processes of authorization and accountability exist, are independent, and activate the constituency in inclusive participatory public opinion.

Another measure of the degrees of democracy, I suggest, is whether people are connected through relationships of authorization and accountability to a few or many representatives. The assumption that representatives should in some fashion be identical to constituents implicitly carries the impossible requirement that a person is only represented if everything about her potentially has a voice in the political process. Since no representative can stand for all the constituents in all the thickness of their individuality, direct democracy, in which each stands only for himself, wrongly appears to be as the only authentic democracy. The representative must be different from the constituents, and a democracy is better or worse according to how well those differentiated positions are related. Democracy can also be strengthened by pluralizing the modes and sites of representation. Systems of political representation cannot represent individuals in their individuality but rather should represent *aspects* of a person's life experience, identity, or activity where she or her has affinity with others. Potentially there are many such aspects or affinity groups. I propose to distinguish here three general modes through which a person can be represented: according to interest, opinion, and perspective. Within a particular political context, a person may be represented in several ways within each of these modes. Explication of what it means to represent perspective in particular will set the basis for a new argument for the special representation of oppressed or disadvantaged social groups.

What do I mean when I say that I feel represented in the political process? There are many possible answers to this question but three stand out for me as important. First, I feel represented when someone is looking after the interests I take as mine and share with some others. Second, it is important to me that the principles, values and priorities that I think should guide political decisions are voiced in discussion. Finally, I feel represented when at least some of those discussing and voting on policies understand and express the kind of social experience I have because of my social group position and the history of social group relations. I will discuss interest and opinion only briefly because these have been much discussed in political theory. I will focus more attention on representing perspectives because this idea is less familiar.

*Interest.* I define interest as what affects or is important to the life prospects of individuals, or the goal-oriented success of organizations. An agent, whether individual or collective, has an interest in whatever is necessary or desirable in order to realize the ends the agent has set for himself, herself, or themselves. These include both material resources and the ability to exercise capacities—e.g., for cultural expression, political influence, economic decision-making power, and so on. I define interest here as self-referring, and as different from ideas, principles, and values. The latter may help define the ends a person sets for herself, where the interest defines the means for achieving those ends.

Interests may and often do conflict, whether in the action of a single agent or between agents. Where agents need resources to accomplish a variety of ends, they are likely to find some of the resources they need to be relatively scarce. Sometimes the means one agent needs to pursue a certain end implies directly impeding another agent's ability to get what he needs to pursue his ends. It is important to note, however, that interests do not necessarily conflict. The pursuit of ends in society and the setting of political frameworks to facilitate that pursuit need not necessarily be structured as a zero-sum relationship among agents.

The representation of interest is familiar in political practice, and there exists more theory of interest representation perhaps than any other kind. I do not here wish to review the entire literature on interest groups and the means by which they can achieve political influence. I only note here that it is part of the free associative process of communicative democracy that people have the freedom to press politically for policies that will serve their interests and to organize together with others with similar interests in order to gain political influence.

*Opinions.* I define opinions as the principles, values and priorities held by a person as these bear on and condition his or her judgment about what priorities should be pursued and ends sought. This is the primary sphere of what Anne Phillips refers to as the "politics of ideas,"[18] on which much contemporary discussion of pluralism also focuses. Rawls's recent discussion of the principles and problems of political liberalism, for example, focuses on the existence of plural ideas and belief systems in modern societies, how these legitimately influence political life, and how people with differing beliefs and opinions can maintain a working polity.[19] By opinion, I mean any judgment or belief about how things are or ought to be, and the political judgments that follow from these judgments or beliefs. Opinions may be religious, or derive from religious reasons, or they may be culturally based in a worldview of the history of social practices. They may be based in disciplinary or knowledge systems, as might be political opinions derived from certain premises of neoclassical economics, or based in a set of normative principles such as libertarianism or radical ecology. While I doubt that most people's opinions on public matters all derive from a single "comprehensive doctrine," I do assume that most people make judgments about particular social and political issues with the guidance of some values, priorities, or principles that they apply more broadly than that case, if not to all cases. Opinions are certainly contestable, and often some can be shown to be more well founded than others. A communicative democracy, however, requires the free expression and challenging of opinions and a wide representation of opinions in discussions leading to policy decisions.

Political parties are the most common vehicle for the representation of opinions. Parties often put forward programs that less express the interests of a particular constituency, and more organize the political issues of the day according to principles, values, and priorities the party claims generally to stand for. Smaller or more specialized associations, however, can and often do form to represent opinions in public life and influence public policy. Traditionally, interest group theory has treated such associations as another kind of interest group, and for most purposes this is a harmless conflation. I think it important to distinguish in general, however, between kinds of political association motivated by an instrumentalist interest, on the one hand, and kinds of association motivated by commitment to beliefs and values, on the other. Whereas the former sort of motivation is selfish, even if selfish for a group, the latter often takes itself to be impartial or even altruistic.

*Perspective.* Social perspectives involve the way people interpret issues and events because of their structural social locations. Structural social locations arise from group differentiations that exist in a society, collective attributions that have cultural and practical meanings for the way people interact or the status they have—such as age, gender, race, ethnicity, caste, religion, physical ability, or health status in some societies, sexuality in some societies, and so on. These structured relations of social action involve the differentiation of at least one category of people from others. In most societies these group differentiations structure some social inequalities of prestige, power, or access to resources. Many structural relations of differentiated groups, that is, are relations of privilege, on the one hand, and oppression or disadvantage on the other.

A well-developed theoretical discourse describes these sorts of social structures as "positioning" individuals. Individual actors find themselves located in certain positions in relation to others, in a web of social relations that varies across societies, and which changes in a particular social history.[20] Contemporary American society positions me as a woman, white, Anglo, professional, and so on. Without my choice, I find myself designated in certain ways by others that imply specific norms and status in relation to others. Any one of us finds ourselves positioned in multiple ways in modern societies. Others are similarly positioned with me who bear similar designations and for whom this implies similar relations with specific others. Social positioning conditions the lives of individuals by posing constraints on action and distributing benefits and burdens. It is a mistake to think that structural positioning forms the *identity* of persons, however. My life is conditioned by my social position of being a woman, but this hardly begins to say anything specific about who I am.[21] In our actions and self-formation, each of us takes an attitude toward the social positioning which both enables and constrains our social possibilities, the way others regard us, the way we regard them, the social norms that guide our conscious and unconscious interaction, and often the formal and bureaucratic status we do or do not have. But "who I am" is a product of my own particular history and active engagement with the multiple facts of social positioning that condition my life. Thus we may say that women or people of color, for example, are similarly positioned in a particular society without attributing to them a common identity.

Because of their social locations, people are attuned to particular kinds of social meanings and relationships to which others are less attuned. Sometimes others are not positioned to be aware of them at all. From their social locations people have differentiated knowledge of social events and their consequences. Because their social locations arise partly from the constructions that others have of them, and which they have of others in different locations, people in different locations may interpret the meaning of actions, events, rules, and structures differently, though not necessarily in incompatible ways. Structural social positions thus produce particular locationally relative kinds of experience and a specific knowledge of social processes and consequences.

Social *perspective*, then, refers to this experience, history and social knowledge derived from social position. To represent a social perspective means to approach public discussion and decision making with the experience and knowledge of those positioned in a structurally specific way. Representing an interest or an opinion, I suggest, usually entails promoting certain specific outcomes in the decision-making process. Representing a perspective, on the other hand, usually means promoting certain starting points for discussion. From a particular social perspective a representative asked certain kinds of questions, reports certain kinds of experience, recalls a particular line of narrative history, or expresses a certain way of regarding the positions of others. These vitally contribute to the inclusion of different people in the decision-making process and attention to effects that proposed policies may have on different groups. Expressing perspective, however, does not usually mean drawing a conclusion about outcomes.

I introduce the idea of social perspective, and the idea of representing a social perspective, in order to begin to address the objection to the idea of group representation with which I began this essay. I wish to retain the intuition that social groups structured by gender, race, nationality, religion, ablement, sexuality, and so on, have some socially specific and politically relevant ways of experiencing and speaking about political issues. Nevertheless, I take seriously the claim that no such groups can be defined by a set of common interests, nor do all their members agree on principles and values to guide political discussion and decision making. African Americans in the United States, for example, have a large number of different and even conflicting interests, and adhere to a broad spectrum of political ideologies and opinions. For this reason, representing African Americans in political life cannot mean representing a particular set of interests or opinions. But I wish to retain the intuition that African Americans may have a reason to claim that they should be specifically represented in the political life of the United States. I believe that the structured position of African Americans in a historically racist society, and the specific social and cultural consequences of this history and position, provides African Americans with specific experiential background and knowledge of the workings of society which makes them attentive to certain issues, questions, or events that others tend not to think about. This is what I mean by perspective.

For more than fifty years, *The Pittsburgh Courier* has been an important newspaper for African Americans in the city of Pittsburgh and in other parts of the United States as well. I think that this newspaper illustrates well the difference between perspective, on the one hand, and interest and opinion, on the other. In the pages of this newspaper each week appear reports of many events and controversies that exhibit the plurality of interests, not all of them compatible, that African Americans in Pittsburgh and elsewhere have. On the opinion pages, moreover, appear editorials that cover the range from right-wing libertarian to left-wing socialism, from economic separatism to liberal integrationism. Despite this variety of interests and opinions, it is not difficult to identify how *The Pittsburgh Courier* nevertheless speaks an African American perspective. Most of the events discussed involve African Americans as the major actors, and take place at sites and within institutions which are are majority African American or otherwise specifically associated with them. When the paper discusses local or national events not specifically identified with African Americans, the stories usually ask questions or give emphases that are particularly informed by issues and experiences more specific to African Americans.

One might object that the idea of an African American perspective, or a female gendered perspective, is just as open to criticism as the idea of interest or opinion. Isn't it just as inappropriately reductive to talk about *one* Native American perspective as one interest? This is in fact so. Each person has his or her own irreducible history which gives him or her unique social knowledge and perspective. I think, however, that we must avoid the sort of individualism that would conclude from this fact that any talk of structured social positions and group defined social location is wrong or incoherent. It makes sense to say that nonprofessional working-class people have predictable vulnerabilities and opportunities because of their position in occupational structures. The idea of perspective is meant to capture that sensibility of group positioned experience without specifying unified content to what the perceptive sees. The social positioning produced by relation to other structural positions and by the social processes that issue in unintended consequences only provide a background and perspective in terms of which particular social events and issues are interpreted; they do not make the interpretation. So you can well have different persons with a similar social perspective giving different interpretations of an issue. Perspective is an approach to looking at social events, which conditions but does not determine what one sees.

I take interests, opinions, and perspectives to be three important aspects of persons that can be represented. None reduce to the identity of either a person or a group, but each is an aspect of the person. I do not claim that these three aspects are exhaustive of the ways people can be represented, moreover. There may well be other possible modes of representation, but I find these three particularly important in the way we talk about representation in contemporary politics and in answering the conceptual and practical problems posed for group representation.

None of these aspects of persons is reducible to the others.

They are logically independent in the sense that from a general social perspective one can derive neither a set of interests nor opinions. Within an individual life, it may be possible to explain why being socially positioned in a certain way has led a person to set certain goals or develop certain values, but such connection among interests, opinions, and perspectives can only be made at the level of the individual case.

Unlike interests or opinions, moreover, social perspectives cannot easily be thought of as conflicting. Put together they usually do not cancel each other out but rather offer additional questions and fuller social knowledge. Perspectives may often seem incommensurate, however. An account of postwar America from the perspective of those now in their eighties cannot be made in the same language and with the same assumptions as an account made from the perspective of those now in their twenties.

## V. New Argument for Group Representation

We are now in a position to return to the problem with which I began this essay. Advocates of inclusive democracy are faced with a certain dilemma. On the one hand, in nearly every society an underrepresentation of less privileged structural social groups can be observed in many dimensions. Women are underrepresented everywhere, racial, ethnic, or religious groups often lack significant political influence, as do poor and working-class people. Many find such underrepresentation wrong, which leads to calls for mechanisms of special representation for excluded groups.

Implementing such measures of group representation, on the other hand, seems to imply that the represented group has or should have a common set of interests or opinions. The fact that such unity of interest or opinion almost never exists seems to imply that social group representation is impossible. The idea of representing the social group perspective, coupled with the argument that representation is a differentiated relationships rather than a condition of identity or substitution, aims to move democracy theory out of this dilemma. A structural social group does not exist as a unity prior to the moment of representation, with a clear set of interests and opinions with which it authorizes the representative's action. Rather, the very mechanisms of authorizing a representative activate members of the social group to discuss with one another their perspective on issues, and perhaps to formulate positions. Representing a social group consists primarily in representing the perspective members of the group have derived from their structured social positioning. Perspective concerns questions, assumptions, and particular experience more than answers or conclusions.

Thus a renewed argument for the special representation of oppressed or disadvantaged social groups runs as follows: Inclusive democracy implies that every structured social group perspective in the polity should be represented. Every perspective should be represented not only for reasons of political fairness but also to maximize the social knowledge needed to reach fair and wise decisions. In societies structured by group based privilege and disadvantage, political processes of procedural liberalism generally result in the dominance of the perspectives of privileged groups in political discussion and decision making. Democratic inclusion thus requires special measures to enable the representation of oppressed or disadvantaged structural social groups. Ensuring the representation of multiple perspectives gives voice to distinctive experiences in the society and relativizes the dominant perspectives which are assumed as normal and neutral.

Does this argument imply that minority or disadvantaged interests or opinions should be specially represented? Before deciding that the same sort of reasoning applies to interests and opinions, we should notice their differences from perspectives. Social perspectives arise from broad social structures that position many people in similar ways whether they like it or not. This makes social perspectives basic in a way that some interests and opinions are not. Interests and opinions may be shared with a large number of others, or they may be quite idiosyncratic. Many are voluntarily formed and organized, and their potential number in a given society is vast.

But the primary relevant difference between interests and opinions, on the one hand, and social perspectives, on the other, is that some asserted interests or opinions may be bad or illegitimate, whereas a social perspective is not in itself illegitimate. In a society of white privilege, for example, the social perspective of white people usually wrongly dominates the making of many public discussions, and it should be relativized and tempered by the social perspectives of those positioned differently in the racialized social structures. But the social perspective of white people is not itself wrong or illegitimate. White supremacist opinions, on the other hand, which would call for the forced segregation of all people of color, are illegitimate. A liberal society in which such opinions are held by a small minority might be obliged to let them express the opinions, but it is not obliged to give any special support to them just because they are at a disadvantage in the marketplace of ideas.

In general, liberal principles of free speech and association govern the representation of interests and opinions. Everyone should have the freedom to express opinions and organize groups to publicize them. Everyone should be free to organize groups to promote particular interests. Both freedoms should be limited by rules that enable a similar freedom for others and which prohibit activities that wrongfully harm others. The content of this harm principle is notoriously contested, of course, and I will not enter that controversy here. The point is that on the whole maximizing liberty of speech and association should be the general principle guiding the representation of interests and opinions.

Some critics of interest group liberalism, however, rightly argue that unbridled freedom of expression and association leads to gross unfairness in an economic system where some interests and opinions have much greater access to resources than others. At this point, some of the reasoning used to argue for special measures to ensure that representation of perspectives might also support special measures to ensure the representation of interests or opinions in public debate. Political equality may require guaranteeing media access to groups with few resources, or limiting the ability of richer groups to dominate public influence. As Joshua Cohen and Joel Rogers suggest, moreover, a fair system of interest group representation ought to subsidize the ability to organize of those with legitimate interests but few resources.[22]

How should a principle of the special representation of silenced or excluded perspectives be implemented? Space permits only a brief answer to this important question. In my previous work on group representation, I argued that oppressed or disadvantaged social groups should be given resources to organize, have special representative seats, and veto power over some issues most directly affecting the lives of those associated with the group. This is a strong interpretation of the requirements of the representation of perspectives. While I do not retract this position, at the moment I will defer it, and here will consider other, weaker practical options for promoting the political inclusion of social perspectives.

Many writers and policy makers concerned with group representation look to legislative districts and/or voting procedures. I believe that it is not wrong to draw representative district boundaries in ways that will increase the likelihood that unrepresented social perspectives are represented. As Lani Guinier and others point out, however, it is nearly impossible to create a homogenous district, and group-conscious districting does tend wrongly to balkanize an electorate. Thus, I agree with her and others that various forms of proportional representation in voting schemes may be the best way to combine choice and fairness with a desire to maximize the representation of social perspective.[23]

It is important recognize that law-making bodies need not be the only governmental sites whose members are elected according to rules of representation. A more democratic representative government would have various layers and sites of elected, appointed, and volunteer bodies serving as agenda setting—advisory commissions and administrative review boards, as well as legislatures. In such bodies, it is possible to give specific representation to particular social group perspectives which might not otherwise be present in the policy-making and review processes. If more attention had been paid to special representation of oppressed or disadvantaged groups in the process of setting up the citizens's discussions that led to Oregon's health care rationing plan in 1990, for example, those citizen discussion groups would probably not have been so white middle-class and college educated.[24]

The processes of authorization and accountability that constitute the representative function, finally, should not be thought of as confined to official government bodies. I have already discussed how the free associative life of civil society is important for the formation and expression of interests and opinions. It is also an important site for the consolidation and expression of social perspectives. Deepening democracy means encouraging the flourishing of associations that people form voluntarily according to whatever interests, opinions and perspectives they find important. A principle of the special representation of oppressed or disadvantaged social perspectives would apply to civil society by subsidizing the organization of members of oppressed or disadvantaged social groups and linking them to processes of policy formation. In order to ensure that the perspectives of migrant groups are represented in the policy-making process, for example, the Dutch government subsidizes the organization of migrant groups and regularly consults with them.[25]

I have argued that the worry that the representation of groups implies that all members of the group must have the same interests presupposes that the representative stands for everyone in the group or somehow unites the group. Conceiving representation as a differentiated relationship whose primary moments are authorization and accountability, I have suggested, helps dispel this logic of identity. Representation of social positions structured by gender, race, nation, class, age, and so on, moreover, should be thought of primarily in terms of perspective rather than interests or opinions. Representing a social perspective means bringing to discussion certain kinds of experiences, questions, and sensibilities, moreover, rather than making positive assertions about policy outcomes. Thus, representing perspectives is less unifying than representing interests or opinions, and a particular perspective may be compatible with a variety of interests and opinions. Special mechanisms for ensuring the representation of perspectives that would not otherwise be represented maximizes fairness and social wisdom.

## NOTES

I am grateful to Linda Alcoff, David Alexander, Will Kymlicka, and Ian Shapiro for helpful comments on an earlier version of this paper. Earlier versions of this paper were presented at conferences sponsored by the Institute of Philosophy of the Czech Academy of Sciences and the Institute of Cultural Studies in Essen, Germany. I am grateful to Jean Cohen and Gertrud Koch for arranging my speaking on those occasions, and this paper benefitted from discussion at both conferences.

1. See Nelida Archenti, "Political Representation and Gender Interests: The Argentine Example," paper presented at the Sixteenth World Congress of the International Political Science Association, August 1994.

2. I. M. Young, "Polity and Group Difference: A Critique of the Ideal of Universal Citizenship," in *Throwing Like a Girl and Other Essays in Feminist Philosophy and Social Theory* (Bloomington: Indiana University Press, 1990); I. M. Young, *Justice and the Politics of Difference* (Princeton: Princeton University Press, 1990), chapter 6.

3. For versions of this objection, see Anne Phillips, *Democracy and Difference* (Cambridge: Polity Press, 1993); Chantal Mouffe, "Feminism, Citizenship, and Politics," in *The Return of the Political* (London: Verso, 1993).

4. See Maria Lugones, "Purity, Impurity, and Separation," *Signs: A Journal of Women in Culture and Society* 19:2 (Winter 1994): 458–79.

5. Benjamin Barber, *Strong Democracy* (Berkeley: University of California Press, 1984), 145–46; Paul Hirst, *Representative Democracy and Its Limits* (Oxford: Polity Press, 1990).

6. Linda Alcoff argues that the position that a person can and should speak only for herself is an abrogation of responsibility. It ignores the fact that people's lives are affected by the congruence of many distant actions, and that the participation of people in institutions here in turn affects others. See "The Problem of Speaking for Others," in *Cultural Critique* (Winter 1991–92): 5–32.

7. Robert Dahl, *Democracy and Its Critics* (New Haven: Yale University Press, 1989), chapter 16.

8. This is the general vision of deliberative democracy. See Joshua Cohen, "Deliberation and Democratic Legitimacy," in A. Hamlin and P. Pettit, ed., *The Good Polity* (London: Basil Blackwell, 1989), 7–34; John Dryzek, *Discursive Democracy* (Cambridge: Cambridge Univeristy Press, 1990); Iris Marion Young, "Communication and the Other: Beyond Deliberative Democracy," in Seyla Benhabib, ed., *Democracy and Difference* (Princeton: Princeton University Press, 1996).

9. This is Hanna Pitkin's criticism of mirror, or what she calls descriptive, representation. See *The Concept of Representation* (Berkeley: University of California Press, 1972); see also Will Kymlicka, *Multicultural Citizenship* (Oxford: Oxford University Press, 1995), chapter 7.

10. See Ann Phillips, *The Politics of Presence* (Oxford: Oxford University Press, 1995). See also Rian Voet, "Political Representation and Quotas: Hannah Pitkin's Concept(s) of Representation in the Context of Feminist Politics," *Acta Politica* (1992–94): 389–403.

11. See Jacques Derrida, *Of Grammatology* (Baltimore: Johns Hopkins University Press, 1974).

12. I derive my account of *differance* primarily from Derrida's essay of that title in *Speech and Phenomena and Other Essays in Husserl's Theory of Signs* (Evanston, Ill.: Northwestern University Press, 1973). My discussion of *differance* no doubt will be thought too simple by those familiar with Derrida's philosophy and perhaps too abstract by those who are not. My purpose is not to explicate Derrida but to borrow and perhaps transform as set of concepts that I believe help build a better description of the function of political representation.

13. Derrida, "Differance," 138. See also Derrida's essay, "Sendings: On Representation," translated by Peter and Mary Ann Caws, *Social Research* 49 (Summer 1982): 294–326.

14. Hanna Pitkin, *The Concept of Representation* (Berkeley: University of California Press, 1972).

15. See Claude Lefort, *The Political Forms of Modern Society* (Oxford: Oxford University Press, 1986), 305–25; see also Chantal Mouffe, "Democratic Citizenship and the Political Community," in *The Return of the Political* (London: Verso, 1993), 74–90.

16. See Brian Seitz, *The Trace of Political Representation* (Albany: State University of New York Press, 1995), especially chapters 4 and 5.

17. Frank Cunningham, *Democratic Theory and Socialism* (Cambridge: Cambridge University Press, 1987), chapter 3.

18. Anne Phillips, *The Politics of Presence* (Oxford: Oxford University Press, 1995).

19. John Rawls, *Political Liberalism* (New York: Columbia University Press, 1993). With the term "opinion," however, I do not necessarily intend something so all-encompassing and fundamental as what Rawls calls "comprehensive doctrine," partly because I doubt that most people in modern societies hold and have most or all of their moral and political judgments guided by a single comprehensive doctrine. See I. M. Young, "Rawls's *Political Liberalism*," in *Journal of Political Philosophy* 3:2 (June 1995): 181–90.

20. See Diana Fuss, *Essentially Speaking: Feminism, Nature, and Difference* (London: Routledge, 1989), chapter 1; Bill Martin, *Matrix and Line: Derrida and the Possibilities of Postmodern Social Theory* (Albany: State University of New York Press, 1992), 149–60.

21. I have developed at length a concept of social collectivity that aims to distinguish membership in socially positioned collectives from group identity. See "Gender as Seriality: Thinking about Women as a Social Collective," in *Signs: A Journal of Women in Culture and Society* 19:3 (1994): 713–38.

22. Joshua Cohen and Joel Rogers, "Secondary Associations and Democratic Governance," *Politics and Society* 20:4 (December 1992): 393–472.

23. Lani Guinier, "The Representation of Minority Interests: The Question of Single-Member Districts," *Cardozo Law Review* 14 (1993): 1135–74; "No Two Seats: The Elusive Quest for Political Equality," *Virginia Law Review* 77:8 (November 1991): 1413–1514. See also Center for Voting and Democracy, *Voting Democracy Report,* Washington, D.C., 1995.

24. See Michael J. Garland and Romana Hasraen, "Community Responsibility and the Development of Oregon's Health Care Priorities," *Business and Professional Ethics Journal* 9:3 and 4 (Fall 1990): 183–200.

25. See Yasemin Nohglu Saysal, *Limits of Citizenship: Migrants and Postnational Membership in Europe* (Chicago: University of Chicago Press, 1994), chapter 6.

# 13

# WHAT IS A BALANCED COMMITTEE? DEMOCRATIC THEORY, PUBLIC LAW, AND THE QUESTION OF FAIR REPRESENTATION ON QUASI-LEGISLATIVE BODIES

## ANDREW STARK

## I. Introduction

In recent years political scientists, writing about fair representation in the legislative and judicial spheres, have noted democratic theory's failure to deal with the profound representational questions that arise in other kinds of forums and institutions.[1] Prominent among such forums and institutions is the quasi-legislative body—where "quasi" implies the capacity to influence but neither make nor (alternatively) simply rubber-stamp government decisions, and "legislative" signifies a concern with law, rule, or policy making. At the federal level, most such bodies comprise private citizens representing various interests; almost all are established or utilized under the U.S. Federal Advisory Committee Act (FACA) to provide advice and recommendations to the executive branch. Federal advisory committees can "exert an enormous influence on government ... decision making," and their concerns span the policy spectrum.[2] The White House Conference on Aging, the National Industrial Pollution Council, the Ad Hoc

377

Committee on Long-Term Care, the President's Commission on AIDS, the National Commission on the Observance of International Women's Year, and the Grace Commission on Cost Control in Government, all would be classified as advisory committees.[3] Despite their diverse topicality, though, most FACA-governed committees can be termed "quasi-legislative" in the sense that they influence the making of law, rules or policy, construed broadly so as to embrace a spectrum from focused technical panels to omnibus bodies with extremely diffuse mandates.[4] But how should we go about the task of ensuring that such bodies exhibit fairness of representation? This question, as a number of scholars have noted, remains both a significant and a wide-open one for democratic theory.[5] There is, simply, no theory of quasi-legislative representation.

There does, however, exist a theoretically rich body of public discourse—court decisions and briefs, legislative debate and attendant journalistic commentary—that has arisen surrounding the issue of fair representation on FACA-governed committees. Pursuant to the intent of FACA's drafters, discourse participants have universally taken a "fairly-representative committee"—or, to use FACA's terms, a "balanced committee"—to be one on which all interests affected by the committee are accorded some representation on it.[6] But by what modes to we judge that all affected interests are represented on any given committee? This question has embarked those concerned with balancing committees on the kinds of inquiries that most engross theorists concerned with group representation: how do we determine what kinds of groups ought to be represented in different kinds of forums (what principles of inclusion and exclusion ought to prevail), and how do we identify both the membership of such groups and those who speak for them? Discourse over fair representation on FACA-governed committees engages these questions and many others central to democratic theory, and it does so in a way immersed in the richness of particular cases and shaped by the constraints imposed by actual democratic practice.

Specifically, those in the political branches responsible for establishing such quasi-legislative bodies—or those who seek representation on them through the courts—have found themselves wrestling with two vexing democratic-theoretic questions: First, given that any such body will affect only a circumscribed set of social issues, how should we approach the question of constructing the boundaries of its mandate? Should a governmental cost-control committee, for example, be understood to affect the interests of the poor, and should the poor therefore have representation on it? This can be called the question of "mandate definition." And second—given that the quasi-legislative realm has at its disposal neither the electoral mechanism for choosing representatives available in the legislative realm, nor the standing criteria available in the judicial realm—how should those who establish or review quasi-legislative bodies approach the question of selecting members to represent (those who hold) various affected interests? Even if a cost-control committee is understood to affect the interests of the poor, that doesn't settle the question of who should be selected to represent them. This can be called the question of "membership selection."[7]

It is worth taking a bit of space at the outset to underscore the distinctiveness of these twin questions of quasi-legislative representation, mandate definition and membership selection, and I do this in part II. The "quasi-legislative," in a manner of speaking, is situated in "representational space" between the pure-legislative and the quasi-judicial, two realms whose representational issues *have* been heavily theorized. Yet it is necessary to set out briefly the preoccupations and constructs emergent in these two neighboring theoretical realms, and not only because doing so helps set in bold relief and lend more definition to the distinctiveness of the quasi-legislative, and what is and is not at issue there. Doing so also shows how little we can draw on established theories in neighboring representational domains, if our task is to theorize the unique quasi-legislative issues of mandate definition and membership selection and the central group-representational questions they implicate. To do so we must turn to actual public discourse over fair quasi-legislative representation and analytically reconstruct it, as I do in part III, before drawing from it, as I do in part IV, a framework theory of fair representation for the quasi-legislative sphere.

## II. Neighbors of the Quasi-Legislative: The "Pure" Legislative and the Quasi-Judicial

### Normative Theories of "Pure" Legislative Representation

Most normative theories of legislative representation—i.e., those concerned with "pure" legislative bodies such as Congress, state legislatures, and town councils—yield theoretical constructs fundamentally inapplicable to the two central issues of fair quasi-legislative representation, mandate definition and membership selection. But a look at normative pure-legislative representation theory is helpful, because it makes vivid the uniqueness of the quasi-legislative and helps, as well, to delineate the boundaries between the two legislative realms, "pure" and "quasi." To see this, consider mandate definition first.

Much pure-legislative representation theory takes the mandate of the legislative body under analysis—whether Congress, state legislature or town council—as given, and instead treats the boundaries of the constituencies to be represented on that body as the principal variable, the instrument most readily manipulable, to the end of achieving representative fairness. After all, the mandates of pure-legislative bodies are constitutionally entrenched, sovereign artifacts—ordinarily unalterable by the political and judicial branches in pursuit of representative fairness, invariably affecting all social interests within a given jurisdiction. By contrast, the pure-legislative constituency is a subsovereign, geographically fungible artifact—capable of being politically made and judicially remade so as to embrace innumerable possible subsets of social interests, with dramatic resultant import for representative fairness. Hence the legislative constituency's centrality as a variable in normative theories of pure-legislative representation concerned with "affirmative gerrymandering."[8]

The structure of the quasi-legislative, however, dictates the reverse focus. For on quasi-legislative bodies, the principal variable—the instrument most readily manipulated in aid of representative fairness—is the mandate of the body itself, while it is the configuration of the constituencies represented on quasi-legislative bodies that must be taken as given. It is, after all, the quasi-legislative body itself—or, more exactly, its mandate—

which can be most readily described as a political-judicial, subsovereign artifact, capable of being politically made and judicially remade so as to embrace any bounded set of interests, with dramatic resultant import for representative fairness. A body's mandate could be struck by agencies or interpreted by courts, for example, so as to deal broadly with all interests affected by AIDS, or more specifically with AIDS and the black community, AIDS and health-care workers, or any combination between and beyond. By contrast, in the quasi-legislative sphere, it is the constituencies represented that must be taken as given. Pursuant to FACA and individual committee charters, each such constituency consists not of a variable agglomeration of manifold interests, as do geographical pure-legislative constituencies, but rather a single, discrete social interest (i.e., a particular environmental interest, consumer interest, business interest, etc.). Such constituencies are "givens" in that they are socially "self-identifying" entities, not political-judicial creations. Hence, they lie beyond the capacity of those establishing and reviewing committees to reconfigure in the quest for representative fairness.[9]

Much pure-legislative representation theory, then, focuses on affirmative gerrymandering—how to manipulate variable legislative constituencies (i.e., constituencies which embrace mutable subsets of social interests) against the backdrop of constitutionally given legislative mandates (mandates which invariably embrace all social interests). The quasi-legislative realm, however, focuses on the reverse ("mandate-definition") question: how to manipulate variable quasi-legislative mandates (mandates which typically embrace mutable subsets of social interests) against the backdrop of socially given quasi-legislative constituencies (constituencies which each encompass single social interests).

Nor does pure-legislative representation theory have much to say about the other major question of quasi-legislative representation, the question of membership-selection. To see this, consider that by no means does all pure-legislative representation theory confine itself to legislative constituencies and bodies as presently constructed. Some theorists would replace the pure-legislative constituency with various forms of proportional representation, so as to enable self-identifying social interests to be represented in pure-legislative deliberations. Others would exchange the majoritarian procedures operative in pure-legislative bodies for norms of consensus or supermajoritarian decision making, so as to ensure that a greatrer range of interests are reflected in pure-legislative decisions.[10]

What appear to be avenues for improvement in the pure-legislative realm, however, are already well utilized in the quasi-legislative domain. First, the quasi-legislative is at the vanguard of the pure-legislative in one of the major purposes of proportional representation; i.e., in the capacity to represent an array of self-identifying social interests.[11] Second, most federal advisory committees already operate according to a variety of informal consensus (unanimity, high-threshold supermajority) decision rules.[12] Hence, the advanced theoretical inquiries of normative pure-legislative theory—so many of which are concerned with incorporating or intimating various features of proportional representation and consensual governance—deal with issues that have long since been settled in the quasi-legislative case. Conversely, it is precisely in an area long-since settled in the pure-legislative domain, and hence essentially unaddressed in normative theories of pure-legislative representation, that the quasi-legislative realm is developmentally primitive, requiring theoretical illumination. Specifically, the quasi-legislative realm cannot generate any analogue for the electoral link between representatives and represented which pure legislative bodies take for granted as the elemental first stage of fair representation. Hence, in addition to the question of "mandate definition," the quasi-legislative realm poses the question of "membership selection": how can we "select . . . and legitimat[e] the membership" of quasi-legislative bodies in a fashion "analogous to what goes on when legislative representatives have been out to the test of an election?"[13]

Taken as a whole, then, contemporary pure-legislative representation theory preoccupies itself with affirmative gerrymandering, proportional representation, and legislative consensus norms. Theories dealing with such problems, however, have little applicability to the quasi-legislative sphere. There, the search is for principles of mandate definition and membership selection—issues that understandably remain unencompassed by pure legislative-representation theory.

A word should also be said about that body of *formal* political theory which, since the publication of Duncan Black's seminal *Theory of Committees and Elections* in 1958, has explicitly concerned itself with representation issues on "committees." For purposes here, all that need be noted is that notwithstanding its explicit concern with "faithfully representative *committees,*" the usual formal-theory focus is on bodies that seem less quasi-legislative—i.e., not really committees at all—and more pure-legislative in their governing characteristics. Specifically, the formal-theoretic focus is on "committees" that are usually imagined to exercise mandates governing all or at least many social issues, and/or are possessed of electoral links to the represented (or are otherwise assumed to possess unproblematic mechanisms for selecting representatives).[14] Formal committee theory, too, thus leaves the central quasi-legislative questions of mandate definition and membership selection unaddressed.[15]

Conversely, the central issue to which formal committee theory does address itself—designing schemes for weighting committee members' votes so as to faithfully reflect the intensity of popular support for different positions—is essentially a closed question for those engaged in the actual practice of establishing faithfully representative quasi-legislative committees.[16] This is so for a couple of reasons. First, because quasi-legislative bodies generally govern themselves according to various forms of consensual decision making, discourse surrounding their makeup reveals few contests over the weighting of votes, as it would if such bodies typically adopted majoritarian modes of governance (as, generally, do most hypothetical "formal" committees). Public-interest groups seeking representation on federal advisory committees, knowing consensus rules normally prevail, rarely request more than one or two representatives, even on bodies that might otherwise consist of over a hundred private-sector members.[17] Second, because quasi-legislative bodies are possessed of no electoral or other cognizable links to the represented, discourse surrounding their composition shows little interest in apportioning seats on the basis of popular support, as it presumably would if any kind of metric for such support were available. Those seeking representation on quasi-legislative committees, in fact, never request representation of the interests they voice in proportion to some assertion about their intensity within the population or the voting share of those who hold them.[18] The presence of consensual norms among committee members, along with the absence of electoral links between committee members and those they represent, means that the only goal plaintiff groups seeking quasi-legislative representation generally harbor is to win representation per se. They seek neither representation in proportion to the size of other delegations, nor representation in proportion to numbers in the population. Yet these are precisely the "weighting" questions with which much formal "committee" theory deals.[19]

### Public Law

One other theoretical body may suggest itself as having some bearing on the question of quasi-legislative representation: public-law jurisprudence dealing with the conjoining realm of the quasi-judicial.[20] While the line between the quasi-judicial and the quasi-legislative is notoriously blurred, there is nevertheless a sufficiently articulable distinction between representation issues raised in trial-type proceedings on the one hand, and those posed by law-, rule- or policy-making bodies on the other, that a theory of quasi-legislative representation cannot easily be coaxed out of theories of quasi-judicial representation.[21] Yet an exploration of their differences becomes useful, again, to refining what is and is not at issue in quasi-legislative representation. And those differences become apparent simply by stating the quasi-judicial analogues for the two main questions of quasi-legislative representation, mandate definition and membership selection.

While the quasi-legislative question of mandate definition centers on whether a particular committee's governing mandate affects a given interest, the quasi-judicial analogue centers on whether a particular trial-type proceeding's underlying statute protects a given interest.[22] The difference here is that while quasi-judicial proceedings apply a statute or regulation the legislature or executive have already enacted, quasi-legislative bodies assist the legislature and the executive in the *making* of law or policy *de novo*. Quasi-judicial discourse—over whether a trial-type proceeding's underlying statute protects particular interests—is thus dominated by legal-theoretic issues of statutory interpretation, Congressional intent and agency precedent. In the quasi-legislative case, by contrast—because there is no analogously underlying law to which to refer—discourse over whether a body's governing mandate affects particular interests takes the form of an uninhibitedly political inquiry into the impact of a particular policy area (AIDS policy; government cost-cutting, etc.) on those interests.

Turning, secondly, to the quasi-legislative question of membership selection—which asks who should be selected to represent (those who hold) a given affected interest—the quasi-judicial analogue here queries: who should be granted standing to intervene on behalf of (those who hold) a given protected interest? [23] Again, the differences between quasi-judicial standing criteria and quasi-legislative selection considerations, as they have evolved, are substantial. Because quasi-judicial proceedings are adversarial, standing criteria require would-be parties to sharpen "that concrete adverseness upon which a case or controversy depends." This, in effect, requires interest groups seeking standing to show that they represent either their own particular interests as an organization "qua organization," [24] or else a class of individuals who hold a protected interest in an acute or special way, to a degree "greater than that possessed by an ordinary citizen." [25] Quasi-legislative bodies, by contrast, are not adversarial but deliberative in character, and standing criteria are hence inapt. Here, a public-interest organization's claim to represent its own organizational interests, or only those individuals who hold the public interest in question in a special or significant way, might actually be disqualifying, since the protection of special, non-widely shared interests is the task of the quasi-judicial. Instead, as we shall see, to be selected in the quasi-legislative setting a public-interest organization must show that it represents the disembodied public interest itself—in environmental protection, say, or consumer safety—and not just the organization's interest qua organization. Or else, it must show that it represents all individuals who possess that interest and not just some. Such approaches would, of course, normally be disqualifying in a quasi-*judicial* setting.

In sum, the issues of quasi-judicial representation—statutory interpretation and standing criteria—flow along relatively legalistic trellises. The analogous issues of quasi-legislative representation—mandate definition and membership selection—have, by contrast, provoked a far more robustly political discourse, suitable to what is a more political realm of representation. While public-law jurisprudence has much to say about the former, it has had little to say about the latter.[26]

## Public Discourse

One might have thought that the neighboring realms of normative pure-legislative representation theory, or formal committee theory, or legal theory dealing with quasi-judicial representation might—whether singly or jointly—have generated theoretical constructs of fundamental bearing on the group-representational issues that dominate the quasi-legislative. This, however, is not the case. Showing in what ways it is not the case, moreover, helps clear the deck for the only remaining approach: a theoretical analysis of public discourse over fair quasi-legislative representation itself. Or, more exactly, an analysis of the discourse of those—courts, litigants, politicians, and commentators—actually concerned with ensuring that federal quasi-legislative bodies conform to FACA's requirement that they be "fairly balanced," meaning that all interests affected by any given committee must be represented on it. Discourse has thus flowed toward the twin questions of (1) how first to determine the range of interests any given committee does affect (the question of mandate) and (2) how then to ensure that those interests are properly represented (the question of selection).

Yet although it addresses these two questions in a rich and multivarious fashion, public discourse has been far from univocal in answering them. Indeed, FACA's "balance provision" has proved to be "the most troublesome aspect of FACA litigation, . . . generat[ing] more lawsuits than any other provision of FACA."[27] The typical FACA balance case involves litigation commenced by a public-interest group seeking representation on a given committee—a committee which, the plaintiff group typically charges, is "seriously imbalanced," lacking members truly representative of all the interests it affects.[28] According to the defendant U.S. government, however, challenged committees are invariably well balanced—appropriately representative of all affected interests.[29] The litigiousness FACA's balance provision has provoked, the absence of any lines of clarity in balance decisions,[30] the vagueness of the balance provision itself,[31] and the difficulties Congress has faced in attempting to render it more concrete—these are each rooted in the same thing: the contestedness of the concept of a fairly representative quasi-legislative body; i.e., a balanced committee. Or, more exactly, in the inaccessibility of the principles on which committee mandates are to be determined and members selected.

In what follows, I reconstruct "balance discourse" in order to yield a framework theory of quasi-legislative representation. In fact, it would be most accurate to characterize this study as a "theorization of public discourse." It should be emphasized, however, that if it is to remain faithful to the shared assumptions of discourse participants *any* such theorization must take a traditional "interest-group liberalism" as its point of departure. And for that reason, the questions of fair quasi-legislative representation escape the concerns not only of much normative theory, formal theory, and legal theory but also many of the more critical democratic theories that engage contemporary political philosophy.

To see this, consider that while FACA's balance provision literally requires committees to be representative of all *"points of view* relevant to their functions," the aim of each party in any given balance case, as noted, has become simply to ensure representation of all *interests* the committee directly affects.[32] Congress, courts and litigants have simply taken "'a direct interest' as proxy for a point of view so that judicial review would be available."[33] In its suit to have consumer interests represented on the National Advisory Committee on Microbiological Criteria for Foods, for example, the plaintiff Public Citizen was concerned to show simply that "the Committee lack[ed] *any* consumer representation, not that it lack[ed] consumer representatives with specific viewpoints"—and least of all that it lacked consumer representatives "who share[d] their own viewpoint." Indeed, Public Citizen conceded that someone like "the economist Milton Friedman—presumably an opponent of most government regulation—might, at least facially, qualify as a consumer representative."[34] All parties to discourse thus agree that representation of affected interests (where the interests concerned can be classified under comparatively "objective" rubrics such as various types of "environmental," "health," "consumer," "business," etc., interests) is simply more manageable, more readily accomplished, than representation of "subjective, amorphous concepts such as viewpoints."[35] Whatever its merits, the balance-of-interests model must be incorporated into any discourse-based theorization of "fair quasi-legislative representation"—a concept contestable enough as it is, so the discourse shows, without bringing in the added difficulties attendant on a need to balance representation not just of affected interests but of viewpoints as to how to realize those "interests."[36]

It must be said, however, that a large question remains closed, and goes wholly unaddressed in balance discourse, as a consequence of this assumed equation of fair quasi-legislative representation with representation of affected interests. That precluded question is whether democratic politics can ever transcend the clash-of-interests model.[37] But even some scholars who advance alternative models of representation agree that at the moment, "[t]he operation of liberal democratic politics corresponds to these assumptions;" i.e., that their conflicting interests are often what the represented seek to have represented.[38] "The very distance of . . . prospects" for reforming the clash-of-interests system, as Anne Phillips has noted, "puts a premium on political prescriptions"—and, presumably, political theorizations of public discourse—"that can be made relevant to representative democracy as currently practised."[39]

To summarize thus far: Normative theories of "pure" legislative representation focus on affirmative gerrymandering, along with various possibilities for enabling the representation of social interests (proportional representation) and enacting consensual legislative decision rules. Formal committee theory concentrates on committees that govern all or many social issues, or else possess unproblematic or presumed links to the represented, or else operate according to majority vote. Public-law jurisprudence concerns itself largely with the issues of statutory interpretation and standing criteria suitable to weighing fair quasi-judicial representation. And a variety of critical democratic theories assume selves variously communitarian, other-regarding, or altruistic. No developed representation-theoretic body, in other words, deals with the quasi-legislative realm—the realm in which central issues of group representation most directly come to a head—where the challenge is to ensure the representation of all affected interests, and the questions are therefore those of mandate definition and membership selection. Yet to explicate the central preoccupations displayed by these other theoretical bodies is, necessarily, to show that only an exploration of public discourse, and not an extrapolation from neighboring theoretical domains, can theorize the group-representational issues central to the quasi-legislative realm.

## III. BALANCE DISCOURSE:
## AN ANALYTICAL RECONSTRUCTION

In this section, I offer an analytical reconstruction of discourse—and in particular, government and plaintiff-group argumentation—in the major "balance" cases, ranged around the separate issues of how to define a quasi-legislative committee's mandate and how to select its members. On both issues, mandate and selection, the government habitually argues in the alternative. That is, it advances two recurrent lines of democratic-theoretic argument on mandate, and two on selection, for a total of four argumentative strategies in its arsenal. Plaintiff groups, accordingly, mount four discernible counterarguments. The structure of balance discourse thus displays four distinct strands, which are reconstructed here as *Discourse over Mandate (1) and (2)* and *Discourse over Selection (1) and (2)*. And although this discourse largely surrounds cases where public-interest groups seek representation on committees dominated by private interests, the theorization it affords can be generalized to instances where this is not the case.[40]

### Discourse over Mandate (1)

In seeking to exclude a plaintiff group from a given committee, the government's first move, typically, is to characterize the committee's mandate as both a well-defined and a narrow one, best understood as touching on issues that affect the particular interests only of those, usually members of the private sector, who are already represented. When the National Treasury Employees' Union sought representation on President Reagan's Commission on Privatization (a body composed exclusively of business representatives), the government contended that the Commission's mandate was "a narrow one, namely, to determine *which* government programs are more appropriately part of the private sector," and "*not* to determine whether or not privatization in general is a good or desirable public policy."[41] "Within these parameters," the Court itself agreed, there was no need for "critics of privatization" such as the plaintiff group "to be present on the Commission to lend it balance."[42] Or consider the National Anti-Hunger Coalition's suit for membership on President Reagan's Private-Sector Survey on Cost Control in Government (the Grace Commission), a body composed of 150 "citizens appointed by the President from the private sector." There, the government claimed that the "line" between the committee's "narrow managerial mandate" and any "broader 'policy' questions . . . was a bright one," and that the interests the Anti-Hunger Coalition claimed to represent were not "directly affected by the work of the committee." Any "imbalances" alleged by the plaintiff, the government contended, would thus be "irrelevant to the ability of the [Commission] to perform its function fairly and impartially."[43] In short, in "some cases the issues to be decided by committees are so bounded that any threat to public values simply disappears."[44] In such circumstances, to include representatives of broader interests would transform "the function of the committee, not lend it greater balance."[45]

For the government, it is thus possible to draw bright, hermetic lines distinguishing a quasi-legislative body's well-defined, relatively narrow mandate—and the delimited range of (private) interests it *does* affect—from anything broader and extrinsic to it. Plaintiff groups, in replying, argue that however narrow or private-sector-oriented a committee's initial concerns may have been, they inevitably broaden beyond their original confines, impelled to do so by the kinds of inner dynamics that typify such bodies. In seeking representation on the Privatization Commission, for example, the Treasury Employees' Union asserted—almost as a general principle of the sociology of committees—that "committees in government seldom operate wholly within their charter, and hence the original representation usually turns out not to be balanced."[46] Similarly, in seeking representation on the Grace Commission, the National Anti-Hunger Coalition argued that "the committee has departed from its narrow mandate and is considering substantive changes in federal programs."[47] All of which amounts to a line of argument running flatly counter to the government's habitual attempt to "justify homogeneous committee membership by a correspondingly narrow definition of a committee's functions."[48]

*Discourse over Mandate (2)*

In the first strand of mandate discourse, then, the government argues that the committee's mandate, at an appropriately fine-grained level of specification and definition, can be deemed sufficiently narrow so as not to affect directly the excluded interest. To be sure, though, at some sufficiently broad level of generality or attenuation anything can be said to affect anything else. But then if we are going to argue at such broad levels of attenuated connection—and this is the government's *second* argument on committee mandate—not only the plaintiff interest, but an "infinite" number of other interests, might be deemed equally affected. The *Treasury Employees' Union* decision, for example, begins—along lines urged by the government's first mandate argument—by characterizing the contested committee's mandate as a "narrow one," affecting at most a very thin range of private-sector interests, and certainly not the putatively excluded public interest. But, the court then opines, if the committee's *de facto* mandate should indeed be understood as sufficiently broad as to affect the excluded interest—in the way the plaintiff union had urged—then it is in fact "so broad" that "it would be impossible to include among [the committee's] members a representative of every [interest] that would or could conceivably be affected by the [committee's] work"—including, *inter alia,* the plaintiff group.[49]

Courts have been as influenced by this second strand of government mandate-argumentation as they have been by the first. When a consumer organization sought membership on an FDA Food Safety Committee, the court—in the form of a general statement about committees *per se*—followed the government brief in opining that if the excluded interest were somehow deemed directly affected, then the similarly relevant interests "to be considered by an advisory committee are virtually infinite . . . I can conceive of no principled basis . . . to determine which . . .

deserve representation on particular advisory committees." Although—pursuant to the first governmental "mandate" argument—at an appropriate level of specification the line between a
committee's "narrow" mandate and any "broader" questions may
be a "bright one," at the level of imputed breadth at which committee mandate *could* be said to affect the excluded interest, the
line between those with "'direct interests' and those with 'tangen-
tial interests'" would turn into a "hopelessly manipulable" one. So
manipulable that judges and agencies "would be obliged to make
an arbitrary decision as to how attenuated an interest must be
before it should be classified as 'indirect,'" and hence exclud-
able.[50]

Underlying this second exclusionary argument are some deter-
minant assumptions about interest pluralism. Specifically, the government assumes that a radical disintegration characterizes the
universe of interests. Once beyond a narrow point of rich-textured
specification, "[n]o principles" exist by which, and there simply is
no impartial perspective from which, one might "draw lines" or
definitively priorize various excluded interests—at least according
to the "directness" or intensity with which any particular committee mandate might affect them. Each "interest" by its own lights
could claim to be so affected, but no intersubjective ordering or
ranking principles prevail whereby agencies or courts could seat
representatives of only a few. As the government brief in the
*National Anti-Hunger Coalition* case put it, "if the Court were to
follow the logic of the plaintiff's argument," "virtually every special interest . . . in the United States [could] claim that it might be
affected" by the cost-control committee; the "churches [would]
have a right [to be represented]. The hospitals [would] have a
right. The schoolteachers [would] have a right. . . . And you can
go on and on."[51] No principles of relationship even exist such
that one or two interests could be said to virtually represent the
affected others, or such that all the excluded but affected interests
might reasonably be asked to coalesce behind one representative.[52] The interest universe is a realm of radical difference, a view
which is no stranger to democratic theory.[53]

The interest universe, plaintiff groups reply, in fact betrays
more definition, contour and lines of inner commensurability
and relationship than the government position assumes—defini-

tion, contour, and commensurability on the basis of which agencies and courts could, within appropriate bounds, determine that a committee's mandate will lead it to affect directly some excluded interests more than others.[54] In support of its claim to membership on the Grace Commission, the Anti-Hunger Coalition claimed to be "unique in the entire universe of possible interests," possessing an "extremely specific, definable disproportionate interest . . . in [the Commission's] activities."[55] Seating the excluded interest need not open the floodgates; it is simply not true that, beyond a circumscribed point, "no principles" are available for intersubjectively ranking, priorizing, or coalescing interests by the extent to which they have import for the committee, or the committee for them.[56] This line of argument, as well, resonates with an important strand in democratic theory.[57]

*Discourse over Selection (1)*

In mandate discourse, then, the government habitually urges that at the most appropriate level of definition, committee mandate is best understood as simply too narrow to directly affect the excluded interest. Or, if we are to conclude that mandate somehow *does* affect the excluded interest, the link must take place at a level of such omnibus generality that there is no way of distinguishing those interests directly affected from those only indirectly affected. Plaintiff groups, for their part, question both claims.

Turning now to the issue of "membership selection," the government typically urges that even if a committee's mandate *can* be said uncontroversially to "directly affect" the excluded interest in question (i.e., it can be understood as not so narrow as to exclude that interest, but not so broad as therefore to include "myriad" others), that in itself provides no reason why the particular plaintiff group—as opposed to some other group or individual— should be "selected" to represent (those who possess) the excluded interest. And here, on the question of selection as well, two strands of discourse—two modes of government argumentation and group response—are discernible.

In the first, the government rejects the group's claim to be selected by arguing that no means exist whereby interest groups can, in a suitably cognizable fashion, establish that they actually represent any real individuals. In the pure-legislative arena, electoral ratification exists as a means to validate parties' claims to speak for constituencies of real individuals. In the quasi-judicial realm, various standing tests are available to validate parties' claims to speak for classes of real individuals. Neither vehicle, however, is accessible in the quasi-legislative setting. It is impossible, one balance jurist urged, to decide which "American[s]" a plaintiff "organization truly represents; [i]n our system of government, that sort of question is implicitly determined by elections."[58] Or, as the government insisted in another case, all that a quasi-judicial standing test shows—indeed, all that it is meant to show—is that an excluded group represents a defined few who harbor the interest in question in a "distinct and palpable" or "specific" way.[59] But while standing tests may thus be suited to advancing a group's claim to represent real individuals in a quasi-judicial setting, they do not suffice to make a comparable claim in the quasi-legislative.

Jeremy Rabkin well articulates the fundamental political-theoretic position lying behind the government's claim that—outside of electoral mechanisms and standing tests—groups cannot claim to represent any real individuals. At most, Rabkin writes, groups can claim to

> represent interests instead of directly representing the people assumed to hold those interests. But just to that extent, they do not really represent anyone ... for it is notorious that people are not always interested in their interests. ... Thus near majorities of union members have ignored the counsel of their union officials in successive presidential elections over the past two decades. And the reason, in all likelihood, was not that they disagreed with union officials about their interests *as* union members but that they did not see this interest as predominant.[60]

The concern here, as Rabkin makes clear, is not that when it comes to the excluded interest in question, the group's view as to how best to serve that interest may simply not represent the views of any actual individuals—that, for example, the group may have a view as to what is in the environmental interest not shared by anyone in the public. For even if a great many individuals *do* share a group's point-of-view as to how best to serve the interest the group claims to represent, a more fundamental problem of representation will still arise because those individuals will invariably have other interests to which they may give "preference" or "predominance"—and they may do so with an innumerable variety of gradations, emphases, and tradeoff formulas.[61] A "steelworker, for example, may like clean air as much as the next person but still prefer to put up with a bit more air pollution rather than see the closing of the plant in which he works"; hence an "environmental group" will not speak for him.[62] Groups, focused as they must be on representing one or (at most) a handful of interests apiece, cannot easily be assumed to represent total individuals—those complicated congeries of manifold conflicting interests.[63] This line of governmental argument is, as well, a prominent one in public law and political theory.[64]

Plaintiff groups predicate their counterargument on the idea that individuals may not be the entities which quasi-legislative bodies ought to represent in the first place. Or (to put it another way) when faced with the government's claim that they can never represent individuals—only at best disembodied interests—plaintiff groups argue that after a point, there *are* only interests. Individuals do not exist, if individuals are conceived as rank orderings of multiple interests, orderings that may well give predominance to interests other than the one the plaintiff group represents.

It is important—before consulting some relevant strands of plaintiff argumentation itself—to frame this argument conceptually. And, in the absence of any theory of quasi-legislative representation that does so directly, it will prove helpful to recur to those minoritarian strands in neighboring political and legal theory which argue—certainly against convention—that disembodied single interests, and not multi-interested individuals, should be the primary constituents represented in *pure*-legislative and *quasi*-judicial forums as well. For in both strands of scholarship one finds the individual deconstructed into an inchoate constellation of unranked and unrankable discrete interests, interests which are themselves deemed to be the basic building-blocks—the entities which truly merit representation—in the legislative body or quasi-judicial proceeding in question, and which single-interest groups *are* eminently capable of representing. In his book on reform in the pure-legislative domain, for example, John Burnheim argues that

> I may well have conflicting interests as a producer and a consumer,
> [but it] is not desirable that I settle in advance for some one
> balance between these conflicting interests. [Better that] my di-
> verse interests each have its own representative. Each representa-
> tive [would] do the best for a specific interest in the circum-
> stances.[65]

The inner realm of the individual is one of conflict, with each
major interest suggesting itself as uniquely important and no
internal, intrasubjective scheme operative for prioritizing them.
Hence, in representing separately the various interests of an individual, groups do not misrepresent the total individual—indeed,
together they represent the total individual. Or, put another way, a
group—focusing as it must on a single interest—does not thereby
misrepresent the priorities individuals may lend to other competing interests, since the concept of enduring, identifiable, individual interest priorizations is deeply problematic.

In *Legal Identity,* the legal theorist Joseph Vining advances a
similar deconstructive conception of the individual—only his focus is the quasi-judicial arena, and his point is that there as well it
is only interests, not individuals, that ought to be represented.
Vining flatly rejects the constitutive conception of the individual
underlying traditional quasi-judicial standing doctrine, namely,
that "[w]e are each one person; we rank our values and order our
loves; we each resolve the conflicts within us and speak with a
single voice"—and that, in representing just one of those "values"
or "loves," groups always risk misrepresenting individual "rank[-
ings]" or "order[ings]" or "voices" *in toto.*[66] Instead, Vining argues
that

> there is no objective necessity ordering an individual's interests. . . .
> There may indeed be no ultimate structure of our wants. The inner
> world no less than the outer is too complex to be centrally ordered.
> . . . It is they who contend in legislatures, courts and agencies,
> pushing for attention, recognition, and realization of "their" inter-
> ests, who must deal with this problem.[67]

What is intriguing about all of this is that while Burnheim
deconstructs the individual as part of a political-theoretic critique
of pure-legislative representation criteria (criteria which traditionally require the represented to be real individuals), Vining does so

as part of a legal-theoretic critique of quasi-judicial representation criteria (which traditionally require the same). Yet it turns out to be something in between Burnheim's and Vining's two separate concerns—namely, discourse over *quasi-legislative* representation—which has given by far the most scope to the idea (and certainly to public-interest plaintiffs to argue it) that the represented need not be individuals but rather their component interests. Absent the possibility of either pure-legislative electoral links with real individuals, or quasi-judicial standing-test links to real individuals, such a move is a much more obvious one for groups to make in the quasi-legislative case. In a much-cited phrase, for example, the original House Report on FACA reified disembodied interests. It converted them into the represented by stipulating that committee members should be "representatives of conservation, environment, clean water," and so forth. The Report quite explicitly conceived of committees as forums for the representation of "competing interests," not of individuals.[68] Plaintiff groups have largely adopted this vocabulary[69] and courts have done so as well: In the *Anti-Hunger Coalition* case, for example, Judge Gerhard Gesell writes of the need to represent "the interests of hunger [and] the interests of the environment" in a way that would jar in a pure-legislative or quasi-judicial setting.[70] Fundamentally, then, this strand of "selection" discourse takes the form of a disagreement over the constitutive nature of the individual and its relationship to its own interests. The government presumes that individuals possess interest hierarchies in which some interests are always "predominant" or "preferred" to the ones groups represent. Groups—unable to avail themselves of traditional pure-legislative or quasi-judicial links to such individuals—essentially argue from a deconstruction of individuals so conceived.[71]

## Discourse over Selection (2)

Finally, assume agreement that quasi-legislative bodies *are* (as plaintiff groups suggest) better conceived as meant to represent pure interests, not individuals. Or, put another way, assume that the only aspects of an individual that *can* be represented are her own disaggregated interests, and not some unique prioritization she imposes on them. Even so, the government recurrently mounts a second line of argument as to why the plaintiff group should not be selected—an argument to the effect that groups are not only incapable of representing real individuals, but that they are incapable of representing disembodied interests (in a consumer, health, or other social area) as well. Specifically, the government contends that groups possess their own private organizational interests, interests that necessarily dilute their capacity to speak full-throatedly for the (public) interests they claim to represent.

The *Microbiological Criteria* case offers a good example of this strand of governmental argumentation. There, Judge Lawrence Silberman denied a plaintiff consumer organization's claim to be selected to represent the (concededly affected) consumer interest on an FDA Food Safety Committee, on the grounds that such an "organization . . . would have an economic interest in the work of the Committee—not shared by the public—and therefore a special interest."[72] At its most expansive, this line of argument has it that public-interest groups—in addition to the consumer, environmental, or other social interests which they were established to advance—also develop a range of private or "special" interests in organizational longevity or ideological positioning, interests analogous to business interests in corporate survival or market share.[73] Within the margins of calculation available to agencies and courts, the government argues, such private or special interests must be seen as incompatible with any kind of dedicated, unalloyed representation of the pure public interest in question. Any given individual consumer whom the government appoints might, despite her other interests (say as a pension-fund member), represent the consumer interest as faithfully as—perhaps more faithfully than—a consumer-group representative, given the group's other interests (e.g., in the group's finances and profile).[74] The government's position here, it is worth noting, resonates with those strands of political-science research according to which groups often "develop . . . interests of their own which they [seek] to realize at the expense of membership interests."[75]

Such a line of argument is rebuffed by plaintiff groups seeking representation on advisory committees ("these arguments are silly on their face").[76] Plaintiff groups routinely state or "imply that their [claims] ought to be . . . accorded higher priority" precisely "because they . . . do not have ordinary 'special interest' attachments," and that they therefore can represent, in a pure and undiluted way, the (public) interests for which they claim to speak.[77] Here, plaintiff groups resolutely identify themselves with those strands of contemporary political science that characterize public-interest organizations as "groups seeking benefits whose achievement will not benefit selectively either the members or the professionals of the organization."[78]

## IV. Toward a Theory of Quasi-Legislative Representation: A Theorization of Discourse

Together, the twin debates over mandate and selection comprise public discourse over the meaning of a balanced committee—or, effectively, discourse uttered by those actually wrestling with fair representation on America's principal quasi-legislative bodies. At its surface level, that discourse takes a fourfold form: First, on mandate definition, the government typically begins by arguing that at the most appropriate level of specification, a particular committee's mandate is best understood as too narrow to affect the excluded interest. Second, if a link is going to be posited between the mandate of such a committee and the excluded interest, it would have to be one of such generality that, having introduced it, it would then be impossible for agencies and courts to exclude—as less than directly affected—"myriad" other interests. Third, turning to the question of membership selection, the government argues that even if the committee's mandate *does* directly affect the excluded interest, there is no way the plaintiff group can establish that it speaks for individuals who hold that interest. After all, individuals may well lend priority to interests of their own *other than* the one for which the group claims to speak. Fourth, even if plaintiff groups need not represent any real individuals—only the disembodied affected interest itself—their claim to do so fails, since any group will inevitably lend priority to interests of its own other than the one for which it claims to speak.

Plaintiff groups counter on all fronts. Mandates almost always broaden beyond their original confines, however narrow, to affect the excluded interest. It is not true, however, that "no principles" exist whereby those a mandate so affects directly can be distinguished from "myriad" others more "tangentially" affected. When it comes to selection, the criteria employed must recognize that in representing isolated, discrete interests, groups do not necessarily misrepresent individuals properly conceived. Finally, groups *are* capable of representing pure public interests—without being distracted by their own concerns.

To theorize such a body of discourse, however, it is necessary to look beneath the surface debate and turn to its deep structure, to the political assumptions animating each side, and to draw from them a small set of political determinants (one could also call them "variables") on which the issues always turn. And, as we shall see, the deep structure of balance discourse—and therefore any resultant theorization of fair quasi-legislative representation—centers on variables at play on four primary levels of democratic politics. Or, more precisely, it centers on the particular way in which diverse and discrete interests are seen to interact—gain priority or primacy—within the polity at large, within those two mediating structures—committees and groups—and, finally, within the individual citizen.

To theorize the question of fair quasi-legislative representation is not, in and of itself, to answer the question of whether any particular committee is in fact balanced—just as theories of pure-legislative or quasi-judicial representation do not generate algorithms telling us, definitively, whether any given legislative or quasi-judicial forum exhibits representative fairness. What such a theorization can do is reveal the fundamental determinants of fair quasi-legislative representation. It can outline how these determinants are implicated in, and carved out of, larger theoretical and empirical issues in democratic politics.

Consider first the two "mediating structures" whose functionings are integral to balance discourse, committees and groups, and the ways in which interests are seen to interact within them. Here it will prove useful to juxtapose discourse over the *first* question of mandate (the extent to which committees are capable of confining themselves to their putative "private-interest" mandates, and so do not affect the excluded interest) with that surrounding the *second* question of selection (the extent to which plaintiff groups are capable of confining themselves to their putative public-interest purposes, and so ought to be selected to represent the excluded interest).

In discourse over mandate, recall, the government's first move is to characterize committee purposes as essentially focused and delineated, concerned exclusively with a set of relatively narrow, well-defined, usually private interests. In response, the plaintiff group suggests that however comparatively narrow or private-interest-focused their initial purposes may have been, it is in the nature of such committees that their concerns and motivations ineluctably expand, so as to embrace a much broader range of (usually) public interests. Now turn to discourse over *selection*, and in particular to its second strand, wherein plaintiff groups characterize their own purposes as essentially focused and delineated, concerned exclusively with a set of broad, unalloyed, public interests. In countering, the government suggests that however "broad" or "public-interest-focused" their initial purposes may have been, it is in the nature of such groups that their concerns and motivations inevitably expand so as to embrace, as well, a variety of essentially private narrow organizational interests.

For the government, the sociology of committees is such that their concerns do not, generally, move from those of relatively narrow or private interest toward those of broad and public interest; hence, committees do not generally affect the excluded interest. The sociology of groups, however, is such that their concerns inevitably do move from those of broad and public interest toward those of narrow or private interest; hence, no group can reliably be selected to represent the excluded interest. For plaintiff groups, the reverse is the case. I am not suggesting that there is anything necessarily paradoxical about either the government or the group position; whether there is will depend on particular arguments and cases, and on relevant theoretical and empirical findings. What I would like to suggest is that the theorization of fair quasi-legislative representation implicates, fundamentally, these two parallel questions in the comparative sociology of mediating structures—concerning the ways in which interests interact and gain primacy within committees and groups.[79]

There are two final theoretical determinants of fair quasi-legislative representation, and each departs—one, as it were, in either direction—from the mediating democratic-theoretic level occupied by committees and groups. Here, the issues surround the differing ways in which interests are arrayed within the external world of politywide interest pluralism on the one hand, and the inner world of individuals' interest hierarchies on the other. To see this, it is necessary to juxtapose the deep structure of the remaining two strands of balance discourse. On the one hand is the *second* question of mandate; i.e., the extent to which—within the public realm of the democratic polity—interests can be ranked and ordered in a sufficiently definitive way that a committee's mandate can be said directly to affect some but not all. On the other hand is discourse over the *first* question of selection; i.e., the extent to which—within the private realm of the democratic citizen—interests are ranked and ordered in a sufficiently definitive way that single-interest groups can be said to represent few individuals if any.

To begin with, recall that in the second strand of mandate discourse, the government contends that even if a principle *is* found on which mandate can be said to affect an excluded interest, it is inevitably one of sufficient breadth such that it would then be impossible to exclude—as less than directly affected— "myriad" others. Here, the government argues that the public world of interests is essentially planar or horizontal, incapable of being priorized or sorted in any meaningful way, at least for the purposes at hand. It is impossible, the government urges with this argument, to look upon the interest universe and exhaustively order or rate its components such that one or more of them might—in any dispositive way—be deemed more directly affected by a committee's mandate than the others.

Now turn to the first strand of discourse over selection, in which the government seeks to exclude the plaintiff group—i.e., urges that it ought not be selected—on the grounds that self-identifying, single-interest groups cannot claim to represent any real individuals. The government here assumes that the individual's internal world of interests is hierarchical and vertical, definitively well ordered, priorized, arrayed, and assorted. Or, at least, sufficiently ordered and ranked that it is impossible to say of any group, concerned as it must be with one or two isolated interests at most, that it can meaningfully represent any real individuals—

who may, after all, lend priority to interests other than the one for which the group claims to speak.

As they inhabit the public world of democratic pluralism, then—so the government's theoretical position here has it—interests simply do not display sufficiently rich and definitive intersubjective lines of relationship and priority such that we can say, within the margins of calculation available to both courts and agencies, that any given committee mandate directly affects some and not others. As they inhabit the private inner world of the democratic citizen, however, interests do display exceedingly rich and definitive intrasubjective lines of relative bearings and priorities—sufficiently rich and definitive such that we *can* say that any group seeking selection, single-interested as it must be, will never completely represent any real individuals. On both scores, of course, the plaintiff group's position is the reverse: The external interest universe is such that, from an intersubjective perspective, the interests within it *are* capable of being ranked or prioritized— at least such that any given committee mandate can be said to directly affect some and only indirectly others. Individuals' inner interest hierarchies, however, are such that from an intrasubjective perspective the interests within them are not meaningfully ranked and priorized; hence groups, in representing individuals' separate interests, do not thereby misrepresent individuals themselves.

Again, I am not suggesting that there is anything necessarily paradoxical about either the government or the group position on these questions. The array of interests in the external, public world may well be thought (whether in any given case or as a general principle) to remain more or less recalcitrant to intersubjective rankings or assortments. Likewise, the array of interests in individuals' inner worlds—for the purposes of any given committee, or else more globally—may well be deemed more or less impervious to intrasubjective orderings or prioritizings. What I would like to suggest is that the theorization of fair quasi-legislative representation implicates, in part, these two parallel questions in democratic theory—having to do with the ways in which interests interact and display lines of priority within the polity and within individuals.

In sum, a theorization of discourse shows that the question of fair quasi-legislative representation implicates fundamental issues in political science. In any given case—or else more globally— the issues hinge on the extent to which certain kinds of interests are thought to display relationships of primacy within committees and within groups, along with the extent to which diverse interests are thought to display relationships of priority within the polity and within individuals. Political science itself is divided on most of these issues (as noted, both government and group argumentation find resonances in the literature) which is why variables such as those at play in balance discourse do not suggest themselves as taking on any obvious value either generally or in specific cases. And, as discourse shows, what one believes about the way interests interrelate within committees and groups, or within the entire polity and sole individuals, will lend itself to a host of ideological and factual considerations.

Nevertheless, research can—in at least a couple of ways—help refine and elaborate such a discourse-rooted theorization of fair quasi-legislative representation. Theoretical and empirical research can, for example, explore the extent to which certain views of interest interaction at various levels of democratic politics cohere with each other. Perhaps a political sociology on which committees remain capable of concerning themselves exclusively with issues affecting a narrow set of (often private) interests is, in certain ways, incompatible with one on which groups invariably stray from an exclusive concern with issues implicating broad sets of (public) interests. Similarly, both theorists and empirical researchers could sharpen a theorization such as this by incorporating into it, for example, their findings regarding the extent to which various views of interest interaction at different levels of democratic politics correspond to political reality. Of central bearing would be work on the extent to which individuals ought to be conceived as monads as opposed to entities deconstructable in some fashion; or the extent to which the polity is one of patterned pluralism as against radical difference. What a theorization of balance discourse *can* do is show how research into these questions may bear on the particular issue of fair quasi-legislative represention. And, in turn, it can offer a set of new, directed lines

of inquiry for political scientists doing work in pertinent areas—
all to the end of further enriching this initial theorization.

### V. CONCLUSION

A central task of political theory is to "provide standards that
would enable us to judge" fairness-of-representation in major "formal structures of policy making." In pursuing this task, "what we
are looking for are principles of political structure that have
essentially the same standing as principles of design in architecture, canons . . . that are not beyond criticism, that necessarily will
reflect diverse schools of thought, but that nonetheless stand as a
basis for appraising the workmanship of any political construction." [80]

A theorization of balance discourse yields just such principles
for approaching the question of fair representation on quasi-
legislative bodies. It is a question whose structural concerns differ
fundamentally from those addressed by theories dealing with
neighboring representative domains: theories of pure-legislative
representation on the one hand; jurisprudence surrounding
quasi-judicial representation on the other. Nor have theories operating on different planes of abstraction or transcendence—
formal committee theories, critical democratic theories—been
channeled by balance discourse's constraints and imperatives.
Even so, in its deep structure, this reconstructed discourse re-
solves itself into, and configures in a particular way, a defined set
of theoretical and empirical questions of ongoing centrality to
political science—questions having to do with the way in which
interests interact and array themselves within the public sphere of
the democratic polity, the private sphere of the democratic citizen, and the mediating private-public sphere of democratic committees and groups. To what extent do different kinds of interests
gain primacy in different kinds of committees and groups? To
what extent do different interests display lines of priority within
the polity as a whole or individuals singly? To pursue the political-
science agenda of answering these questions, both generally and
for the purposes of specific cases, is to continue building the
theory of fair quasi-legislative representation.

## NOTES

An earlier version of this chapter was presented to the Fellows' Seminar in the Harvard Program in Ethics and the Professions. I am grateful to all those who participated, and additionally to Patti Goldman, Rob Howse, Don Herzog, Keith Krehbiel, Will Kymlicka, and Melissa Williams for their helpful comments. I would also like to acknowledge the financial support of the Harvard Program in Ethics and the Professions, the Woodrow Wilson International Center for Scholars, and the Connaught Fund at the University of Toronto.

1. See, for example, Iris Marion Young, *Justice and the Politics of Difference* (Princeton: Princeton University Press, 1990), 185–91; Joshua Cohen and Joel Rogers, "Secondary Associations and Democratic Governance," *Politics and Society* 20 (1992):393–472; and Charles W. Anderson, "Political Design and the Representation of Interests," *Comparative Political Studies* 10 (1977): 132.

2. See Eric R. Glitzenstein and Patti A. Goldman, *The Federal Advisory Committee Act at the Crossroads* (Washington, D.C.: Public Citizen, 1989), 1.

3. Henry Perritt, Jr., and James A. Wilkinson, "Open Advisory Committees and the Political Process," *Georgetown Law Journal* 63 (1975): 728–29.

4. See Bruce L. R. Smith, *The Advisers: Scientists in the Policy Process* (Washington, D.C.: Brookings, 1992), 200–201; and Sheila Jasanoff, *The Fifth Branch: Science Advisers as Policymakers* (Cambridge: Harvard University Press, 1990), 47. While there are exceptions to both the "legislative" characteristic of federal advisory committees (peer-review committees are also covered by FACA, for example), and to the "quasi" aspect (some committees do essentially make, while others rubber-stamp, government law and policy), for purposes here, "federal advisory committee" and "quasi-legislative body" will be treated as equivalent. See Congressional Research Service, *Federal Advisory Committee Act Sourcebook: Legislative History, Texts and Other Documents* (95th Congress: 2nd Session, 1978), 288–89.

5. Robert C. Grady, *Restoring Real Representation* (Urbana and Chicago: University of Illinois Press, 1993), 145–46; see also Mark P. Petracca, "Federal Advisory Committees, Interest Groups and the Administrative State," *Congress and the Presidency* 13 (1986): 106; and Thomas E. Cronin, "Political Science and the Executive Advisory System," in Thomas E. Cronin and Sandford D. Greenberg, eds., *The Presidential Advisory System* (New York: Harper and Row, 1969), 321–35.

6. *National Anti-Hunger Coalition*, 1074.

7. Or, as James A. Morone and Theodore R. Marmor observe in discussing the particular case of representation on local Health Systems Agencies, "designation of interests deserving representation is . . . one part of the representational difficulties of such committees. The other part relates to the mechanisms that will guarantee that those interests are faithfully represented." See "Representing Consumer Interests: The Case of American Health Planning," *Ethics* 91 (1981): 445; see also Jasanoff, *The Fifth Branch*, 2.

8. See, for example, Robert B. McKay, "Affirmative Gerrymandering," in Bernard Grofman, Arend Lijphart, Robert B. McKay, and Howard A. Scarrow, eds., *Representation and Redistricting Issues* (Lexington, Mass.: Heath, 1982), 91–94; Ronald Rogowski, "Representation in Political Theory and Law," *Ethics* 91 (1981): 420–26; and Abigail Thernstrom, *Whose Votes Count?* (Cambridge: Harvard University Press, 1987), 7.

9. For a more complex treatment of the extent to which "social interests" can be said to "lie beyond politics"—can be understood as "givens" as opposed to "political constructs"—than I am able to offer here, see Cohen and Rogers, "Secondary Associations and Democratic Governance"; and Paul Q. Hirst, "Comments on 'Secondary Association and Democratic Governance,'" *Politics and Society* 20 (1992): 473–80. But even though social interests can in some ways be affected by political and judicial institutions, they are not the political-judicial artifacts that geographical legislative constituencies have come to be.

10. The literature here is vast. See, for example, Lani Guinier, "The Triumph of Tokenism: The Voting Rights Act and the Theory of Black Electoral Success," *Michigan Law Review* 89 (1991): 1077–1154; Douglas J. Amy, *Real Choices/New Voices: The Case for Proportional Representation Elections in the United States* (New York: Columbia University Press, 1993); and John R. Chamberlin and Paul N. Courant, "Representative Deliberations and Representative Decisions: Proportional Representation and the Borda Rule," *American Political Science Review* 77 (1983): 718–33.

11. To be sure, advocates of proportional representation in the pure-legislative realm urge not only "that a representative assembly should represent [social] interests," but that it should do so "in proportion to their numerical strength in society" (see Robert Sugden, "Free Association and the Theory of Proportional Representation," *American Political Science Review* 78 [1984]: 31). Because *quasi*-legislative bodies are unelected, however, the only essence of proportional representation they reasonably can conserve is the idea of socially self-identified interest constituencies, and not the more refined notion of proportionality.

12. Nicholas A. Ashford, "Advisory Committees in OSHA and EPA: Their Use in Regulatory Decision-Making," *Science, Technology and Human*

*Values* 9 (1984): 77; Thomas R. Wolanin, *Presidential Advisory Commissions: Truman to Nixon* (Madison: University of Wisconsin Press, 1975), 196. On many such quasi-legislative bodies, dissents actually either preclude or else—by comparison with the *modus operandi* of American "pure" legislative bodies—they effectively delegitimize decisions. See, for example, Glitzenstein and Goldman,*The Federal Advisory Committee Act at the Crossroads*, 33; *National Anti-Hunger Coalition v. Executive Committee of the President's Private-Sector Survey on Cost Control,* 557 F. Supp. 524 (1983): 524–25.

13. Joseph W. Witherspoon, "The Bureaucracy as Representatives," in J. Roland Pennock and John W. Chapman, eds., *NOMOS X: Representation* (New York: Atherton, 1968), 240.

14. See, for example, Duncan Black, *Theory of Committees and Elections* (Cambridge: Cambridge University Press, 1958); Chamberlin and Courant, "Representative Deliberations," 718–21; and Scott L. Feld and Bernard Grofman, "On the Possibility of Faithfully Representative Committees," *American Political Science Review* 80 (1986): 863, 874.

15. Chamberlin and Courant ("Representative Deliberations," 720 n. 4), for example, while noting that the composition of the committees they analyze would have to "vary from issue to issue," do not deal with the question of how to define an issue-specific committee's particular mandate. Instead, their purpose is to offer a general theory applicable to "representative bod[ies] that must decide many issues." As far as membership-selection is concerned, Feld and Grofman ("On the Possibility of Faithfully Representative Committees," 874) refer to members of the committees they discuss as "legislators" and the represented as "voters"—evidently assuming, for their purposes, the existence of an electoral mechanism with which to choose committee members—while Chamberlin and Courant (718) note that "social choice theorists have paid almost no attention to methods of selecting" committee members. William A. MacEachern ("Federal Advisory Committees," *Public Choice* 54 [1987]: 313, 343) observes that "[d]espite the prevalence and potential importance of these . . . bodies, their role . . . has largely been overlooked in the public choice literature."

16. Feld and Grofman, "On the Possibility of Faithfully Representative Committees," 863, 874; Chamberlin and Courant, "Representative Deliberations," 731–32.

17. Glitzenstein and Goldman, *The Federal Advisory Committee Act at the Crossroads*, 33.

18. Common Cause, *Public Advisers/Private Interests: A Common Cause Study of Imbalance on Federal Advisory Committees* (Washington: Common Cause, 1984), 14.

19. A related area of scholarship *prima facie* suggests itself as having some bearing on quasi-legislative representation, namely, that surrounding representation on Congressional committees. Once again, though, a number of important differences obtain which limit the bearing of the Congressional committee situation on the quasi-legislative committee situation (the former concern subsets of pure-legislative bodies, the latter executive-branch entities). What appears as the problem of quasi-legislative *mandate-definition* is transformed, in the case of Congressional-committees, by the fact that—while only a fraction of the issues before the executive branch go to quasi-legislative committees—a far larger preponderance of issues before the legislative branch go to committee, creating intercommittee jurisdictional or "mandate" battles of a sort that do not exist in the quasi-legislative case. And what appears as the problem of quasi-legislative *membership-selection* is lent a different coloration, in the Congressional-committee case, by criteria such as party, geography, seniority, fairness of task-distribution among members, members' electoral needs, and the capacity for (albeit) limited *self*-selection by members—none of which emerge as part of the selection process for quasi-legislative bodies. For some good discussion, see Richard L. Hall and Bernard Grofman, "The Committee Assignment Process and the Conditional Nature of Committee Bias," *American Political Science Review* 84 (1990): 1151, 1164; and Steven S. Smith and Christopher J. Deering, *Committees in Congress,* Second Edition (Washington: Congressional Quarterly, 1990), 61–117.

20. I shall here use the term *quasi-judicial* as if it read *(quasi-)judicial;* that is, to refer to both "pure" judicial and quasi-judicial—i.e., any trial-type—proceedings.

21. Of course, as well as dealing with representation issues that arise at trial-type proceedings, public law also deals with representation issues that arise at rule-making proceedings; i.e., those that are in important ways quasi-legislative in character. Even in the case of these quasi-legislative *proceedings,* however, the representation issues differ dramatically from those raised by quasi-legislative *bodies.* Principally, to represent an interest in a rule-making proceeding is to engage in a one-shot appearance before a body, whereas to represent an interest on a quasi-legislative committee is to be a permanent member on a body. And proceedings are simply seen to be able to accomodate a great many more one-shot appearances than committees can accomodate permanent members. Hence, the constraints which force the greatest contentiousness in litigation over representation on quasi-legislative bodies do not exist in cases concerning quasi-legislative (rule-making) proceedings. See Perritt and Wilkinson, 727; for an analogous discussion of the differences between

the representational issues on "ongoing advisory bodies" and "one-shot regulatory negotiations" of the negotiated rule-making sort, see Steven Kelman, "Adversary and Cooperationist Institutions for Conflict Resolution in Public Policymaking," *Journal of Policy Analysis and Management* 11 (1992): 200–201.

22. Karen Orren, "Standing to Sue: Interest-Group Conflict in the Federal Courts," *American Political Science Review* 70 (1976): 723–41.

23. The recent Supreme Court decision *Lujan* v. *Defenders of Wildlife* (112 S. Ct. 2130, 1992), it should be noted, may or may not have significantly altered standing jurisprudence in this area. But even those jurists who believe *Lujan* represents a major rupture tend to regard it as simply the latest, but by no means last or dispositive, high-court entry into the ongoing debate over constitutional issues of standing. In any case, *Lujan* has little bearing on the set of quasi-judicial/quasi-legislative distinctions set out here. For some good discussion, see Cass R. Sunstein, "What's Standing after *Lujan?* Of Citizen Suits, 'Injuries,' and Article III," *Michigan Law Review* 91 (1992): 163–236; and Marshall J. Breger, "Defending *Defenders:* Remarks on Nichol and Pierce," *Duke Law Journal* 42 (1993): 1202.

24. Orren, "Standing to Sue," 727.

25. Sunstein, "What's Standing after *Lujan?*" 174.

26. In this short explication, I have necessarily glossed over some complicating issues. One of these emerges from the jurisprudence advanced by those scholars and jurists who believe that quasi-judicial proceedings either do—or else explicitly should—function as if they were essentially quasi-legislative affairs. Or, put another way, those who believe that a more overtly political set of criteria should be imported into the quasi-judicial realm than is allowed by a reference to the underlying statute to determine whether an interest ought to be represented, and traditional standing criteria to determine who should represent it. In arguing that the quasi-judicial should function more explicitly along quasi-legislative lines, however, such jurists and scholars actually reinforce the analytic distinction between the two modes of representation. They simply argue that the applicability of the quasi-legislative mode should be extended from the space of policy and rule making to the space of adjudication. See, e.g., Sunstein, "What's Standing after *Lujan?*; Joseph Vining, *Legal Identity: The Coming of Age of Public Law* (New Haven: Yale University Press, 1978); and William A. Fletcher, "The Structure of Standing," *Yale Law Journal* 98 (1988): 245.

27. U.S. Senate, Committee on Governmental Affairs, *The Federal Advisory Committee Act Amendments of 1992* (100th Congress: 1st Session, December 3, 1987), 9.

28. Common Cause, i; see also Terrence R. Tutchings, *Rhetoric and Reality: Presidential Commissions and the Making of Public Policy* (Boulder, Colo.: Westview, 1979), 37–48.

29. *Metcalf* v. *National Petroleum Council* 553 F. 2d 176 (1977), 179. The meaning of the term "public-interest group" is of course contestable. Here, following actual discourse, I use the term to refer to (1) non-business groups whose interests are (2) arguably non- or underrepresented on the committees in question. For scholarly definitions of public-interest groups along these lines, see Andrew S. MacFarland, "Interest Groups and Theories of Power in America," *British Journal of Political Science* 17 (1987): 129–47; David Vogel, "The Public-Interest Movement and the American Reform Tradition," *Political Science Quarterly* 95 (1980): 625; Jeffrey M. Berry, *The Interest Group Society* (Boston: Little Brown, 1984), 28–30; and John P. Heinz, Edward O. Laumann, Robert L. Nelson, and Robert H. Salisbury, *The Hollow Core: Private Interests in National Policy Making* (Cambridge: Harvard University Press, 1993), 133.

Another characteristic often attached to "public-interest" groups is that they be "organized around a status or role which virtually all persons in the community are thought to share in common—the status of consumer, citizen, taxpayer, member of the biosphere"; see Peter H. Schuck, "Public Interest Groups and the Policy Process," *Public Administration Review* 37 (1977): 133, and Michael W. McCann, *Taking Reform Seriously: Perspectives on Public Interest Liberalism* (Ithaca: Cornell University Press, 1986), 15–26. And, in fact, almost all major balance-case plaintiffs do fall into this category. But regardless, the problem posed for "public-interest" groups who seek quasi-legislative representation is not whether all—as opposed to only some—of the public hold the interest in question; after all, business representatives on quasi-legislative bodies represent interests held by only some of the public. Rather, the issue is how the group can establish that it speaks for all (or at least a preponderance of) that set of individuals who do hold the interest, and not just some few who hold it in a "special way" (as is required in the quasi-judicial case).

30. *Public Citizen* v. *Department of Health and Human Services* 795 F. Supp. 1212 (D.D.C. 1992), 1212, 1223.

31. *National Association of People with AIDS* v. *Reagan,* Civil No. 87–2777–OG (D.D.C., May 13, 1988), slip op., 6.

32. *National Anti-Hunger Coalition,* 1074; Mary Kathryn Palladino, "Ensuring Coverage, Balance, Openness and Ethical Conduct for Advisory Committee Members under the Federal Advisory Committee Act," *Administrative Law Journal* 5 (1991): 254.

33. "Although [FACA] does not define the term 'fairly balanced,' . . . the Senate report on the Act states that legislation [establishing an advi-

sory committee] shall . . . require that membership of the advisory committee be representative of those who have a direct interest in the purpose of such committees. . . . Nothing in the Act or its legislative history even slightly indicates that Congress intended the presence or absence of balance to turn on an inquiry into the opinions of individual members." See *Public Citizen* v. *National Advisory Committee on Microbiological Criteria for Foods* 886 F. 2d 419 (D.C. Cir., 1989), 423, 427.

34. Ibid., 429.

35. Glitzenstein and Goldman, *The Federal Advisory Committee Act at the Crossroads*, 29, 32.

36. The exclusion of considerations concerning viewpoints—i.e., viewpoints as to how represented interests are best served—also removes from balance discourse the kinds of debate surrounding the delegate-trustee polarity that engages, albeit fitfully, normative pure-legislative representation theory.

37. Jane J. Mansbridge, "A Deliberative Theory of Interest Representation," in Mark P. Petracca, ed., *The Politics of Interests: Interest Groups Transformed* (Boulder, Colo.: Westview, 1992), 36–37.

38. Anne Phillips, "Dealing with Difference: From a Politics of Ideas to a Politics of Presence," paper written for the conference on "Democracy and Difference," Yale University, April 16–18, 1993, p. 31.

39. Ibid., 31.

40. Following the tradition of most contemporary political-theoretic analysis of public discourse, I concentrate on the ideological structure and public strategy of argumentation, and will not pursue the twin questions as to whether the various positions discourse-participants take are (1) capable of being rationally or empirically justified or else controverted (in any case, as will be seen, the issues in balance discourse remain radically open), and (2) capable of being instrumentally or reductively explained by reference to participants' private interests or psychological makeups. For a methodological elucidation of the enterprise of political-theoretic analysis of public (and especially judicial) discourse along the lines I undertake here, see Rogers M. Smith, "Political Jurisprudence, the 'New Institutionalism,' and the Future of Public Law," *American Political Science Review* 82 (1988): 90, 102. Smith shows that "if one is trying to ascertain the presence" of "certain traditions of political discourse" within judicial texts, one can do so effectively by drawing upon "a few major cases that seem representative . . . instead of documenting how those structures are visible in all or most of the relevant cases."

41. *Defendant's Opposition to Plaintiff's Motion for a Preliminary Injunction, National Treasury Employees' Union* v. *Reagan* (D.D.C., February 12, 1988), 2–3.

42. *National Treasury Employees' Union* v. *Reagan* Civil No. 88–0186 (D.D.C., February 26, 1988), 6.

43. *National Anti-Hunger Coalition* v. *Executive Committee of the President's Private Sector Survey on Cost Control* 557 F. Supp. 524 (1983), 526, 528.

44. William Funk, "When Smoke Gets in Your Eyes: Regulatory Negotiation and the Public Interest—EPA's Woodstove Standards," *Environmental Law Review* 18 (1987): 97.

45. *Public Citizen* v. *National Advisory Committee*, 423.

46. *Memorandum in Support of Plaintiff's Motion for a Preliminary Injunction, National Treasury Employees' Union* v. *Reagan* Civil Action No. 88–086 (D.D.C., February 5, 1988), 17.

47. *National Anti-Hunger Coalition* v. *Executive Committee of the President's Private Sector Survey on Cost Control,* 557 F. Supp. 524 (1983), 528; *Public Citizen* v. *National Advisory Committee,* 423; *Plaintiff's Motion for Relief from Judgment, National Anti-Hunger Coalition* v. *Executive Committee of the President's Private-Sector Survey on Cost Control* (D.C.C., June 27, 1983), 9.

48. Richard O. Levine, "The Federal Advisory Committee Act," *Harvard Journal on Legislation* 10 (1973): 229.

49. *National Treasury Employees' Union,* 7, 8; *Defendant's Opposition to Plaintiff's Motion for a Preliminary Injunction, National Treasury Employees' Union* v. *Reagan,* 17.

50. *Public Citizen* v. *National Advisory Committee on Microbiological Criteria for Foods,* 426, 427; *Defendant's Opposition to Plaintiff's Motion for a Preliminary Injunction, Public Citizen* v. *National Advisory Committee on Microbiological Criteria for Foods* (D.D.C., July 25, 1988), 24; *National Association,* 10–11.

51. *Proceedings, National Anti-Hunger Coalition* v. *Executive Committee of the President's Private-Sector Survey on Cost Control* 557 F. Supp. 524 (February 17, 1983), 55; *Proceedings, National Anti-Hunger Coalition* v. *Executive Committee of the President's Private-Sector Survey on Cost Control* 711 F. 2d 1071 (D.C. Cir., aff'd, July 20, 1983), 83, 30 ("[f]or every one of those groups to be seated [we would require] an Executive Committee of thousands of members"); *National Association,* 11.

52. *Proceedings, National Anti-Hunger Coalition* v. *Executive Committee of the President's Private-Sector Survey on Cost Control* 557 F. Supp. 524 (February 17, 1983), 55; *Proceedings, National Anti-Hunger Coalition* v. *Executive Committee of the President's Private-Sector Survey on Cost Control* 711 F. 2d 1071 (D.C. Cir., aff'd, July 20, 1983), 83, 30.

53. On the difficulties theorists have in determining "what the appropriate interest system should be for each policy arena," see Philippe C. Schmitter, "The Irony of Modern Democracy and Efforts to Improve Its Practice," *Politics and Society* 20 (1992): 509; and Ellen M. Immergut,

"An Institutional Critique of Associative Democracy: Commentary on 'Secondary Associations and Democratic Governance,'" *Politics and Society* 20 (1992): 484–85. Some analogies also exist here with problems faced in class-action jurisprudence, although the comparison has its substantial limitations (see Orren, "Standing to Sue," 725).

54. *Plaintiff's Reply Memorandum in Support of Their Motion for a Preliminary Injunction, Public Citizen v. National Advisory Committee on Microbiological Criteria for Foods* (D.D.C., July 27, 1988), 4; *Brief for Appellants, Public Citizen v. National Advisory Committee on Microbiological Criteria for Foods*, U.S. Court of Appeals for the District of Columbia (January 27, 1989), 30–31; *Reply Memorandum in Support of Plaintiff's Motion for a Preliminary Injunction, National Treasury Employees' Union v. Reagan* (D.D.C., February 18, 1988), 4–5.

55. *Proceedings, National Anti-Hunger Coalition v. Executive Committee of the President's Private-Sector Survey on Cost Control*, 711 F. 2d 1071 (D.C. Cir., aff'd, July 20, 1983), 66, 56 ("if you were to take [a] sharp focus . . . you would really dismiss tremendous numbers of groups which would claim some type of theoretical, hypothetical interest in what is going on, and really be left with a relatively small number such as plaintiffs . . . who have a direct stake").

56. Whatever these principles are, though, they do not seem to be generalizable; rather, their nature is immanent within plaintiff-group argumention in particular cases (*National Treasury Employees' Union*, 7; *Public Citizen v. National Advisory Committee*, 436; Glitzenstein and Goldman, 33). Iris Marion Young puts the same point more theoretically. Young asks what principles ought to govern whenever we must decide whether "the interests of [a particular group's] members are specifically affected" by a particular "policy discussion." And her answer is that in fact "[n]o . . . set of principles can found [such] a politics, because politics is always a process in which we are engaged"; hence no such principles "can . . . replace that discussion or determine its outcome." See "Polity and Group Difference: A Critique of the Ideal of Universal Citizenship," *Ethics* 99 (1989): 266; see also Cohen and Rogers, "Secondary Associations and Democratic Governance," 451.

57. Grady, *Restoring Real Representation*, 146–48; Burdett A. Loomis, "Coalitions of Interests: Building Bridges in the Balkanized State," in Allan J. Cigler and Burdett A. Loomis, eds., *Interest Group Politics*, 2d ed. (Washington: Congressional Quarterly Press), 258–74; W. Douglas Costain and Anne N. Costain, "Interest Groups as Policy Aggregators in the Legislative Process," *Polity* 14 (1981): 256–57.

58. *Public Citizen v. National Advisory Committee*, 429.

59. *Mulqueeny v. National Commission on the Observance of International*

*Women's Year* 549 F. 2d. 1115 (1977), 1121; see also *Warth* v. *Seldin* 422 U.S. 490 (1974), 501; and *Laird* v. *Tatum* 408 U.S. 1 (1972), 13–14.

60. Jeremy Rabkin, *Judicial Compulsions: How Public Law Distorts Public Policy* (New York: Basic Books, 1989), 75; see also Richard Stewart, "The Reformation of American Administrative Law," *Harvard Law Review* 88 (1975): 1767.

61. See also David Vogel and Mark Nadel, "Who Is a Consumer? An Analysis of the Politics of Consumer Conflict," *American Politics Quarterly* 5 (1977): 29–30, 41; and Kay Lehman Schlozman and John Tierney, *Organized Interests and American Democracy* (New York: Harper and Row, 1986), 22. In any case, such a concern—i.e., with whether a group's particular viewpoint most appropriately represents the interest for which it claims to speak—is, as noted earlier, explicitly excluded from balance discourse. The question here is more basic: not whether a group's particular viewpoint most appropriately represents the interest for which it claims to speak, but rather whether, in representing only that particular interest (with whatever viewpoint), the group can claim to represent any real (multi-interested) individuals.

62. Rabkin, *Judicial Compulsions,* 10.

63. *Transcript of Preliminary Injunction Before the Honorable John Garrett Penn, United States District Court Judge, Public Citizen* v. *National Advisory Committee on Microbiological Criteria for Foods* (D.C. Cir., November 18, 1988), 26.

64. See, e.g., Sylvia Tesh, "In Defense of Single-Issue Politics," *Political Science Quarterly* 99 (1984): 27–44; D. Stephen Cupps, "Emerging Problems of Citizen Participation," *Public Administration Review* 37 (1977): 481; and Michael Rogin, "Nonpartisanship and the Group Interest," in Philip Green and Sanford Levinson, *Power and Community: Dissenting Essays in Political Science* (New York: Random House, 1970), 115.

65. John Burnheim, *Is Democracy Possible? The Alternative to Electoral Politics* (Berkeley: University of California Press, 1985), 195, 112.

66. Traditional standing criteria, as Vining (*Legal Identity,* 150, 151) points out, enable single-interest groups to claim to represent at least some individuals—even individuals who possess manifold coherently ranked interests (or values or loves)—if those individuals happen to have lent the interest in question a special, distinctive, or paramount place in their orderings. So distinctive or paramount that—for the limited purposes of the proceeding and within the margins of calculation available to the courts—that interest approaches being as all-engrossing and constitutive for those individuals as it is for the group itself, enabling the group to speak for them. There is, in other words, a metaphysical as well as a jurisprudential ("abetting a case or controversy") rationale for

standing criteria, on which single-interest groups, seeking quasi-judicial representation, claim to represent only "specially interested" individuals; i.e., those individuals who harbor the interest in question to a "greater degree than ordinary citizens."

67. Ibid., 149, 155.

68. U.S. House of Representatives, *Report No. 1017* (92nd Congress, 2nd Session, 1972), 6; see also U.S. Senate, *Report No. 92–1098* (92nd Congress, 2nd Session), 5.

69. *Plaintiff's Reply Memorandum in Support of Their Motion for a Preliminary Injunction, Public Citizen* v. *National Advisory Committee on Microbiological Criteria for Foods* (D.D.C., July 27, 1988), 7, 8; *Reply Memorandum,* 7; *Memorandum in Support of Plaintiff's Motion, National Treasury Employees' Union* v. *Reagan,* 3, 15, 16; *Proceedings, National Anti-Hunger Coalition* v. *Executive Committee* 711 F. 2d 1071 (D.C. Cir., aff'd, July 20, 1983), 20; *Plaintiff's Motion for a Preliminary Injunction, Public Citizen* v. *National Advisory Committee on Microbiological Criteria for Foods,* 20.

70. *Proceedings, National Anti-Hunger Coalition* v. *Executive Committee* 557 F. Supp. 524 (February 17, 1983), 60. Groups here can be understood to argue that the quasi-legislative realm ought to be a functionally representative one. "[B]y not requiring each citizen to sort out his whole philosophy of life," as Elaine Spitz puts it, "a functional system divides up a person's interests for him, giv[ing] him a chance to choose meaningfully"; see Spitz, *Majority Rule* (Chatham, N.J.: Chatham House, 1984), 43. Because their governmental interlocutors do not agree, however, any theorization of this strand of discourse cannot derive from functional-representation theory, but instead must take account of discourse-participants' fundamental disagreement over the relationship between individuals and interests.

71. An interesting question—one which, curiously enough, plaintiff groups have not raised—is whether those the government selects to committees can justify *their* membership by pointing to real individuals they represent. Discourse has not flowed in this direction, although one can imagine a couple of governmental responses. With respect to committee members the government appoints to represent a private or business interest, the government might argue that *all* who possess that interest in fact lend it such a special and distinctive place in their own interest-hierarchies that, in representing that interest alone, the designated committee member (at least for the purposes of the proceeding at hand, and within the margins of calculation available to agencies and courts) can be assumed to represent *all* who hold it. With respect to committee-members the government appoints to represent public interests, they are at least derivatively answerable to the appropriate public

constituencies through (for what it's worth) the public's electoral control over the appointing government—whereas those appointed by groups are not. These of course are very open questions. But in any case—and what is of importance here—a properly generalizable theorization of balance discourse is not affected by the fact that it is only the government which challenges plaintiff-group claims to selection on these grounds, and not plaintiff groups that so challenge government appointees.

72. *Public Citizen* v. *National Advisory Committee*, 430.

73. Ibid., 430.

74. *Defendant's Opposition, Public Citizen* v. *National Advisory Committee*, 23; *National Association*, 6.

75. Rogin, "Nonpartisanship and the Group Interest," 112; Vogel, "The Public-Interest Movement," 627.

76. *Plaintiff's Reply*, 8.

77. Cupps, "Emerging Problems of Citizen Participation," 480; *Memorandum in Support of Plaintiff's Motion for a Temporary Restraining Order, Pension Rights Center* v. *Advisory Council on Employee Welfare and Pension Benefit Plans* (D.D.C., March 14, 1986), 19; *Brief*, 15.

78. Berry, *The Interest Group Society*, 29; Jeffrey M. Berry, *Lobbying the People* (Princeton: Princeton University Press, 1977), 7; Schlozman and Tierney, *Organized Interests and American Democracy*, 29; Harry C. Boyte, *The Backyard Revolution: Understanding the New Citizen Movement* (Philadelphia: Temple University Press, 1986). A particular contrariety between the quasi-legislative and the quasi-judicial is worth underlining here. In the quasi-judicial setting, groups often attempt to gain standing precisely by showing that the proceeding will affect their own organizational interests; the government—or others—attempt to defeat that claim by insisting that the group's real aim is to represent not its own but a pure public interest. In the quasi-legislative setting, selection criteria thus invert standing criteria, and the government and groups exchange arguments. See some of the discussion in Heidi Li Feldman, "Divided We Fall: Associational Standing and Collective Action," *Michigan Law Review* 87 (1988): 733–53.

79. Balance discourse, as noted, centers on plaintiff *public*-interest groups challenging the representative fairness on committees that, themselves, are largely composed of *private*-sector representatives and whose initial mandates deal with concerns central to *private*-sector interests. Cases, though, could (and in fact occasionally do) arise where the group seeking selection represents a private-sector interest, or where the challenged committees are largely composed of public-interest representatives and are possessed of mandates to deal with issues of broad public interest; see e.g., *Lead Industries Associations, Inc.* v. *U.S. Center for Disease*

*Notice Control* No. C84–1203 (N.D. Ga., 1984). It is precisely on a point like this, however, that a discourse-rooted theorization is capable of abstracting beyond the particular contours of the discourse itself. For whether the plaintiff group claims to represent public (consumer, environmental) interests, private (business, industrial) interests, or interests that fall into some intermediate class, the question will still arise as to whether the group's focus may have shifted, at least to some extent, toward its own narrow, special concerns—incapacitating it from representing the interest in question. Conversely, whether the original committee mandate is meant to affect a delimited range of private interests, public interests, or some mixture, the question will still arise as to how rigorously the committee is observing its original confined mandate, or whether, in effect, its focus has broadened and become even more general.

80. Anderson, "Political Design and the Representation of Interests," 131; see also Mary Grisez Kweit and Robert W. Kweit, "The Politics of Policy Analysis: The Role of Citizen Participation in Analytic Decision Making," in Jack DeSario and Stuart Langton, eds., *Citizen Participation in Public Decision Making* (New York: Greenwood, 1987), 19–37.

# PART VI

# DYNAMICS OF INCLUSION AND EXCLUSION

# 14

# SELF-DETERMINATION:
# POLITICS, PHILOSOPHY,
# AND LAW

## DONALD L. HOROWITZ

It has been said of Mikhail Gorbachev that he had the distinction of having lost three world wars. He lost the Cold War, of course. He also lost World War II, because he lost Eastern Europe. And he managed to lose World War I, because he presided over the end of the Russian Empire. This triple defeat produced great changes in the relationship of ethnic groups to territory. Not only did Eastern Europe become free of the Soviet Union but steps were taken to free Slovaks from Czechs, as well as various Yugoslavs from each other, to unite (in various ways) East Germans, Volga Germans, and Romanian Germans with West Germans, and to create new relations between Bulgarians and Turks, between Albanians and Serbs, and between Hungarians, on the one hand, and Romanians, Ukrainians, Slovaks, and Serbs, on the other. Within the former Soviet Union, the Baltic, the Central Asian, the Caucasian, the Ukrainian, and some Middle Volga republics all sought to or did disengage their fate, to a greater or lesser degree, from that of the Russian Republic and often from that of their neighbors as well. These movements have generally been painful, and they have recurring, generalizable implications for the relations of ethnic groups to territories, to other proximate ethnic groups, and to their territories in turn.

To be sure, not all ethnic conflict has a significant territorial side. In some countries, groups are territorially so intermixed that political claims reflect aspirations to power within the existing territory, rather than ripening into movements for a change of state boundaries. (Neighborhood and electoral boundaries are another matter, of course.) Yet, in many parts of the world, groups make claims to homelands that produce demands for ethnically induced boundary alterations. The conflicts in Bosnia, Chechnya, and Nagorno-Karabagh—not to mention Georgia-Abkhazia, Moldova-Transniestria, or Crimea-Ukraine—all make these issues timely. Nevertheless, they have enduring features that easily transcend current controversies, raising important and, as I shall suggest, intertwined questions about patterns of ethno-territorial politics, about the status of ethnic self-determination in philosophy, and about rights to a territorially conceived ethnic self-determination in international law. In pursuing these related questions, my theme will be that a fuller understanding of the patterns of ethnic politics can—and assuredly should—inform emerging debates about self-determination in politics, philosophy, and law.

What a fuller understanding discloses, above all, are the limits of territorial solutions to ethnic conflicts. The limits to territorially based ethnic aspirations have often been obscured, because the world has just emerged, as I shall explain, from a period of unusual stability in state boundaries. Now that territorial boundaries seem more generally adjustable, it has become plausible to inquire into the purposes for which boundaries ought to be changed. Moral and legal theories have been laid on the table, and the norm of ethnic self-determination is being revitalized after a period of dormancy. The theories have been cascading more quickly than has understanding of patterns of ethnic conflict in general or of ethnoterritorial movements in particular. As a result, the emerging norms risk being seriously out of joint with the phenomena that form their subject matter. The norms may even foster the acceleration of conflict, without the attenuation of ethnic domination to which they aspire.

## IRREDENTAS, SECESSIONS, AND STATE BOUNDARIES

There are two main forms of ethnically induced territorial adjustment: irredentas and secessions.[1] Secession involves the withdrawal of a group and its territory from the authority of a state of which it is a part. Irredentism entails the retrieval of ethnically kindred people and their territory across an international boundary, joining them and it to the retrieving state. The difference is between subtracting alone and subtracting and then adding what has been taken away to an adjacent state.

From these differences follow others. Secession is a group-led movement. Irredentism, on the other hand, is state-initiated, although groups, of course, lobby the retrieving state to take irredentist action. In the post-World War II period, there have been few actively pursued irredentas but many attempted secessions, some of them eventuating in warfare lasting decades, as in Burma since 1949 or the Southern Sudan on and off since 1963.

Irredentism is inhibited by all the forces that prevent rash action by states. An irredentist movement can be deterred by displays of force. It can be requited by concessions made by the state that is the target of the irredenta, even by concessions on unrelated matters of interstate relations.

Moreover, irredentist states are unlikely to be ethnically homogeneous, so successful pursuit of the irredenta would change ethnic balances in the retrieving state. Pursuit of the Somali irredenta against the Ethiopian Ogaden would, if it resulted in a transfer of people and territory, greatly augment the proportion of Darood, already the largest group in Somalia. Not surprisingly, Hawiye and Isaq have been less enthusiastic about the movement. Successful irredentism might alter subethnic or political balances within the kindred group in the retrieving state. An Albania that managed to add Kosovo to Albania would also turn the balance of Ghegs and Tosks upside down in Albania, for while Tosks are the leading subgroup in the home country, Ghegs predominate on the Yugoslav side of the border. A Malaysia that got seriously interested in transferring Malays and their territory in southern Thailand to Malaysia would soon find that the affinities of Malays in Thailand to Malays in the Malaysian state of Kelantan would likely produce a dramatically unsettling change in the balance of party politics, in favor of the opposition Pan-Malayan Islamic Party that runs the Kelantan state government. All of these apprehensions operate to inhibit active irredentism. There are others as well.

A separate question relates to whether the group to be retrieved will wish to be retrieved. Often the answer is negative, as the Taiwanese, among many others, have made clear. The retrieving state may be poorer, or more authoritarian, or otherwise undesirable. The group to be retrieved may be seen at the center of the irredentist state as consisting of country bumpkins or people who lived too long under the corrupting cultural influences of an alien regime. The group to be retrieved is, by definition, peripheral, and it needs to be saved from the effects of being located in what is viewed as the wrong state. These characteristics often produce a stigma. Members of the peripheral group surely know the stigma exists and may have experienced it on visits to the irredentist state, where they perhaps displayed the wrong accent, the wrong manners, or an inadequate knowledge of the group's destiny and history. If they know they are patronized as rustics, their enthusiasm for reunion may be diminished.

Politicians in the region to be retrieved have their own reservations. They can easily imagine that their position will not improve if their constituents and territory are transferred to a new, larger state. They will have to break into an already crystallized political situation in the annexing state from a merely regional (and in many ways still foreign) base. Their existing clientele will be vulnerable to absorption in a larger political party that serves the whole ethnic group, particularly if overarching group sentiment—pan-whatever-it-is—rises before and during the transition, as it surely will. They, however, will have little ability to expand their influence outward; they will need to worry about keeping the support they have. These leaders are therefore small fish jumping from one big pond, in which their clientele is at least secure—since they act as representatives of the minority that their group constitutes in the existing state—into another big pond, in which that security is gone.

As a result of all of these inhibitions, there have been few active irredentas, compared to the many possibilities raised by the dissonance between territorial boundaries and ethnic boundaries.

Yet there are some. Armenia's claim to Nagorno-Karabagh is one, and Pakistan's claim to Kashmir is another. Even those that have been active at some time in the past tend to be on back burners: Somalia and the Ogaden; Albania and Kosovo; Hungary and Romanian Transylvania, the south of Slovakia, and the Vojvodina region of Serbia; until recently, China and Taiwan. In virtually all, there are restraints. If Kashmir were, with Pakistani aid, to free itself from Indian rule, the result would likely be, not accession to Pakistan, but an independent Kashmir, with major disintegrative consequences within Pakistan itself. With Somalia and Albania, there are restraints deriving from composition that I referred to earlier. With Hungary and Romania, any serious Hungarian irredentism would quickly confront the facts that Transylvania is itself heterogeneous and that Romanians are generally closer to the Hungarian border than are the centers of Hungarian population in Romania. The frequent heterogeneity of the region to be retrieved creates yet another inhibition on irredentism.

Secession, by contrast, is usually a more precipitously undertaken decision. Most secessionist movements (but only most, not all) are begun by groups stigmatized as backward.[2] Convinced that they cannot compete in the undivided state of which they are a part, colonized by civil servants from other regions, and subjected to uncongenial policies on language, religion, or other symbols of state ownership, the patience of such groups is quickly exhausted. Many attempt independence, often heedless of economic costs, including the loss of subsidies from the center.

One reason for the relative attractiveness of secession, compared to the status quo or to irredentism, resides in the position of ethnic group leaders. In contrast to what they can expect if their group and territory are annexed by their irredentist cousins, secessionist elites can expect to become big fish in a small pond. In a secessionist state, they can easily push aside the queue for civil service positions and for political leadership that exists in the undivided state. When the Sudan became independent and senior civil service positions were "Sudanized," Southerners were, by dint of their relatively low educational standing and seniority, allocated only about six of the eight hundred positions vacated by the departing British. Other relatively poorly educated groups have had comparable experiences. Similarly, political party leaders

who, in the undivided state, head an ethnic minority party that is
likely to be shut out of power permanently, can expect, with
secession and independence, to see their minority status transformed overnight. That is the very meaning of ethnic secession,
after all. For ethnic elites, small is indeed beautiful; it provides
them with the prerogatives, the perquisites, and the trappings of
power. Better to be the president of Abkhazia or Transniestria
than to be the leader of an ethnically differentiated, permanent
opposition party in Georgia or Moldova.

A good many transborder groups have the potential choice
to be retrieved by an irredentist neighbor or to secede.[3] The
convertibility of claims means that, all else equal, the fewer the
irredentas, the more the secessions.

Secessionist movements persist despite the many obstacles to
their success. For nearly fifty years after World War II, only one
state was created by a secessionist movement through force of
arms: Bangladesh.[4] Bangladesh had crucial assistance from India,
which acted out of two idiosyncratic motives.

First, quite obviously, by detaching East Bengal from Pakistan,
India could achieve an important strategic objective: the breakup
and reduction in power of a menacing neighbor. Few states in a
position to aid separatists in adjacent territories have such an
overwhelming motive.

Second, India acted to avert the growth of pan-Bengali sentiment that might have produced alternatives to a secessionist Bangladesh. At the time of the insurgency in East Bengal, pan-Bengali
sentiment was growing. If, as it then seemed, religion was an
inadequate basis for statehood in Pakistan, perhaps ethnic affinity
and the strong cultural links that bind all Bengalis might provide
a more durable foundation. Had this sentiment been allowed to
grow, it might have produced a movement to reincorporate East
Bengal into India or to create a separate pan-Bengali state out of
Pakistani East Bengal and Indian West Bengal. Either possibility
would have been enormously destabilizing for India. The first
would have unbalanced India in religious and ethnic terms, by
adding some seventy million more Muslims (most Hindus having
already fled to India) and some seventy to eighty million Bengalis
altogether to the population and political mix of India. The
second would have created a precedent for other states to detach

themselves from the Indian federation. Given these devastating possibilities, India did not wait for them to develop: it aided Bangladesh to achieve its independence by force.

Most secessionists, however, receive insufficient aid to do the same. Many neighboring states will aid secessionists in order to achieve some gain by meddling in the affairs of their neighbors, but few will provide sufficient assistance over a period long enough to help the secessionists through a protracted war.[5] Most states have more limited motives for supporting secessionists than the secessionists do for fighting. An assisting state is vulnerable to the quid pro quo, to domestic pressure to end support, or to some weak spot (perhaps an ethnic-minority vulnerability of its own) that makes it recalculate the costs of involvement. Most long-standing secessionist movements receive support from multiple sources. The support comes and goes; it is rarely enough. By contrast, the international system has a strong bias toward central governments; these are able to augment their own military resources with external assistance for which they are likely to be able to give more than separatists are in return. For all these reasons, secession is usually a long shot.

Most of the time, then, irredentism is unattractive, and secession is impossible. Nevertheless, no one could have anticipated the extraordinary degree of territorial stasis in the fifty years since World War II. Given the considerable incidence of peoples divided by existing boundaries, the prospects for irredentism seemed, a priori, to be enormous. The number of aggrieved groups willing to resort to secessionist warfare has been large. In Asia and Africa, colonialism, which created the boundaries of inherited states, was unequivocally repudiated as illegitimate, thus opening the question of boundaries.[6] In the end, however, irredentism was subdued, secessionists were unable to make good their claims despite their heroic willingness to sacrifice for them, and successor states accepted and even legitimated the inherited colonial boundaries. Together with the European status quo induced by the Cold War, the confluence of these forces produced the most remarkable stability in state boundaries during the past half century—a half century marked, paradoxically, by severe and growing ethnic conflict within states that might have been expected to spill over boundaries and contribute to the disintegration of many states. None of the entirely reasonable expectations for state disintegration and boundary change was fulfilled.

## SEPARATISM: A NEW WATERSHED

Several recent developments enhance prospects for a proliferation of states arising out of ethnic movements. Underpinning these developments are changes in thinking about self-determination, but the developments have also precipitated the changes in thought, and so I shall deal with the events before turning to explicit theoretical justifications. This is not merely to satisfy a general curiosity about a changing landscape. Rather, I shall argue that any legal or moral response to these phenomena that elides some of their recurrent characteristics will be inapt, inadequate, or counterproductive.

Sequencing is an underrated explanatory factor in social life. Whether one event precedes another and whether several events are confluent often shapes outcomes and certainly has in this field. In the case of secession and state dissolution, critical events have been confluent and capriciously sequenced. They came thick and fast, and easy cases came first, setting precedents for what should have been seen as harder cases.

First there was the victory of the Eritrean secessionists by force of arms—a victory unprecedented in independent Africa. It was a victory won in fortuitous ways and at a fortuitous time. The Eritrean war against Ethiopia was fought in conjunction with other insurgent movements within Ethiopia proper and was probably won for this reason. The victory and the secession came at the same time as the fragmentation of Liberia and Somalia. North Somalia, the former British Somaliland, a predominantly Isaq region, has declared its independence. The confluence of these movements may ultimately produce increasing instability in African boundaries, which have been remarkably stable.

On the other hand, perhaps not. North Somalia is unrecognized. Liberia has experienced territorial stalemate rather than the emergence of new polities. Eritrea was, like the Baltic states, a case of illegitimate incorporation. Haile Selassie disregarded his promise to maintain a federal relationship with the former trust territory of Eritrea. Equally important, the Tigrean and Oromo movements, which also defeated Addis Ababa, actually agreed that Eritrea could have its independence. Central governments do not generally agree to regional secession.

Idiosyncratic or not, successful secessionist movements are likely to have demonstration effects. The unsuccessful Biafra movement catalyzed separatists among the Agni and the Bété in the Ivory Coast. Bangladesh had a stronger effect, especially on the Baluch of Pakistan, on the Sri Lankan Tamils, and on the Mizo and Naga in northeast India. Africa has many weak states that might be vulnerable, although most African secessionists will be unable to call upon a strong neighboring state with motives for assistance as powerful as India's in Bangladesh.

The second critical event, the dissolution of the Soviet Union, more or less by consent, proliferated new states. In the wake of this fragmentation, there are many actual and potential subsecessions—within Moldova, Georgia, and Tajikistan, in Chechnya, perhaps in the north of Kazakhstan or in the Narve area of Estonia, among others. Some twenty-five million Russians reside outside Russia, where they are subject to discrimination and sometimes clustered in compact areas adjacent to a Russian border that is subject to dispute. In a number of autonomous republics of the Russian Federation, there are so-called titular nationalities that aspire to independence.[7] In turn, Russian minorities or majorities in these republics may nurse their own aspirations or will when they feel the brunt of the hostility against them.

The more or less peaceful and consensual parting of the ways in the former Soviet Union was remarkable. Again fortuitously, the Baltic states, with indisputably legitimate claims, led the way, and the Central Asian republics, at first reluctant, soon joined in. The domino effects of secessions within states are considerable, which is one major reason central governments almost universally fight them. In Russia, however, the central government did not fight. Instead, it acquiesced in the movement to break the Union.

Two changes underlay the assent of Moscow. The first involved sentiment at the bottom. The second was a function of rivalry at the top.

During the predissolution period of the late 1980s and very early 1990s, many Russians were abandoning Soviet imperial pretensions and identification with the Soviet Union in favor of

identification with Russia. This contraction in identity was coupled with and fostered by the growth of anti-Southern (especially
anti-Caucasus) and anti-Muslim sentiment. Food markets in Moscow were dominated by migrants from the Caucasus, many of
whom were later expelled from Moscow. Ethnic clashes in the
South were regarded with extreme distaste, and the prevailing
Russian view of Southerners—especially Chechens and Azeris—
was of corrupt and criminal influences. The results of these prejudices was a demand to "cast off ungrateful neighbors."[8] Here is
an unusual case in which ethnic antipathy was conducive to a
peaceful outcome.

Such an outcome was also the unintended consequence of
leadership rivalry in what was formally a federal system. When
Boris Yeltsin ascended the presidency of the Russian Federation,
he was able to use his office as a platform to pursue his conflict
with Gorbachev. The means to do this was for Russia to oppose
the Soviet Union.[9]

In the background to these developments lay the crumbling
legitimacy and diminished capacity of the Soviet regime.[10] No
longer able to steer a course, Moscow vacillated between attempting to keep the Union together by force and speaking a
wholly new language of consent. The decline of the center enabled people to act on their sentiments and politicians to pursue
their rivalries. As a consequence, what might have been a series
of cataclysmic secessionist wars became instead a dissolution by
something close to mutual consent. This is, as I have said, highly
unusual.

It is not unusual for more than one region in a political unit
to entertain secessionist aspirations. Often these aspirations are
conceived as embodying the desire to separate from another region, not merely from the undivided state. Reciprocal secessionist
movements result.[11] A year before the attempted secession of
Biafra, the Ibo-dominated Eastern Region of Nigeria, there was a
serious possibility of a Northern secession, at a time when the
Nigerian regime viewed itself as having been controlled by Ibo
military officers. Only after these officers were overthrown by a
Northern coup did the Biafra movement take shape. By then,
Northerners became committed to and fought for an undivided
Nigeria. Likewise, in the Indian state of Andhra Pradesh, there

was a strong secessionist movement in the Telangana region in the 1960s. When policies were put in place to respond to the movement and keep the Telanganas attached, there was a secessionist reaction to those policies by people from the coastal region, who saw themselves disadvantaged by them. Reciprocal secession is part of the zero-sum game of ethnic conflict. It is therefore an alternating rather than a simultaneous phenomenon. The alternating character of the sentiment explains why secession so often produces warfare rather than amicable agreement to part. And that in turn is why the Soviet case is so truly exceptional.

The effect of a peaceful dissolution of the U.S.S.R. was to create at a stroke an array of new states, as well as to pave the way for secessionist warfare within several of them. Had the Soviet dissolution not been consensual, it would have had much less profound, albeit much less peaceful, results. Perhaps some republics would have freed themselves, while others remained repressed. The Soviet Union would have reinforced rather than undermined existing boundaries.

The third event, the dissolution of Yugoslavia and the creation of independent Slovenia, Croatia, Macedonia, Montenegro, Bosnia, and Serbia, occurred along the more usual—that is to say, nonconsensual, violent—lines. Although Bosnia is a state with no history of independence,[12] the disintegration of Yugoslavia was followed by international recognition of the new states. Led by Germany, European and American recognition of the former Yugoslav republics was accomplished in disregard of international-law doctrine forbidding recognition of secessionist units whose establishment is being resisted forcibly by a central government.[13]

The recognition of the Baltic states, which was inevitable, may have affected recognition practice when it came to Yugoslavia. It seems clear, however, that there has been a sharp change in the willingness of Western states to recognize secessionists. It is not a uniform change, as nonrecognition of Northern Somalia makes clear, but it is palpable, and it can be sensed by contrasting Biafra. Biafra was a cause with great sympathy in the West, particularly in the United States. Many Ibo had studied in the United States, and Biafran propaganda about ethnic oppression, wartime suffering, and infant starvation was extremely skillful. In spite of this, not only did Western countries, excepting France, which aided Biafra militarily, refuse to recognize Biafra, but the United States, Britain, and the Soviet Union all assisted the Nigerian central government in its military efforts, despite its culpability in creating the conditions that led to war. Barely a glimmer of such Western central-government bias was in evidence in the Yugoslav case. As we shall soon see, this change in the willingness to recognize secessionists may slowly be felt in international law.

If Eritrean independence and the dissolution of the Soviet Union and Yugoslavia are watershed events shaping prospects for the proliferation of states—and, to that extent, for a territorially based doctrine of self-determination—it is nonetheless possible to draw too much from them. The Eritrean and Soviet experiences are, in some ways, special cases, even if major special cases. The recognition of the Yugoslav secessionists took place at an especially weak moment for Western diplomacy and will surely not be seen everywhere as a successful policy.

Even so, there are now new incentives to secession. Secessionists have defeated central governments, and one central government has recognized the legitimacy of multiple national separations. Even in the case of Yugoslavia, it could be said that the resulting war was not about secession per se but about the boundaries and the ethnic composition of the successor states.

All of this surely means that people who were resigned to living together, no matter how uncomfortably, may now think they no longer need to be so resigned. Secessionist movements did not need much encouragement before, when their prospects for success were very slim. Now they need less.

The background to this development is, as mentioned earlier, a surprising degree of firmness of inherited boundaries, an international law that countenanced no real departures from them, and an insistence by affected states—particularly strong in the Organization of African Unity[14]—that legal doctrine reinforce them by inhospitability to secession. International actors generally took a hard line against secession except in the rarest case (Bangladesh), and then only when it became a *fait accompli*. To put the point sharply, the former view was that international boundaries were fixed and regimes could do what they wished within them. This was the international framework for a good deal of tyranny.[15]

### THE ILLUSION OF THE CLEAN BREAK

Although the incentives to secession may be changing, the demographic and political relations of ethnic groups within secessionist and rump regions are not changing. The assumption has usually been that secession produces homogeneous states. In point of fact, neither secessionist states nor rump states are homogeneous. They can be made more homogeneous only by the clumsiest and most unfair methods of population exchange or by policies of expulsion, always carried out with a massive dose of killing. Like Bosnia and Croatia, even after ethnic cleansing, the Southern Sudan, Eritrea, and areas claimed by the Tamil Tigers in Sri Lanka and countless other secessionist movements are ethnically heterogeneous, and so are the states they would leave behind. There used to be a tendency to think of secession as a form of "divorce," a neat and clean separation of two antagonists who cannot get along. But if a crude household analogy could be applied to large collectivities, then, as in domestic divorces, there is nothing neat about it, and there are usually children (smaller groups that are victims of the split). Sometimes secession or partition is the least bad alternative, but it is rarely to be preferred. As I shall suggest, the opposite course, international regional integration and the amalgamation of states, is likely to produce far better results in many (though not all) cases of ethnic conflict. Unfortunately, it is a course unlikely to be pursued.

Secession or partition usually makes ethnic relations worse, because it simplifies intergroup confrontations. Instead of six groups, none of which could quite dominate the others—call this Yugoslavia—it is possible, by subtracting territory, to produce various bipolar alignments of one versus one or two versus one, together with the possibility, even the likelihood, that one side will emerge dominant. Simplification by secession reverses the benign complexity of states such as India or Tanzania that are fortunate enough to contain a multitude of dispersed groups, none with the power to control the others or to take possession of the state for its own ends.

Furthermore, not only are secessionist regions heterogeneous, but secession is often conceived as affording the means of "dealing with" precisely that irritating heterogeneity. For if Group *A*,

no longer in the undivided state, now holds power over the secessionist state, it can regulate the rights available to Group *B*, expel
Group *B* if it is an immigrant group, oppress it, or even take
genocidal measures against it. It is insufficiently appreciated that
concern about demographic changes from in-migration to the
secessionist region often motivates secessionist sentiment, as it has
historically, for example, in the Basque country, in Catalonia, in
the southern Philippines, and in the Shaba province of Zaire.
None of this should surprise observers in the United States. The
secession of 1861 in the United States South was, in part, designed
to permit Group *A* to "deal with" Group *B*, without impediments
from the North. Theories that rest on the reduction of the incidence of domination by means of territorial separation need to
be treated with utmost skepticism. There is no clean break.

The clean-break theorists have another problem that derives
from an inadequate analysis of the character of ethnic affiliations.
Ethnicity is a contextual and therefore mutable affiliation. As I
shall show later, what looks homogeneous today in an undivided
state in which large groups oppose each other can look quite
different after a secessionist state establishes itself. The benefits of
secession and partition for the reduction of ethnic conflict are
very easy to exaggerate. Those writers who, with increasing frequency and decreasing caution, advocate partition as the "solution" to ethnic conflict[16] neglect the contextual character of ethnic affiliations at their peril.[17]

## THE CONSEQUENCES OF TERRITORIAL DIVISION

If the break is not clean, perhaps it can be cleaned up by further
territorial adjustments incidental to secession. In the Biafra case,
for example, severing the territory of the non-Ibo minorities
would certainly have reduced heterogeneity within Biafra as well
as in the severed territory (particularly after the massacre and
flight of Ibo from Port Harcourt). Apart from the fact that populations are more intermixed than many people imagine, such possibilities encounter two major obstacles.

The first is the common desire to limit the damage done by a
secession. If secession is unavoidable, if it becomes a *fait accompli*,
the undivided state will not necessarily be interested in multi-

plying the effects of secession by encouraging further territorial division, except to reclaim for itself part of the secessionist region. Identifying those who get to opt out becomes a new source of conflict.

The second obstacle to realigning groups and territories after secession derives from the confusion buried in the concept of self-determination when the expression of self-determination takes a territorial form. While self-determination refers to people, secession refers to territory. (As I shall suggest, this confusion reflects a deeply rooted ambiguity in the Western political tradition.) Despite the ethnic sources of most secessions, secessionists themselves generally claim independence for the whole territory and for everyone in it, just as the undivided state did.

There is to be, then, no secession from secession. This matter was made as clear as any such confusion can be made by the Arbitration Committee attached to the International Conference on the Former Yugoslavia. The conference had asked the committee to determine the lawfulness of the secessions from Yugoslavia. The committee pronounced Yugoslavia to be a federation "in the process of dissolution,"[18] and it therefore concluded that new states could emerge within the previous republican boundaries (Croatia, Bosnia, Serbia, etc.) but not within any other boundaries.[19] Croatia and Bosnia may thus secede but only intact.

The permissibility of disintegration of federations along the lines of their constituent units is profoundly important. This new doctrine appears to legitimate the secession of Eritrea, which earlier had a federal relationship with Ethiopia, and it could conceivably justify secession of intact units from other federal states, such as India, Pakistan, Malaysia, Canada, Belgium, Nigeria, and the Russian Federation. To the extent that the newly articulated rule means that the cessation of participation of a constituent republic in a federal government sets in motion the process of disintegration, the committee's decision puts in place an enormous disincentive for the creation of federal arrangements to ameliorate ethnic conflict in the first place. Inadvertently, it confirms the otherwise unfounded but very common fears of central policymakers that devolution to regional units constitutes the first step to secession. Confining the lines along which dissolution of federal states can take place to the boundaries of the constituent units limits the possibility of further secession within those constituent units.[20] "[W]hatever the circumstances," pronounced the committee, "the right to self-determination must not involve changes to existing frontiers at the time of independence," barring agreement to the contrary.[21] In short, the minorities in Croatia and Bosnia are entitled to minority rights,[22] but they may not lawfully alter the boundaries of the states in which they find themselves, either to secede or to accede to the adjacent republics. So a liberal rule legitimating secession of constituent federal units is matched by a strict prohibition on any further territorial change.

One of the most prominent effects of secession (or partition) is to place an international boundary between former domestic antagonists, thereby transforming their domestic conflicts into international conflicts, as partition did for India and Pakistan. Without further boundary change, warfare is made more likely, because kindred minorities, formerly within the same state, are placed beyond the reach of their cousins across the border, where their plight elicits sympathy and urgency. This applies to Croats in Bosnia as well as to Serbs in Bosnia and Croatia; it applies to Russians in Transniestria, Estonia, and Kazakhstan, and to Uzbeks in Kirghizia, among many others.

To be sure, irredentism will still be considered illegitimate. The prohibitions of Article 2 of the United Nations Charter on the acquisition of territory by force will still have some effect. Irredentism will thus be seen as different from withdrawal of a group and its territory from a state controlled by others. Consequently, the Serbian and Russian temptations will not be regarded with favor. But the Arbitration Committee rules and the generally growing receptivity to secession create the conditions that make irredentism tempting. While there have been surprisingly few active irredentas in the post-World War II period, the secessions of heterogeneous regions will provide new reasons for irredentas to recapture territory lost as a result. Not only will there be more groups straddling boundaries (as there are more boundaries created), but, as these are fresh losses of people and territory, the usual inhibitions on pursuing irredentas will often be overcome. Irredentism thus can follow smoothly from secession.

### THE BASES OF COMMUNITY AND THE PROBLEM
### OF PLURALISM

If new secessions are likely to produce lower-level ethnic tyran-nies,[23] this is the result of pervasive ambivalence about principle. The international community seems to value simultaneously self-determination, increasingly defined in ethnic terms, and the sanc-tity of frontiers—principles that are in collision. Some people therefore get to determine the future of others.

Much of this problem comes from mixing two different ideas of social organization. In Western political thought, which has influenced political practice far beyond the West, there is, on the one hand, the familiar idea of the social contract between individuals, and there is, on the other, the contending idea that society grows out of the family. Writers like Sir Henry Sumner Maine, who superimposed on this duality an evolutionist bent, identified contract with progress and status (including, promi-nently, birth-derived status) with "primitive society."[24] Not all nine-teenth-century writers, however, accepted Maine's teleology; some were influenced by German notions of *Volksgeist*, which were de-cidedly anticontractarian. As organizing principles, territorial proximity and contract form only one part of the Western tradi-tion. The other part, informed by German Romanticism, consists of concepts of community based on birth. Contemporary evidence of the alternative can be found in citizenship law and practice. Until very recently, citizenship in Germany was almost entirely based on *jus sanguinis,* or descent, and naturalization was exceed-ingly difficult.[25] Alternative ideas about the bases of community remain, and they show up in many places.

Self-determination is one of those places. The theory and prac-tice of self-determination oscillate between the two conceptions. The post-World War I Wilsonian idea of the self-determination of nations was applied, albeit far from completely, to national—or, for present purposes, ethnic—groups. The post-World War II version was applied to "peoples" in colonial territories. Every-one in the territory was supposed to form part of the people, and the right or principle of self-determination (such as it was) was deemed to be spent upon the attainment of independence.

In this phase, self-determination did not have an ethnic dimension.[26]

In fact, there are two kinds of states in the world as well as a good many hybrids. Often self-determination of the Wilsonian sort produces states that are supposed to belong to particular peoples, those whom the Russians call the titular nationality because their name is reflected in the name of the republic: the Tatars in Tatarstan, the Bashkirs in Bashkortostan, and so on, even if they are a minority in the republic, as they frequently are. And so Romania is said to belong to the Romanians, Fiji is said to belong to the Fijians, and Kazakhstan is said to belong to the Kazakhs. Such notions legitimize the status of one group that purports to be at the core of the state. The problem is that others also live within the bounds of such states, and their position is, more often than not, tenuous. Each of the new states of the former Yugoslavia is based on a constitutional structure that accorded sovereignty to one group and so quickly threatened the future of others in the territory.[27]

In states based ostensibly on territorial proximity—which includes, among others, virtually all African states—different problems arise. Some ethnic groups may have claims to priority in the state, notwithstanding and even in defiance of its inclusive character. The conflict between competing principles of community is likely to be sharp in such cases.[28] With or without such explicit claims, the territorial-proximity state still has the problem of majority rule. In severely divided societies, under free elections, ethnic conflict produces ethnically based parties, and eventually one or more of them typically come to dominate the rest. Those who are excluded sense that their exclusion is permanent, since it is based on ascriptive identity, and they may resort to violence.

To put it starkly, then, the self-determination view makes birth-based identity the cornerstone of political community and produces a state with ethnic characteristics and minority exclusion (or occasionally majority exclusion). The territorial-proximity view, based on undifferentiated majority rule, also produces an ethnically exclusionary state. In the first instance, elections in such a state (for example, Nigeria, Sri Lanka, or Bosnia) look as if they are textbook illustrations of democracy in action. On closer inspection, however, their purpose is to determine who will be included in the governing institutions of the polity and who will be excluded.

In the end, then, the results of the two views are not much different. In fact, the domination of the territorial-proximity state by a single ethnic group may lead to its transformation into a state that increasingly belongs to a single ethnic group, as, for example, Sri Lanka after 1956 began to assume characteristics of a state belonging to the Sinhalese.

Now, to this predicament of inclusion and exclusion, rarely articulated quite so explicitly, several answers are possible. The first is consociation, a prescription for treating the multiethnic state for some purposes as if it is more than one polity and for according to each of the subpolities a considerable degree of veto power and autonomy.[29] Few states outside Western Europe have gone in this direction, and some that have been coerced into following this course (such as Cyprus) have rapidly turned away from doing so.

There are some obvious and nonobvious reasons for the unpopularity of parceling out sovereign power in divided societies. It seems plain enough that those who have all of state power within their reach have no incentive to take a large fraction of it and give it away. The most likely motive advanced, the awareness by leaders of the risk of mutual destruction,[30] is based on a time horizon not generally employed in the calculations of political leaders; and, in any case, it certainly is not clear to them in advance that disintegrative conflict is not best deterred by a system that keeps power in their own hands. Furthermore, the sentiments of leaders and followers in divided societies are hardly conducive to what are regarded as concessions to the other side. If statesmanship is required, then it needs to be pointed out that the assumption that elites are invariably less ethnocentric than their supporters is without foundation. Most studies do not show leaders to be less ethnocentric than their followers, and some studies show that ethnocentrism actually increases with education.[31] Whatever the dispositions of leaders may be, when leaders have tried to compromise, it has been shown repeatedly that leadership leeway is very narrow on issues of ethnic power in severely divided societies. Compromisers can readily be replaced by extremists on their flanks, once the latter are able to make the case that a sellout of group interests is in progress.[32] In short, no mechanism can be adduced for the adoption or retention of consociational institutions, particularly no reason grounded in electoral politics.

A rather different approach is to make multiethnic participation at the center of power rewarding to all the participants who espouse it. The approach is different, because it does not require that elites entertain and act on conciliatory feelings that may not exist but assumes only that they will follow their interests. Since such an approach is based on political incentives, it requires some institutions, particularly electoral institutions, that are specially tailored for severely divided societies.[33] In severely divided societies, parties typically break along ethnic lines. The identification of party with ethnic group eliminates any significant number of floating voters. Where there are few, if any, floating voters, democratic business-as-usual results in the bifurcation of the included and the excluded. Some multiethnic states have stumbled across apt institutions to mitigate polarization of this kind, but it will require coherent packages of institutions, not partial adoptions that can be neutralized by countervailing institutions,[34] to make such incentives to intergroup accommodation effective.

Because this approach is designed to reward political leaders for interethnic moderation, sustaining the system, once it is adopted, will be much easier than sustaining consociational arrangements that are based merely on exhortations and constitutional constraints, devoid of political incentives. Still, the threshold problem of adoption remains. Rather than innovate with an explicit view to conciliation, most states, most of the time, have adhered to institutions associated with their former colonial power or to institutions that were otherwise familiar to them. Hardly any state has learned from the actual experience with ethnic conflict of any other state.

A third, neglected approach is territorial, entailing the opposite of secession: international regional integration, to build larger, more complex multiethnic states, for reasons familiar to readers of the *Federalist Papers* and exemplified, for severely divided societies, by India. Scale, as Madison wrote in the *Federalist* number 10, proliferates interests and makes it more difficult for any single interest to dominate. India is a federal state with so many compartmentalized ethnic cleavages that no single group can be said to dominate the state at the center.[35] Nevertheless, it is perfectly obvious that the prevailing worldwide trend is in the opposite direction, toward smaller states, for reasons already explored.

Had any of these three approaches gained widespread popularity and displayed significant efficacy in mitigating severe ethnic conflict, self-determination—especially ethno-territorial self-determination—would not be the genuinely burning issue it has become. Largely in response to disintegrative events, there is a revived interest among philosophers in the political significance of ethnicity and among international lawyers in the law of secession and minority rights. Philosophers and international lawyers have been engaged in a dialogue about self-determination, a subject on which the international lawyers and foreign policy makers have also had exchanges. Here, then, is a case in which evolving ideas may soon matter in practice.

### Philosophical Arguments about Secession

Recent philosophical writings on self-determination would provide more latitude for secession than state practice has customarily afforded.[36] While the philosophical arguments vary, many have a core of similarity in their starting assumptions. Self-determination is to important groups (mainly birth groups) what moral autonomy is to individuals. Just as individual autonomy is an important value, argues Neil MacCormick, so is "some form of collective self-constitution"[37] for those groups that share a consciousness of kind. For Margalit and Raz, groups important to the well-being of their members have rights to political expression, because collective welfare and individual welfare are linked; hence there is "an intrinsic value" to self-government on the part of groups as "an extension of individual autonomy."[38] For David Miller, the relation of individual and group autonomy is most direct; he speaks of exercising "at the collective level the equivalent of autonomy at the individual level."[39] In such starting points, the roots of contemporary thinking on this subject in Kantian conceptions of individual autonomy are apparent.[40]

Viewing ethnic self-determination as simply the collective equivalent of the moral autonomy of individuals produces some fairly sweeping presumptions that groups from which people de-

rive satisfaction and self-esteem should be able to govern themselves. Almost by virtue of their existence, such groups entertain
political aspirations that require recognition.[41] Group membership, if it is to be fruitful, requires "full expression," which is best
assured through self-government.[42] Morally autonomous beings
should have their political preferences respected, and territory
easily follows.[43]

A free-flowing right to secede is sometimes qualified by concerns deriving from respect for the interests of other groups. If,
for example, an "illiberal regime" were to result, then secession
might not be sanctioned.[44] And if there are minorities in the
secessionist regime—a matter rarely touched on in these treatments[45]—then minority rights must be guaranteed.[46]

It hardly needs to be said that many ethnic movements have
illiberal aspects, for reasons that derive from their focus on ancestry, on blood and soil, and on the mystification of group identity
that often accompanies ethnic conflict. As mentioned previously,
secessionist movements sometimes gain much of their energy
from a desire to "deal with" regional minorities, free from the
intrusion of the center. Even movements that do not begin this
way can, nevertheless, produce illiberal, intolerant regimes. The
inability to forecast the emergence of an illiberal regime with any
degree of reliability renders this qualification on the right to
secession illusory.

Neither does the assurance of minority rights assure much. The
historical experience with minority rights is not reassuring, as I
shall soon show. Since secessions are fostered precisely by the
difficulty of accommodating minorities, the presumption that the
situation will be different in the new state cannot be accepted
without substantial evidence that it will.

I noted earlier that much of the recent philosophical literature
is based on projection of claims to individual autonomy onto a
larger collective canvas, rather than on any sense of qualitative
distinctiveness about ethnic groups. These are liberal, individualistic theories. It may seem curious that such a thin understanding
of the nation as an extension of the individuals comprising it
quickly gives rise to territorial claims on behalf of such collectivities. Even more curiously, thicker and generally more conventional understandings of nations as differentiated, culture-bearing

units, with an interest in expressing and preserving their distinctiveness—rather than as groups simply pursuing an extended version of individual freedom—do not necessarily lead to territorial claims.[47] Curious or not, sharply individualistic justifications of a collective right to secede appear to be ascendant.[48]

A few liberal philosophers are more circumspect and less generous to secessionists. Will Kymlicka finds secession acceptable when it is voluntary and mutual, but he acknowledges that secession "is not always possible or desirable," because some states might not be "viable," some movements would produce warfare, and "there are more nations in the world than possible states."[49] Kymlicka's focus, however, is not on secession but on the problems of undivided multiethnic states, and his consideration of the issues is hardly plenary. Allen Buchanan, who is focused squarely on the morality of secession, argues that secession is justified only where the undivided state refuses to cease perpetrating serious injustices or where a group's survival is threatened.[50] Even in the latter case, he would inquire about the availability of lesser alternatives, such as a loose federalism.[51] Per Bauhn would not countenance secession in the absence of serious discrimination and, like Buchanan, would seek less drastic alternatives, unless the undivided state resorts to repression.[52] The caution of Buchanan and Bauhn underscores the incaution of others, including some influential philosophers, who would not require any such inquiry.

The renewed activity of philosophers in this field derives, of course, from events. The claims of oppressed ethnic groups to self-determination are bound to have considerable *prima facie* appeal when ethnic warfare and genocide are recurrent. Added to this is the great failure of imagination in adapting democratic institutions to the predicament of severely divided societies. But if interest in the problem is driven by events, the methodology is not, for much of the literature thus far often displays a thoroughgoing ignorance of the complexities of ethnic interactions. To say this is not to exhibit hostility to the efforts of philosophers on such issues in general—for moral reasoning is needed—but a priori methods that seem appropriate to other issues are utterly unsuitable to this problem.

Consider a recurrent set of empirical assumptions. It is sometimes, albeit rarely, noted that secession could create a new set of minority problems in the secessionist region. The response is, as Margalit and Raz say, that this is a "risk [that] cannot be altogether avoided."[53] This puts the problem rather mildly, since, nine times out of ten, the creation of a new set of minority problems is a "risk" that will come to pass. In Biafra, there were the Rivers and Cross River people who were understandably hostile to Biafran independence. Bosnia has minorities everywhere; Croatia has Serbs in Krajina; Serbia has Hungarians in Vojvodina and Albanians in Kosovo; Kosovo in turn has Serbs. Slovakia has a large minority of Hungarians. Even relatively homogeneous Bangladesh had the Biharis, who were victimized immediately upon independence, and the Chakma in the Chittagong Hills, who soon resorted to arms. Beyond this, ethnic identities are extraordinarily responsive to context. A new, lower-level context will stimulate the salience of dormant, subethnic cleavages, usually submerged while common struggles are being played out on a larger canvas. Eritrea has Christian Eritreans and Muslim Eritreans, who fought each other intermittently even as both were fighting Ethiopia. The secession of South Kasai in Zaire in 1960 immediately produced a prominent, polarizing cleavage between Tshibanda and Mukuna. Both were subgroups of the Luba, who had suffered at the hands of the Lulua and had hoped South Kasai would be "an all-Luba polity," only to discover that "the constriction of a political field may . . . generate new fissiparous tendencies."[54] The same was true of the Ibo, solidary in the all-Nigeria context but in their home region divided by subregion into Owerri, Onitsha, Aro, and other subgroups that sought power along ascriptive lines. Aside from the Efik, Ijaw, and other Eastern-Region minorities that resisted Biafran independence, the Ibo themselves would have produced ethnic heterogeneity and conflict, merely on a smaller scale, just as Pakistanis have done, in an ever-more-bloody way, since the partition of India. Underestimating the continuing problems of pluralism following secession, philosophers end up on this question just about where the Arbitration Committee did in the Yugoslav secession case: they make no provision for subsequent secessions or, for that matter, for thinking about the adjustment of interethnic rights and duties in the new state. They also accord no weight to the interests of those left in the rump state in having access to people, property, and opportunities now to be located in the secessionist state.

## THE EMERGING INTERNATIONAL LAW OF SECESSION
## AND MINORITY RIGHTS

International lawyers have so far been generally more cautious than philosophers but hardly more helpful. The evolving standards of international law bear close watching, because the end of the Cold War has produced, among other things, an intersection of two different trends. First, there has been more ethnic conflict in the former Soviet Union and Eastern Europe. Second, there has been a great reduction in, if not an end to, the impasse that blocked so much international action. As a result, there is likely to be more rapid development of international law and a more rapid development of international law pertinent to ethnic conflict, particularly, of course, self-determination claims, which so often implicate international actors. As the experience of the Yugoslav arbitral decisions already suggests, this is hardly a guarantee that the emerging legal norms will be crafted or enforced appropriately.

Some states respect the rights of minorities, but this respect cannot be attributed to international legal protections. The international law of self-determination and of minority rights has done very little to afford effective protection to minorities in undivided states or minorities in states created out of undivided states. Nevertheless, the efforts of international bodies and international lawyers have been directed disproportionately toward the creation of rarefied versions of new rights, often with a self-determination component to them. To the extent the new rights take hold in the consciousness of those they are to benefit, they are likely to prove disintegrative influences within states, without providing protection for minorities or any incentives for groups to find ways to live together.

The starting point for any inquiry remains the law of self-determination. There is a lively and long-standing debate over whether self-determination is still merely a principle or is now a right.[55] If it is a right, that does not determine who holds the right or what the right entails when exercised, particularly whether it embraces a right to secede. United Nations instruments speak variously of both the right and the principle of self-determination,[56] but there remains a consensus that there is no general right of ethnic groups to secession.[57] Even the self-determination exercise at Versailles following World War I did not produce a general acknowledgment of a right to secede. Thus far the emphasis has been on the need to ascertain the freely expressed will of peoples, particularly colonized peoples; and *peoples* include all those occupying a territory.[58]

There have been many efforts to undermine the prevailing consensus. For some, the case for a legal conception of self-determination that includes ethnic groups, with the attendant possibility of secession, rests on cultural preservation as a collective good that is insufficiently cultivated by the present doctrine.[59] For others, the argument turns on the illegitimacy of a set of boundaries in the light of a historic grievance connected to the territory and how it came to be defined.[60] For a number of writers, the difficulties encountered by groups in living together in multi-ethnic states, with resulting discrimination, deprivation of human rights, and even genocide, have made recognition of a right to self-determination, including the creation of separate states on an ethnic basis, a matter of urgency.[61] A new openness to secession among writers on international law is unmistakable.

In an international system that remains, for most purposes, state dominated,[62] however, no broadly based rights of ethnic groups to secession seem likely to be recognized. Much more likely are post facto rationalizations of territorial separation on the basis of whatever attributes seem to fit particular cases, such as insurgent control over territory and consequent entitlement to recognition, as in Bangladesh,[63] or the dissolution of federal units along the lines of constituent republics, as in Yugoslavia. Since no such decision will affect a majority of states, what can be expected is incremental change in the rules of self-determination, with attendant and growing inconsistency of application. That, after all, is the common fate of flat rules in the face of what are seen to be changing circumstances.

An example of the inconsistency relates to those groups living under "alien" or "racist" regimes. Such groups are said to have a right to self-determination,[64] but the category of people living under "alien" or "racist" regimes turns out to embrace only one case for each adjective: Palestinians living under Israeli occupation and nonwhite South Africans living under apartheid, respectively. Other peoples living in territory acquired in warfare—Tibetans, for example—or peoples living under analogously exclusive regimes—such as Hutu living under the more violent version of apartheid prevailing in Burundi—are not included. To be sure, changes in Israeli-Palestinian relations and in the South African regime may vitiate these particular exceptions, but others may replace them. The categories are there for future invocation, even if for the moment "alien" and "racist" regimes constitute a limited edition.

The same cannot be said for the Draft Declaration on the Rights of Indigenous Peoples,[65] which spells out rights expansively and has considerable possibility for widespread application to divided societies in which one group claims to be indigenous and claims that others are immigrants, even though none is a so-called tribal people of the sort the Declaration aims to protect.[66] The effects on claims to a territorially based self-determination will, again, be incremental, but the prospects are assuredly considerable. The rights conferred by the Declaration constitute a combination of minority rights, such as the rights to practice and transmit distinctive customs and to provide education in the indigenous group's language,[67] and rights to self-determination, most notably provisions limiting the authority of states to take measures affecting indigenous peoples without their informed consent.[68] Their expressly recognized "right of self-determination" includes the right to "freely determine their political status."[69] The Declaration stops short, however, of providing for independence.[70]

The Declaration purports to create dozens of new rights for an indeterminate category of beneficiary-group. The Declaration does not attempt to define the term *indigenous people,* and the work of a United Nations Sub-Commission's Special Rapporteur on the problem of discrimination against indigenous peoples provides a conception sufficiently elastic to permit many groups to claim indigenous status.[71] The impact of the Declaration will prove difficult to confine. Interpreters close to the drafting of the document have made very broad claims for it.[72] Since all groups

ultimately have their origin somewhere else, indigenousness is a
concept that eludes definition, unless it merely refers to earlier
arrival. Many groups claim to have arrived before others, in the
state as a whole or in a single region. Sinhalese have often claimed
priority in Sri Lanka by virtue of their arrival before the Tamils,
but Tamils make contrary claims with respect to the Northern and
Eastern Regions. Both groups may find support in the Declaration
for their mutually exclusive aspirations, Sinhalese in the whole of
Sri Lanka, Tamils in the regions they inhabit. The same applies in
many other countries in which such claims are made. The likely
disintegrative effects on territorially based ethnic conflict are not
difficult to anticipate.

Attempts to protect the rights of minorities in general are not
likely to have such effects. Rather, they are likely to have few, if
any, effects at all. At various times, going back to the Treaty
of Westphalia (1648), with its provisions regarding the rights of
religious minorities, efforts have been made to breathe life into
the international law of minority rights. Because the Wilsonian
exercise in self-determination in Eastern Europe was incomplete,
minorities treaties were imposed on the remaining multiethnic
states that found themselves on the losing side of World War
I. The treaties were accepted reluctantly, enforced poorly, and
undermined quickly as the Versailles order declined and World
War II approached.[73]

The assertion of philosophers that secession may have to be
accompanied by the provision of minority rights *tout court* needs
to be viewed against this experience. International regimes for
minority rights have generally failed to achieve even minimal
objectives, and the frequency of secessionist movements themselves suggests the common inefficacy of measures within states to
protect minority rights.

Following World War II, several minorities treaties were concluded: the Austro-Italian Treaty on the South Tyrol, relating to
Austrians in Italy; the Austrian State Treaty, providing guarantees
for Slovenes and Croats; and the Aaland Islands Treaty, protecting
Swedes in Finland. These special regimes often allow a generous
measure of minority protection. Because the treaties were concluded voluntarily, it stands to reason that their provisions, more

generous than those of customary international law,[74] have had far more benign results.

There is no shortage of formal provisions to protect minorities. United Nations conventions are frequently inclusive in their coverage. The Convention on the Elimination of All Forms of Racial Discrimination (1969) covers groups based on "national or ethnic origin,"[75] and the Genocide Convention (1951) applies to national, racial, ethnic, and religious groups.[76] The protections afforded are often framed in general terms and, as recent experience indicates, often honored in the breach. Some conventions, however, withdraw in one phrase what they accord in another. The UNESCO Convention against Discrimination in Education (1960), for example, recognizes the rights of minorities to maintain their own schools and teach in their own languages, but subject to the educational policy of each state.[77] The minority rights philosophers have assumed into their schemes, if and as necessary, turn out to be contradictions in terms when they are specific and to be ineffective when they are general.

In 1992, the General Assembly adopted a Declaration on the Rights of Minorities.[78] It provides, simultaneously, too little and too much. Like the Convention against Discrimination in Education, the Minorities Declaration takes as it gives: it allows minorities "the right to participate effectively in decisions on the national and, where appropriate, regional level" but "in a manner not incompatible with national legislation."[79] The Declaration also accords members of minority groups "the right to establish and maintain their own associations."[80] If the term *associations* is meant to include ethnically based political parties, that is more than some states—especially African states—have been willing to allow. The Declaration exhorts states to "create favourable conditions" for minority cultures to flourish.[81] It reaffirms the territorial integrity of states[82] but is silent on methods of implementing the one "right" that might help preserve territorial integrity from challenge: the right not to be shut out of political power permanently by virtue of the ethnic exclusion of minorities, whether that exclusion is accomplished by ordinary electoral processes meant to produce democratic outcomes or by authoritarian means. The Declaration is a hortatory document.

Undaunted by the inability to effectuate even rudimentary guarantees of nondiscrimination, international bodies have crossed new frontiers. The Conference on Security and Cooperation in Europe, meeting in Copenhagen in 1990, adopted a final document that included a provision obliging participating states to "respect the right of persons belonging to national minorities to effective participation in public affairs" and mentioning local autonomy as one "possible means" for meeting the obligation.[83] Other European bodies, notably the Council of Europe, have been active on the same front.[84] Despite all this activity, it is difficult to disagree with Hurst Hannum's conclusion that "the substantive development since 1945 of international law related to minorities has been minimal."[85]

International law has always been much influenced by academic writing, and academic writing has now moved toward a new emphasis on popular sovereignty. Thomas M. Franck has suggested that there may be an emerging international "entitlement" to democracy.[86] Among the sources of this "entitlement," its "first building block," is the principle of self-determination,[87] and among its most prominent features is "the emerging normative requirement of a participatory electoral process."[88] Earlier, Antonio Cassese, who in 1993 became chief judge of the Yugoslav War Crimes Tribunal, had argued that the emerging meaning of self-determination is to provide the "possibility for a people to choose a new social and political regime."[89] Nondemocratic governments deny self-determination, conceived broadly "as the right of peoples or minorities to be free from any form of authoritarian oppression."[90]

With widespread movements of democratization, these formulations will undoubtedly be influential in international law. What needs emphasis, however, is exactly how unresponsive they are to the political problems of severely divided societies.[91] To begin with, Cassese's formulation opens the door to a territorial fulfillment of the right to be free of oppression and to choose a new regime, without any criteria justifying its exercise. Much more fundamentally, both the Cassese and Franck formulations, with their intuitive emphasis on democracy and elections, miss completely the electoral paradox in divided societies. What is usually thought of as ordinary democracy is inadequate in societies in which Group *A*, with 60 percent of the voters and often at least 60 percent of the seats, can, under most democratic systems, shut out Group *B*, with 40 percent. In such conditions, democracy is more the problem than the answer to a problem.[92]

The new declarations of minority rights, numerous though they are, are unlikely to contribute to the recognition of minority rights and in many cases are likely to stimulate further conflict, with unfortunate effects on minority rights. The same is surely true for newly invented rights to democratic governance, which are conceived too broadly to cope with the institutional difficulties encountered by divided societies.[93] International law can hardly be expected to prescribe appropriate and exact solutions to what is really a complex problem of electoral engineering.

A final area of international law with a heavy bearing on self-determination relates to recognition practice. Morton H. Halperin and David J. Sheffer have argued that international recognition ought to be the hook on which to hang certain international norms that are otherwise unenforceable.[94] Halperin and Sheffer contend that, before a secessionist state is recognized, the United States and international organizations ought to secure commitments from that state to democracy, minority rights, the inviolability of borders, the renunciation of force, the peaceful settlement of disputes, a market economy, the freedom for transborder minorities in the new state to decide on their own citizenship, and provisions for local autonomy and shared sovereignty over regions inhabited by such minorities.[95] It is left unsaid by Halperin and Sheffer that nearly all such new states have minorities, often minorities they wish to "deal with" in their own way; that nearly all such states come into being by force; that nearly all are dissatisfied with their borders—or else the rump state is—and see those borders as eminently violable; that the drawing of any new boundary invites further conflict rather than shared sovereignty; and that, as already mentioned, democracy in divided societies is part of the problem, the 60–40 problem.

In any case, recognition practice hardly responds to such questions and is difficult to turn in these directions. Yugoslavia provides a convenient example.[96] Britain and France, concerned, respectively, about separatism in Scotland and Wales and in Corsica, were reluctant to recognize the dissolution of Yugoslavia. The

Federal Republic of Germany, with East German unification on its agenda (not to mention longstanding ties with Croatia), led the way to recognition. In each case, apprehensions about fission or aspirations to fusion, as well as various other considerations based on interest, drove recognition policies that had major effects for the future of post-Soviet Eastern Europe and potential effects on European security overall. Given the idiosyncratic determinants of recognition policy, even in the face of the magnitude of the consequences of warfare in Yugoslavia, it is difficult to imagine how recognition could be turned to Halperin and Sheffer's objectives when the general stakes are, as they usually will be, much lower.

Even if recognition does not respond to idiosyncratic national interests and if Yugoslavia has more general significance, then recognition practice is going the other way—toward fewer conditions and faster recognition of secessionists. (By "Yugoslavia," I mean both state practice and the arbitral award.) Obviously, this augurs ill for the imposition of conditions.

It seems perverse to start at the rear end of the problem— with secession and the demand for recognition—rather than to encourage domestic measures of interethnic accommodation. Early, generous devolution, coupled with abundant opportunities for a regionally concentrated group outside its own region, is generally a considerable disincentive to secession, since departure from the undivided state would forfeit those opportunities or leave a large fraction of the group's extraregional population outside any new state. (To be sure, for reasons specified earlier, these are not guarantees against secession. There are no guarantees.) Autonomous regions, provinces, or states in a federation that group people together homogeneously typically foster subethnic divisions, if some are already present, thereby serving a variety of functions in interethnic conciliation. Politicians who have self-interested incentives to work in a conciliatory way across group lines will ordinarily do so, regardless of personal prejudice. But most constitution makers, and certainly most international bodies, have not been diligent in creating those incentives.

Hardly any aspect of international law, save perhaps emerging rights to autonomy, is any more attuned to these domestic problems than recognition doctrine is. The problems are not aptly captured by the concept of minority rights, they do not really respond to the category of discrimination, and they are assuredly not within the province of a general entitlement to democracy or a right to be free from authoritarian rule. Ethnic conflict within states has international consequences, but it is not principally a problem for international law.

SELF-DETERMINATION OR
INTERETHNIC ACCOMMODATION?

Self-determination is a magnificently resonant term, especially in the United States, where it conjures up notions of popular sovereignty. But there is no blinking the fact that, as things now stand, some people have managed to determine the fate of others. As that recognition has dawned, various extensions of the attractive doctrine of self-determination seem tempting, but the temptation should be resisted. What is needed is to substitute interethnic accommodation within borders for a self-determination that either creates new borders or legitimates ethnic exclusion within old ones. No doctrine of minority rights can be adequate to the task, and no amount of self-determination can give territorial expression to more than a small fraction of dissatisfied groups.

Still, the invention of new rights proceeds apace, confirming that civilized declarations are uttered in direct proportion to the commission of brutal acts. Rights will form only a small part of the solution to the problems of ethnic conflict. Most people will have to find political techniques to enable them to live together within existing states, unless they are prepared to do so much ethnic cleansing that the world will soon run out of soap.

NOTES

Portions of this essay were first presented at the Harvard-MIT Joint Seminar on Political Development, and various versions were then delivered as lectures at Colorado College, Emory University, the London School of Economics, Stetson University, the University of California at Santa Barbara, the University of Lund, Rutgers University, the University of Auckland, the University of Melbourne, the Massachussets Institute of Technology, and the University of California at Berkeley. I am grateful to my hosts at these various institutions—respectively, Samuel P. Huntington and Lucian W. Pye, David Hendrickson, Juliette R. Stapanian-Apkarian, Anthony Smith, Eugene Huskey, Cynthia S. Kaplan, Kajsa Eckholm-Friedman and Jonathan Friedman, Robert R. Kaufman, Thomas Telfer, Andrew Christie, Brian Hehir and Steven Van Evera, and Edward Walker—for their hospitality and for the occasion to think and rethink these issues. I am greatly indebted to Layna Mosley for research assistance.

1. There are many theories of secession. E.g., Ralph R. Premdas, "Secessionist Movements in Comparative Perspective," in Ralph R. Premdas, S. W. R. de A. Samarasinghe, and Alan P. Anderson, eds., *Secessionist Movements in Comparative Perspective* (London: Pinter Publishers, 1990), 12–29; Joane Nagel, "The Conditions of Ethnic Separatism," *Ethnicity* 7 (1980): 279–97; John Wood, "Secession: A Comparative Analytic Framework," *Canadian Journal of Political Science* 14 (1981): 107–34; Alberto Alesina and Enrico Spolaore, "On the Number and Size of Nations," National Bureau of Economic Research, Working Paper No. 5050, March 1995. There is much less theoretical literature on irredentism. But see Naomi Chazan, ed., *Irredentism and International Politics* (Boulder, Colo.: Lynne Rienner, 1991). And there is even less on the interrelations of the two phenomena. I have dealt with secessions and irredenta, and with relations between them, in, respectively, Donald L. Horowitz, *Ethnic Groups in Conflict* (Berkeley: University of California Press, 1985), 229–88, and "Irredentas and Secessions: Adjacent Phenomena, Neglected Connections," in Chazan, ed., *Irredentism and International Politics*, 9–22. In this section and occasionally elsewhere, I am borrowing from my essay, "A Harvest of Hostility: Ethnic Conflict and Self-Determination after the Cold War," *Defense Intelligence Journal* 1 (1992): 137–63.

2. The evidence for this is presented in Horowitz, *Ethnic Groups in Conflict*, 233–62.

3. We shall see very shortly, in the case of India vis-à-vis the emergence of Bangladesh, that this can present a problem for a putative irredentist state that wishes to forswear irredentism. In India's case, it helped push India toward aiding the secessionist alternative to irredentism.

4. The Turkish invasion of Cyprus in 1974 was something else altogether and has not produced a state, certainly not a recognized one. The separation of Singapore in 1965 was peaceful and was the result of expulsion, not secession.

5. See Alexis Heraclides, "Secessionist Minorities and External Involvement," *International Organization* 44 (1990): 341–78.

6. See generally Rupert Emerson, *From Empire to Nation* (Cambridge: Harvard University Press, 1960).

7. For a useful survey, see *Fact Sheet on Ethnic and Regional Conflicts in the Russian Federation* (Cambridge: Strengthening Democratic Institutions Project, Harvard University, September 1992).

8. This account follows that of Victor Zaslavsky, "The Evolution of Separatism in Soviet Society under Gorbachev," in Gail W. Lapidus, Victor Zaslavsky, and Philip Goldman, eds., *From Union to Commonwealth: Nationalism and Separatism in the Soviet Republics* (Cambridge: Cambridge University Press, 1992), 71–97, at 83–85.

9. I am indebted to Gail Lapidus for a helpful conversation on this point.

10. I am grateful to Ian Shapiro for stressing this point to me.

11. For a discussion, see Horowitz, *Ethnic Groups in Conflict*, 278–79, 672–75.

12. See Aleksa Djilas, *The Contested Country* (Cambridge: Harvard University Press, 1991).

13. For a careful treatment, see Hurst Hannum, "Self-Determination, Yugoslavia, and Europe: Old Wine in New Bottles?" unpublished paper, n.d. For a scathing critique of German diplomacy on this issue, see Henry Huttenbach, "Post-Factum Diplomacy: Bonn's Revisionist Apologia for Its Policy of Recognizing Croatia," Association for the Study of Nationalities, *Analysis of Current Events* 5 (September 4, 1993): 1–3. Again, a fortuitous confluence took place, for the German government, interested in the reunification of East and West Germany, had a momentary stake in fostering the instability of boundaries. In this, its interests were at odds with those of France (*re* Corsica), Spain (*re* the Basque Country and Catalonia), and Britain (*re* Scotland, Wales, and Northern Ireland).

14. Organization of African Unity, Resolution 16 (1) of July 1964, cited in Hurst Hannum, *Autonomy, Sovereignty and Self-Determination* (Philadelphia: University of Pennsylvania Press, 1990), 23 n. 65, 47.

15. See, e.g., Leo Kuper, *Genocide: Its Political Uses in the Twentieth Century* (New Haven: Yale University Press, 1981), 183. J. Brian Hehir, "Intervention: From Theories to Cases," *Ethics and International Affairs* 9 (1995): 1–13, at 4, traces the roots of nonintervention to the Treaty of Westphalia, designed to end the interventionism of the religious wars.

16. See, e.g., Chaim Kaufman, "Possible and Impossible Solutions to Ethnic Civil Wars," *International Security* 20 (1996): 136–75.

17. David D. Laitin, "Ethnic Cleansing, Liberal Style," MacArthur Foundation Program in Transnational Security, Working Paper Series, M.I.T. Center for International Studies and Harvard Center for International Affairs, 1995. Laitin points out that those who are rewarded with

states for making claims to nationhood will perforce have reason to make such claims in order to benefit from what he calls "Wilsonian ethnic cleansing."

18. Opinions of the Arbitration Committee, reported by Alain Pellet, "The Opinions of the Badinter Arbitration Committee: A Second Breath for the Self-Determination of Peoples," *European Journal of International Law* 3 (1992): 178, Appendix, at 183.

19. Unless the republics agree otherwise, which obviously they did not. Ibid., 183–84.

20. As Hurst Hannum remarks, this is the first time that the domestic constitutional structure of a state was deemed relevant, as a matter of international law, to its continuing existence and to the lines of its possible dissolution. Hannum, "Self-Determination, Yugoslavia, and Europe," 11.

21. Opinions of the Arbitration Committee, at 184.

22. Ibid.

23. The framers of the United States Constitution understood that lower-level tyranny was more difficult to control than higher-level. This is a reason they advanced for a large republic. See *The Federalist* no. 10 (New York: G. P. Putnam's Sons, 1888).

24. Sir Henry Sumner Maine, *Ancient Law* (London: Oxford University Press, 1931; originally published 1861).

25. See Rogers Brubaker, *Citizenship and Nationhood in France and Germany* (Cambridge: Harvard University Press, 1992).

26. For helpful surveys, see Hurst Hannum, *Autonomy, Sovereignty, and Self-Determination: The Accommodation of Conflicting Rights* (Philadelphia: University of Pennsylvania Press, 1990), 28–49; Lee Buchheit, *Secession: The Legitimacy of Self-Determination* (New Haven: Yale University Press, 1978), 8–20; Rupert Emerson, *Self-Determination Revisited in an Era of Decolonization,* Occasional Papers in International Affairs no. 9 (Cambridge: Harvard University Center for International Affairs, 1964).

27. See Robert M. Hayden, "Constitutional Nationalism in the Formerly Yugoslav Republics," *Slavic Review* 51 (1992): 654–73; Robert M. Hayden, "Constitutional Nationalism and the Wars in Yugoslavia," paper prepared for the conference in Post-Communism and Ethnic Mobilization, Cornell University, April 21–23, 1995.

28. See, e.g., the interesting discussion in Mahathir bin Mohamad, *The Malay Dilemma* (Singapore: Donald Moore, 1970), 115–53, lamenting the demise of *Tanah Melayu* (the Malay land) in favor of Malaysia, which includes citizens of all ethnic origins.

29. For the argument, see Arend Lijphart, *Democracy in Divided Societies* (New Haven: Yale University Press, 1977).

30. Ibid., 165.

31. I have gathered much of the evidence in Donald L. Horowitz, *A Democratic South Africa? Constitutional Engineering in a Divided Society* (Berkeley: University of California Press, 1991), 140–41 nn. 44–50. There is, however, more. In Romania and in Moldova, university-educated people exhibit the strongest hostility to minorities; and in Moldova, hostility increases directly with level of education. William Crowther, "Exploring Political Culture: A Comparative Analysis of Romania and Moldova," unpublished paper, University of North Carolina at Greensboro, n.d., 16, figures 1–3. For similar results for Eastern Europe in general, see Radio Free Europe/Radio Liberty, "Stereotypes Projected to Jews, Blacks, and Gypsies by East Europeans and Austrians" (unpublished paper, July 1980). In the European republics of the former Soviet Union, on the other hand, education is negatively associated with anti-Semitism. James L. Gibson and Raymond M. Duch, "Attitudes toward Jews and the Soviet Political Culture," *Journal of Soviet Nationalities* 2 (1991): 77–117, at 98–100. In Guyana, education mitigates Indian prejudice toward Africans but has no significant effect on African prejudice toward Indians. Joseph B. Landis, "Racial Attitudes of Africans and Indians in Guyana," *Social and Economic Studies* 22 (1973): 427–39, at 436. The United States cannot be regarded as typical. See generally Paul M. Sniderman and Thomas Piazza, *The Scar of Race* (Cambridge: Harvard University Press, 1993); Howard Schuman, Charlotte Steeh, and Lawrence Bobo, *Racial Attitudes in America* (Cambridge: Harvard University Press, 1985). Cf. Frederick D. Weil, "The Variable Effects of Education on Liberal Attitudes: A Comparative-Historical Analysis of Anti-Semitism Using Public Opinion Survey Data," *American Sociological Review* 50 (1985): 458–74.

32. Sri Lanka recurrently illustrates this pattern. Every time a Sinhalese-dominated government proposes compromise with the Tamils, a Sinhalese opposition party gathers support by opposing it. For examples, see Chandra Richard de Silva, *Sri Lanka: A History* (New Delhi: Vikas Publishing House, 1987), 238–45.

33. See, e.g., Horowitz, *A Democratic South Africa?* 154–60, 163–203; Donald L. Horowitz, "Making Moderation Pay: The Comparative Politics of Ethnic Conflict Management," in Joseph V. Montville, editor, *Conflict and Peacemaking in Multiethnic States* (Lexington, Mass.: Lexington Books, 1990), 451–75.

34. In 1979, for example, the Nigerians returned to civilian rule under a constitution containing a presidential electoral system that made the president a conspicuously pan-ethnic, conciliatory figure. The legislature, however, was elected under a formula that did nothing for ethnic conciliation and turned legislators into representatives of mutually

exclusive ethnic interests. One institution more than canceled the other out.

35. This remains true despite the disturbing growth of a great Hindu-Muslim cleavage that threatens to rend the whole society.

36. See Per Bauhn, *Nationalism and Morality* (Lund: Lund University Press, 1995), 104–13; Allen Buchanan, *Secession: The Morality of Political Divorce from Fort Sumter to Lithuania and Quebec* (Boulder, Colo.: Westview Press, 1991); Allen Buchanan, "Self-Determination and the Right to Secede," *Journal of International Affairs* 45 (1992): 347–65; Mary Maxwell, "Normative Aspects of Secession and Supranationalism," unpublished paper presented at the annual meeting of the American Political Science Association, 1992; Daniel Philpott, "In Defense of Self-Determination," *Ethics* 105 (1995): 352–85; Neil MacCormick, "Is Nationalism Philosophically Credible?" in William Twining, ed., *Issues of Self-Determination* (Aberdeen: Aberdeen University Press, 1991), 8–19; Yael Tamir, "The Right to National Self-Determination," *Social Research* 58 (1991): 565–90; Avishai Margalit and Joseph Raz, "National Self-Determination," *Journal of Philosophy* 87 (1990): 439–61; David Miller, "The Ethical Significance of Nationality," *Ethics* 98 (1988): 647–62.

37. MacCormick, "Is Nationalism Philosophically Credible?" 14.

38. Margalit and Raz, "National Self-Determination," 451. For the foundations of such views in Raz's conceptions of collectivities as aggregates of individuals, see Joseph Raz, *The Morality of Freedom* (Oxford: Clarendon Press, 1986), 207–9.

39. Miller, "The Ethical Significance of Nationality," 659.

40. Perhaps less obvious are the similarities to John Stuart Mill's sympathetic speculations on the same subject. At least with respect to what he called "civilized" nations, Mill advocated sweeping support for the efforts of peoples to free themselves from foreign rule or from "a native tyranny upheld by foreign arms." Mill, "A Few Words on Non-Intervention," in Mill, *Dissertations and Discussions,* vol. 3 (London: Savill and Edwards, 1867), 153–78, at 176. For a helpful exposition, suggesting that the analogy of communities to individuals was also on Mill's mind, see Michael Walzer, *Just and Unjust Wars* (New York: Basic Books, 1977), 87–91. Mill was extremely doubtful that democratic regimes could survive in what would be called today conditions of ethnic pluralism; he described the prospect as "next to impossible," and this may have colored his receptivity to collective opting out. Mill, "Considerations on Representative Government," in Mill, *Utilitarianism, Liberty, and Representative Government* (New York: E. P. Dutton, 1951; originally published 1861), 486. For a critique of Mill's views on the prospects for plural societies, see Stanley French and Andres Gutman, "The Principle of National Self-Determina-

tion," in Virginia Held, Sidney Morgenbesser, and Thomas Nagel, editors, *Philosophy, Morality, and International Affairs* (New York: Oxford University Press, 1974), 138–53, at 142–44.

41. MacCormick, "Is Nationalism Philosophically Credible?" 17.

42. Margalit and Raz, "National Self-Determination," 451–54.

43. Philpott, "In Defense of Self-Determination," 355–62.

44. Ibid., 371–75.

45. The matter is, for example, never mentioned in Per Bauhn's treatment (*Nationalism and Morality*) and in most others; it is passingly acknowledged in a few.

46. Ibid., 27.

47. Yael Tamir, "The Right to National Self-Determination." Tamir explicitly rejects the reduction of self-determination to the quest for freedom or autonomy, ibid., 584, insisting that national self-determination is "attained only when certain features, unique to the nation, find expression in the political sphere." Ibid., at 584, 586. Yet she finds it possible to achieve adequate expression of cultural identity through many political institutions that fall far short of territorial separation. Ibid., 587.

48. In a striking reversal of the usual parlance, MacCormick states flatly that groups are "constitutive" of individuals. "Is Nationalism Philosophically Credible?" 17. One problem, at least, that is obviated by such an approach relates to the ascertainment of the will of an abstract entity, such as a nation. See the critique of French and Gutman, "The Principle of National Self-Determination," 148–53; and compare the solution of Margalit and Raz, "National Self-Determination," 458.

49. Will Kymlicka, *Multicultural Citizenship: A Liberal Theory of Minority Rights* (Oxford: Clarendon Press, 1995), 186.

50. Buchanan, *Secession*; Buchanan, "Self-Determination and the Right to Secede."

51. Buchanan, *Secession,* 61.

52. Bauhn, *Nationalism and Morality,* 111–13.

53. "Nationalism and Self-Determination," 458.

54. René Lemarchand, "Ethnic Violence in Tropical Africa," in John F. Stack, Jr., editor, *The Primordial Challenge: Ethnicity in the Contemporary World* (New York: Greenwood Press, 1986), 199–200. For further empirical cautions regarding secessionist solutions, see Valery A. Tishkov, "Nationalities and Conflicting Ethnicity in Post-Communist Russia" (Conflict Management Group, Working Papers on Ethnic Conflict Management in the Former Soviet Union, Cambridge, Massachusetts, April 1993), 17–20.

55. See, e.g., Richard T. DeGeorge, "The Myth of the Right of Collective Self-Determination," in Twining, ed., *Issues of Self-Determination,* 1–7;

Anna Michalska, "Rights of Peoples to Self-Determination in International Law," in ibid., 71–90; Patrick Thornberry, *Minorities and Human Rights Law* (London: Minority Rights Group, 1991), 9–10.

56. See Malvina Halberstam, "Self-Determination in the Arab-Israeli Conflict: Meaning, Myth, and Politics," *New York University Journal of International Law and Politics* 21 (1989): 465–87, at 465 n. 3.

57. See Hannum, *Autonomy, Sovereignty, and Self-Determination*, 28–49; Max M. Kampelman, "Secession and the Right of Self-Determination: An Urgent Need to Harmonize Principle with Pragmatism," *Washington Quarterly* 16 (1993): 5–12. Michalska, "Rights of Peoples to Self-Determination in International Law," 78–79; Ralph G. Steinhardt, "International Law and Self-Determination" (unpublished paper, Atlantic Council Project on Individual Rights, Group Rights, National Sovereignty, and International Law, n.d.), 41–43. Buchheit, *Secession,* argues for a right to secede but concedes it does not yet exist.

58. See, e.g., Western Sahara (Advisory Opinion), 1975 I.C.J. 12, 80–81 (Opinion of Nagendra Singh, J.).

59. Guyora Binder, "The Case for Self-Determination," *Stanford Journal of International Law* 29 (1993): 223–70. For an extreme and ill-considered version, see Michael Kirby, "The Peoples' Right to Self-Determination," *New Zealand Law Journal* (September 1993): 341–44. Kirby suggests simply that "peoples should ordinarily be allowed to live together in a group identity which is congenial to them," provided they are "respectful" of minorities (343).

60. Lea Brilmayer, "Secession and Self-Determination: A Territorial Interpretation," *Yale Journal of International Law* 16 (1991): 177–202.

61. For numerous ways of arriving at a similar destination, see Robert McCorquodale, "Self-Determination beyond the Colonial Context and Its Potential Impact on Africa," *African Journal of International and Comparative Law* 4 (1992): 592–608; James E. Falkowski, "Secessionary Self-Determination: A Jeffersonian Perspective," *Boston University International Law Journal* 9 (1991): 209–42; Lung-Chu Chen, "Self-Determination and World Public Order," *Notre Dame Law Review* 66 (1991): 1287–97. Cf. Eric Kolodner, "The Future of the Right to Self-Determination," *Connecticut Journal of International Law* 10 (1994): 153–67.

62. But see Benedict Kingsbury, "Claims by Non-State Groups in International Law, *Cornell International Law Journal* 25 (1992): 481–530.

63. For one such, badly strained effort, see Susan Marks, "Self-Determination and People's Rights," *King's College Law Journal* 2 (1991–92): 79–94, at 91.

64. Hannum, *Autonomy, Sovereignty, and Self-Determination*, 97, 103; Mi-

chalska, "Rights of Peoples to Self-Determination in International Law," 80.

65. U.N. Doc. E/CN.4/Sub. 2/1994/2/Add. 1 (Economic and Social Council, Commission on Human Rights, Sub-Commission on Prevention of Discrimination and Protection of Minorities, 20 April 1994).

66. See Ved P. Nanda, "Ethnic Conflict in Fiji and International Human Rights Law," *Cornell International Law Journal* 25 (1992): 565–77.

67. Draft Declaration on the Rights of Indigenous Peoples, articles 12–16.

68. Ibid., article 20.

69. Ibid., article 3. Other articles reinforce their political independence. E.g., articles 4, 23, 31–33.

70. Article 31 refers instead to "the right to autonomy or self-government." After vigorous controversy, the language was chosen deliberately. I am indebted to Benedict Kingsbury for this background.

71. See Benedict Kingsbury, "Self-Determination and 'Indigenous Peoples,'" in *Proceedings of the American Society of International Law*, 86th Annual Meeting (1992): 383–94, at 385–86. See also Benedict Kingsbury, "'Indigenous Peoples' as an International Legal Concept," in R.H. Barnes et al., editors, *Indigenous Peoples of Asia* (Ann Arbor, Mich.: Association for Asian Studies, 1995), 13–34.

72. See Erica-Irene A. Daes, "Consideration on the Right of Indigenous Peoples to Self-Determination," *Transnational Law and Contemporary Problems* 3 (1993): 1–11. Daes wrote as Chairperson and Special Rapporteur of the U.N. Working Group on Indigenous Populations. Ruth Lapidoth, "Autonomy: Potential and Limitations," *International Journal on Group Rights* 1 (1994): 269–90, at 274, noting the "far-reaching claims" supported by the convention, suggests the need to limit its scope if it is to be acceptable to states. For a more circumspect view of the claims of indigenous peoples, see Allen Buchanan, "The Role of Collective Rights in the Theory of Indigenous Peoples' Rights," *Transnational Law and Contemporary Problems* 3 (1993): 90–108.

73. Hannum, *Autonomy, Sovereignty, and Self-Determination*, 50–54; Salo Baron, "Ethnic Minority Rights: Some Older and New Trends," the Tenth Sacks Lecture, 26 May 1983, Oxford Centre for Postgraduate Hebrew Studies, 1985.

74. Which accords them, in principle, the rights to equality and non-discrimination. Hannum, *Autonomy, Sovereignty, and Self-Determination*, 69.

75. *United Nations Treaty Series* 660 (1969): 195.

76. International Convention on the Prevention and Punishment of the Crime of Genocide (1951), *United Nations Treaty Series* 277 (1951): 78.

77. UNESCO Convention Against Discrimination in Education (1960), *United Nations Treaty Series* 429 (1960): 93.

78. *Declaration on the Rights of Persons Belonging to National or Ethnic, Religious and Linguistic Minorities,* United Nations General Assembly, A/RES/47/135, 3 February 1993 (adopted 18 December 1992).

79. Ibid., art. 2(3).

80. Ibid., art. 2(4).

81. Ibid., art. 4(2).

82. Ibid., art. 8(4).

83. Document of the Copenhagen Meeting of the Conference on the Human Dimensions of the Conference on Security and Cooperation in Europe, June 29, 1990, art. 35. The text of article 35 can be found in Thornberry, *Minorities and Human Rights Law,* 29. For a commentary, see Hurst Hannum, "Contemporary Developments in the International Protection of the Rights of Minorities," *Notre Dame Law Review* 66 (1991): 1431–48, at 1439–43.

84. See Hannum, "Contemporary Developments in the International Protection of the Rights of Minorities," at 1439–43. See also Morton H. Halperin and David J. Sheffer, *Self-Determination in the New World Order* (Washington, D.C.: Carnegie Endowment for International Peace, 1992), 59.

85. Hannum, "Contemporary Developments in the International Protection of the Rights of Minorities," at 1444.

86. Thomas M. Franck, "The Emerging Right to Democratic Governance," *American Journal of International Law* 86 (1992): 46–91.

87. Ibid., 55–56.

88. Ibid., 63 (emphasis omitted).

89. Antonio Cassese, "Political Self-Determination: Old Concepts and New Developments," in Antonio Cassese, editor, *UN Law/Fundamental Rights: Two Topics in International Law* (Alphenaanden Rijn, Netherlands: Sijthoff and Noordhoff, 1979), 137–65, at 158.

90. Ibid., 160 (emphasis omitted). Cf. Morton H. Halperin and Kristen Lomasney, "Toward a Global 'Guarantee Clause,'" *Journal of Democracy* 4 (1993): 60–69.

91. For a trenchant critique, based on an analysis of the international instruments relied on by Franck and Cassese, see Steinhardt, "International Law and Self-Determination," 38–43.

92. Compare ibid., 43: "Popular sovereignty, to the extent that it translates into majority rule, does not necessarily reflect any commitment to minority rights and may well work against them."

93. The occasional international law treatment that descends to institutional particulars is typically far too imprecise and cavalier to be help-

ful. See, e.g., John B. Attanasio, "The Rights of Ethnic Minorities: The Emerging Mosaic," *Notre Dame Law Review* 66 (1991): 1195–1217, at 1205–8, blithely proposing electoral arrangements deemed a priori to be favorable to minorities and a variety of protective arrangements for regional minorities in autonomous provinces.

94. Halperin and Sheffer, *Self-Determination in the New World Order.*

95. Ibid., 84–93.

96. See generally Stuart Kaufman, "The Irresistible Force and the Imperceptible Object: The Yugoslav Breakup and Western Policy," *Security Studies* 4 (1994–95): 281–329, at 311–14. See also note 13, above.

# 15

# TRIBES, REGIONS, AND NATIONALISM IN DEMOCRATIC MALAWI

## DEBORAH KASPIN

### Introduction: African Tribalism on the

### International Stage

When African political conflicts are reported in the press, the word "tribalism" is usually reported too, lying at the heart of political parties, territorial disputes, and when they have them, national elections. Whether they are defined by language, culture, or physiognomy, tribes seem to be fundamental to Africa's social geography, originating in the precolonial past and persisting within and across the borders of modern nations. Tribal identities are thus prior, indigenous, and totalizing, while nation-states are recent, imposed, and superficial. And because tribes and nations are not coterminous, tribalism seems to pose the single greatest threat to national stability.

These assumptions are the legacy of nineteenth-century social theory which sought stages in the evolution of civilization and placed the tribe, synonymous with the primitive, near the front end of the evolutionary continuum. Modern primitives of the colonial world were thought to be frozen in evolutionary time, unable to become politically modern without external assistance.

Twentieth-century anthropology disputed social evolutionism but retained the "tribe" within its lexicon as it sought greater specificity in the ethnographies of particular primitives. Ultimately the "tribe" was challenged as a unit of study because of its linkages to evolutionary essentialism and the conspicuous invisibility of colonialism which required this category of subordinate and essential "other." A new vocabulary used such terms as "ethnicity" and "peasant," separating identity from political economy and putting first and third world politics in the same conceptual framework.[1]

But African tribes still appear in the public media, especially when they threaten to wreak havoc upon new nations. Warfare between Zulus and Xhosas nearly scuttled the South African election; skirmishes between Kalengin and Kikuyu threatened the security of Kenya; and ancient enmities between Hutu and Tutsi led to new episodes of genocide in Rwanda and Burundi. The conflicts are certainly real, but by describing them all as "tribalism," the press conflates a variety of political situations into a single type of stereotypic behavior, that of the primitive African.

Western media are not, however, wholly to blame for the stereotypy, since it is used with equal facility by African presses and intelligentsia. Certainly elites raise the specter of tribal violence to advance and conceal their political agendas, such as Gatsha Buthelezi, who cloaks the conflict between the Inkatha Freedom Party and the African National Congress in the language of tribal warfare by misrepresenting the ethnic composition of the two organizations; and President Moi of Kenya who warns that tribal violence can erupt in his country at any time, and that the best way to circumvent it is to maintain ironclad rule under his government.

But not all Africans are so calculated in their use of the terms. More often, they are simply using local vernaculars that have absorbed the same colonial culture that produced social evolutionism and that now include the vocabulary of tribalism. In Africa today, the question "What is your tribe?" is readily understood and promptly answered, and the suggestion that ethnicities are artifacts of European conceptual schemas, colonial politics, and postcolonial nation-building may be met with laughter and derision. At a fundamental level, the discourse of tribalism coincides with the experience of political identity, a coincidence that cannot be ignored.

The Republic of Malawi is a case in point. In 1993, President Hastings Banda, once proclaimed President for Life in a one-party state, yielded to local and international pressure to hold a referendum for multiparty democracy, leading to presidential and parliamentary elections in 1994. In the year leading up to the election, numerous presidential candidates stepped forward and seven new political parties were formed in anticipation of the fall of President Banda and the Malawi Congress Party. Although no one was surprised that Banda lost the election, many were shaken when the electorate divided on regional lines, with each of the three administrative regions supporting its home candidate for president and his party for parliament. Bakili Muluzi and the United Democratic Front won the presidency and parliamentary majority because Muluzi's home region, the south, represented almost half the population of Malawi.

If regional factions revealed a disappointing absence of ideological commitments, the Malawi press and intelligentsia saw in it more sinister implications: multiparty democracy had exposed the tribal divisions that ran through the heart of Malawi civil society. Bakili Muluzi, a Yao from the south, claimed a Yao constituency; Hastings Banda, a Chewa from the center, claimed a Chewa constituency; and Chakufwa Chihana, a Tumbuka from the north, claimed a Tumbuka constituency. It was especially disturbing because ethnic loyalties had not been explicitly solicited in preelection campaigns, at least not in ways that journalists and observer groups could detect. Tribal politics seemed to emerge on their own from the sentiments of the grass roots, suggesting that Malawi was, at its core, another Kenya or Rwanda.

The consensus among Malawians was that tribalism drove voter choice, casting an ominous cloud over the country's political future. But is this an accurate assessment of regional coalitions? The ethnic composition of Malawi is complicated at best, for aside from the Chewa-dominated central region it is hard to pinpoint coherent tribal areas, much less identify them with administrative regions. In reality the voting blocks were multiethnic, their boundaries corresponding to administrative units that were never based on tribal composition. As such, the real revelation of the election is that the seemingly arbitrary divisions produced by colonial administrators provided the basis of political mobilization thirty years after the end of colonial rule. Regional constituencies were so consistent that Malawians referred to them as tribes, that is, as primordial identities rooted in precolonial cultural history. (See map 1.)

NATIONALITY AND ETHNICITY IN
POSTCOLONIAL AFRICA

This chapter locates Malawi's "tribalism" in the first thirty years of national history, the period of President Banda's one-party state that ended in 1994. It will show that Malawi's regional factions and ethnic discourse are the result of the president's program for nation-building. I take as my starting point Crawford Young's taxonomy of third world nation-states and cultural pluralisms, placing Malawi in a group typical of post-colonial Africa. These are "entirely arbitrary colonial creations, without historic antecedents or sanction but where new territorial elites representing the populace within its boundaries have inherited power . . . . Their shared historic memory is limited to the common experience of a single colonial ruler and the collective struggle to secure independence."[2]

Malawi is also "multipolar", a type of cultural pluralism "particularly characteristic of the African scene [which] contains . . . a single type of cultural cleavage, normally ethnic but with at least three, and often many, identity groups in the political arena."[3] According to Young, nation-building under this type of emergent state "involves a dual imperative":

> to define a new cultural identity linked to the dimensions of the polity and related to commonalities among the polity's populace, while eschewing identification of the state with any one of the cultural segments within it, which would immediately threaten the identity of other collectivities.[4]

> Multiplicity of cultures almost necessarily means removing the state itself from the cultural arena and preserving its institutions in a status of neutrality, distinct from any of the component cultures.[5]

MAP 1    MALAWI'S 1994 ELECTION

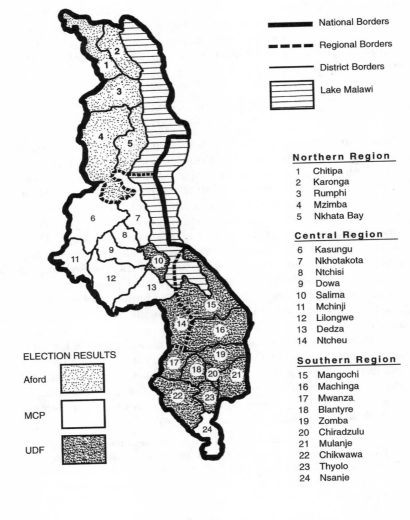

National Borders
Regional Borders
District Borders
Lake Malawi

**Northern Region**

1  Chitipa
2  Karonga
3  Rumphi
4  Mzimba
5  Nkhata Bay

**Central Region**

6   Kasungu
7   Nkhotakota
8   Ntchisi
9   Dowa
10  Salima
11  Mchinji
12  Lilongwe
13  Dedza
14  Ntcheu

**Southern Region**

15  Mangochi
16  Machinga
17  Mwanza
18  Blantyre
19  Zomba
20  Chiradzulu
21  Mulanje
22  Chikwawa
23  Thyolo
24  Nsanje

ELECTION RESULTS

Aford

MCP

UDF

Malawi illustrates the dual imperative that Young has described, but in this case the state sacrificed objective neutrality vis-à-vis cultural cleavages in order to consolidate a national identity and legitimate the ruling elite. Thus while its rulers claimed to be neutral arbiters over the affairs of their citizens, they also sought allies in specific constituencies and legitimated themselves in terms of contrived ideologies of identity. Internal cleavages became more not less acute, and some, in fact, emerged anew, engendered by the government that purported to meld the whole together.

Nation-building in Malawi is reminiscent of what Benedict Anderson has called official nationalism.[6] This is the process by which states create fictions of national identity by disseminating the cultural characteristics of the elite—their language, customs, and history—to the citizenry, and reciprocally, by proclaiming the ethnicity of the elites as prototypically national. Although Anderson finds his paradigmatic examples among nineteenth-century European dynasts, the lessons of official nationalism are available to the postcolonial third world. Certainly Malawi's new elites sought to naturalize both the state and the citizenry through "a systematic, even Machiavellian, instilling of nationalist ideology through the mass media, the educational system, administrative regulations, and so forth,"[7] ornamenting that ideology with the cultural attributes of the president's ethnic group.

Nationalist ideologies are, however, a double-edged sword, insofar as they use ethnic particularities to characterize a diverse citizenry. As several studies of nationalism have shown, iconographies of nationality in multiethnic nations are usually derived from one ethnicity in the mix that is assumed to be mainstream.[8] The result is that the discourse of nationality contains the seeds of its own undoing, not because it embraces irreconcilably diverse populations but because it hierarchizes ethnicities vis-à-vis a national patrimony: ethnic identity becomes more not less critical, if conformity to the national norm determines access to public resources.[9]

The Malawian case is, therefore, a chapter in the story of official nationalism and its internal breakdown. The state under President Banda claimed to transcend "tribalism" and to act on behalf of the nation, when in fact development policies were regionally biased, while the state-generated national culture was steeped in ethnic particularities. Because the economy was small, and the government the principal agent of development, the promotion of one ethnicity—the Chewa—as the national mainstream, and one region—the center—as Malawi's heartland had serious consequences for the rest. This was expressed in the general elections when the President's party drew its support from Chewa central region, and the two opposition parties drew their support from the non-Chewa north and south. (See map 1 and tables 1 and 2.)

The Malawian case also adds an instructive twist to the story of ethnic solidarities, for although tribalism is the name of the political game, regional coalitions are the fact of it. While the central region is (more or less) ethnically homogeneous, the northern and southern regions are not, and while ethnic solidarity gained support for the three presidential frontrunners, multiethnic voting blocks dominated the election. Insofar as the regions, like the nation, are administrative conventions created under colonial rule, the Malawi election is a lesson in how quickly collective solidarities can be formed and naturalized. Evidently the fervor of group identity need not be a function of its historical depth, and at least in emerging nations, the state has great latitude to invent both its national community and the lines of cleavage within it.

The following essay explains Malawi's so-called tribalism in terms of its history of nation-building. The first section discusses Malawi's ethnic composition and the disputes about it; the second section, describes political and economic development under the first president and its relation to his policy of official nationalism; the third section discusses the mobilization of regional factions that state policies of nation-building engendered; the fourth section briefly recounts the events leading up to the election; and the fifth section reconsiders the interplay of regional and ethnic solidarities among Malawi's electorate. The sixth section speculates briefly about identity politics under a democratic order.

## LANGUAGE AND ETHNIC CATEGORIES OF MALAWI

When the Malawian press refers to the ethnicities and languages that dominate the social geography of their country, they usually

TABLE 1. THE 1993 REFERENDUM

| | MULTI-PARTY | SINGLE PARTY |
|---|---|---|
| *National* | 63% | 35% |
| *North* | 88% | 11% |
| Chitipa | 90% | 9% |
| Karonga | 93% | 6% |
| Nkhata Bay | 91% | 7% |
| Rumphi | 86% | 13% |
| Mzimba | 91% | 8% |
| *Center* | 31% | 66% |
| Kasungu | 27% | 70% |
| Nkhotakota | 45% | 51% |
| Ntchisi | 22% | 77% |
| Dowa | 15% | 83% |
| Salima | 44% | 54% |
| Lilongwe | 27% | 69% |
| Mchinji | 30% | 64% |
| Dedza | 25% | 72% |
| Ntcheu | 74% | 25% |
| *South* | 84% | 15% |
| Mangochi | 89% | 9% |
| Machinga | 90% | 9% |
| Zomba | 86% | 13% |
| Chiradzulu | 86% | 10% |
| Blantyre | 86% | 13% |
| Mwanza | 70% | 28% |
| Thyolo | 80% | 18% |
| Mulanje | 70% | 28% |
| Chikwawa | 75% | 23% |
| Nsanje | 81% | 17% |

Figures are taken from *International Observers Briefing Manual.*

name Tumbuka, Chewa, and Yao, identifying Tumbuka and Chewa with the north and the center (as in the phrases, "the Tumbuka north" and "the Chewa center"), and Yao as one of several groups indigenous to the south. But ethnic dominance and regional identification are peculiar notions here, for no sur-

TABLE 2. THE 1994 PRESIDENTIAL ELECTION

| | MCP BANDA | AFORD CHIHANA | UDF MULUZI | REG. VOTERS AS % OF POP | VOTES CAST AS % OF POP |
|---|---|---|---|---|---|
| *National* | 33.45% | 18.00% | 47.16% | 47.20% | 38.10% |
| *North* | 7.30% | 87.80% | 4.52% | 59.80% | 51.30% |
| Chitipa | 9.57% | 88.26% | 1.82% | 55.20% | 47.50% |
| Karonga | 5.21% | 91.55% | 2.89% | 57.10% | 48.30% |
| Nkhata Bay | 6.21% | 84.68% | 8.45% | 52.10% | 43.40% |
| Rumphi | 5.58% | 85.36% | 4.70% | 65.60% | 56.90% |
| Mzimba | 8.15% | 87.02% | 4.50% | 62.90% | 54.60% |
| *Center* | 64.31% | 7.50% | 27.81% | 47.00% | 38.10% |
| Kasungu | 65.55% | 18.91% | 15.13% | 55.80% | 45.40% |
| Nkhotakota | 46.57% | 15.20% | 37.85% | 55.60% | 47.10% |
| Ntchisi | 65.18% | 3.45% | 30.87% | 46.90% | 37.60% |
| Dowa | 80.51% | 3.75% | 15.04% | 45.90% | 37.60% |
| Salima | 47.31% | 4.35% | 47.73% | 49.10% | 38.00% |
| Lilongwe | 71.66% | 7.79% | 20.22% | 46.90% | 40.10% |
| Mchinji | 69.54% | 3.25% | 26.79% | 50.00% | 39.70% |
| Dedza | 71.60% | 2.28% | 26.28% | 44.40% | 32.90% |
| Ntcheu | 23.77% | 3.65% | 71.97% | 36.20% | 27.70% |
| *South* | 16.09% | 5.23% | 78.04% | 44.60% | 35.00% |
| Mangochi | 7.50% | 3.31% | 88.70% | 51.60% | 41.80% |
| Machinga | 6.93% | 4.52% | 91.17% | 50.20% | 42.30% |
| Zomba | 11.24% | 4.05% | 84.13% | 48.50% | 40.00% |
| Chiradzulu | 8.99% | 1.54% | 89.06% | 46.80% | 32.80% |
| Blantyre | 13.15% | 7.86% | 78.43% | 45.40% | 37.60% |
| Mwanza | 25.14% | 4.60% | 69.05% | 40.50% | 32.30% |
| Thyolo | 19.87% | 7.66% | 71.94% | 40.40% | 31.30% |
| Mulanje | 20.83% | 11.83% | 66.71% | 40.30% | 26.70% |
| Chikwawa | 38.54% | 3.36% | 56.76% | 38.30% | 29.10% |
| Nsanje | 52.89% | 2.87% | 42.65% | 34.90% | 28.40% |

Election results were taken from *Malawi Government Gazette.* Rates of voter turnout were calculated as a percentage of population, using the *Malawi Population and Housing Census for 1987* (Zomba, Malawi: National Statistics Office, 1993). In 1987, population distribution above age fifteen (the voting public in 1994) was fairly uniform across all districts, making it a stable baseline for calculating voter turnout.

vey, census or ethnography has ever shown that these represent demographic majorities or distinct cultural types. The record shows instead that Malawi's population is made up of Bantu peasants whose social practices are so similar that only modest differences distinguish them from each other; as a Ngoni man working in a Chewa area once told me, "we Malawians are eighty percent alike." In the absence of "hard" cultural boundaries, there is also little documentary agreement about the number of groups in Malawi. Mary Tew's 1950 survey, for example, describes a very intricate ethnic mosaic in the area of Lake Malawi and locates some twenty-five groups within Malawi. (See map 2). Other mapmakers, however, use far fewer ethnic categories and draw a simpler social landscape, such as Pike and Rimmington who reduce Tew's twenty-five groups to nine by subsuming the northern groups within four categories and the southern groups within five.[10] (See map 3.)

The logic of the simpler ethnographic maps can be found in part in the 1966 census,[11] which tabulated the speakers of thirteen African languages in use in Malawi. Speakers of Nyanja (which includes Chewa, Mang'anja, and Nyanja), Lomwe, Yao, Tumbuka, Tonga, and Sena outnumber speakers of Kokola, Ngoni, Nkonde, Lambya, Sukwa, Nyakyusa, and Swahili, in some instances so dramatically as to justify eliminating from the cartographer's template some of the categories that Tew uses. But it does not fully explain those that remain. Why do Pike and Rimmington differentiate Nyanja from Chewa but not from Mang'anja? Why do they retain "Ngoni" as an ethnic category, when Ngoni-speakers are so few in number?[12] And why does the press describe Chewa, Tumbuka and Yao as Malawi's "main" languages, when the census clearly shows that Tumbuka- (9.1 percent) and Yao-speakers (13.8 percent) are each outnumbered by Lomwe-speakers (14.5 percent), a group that never figures in any Malawian's account of ethnic dominance? (See table 3.)

In Malawi, ethnic "dominance" means cultural visibility, not demographic majorities, and is the result of social policies under colonial and independent administrations and the mobilization of ethnic consciousness during this century. An outline of this history is recounted by Vail and White[13] who show how Tumbuka, Chewa, and Yao identities took shape under colonial rule as a

MAP 2    ETHNIC GROUPS OF MALAWI
Adapted from *Peoples of the Lake Nyasa Region*
by Mary Tew (1950)

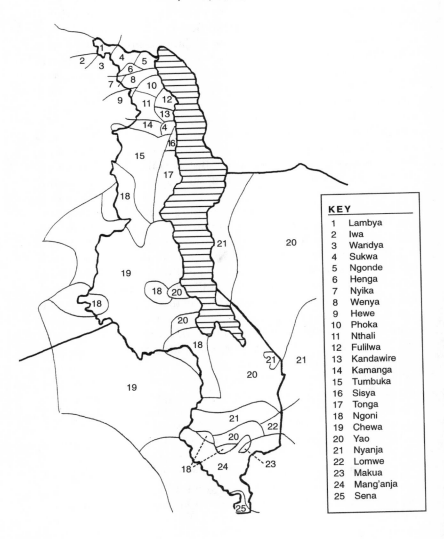

| KEY | |
|---|---|
| 1 | Lambya |
| 2 | Iwa |
| 3 | Wandya |
| 4 | Sukwa |
| 5 | Ngonde |
| 6 | Henga |
| 7 | Nyika |
| 8 | Wenya |
| 9 | Hewe |
| 10 | Phoka |
| 11 | Nthali |
| 12 | Fulilwa |
| 13 | Kandawire |
| 14 | Kamanga |
| 15 | Tumbuka |
| 16 | Sisya |
| 17 | Tonga |
| 18 | Ngoni |
| 19 | Chewa |
| 20 | Yao |
| 21 | Nyanja |
| 22 | Lomwe |
| 23 | Makua |
| 24 | Mang'anja |
| 25 | Sena |

MAP 3   ETHNIC GROUPS OF MALAWI
Adapted from *Malawi: A Geographical Survey*
by J. G. Pike and G. T. Rimmington (1965)

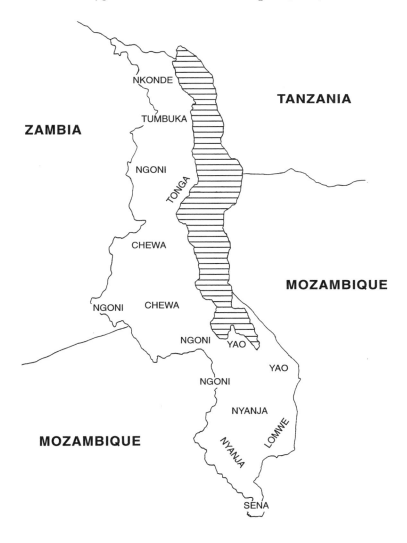

TABLE 3. LANGUAGE GROUPS OF MALAWI*

| | FIRST | % | SECOND | % | THIRD | % | FOURTH | % |
|---|---|---|---|---|---|---|---|---|
| *National* | Nyanja | 50.2 | Lomwe | 14.5 | Yao | 13.8 | Tumbuka | 9.1 |
| *North* | Tumbuka | 63.9 | Tonga | 12.5 | Nkonde | 7.5 | Lambya | 0.6 |
| Chitipa | Lambya | 36.7 | Sukwa | 32.2 | Tumbuka | 20.6 | Nyanja | 0.3 |
| Karonga | Nkonde | 46.4 | Tumbuka | 15.2 | Sukwa | 4.3 | Nyakyusa | 4.2 |
| Nkhata Bay | Tonga | 70.2 | Tumbuka | 18.4 | Nyanja | 10.3 | Yao | 0.2 |
| Rumphi | Tumbuka | 97.0 | Nyanja | 0.7 | Swahili | 0.5 | Tonga | 0.2 |
| Mzimba | Tumbuka | 95.0 | Ngoni | 2.0 | Nyanja | 1.1 | Tonga | 0.9 |
| *Center* | Nyanja | 91.1 | Yao | 3.6 | Tumbuka | 2.9 | Tonga | 0.7 |
| Kasungu | Nyanja | 61.6 | Tumbuka | 37.0 | Tonga | 0.3 | Yao | 0.2 |
| Nkhotakota | Nyanja | 82.5 | Tonga | 14.5 | Tumbuka | 2.2 | Yao | 1.0 |
| Ntchisi | Nyanja | 98.0 | Yao | 0.2 | Tumbuka | 0.1 | Tonga | 0.1 |
| Dowa | Nyanja | 97.7 | Yao | 0.8 | Tumbuka | 0.7 | Lomwe | 0.1 |
| Salima | Nyanja | 82.9 | Yao | 14.1 | Tumbuka | 0.5 | Lomwe | 0.4 |
| Lilongwe | Nyanja | 95.7 | Yao | 2.2 | Tumbuka | 0.6 | Lomwe | 0.3 |
| Mchinji | Nyanja | 89.9 | Yao | 0.9 | Ngoni | 0.8 | Tumbuka | 0.5 |
| Dedza | Nyanja | 89.5 | Yao | 9.7 | Lomwe | 0.1 | Tumbuka | 0.1 |
| Ntcheu | Nyanja | 95.5 | Yao | 2.2 | Ngoni | 0.5 | Lomwe | 0.5 |
| *South* | Nyanja | 32.8 | Lomwe | 28.1 | Yao | 24.3 | Sena | 6.8 |
| Mangochi | Yao | 79.7 | Nyanja | 14.3 | Lomwe | 4.5 | Ngoni | 0.4 |
| Machinga | Yao | 50.7 | Lomwe | 24.4 | Nyanja | 19.7 | Ngoni | 3.7 |
| Zomba | Nyanja | 41.3 | Lomwe | 29.2 | Yao | 26.1 | Ngoni | 1.3 |
| Chiradzulu | Lomwe | 38.0 | Nyanja | 36.3 | Yao | 23.1 | Ngoni | 1.3 |
| Blantyre* | Nyanja | 57.5 | Yao | 23.4 | Lomwe | 7.8 | Ngoni | 5.0 |
| Thyolo | Nyanja | 34.1 | Lomwe | 32.2 | Kokola | 23.9 | Yao | 5.0 |
| Mulanje | Lomwe | 66.7 | Nyanja | 21.4 | Kokola | 6.6 | Yao | 3.9 |
| Chikwawa | Nyanja | 52.1 | Sena | 33.6 | Lomwe | 6.1 | Yao | 1.4 |
| Nsanje | Sena | 72.9 | Nyanja | 20.4 | Kokola | 2.3 | Lomwe | 1.9 |

Figures are taken from *Malawi Population Census 1966*. Although this table only includes four languages per ares surveyed, there were many more reported in the census. The complete list of languages is: Nyanja (50.2%), Lomwe (14.5%), Yao (13.8%), Tumbuka (9.1%), Sena (3.5%), Kokola (2.3%), Tonga (1.9%), Ngoni (1.1%), Nkonde (0.9%), Lambya (0.6%), Sukwa (0.6%), Nyakyusa (0.1%), Swahili (0.1%), and English (0.0%).

*In 1966, Mwanza was part of Blantyre District and was surveyed as such for the census.

result of the following practices: (1) the creation of written forms of Chewa and Tumbuka languages by missionaries, and their establishment as lingua franca by colonial administrators; (2) the training of Tumbuka and Yao intelligentsias by missionary schools; and (3) indirect rule which designated relations of domination and subordination among Africans along ethnic lines, such as Yao over Lomwe. These developments gave some people greater access to social resources than others, while also providing them with the insignia, such as standardized languages, of their collective identities as tribesmen. The result was the high visibility of the Chewa, the Tumbuka, and the Yao people, but not the Ngonde, the Tonga, the Lomwe, the Sena, and so on.

This account of ethnic mobilization exposed the underpinnings of political identity in colonial Nyasaland and forecast with eerie precision the outcome of Malawi's 1994 elections. Tumbuka, Chewa, and Yao candidates did move to the front of the pack, while candidates of other ethnicities seemed not to exist, a testimony to their invisibility in the public imagination and to their lack of access to resources that give entry to national politics. This does not mean, however, that *regionalism* and *tribalism* are synonymous, for although the three candidates drew voters of their own ethnicity to the polls, more than 40 percent of the electorate were not Tumbuka, or Chewa, or Yao and supported candidates outside their own ethnicities. That 40 percent was decisive in determining the outcome of the election. (See table 4.)

Two questions must be addressed: What were the forces driving *regional* constituencies? And why do the press and the public believe that ethnic loyalties were decisive? The answers are to be found in the political era preceding the election, when President Banda took over the reins of power from the British colonial office and set out to consolidate a new nation with himself securely at the helm. Two aspects of his program for nation-building were critical in shaping the political landscape. The first was his decision to rule with absolute authority, shutting out all voices of opposition and generating pervasive sentiments of disaffection in government and in civil society. The second was his program for social development which was predicated on regional and ethnic favoritism, promoting the Chewa center to the detriment of the

TABLE 4. PRESIDENTIAL CANDIDATES, ETHNICITY
AND VOTING BLOCKS

| CANDIDATE | CANDIDATE'S ETHNICITY | SIZE OF ETHNIC GROUP AS % OF POPULATION | | VOTES WON AS % OF VOTES CAST |
|-----------|----------------------|-------------|-------------|-----------------|
|           |                      | *1946*      | *1966*      |                 |
| *Muluzi*  | Yao                  | 11.2        | 13.8        | 47.2            |
| *Banda*   | Chewa [Nyanja]       | 28.3        | [50.2]      | 33.5            |
| *Chihana* | Tumbuka              | 7.4         | 9.1         | 18.0            |

The electoral results are taken from the *Malawi Government Gazette*, the 1946 ethnicity figures from Pryor (25), and the 1966 ethnicith figures from *Malawi Population Census 1966* (see table 3). I include the 1946 figures because the 1966 census does not differentiate Chewa from other languages in the Nyanja cluster and does not specify the number of Chewa-speakers within the 50.2% of the population who are Nyanja-speakers. The fact that the totals for Yao and Tumbuka differ for the two periods is additional evidence of the imprecision of linguistic and ethnic boundaries. (See n. 19.)

non-Chewa north and south. The result was a nation attuned to the language of tribalism and divided on regional lines, the language and the lines emanating from the state which purported to be the sole agent of national unity.

PRESIDENT BANDA AND THE MALAWI CONGRESS
PARTY, 1964–1994

Dr. Hastings Kamuzu Banda and the Malawi Congress Party assumed control of Malawi in 1964, inheriting a polity and administrative system created under British colonial rule. International, regional, and district boundaries were already established as was the system of governance. The only thing that distinguished the new regime from the old one was the widespread popular support it enjoyed, an expression of pervasive anticolonialism that had fueled the rise of Malawi nationalism.[14] However, that support eroded as competing political interests within the nationalist coalition began to lobby the Banda government for recognition and as President Banda made clear his intention to tolerate no criticism from within.

The first rupture was the Cabinet Crisis of 1964 when Banda

dismissed founding members of the Nyasaland African Congress, then Cabinet Ministers, for opposing his policy direction and his pretensions to absolute rule.[15] Some fled the country, and some were pursued by MCP special branch officers who targeted them for assassination or abduction. This proved to be the first episode of what became a fixed feature of the MCP government: the banning, detention, maiming and murder of Banda's rivals within government and his critics outside it.[16]

In addition to these well-publicized assaults against his rivals, President Banda developed complex instruments of social control in order to maintain broad-based political security. To establish the reach of the MCP into the countryside and into specific loci of potential disaffection, the architecture of the party was extended throughout the country through a network of local committees and representatives. This network linked all Malawians, villagers and university professors, teapickers and estate managers, to a chain of communication that led ultimately to the party elite: whispers of sedition at the bottom could be repeated at the top. The Malawi Young Pioneers (MYP) were also created as a cadre of Banda enthusiasts who ran high-profile development projects while also providing the manpower for the party's paramilitary wing. A formidable organization, the MYP were empowered to intimidate lawbreakers and to harass any citizens earmarked as "troublemakers" by the MCP. Typically Young Pioneers could be seen manning roadblocks and policing markets to sell the party cards that Malawians were required to buy. The constant presence of MYP and MCP representatives guaranteed the high visibility of the Banda government in everyday life, while reminding everyone of the high price to be paid for disloyalty.

While the elite core of the MCP perfected the mechanisms of control and coercion, they also sought to shore up their bases of support. Patronage was extended to loyal cabinet ministers and members of parliament by subsidizing their entry into Malawi's small commercial economy, especially tobacco and sugar production. The meant offering low interest loans to new African-owned estates, using moneys gleaned from the Agricultural Development and Marketing Board (ADMARC); giving the estate sector a monopoly on the most profitable crops; and cutting off the flow of migrant labor to South Africa to create a cheap supply of farm labor at home.[17] The result was a rising class of politicians cum capitalists who owed their fortunes to the Banda regime.

Banda also solicited loyalty from rural Malawians by developing lines of patronage among them. First, he cultivated the territorial chiefs, known as Traditional Authorities, who administered the countryside and served as judges in the Traditional Courts. The chiefs were an important mechanism for ensuring the passivity, if not the enthusiasm, of the village population, and for exerting leverage against his political opponents, since the Traditional Courts were empowered to try treason cases and the accused came primarily from the ranks of government.[18] Second, he sought specific constituencies of so-called ordinary Malawians within the country's vast peasant population. In this effort, the regime turned its gaze primarily to the central region and its majority Chewa population, seeking there the quintessential Malawian citizen and party loyalist. In this context, Chewa ethnicity and regionalism acquired political importance.

The decision to develop a Chewa base of support was based on Banda's own ethnic origins and the fact that though a minority, Chewa are Malawi's single largest ethnic group (see maps 2 and 3). In fact, under Banda, Chewa, Nyanja, and Mang'anja were consolidated within a single language group, allowing him to claim that Chewa were the majority population. (See table 3.) [19] Whatever their numbers, Chewa were not, however, politically central at the time of independence. The heart of Malawi's commercial economy lay in the south, the best educational facilities in the north, and as a consequence the party and the civil service were dominated by northerners (especially Tumbuka and Ngoni) and southerners (especially Yao). The most significant characteristics of the Chewa center were its ethnic homogeneity and the relative *im*mobility of its population. Cultivating the Chewa as a support group had to be done against the prevailing concentrations of political and economic influence already in place.

The creation of a rural Chewa constituency was undertaken at three levels: the investment of capital into the central region to develop its economy from the ground up; the creation of differential educational standards to give central region pupils a leg up in urban employment; and the Chewalization of a Malawian national identity through language policy and political iconography. The single most important program for economic development was the relocation of the national capital from Zomba in the south to Lilongwe in the center. A minor provincial trade center at the time of independence, Lilongwe was built up almost entirely from scratch, requiring substantial investment in infrastructure to support government services, international offices, new commercial ventures, and a massive influx of population. Within a few years, Lilongwe City had acquired the futuristic "new city center," a new government hospital, two of the four campuses of the University of Malawi, an international airport, several development and research stations, and acre upon acre of suburban neighborhood. This rapid build-up made the Chewa heartland highly visible as the political center of a modernizing nation, while also creating a locus of economic opportunity for the surrounding population. Suddenly rural Chewa had a major market for their goods and labor in their own backyards.

Although the new capital city was the most conspicuous effort to develop the central region, other projects revealed a similar interest in stimulating the economy there. Early in Banda's administration, national policy objectives for rural development were drafted that aimed to raise the standard of living of the peasantry by increasing cash-crop production among them.[20] The policy was tested in four projects initiated between 1968 and 1972, distributed among the country's three regions, with the Lilongwe and Lake Shore (Salima) projects in the center, the Shire Valley project in the south, and the Karonga/Chitipa project in the north. Although the policy was explicitly national, and the projects geographically dispersed—one north, one south, one east, one west—the regional bias was evident in the unequal allocation of project resources to the center. Not only was the central region the site of two projects, but these two were the first initiated, the longest in operation, and the recipients of the most money. Greatest attention was given to the Lilongwe project near the national capital which received forty-two of the sixty-six farmer training centers distributed among the four projects.[21]

The ten years of rural development inputs had a measurable impact on the peasant economy, to wit, a fourfold increase in smallholder production of cash crops, contributing 36 percent to Malawi's agricultural export earnings. These improvements were owed primarily to rises in tobacco and groundnut production in the central region which in 1971/72 accounted for 86 percent of ADMARC's profits. As a consequence the Lilongwe project was held up as a showpiece of market-oriented rural development planning to World Bank funders.[22] Thereafter the projects were absorbed within the National Rural Development Programme (NRDP), which divided the country into nine Agricultural Development Divisions with the aim of investing additional capital into rural development on a more broadly national basis. However, the level of funding under NRDP never matched that of the Lilongwe and Lake Shore projects, as a result of which the boom of the project years was shortlived. Still the farmers who had benefited from those projects had received a sufficient leg up in commercial production to set them ahead of their neighbors in subsequent years.

The investment of state resources in the Chewa peasantry cannot be taken at face value as the process by which a poor peasantry was transformed into a wealthy one, nor can one assume that the state had cultivated a broadly inclusive and loyal clientele among all Chewa. It is not clear how many households actually received the patronage that flowed from project resources, nor is it clear that cash-crop farmers enjoyed a dramatic rise in their standards of living.[23] Still, rural development provided the means for extending patronage along specific lines into the Chewa peasantry by targeting its most high status members, namely, territorial chiefs and village headmen who were invariably the first and most frequent recipients of state aid.[24] As such, development aid flowed along the same channels as the administrative hierarchy and the MCP cell structure, strengthening the government's base of support among a strategic group of clients within the Chewa population and securing them as an instrument through which the state could control the rest. In the meantime, the economic productivity of the central region did rise, thanks to rural development inputs, enhancing the impression, north and south, that all Chewa were recipients of the state's largesse to the neglect of everyone else.

The same message of ethnic privilege was conveyed by the promotion of Chewa through the educational system and by Banda's decision to Chewalize a national identity. The first was accomplished by establishing different grading standards for the three regions, allowing Chewa students to matriculate to secondary schools with much lower test scores than those required of northern and southern students.[25] The result was increasing numbers of Chewa in the civil service and in the personal debt of the Banda government. The second was accomplished primarily by establishing Chichewa as the national language. This was a departure from colonial policy which had recognized two languages, Chinyanja and Chitumbuka, as lingua franca, both of which were written and in use in the media and the civil service. In 1968, Chinyanja, renamed Chichewa, became the only African language in official use, while all others, including Chitumbuka, were forbidden in government offices, schools, the press, and radio.[26]

Although the new language policy was explained as a practical mechanism to foster communication and national unity, the extent to which it entailed a new mythology of Malawi's cultural identity soon became apparent. In the 1970s, the Office of the President established the Department of Linguistics and Chichewa at Chancellor College in Zomba, against the recommendation of the linguists who sought a more inclusive Department of African Languages.[27] At the same time, the president was referred to as permanent head of department, in which capacity he would occasionally address the nation on Malawi radio to clear up questions about Chichewa syntax, vocabulary, and pronunciation, even though decades of living in America and England had long since eroded his fluency.[28] Linguistic incompetence notwithstanding, Chewa identity was Malawi identity, and the president was the embodiment of both.

The promotion of Chichewa went hand in hand with the promotion of Chewa culture as the cornerstone of nationhood and the source of its political iconography. The term *Nkhoswe* or "Mother's Brother" Number One became Banda's epithet, identifying him as the guardian of the nation, while the reciprocal term *mbumba* or "female dependency group" was given to the women who danced for him at political rallies. This was part of an effort to naturalize the relationship between ruler and ruled in terms meaningful to a matrilineal people (i.e., the Chewa) while also establishing for the many patrilineal areas of Malawi (especially the north) the authority of Chewa categories for all of them.

Similarly the Chewa masked dancers known as *Nyau* or *Gule Wamkulu* were solicited to perform for the president at these same rallies, giving a Chewa cultural institution pride of place on a national stage. Although the same honor was given to the Ngoni war dance, Ngoma, only the Chewa dancers became popularly identified with the authority of the state, reflected in the colloquial use of the term "Gule Wamkulu" to refer to MCP supporters.

## CHEWALIZATION AND THE NON-CHEWA NORTH AND SOUTH

President Banda's attempt to create a national identity through language policy and cultural promotion is a form of official nationalism described by Anderson as "the means . . . for stretching the short, tight, skin of the nation over the gigantic body of the empire."[29] Although Malawi can hardly be called gigantic, its ethnic and linguistic diversity ran counter to the President's claims of national cohesion and justified his decision to nationalize Chichewa in order to homogenize the citizenry and bind it to the political elite. Similarly, the relocation of the capital in Lilongwe was a credible strategy for promoting national unity, since with the seat of government exactly midway between the north and south, the center could stand for the whole.

Official nationalism was not, however, simply an exercise in the symbolism of unity, for it was communicated alongside policies of political and economic favoritism that belied the symbolic message and revealed its seamy underside. As Williams and Foster[30] have argued, when one ethnicity is privileged above many as a nation's mainstream citizenry, national cohesion exists only from the standpoint of the mainstream, while the rest must negotiate ambiguous identities as citizens who are not fully national. In Malawi, the privileges were neither subtle nor ambiguous, for President Banda identified Malawi's mainstream in explicit opposition to marginal groups, celebrating Chewa language and culture, investing heavily in the Chewa rural economy, and opening the doors of higher education more widely to Chewa than to anybody else. The result was lines of fission through the allegedly seamless whole, with the rifts between Chewa and non-Chewa, center and non-center, growing ever wider beneath and in spite of Banda's pronouncements of national unity.

This was most apparent in the "Tumbuka north." At the time of independence, not only was Chitumbuka already a written language, but a Chitumbuka-speaking intelligentsia, some of the original organizers of the Malawi Congress Party, occupied key positions in government. They were among the elites swept out during the Cabinet Crisis of 1964.[31] Chitumbuka-speakers continued to enter the ranks of Malawi's intelligentsia, thanks to the educational facilities of the Livingstonia mission in Rumphi and its satellite schools in the north, but they became the repeated target of Banda's accusations of tribalism and of punitive acts by the state. As recently as 1988 northerners on the Malawi National Examination Board were accused of skewing the results of the Certificate of Education exams and were dismissed. Similarly in 1989, northerners teaching in central and southern region schools were accused of deliberately miseducating their students in order to give northern children an unfair advantage; they were removed from their positions and relocated in northern schools.[32]

Neither language policy nor political abuse, however, account for the politicization of the north as a whole, for the harassment of teachers and civil servants involved only a small, relatively elite group, the majority of whom were probably Tumbuka and Ngoni from the immediate vicinity of the Livingstonia mission. But the vilification of educated northerners occurred alongside the economic stagnation of the region as a whole, not only the Tumbuka/ Ngoni districts of Rumphi and Mzimba, but the non-Tumbuka districts of Chitipa, Karonga, and Nkhata Bay as well. The region's depressed economy was already in evidence during the colonial period, a function of inadequate farmland, lack of commercial development, and the drain of labor out of the region. The northern economy continued to stagnate under the Banda government in part because there was no fledgling commercial industry (like tobacco production) to cultivate, and in part because there was no effort made by the state to fuel development: its one project was not well subsidized, roads and communications were modernized grudgingly or not at all, and the medical and educational facilities received little attention. Whatever the source of the north's dead economy, the fact of it was amply indicated by the sparsity of its population.

The dead economy was critical in consolidating the region as a cohesive seat of opposition to the regime. Thus the abuse of Chitumbuka-speaking elites took place alongside the economic deprivation of the northern peasantry, making the experience of marginalization as acute in the non-Tumbuka areas of the extreme north as in the Tumbuka area closer to the Chewa heartland. So too, when Banda spoke of the achievements of his National Rural Development Programme, they were not in evidence in northern villages, and when he spoke ill of "northerners," though he had Tumbuka-speaking professionals in mind, Tonga and Ngonde villagers were implicated.

The southern region also became a seat of political opposition, although less cohesively than the north, a function of its more ambiguous relationship with the Banda government. On the one hand, the south was subject to the same inequities as the north: higher test scores were required of southern school leavers, little state aid was invested in peasant production, and local elites were subject to Banda's relentless search for the enemy within. But unlike the north, the south was not subject to repeated accusations of tribalism nor to any other stereotypy as southerners. In fact, Banda went to some pains to define "Chewa" broadly enough to include much of the southern population within the national mainstream: "Chewa" referred also to Nyanja, Mang'anja, and even Lomwe, suggesting that a commonality of language, culture, and history bound the south to the center and both to Banda's own cadre of elites.[33] This expansive definition of "the Chewa" was not wholly absurd, since dialects of Nyanja were in common usage in the south, and since, therefore, the new language policy did not automatically exempt all southerners from cultural citizenship, as it did northerners. But aside from the resurrection of one Mang'anja paramountcy,[34] Banda's claims of cultural inclusion were not backed up with any material benefits for the so-called southern Chewa. As southerners they were afforded none of the privileges extended to the central region, making the claims of cultural brotherhood an empty gesture.

If the efforts to embrace some southerners as Chewa was an exercise in rhetoric only, the failure to extend that courtesy to Yao marked them as the most marginal of the marginalized. Yao were regarded always as emigres from Mozambique who were distinguished from "true Malawians" by language, custom, and origin.[35] They are also the only predominantly Muslim group (among Africans) in this officially Christian country and were, therefore, "other" by virtue of religion as well as ethnicity. Yao thus became Malawi's quintessential resident outsider, a position of structural ambiguity of precisely the type noted by Williams. And although in principle Yao were no more the victims of regional inequities than any other southerner, according to Human Rights Watch observers, they figure largely as targets of political reprisals perpetrated under President Banda.[36]

The manipulations of ethnic and national identities may have been enough to discredit the Banda regime in the eyes of southerners, but his economic policies toward the region were probably more serious sources of disaffection. Unlike the underpopulated north, the south is overpopulated, owing to its rich landscape which sustains peasant production, estate agriculture, and Malawi's largest urban population. Banda's development policies took heed of the south's strategic position within the national economy. On the one hand he deemphasized peasant production and urban expansion, concentrating development resources in the central region where capital investment could increase productivity and decrease out-migration. On the other hand, he supported the interests of south's plantation economy, seeking to expand the estate sector by turning more land over to new estate owners— primarily his political clients—and by securing for them a cheap source of local labor. This meant closing off labor migration to South Africa, outlawing labor unions, and refusing to raise wages of migrant and tenant labor. A dramatic reversal of his preindependence politics, Banda allied himself with plantation owners, white and black, and reneged on all promises to poor black farm workers.

The expansion of plantation agriculture was not limited to the south, for new estates were opened up in all three regions, doubling the acreage of that sector during Banda's rule.[37] But because the infrastructure (roads, transport, auction floors) was already in place in the south, it was the preferred site of estate farming, even though its high population density meant that the region could least afford the expansion. As a consequence, southern estate owners enjoyed state subsidies and protections, while their work force endured ever diminishing resources and alternative liveli- hoods. This in turn produced large pockets of disaffection among the southern poor, securing them, regardless of their ethnicity, as voices of opposition to the regime.

## DEMOCRATIZATION AND THE 1994 ELECTIONS

Many African dictators like President Banda were able to with- stand internal pressure for democratization for the duration of the cold war, given the international community's collective disin- terest in African domestic politics; as long as their statesmen were on the "right" side of global alignments, they were free to pursue any political strategies they liked within their own borders. Cer- tainly Banda, who championed capitalism, repudiated commu- nism, and maintained open trade relations with South Africa, ruled securely for nearly thirty years, while protecting Malawi from the military interferences visited upon his neighbors to the east and west. But the end of the cold war altered the African political landscape, in part because civilians were inspired by the collapse of one-party states in eastern Europe to agitate for liberalization in their own, and in part because international observers would no longer ignore human rights violations among their third-world clients.

Popular agitation against the Banda regime began in 1992 with a public letter of protest by the Catholic Bishops of Malawi against the president. Despite—or because of—Banda's threats to banish the bishops and rumors of a plot to assassinate them, the letter inspired protest rallies on college campuses and led ultimately to rioting in Malawi's cities. Although police were able to contain the unrest, they were not able to quell the spirit of rebellion, and with unprecedented recklessness, university personnel, civil servants and factory workers became active agitators for reform. Chief among the protestors was Chakufwa Chihana, a Tumbuka trade unionist from the north and founding member of the MCP. Long since exiled by Banda, Chihana returned to Malawi in 1992 to assist in the organization of the resistance and was promptly jailed for his efforts, a move that only increased his popularity in the public eye. A less notorious but still important voice of protest came from Bakili Muluzi, a Yao businessman from the south and former Secretary General of the MCP who had been expelled from the party in 1980 under (unproven) allegations of embezzling party funds. Now pursuing private business interests, Muluzi also emerged from the political shadows to join the anti-Banda resistance.[38]

The reform movement would have been just another aborted episode of internal agitation had the international community not interceded, but Malawi's foreign allies did declare their support for the protestors, lobbied for the release of Chihana and other political prisoners, and ultimately held foreign aid hostage to democratization. President Banda was forced to yield, freeing Chihana in 1993 and holding a referendum for multiparty elections the same year. The referendum proved to be a vote of no-confidence in the regime, with 63 percent supporting a multiparty democracy in opposition to Banda, 35 percent supporting a single-party state in support of Banda. Multiparty voters came mainly from the north and south, single-party voters from the Chewa center. (See table 1.)

If democratization was now inevitable, the outcome of the upcoming elections was not, as evidenced by the democratization movements taking place elsewhere in Africa. In Zambia, where general elections followed the referendum by just a few months, the sitting President Kaunda lost his bid for reelection to a resoundingly cohesive opposition. In Kenya, in contrast, where a full year lapsed between the legalization of opposition parties and the general elections, the opposition fragmented into numerous ethnically particular constituencies, allowing the sitting President Moi to win reelection with a minority vote. President Banda knew that with 35 percent of the vote—his Chewa constituency—he was guaranteed a second place finish, and that he could win reelection outright if the opposition fragmented into many small pieces. Hoping to emulate the Kenyan example, he chose to delay the election as long as possible, setting the date for May 1994, one year after the referendum.

During the intervening year the MCP set out to shore up its base of support in the center, to extend its influence north and especially south, and to discredit and intimidate its opponents.

This meant investing its considerable resources into rallies, gifts, and political bribes, and using the media that Press Inc. monopolized—the printers, the newspaper outlets, and the radio—to obstruct the opposition's access to the public. They also ordered the Young Pioneers to intimidate opposition organizers by breaking up political rallies, seizing voter registration cards, and assaulting citizens who dared to wear the wrong party buttons. As a campaign strategy the last effort backfired, since it led the Transition Council to disband the paramilitary, and prompted the Army to rout and disarm them when President Banda failed to heed the directive.[39] But even without its muscle, the MCP still held a near monopoly on campaign resources, enabling them to coerce many voters into silence where it could not garner their support.

In the meantime, several opposition parties were formed, beginning with Chihana's Alliance for Democracy and Muluzi's United Democratic Front. Eventually seven opposition parties and five presidential candidates emerged, suggesting that the opposition was in fact in turmoil. The fragmentation did not, however, reflect any ideological disputes, as indicated by the remarkable similarities among the party platforms: all promised to alleviate poverty, control inflation, and protect human rights, and all were similarly unspecific about their methods to do so. Nor did the fragmentation reflect further ethnic particularization. Of the five presidential candidates, two were Tumbuka, two were Chewa, and one was Yao, the same three ethnicities overrepresented among Malawi's intelligentsia whence presidential hopefuls emerged. The proliferation of opposition parties was simply an expression of political enthusiasm, self-igniting in a country where political discussion had been too long suppressed. More significant was the fact that as the election drew near, an opposition coalition girded itself together against their common enemy, persuading one of the presidential candidates to withdraw from the race in order to prevent a Kenya-like victory for Banda.[40]

The MCP did in the end hold onto most of its constituencies, but the opposition was sufficiently cohesive to resist disintegration, dividing not into many pieces based on ethnicity, but into two pieces based on region. Chihana and Aford won the northern districts, Muluzi and UDF won all but one of the southern districts, and Banda and MCP took most of the central region (see map 1 and table 2). The cohesion of the opposition was also reflected in the breakdown of the votes district by district, where significant contests were waged between not opposition parties but one of two opposition parties and the MCP: in all districts but one MCP came in either first or second,[41] and in only one district was the split between opposition parties decisive in securing a victory for MCP.[42] With the opposition split into regional blocks, the election outcome was simply a function of population distribution, dense in the south and sparse in the north. Thus UDF won with 47 percent, MCP came in second with 33 percent, and Aford came in third with 18 percent.

## REGIONALISM VERSUS ETHNICITY IN THE ELECTION

Why did regionalism have so profound a claim on political loyalties? If the north and the south were alike in their opposition to the MCP, why was Chihana unable to win any constituencies in the center or the south, and Muluzi unable to win any in the north? The answer lies in the historical relationships of the two regions to the Banda government. The north was despised and disadvantaged by the regime on all counts, for it was neglected economically, obstructed politically, and vilified publicly as the "wrong" ethnicity. This was symbolized by the promotion of Chichewa as the national language, scarcely in use anywhere in the north. The advantages that the north did enjoy, namely, the superior educational facilities at Livingstonia and the highest rate of literacy in the country, were overridden by an educational policy that obstructed the path of northerners into the civil service and government. The result was broad-based solidarity across all northern districts in opposition to the regime to such a degree that only their own candidate, the highly educated and much abused Chihana, could represent their collective identity vis-à-vis the state. This was borne out in the election when Chihana won almost 90 percent of the northern vote and drew the highest rate of voter turnout in the country, with little variation in the region's five districts. (See table 2.)

The south had a more ambiguous relationship with the Banda government. Instead of suffering political exclusion, economic neglect, and ethnic denigration as a whole, the south was home

to numerous subregional communities whose relations to the
regime were shaped by local particularities of class structure and
ethnic composition. Some southerners were typical Malawians,
others were not; some were successful rural entrepreneurs, others
were exploited plantation labor; some made significant educational achievements only to be cut off by unfair testing standards,
others had never had educational advantages and were unaffected
by the state's educational policies. The south's more variegated
economy meant more complex social strata and more ambiguous
interactions with government policies, and this in turn meant less
political cohesion as a region and less consistent support for the
home candidate. Thus, unlike the north, voter behavior in the
south varied considerably district by district: turnout ranged between eleven percentage points below the national average to four
points above it,[43] and support for the home candidate ranged
between 43 percent and 91 percent.[44] So too, while Muluzi won
the south, he did so with a less exceptional 78 percent of the
regional vote and the lowest voter turnout in the country—about
three percentage points below the national average. He also drew
the lowest rate of voter turnout in the country, ranging at the
district level from over eleven percentage points below the national average (the lowest turnout in the country) to over four
percentage points above it. These figures suggest not that Muluzi's
southern constituencies were ambivalent, but that the south was
less cohesive than the north as a political entity. By the same
token, Chihana's reputation as a champion of the *north* must
have cost him political credibility outside his home region: as a
northerner first and Malawian second, Chihana's represented a
version of citizenship that was too reminiscent of Banda's.

The political importance of regionalism becomes even more
apparent when we examine the election data for evidence of
ethnic alignments. All three presidential frontrunners were supported by their own ethnic groups,[45] and ethnic mobilization
was especially noticeable in Tumbuka and Yao areas where voter
turnout was unusually high, and where Chihana's and Muluzi's
margins of victory were greatest.[46] Evidently, a candidate who
appealed to oppositional politics *and* ethnic solidarity enjoyed an
enthusiastic support base. But ethnic backing was decisive only for
President Banda, who would not have made a credible showing

without his Chewa constituencies. For the opposition candidates, ethnic loyalty was statistically insignificant, accounting for fewer than half the districts they won, and securing neither Aford's victory in the north nor UDF's victory overall.[47]

Still, ethnicity may have been an important variable for the opposition parties insofar as ethnic minorities consistently voted against MCP. Thus, districts without Chewa, Tumbuka, or Yao majorities went to opposition candidates,[48] while those with large minority populations gave them large minority support.[49] This suggests that Malawians who did not self-identify as Chewa, Tumbuka, *or* Yao found a point of commonality with an opposition candidate by virtue of the fact that they were not Chewa. This is ethnicity in the negative, reactive rather than proactive, motivated by a relationship of contrast to the hegemonic group as the significant, self-defining "other."

However, even if reactive ethnicity motivated voter choice, regionalism modified its expression. First, opposition voters consistently supported the candidate from their own region, with the north's non-Tumbuka voters backing Aford, the south's non-Yao voters backing UDF. More significantly, minority groups—non-Chewa, non-Tumbuka, non-Yao—who were divided by regional borders backed the opposition candidates of their own region. Thus, while Ngoni areas consistently voted opposition, northern Ngoni supported Aford, while central and southern Ngoni supported UDF; similarly, while northern Tonga supported Aford, central Tonga—a population contiguous with the northern group—supported UDF. (Compare maps 1 and 3, and tables 2 and 3.) Evidently when ethnic cohesion was mobilized solely in opposition to "Chewaness," it was easily pulled apart by regional affiliation.

Second, regional cohesion was more effective than minority ethnic cohesion in drawing voters to the polls. Thus, voting behavior in the north varied only slightly along ethnic lines: although turnout was highest in the two predominantly Tumbuka districts, it was well above the national average in the other three, with Chihana's margin of victory comparably high in all five districts. In contrast, voting behavior in the south varied noticeably along ethnic lines. Predominantly Yao districts had high voter turnout and gave Muluzi his widest margins of victory, while minority districts had very low turnout and gave Muluzi his narrowest margins of victory and one defeat.[50] Evidently, voter enthusiasm owed more to regional solidarity than to minority ethnic antipathies.[51]

Given the political cohesion of the north, it is tempting to say, as many Malawians do, that the north *is* an ethnicity. However, ethnicity in this case is based not on a common culture or language, but on a common experience of marginalization that became acute during the thirty years of Banda's rule.[52] In fact, insofar as voters throughout Malawi were mobilized for or against Banda, ostensibly ethnic bases of support were manifestations of the state's engagement with particular communities and may not be driven by sentiments of ethnic loyalty at all. Thus, support for UDF among Lomwe and Nyanja plantation labor may have owed less to reactive ethnicity than to class interests as a captive and underpaid work force long abused by the Banda government. By the same token, Chewa support for MCP was shored up, if not wholly engineered, through coercion and control, suggesting that Chewa tribalism owed more to political manipulations by party elites than to grass-roots solidarity.[53] While it may be too much to argue that ethnic loyalty was never a self-generating political force, the evidence indicates that the machinery of Malawi's old regime consistently lay behind appearances of tribalism, acting as the center from which lines of political cleavage radiated.

## CONCLUSION

The forces behind Malawian political identities emanate not from ancient African societies, but from the colonial administration and more recently the independent government which, through its efforts to consolidate the nation and to entrench itself within it, created the conditions and the content of factionalism. In so doing, the Banda government undermined itself and its own program for nation-building. Or did it? For thirty years, Banda's government was the main mover of capital in Malawi, the principal source of urban employment, and the uncontested voice in policy formation and implementation. In this location, it trained the eyes of all Malawians on itself, establishing the fact of a national community even as it drew the faultlines within it. Thus regionalism surfaced in the context of a *national* election, when Malawian voters considered who they were and where their interests lay vis-à-vis the state and each other. In this sense, official nationalism accomplished its purpose, impressing upon Malawians the fact of their common identity as citizens, whether or not they liked the cultural content of citizenship. This is not to deny that Malawianness was problematic, for by privileging the center over the north and the south, and the Chewa over everyone else, Banda made some citizens more Malawian than others and gave some citizens greater access to public resources than others. But notwithstanding the fissioning of the electorate and murmurs of a pending northern secession, Malawi remained intact, revealing that an unpopular regime did not betoken a fragile state or a fractile nation.

This suggests that nationality, regionality and ethnicity are not intrinsically incompatible as loci of identity, but are equally "imaginable" as political communities. As such, Malawians are not hopelessly divided, but oriented around categories of identity that are fluid, overlapping and mobilized in oppositional contexts. This is illustrated by friends of mine who, in the 1980s, distinguished themselves from each other as Ngoni *or* Tumbuka, but in 1994 self-identified as "northerners" who voted together against the Banda government. Similar positionalities drove political coalitions throughout Malawi as voters declared themselves in sympathy or antipathy with the MCP and chose their candidates on the basis of region and ethnicity, proactive and reactive.

Still, if identity shifts according to context, it is not infinitely elastic, for it assumed a form in the elections that the new democratic order will retain. The three national parties now see themselves as regional organizations and have reorganized their elite core on that basis. Admittedly Muluzi's failure to win an absolute parliamentary majority forced him to seek support outside his regional base, but he did so by appealing to regional interests. He courted northerners by reinstating Chitumbuka in the media and by promising them improved roads, a new hospital and a university campus of their own. And he courted the central region by declaring his intention *not* to prosecute the MCP for past political abuses, and by publicly embracing former President Banda as the father (or mother's brother) of the nation. Ultimately, he consolidated an inter-regional regime within government through a coalition agreement with Aford which gave southerners the Presidency, the First Vice-Presidency, and twenty-eight Cabinet posts, and northerners the Second-Vice Presidency, and seven Cabinet posts. The MCP and their central region constituencies were the losers, indicated by Muluzi's abrupt reversal of his promise not to prosecute MCP elites for past political abuses: days after the coalition agreement, former President Banda and his close associates were arrested for the 1984 murders at Mwanza.

It remains to be seen how regional politics will be played out in the formation of social programs, and how the celebration of national identity will be enacted in the wake of Banda's policies of official nationalism. On the first issue it is clear that Muluzi's initial promises to invest in schools, roads and hospitals were ill-conceived, since the resources do not exist for such expenditures, and since high inflation, low productivity, and a balance of payment crisis are forcing cutbacks on programs and offices already in existence. At the same time, as public discontent with the economy increases, so too will pressure to funnel state resources into specific constituencies to secure political support for beleaguered MPs. It seems likely that patron/client flows will increase not decrease, albeit along lines unrepresented under the previous government.

The fate of national culture is another question. On the one hand, Banda's version of official nationalism has already ended. Chitumbuka has returned to the public media and may emerge as an alternative national language; and the Chewalization of Malawian nationality is not politically practicable, since it cannot be attached to the current head of state nor to the constituencies who supported him. On the other hand, it is unlikely that an alternative national culture can be fashioned around President Muluzi, since as a Yao and a Muslim he is not a sufficiently mainstream to embody an archetypal Malawian identity even for his own support base. It may well be that Muluzi has no choice but to subscribe to the program suggested by Crawford Young: to remove the state from the cultural arena and represent itself as a neutral player according to an iconography of nationalism that is not ethnically marked.

## NOTES

Research in Malawi was supported by the Southern African Research Project of Yale University. I wish to thank Kings Phiri who gave me invaluable help in Malawi, and Bill Foltz, Eric Gable, Angelique Haugerud, Ben Kiernan, Ian Shapiro, Leroy Vail, and Tina West who commented on earlier drafts of the essay. I am also grateful to the participants of the Spring 1995 Workshop of the Southern African Research Project at Yale where a draft of this chapter was discussed, and to Sue Cook who helped prepare the maps.

1. Nineteenth-century social evolutionism and its critique by twentieth-century social anthropology are described by J. W. Burrow in *Evolution and Society* (New York: Cambridge University Press, 1974) and by George W. Stocking in *Race, Culture, and Evolution* (New York: Free Press, 1968) and *Victorian Anthropology* (New York: Free Press, 1987). The "tribe" is deconstructed by Aidan Southall in "The Illusion of Tribe," *Journal of Asian and African Studies* 5 (1970): 28–50; and the argument is incorporated into a general critique of anthropological reifications in Richard Fox, ed., *Recapturing Anthropology* (Santa Fe, N.M.: School of American Research Press, 1991).

2. Crawford Young, *The Politics of Cultural Pluralism* (Madison: University of Wisconsin Press, 1976), 93.

3. Ibid., 97.

4. Ibid., 93.

5. Ibid., 97.

6. Benedict Anderson, *Imagined Communities: Reflections on the Origin and Spread of Nationalism* (New York: Verso, 1991).

7. Ibid., 114.

8. See Robert Foster, "Making National Cultures in the Global Ecumene," *Annual Review of Anthropology* 20 (1991): 235–60; and Brackette Williams, "A Class Act: Anthropology and the Race to Nation Across Ethnic Lines," *Annual Review of Anthropology* 18 (1989): 401–44.

9. As Williams notes, this is not limited to third world nations; for example, the typical British national is white and not black, and more specifically, English and not Scottish, Welsh, or Irish.

10. Mary Tew, *Peoples of the Lake Nyasa Region* (London: Oxford University Press, 1950), leaf.; J. G. Pike and G. T. Rimmington, *Malawi: A Geographical Study* (Oxford: Oxford University Press, 1965), 139.

11. *Malawi Population Census for 1966* (Zomba, Malawi: National Statistics Office, 1966).

12. The Ngoni are a good example of the lack of fit between ethnic

identity and language. The Ngoni came as immigrants from South Africa in the nineteenth century and were a highly visible group under colonial and independent rule, the result of the prominence of Ngoni paramounts during the initial British colonization, rural mobilization around these paramounts against colonial rule, and ethnographic attention by anthropologists. However, the Ngoni language disappeared from use, displaced by Chichewa and Chitumbuka, the languages of the regions where they settled. For this reason, they are barely noticeable in the language census, even thought they are very vocal about their identity as Ngoni, not Tumbuka or Chewa.

13. Leroy Vail and Landeg White, "Tribalism in the Political History of Malawi," in *The Creation of Tribalism in Southern Africa* (Berkeley: University of California Press, 1991).

14. Robert Rotberg, *The Rise of Nationalism in Central Africa: The Making of Malawi and Zambia 1873–1964* (Cambridge: Harvard University Press, 1971).

15. Ibid., 317–21.

16. Among the more celebrated victims of Banda's "thugs" were Orton and Vera Chirwa who were abducted from Zambia and tried for treason in 1981; three cabinet ministers and an MP who were assassinated in the "Mwanza Incident" of 1983; and Jack Mapanje, author of "seditious" poetry, who was detained in 1987 and held in prison without trial for five years. These and other human rights abuses are reported by Africa Watch in *Where Silence Rules: The Suppression of Dissent in Malawi* (New York and Washington, D.C.: Human Rights Watch, 1990).

17. Jonathan Kydd and Robert Christiansen, "Structural Change in Malawi Since Independence: Consequences of a Development Strategy Based on Large-Scale Agriculture," *World Development* 10:5 (1982): 355–75.

18. Africa Watch, *When Silence Rules*, 30–33.

19. These were the categories used in the *Malawi Population Census 1966* , which established that Nyanja is the first language of over half the Malawian population and is understood by more than three-fourths of it. Although this amply justified using Nyanja as an official language, Vail and White claim that these figures were far in excess of standard calculations of the time—how far they do not say—and were inflated to support a language policy that the Banda elite had already made (Vail and White, "Tribalism in the Political History of Malawi," 180, 191 n. 157). Language use has not been resurveyed in 1966, so there is no way to test the veracity of either the Malawi Census or Vail and White's counter claim.

20. These objectives were described in *Nyasaland Government Development Plan 1962/65* (Zomba Government Printer, 1962), *A Statement of*

*Development Policies 1971–80* (Zomba Government Printer, 1971), and *A Foreword to Development Policies 1971–82* (Zomba Government Printer, 1971).

21. The following table is taken from Richard Mkandawire, "Markets, Peasants and Agrarian Change in Post-Independence Malawi" (Research Paper, Bunda College of Agriculture, Lilongwe, Malawi, 1985), and shows the resources in Malawian kwacha allocated to the four projects.

| PROJECT | PHASES | COST (K. MILL) | FAMILIES IN PROJECT AREA | TARGET OF ADOPTING FARMERS |
|---------|--------|----------------|--------------------------|----------------------------|
| Lilongwe | I-III | 22.8 | 104,000 | 45,900 |
| Shire | I-II | 15.1 | 70,000 | 28,000 |
| Lake Shore | I-III | 20.2 | 67,000 | 21,000 |
| Karonga | I-II | 13.6 | 36,000 | 12,900 |

Mkandawire also reports that the sixty-six farmer training centers were distributed among the four projects as follows: forty-two were built in the Lilongwe project, eleven in the Lake Shore project, seven in the Shire Valley project, and six in Karonga/Chitipa. This amounts to one training center per 2,500 families in Lilongwe, one per 6,000 in Shire Valley and Lake Shore, and one in 10,000 in Karonga. See Richard Mkandawire, "Markets, Peasants, and Agrarian Change in Post-Independence Malawi" (Research Paper, Bunda College of Agriculture, Lilongwe, Malawi, 1985).

22. The pilot projects were evaluated by Simon Thomas in "Economic Development in Malawi since Independence," *Journal of Southern African Studies* 2:1 (1975): 30–51; S. N. Acharya, "Perspectives and Problems in Development in Sub-Saharan Africa," *World Development* 9:2 (1981): 109–47; and Richard Mkandawire, "Markets, Peasants and Agrarian Change" (ibid.), and "Agrarian Change and Rural Development Strategy in Malawi: A Case Study of the Chewa Peasantry in the Lilongwe Rural Development Project" (Ph.D. diss., University of East Anglia, 1984). Mkandawire is the most critical of the project approach and disputes Acharya's claim that the Lilongwe Project was an economic success.

23. According to Kydd and Christiansen, the real return for labor among cash-cropping peasants actually declined under Malawi's rural development projects, owing to the constraints they faced in marketing their crops. Thus, they were required to sell to ADMARC, a parastatal that fixed the purchase price and resold the crop at auction with as much as a 300 percent profit. (Also in Mkandawire, "Markets, Peasants, and Agrarian Change," 13.) ADMARC in turn reinvested most of its assets into estate farming and large commercial enterprises, so that the profits

of peasant production were actually subsidizing Malawi's financial elites. With President Banda serving both as the chairman of ADMARC and the Minister of Agriculture, we can detect his hand behind this strategy for expanding commercial agriculture and infer the relative importance to him of one set of clients over another: the party and political elite who owned the estates commanded greater patronage from him than did any group of peasants.

24. While it was never expressly stated that chiefs and headmen should be targeted, credit facilities were only offered to those farmers deemed "creditworthy." As Mkandawire ("Agrarian Change") reports, the criteria for creditworthiness favored those Chewa who already had substantial resources, like good garden land and other sources of cash income. This invariably led the projects to favor chiefs and headmen.

25. Vail and White, "Tribalism in the Political History of Malawi," 183.

26. Ibid.

27. P. Kashindo (Dept. of Chichewa and Linguistics, University of Malawi), personal communication, 1994.

28. L. Msukwa (Centre for Social Research, University of Malawi), personal communication, 1983.

29. Anderson, *Imagined Communities,* 86.

30. Williams, "A Class Act"; Foster, "Making National Cultures in the Global Ecumene."

31. Rotberg, *The Rise of Nationalism in Central Africa,* 317–21; Vail and White, "Tribalism in the Political History of Malawi," 179.

32. Africa Watch, *When Silence Rules,* 58–59.

33. Vail and White, "Tribalism in the Political History of Malawi," 179.

34. This was the Lundu chiefship of Chikwawa East, defunct since colonial rule and one of the few southern constituencies to support MCP in the general election.

35. Although Lomwe were more recent Mozambican emigres than Yao, they were included within the category "Chewa." This might be explained by the use of Chichewa as a lingua franca in Lomwe areas, but it is also consistent with the different social attainments of Yao and Lomwe as merchants and plantation labor, and as more and less educated respectively: Yao emerge in greater numbers than Lomwe in university, civil service, and government. This suggests that Banda's intention in identifying a mainstream ethnicity was to consolidate a *common* folk as his allies positioned in opposition to his elite rivals, real and imagined, defined increasingly as Tumbuka and Yao.

36. Africa Watch, *When Silence Rules,* 58–59.

37. Frederic Pryor, *Malawi and Madagascar: The Political Economy of Poverty, Equity, and Growth* (Oxford: Oxford University Press, 1990), 86.

38. Catholic Bishops in Malawi, "The Pastoral Letter," *Southern Africa* 5:8 (June 1992); Chakufwa Chihana, "Malawi: Prospects for Democracy," *Southern Africa* 5:8 (June 1992); Mapopa Chipeta, "Malawi: The Current Situation," *Southern Africa* 5:8 (June 1992); Lloyd M. Sachikonye, "Movements for Democracy in Kenya and Malawi," *Southern Africa* 5:8 (June 1992); Tony Woods, "The High Cost of Obstinacy: Banda Hangs On," *Southern Africa Report* 8:2 (November 1992).

39. The transition council voted to disband the MYP in September 1993, and when the MCP failed to do so, the Army routed the Young Pioneers the following December and January. This included shelling and burning MYP barracks, the Kamuzu Institute of Youth, and Malawi Congress Party Headquarters in Lilongwe, sending Young Pioneers members into flight. The Army pursued and disarmed them in Operation Bwezani (Operation "Get Back the Arms"). The operation was reported in several Malawi newspapers, including the Malawi Daily Times which is owned by the MCP and downplayed the events, and the Malawi Monitor which is pro-opposition and reported every encounter and rumor thereof among MYP, the Malawi Army, the Malawi police and Renamo.

40. The seven opposition parties were the Alliance for Democracy (Aford), the United Democratic Front (UDF), the Malawi Democratic Party (MDP), the United Front for Multiparty Democracy (UFMD), the Congress for the Second Republic (CSR), the Malawi Democratic Union (MDU) and the Malawi National Democratic Party (MNDP). (*International Observers Briefing Manual for the Malawi Parliamentary and Presidential Elections May 17, 1994.*) The two other presidential candidates were Kamlepo Kalua (Malawi Democratic Party) from Rumphi District (same as Chihana), and Tim Mangwaza (Malawi National Democratic Party) described as a "nephew" of President Banda. Mangwaza withdrew his candidacy within two weeks of the election. Of the seven opposition parties, only Aford and UDF won seats in parliament and survived the election. (*Malawi Government Gazette* 2,097: 21.40 (24 June 1994).

41. The exception was Nkhata Bay (north), where Aford won (85 percent), UDF came in second (9 percent), and MCP was third (6 percent). See table 2.

42. The exception was Nkhotakota (center) where MCP won with 47 percent, because the opposition split into two smaller segments giving UDF 38 percent and Aford 15 percent. It was a different scenario in Salima (center), where MCP also took 47 percent of the vote, but was edged out by UDF with 48 percent, while Aford trailed in third with 4 percent. See table 2.

43. Average voter turnout for the country was 38.1 percent of the population; broken down by region, voter turnout was 51.3 percent in

the north, 38.1 percent in the center, and 35 percent in the south. The lowest turnout was in Mulanje District in the south with 27 percent, while the highest was in Rumphi District (Chihana's home district) in the north with 57 percent. The highest turnout in the south was in Machinga, a Yao district, with 42 percent. See table 2.

44. Muluzi got 43 percent of the vote in Nsanje District in the extreme south, losing to Banda, while he got his smallest margin of victory (57 percent) in the neighboring district of Chikwawa. He won his largest victory (91 percent) in Machinga District with a predominantly Yao population. See table 2.

45. Ethnic mobilization can account for Banda's constituencies in the central region, Chihana's constituencies in two northern districts (Rumphi and Mzimba), and Muluzi's constituencies in one central and two southern districts (Salima, Mangochi, and Machinga). It can also account for some minority support where these cadidates came in second. Chihana took second with 19 percent in Kasungu where there is a minority Tumbuka population, and Banda took second with 47 percent in Salima where there is a large Chewa minority. See tables 2 and 3.

46. The Tumbuka stronghold of Rumphi and Mzimba (north) had the highest voter turnout in the country, while the Yao stronghold of Mangochi and Machinga had the highest voter turnout in the south and higher rates than the national average overall. See tables 2 and 3.

47. Chihana's Tumbuka support in Rumphi and Mzimba accounts for only two of the five districts he won and was not sufficiently higher in those two districts to identify him as a quintessentially Tumbuka candidate. Although Muluzi's Yao coalition secured him an important upset victory over Banda in Salima, Yao solidarity can account for only three of the ten districts that he won. See tables 2, 3, and 4.

48. In the north, Chitipa and Karonga Districts with Ngonde, Asukwa and Nyakyusa populations supported Aford, as did Nkhata Bay District with a large Tonga population. In the center, Ntcheu District with a majority Chichewa-speaking Ngoni population supported UDF, and in the south Mwanza, Mulanje, Chiradzulu, and Chikwawa Districts with mixtures of Nyanja, Lomwe, Mang'anja, and Sena populations supported UDF. See tables 2 and 3.

49. Nkhotakota District in the central region has a large Tonga population and voted 53 percent for the two opposition parties; but with the opposition divided 38 percent (UDF) and 15 percent (Aford), MCP won the district with 47 percent. Dedza District, also in the center, has a large Ngoni minority, and voted 26 percent for UDF. See tables 2 and 3.

50. Mwanza, Chiradzulu, Thyolo, Mulanje and Chikwawa Districts in the southern region have populations of Nyanja, Lomwe, Mang'anja and

Sena; levels of voter turnout were from eight to eleven percentage points below the national average. Ntcheu District of the central region has a majority Ngoni population and had the second lowest rate of voter turnout in the country at 10 percent below the national average. See tables 2 and 3.

51. This is best illustrated by comparing the northern district of Nkhata Bay and the southern district of Machinga. Nkhata Bay is populated primarily by Tonga, and although they gave 85 percent of their vote to Aford, they had the lowest rate of voter turnout in the *north*. Nevertheless, voter turnout in Nkhata Bay was higher than voter turnout in Mangochi which is populated primarily by Yao, gave 91 percent of its vote to UDF, and had the highest level of voter turnout of all the *southern* districts. See tables 2 and 3.

52. I raise this point in response to an argument I heard in Malawi that the cohesion of the north is "ethnic" insofar as it is broadly Tumbuka, a function of its use as the lingua franca of the region that subsumes all the other languages spoken there. While it may be true that Tumbuka has widespread usage in the north as a language of commerce, to assert that this is the basis of widespread ethnic identity forces a redefinition of ethnicity to fit the northern case. If we accept it, then we are forced to ask why the south, whose lingua franca is Chichewa, did not vote for the Chewa candidate, Hastings Banda.

53. Although the Malawi Young Pioneers were disbanded, an extensive armature of MCP control remained in place through the party's cell structure and the linkages to chiefs and headmen, enabling the MCP to indulge in numerous methods of voter coercion. Nyau dancers broke up opposition rallies, territorial chiefs seized voter registration forms and ballots from villagers, and village headmen were bribed by party officials to threaten to reclaim garden land from anyone who voted against "the black cock." Given a land-poor peasantry, the last tactic must have been an especially effective weapon for intimidating disaffected voters.

# 16

## "THAT TIME WAS APARTHEID, NOW IT'S THE NEW SOUTH AFRICA": DISCOURSES OF RACE IN RUYTERWACHT, 1995

### COURTNEY JUNG AND JEREMY SEEKINGS

South Africa's apartheid system, which structured politics, economics, and society on the basis of race from 1948 to 1994, has made South Africa an important case study for racial discourse. The 1950 Population Registration Act separated South Africans into whites, Asians, coloureds, and blacks, roughly in that hierarchical order. Although separate development meant officially that each racially defined group could exercise political rights in its "own area," only whites had a political voice for most of the apartheid era. Petty apartheid—those laws, including access to movie theaters, beaches, public restrooms, hospitals, and so on, which structured contact among race groups—differentiated primarily between whites and nonwhites.

In the aftermath of the country's first nationwide, nonracial elections in April 1994, South African society remains deeply structured by race. The advent of a nonracial political system in a racially structured society draws our attention to how little social scientists have had to say about race in contemporary South Africa. While "race relations" was a prominent research topic until the mid-1960s,[1] critical research virtually disappeared thereafter as social scientists focused instead on class relations, consciousness, and conflict. Only recently have historians led a wave of renewed interest in race, racial imagery, and racial identity.[2] Scholars routinely apologize for "having" to employ racial categories but avoid exploring the categories themselves.

Most work on race in late-twentieth-century South Africa falls into two broad areas. On the one hand, there are a number of studies of official discourse, focusing on broad changes in the character of official discourse and ideology on black South Africans.[3] On the other hand, psychologists—together with the occasional sociologist and political scientist—have investigated interracial attitudes through the use, particularly, of social distance scales.[4] The former are crucial to understanding the state and state policy, but we should not assume that elite or official ideology matches popular sentiment. The latter highlight variation and change in attitudes to racially defined groups over time but rarely disaggregate the category of "attitudes" (according to different issues, for example), and the research is generally limited to readily accessible subjects such as university students. The practice of interracial contact, and the relationships between racial identities, sentiment, and behavior, remain almost entirely uncharted.[5]

The gaps in the existing literature make it impossible to either confirm or contest stereotypes about race and racism. Are black South Africans hostile to their white compatriots, or are they committed to non-racialism (whatever that might mean)? Are white South Africans—and especially the white working class—as racist as they are often made out to be? These are surely important questions now, in 1995, as South Africa's political, economic, and social landscape is being transformed. Apartheid has been declared "abolished"; the two leading political parties (the African National Congress, ANC, and the "new" National Party, NP) both claim nonracial credentials; the country has a democratically elected black president and a predominantly black parliament; and everyone supports the government's Reconstruction and Development Programme. But racial identities are still significant and play some role in shaping political, social, and economic identities.

Studies of racism in other parts of the world suggest that we should beware the persistence of racism, even in changing contexts. It is precisely the fluidity and flexibility of racist discourse (and ideology) that enables it to adjust and retain broad popular appeal.[6] A wealth of research exists on the "new" faces and languages of racism. In the former imperial powers of Europe and in some of their former dominions (e.g., New Zealand), racism has become wrapped up in cultural nationalism.[7] In the United States, in the aftermath of the civil rights movement and the abolition of formal segregation and discrimination, very few Americans continue to believe that black people are inherently inferior or that they should not enjoy the same opportunities as white people. But many white Americans continue to hold pejorative views about their black compatriots' behavior—views which have been labeled as "modern racism" or "new racism."[8]

What forms might racism take among white South Africans after apartheid? This chapter examines contemporary discourses of race in a small, mostly white working-class suburb of Cape Town: Ruyterwacht. Ruyterwacht hit the headlines in February 1995 as residents protested against black pupils being bused into the suburb to attend school. Television and press reports depicted violent and racist white men and women denying black school children access to school. Our interviews with residents suggest that this picture of racial bigotry was misleading: it misunderstood the reasons for the residents' protest, and the character of their racism. Racial discourse in Ruyterwacht shares many of the features of "modern racism" in contemporary America in that it focused more on patterns of behavior rather than on biological or other inherent characteristics. This reflects, as we argue in the final section of this essay, the ambiguities and changes in official discourse together with changes in the political and economic context in the "new" South Africa.

This chapter is concerned with "mapping the language of racism" in one part of white South Africa during events which reflected and symbolized the transition away from apartheid. We are primarily concerned with examining the ways in which people talk about the arrival and presence of black pupils in this formerly white suburb. But this issue allows us to explore discourses of race more broadly, exploring the ways in which people talk about race, about racism, and about other people whom they categorize as members of a different race.

We argue that discourses of race in Ruyterwacht in 1995 reflect changes in the wider context of the new South Africa. What we cannot determine is the extent to which the discourses were independent of the school crisis itself. The discourse analyzed here is framed by, as well as focused on, the arrival of black pupils, and it is possible that the crisis served as a catalyst for the emergence of new forms of discourse. Insofar as the events in Ruyterwacht were just an extreme example of changes occurring throughout South Africa, we can expect that the character of discourses in Ruyterwacht were at least indicative of discourses in the country as a whole.

## RUYTERWACHT

Ruyterwacht is a clearly defined suburb with about six thousand residents about ten kilometers from central Cape Town. It is bounded by the Goodwood showgrounds to the west, a railway line (and beyond it Goodwood) to the north, the old coloured residential area of Elsies River to the east, and the Epping industrial area to the south. The only road access is from the south. Ruyterwacht is, in the words of one resident, "a small place for poor people." It initially comprised public housing for "poor whites," and remained a white working-class area until very recently—as one resident told us, "dis 'n armsmans dorp die; dit is net vir mense wat sukkel" (this is a poor man's town; it's only for people who are struggling). In the past three years, there have been some changes, with an influx of slightly better-off white and coloured families, many of whom have bought their homes. But pensioners continue to comprise a high proportion of the population, unemployment is high, and incomes are generally low.

In this bleak environment stand the attractive school buildings that once housed a primary school for local white children, and

for the last five years or so were used as offices by the South
African Army. In January 1995, faced with an apparent shortage
of classrooms in Cape Town, the army moved out. On January 30,
about 3,800 black pupils were bused in to Ruyterwacht from the
black townships of Nyanga, Langa, Guguletu, and Khayelitsha.
Two weeks later, several hundred white residents of Ruyterwacht
picketed the school, blocking the school buses' access, in an
attempt to keep the black pupils out of the school and out of the
suburb.

The media seized on images of white racist bigotry. Ruyterwacht became synonymous with white racism, vilified not only as
an unacceptable outpost of apartheid in the new South Africa but
also as a portent of trouble to come if white racism sparked
a black reaction. As one letter-writer warned, "the provocative
behaviour of the Ruyterwacht residents could trigger a cata-
strophic sequence of events in the Western Cape and the rest of
the country."[9] The images of barbaric, racist white protesters
persisted. When Nelson Mandela visited the school in Ruyterwacht in early March, residents gathered to watch. Press photos
showed matrons in Sunday best, but the accompanying text wrote
of police keeping Ruyterwacht residents "at bay." Ruyterwacht is
now cited as an example of the "rightwing" trying to cause
"chaos,"[10] with "rightwing" violence provoking incidents of count-
erviolence.[11] These images are apparently so ingrained that contrary interpretations are sometimes acknowledged but inexplica-
bly disregarded.[12]

In the middle of the "crisis" we conducted a series of discussions and interviews with residents of Ruyterwacht. Between February 23 and March 3 we spoke to over fifty residents, in some
cases for just five or ten minutes, in others for up to two hours.
We spoke to a wide range of people in different parts of Ruyterwacht, during the day, at night (including "on patrol" with the
neighborhood watch), and over the weekends; on the "picket
line" outside the school, in the street, and in their homes; and
including both participants and nonparticipants in the protests.
We ended up with what seemed to be a reasonable cross section
of the local population in terms of age, race, class, and gender,
although our sample cannot be assumed to be "representative" of
the local population.

## Defining the Threat

The way in which Ruyterwacht residents articulated the "problem" that prompted their protests reflects their understanding and representation of the Other. A crucial element of the "threat" or danger facing the "community" was uncertainty. The absence of any prior consultation or warning was repeatedly cited as a major cause for concern. Residents say that they were taken completely by surprise when black pupils were bused into Ruyterwacht:

> "The first we knew about it was when we saw them here, that was the first we knew about it. The street here was full of everybody, walking up and down all the time." [older man— all interviewees were white unless indicated otherwise]

> "I didn't know anything about it, I phoned my husband [at work] and said I don't know what was going on here." [young mother]

> "See, what upsets the community the most is that they haven't informed anybody about this whole situation: What was going to happen, that it's going to be a school, or anything like that.. . . The next day a bunch of school kids arrive and they bring it in a very wrong way." [young man]

The change was accentuated by the fact that the school's prior occupants—the army unit using the buildings as offices—had been particularly unobtrusive and ordered. Residents point to the care and regularity with which the army tended to the lawns and flowerbeds, as symbols of the unit's orderliness.

Residents report that the pupils were very disorderly, in contrast to the army:

> "This just happenned. Not one person in the neighbourhood had any idea that this was going to happen. Thirty-eight buses just pulled in here, and they just piled out. And then there was total and absolute chaos. You had them marching up the street. There were like an uncontrollable rabble." [young mother]

> "I came back from hospital, and thought what is going on here?. . . It's covered with them, they were walking up and

down here, you would have thought it was Khayelitsha." [old man]

These quotations represent clear evidence of racist discourse: black pupils are described as an "uncontrollable rabble," transforming Ruyterwacht into Khayelitsha, Cape Town's largest black residential area. But residents' explanations of their own attitudes and discursive moves render charges of plain old-fashioned racism less compelling. Residents focused on the perceived threat to their community and on pupils' behavior, rather than on inherent characteristics that made black people "unacceptable."

The 3,800 pupils bused to the school far exceeded the five hundred students that the school buildings could accommodate. Furthermore, there were no desks or other teaching facilities, and no teaching took place. In a sense, there was no "school," just buildings. The pupils, unsupervised and presumably bored, inflicted minor damage on the buildings, damaging the floor of the gym and some of the toilets. For the most part the pupils just milled around the school grounds and the surrounding streets. Ruyterwacht residents recall that they felt overwhelmed by this massive and unexpected influx into their streets.

"They were walking up and down and blocking the whole road, people couldn't get through. . . . And making a noise, you know. Our children were so scared. . . . Because when my child comes back from school, he doesn't know what he has run into. They were scared to come home from school." [young coloured mother]

"There are non-European people, there are Africans living here, it's fine. But if you wake up one morning and look out of your window and there are four thousand, regardless of what . . . right outside your door, you want answers, you want to know what's going on here." [young husband]

"One day the police had to escort her [our daughter] home, it was just black; she was afraid; they pull down their pants. . . ." [middle-aged father]

Residents refer to the pupils as "black" or "African," suggesting that color is part of their perception of the problem, but they focus less on the *race* of the pupils than on their alleged *behavior*. Residents claim that pupils wandered into their yards, helped themselves to or demanded tapwater, sat in the shade, urinated, and left their litter. Residents complain that pupils obstructed them in the street and jeered at them and their children. "Hulle het in my gesig gespoeg en my nat gepee" (they spat in my face and peed on me), charged one middle-aged woman! Pupils allegedly smoked marijuana. Some pupils stole food from a local shop. All in all, pupils did many "naughty things," said one pensioner.

> "They called us you boere (slang for Afrikaner), things like that." [old man]

> "I was walking home from school, and one youth came running past me, riding in the bus, and called me my mother's pee, and he spat at me. He missed, so I went home. . . ." [boy]

> "This woman over the road, she was working in the kitchen, when she turned round there were six people standing behind her; they didn't knock, they just walked right in. . . . When the girls came back from school, the boys showed the girls what they wanted to do with them." [middle-aged father]

Many residents spoke of the need to protect older residents and children, in particular. Depersonalizing the threat—which was to other people, and to an entire community that included people perceived to be vulnerable—increased the level of danger and the validity of feeling threatened.

Rumors of particular incidents spread rapidly. An eight-year-old girl was allegedly offered twenty cents if she got into one of the buses with the (much older) black pupils. Pupils were said to have had sex in the school grounds or between parked buses. Many people repeated the story of the invalid who was tipped out of her wheelchair by a gang of jeering pupils. When asked "did you see that yourself?," most of our informants retreated: "well, no, but my neighbor told me she saw it." Others claimed to have witnessed things themselves: "I saw, with my own eyes: they had sex between the buses, on the ground." We tracked down the woman who claimed to have been tipped out of her wheelchair. Whether or not all of these allegations were true, they were widely repeated and apparently believed to be true within Ruyterwacht.

The perceived age of the (supposed) pupils was seen as an important factor:

> "Some of the black pupils are our age—25, 26. How can you put a bloke of 26 in a class with a girl of 15? No way." [young father]

The legacy of inadequate and disrupted schooling is that many black pupils are older than their white counterparts in each grade (although there are not usually pupils as old as 25 or 26). But residents were not just concerned that there were old pupils; they claim that some of the youngsters were not pupils at all—they were what one man called "walk-alongs," calling into question the legitimacy of their status as students at all.

> " ... there were people my age. ... They made people scared. We don't know where they come from, what they're going to do here. ... Here, I leave the windows open, I have no burglar bars. I'm in the backyard, when I come in, everything's gone. ... This is why most of the people are scared. It wasn't just children, it was big people as well, big guys. ... That's why people were scared." [young coloured woman]

> "They were supposed to be schoolchildren. There were some youngsters among them—25, 26, 27. ... The way they were dressed. ... In American films, blokes from Brooklyn area, in American films, in New York, the way they walk, swagger about, hats back to front, half-length jackets." [old man]

Members of the residents' committee—which took the lead during the picketing—further claim that pupils were brought in from other schools to inflate the numbers in Ruyterwacht:

> "You know what they did?. ... They brought more students in, from other schools, to support these students. Busloads. And they admitted they were just supporting. They were fetched from Guguletu, Langa, Nyanga, all over. They actu-

ally went and took them out of school." [committee member]

"Their people, that were already in school, were picked up from school and were brought here to support those pupils. Just to support them." [committee member]

By casting doubt over whether the young black people were in fact pupils, or were pupils with no school to go to, Ruyterwacht residents tried to delegitimize the exercise.

Residents portrayed the threat in terms of deviant and hostile behavior but many linked this to broader issues of power. Some argued that the the "pupils" (or some of them) had no right to be there. Others dramatized the alleged threat that the pupils presented to them, representing the takeover of the school buildings as just the first step in a process of forced redistribution.

"They want twenty houses, near to the school; they want the hostel. . . . to live near the school. They want the impossible, because all the houses are taken. People would have to be thrown out of the houses. . . . If they can break up the school they can break up the houses." [boy]

"That school is our school; we say that school must be an old age home. . . . That school is not for the darkies. If you give in, the next place is Parow, the next place is Bellville (nearby white suburbs). You must draw the line. . . . They want the other school as a hostel. . . . And they want twenty-five houses too. They want them, we must give it to them." [middle-aged man]

"There was a section in one of the newspapers that said they want the school and fifty houses. The houses around the school, so that means my house is gone." [young mother]

Ruyterwacht residents quite clearly saw the presence or behavior of large numbers of black pupils as a threat. To what extent, however, were their discourses of threat also discourses of race? The available testimony does not allow us to reach firm conclusions on the precise significance of the pupils' race in the residents' definition of the problem. The "blackness" of the pupils seems integral to the definition of the problem as a threat—large numbers of ill-behaved white pupils would also have been defined as a problem but probably not a threat. Pupils, individually unknown to Ruyterwacht residents, present in large numbers, and behaving in ways seen as antisocial, would have constituted the Other regardless of their race. But the fact that these pupils were black rendered them a different kind of Other, linking their presence not to a problem of generational authority but to the broader issues of social and political transformation in the country as a whole. The political significance of race in South Africa translated the presence of specifically black pupils into an issue of power.

## THE RESPONSES OF RUYTERWACHT RESIDENTS

The significance of the pupils' race also became clear in terms of the residents' responses.[13] The pupils first arrived on January 30 and returned daily thereafter. For two weeks, there was no collective response from residents. Residents explain this passivity in terms of fatalism—"I was flabbergasted, but what can you do?," said one old man. But this must be understood in terms of a population with no recent history of civic action. Moreover, the existing civic leaders had their own ways of doing things, which did not include collective action. Four leaders, including a Dutch Reformed Church minister and the local National Party organizer, met with the Department of Education and the National Election Crisis Committee. They asked that the number of pupils be reduced, but their requests were ignored. On February 13—by which date Ruyterwacht's streets had been filled with unoccupied and unsupervised pupils for two weeks—they reported their failure to residents at a packed public meeting. After the meeting some people decided to hold a protest outside the school the next morning.

Early on February 14, several hundred residents gathered at the school, some with sticks and dogs. One worried community leader called the police. When the buses arrived, protesters and pupils traded verbal abuse. A few stones were thrown by both sides and there were a few minor scuffles but no injuries. (One pupil was later killed inside the school grounds in an apparently unrelated incident.) Some residents employed a classic technique of nonviolent direct action, lying down in front of the buses to prevent them driving to the school. The local minister appealed for peace and calm. The police eventually escorted the buses into the schoolyard. For the remainder of the day pupils and residents squared off across the fence. Police kept them apart, while Ruyterwacht community leaders strategically drew some of the most voluble protesters into a committee to negotiate and to help maintain order among the protesters. This situation continued for another day and a half, after which the pupils stayed away. A small group of residents continued to keep a watch on the school, ready to act if the buses—and pupils—returned.

Residents who participated in the limited confrontation claim that it resulted from provocation by the pupils. There was

" . . . shouting and swearing and spitting from the buses—so we thought, if that's the way they want to handle it, we thought we want to handle it in a better way." [middle-aged woman]

"And they started throwing stones. I mean mega stones like this [indicates a large stone]. And there was old people there. There was an old tannie of sixty years old standing right there in the front line. . . . And we went through there and we got this old tannie out of the way because she were hit by a stone. And then the people retaliated." [committee member]

But the use of even limited and retaliatory violence was not endorsed by many nonparticipants. The most serious incident, in which one pupil was hit with a sjambok, was condemned by all of the respondents, in part because it was too much like the misbehavior of the pupils themselves.

Residents insist that the protest was entirely local and nonpolitical. Civic leaders said that they did not want political parties to be involved because "this whole thing wasn't a political thing." Local NP supporters probably wanted to depoliticize the issue because it could easily play into the hands of the far right-wing parties. As one community leader put it, they did not want to "be used as political pawns." Most residents were, historically, NP supporters, suspicious of the Afrikaner Weerstandbeweging (AWB) and other far right-wing groups. Residents expressed doubts about the AWB on racial grounds.

> "The AWB say it's blacks and whites, but what about the coloureds? Coloureds are half white." [young man]

The general feeling, even among supporters of the AWB, was that it was inappropriate for groups like the AWB to get involved because it was a local issue.

Although the issue was seen as nonpolitical, the responses of the NP leadership served to alienate many lifetime NP supporters who had continued to vote for the National Party even after the transition:

> "Kriel [the NP Western Cape premier] said he would come here but he never came. . . . I'm not a bloke for politics. . . . Now people like De Klerk, and Mandela, and Kriel force you to do so, we just want to live quiet. . . . These are things which de Klerk and Mandela and Kriel don't know because they don't come here." [middle-aged man]

> "Nobody's ever been here. The ANC, or the National Party, or somebody, . . . surely they send out a little pamphlet or notice to the residents? Nothing. The first person to mention anything about this was Mandela, when he was opening parliament. That's the first one that ever said anything about this. And he had no idea what happened here." [young man]

Both NP and ANC politicians were seen in much the same light: out of touch and unresponsive to residents' concerns.

NP and ANC leaders were said to have relied on "what they saw on TV," but television (and to a lesser extent press) coverage was widely condemned. One community leader related that a cameraman had called two white women "whores" in order to provoke them and get his desired shots of angry and aggressive white protesters! Many residents said that television reports were "definitely" biased:

> "The media were inside the grounds, with the cameras on us, not on the pupils. They wanted to see how the white

people are behaving. . . . There were coloureds and muslims fighting with us but they only showed the whites." [middle-aged woman]

" . . . the TV, it doesn't show the facts. They show what happens there, but they don't show what happened along the streets or in the shops or anywhere else." [old man]

One resident drew a parallel with a fight between his two young children:

"One says, 'daddy he pulled my hair,' 'daddy he bit me.' I say 'why?' The TV shows the fight, fair enough, but they don't show *why* there was a fight." [old man]

Newspapers were said to be "talking rubbish." The media, like the NP and ANC leadership, were not seen as being on the side of the "community." But what did the community comprise?

## Us, Them, the Other

In their testimonies, residents offered a variety of versions of who or what constituted "us" or the "community." The most common version was of a local "community" bounded by space—people called themselves "residents," thereby emphasising the primacy of their claims in the area. Race was woven into this representation, but it was neither the foremost nor the most consistent aspect of it.

Crucially, the local "community" was represented as being racially inclusive in that it explicitly embraced nonwhite families living in Ruyterwacht. By 1995, about one in five families in the suburb were coloured (or were formerly illegal, so-called mixed couples), and the first few black families had moved in. A racially inclusive discourse of "community" that accommodated these residents stood in stark contrast to the racially exclusive discourse of apartheid that accompanied the rigid separation of white from coloured people and coloured from black people. The concept of the racially exclusive "community" was the goal of apartheid policies that prohibited members of different race groups from worshiping together, intermarriage, using the same public transport, sharing public amenities, and voting in the same elections.

The racially inclusive understanding of the "community" was explicitly and often offered in a denial of personal racism:

> "We have black people living here; we have white people living here; at the school there are black and white and coloured people, and there's no problems. At any one of these schools, you can see, it's not only whites, there are coloured children, there are black children. And they're all happy, no complaints, no arguments. Even the public, the residents, we are quite happy." [older man]

> "In this town we are not racist: we are whites, coloureds, Muslims, blacks also; I'm on the rugby and cricket committees; we have coloureds on the committee; we have no problems; we have no racism. The media, the government says we are racist; it's not true." [middle-aged man, said to be an AWB member]

Coloured residents of Ruyterwacht are said to have supported the protests. At one of the meetings in the community hall, for example:

> "They got up on their own to go and say how they feel about the situation. It was a coloured guy and a coloured lady. . . . And a very good point that he said there, he said we—and he said WE—we don't mind if they come to the school, provided they stay here, they're residents of the area. And that came out of a coloured man—one of the so-called oppressed." [young man]

> "The coloureds are with us. Last night we even had a coloured chap that was working with us [on the neighborhood watch], even they offer up their time because they are part of our community and they are involved with us. They also stay here." [young woman]

> "Even the black people that live here were standing there with sticks and pipes and everything to chase those people away; you can't call that racism." [boy]

Some white residents say that coloured residents actually encouraged them to take a stand:

"They [i.e., coloured people] are the people who are . . . starting this; they don't want these people here because they know what they're like; they fired us up." [middle-aged man]

"A coloured lady told us we were cowards, because if this was our township we wouldn't even allow them into the area. One coloured man, he came from Mitchell's Plain, he said you stupid people, you mustn't just stand here with your batons, you must get in there and drive them out." [middle-aged woman]

Coloured families might be part of the "community," but few white residents seem to have reached the point of disregarding their "colouredness" (any more than they would their own "whiteness"). We didn't probe into attitudes on, for example, white family members having relationships with members of coloured families, nor did we probe attitudes towards "mixed" couples. But peoples' comments on neighbors points to an emphasis on "respectability."

"There's lots of coloured people here, but they're decent. They stay in their yards, they don't mix with us, they stay on their one side." [Would you mind if coloured people moved in next door?] "Not if they're decent people. They stay in their yard, and I stay in my yard. But if there's trouble. . . . I must think of my two kids. . . . If there's skollies (hoodlums)." [middle-aged man]

Or, to quote a ten-year-old boy decribing black children at his school (and it is unclear what he understood by "black" as some whites call all nonwhites black):

"They're OK. As long as they don't think they're like the main manne. . . . Some of them, not all of them, most of them are nice. . . . The black people [i.e., pupils at school] are behaving themselves like normal people. They're not like the people here [i.e., the pupils in the street]." [boy]

Antiblack sentiment was directed primarily against the pupils and rarely against black people in general, and was usually couched in terms of their bad behavior. The black pupils were not "decent."

On one level, "us" and "them" were understood in terms of perceived behavior.

At the same time, however, "us" and "them" were widely understood in terms of broader concerns. The black pupils were seen as representing black people in general, who wanted

> " . . . to show the white people, 'you are out, we are running the country, . . . you are white but you're no longer in charge'; they want to put the ANC flag there, just to show the white people. . . . " [middle-aged man]

> "We've all got to live together, it's the new policy. But they [black people] can sort of be with us instead of trying to work against us. . . . They are trying to be better than what we are." [young woman]

Just as the ill-behaved black pupils were representative of a much broader, and hence more threatening and dangerous Other, so Ruyterwacht residents were members of a broader "community." The "community" was constructed in terms of white or decent people in other parts of Cape Town, elsewhere in South Africa, and even beyond South Africa's borders—with the scope or even universality of the "community" providing another thread of a fabric of legitimation:

> "I'm an outsider; I'm not from here. I'm from Goodwood. But they get their way here, they're not going to stop here. . . . I can assure you, from what I've seen here, it's not only residents of Ruyterwacht. It's Kraaifontein, Goodwood, Brackenfell, all over the show." [young man]

> "This country must come together now and make a decision that the ANC cannot get everything it wants with mass action." [committee member]

> "We've had calls from all over the world, from Pretoria, from Johannesburg. We had a guy here yesterday from Japan. That's why we said to Mr. Kriel you must watch out what you do here because the whole world is watching you. If he's going to give in to the ANC now it's the end of the National Party." [committee member]

One activist said he would switch his support to a firmer leader:

"Dr. Mangosuthu Buthelezi. . . , although he's a black man, I'm prepared to be behind him because he agrees; he's got something like what he stands for. He doesn't allow the ANC to do what they want to do. You see what they (Buthelezi's Inkatha Freedom Party) did in parliament the other day? They just walked out." [young man]

While the struggle was largely symbolic, it was fought out over resources that were real enough—resources like the school. For both material and symbolic reasons, therefore, "you can't take the white people's stuff and give it to the darkies" (as one man put it, unusually crudely).

### DENIALS OF RACISM

Ruyterwacht's residents uniformly deny being prejudiced or racist. This in itself is not uncommon: in the late twentieth century, racism is generally seen as a bad thing, and unambiguously racist views are usually presented in terms of "facts" (about black people) rather than prejudice (among white people). There need not be any relationship between the denial of racism and the absence of racism. But the *ways* in which people deny charges of racism— i.e., the discourses of denial—constitute important elements in broader discourses of race.

People in Ruyterwacht present evidence of their supposed tolerance and fair-mindedness in support of their denials of racism. White residents stress their acceptance of coloured or black people living in Ruyterwacht—and their claims are corroborated by many of the coloured residents with whom we spoke. According to one "mixed" couple, for example:

"When we moved in here nobody gave us dirty looks, or anything like that." [old man]

"Since I lived here I never had any problems—had lots of problems before, in other areas, people wanted to chuck me in the street or whatever. . . . When we moved in here, people were quite happy. . . . Nobody worried me. . . . When I walk down the street, nobody looks at me like I'm an alien or something. You know when people look at you like that, you feel very uncomfortable." [young coloured woman]

They and others claimed that even black families were accepted:

"I know of three black families, their children go to school with my young daughter. There's never any hassles there. Everybody's happy, everybody talks to one another." [young coloured woman]

"We accepted this new South Africa and it was a hell of a big surprise to me. I mean, coloureds moving in, blacks moving in, Muslims, all these other races, and there was not one single . . . there was no complaint from a white against a black, an unreasonable or racist thing, incident, no racist incident." [community leader]

Aspects of this kind of discourse were common, but they often coexisted with representations that distinguished between black and coloured people.

Under apartheid, coloured people were accorded higher status than black people. At the same time, however, apartheid policies sought to impose rigid segregation between white and coloured people. In the Western Cape, where coloured people comprised a majority of the population, apartheid policies led to the massive forced removal of coloured families from "mixed areas" and the exclusion of coloured voters from the common voters roll, as well as prohibition of white/coloured marriage and sex. Thus while coloured people retained some privileges relative to black people, they were comprehensively discriminated against compared to white people.

Unfortunately there is very little data on the extent to which white South Africans differentiated black from coloured people during the apartheid era. Surveys asking about residential desegregation, opening public amenities, or sharing power, for example, did not ask separate questions about coloured and black people.[14] Social distance scales indicate that Afrikaans-speaking white South Africans felt marginally closer to coloureds but that English-speakers felt marginally closer to blacks. In both cases, the gulf between white and coloured or black people was vast.[15]

In Ruyterwacht, in 1995, many residents represented coloured people more favorably than black people. They claimed that this was because their own attitudes toward coloureds had changed through increased contact with well-behaved coloured families, while their partial (or uneven) hostility toward black people was linked to the behavior of the black pupils. Indeed, the context of black and coloured residents together resisting ill-behaved black pupils no doubt shaped the representations of racial groups at the time that we conducted interviews in the suburb.

> "Some of the old people had a problem, but . . . they changed. I mean, ten years ago I also thought . . . , most of us, 99 percent of the people in this town, we've changed. You must just look at the coloured people here, they are building on, they showed us they are prepared to go forward in life—but these black people are not prepared, if they were like that they wouldn't damage the school like that." [young man]

> [Were white residents' attitudes to coloured people better or worse than they had been a decade before?] "Yes, better. . . . That time was apartheid; now it's the new South Africa. Coloureds can stay here, I don't worry. But the school. . . . It should be a old age home, for white people, coloured people, I don't care. But not a school for African children." [middle-aged man]

> "That's why we say we've got nothing against the coloureds, we've got nothing against the Indians and the Malays. But the blacks! Look what they've done here!" [young man]

Some residents welcomed black neighbors:

> "Let me put it this way: if a black family has to buy the house next door, and move in there tomorrow, neither my wife nor myself would complain about that." [old man]

But others were more prejudiced. One resident told us that "you can't pick and choose between color," but resorted to pejorative stereotypes when asked how he would feel if his new neighbors turned out to be black:

"If you let some stay, others will follow. Within a month or two there will be a hokkie (shack) outside . . . the whole family . . . " [middle-aged man]

Representations of coloured people in discourse in Ruyterwacht are clearly different from those of black people in important respects. Coloured people are more likely to be considered respectable than black people. For some white people in the suburb, it seems that coloured people have been incorporated alongside white people into a "nonblack" category. For these people the parameters of the in-group have shifted while the status and meaning of the out-group has remained the same. Such residents might retain an essentialist conception of race, but now represent coloured people as innately respectable, like white people, in contrast to innately uncivilized or barbaric black people. More generally, however, our research suggested that essentialist racist discourse was deprivileged and replaced by discourses of respectability and community that explicitly or implicitly transcended racial lines. Although most of the people admitted to respectability and community were coloured, this new discourse opened up the possibility of more benign representations of black people as well.

Residents acknowledge that there are some people in the suburb whose views are racist:

"There are a few people who are very rude, they talk about kaffir and all that jazz. It's not right. The same with the black people, they're talking about boers." [young man]

"You get your one or two elements, but we won't accept them because it's the new South Africa and we accepted the new South Africa. And we don't want them here. . . . There are some people in Ruyterwacht who are racists. Obviously. You get them everywhere. But we kicked them out [i.e., off the picket line]. There was only a few, I would say four or five, but we kicked them out." [committee member]

"[They were] throwing racist remarks like 'kaffir,' 'we don't want you kaffirs here,' 'we don't want blacks in this town.' Those are racist comments. We don't need that.' [committee member]

White residents thus deny their own racism through both emphasizing their acceptance of coloured (or at least "decent" coloured) families, their acceptance of the "new South Africa," and their disassociation from "actual" racism and the small number of acknowledged racists in the area. At the same time, many of these same residents express pejorative views of black people based on observed or imagined behavior that contravened "acceptable" standards.

Residents are insistent that the issue was not race, or racism, but something else—the behavior of the black pupils, the lack of consultation, crime, and so on. The question "It's not a race issue?" prompted the following responses from two elderly men:

"No, definitely not."
"No. Look here, my friend, we can't afford to be that, we are trying to make a new South Africa, we are trying to build, getting better."
"You're living in this house. Tomorrow morning, I bring all my pals down here, heh, they're spending the day in your home. How do you feel about it? Are you happy? That's the way it was. In our quiet community, then all of a sudden you get this whole crowd just being dumped on your doorstep. They don't ask you can we do this, or do you mind? They just take over." [old men]

Similarly, a woman insisted:

"We are not racists. We are going on like that because of what they did." [young woman]

Some people countered charges of racism by saying that black people were the real racists. They pointed to press reports that there were vacant classrooms in schools in coloured areas, which black pupils allegedly did not want to go to.

"I don't know how much you know about the African blacks? If you look into the matter you find they are more racist than anybody, than any white, coloured. . . . They are racist because they don't want schools in coloured areas." [old man]

"I'm not racist or anything—they are more racist than us, they didn't want to go to schools in Mitchell's Plain." [young mother]

"The racism is among the black people, not among us. Because they want the school for themselves. They don't want it as a mixed school, they want it just for themselves. All of this they want for themselves. They just want everything for themselves at this stage." [committee member]

Other residents disputed this view. As one young mother put it, "in every community you get the bad and the good—I think there was a bad element among them [the pupils]."

Ruyterwacht residents nonetheless claimed great confidence in the ability to resolve conflicts through orderly negotiations. "Let's take it step by step, in an orderly manner," one old man told us, endorsing a negotiated settlement. Civic leaders related that they argued at community meetings that "we're going to stay within the law and have a proper way of doing things," "that people would protest in a behaved way, in such a way that the people that saw them would not think they were ill-behaved or racist." The emphasis was put on negotiations and orderly protest.

By counterposing the rationality of negotiations and legality against the irrationality of racism, residents were simultaneously distancining themselves from racism and affirming that the issue was about order not race. Both their grievances and their preferred strategy of negotiations within the law were represented as reasonable and not racial in nature, and stood in contrast to the undemocratic initiation of busing and the disorderly behavior of the pupils. The residents represented the difference between "us" and "them" as not one of color (they were black, we were white), nor as simply about the legitimacy of claims (they were outsiders; we were residents of the "community"); the difference was one of behavior (they were rude and criminal, we were polite and law-abiding).

Most residents asserted that they would accept a reasonable number of well-behaved black pupils in the school.

"If you had a normal amount of students, . . . they go to school in the morning, the gates are locked, they cannot go in and out whenever they like, at lunchtime they open the gates. After lunch the gates are locked again. . . . You can't just walk in and out. Here, they walk in and out when they like, there's no control. . . . If you had a normal amount of students. They go in, the gates are closed, like other schools are, when they have their breaks they can come out, go to the shop—that's normal, like any school. . . . " [older man]

Some residents dissented from this view, saying that "they had the chance and they abused it." But when five hundred or so black pupils did return to Ruyterwacht at the beginning of March, and desks and teachers were provided, the more vocal and defiant activists in the suburb were unable to mobilize more than fifteen or twenty residents in protest.

Discourses of race in Ruyterwacht are not uniform. There are some residents who consistently use racist representations. But most residents offer a complex and contradictory discourse. Elements of crude bigotry are mixed with a different language about rights, democracy, and legalism. Talk of decent versus unacceptable behavior is linked to talk about the "community," but both can be offered in racially inclusive as well as racially exclusive ways. Pejorative characterizations of black people are couched in terms of their behavior and demands, as well as the injustice of their treatment of residents. The predominant discourse of race was quite different to the apartheid-style bigotry we had expected on the basis of media reporting.

## From Racial Bigotry to Modern Racism

Research on racial attitudes in America contrasts the "old-fashioned" or "red-necked" forms of racial bigotry that were common up to the 1960s with what has been termed "modern" or "new" racism in the 1980s. A comparison of the limited evidence on discourses of race in apartheid and postapartheid South Africa suggests that a similar shift may have occurred here.

Old-fashioned racism in America generally imputed a biological basis to race, and to the negative stereotypes associated with black people. White Americans considered black people to be inherently inferior—stupid, lazy, or dishonest—and supported discrimination and segregation.[16] Such "old-fashioned" racism was surely common in the past among white South Africans, most of whom repeatedly voted for parties that espoused segregation and discrimination. One study of white South Africans' attitudes, conducted in the mid-1960s, found a variety of attitudes toward racial issues and black people, but that the majority of people interviewed saw black people as inferior and supported apartheid as the solution to the country's "problems."[17] The study reports examples of the discourse of race which prevailed then:

> "To me the bantu is a child—a grown-up child in a manner of speaking."[18]

> "You can't speak to a Native as to a European."[19]

> "On the farm I always played with the piccanins but he was always kaffir and I was the boss."[20]

> "The Native in our land is still the hewer of wood and the drawer of water."[21]

> "The Bantu cannot really think for himself. It will take many centuries for him to develop."[22]

> "He is uncivilised, unintelligent."[23]

> "He belongs in his place and the whites in theirs."[24]

> "A kaffir is a kaffir, and a White person is a White person—there is a clear difference between the two and there is no question of social integration."[25]

Such views were repeatedly affirmed in church, cultural associations, the press, and the business world. While we should beware treating discourse and attitudes as stable or uniform, it seems likely that these views were widespread.

In the United States, the incidence of such "old-fashioned" forms of racism fell sharply in the second half of the twentieth century. Ever smaller numbers of white people employed the old racial stereotypes, or supported formal segregation or discrimination. But racial prejudice persisted in other, perhaps subtler, forms. These "modern" forms of racism incorporate antiracist, egalitarian, and humanitarian sentiments alongside strands of racial prejudice.[26] Overt racism is condemned, and discrimination is seen as a thing of the past. Individually, black people have the same rights and legitimate claims as anyone else. But black people collectively are viewed as "pushing too hard, too fast and into places where they are not wanted," their tactics and demands are seen as unfair, and they are judged to receive more attention and help than they deserve.[27] Modern racists in America thus combine opposition to formal discrimination or segregation with opposition to policies such as busing (i.e., busing black school pupils to schools in predominantly white areas, and vice versa) and affirmative action.[28]

The discourses of race used by people in Ruyterwacht mirror some of these themes. Black people are not represented as inferior, and nobody voiced support for discrimination or statutory segregation. Racism was denounced and instances of nonracism emphasized. There seemed to be an acknowledgement that black people had legitimate rights. Coloured or black people living in Ruyterwacht were portrayed as members of the "community," and most residents agreed that black chidren should in principle be allowed to use the school buildings. But at the same time the black pupils were seen as a threat, in part because of their large numbers in the small suburb, in part because of their supposedly bad behavior, and in part because black people collectively were represented as making unfair demands and using unreasonable tactics. Coloured people were seen as more "decent" than black people. Black people were said to be the real racists. While the residents were fair, reasonable, and orderly, the authorities were disregarding them and supporting injustice and disorder.

### EXPLANATIONS OF MODERN RACISM

One approach to "modern" racism suggests that racists have simply learned to give "socially desirable answers" and to avoid blatant displays of racial bigotry. According to this view, racist views are "disguised" in ostensibly nonracial language, perhaps allowing racist messages to be communicated while denying that this is being done. This argument has intuitive appeal, fitting the "commonsense understanding that people tailor their words and deeds to their social circumstances, concealing ideas or attributes that would evoke disapproval."[29] And analyses of "modern" racists' discourses show that they employ "standard discursive moves for

coping with negative evaluations," i.e., for denying charges of
racism, such as avoiding explicit generalizations and redirecting
charges of racism at others.[30]

Ruyterwacht residents used many such "discursive moves" in
their denial of racism, and there are some indications that residents—and especially activists on the picket line—tailored their
discourses to the particular interviewers. Some residents used
more overtly racist vocabulary when they were speaking Afrikaans,
in our presence but not to us, than when they addressed us in
English. We were presumably identified with a "liberal" academic
institution (the University of Cape Town); moreover, most of us
were identifiably foreign (American or British). Two recent South
African studies have argued that white South Africans employ
supposedly race-neutral discourses to disguise their racism.[31] Perhaps people in Ruyterwacht did likewise.

But to understand "modern" racism simply in terms of disguise
is to exaggerate the weakness of prejudice:

> In fact, race prejudice owes its strength to the fact that, from the
> point of view of the person who subscribes to it, it is not prejudice
> at all. The racial bigot does not see *himself* as a bigot, merely as a
> person who sees blacks as they are, for what they are; and there is
> nothing he has to be ashamed about just because blacks (in his
> eyes) have much about which to be ashamed. The failings are
> theirs, not his. To suppose that a controlling desire of racists is to
> hide their racism is to misread racism altogether.[32]

In Ruyterwacht, several of the people we spoke to were candid in
their criticisms of black people. Moreover, many of the people we
spoke to seemed to assume that we were sympathetic—perhaps in
part because we voiced our disquiet over the unfavorable media
reporting—and appealed to our "reason" to acknowledge that
what they had done, or what they thought, was "reasonable."
Moreover, we were in Ruyterwacht at a time when race had become the most salient issue and emotions ran high, making it
unlikely that residents who held old-fashioned racist views would
have restrained themselves. We think it unlikely that informants
successfully sublimated "natural" discourse throughout days of
continuous interviewing and contact. Moreover, their insistence
that they were not racist went deeper than a performance for our

benefit. Community leaders actually organized a march through the suburb in which some two hundred residents carried banners proclaiming that they were not racist and protesting against the media portrayal of them as such.

If Ruyterwacht residents' discourses of race are more ambiguous than the views associated with white South Africans in the heyday of apartheid, then we must ask "why?" The American literature on "modern" racism offers three broad, and possibly overlapping, explanations, each of which raises issues pertinent in the South African context.

Firstly, this "ambivalence" about race is said to be rooted in underlying, core values. The complexity of "modern" racism in America reflects the tensions between the "core American values" of egalitarianism and individualism. Egalitarianism leads people to oppose discriminatory policies and restrictions on the freedom of black people; individualism leads people to oppose policies (such as affirmative action) which are seen as serving to offset the qualities or failings that people have as individuals.[33] Discourse theorists similarly suggest that the contradictory nature of "modern racism" should be explained in terms of the competing "argumentative and rhetorical resources available in a 'liberal' and 'egalitarian' society."[34]

There are no obvious "core South African values" corresponding to these American ones. We found no references to Christianity or Afrikaner nationalism in popular discourse in Ruyterwacht, nor was there any appeal to history. There are, however, competing public discourses which could inform popular discourse and sentiment. Even under apartheid, public discourse was not monolithic. On the one hand, black and coloured people were said to be inferior, warranting discrimination. On the other hand, black people were said to be different, warranting segregation—but not necessarily inequality, as black people could exercise democratic rights in "their own" countries, and coloured people through "their own" institutions. Apartheid policy gave precedence to the former while its rhetoric, after 1960, emphasized the latter. The limited extant research suggests that notions of black inferiority (and criminality) had a much deeper hold on popular sentiment among white South Africans.[35] But the latter may have retained some purchase, providing some basis for the resurgence of public democratic and nonracial discourses since 1990, and especially since mid-1993.

Now, in the "new" South Africa, white South Africans are much more widely exposed to the discourse of nonracial democracy, equality, and rights. Negotiations are represented as preferable to violence, consultation to coercion. Even the National Party proclaims itself to be reborn as the "new," nonracial NP. This public discourse is reflected in discourse in Ruyterwacht. People in Ruyterwacht use the discourse of democracy, rights, and negotiations to support their claims to quiet streets and an orderly neighborhood—free, that is, of any rabble of young black people. It is perhaps the "newness" of the "new" South Africa which explains the absence of the key apartheid-era values in contemporary discourse.

But there is still a public discourse of black deviance, albeit muted, in the new South Africa. In its 1994 election campaign in the Western Cape, the National Party appealed to white and coloured voters primarily on the basis of allusions to the threat posed by black people and the ANC. White and coloured voters were represented as having common values and interests, which were threatened by the party of black South Africans, the ANC. The spectre of the "swart gevaar" was invoked by NP statements such as "the ANC want to take South Africa back to the dark ages" and the NP's condemnation of the ANC as being destructive rather than constructive. ANC supporters—black, of course—were said to be "uncontrollable"; they were linked to "no-go areas," "kangaroo courts," and "necklacing." The NP publicized the illegal occupation by black squatters of housing intended for coloured people, and portrayed a prominent, but unknown, murderer as a black man. Each of these themes is reflected in discourse in Ruyterwacht. Indeed, the ambivalence of racism in Ruyterwacht corresponds to the ambivalence of the National Party's position.

Finally, South African public discourses are still couched in terms of racial difference—not in the sense that races are necessarily or innately different but in the sense that in contemporary South Africa race is a crucial factor. When political leaders, religious leaders and the media pepper their pronouncements with references to "white," "coloured," and "black" South Africans, it is hardly surprising that racial categorizations are regarded as legitimate at the local level. Of course, South Africa is a racially structured environment, and it is far from being necessarily racist to acknowledge this. But the acknowledgement of the importance of race serves to legitimate the continued use of discourses of race.

A second approach to "modern" racism in America points to the changing nature of the debate about race. Black Americans' basic political and social rights are no longer at issue; ideologies of black racial inferiority no longer have their former purchase; and "old-fashioned" racism is rare. Public debate has shifted to the question of equality, and especially to public policies such as affirmative action. The complexity of "modern" racism reflects the fact that people hold contrasting views on these different issues, and indeed their views may differ between public policies. Thus white Americans might believe that segregation was wrong, that black and white Americans should have the same rights, but that affirmative action is wrong and the poor economic position of most black Americans is due to "their" lack of any work ethic and other personality failings. This is "modern racism."[36]

In South Africa, the issues have also changed. Black, coloured, and white South Africans enjoy the same rights before the law, and in terms of voting in national and provincial elections. We did not ask people about their views on formal segregation or discrimination, but nobody volunteered segregationist views. Indeed, several people made a point of emphasizing that "this is the new South Africa," apparently indicating their acceptance of formal equality. The issue now is not even *whether* black people should be allowed to move into the suburb, or black pupils into the school. Rather, the issue is *how* such changes are to be effected, in terms of both policy or procedure and the effects of change. In the view of Ruyterwacht people, black South Africans should not seize the school or invade the streets without proper consultation, nor should they behave improperly once they are there.

A third explanation of "modern" racism emphasizes rational competition over resources between groups rather than individual feelings of latent prejudice. According to this view, the new politics of race involves the defense of perceived group interests.

Members of defensive, dominant groups "tend to develop and adopt attitudes and beliefs that defend their privileged, hegemonic social position."[37] An individual need not be personally and directly threatened to feel that the social group with which he or she identifies is threatened. Any change in the power structure that affects the relative position of dominant and subordinate groups is likely to trigger anxiety, fear, and negative affect toward the subordinate groups. Racism is thus likely to be intensified when the victims of discrimination protest or rebel against it.

This is clearly plausible in the contemporary South African context, where white people are presumably concerned to protect existing privileges in the face of social and economic as well as political transformation. We can interpret the discourses and actual responses of Ruyterwacht residents in terms of perceived threats to their interests. Few white residents objected to the presence of growing numbers of "decent" coloured families in the area or of black and coloured pupils in the predominantly white schools. Nor did residents represent these families or pupils in negative terms. They were not seen as posing any threat, and could be absorbed into the "community"—a "community" of residents with common interests. Most residents even accepted the idea of five hundred orderly black pupils using the contested school, as long as it was done in the "right way," i.e., after consulting or at least informing the "community." But people in Ruyterwacht felt deeply threatened by the loss of control over their streets, the loss of any say over the school, and the projected loss of their rights to their own homes. It was not simply the fact that the pupils were black that prompted opposition and negative characterizations. Rather, it was the way in which black pupils were brought into Ruyterwacht that posed a threat to the residents' material interests (quiet streets, safety, housing), control, and power.

## CONCLUSION

Explanations of "modern" racism in America should not be imported wholesale into the contemporary South African context. There are similarities between the settings: both shifted away from institutionalized racism through statutory segregation and legal discrimination, and overt racism was generally excised from public discourse in both. But there are also differences: black people constitute a small minority of the American population but an overwhelming majority in South Africa (although the picture is complicated in greater Cape Town, with its large coloured population). The literature on "modern" racism in America suggests possible interpretations of the complexity and ambiguity of discourse in Ruyterwacht, but our evidence is insufficiently broad to allow conclusive answers.

We can say definitively that South Africa's transition to democracy has changed the context of discourses of race throughout South Africa, and especially in places like Ruyterwacht which are vulnerable to real and immediate change. Public discourse in the new South Africa is infused with references to democracy, human rights, and negotiations. And it exists alongside a public discourse of black criminality and barbarity. The issues at the heart of debates about race no longer concern basic political and civil rights. Most of the white residents of Ruyterwacht accept that these rights have been extended to their black compatriots, and that (decent) nonwhite families can therefore move into the area, and (well-behaved) nonwhite children can attend local schools. The controversial issues in 1995 concern social and economic transformation. What transformation and redistribution will there be, and how will this be effected? These questions can clearly involve conflicts over rescources—material and political—which coincide with perceived racial groupings.

It seems likely that the confused, uneven, and unfinished transition to the "new" South Africa underlies much of the ambiguity that characterized discourses of race in Ruyterwacht. Our chapter is a case study, though, limited in time and in space. It suggests the need for much better longitudinal evidence to assess the state of racial discourse before the transition, and broader empirical work on racial discourse in other areas of South Africa. We cannot conclude that Ruyterwacht is typical of the "new" South Africa. A study of the views of black South Africans in November 1994 concludes that they "perceive substantial improvements in white views and treatment of blacks"; overt racism was felt to have diminished, and social interaction had increased.[38] Studies of racial discourse elsewhere in South Africa would shed light on the social, economic, and political bases of racial representations, and on the causes and meanings of discursive shifts.

Nevertheless, we may take comfort that in Ruyterwacht—and perhaps elsewhere—racial identities are less prominent, racial stereotyping less hostile, and interracial contact more acceptable, than media reports would have led us to believe. Discourses of race in Ruyterwacht are rich with irony, surprisingly full of hope, and not without generosity—all of which surely bode well for the peaceful functioning of democracy in South Africa.

## NOTES

Research for this paper was conducted by the authors with the assistance of Devah Pager, Carol Jane Talbut, Zubair Sayed, Andre Malhoney, Ben Morgenthau, and Nicoli Natrass. We wish to thank Andre du Toit, Mike Morris, Hermann Giliomee, Ian Shapiro, and Will Kymlicka for helpful comments. Funding for this project was provided by the University Research Committee at the University of Cape Town and by the Centre for Social and Development Studies at the University of Natal, Durban.

1. A.G.J. Crijns, *Race Relations and Race Attitudes in South Africa* (Nijmegen: Drukkerij Gebr. Janssen N.V., 1959); Leo Kuper, Hilstan Watts, and Ronald Davies, *Durban: A Study of Racial Ecology* (London: Jonathan Cape, 1958); I. D. MacCrone, "Race Attitudes: An Analysis and Interpretation," in E. Hellman, ed., *Handbook on Race Relations in South Africa* (London: Oxford University Press, 1949); Margo Russell, *Study of a South African Interracial Neighborhood* (Durban: University of Natal, Institute for Social Research, 1961); Pierre van der Berghe, *Race and Racism: A Comparative Perspective* (New York: John Wiley, 1967).

2. Shula Marks and Stanley Trapido, eds., *Race, Class, and Nationalism in Twentieth-Century South Africa* (London: Longmans, 1987); Saul Dubow, *Scientific Racism in Modern South Africa* (Cambridge: Cambridge University Press, 1995); Ran Greenstein, "Racial Formation: Towards a Comparative Study of Collective Identities in South Africa and the United States," *Social Dynamics* 19:2 (1993); Jeremy Krikler, "Lessons from America," *Journal of Southern African Studies* 20:4 (December 1994).

3. Heribert Adam, "The South African Power Elite: A Survey of Ideological Commitment," in H. Adam, ed., *South Africa: Sociological Perspectives* (London: Oxford University Press, 1971); Adam Ashforth, *The Politics of Official Discourse in Twentieth-Century South Africa* (Oxford: Ox-

ford University Press, 1990); Stanley Greenberg, *Legitimating the Illegitimate: State, Markets, and Resistance in South Africa* (Berkeley: University of California Press, 1987); Deborah Posel, "The Language of Domination, 1978–83," in Shula Marks and Stanley Trapido, eds., *Race, Class, and Nationalism in Twentieth-Century South Africa* (London: Longman Press, 1987).

4. Don Foster, "On Racism: Virulent Mythologies and Fragile Threads," Inaugural Lecture, University of Cape Town, 1991, in Don Foster and Joha Louw-Potgieter, eds., *Social Psychology in South Africa* (Johannesburg: Lexicon, 1991).

5. For preliminary suggestions, see Eleanor Preston-Whyte, "Race Attitudes and Behaviour: The Case of Domestic Employment in White South African Homes," *African Studies* 35:2 (1976); Don Foster and Gillian Finchilescu, "Contact in a Non-Contact Society: The Case of South Africa," in M. Hewstone and R. Brown, eds., *Contact and Conflict in Intergroup Encounters* (Oxford: Basil Blackwell, 1986); Pierre Hugo, "Towards Darkness and Death: Racial Demonology in South Africa," in Hugo, ed., *South African Perspectives* (Pretoria: Die Suid Afrikaan, 1989); and Pierre Hugo, "The Greatest Evil of Our Time: Race and Rape Scares in South Africa," in C. J. Groenewald, ed., *Sociological Perspectives: Essays in Honor of S. P. Cilliers* (Stellenbosch: University of Stellenbosch, Department of Sociology, 1992).

6. Margaret Wetherell and Jonathan Potter, *Mapping the Language of Racism: Discourse and the Legitimation of Exploitation* (New York: Havester Wheatsheaf, 1992), 176.

7. John Solomos, *Race and Racism in Contemporary Britain* (Basingstoke: Macmillan, 1989); Ali Rattansi and Sallie Westwood, *Racism, Modernity, and Identity on the Western Front* (Cambridge: Polity Press, 1994); Wetherell and Potter, 1992.

8. Howard Schuman, Charlotte Steeh, and Lawrence Bobo, *Racial Attitudes in America: Trends and Interpretations* (Cambridge, Mass.: Harvard University Press, 1985); John Dovidio and Samuel Gaertner, eds., *Prejudice, Discrimination, and Racism* (San Diego: Academic Press, 1986); Phyllis Katz and Dalmas Taylor, eds., *Eliminating Racism: Profiles in Controversy* (New York: Plenum Press, 1988); Paul Sniderman, Richard Brody, and Philip Tetlock, *Reasoning and Choice: Explorations in Political Psychology* (Cambridge: Cambridge University Press, 1991); Paul Sniderman and Thomas Piazza, *The Scar of Race* (Cambridge, Mass.: Belknap Press, 1993).

9. *Sunday Times,* February 26, 1995.

10. *Cape Times,* March 9; *Sunday Times,* April 2, 1995.

11. Human Rights Committee, *Monthly Report* (February 1995): 14.

12. For example, "Outlook on the Month," *South African Outlook* 125:1/2 (January/February 1995): 2.

13. We expect to discuss the residents' responses more fully in a separate paper on the rise and decline of civic protest in Ruyterwacht.

14. N. J. Rhoodie and W. L. Du P. Le Roux, *A Sample Survey of the Attitudes of White Residents towards the Opening of Public/Municipal Amenities to All Races.* Report S-101 (Pretoria: Human Sciences Research Council, 1983); N. J. Rhoodie, *White Perceptions of Black-White Power-Sharing in South Africa's Central Government Institutions,* Occasional paper no. 43 (Pretoria: Human Sciences Research Council, 1989).

15. J. M. Niewoudt and C. Plug, "South African Ethnic Attitudes: 1973 to 1978," *The Journal of Social Psychology* (1983): 121, 163–71.

16. Schuman et al., *Racial Attitudes in America;* Dovidio and Gaertner, *Prejudice, Discrimination, and Racism.*

17. William Hudson, Gideon Jacobs, and Simon Biesheuvel, *Anatomy of South Africa: A Scientific Study of Present-Day Attitudes* (Cape Town: Purnell and Sons, 1966).

18. Ibid., 43.

19. Ibid., 74.

20. Ibid., 76.

21. Ibid.

22. Ibid., 78.

23. Ibid., 80.

24. Ibid.

25. Ibid.

26. Dovidio and Gaertner, *Prejudice, Discrimination, and Racism;* Schuman et al., *Racial Attitudes in America.*

27. John McConahay, "Modern Racism, Ambivalence, and the Modern Racism Scale," in Dovidio and Gaertner, *Prejudice, Discrimination, and Racism,* 92–93.

28. Sniderman and Piazza, *The Scar of Race.*

29. Ibid., 39.

30. Wetherell and Potter, *Mapping the Language of Racism,* 212–13; Teun van Dijk, "Discourse and the Denial of Racism," *Discourse and Society* 3:1 (1992).

31. John Dixon, Don Foster, Kevin Durrheim, and Lindy Wilbraham, "Discourse and the Politics of Space in South Africa: The Squatter Crisis," *Discourse and Society* 5:3 (1994); Raymond Koen, "The Language of Racism and the Criminal Justice System," *South African Journal of Human Rights,* forthcoming.

32. Sniderman and Piazza, *The Scar of Race,* 167.

33. Irwin Katz, Joyce Wackenut, and R. Glen Hass, "Racial Ambiva-

lence, Value Duality, and Behavior," in Dovidio and Gaertner, *Prejudice Discrimination, and Racism;* David Sears, "Symbolic Racism," in Katz and Taylor, *Eliminating Racism.*

34. Wetherell and Potter, *Mapping the Language of Racism,* 196–200, 217.

35. See Hudson et al., *Anatomy of South Africa.*

36. See Sniderman and Piazza, *The Scar of Race,* 167.

37. Lawrence Bobo, "Group Conflicts, Prejudice, and the Paradox of Contemporary Racial Attitudes," in Katz and Taylor, *Eliminating Racism,* 95.

38. Craig Charney, "Voices of a New Democracy: African Expectations in the New South Africa" (Johannesburg: Centre for Policy Studies, Research Report No. 38, 1995).

# 17

## FROM ETHNIC EXCLUSION TO
## ETHNIC DIVERSITY: THE AUSTRALIAN
## PATH TO MULTICULTURALISM

### JOHN KANE

Joseph Raz argues that multiculturalist policy is a response of liberalism to the fact of ethnic diversity.[1] Yet it is a response which troubles many liberals. This is, in part, because its collectivistic bias can seem at odds with the defence of individual rights, and in part because its sanction of multiple sites of loyalty and identity appears threatening to social unity.[2]

Australia is one nation which has not been dissuaded by such threats and tensions from adopting the multiculturalist alternative. Its commitment to multiculturalism is founded on the clear hope that cultural diversity can be recognized, respected, and even encouraged without undermining individual rights or impairing social unity. Indeed, it is fundamental to its rationale that respect for individual rights must include respect for the particular cultures to which individuals owe important allegiances. This clear and continuing commitment to the policy by government, and the dramatic historical shift it marks in Australian attitudes to ethnic minorities, make it an interesting case for study in the context of a discussion on group rights.

In this essay, I want to examine the historical trajectory of

Australian politics from an insistence on singular values and social homogeneity to an acceptance of value pluralism and cultural heterogeneity. I do so in the hope that the journey from White Australia to Multicultural Australia will provide a useful practical ground on which to explore some of the general themes raised by issues of ethnic diversity.

I must note at the start, however, that my focus will be upon policies toward *immigrant groups,* rather than on those toward Australia's indigenous populations. I justify this partly from considerations of space, but also with regard to an observation made by Kymlicka and Norman concerning different kinds of groups and group rights that tend to be run together by commentators on these matters.[3] The three types of rights in question are (1) special representation rights for disadvantaged groups; (2) multicultural rights for immigrant and religious groups; and (3) self-government rights for national minorities. Aboriginal Australians (themselves very culturally diverse),[4] may and do assert rights under all these forms, and insofar as they seek the general multicultural rights, (2), with which this chapter is largely concerned, then general observations apply also to them. Multiculturalism is an essentially *integrative* ideal,[5] and as such the issues with which it deals must be clearly distinguished from those that arise in contexts where national groups seek either autonomy from or domination over other groups, sometimes with disastrous consequences. The problems involved in building a unified polity out of separate, preexisting, and entrenched nationalities are quite different from those of creating an integrated and harmonious society out of a polyglot immigrant population, and it is essential not to confuse the two. I will not, therefore, be taking up the larger issues of autonomy and sovereignty which arise, inevitably, in the politics of indigenous peoples.

### Toward "Affirmative Multiculturalism"

Joseph Raz identifies a progression of liberal responses to "multiculturalism" (by which he means the *fact* of an existent multicultural society).[6] The three stages in this progression are, respectively, toleration, nondiscrimination, and affirmation. *Toleration,* the key Millian liberal value, consists of leaving minorities to conduct themselves as they wish without being criminalized, as long as they do not interfere with the culture of the majority. *Nondiscrimination* goes further than toleration and is based on the assertion of the traditional civil and political rights of liberalism, which forbid discrimination against any individual on the grounds of race, religion, ethnicity, gender, or sexual preference. Under a regime of scrupulous nondiscrimination, Raz says, "a country's public services, its education, and its economic and political arenas are no longer the preserve of the majority, but common to all its members as individuals."[7] The *affirmation of multiculturalism,* finally, transcends the individualistic approach of nondiscrimination and asserts the value of groups possessing and maintaining their distinct cultures within the larger community; the affirmatively multicultural society not only permits but actively encourages and assists different cultures to preserve their separate identities as best they may.

If we examine the Australian record in the light of this categorization, we may conclude that the nation skipped entirely, or at least hardly practiced, the first approach, toleration. It moved, after World War II, directly from an exclusivist policy that was intolerant of cultural and racial minorities[8] (and whose great institutional expression was the White Australia Policy on immigration) to an inclusivist one based on nondiscrimination; and finally, in more recent times, to one of affirmative multiculturalism.

Whether the policy of nondiscrimination was more tolerant of difference than the policy of exclusion it displaced is an arguable point, given that the goal of the former was to achieve the most complete assimilation of minorities to the dominant culture possible. Though "assimilation" could have implied a mixing of cultures and a newly emergent identity, somewhat on the "melting pot" model,[9] the prime concern of most Australians, at least until the 1960s, appeared to be that "New Australians" *fit in* with what already existed without changing it significantly. White Australia might have languished as an explicit policy of government in the postwar period, but the attitudes underlying it lingered on, and chief among these was a belief in the intrinsic superiority of white, British culture.

It was this belief that the new policy of multiculturalism questioned and found wanting. Multiculturalism, with its implicit commitment to value pluralism, sought to make Australia's welcome of migrants not conditional upon their utter conformity to the existing culture. In so doing, it signaled, among other things, the complete repudiation of the nation's racist past. No doubt there existed a variety of motives here. Nonracist policies[10] carry a strong signal of welcome, for example, to Australia's southeast Asian neighbors. Given the recent "discovery" of Asia as a potential market and trading partner for the twenty-first century, and its revised status as opportunity rather than threat in the Australian mentality, this is undoubtedly part of their intention.[11] But however mixed the motives, the moral case presented by multiculturalism's initiators and supporters[12] had to be made convincingly if it were to gain public acceptance. The psychological distance to be travelled by Anglo-Celtic Australians before reaching the point of acceptance was great (for some, of course, it was altogether *too* great). It implied a rejection of much of their history.[13] To appreciate the magnitude of the reversal of attitude that multiculturalism represents, some understanding of the past of White Australia is necessary.

## WHITE AUSTRALIA

The Australian past is one in which a national identity based on a presumed racial and cultural superiority was strongly asserted and legislatively defended by an immigration policy that served effectively to exclude members of so-called inferior races—that is, anyone whose skin color was other than white.[14]

Whiteness was absolutely fundamental. Australians were, as Donald Horne put it, "not only white, but whiter than white: the best people in the world at being white."[15] But as well as whiteness, the "thick" conception of national identity also contained equal parts of Britishness and Australianness. The former reinforced the superiority claim of whiteness, for if the white "races" were manifestly at the peak of evolutionary development, then the British were manifestly at the peak of the white races.[16] The claim of Australianness, on the other hand, indicated that the British character in the Australian environment had been modified by colonial leveling and toughening—though whether toward improvement or degeneration was sometimes a matter of debate.[17]

This tripartite identity functioned at each level to guard security and assert dominion.[18] Whiteness could be asserted against all the colored races of the world who might, by sheer force of numbers, displace the tiny colony from the vast land it had claimed at the southern end of the world, so far from the British "home." (It would be difficult to underestimate the importance of the persistent and terrifying pressure exerted on the minds of most Australians since the early days of colonization by the "teeming hordes"[19] of Asia, always imagined as jealously covetous of the vast, near-empty land to their south.) Britishness could be employed to summon imperial naval and military protection against threats from either the Asian multitudes or rival European powers. (In addition to such pragmatic factors, it should be noted that the psychological attachment of *Anglo*-Australians—as opposed to those of Celtic origin—was very strong; this is demonstrated by the fact that the concept of specifically Australian *citizenship* did not exist until 1948. Prior to that date, Australians were legally classified simply as British subjects.) Australianness, on the other hand, could be asserted against the whole world including, if needs be, against Britain itself, on those occasions when local interests varied from imperial ones.

The importance, to the majority of Australians, of defending this identity is evident in the fact that the immigration legislation which became known as the White Australia Policy was the first item on the agenda of the new Commonwealth parliament in 1901, following federation of the six colonies. A reading of the parliamentary debates on the matter reveals the virtual unanimity it commanded at all points of the political spectrum.[20] Most of the objections raised were not against the legislation itself but against what the protesters saw as its pusillanimous form. To avoid giving offence to the newly powerful and expansionist nation of Japan,[21] direct means of racial exclusion were eschewed and a "dictation test" established, whereby an "undesirable alien" could be required to write out a passage of fifty words in any European language directed by an officer.[22] Some members viewed this subterfuge as cowardly and opposed it on those grounds.[23] Nevertheless, it proved a remarkably effective device over the years.

Between 1901 and 1958, when the dictation test was abolished, the proportion of foreign-born non-Europeans actually declined from 1.25 percent (47,014) to 0.11 percent (9,973).[24] By 1966, when the policy was officially abandoned, Australia (excluding Aborigines) was calculated as being 99.7 percent white.[25]

The desired homogeneity had apparently been achieved.[26] This imperative drive towards homogeneity needs to be further explored, however, if we are to understand its political significance for white Australians during most of this century. Myra Willard put the matter clearly more than seventy years ago when she wrote:

> For the maintenance of their free social and political institutions— the concrete expression of democracy—Australians felt that all resident peoples must be treated alike. But to grant equality of social and political status to resident Asiatics, allowed to enter freely, would destroy the very conception that made such a society possible.[27]

It may seem paradoxical that a policy imbued with notions of human inequality should be pursued for the sake of equality, but to the thinking of the time it appeared perfectly reasonable. The late nineteenth century was the heyday of "scientific" racialism and of social Darwinism, and the racialist attitude was ubiquitous among white colonial nations.[28] Racial inequality was regarded by most people as *fact,* and the "inferior" races seen as fit only for protection—the "white man's burden"—or subjection. When measured against these alleged facts, the Enlightenment doctrine of the "equality of man" seemed invalid except as it might apply *within* races, and then only within those races sufficiently advanced in evolutionary terms to warrant and demand equality.[29] By such reasoning, the realization of egalitarian ideals could be made to seem dependent precisely on the preservation of racial and cultural homogeneity.

Intermarriage between races was believed to lead to the deterioration of the superior group with no compensating improvement in the inferior. In this worldview, whiteness was synonymous with purity, and the great fear was loss of purity (and of supremacy) through promiscuous mixing of races. Many of the defenders of White Australia appear, on the written records, to be obsessed with this notion of racial purity.[30] Even if intermarriage could be prevented, it was held that neither dominant nor inferior groups would benefit from close association. There were, it was true, always those plantation owners who argued that the importation of cheap "coolie" labor—Asian, Indian, or Pacific Islander—was the surest cure for scarce, expensive (and uncontrollable) white labor, but these were never politically dominant. Labor organizations regarded the "coolie option" as a ploy to drive down wages, and liberals feared the moral and political effects that a plantation economy would have on society. The white race would be removed from a healthy contact with labor, and society would become one of virtual slaves and slave owners,[31] with the consequent danger of the sort of civil strife that had rent the United States in the mid-nineteenth century.[32]

In any case, the sort of democratic polity which the majority of Australians wished to see preserved and developed was unthinkable, it was argued, in a mixed race society. Such a polity implied the maintenance of political liberty and equality, and this was only possible in a unified society of united race. According to Australian leader Arthur Deakin:

> A united race means not only that its members can intermix, intermarry and associate without degradation on either side, but implies one inspired by the same ideals . . . a people qualified to live under this Constitution—the broadest and most liberal perhaps the world has yet reduced to writing—a people qualified to use it without abusing it.[33]

The suggestion was that "inferior" races were not competent to fulfill the political duties that a democracy imposes.[34] White Australians had, here, both racial and cultural advantages. As members of the British "race," they believed themselves naturally endowed with physical, mental and moral qualities absent from or less developed in other races. As inheritors, also, of British political traditions and values, they felt themselves possessed of certain ingrained capacities for living under a democratic constitution. The racial and cultural strands were, to their minds, inextricably linked: it was precisely the possession of unique racial characteristics that had enabled the British constitutional achievement, and which also ensured that white Australians were morally and psychologically fit to appropriate that achievement and to develop it further in distinctive and progressive ways.[35] The same could not be hoped for from lesser races.

### DEMOCRACY AND SOCIAL CLEAVAGE: SIMPLIFYING THE ENVIRONMENT

However misguided or distasteful such racialist beliefs may now appear to us, it would be a mistake to judge the fears that Australians historically entertained as wholly without foundation. In particular, the existence of irreconcilable social differences is inevitably a genuine threat to democratic politics. Democracy attempts to contain and moderate social cleavages and conflicts within a structure of shared cultural values. It seeks to domesticate and naturalize conflict, allowing it to be played out with minimal destructive force in a political sphere characterized by mutual respect and tolerance. Democracy endeavors to defuse the threat of violence without succumbing to the temptation of suppression, thus steering a course between the Scylla of anarchy or civil war, on the one hand, and the Charybdis of totalitarianism on the other.[36] It should hardly be necessary to gesture towards those historical and contemporary examples which prove the danger of either rejecting this middle course or failing to navigate it successfully. Persistently effective democratic regimes are still, indeed, a historical rarity, partly no doubt because the conditions of their existence are so difficult to establish. Among other things, they require a populace which is both willing and able to play the civic game, and one which is undivided by differences too deep to be contained within its rules.

This was the problem facing Australians at the foundation of their nation, and the choices appeared to them stark. They sincerely desired the maintenance and strengthening of their democratic rights and recognized unreservedly that this implied a free and equal citizenry. But this ideal had to be accommodated to beliefs and fears which portrayed humanity precisely in terms of radical *in*equality. To admit large numbers of colored people for economic purposes but to deny them citizenship was unacceptable for the moral and prudential reasons already noted (and white Australians always had the great negative examples of South

Africa and the United States clearly in mind here). On the other hand, to admit colored immigrants and to *grant* them citizenship rights appeared equally unthinkable; here all the social, spiritual, and sexual fears associated with racialism came into play. The obsession with "purity" and the belief in the essential incapacity of "inferior" races for responsible citizenship meant that the mutual tolerance that democratic government required for its operation would not exist. Australians might seem historically culpable here, but the fact remains that, given the prevailing racialist climate, the possibility of creating a permanent underclass defined by color was undoubtedly real, as was the danger, in difficult economic times, of racial scapegoating and riot, such as had occurred on the goldfields a half-century earlier.

White Australians opted, therefore, for a policy of radical simplification. They would foster and maintain a society which was as racially and culturally homogeneous as it was possible to attain, by using a selective and discriminatory immigration policy and by encouraging already resident "aliens" to depart. Only thus did they think it possible to prevent the formation of social cleavages that might prove fatal to the preservation of the democratic social order. There was also, of course, that perennial fear of an under-populated nation in a vastly populous region, the belief that to open the doors to colored immigration was to risk being "swamped" and "Asianized." White Australians were insecure in their dominion of the great south continent but determined to maintain it, defending their right, at times vaingloriously, by the need to preserve white, British civilization.[37] It was for these reasons that White Australia was frequently described not as a policy but as a "religion," and that Sir Frederick Eggleston, writing in 1924, could describe it as "the formula which the Australian people have framed as the only solution of a number of very complex problems which affect their security and welfare."[38]

## From White Australia
## to Multicultural Australia

It was a solution that, however effective, would no longer answer in the latter half of the twentieth century. Even by the 1930s the very name of "White Australia" had shifted from being a boast to an embarrassment. In the post-World War II world it could no longer retain whatever respectability it might still have had. It fell victim to the rational discrediting of "scientific" racialism, to the terrible lessons of Nazism, and to a better and more liberally educated population, sections of which began vigorously to assert a revivified belief in the moral equality of all humankind.

The war had other consequences. The fact of Australian vulnerability seemed proven by the success of the Japanese sweep through the South Pacific and by what appeared for a time to be the imminence of invasion. After the war, under the alarmist slogan *Populate or Perish,* a program of massive assisted immigration was undertaken. The Labor Minister responsible for launching it, Arthur Calwell, remained adamantly committed to the policy of White Australia (and opposed to what he termed a *mongrel* Australia).[39] The immigration program was correspondingly targeted overwhelmingly at the population of Great Britain, and, as a second-best option, at Europe. At length, with immigrant numbers still regarded as insufficient, the program turned (somewhat desperately) to the peoples of other nations, mainly Italy and Greece, whose swarthier skins and lack of English made them objects of some suspicion and frequently of racist abuse.[40]

For many, the entry of these people in large numbers compromised the strict doctrine of White Australia, but they were all greeted as "New Australians" and expected to "assimilate." This implied the adoption of dominant cultural norms and practices, an imperative to become indistinguishable from the existing population. Education and employment programs were designed to assist and hasten this assimilation. Nevertheless, it was evident that, even before the official abandonment of the White Australia Policy, the ethnic composition of the nation had altered dramatically. The diverse traditions and characteristics of the new groups were not those of Anglo-Celtic Australia nor, however well they might adapt to the dominant culture, ever wholly would be.[41] A national identity based on the possession of distinctive racial-cultural characteristics ceased, in these circumstances, to be viable as a political option. This was even more the case after 1966, when entry was at last allowed to people of non-European descent,[42] and after the constitutional referendum of 1968 which granted Aborigines full citizenship rights for the first time. Nowhere more than among this latter group were the limitations of an assimilationist policy so clearly evident.[43] To some extent, then, the subsequent adoption of multiculturalist policy was merely a recognition of contemporary Australian reality, though its introduction involved the usual mix of philosophical justification and political calculation.

As an explicit policy of government in Australia, multiculturalism dates from the late 1970s. It was introduced by the ruling Liberal (conservative) Party, whose leaders had discerned in it the chance of securing a decisive portion of the "migrant" vote from their Labor Party opponents. The Galbally Report of 1978 commissioned by the Liberals asserted: "We are convinced that migrants have the right to maintain their cultural and racial identity and that it is clearly in the best interests of our nation that they should be encouraged and assisted to do so if they wish." [44]

Implementation was effected by a restructuring of the welfare system toward more "ethnic specific" services, such as the funding of ethnic schools and various community self-help programs. Other measures included the foundation of the Australian Institute of Multicultural Affairs, and the inauguration of a television and radio service, SBS, with a specific charter to serve Australia's ethnic communities.[45]

The Labor Party's commitment to ethnic groups had taken the traditional form of laborist welfare programs targeted at the "disadvantaged," of whom migrants formed a particular subset. The Minister of Immigration of the previous Labor government had been wont to stress the need for unity rather than diversity within the "family of the nation," though there was an expectation that immigrants would enrich the national life with their distinctive contributions.[46] Nevertheless, the Labor government that came to power in 1983 tolerated, for a while, the multiculturalist programs that were in place despite suspicion of their right-wing origins. But, in 1986, these programs were heavily slashed in a round of budget cuts, and the philosophy underpinning them was simultaneously questioned in a commissioned report which reasserted Labor's traditional welfare reformist attitude under the slogan "equitable participation." [47]

The vigorous criticism these changes evoked, however, led to reversals and partial restorations, and to the setting up in the

Prime Minister's Department of an Office of Multicultural Affairs. In the years that followed, the Labor government began to rethink its attitude to multiculturalism, and to develop its own version of Multicultural Policy, launched in 1989 as the *National Agenda for Multicultural Australia*. This was described as a "policy for managing the consequences of cultural diversity in the interests of the individual and society as a whole," and it combined the traditional social justice objectives of equal treatment for all with a new emphasis on cultural identity.[48] It also, as befitted an era of economic reconstruction, asserted a novel and pragmatical consideration, namely the efficiency dividends to be expected from utilizing the skills and talents of all Australians. The variety of these Australians was, in the meantime, becoming ever greater, as immigration from Vietnam, China, Taiwan, and the Philippines increased dramatically, with smaller numbers coming from such places as India, Fiji, Chile, and Korea.[49]

Labor's *National Agenda* guided multicultural policy in the federal arena until the party lost government in 1996.[50] The mix of policies that issued forth included those which attempted to provide equitable treatment for ethnic individuals, those which generously funded ethnic organizations to enable them to provide services to their members, and those dealing with specific problems arising in the state's dealings with various ethnic groups. The coalition government that came to power in 1996, though it grumbled at the "excesses" of multiculturalism, seemed intent on changing little but the name of the policy, with perhaps a few cuts to multicultural projects as part of a general policy of budget cutbacks. There was no question of a substantial change of direction. The overall aim was, as it had always been, to fully integrate Australia's immigrants into the nation's social and political life, but now with an insistence on the propriety and (by implication) possibility of achieving this via the recognition and even encouragement of continuing cultural diversity. The policy of "assimilation" which had reigned supreme for more than half a century seemed comprehensively overthrown.

Former Liberal Prime Minister Malcolm Fraser put the positive case for multiculturalism clearly, and at the same time emphasized the distance that official thinking has traveled in these matters: "We cannot demand of people that they renounce the heritage they value, and yet expect them to feel welcome as full members of our society. . . . [Multiculturalism] sees diversity as a quality to be actively embraced, a source of wealth and dynamism."[51] This, presumably, is as far as one can go from the formerly prevailing view of white identity and responsible democratic citizenship as logically conjoined. Identity, in the thick descriptive sense at least, has now been dissociated from citizenship rights, and multiple identities are expected peacefully to coexist within the bounds of a common citizenship. It is worth noting again, here, that the encouragement of diversity is not intended, nor expected, to result in the development of separatist, quasi-nationalist sentiment among immigrant groups and the fragmentation of society. Quite the contrary. It is intended to make such groups feel welcome *as full members of society,* and thereby to bind them within the larger society with ties of mutual respect and to their mutual advantage.

## THE LIMITS OF MULTICULTURAL TOLERANCE

The repudiation of racism implied that no person should, on the grounds of color or ethnicity, be excluded from participative citizenship in the democratic polity. This, when extended to matters of gender, religion and so on, is the essence of the nondiscriminatory approach. It is essentially an assimilative ideal, regarding individuals as strictly indistinguishable in social and political terms, however polyglot their attributes.[52] Affirmative multiculturalism in Australia seeks to go further than this. Nondiscrimination, it argues, may be necessary but is insufficient for the fulfilment of adequate citizen rights.

Multiculturalism agrees with its predecessor, the White Australia Policy, on the salience of cultural difference. Unlike its predecessor, however, it regards the portrayal of difference in terms of moral superiority and inferiority as invidious and rationally unwarranted. White Australia stressed difference in order to exclude; multiculturalists stress it in order to allow a more just and comprehensive accommodation of groups in a polity. As Kymlicka and Norman rightly point out, the demand for multicultural rights, like the demand for special representation rights, is generally a demand for *inclusion* in the larger society.[53] We are not, as I stressed at the outset, dealing here with separatist national minorities seeking political autonomy but with immigrant groups who desire to be full and bona fide members of their adopted nation. The point of paying attention to the differences that multiculturalist policy signifies is to promote a greater integration of these disparate groups. The integrative intention is clearly signaled in the Liberal government's Galbally Report of 1978: "Provided that ethnic identity is not stressed at the expense of society at large, but is *interwoven into the fabric of our nationhood* by the process of multicultural interaction, then the community as a whole will benefit substantially and its democratic nature will be reinforced."[54]

The Labor government's *National Agenda for Multicultural Australia* flags the same intention in its description of a "policy for managing the consequences of cultural diversity *in the interests of the individual and society as a whole.*"[55] Labor's *National Agenda,* however, when it asserts the right of all Australians, to express and share their individual cultural heritage, including their language and religion, also adds the important proviso "within carefully defined limits". If disparate cultures are to be accommodated (and are to accommodate themselves) more or less harmoniously within a common framework, then clearly each must be subordinate to the values expressed by that framework, in this case the values of a liberal-democratic polity. An individual culture or an individual cultural practice is acceptable only insofar as it does not significantly transgress key values as these may be expressed in institutions, traditions, and laws. Thus, mutual toleration is fundamental and required even of groups not marked by traditions of tolerance. Thus, the fulfilling of a *fatwa* proclaimed upon an individual citizen is unacceptable (and, of course, illegal) however eminent and holy the proclaimer may be. Thus, the infibulation of female children is a practice to be legally and practically discouraged, however deeply embedded it may be within a particular culture. And so on.

It is necessary to note here a theoretical issue of some importance, though it is one that I cannot begin adequately to address within the confines of this essay. This is whether the concept of multiculturalism finds its securest foundation within liberal or within democratic theory. I began this essay with Raz's view of multiculturalism as a liberal response (albeit an uncomfortable one for many liberals) to diversity, one which tries to extend the liberal principle of toleration to the cultural groups within which individual identities are acquired. On the other hand, I have dwelt upon the way in which democratic institutions function to create a political realm in which social conflicts can be both expressed and contained; in recounting the Australian experience, I have referred to the felt need, repeatedly expressed by Australians, to preserve and strengthen their *democratic* institutions, first by a policy of homogeneity, and then through a policy of multiculturalism. The question encountered in considering the *limits* to multicultural toleration is whether these are imposed by strictures inherent in liberalism or in democracy itself.

Australian democracy is, in common with most other Western democracies, precisely a *liberal* democracy. This was the form of representative democratic polity most acceptable to (or least threatening to) economic liberals who, despite a set of overlapping values between democracy and liberalism, historically regarded the extension of the franchise to the laboring classes with suspicion and fear. So long as economic liberalism remains central to liberal ideology (and to the capitalist system), the hybrid liberal-democratic polity will always be subject to a certain tension: the possibility will always exist that a democratic majority may dismantle the economic structures that liberalism seeks to preserve. The federal structure set up by the Australian Constitution was seen by its designers (among whom the labor movement was unrepresented) as a further means of taming the democratic polity to safeguard against just such a possibility.[56] When Australian leaders and commentators have spoken of the need to defend or enlarge democracy, then, it is always this fragmented liberal-democratic polity that is intended.

Multiculturalism, insofar as it poses no discernible threat to the free market system, is to that extent acceptable to liberal democrats. As we have seen, it was a Liberal[57] government in Australia which first proposed the adoption of a multicultural policy and Labor which, at first, distrusted it (though today it has become closely identified with Labor, and its most vocal opponents are largely Liberal). If multiculturalism runs into limits imposed by liberalist philosophy, it is at points where specific cultural values may clash with liberal values wider than the purely economic, values like the defence of individual liberty and choice, the toleration of different opinions and beliefs (including beliefs about the good life) and the location of human worth in individual human beings rather than in collectivities. It is in these areas, however, that we find the greatest overlap between liberal and democratic values, and it is possible that the best version of both the virtues and limits of multiculturalism may be found in some version of democratic theory rather than in a version of liberalism.[58] It is not my intention to attempt to pursue this question here. I will merely note that, whatever the theoretical solution to the problem, the fact is that the Australian polity embodies and is committed to certain values, typical of, though perhaps not fully coherently expressed in, liberal-democratic governments. These values, whatever their ultimate origin or justification, serve to draw a line in the ground across which the contradictory values of groups or individuals within society ought not to pass.

In other words, the rights that groups in a multicultural liberal-democratic polity may properly assert, either internally with regard to their own membership or externally with regard to other groups,[59] are limited to those which do not interfere with fundamental rights granted to, and obligations imposed on, individuals by that polity. The granting of group rights is governed by the integrative intent of such rights. That is, special rights or dispensations may be granted to individuals as members of particular groups in order that may fully participate in the life of the general society. In terms of Marshall's classic formulation on citizenship,[60] such rights aim at enabling members of particular groups to better translate their formal civic rights into active political participation or into an equitable share of material social benefits.

Insofar as multiculturalism may seem to liberals a threat rather than a fulfilment, it is perhaps pertinent to note, in the light of the limits expressed above, that affirmative multiculturalism can be interpreted as representing a widening of the individualistic premises of liberalism and not a rejection of them. Multiculturalism recognizes that individuals are neither abstractions nor are they *sui generis;* they spring from specific and diverse cultures which may be valued by and be of value to them in any number of ways,[61] and which they may therefore cherish and wish to preserve. Multiculturalism asserts that individual well-being is importantly related to cultural integrity, and thus argues that the state has a role in guarding that integrity. But the limit to this safeguarding is struck as soon as a civic, social, or political right of any individual, group member or otherwise, is transgressed. Raz argues that the moral claim of groups to respect and prosperity "rests entirely on their vital importance to the prosperity of individual human beings. This case is a liberal case, for it emphasizes the role of cultures as a precondition for, and a factor which gives shape and content to, individual freedom."[62] Nor is the value pluralism implicit in multiculturalism necessarily incongruent with liberalism insofar as the latter traditionally seeks to avoid imposing on individuals any particular conception of the good life.[63] Different cultures embody different values, and the essence of individual freedom means being able to choose among plural and competing values. However, the liberal adherence to the value of individual liberty above all others places severe enough limitations upon the values that any particular culture in a liberal democracy may pursue or the manner in which it may seek to fulfill them.

Whenever a particular culture rubs up against one of these liberal-democratic limits to multicultural tolerance, conflict can be anticipated. Multiculturalism, with the best will in the world, inevitably encounters difficulties of adjustment when trying to fulfill its dream of unity within diversity. The hope of multiculturalists is that conflict can be better managed and contained by their policy than by any other.

## MULTICULTURALISM IN AUSTRALIA

In Australia, at any rate, multiculturalism appears to have been marked by a notable success. The fact that an important international Global Cultural Diversity Conference in April 1995 was convened in Sydney, was taken by the local media as "testimony to Australia's growing international profile as a largely harmonious, multicultural society."[64] It was a conference at which United Nations secretary-general Boutros Boutros-Ghali lamented the "new and troubling phenomenon" of micronationalism, characterized by ethnic, religious, and cultural separatism, and at which concern was expressed over "explosive" tensions in a Europe hostile to migrants within its borders. In a world where the pressures of globalization, modernization, and large migration threatened increasing ethnic conflict, Australia was held up by many speakers, including the director general of UNESCO, Federico Mayor, as an example worthy of emulation. At a colloquium on multiculturalism in Melbourne in August 1995, it was pointed out that the Australian population had increased by 7.5 million to 18 million since World War II, 6.4 million of this being due to immigration, and more than 4 million of the latter being non-Anglo-Celtic. Professor Charles Price argued that no other country had absorbed such a high proportion of migrants so successfully.[65]

Cynics might be tempted to argue that it is easier for Australia to be multicultural after a couple of centuries during which white hegemony was thoroughly accomplished by policies of virtual extermination of indigenes and exclusion of foreigners.[66] In such circumstances, nonwhite minorities are scarcely in a position to do other than assimilate or be marginalized. Indeed, this view seemed to be confirmed at the colloquium mentioned above when Professor Price argued that the relative tolerance of postwar Australian society could be attributed to the fact that, Anglo-Celts aside, no single ethnic group comprises more than 4 percent of the population. He claimed that "this balance of nationalities has saved Australia the problems of large minority groups, such as Canada has with the French, and the United States with the African and Spanish minorities."[67]

It may also be, of course, that the absence of newsworthy episodes of intercommunal strife in Australia is a consequence of luck rather than of policy, a point other nations will need to decide before adopting the "Australian approach" to multiculturalism. No clear and comprehensive picture has yet emerged of either the problems or the successes of multiculturalism in this country that would enable such a judgment to be accurately made.

There is, however, no absence of less spectacular problems.[68] Ethnic groups in Australia are just as liable as those elsewhere to suffer the sort of value clashes noted above, and these can be very painful for communities trying to defend traditional ways in a liberal democratic, capitalist environment. No culture is immune to change, especially when confronted not just with adjacent cultures but with the powerful forces of modernity. It hardly needs to be said that the modern industrial state, whether democratic or not, tends to dissolve or reshape the ties that bind "traditional" groups. The generations grow apart, as first generation immigrants try to maintain their ways while the young feel the pull of more material and libertarian values. The north of England riots of June 1995 were attributed to just this phenomenon, as second-generation Indian and Pakistani youth rebeled against family and religious strictures, and against their parents' traditional attitude of quiescence and retreat in the face of societal racism.[69]

Australian immigrant youth similarly protest, though short of riot so far, at finding themselves inhabiting, not so much a harmonious multicultural society, as a cultural limbo. According to Kate Legge, the problem "is particularly pressing for young girls, who acculturate more quickly to the values and practices of a new society than adolescent boys, yet whose freedom is more strictly curtailed."[70] Legge cites disturbing cases of the brutal beating and even murder of teenage girls by their families when the former have seemed to "dishonor" the latter by behavior condoned or tolerated by Anglo-Australian society but a cause of shame in the tradition to which the family belongs.[71] (Even as I write this, a case is before the Australian courts in which a father, a prominent member of Melbourne's Lebanese-Arab community, admitted paying two undercover policemen to murder his daughter because of her refusal to participate in an arranged marriage, to preserve, he said, his own reputation in the community.)[72] The problem for a Community Services Department trying to deal with such cases is to develop practices which are culturally sensitive but which do not compromise general societal standards of acceptable behavior. The New South Wales Child Protection Council, after consulting with Non-English Speaking Background groups, identified a need for a uniform definition of child abuse, and said in a report entitled "Culture—No Excuse" that "this was especially true in relation to physical abuse and neglect which was more likely to be discounted as a "cultural practice," leaving children potentially at risk."[73] The difficulties are multiplied because, as Community Services officer Alan Raison notes, "the issues are all so different from culture to culture."[74]

Similarly in the matter of arranged marriages of underage girls, and also of female circumcision (legal actions on both of which have attracted sensationalized reporting in Australia), the rights attributed to individuals[75] by a liberal democratic polity come into collision with older attitudes of particular communities. Jenny Burley, who has researched the Vietnamese community of South Australia, notes that in such communities individual interest is subordinate to the welfare of the group, and family honor is paramount.[76] Hien Le, coordinator of the Bankstown Vietnamese Community Resource Centre, says that the degree of freedom given to an individual in Vietnamese society is very small, and children are considered to be "human properties" of the family, to whom anything may legally be done.[77] Intergenerational conflict is inevitable when Vietnamese youth attempt to exercise the same freedoms and rights as their Anglo peers. Immigrant groups may, indeed, have no clear conception of what rights their own children have in this society. The Bankstown police, reportedly, receive calls from Muslim families demanding action over daughters who, quite legally at age 18, have gone to live with boyfriends.[78] In these circumstances, both parents and children experience the agonies of trying to reconcile traditional values with freer Western ways.

This is the stuff of multicultural contact everywhere, of course, though some argue that in Australia the problems are exacerbated precisely by a multicultural policy which encourages the maintenance of cultural difference, thereby slowing the cultural change or dissolution which must inevitably occur. This may be especially the case if cultural assistance becomes politicized. Jerzy Zubrzycki, one of the intellectual architects of multicultural policy, claims that commonwealth and state grants to ethnic groups are often based not on a community's social need but on its voting strength.[79] This "blatant wooing" of an ethnic vote represents a grave distortion of multiculturalism, he argues, in that special funds and programs are directed to groups "irrespective of whether they lead to a cohesive or a fragmented society."[80] Zubrzycki believes these are serious charges, given the integrative intent of multicultural policy.

Because of Zubrzycki's founding role, his comments on this occasion received wide attention in the press. They were regarded as a significant contribution to the debate concerning multiculturalism that goes on daily, and often heatedly, in the Australian media. Zubrzycki, in fact, claims that the term itself has outlived its usefulness, because of inherent ambiguities and certain negative associations, and proposes its replacement with the motto "Many Cultures. One Australia."[81] This seems unlikely to catch on, though Zubrzycki argues that it expresses the ideal better, and that the One Australia side of the equation must define the "core values" that will hold the disparate groups together. These turn out to be, of course, the linguistic, political and legal heritage of the English past, traditionally associated with Australian liberal democracy. Indeed, analysis of Zubrzycki's current position reveals it to be virtually indistinguishable from Labor's old, assimilative nondiscrimination policy, though with a few rhetorical gestures toward "ethnic pluralism" thrown in. It argues that ethnic grants should be confined to short-term measures to raise particular communities to a position of equal opportunity and not extended to assist community preservation which (the fear is clearly expressed) may encourage social fragmentation.

And it may be, given the limits which liberal democratic values necessarily place on cultural tolerance, and the stresses that modern Western culture places on traditional communities, that the reality of multiculturalism turns out to be not so distant from this older doctrine. Certainly, there has always been a great deal of rhetoric in the arguments of both opponents and supporters of the newer policy. It is quite possible, indeed, that Australian multiculturalism's greatest importance is less in its practical policy manifestations than in its symbolism, in the clear declaration it makes of the distance traveled from the old days of the White Australia Policy. It is the nation telling itself, telling its immigrant populations and telling the world, "We are no longer what we were. We have changed, and what is more we do not regret the change but embrace it, for it has made us better than we were."

Such symbolism should not be underestimated, nor misunderstood as an exercise merely in self-congratulation. The assurance that multiculturalist propaganda conveys to immigrant groups within the nation may be profoundly important to their sense of welcome and security, to their sense of rightful belongingness in the nation they have adopted as their own, and to the protection the state is willing to extend to them against abuse. Such assurances, indeed, may be ever needful. The strength with which the multiculturalist message is propagated betrays, perhaps, the real fear which underlies it. This is the fear of a persistent racism, assumed to be always simmering just below society's relatively unruffled surface, and wanting only the occasion to be unleashed in all its ugly splendor.[82] Certainly, the electoral success of organizations such as Australians against Further Immigration, and periodic outbreaks of xenophobia in the press, lend credence to such fears. White Australia may be down, but is not yet dead, and multiculturalism seeks to drown its voice by its own insistent clamor.

## Conclusion

Then Prime Minister Paul Keating, in his address to the Global Cultural Diversity Conference,[83] indulged the now familiar sentiment of Australia as "among the most successful multicultural societies in the world." He argued that the cement which holds Australians from more than 150 ethnic backgrounds together is made of "core Australian values and beliefs," namely, an easy egalitarianism, a profound belief in democracy, tolerance, pragmatism, and a deep commitment to Australia. For over two hundred years, waves of settlers have been enriching Australia, he said, and each wave has "extended the reach of our egalitarianism and tolerance, our understanding of what Australian democracy is."

Making allowances for rhetoric, this view may not be too far from the truth. It expresses the truth of *intention*, at any rate, of multicultural policy. The core values of the Australian polity have, in fact, changed very little since the foundation of the nation; what has changed is the range of persons, and of cultural groups, deemed fit and entitled to share in these values. The reach of egalitarianism and tolerance have indeed been extended. Where once it seemed to Australians that the values could only be defended by a policy of exclusion and enforced homogeneity, it is now argued that these same values can bind together a heterogeneous society composed of many and varied cultural groups. The presumed logical link between white identity and democratic political values has been broken; cultural variety can be, not merely tolerated, but encouraged without risk to these central values.

Whether hope will match reality, whether Australia has found the formula for achieving ethnic harmony remains to be seen. It would be naive to think that serious racial violence or inter-communal strife is impossible there but pessimistic to presume it is absolutely inevitable. Indeed, I would not wish to discredit the view, which appears accurate enough, that Australians of many different backgrounds live side by side in many localities quite amicably. But some realism is nevertheless in order. Australian multicultural rhetoric often paints too rosy a picture of a cheerfully and colorfully integrated society of peoples whose complementary gifts and talents will create and enrich a dynamic young nation. (There is also a tendency for multiculturalism to become infected with a fashionable "political correctness" with sometimes farcical results.) [84] The nonutopian hopes of Joseph Raz for a liberal multicultural society seem preferable.[85] Raz presumes that a genuine commitment to the value pluralism implied by multiculturalism means accepting that tension and conflict between incompatible values will be endemic. What the policy requires, however, is not that we all love each other but that we coexist fruitfully *however* we feel about one another.[86] But tension and conflict exist in all societies, homogeneous or heterogeneous; it is recognition of this inevitability that democratic politics embodies, seeking to constrain conflict within its forms without annihilating it.[87] If the difficulty of accomplishing this is greater in a polyethnic society, then the need is all the greater for ensuring that democratic values are instilled, observed and extended by all groups within the society.

Which brings us again and finally to the limits that liberal democratic politics necessarily impose on multicultural tolerance and multicultural rights. A multicultural liberal-democratic polity is required to respect the values of various cultures only to the extent these do not infringe that polity's own core values. It is not, of course, required to sustain the values of any particular group.[88] Communities must survive and adapt as best they may in a changing world, as must liberal democracy itself. It would be pointless, and futile, to privilege a particular statically and homogeneously conceived cultural formation by trying to shield it from the pressures of change, especially as many members of particular communities may themselves be working towards change. And in a clash between the individual rights of a person and the demands placed upon them by their ethnic community, multiculturalism must find ways, within the borders of the respect it extends, to defend the rights of the individual, whatever the long-term consequences for the community.


## NOTES

I would like to thank Ian Shapiro and Will Kymlicka for their generous and useful comments on an earlier draft of this essay. I would also like to thank Geoff Stokes for his comments and contributions to an earlier paper which are also relevant to the present chapter.

1. J. Raz, "Multiculturalism: A Liberal Perspective," in *Ethics in the Public Domain: Essays in the Morality of Law and Politics* (Oxford: Clarendon Press, 1994), 157–60.

2. See ibid.

3. Will Kymlicka and Wayne Norman, "Return of the Citizen: A Survey of Recent Work on Citizenship Theory," *Ethics* 104 (1994): 372.

4. See Tim Rowse, "Aboriginal Citizenship," in W. Hudson and J. Kane, eds., *Rethinking Australian Citizenship*, (Sydney: University of New South Wales Press, forthcoming).

5. I owe this phrase to Will Kymlicka; see his book *Multicultural Citizenship: A Liberal Theory of Minority Rights* (Oxford: Clarendon Press, 1995).

6. Ibid., 157.

7. Ibid., 158.

8. Until the 1960s, Australia was generally regarded by its critics, internal and external, as highly conformist and intolerant of *all* difference, from whatever this difference may have sprung. It was, in short, a highly parochial society. See Manning Clark, *A Short History of Australia* (Ringwood, Victoria: Penguin, 1986), 205–7, 216–17.

9. See R. Takaki, *A Different Mirror: A History of Multicultural America* (New York: Little, Brown, 1993) for a history of the "melting-pot" idea.

10. There have been a number of antiracialist policies in recent years, the most important of which are the ending of the White Australia policy on immigration (1966), the passage of the national Racial Discrimination Act (1975), and multiculturalist policy itself.

11. Australian sincerity in this respect may be treated by South-East Asian nations with more than a measure of scepticism, and perhaps

cynicism. See Julia Suryakusuma, "Can the Eagle and the Kangaroo Co-Exist?" *The Australian, Special Review, Asians in Australia* (15 March 1994): 3.

12. It need not be imagined that multiculturalism commands complete and utter assent from all Australians. It has had its vociferous critics from the start, the chief of whom, perhaps, is Professor Geoffrey Blainey, last great prophet of White Australia. See, for example, his Speech to Rotarians at Warrnambool, Victoria (17 March 1984), and *All for Australia* (Nth Ryde, NSW: Methuen Haynes 1984), 25–35.

13. For an examination of Australia's ambivalent historical legacy in this regard, see my paper, "Racialism, Democracy, and National Identity: The Legacy of White Australia," in G. Stokes, ed., *The Politics of National Identity in Australia* (Melbourne: Cambridge University Press, forthcoming).

14. Or, indeed, any undesirable member of a "superior" race, for example, suspected communists.

15. Donald Horne, "Identity Lies in Beliefs We Must All Uphold," *The Australian* (8 February 1994): 12.

16. There was a tendency to describe the British, French, and Germans as different "races." See R. A. Huttenback, *Racism and Empire: White Settlers and Colored Immigrants 1830–1910* (Ithaca: Cornell University Press, 1976), 15.

17. D. Cole, "'The Crimson Thread of Kinship': Ethnic Ideas in Australia, 1870–1914," *Historical Studies* 14:56 (1971): 518–22.

18. Ibid.

19. The populations of Asia were almost invariably described in such terms, with all their verminous connotations.

20. The deep racialist sentiments characteristic of the age cut across all social classes and infected even the most radical of labor leaders. See B. C. Mansfield, "The Origins of White Australia," *The Australian Quarterly* 26:4 (1954); and A. Markus, "White Australia? Socialists and Anarchists," *Arena* 32–33 (1973). The first Prime Minister of the new nation, Edmund Barton, found the policy politically useful precisely *because* it commanded universal assent and thereby ensured an harmonious inauguration of parliament, something that would have been impossible had he focused immediately on the burning issue of the day, which was protection versus free trade; see A. T. Yarwood, "The 'White Australia' Policy: A Reinterpretation of Its Development in the Late Colonial Period," *Historical Studies* 10:39 (1962): 258.

21. Indeed, Japan was a principal target of the legislation, the Chinese having been effectively excluded during the 1880s by coordinated colonial legislation. The Japanese did not object in principle to the policy,

but did not wish to see themselves classified with races they themselves held to be "inferior." Pressure from the Japanese government and from the Colonial Secretary in Whitehall, Joseph Chamberlain, who was concerned at the slight implied on Indian subjects of the Empire, ensured that the indirect "Natal dictation test," pioneered in South Africa precisely to exclude Indians, won the day. See Yarwood, "The 'White Australia' Policy," 258.

22. The ploy did not *always* work, as the farcical 1934 case of Egon Kisch demonstrates. Kisch, an alleged communist, was given (and failed) the dictation test in Scottish Gaelic, but the High Court overturned the decision on the grounds that Gaelic was not a European language! See A. T. Yarwood, "The Dictation Test—Historical Survey," *The Australian Quarterly* 30:2 (1958): 27.

23. George Reid, Member for East Sydney, declared that "The effect of this ministerial device is that instead of putting 'White Australia' before the world, we put 'funky Australia' before it—an Australia shivering at the very shadow of the Japanese bogey," *CPD* V-5812, cited in D. M. Gibb, *The Making of "White Australia"* (Melbourne: Victoria Historical Association, 1973), 108.

24. A. C. Palfreeman, "The End of the Dictation Test," *Australian Quarterly* 30:2 (1958): appendix I, p. 50.

25. A. C. Palfreeman, *The Administration of the White Australia Policy* (Melbourne: Macmillan, 1967), 2.

26. Though these figures conceal a large proportion of postwar immigrants from southern Italy, Greece, and other European countries whose "assimilation" into the dominant culture was seldom regarded by Anglo-Celtic Australians as ideal. See later in this essay.

27. Myra Willard, *History of the White Australia Policy* (Melbourne: Melbourne University Press, 1923), 196.

28. See C. D. Goodwin, "Evolution Theory in Australian Social Thought," *Journal of the History of Ideas* 25 (1964): 393–416; and Huttenback, *Racism and Empire*.

29. Bruce Smith's was a rare voice raised in the parliamentary debates of 1901 to oppose this narrow reading of the doctrine. He criticized colleagues' liberal use of the phrase "equality of man" because, when asked "What man?" the reply was "Australians," and beyond that "important distinctions" were invoked. Cited in A. T. Yarwood, *Attitudes to Non-European Immigration* (Melbourne: Cassell, 1968), 99–100.

30. The theme is repeated indefinitely in newspapers of the period. Even when racialism is being apparently disavowed, the theme emerges, as when the *Bulletin*, Sydney, of 22 June 1901 declares that if there could be found "a black, or brown, or yellow race, in Asia or Africa, that has as

high a standard of civilisation and intelligence as the whites, that is as progressive as the whites, as brave, as sturdy, as good nation-making material, and that can intermarry with the whites without the mixed progeny showing signs of deterioration, that race is welcome in Australia regardless of color. . . . But there is no such race."

31. See the extract from an *English Review* article by F. W. Eggleston, reprinted in Yarwood, *Attitudes to Non-European Immigration*, 120–23.

32. The *Age* newspaper of 2 June 1898, for instance, expressed a wish "to see Australia the home of a great homogeneous Caucasian race, entirely free from the racial problems which have plunged the United States into civil war."

33. Cited in Gibb, *The Making of "White Australia*,*"* 103–4.

34. This argument was also advanced, by Sir Henry Parkes, to justify the *withholding* of political rights. See Yarwood, *Attitudes to Non-European Immigration*, 94.

35. Huttenback, *Racism and Empire*, 15.

36. See Alain Touraine, "What Does Democracy Mean Today?" *International Social Science Journal* 128 (1991): 250–59.

37. According to one of the leading exponents of White Australia, Charles Henry Pearson, Australia might prove a final bastion of the whole of white civilization, if history went as he foresaw, when "the European will look round to see the globe girdled with a continuous zone of black and yellow races"; from *National Life and Character: A Forecast*, extracted in Gibb, *The Making of "White Australia*,*"* 23–35. This work was cited approvingly by Prime Minister Edmund Barton in the Commonwealth Debates on the immigration question (7 August 1901, p. 3503).

38. In Yarwood, *Attitudes to Non-European Immigration*, 121.

39. "We can have a white Australia, we can have a black Australia, but a mongrel Australia is impossible, and I shall not take the first steps to establish the precedents which will allow the flood gates to be opened." A. A. Calwell, Minister for Immigration, *Commonwealth Parliamentary Debates*, vol. 201 (9 February 1947): 63–64. Calwell professed to respect "Asiatics" and to regard them as equal but "too different from us." A famous remark allegedly revealing his racism was made of a certain Mr. Wong who the press said was being expelled after twenty years of residency: "There are many Wongs in the Chinese community, but I have to say . . . that two Wongs don't make a White." *Commonwealth Parliamentary Debates*, vol. 195 (2 December 1947): 2948. Attempts have been made recently to reinstate Calwell as a courageous protomulticulturalist rather than as a racist, with much of his rhetoric being aimed at "softening up" the Australian people to accept large-scale non-Anglo-Celtic immigration to which they were not predisposed. In fact the two positions are not

either/or. It is impossible to read much of Calwell's output without realizing he was deeply imbued with the racism of his age, but it is also quite probable that his view of Australia's security needs led him to modify a strict exclusionist principle to admit persons who were a little less than white, and that he consciously set about to turn the Australian people toward accepting this "reality."

40. Forty percent of population growth between 1946 and 1983 was due to immigration. By 1981, 21 percent of the population had been born outside Australia. Between June 1947 and June 1959 assisted British immigrants numbered 360,156 and other Europeans 341,685. Between June 1959 and December 1968, British migrants numbered 658,236 and European (mostly Italians, Greeks, Dutch, Germans and Yugoslavs) 468,275. See Clark, *A Short History of Australia,* 217.

41. The cultural influence could not, of course, be unidirectional. Manning Clark writes: "By 1969 the European minorities were influencing not only the eating and drinking habits, but also the mental horizons of the "dinkum Aussie. . . . By the 1960s the migrants from Europe, and the revolution in communications, had broken down the cultural isolation, left the bush culture as a historic survival [and] liberated some from the dead hand of their puritan past." Clark, *A Short History of Australia,* 217.

42. Provided they had recognized qualifications which were in demand in Australia.

43. "Assimilation" policy in relation to Aborigines had included the forced removal and adopting out to white families of Aboriginal children. For a review, see Rowse, "Aboriginal Citizenship."

44. F. Galbally et al., *Review of Post-Arrival Programmes and Services to Migrants* (Canberra: Australian Government Publishing Services, 1978), para. 9.6.

45. These measures were more than funded by the abolition of tax rebates for overseas dependants. In fact, multiculturalism was in large part an exercise in "new right" cut-backs to government spending, which shifted the burden of implementing welfare from state agencies onto the communities themselves.

46. See, for example, the official statement by Mr. A. J. Grassby, 11 October 1973, *Australian Foreign Affairs Record,* where he says that "Unless we achieve unity of purpose . . . how can we succeed as a nation? It is not only a question of ensuring economic opportunity for migrants, but also a question of providing whatever assistance is necessary to place them on an equal footing with the Australian born. The only question that should ever be asked in law is whether a person is a citizen or not. . . . It is not merely a question of helping them to share what we already have, but of

encouraging them to add to it, helping them to enrich our national life and to contribute towards the creation of a new and distinctive Australia."

47. Known as the Jupp Report. James Jupp et al., *Don't Settle for Less* (Canberra: AGPS, 1986).

48. Office of Multicultural Affairs, Department of the Prime Minister and Cabinet, *National Agenda for a Multicultural Australia . . . Sharing Our Future* (Canberra: AGPS, 1989).

49. See G. Bottomley, C. Price, and M. Clyne, "Social Studies Hold up a Mirror Revealing Nation's Multicultural Face," in *Higher Education Supplement, The Australian* (12 October 1994): 34–35. The authors point out that the overwhelming majority of these immigrants, following the traditional pattern, settle in Sydney or Melbourne.

50. The separate States, with greater or lesser enthusiasm, have also taken up the multicultural challenge and established commissions and bureaus of their own for delivering specialist ethnic services or for redirecting mainstream services along ethnic lines.

51. J. M. Fraser, *Multiculturalism: Australia's Unique Achievement,* Inaugural Address to the Australian Institute of Multicultural Affairs (Melbourne: 30 November 1981).

52. The liberal civic notion of "undifferentiated," equal citizens has been attacked, particularly by feminists, for concealing beneath its mask of "neutrality" a middle-class white male; see, for example, Iris Marion Young, "Polity and Group Difference: A Critique of the Ideal of Universal Citizenship," *Ethics* 99 (1989); Ursula Vogel, "Is Citizenship Gender Specific?" in Ursula Vogel and Michael Moran, eds., *The Frontiers of Citizenship* (London: Macmillan, 1991). I will not be taking up these arguments here.

53. Kymlicka and Norman, "Return of the Citizen," 373.

54. Ibid. (my emphasis).

55. Ibid. (my emphasis).

56. See Brian Galligan, *Politics of the High Court: A Study of the Judicial Branch of Government in Australia* (St. Lucia: University of Queensland Press, 1987), chapter 1.

57. The Liberal Party is, as I have indicated, a conservative party somewhat akin to the American Republican party. Its liberalism is largely confined to, or identified with, *economic* liberalism.

58. See, for example, I. Shapiro, "Three Ways to Be a Democrat," *Political Theory* 22:1 (1994). I am indebted to Ian Shapiro for pointing out this issue after reading a draft of the present chapter.

59. Will Kymlicka (*Multicultural Citizenship: A Liberal Theory of Minority Rights,* 325 n. 30, and "The Rights of Minority Cultures: Reply to Kuka-

thas," *Political Theory* 20 [1992]) distinguishes between "internal" rights that a group may exert against its own members to enforce authority, and "external" rights the group may assert against the larger society, arguing that multicultural rights are normally of the latter kind. This is undoubtedly so, but it is not entirely clear, as Kymlicka asserts, that all internal rights are inevitably inconsistent with liberal-democratic norms. Obviously, neither is *any* external right which a group may wish to assert (for example, a right to do violence to another group to which it is hostile) going to be acceptable to these norms. It seems preferable, rather than prejudging the issue, to regard the norms as governing the acceptability of any claimed right, external or internal.

60. T. E. Marshall, *Citizenship and Social Class and Other Essays* (Cambridge: Cambridge University Press, 1950), 72.

61. See Raz, "Multiculturalism: A Liberal Perspective," 162–63.

62. Ibid.

63. Ibid., 159.

64. Rosemary Neill and Catherine Armitage, "New World Disorder," *The Australian* (1 May 1995): 9. This was despite the fact that groups of mutually hostile Australian Greeks and Macedonians demonstrated noisily outside the conference.

65. Cited in John Hyde, "Multiculturalism: A Good Idea Gone Wrong," in *The Australian* (1 September 1995): 15.

66. I owe this point to Ian Shapiro, made upon his reading of the original draft of this essay.

67. Cited in Hyde, "Multiculturalism," 15.

68. Not all the professed problems need be taken equally seriously. For example, Professor Helen Hughes of University of Melbourne's Institute of Applied Economic and Social Research asserted in a speech to a National Immigration and Population Outlook Conference in February 1995 that "Multiculturalism has come to mean . . . that Australia does not have, and does not need, a common language. . . . [T]he presumption that English is no longer an essential common language is undermining essential democratic values of Australian society." ("Migrant Policy Must Leap Language Barrier," *The Australian* [23 February 1995]: 9.) This view can be most kindly described as utter nonsense. Hughes's article, long on rhetoric and short on substance, with an apparent antimulticultural (if not antiimmigrant) agenda, is unfortunately all too typical of what passes for "debate" over the issue of multiculturalism.

69. See *The Australian* (15 June 1995): 9.

70. K. Legge, "Living Two Lives," *The Australian Magazine* (3–4 September 1994): 26.

71. A Syrian-born father admits he would kill his fourteen-year-old

daughter if she fell pregnant because "I would rather go to jail a proud man than have my family live in shame." Legge, "Living Two Lives," 20.

72. Reported in *The Australian* (17 August 1995): 3. Defense counsel for Mr. Shoukan said the latter had been shamed and angered by his daughter's relationship with an "Australian boy" when he had organized for her to marry a Muslim. The court was told that the Mr. Shoukan was a marriage counselor with the status of "priest" in the community. In 1993, he had become upset by his daughter's "preparedness to socialize" and go out with Anglo-Saxon males, and shackled her to a bed, threatening to kill her slowly. He had beaten her with a garden hose and forced her to write her own suicide note. The daughter obtained a restraining order and moved out of the house, at which point Mr. Shoukan felt that she was "no longer his daughter" and decided his honor demanded her death (he instructed the undercover officers that it was to be a "clean death," such as a drug overdose).

73. Cited in Legge, "Living Two Lives," 27.

74. Cited in ibid.

75. The rights of women and children, rather neglected in Australia in the past, have been given ever increasing recognition in recent years.

76. Cited in Legge, "Living Two Lives," 26.

77. Cited in ibid.

78. Ibid., 27.

79. J. Zubrzycki, "How Politics Poses a Threat to Ethnic Harmony," *The Weekend Australian* (8–9 April 1995): 31.

80. Ibid.

81. Ibid.

82. Legge notes that, when researching her above-cited article, she was accused by several Anglo-Australians of "culture bashing." She also quotes Baronia Halstead, a researcher for the Australian Institute of Criminology, who admits toning down her reports on ethnic crime for the Office of Multicultural Affairs for fear of inflaming racist sentiment. Legge, "Living Two Lives," 22.

83. Reprinted as "Common Values the Cement that Preserves Our Diversity," *The Weekend Australian* (8–9 April 1995): 31.

84. I am thinking particularly of a recent national scandal in which a work of literature, ostensibly written by a young woman of Ukrainian parentage named Helen Demidenko, won several prizes including the most prestigious Australian literary award, the Miles Franklin, for a work reportedly based on family memories but which seemed to many an anti-Semitic apologia for Ukrainian participation in the holocaust. Judges in their appraisals spoke of the book *The Hand that Signed the Paper* as a "hitherto unspeakable part of the Australian migrant experience," and as

"a text that positions itself within the wider questions posed by multiculturalism." This led some critics of the book to accuse judging panels of "sentimental multiculturalism" which destroyed their critical sense (*The Australian* [22 August 1995]: 11). Meanwhile, at a literary conference, Ms. Demidenko, dressed in national costume, was persuaded to perform a Ukrainian folk dance. As it later emerged, Helen Demidenko was actually a (probably involuntary) fantasist of pure English parentage, real name Helen Darville; since the book's imagined ethnic authenticity has been touted as a significant part of its value, this was a blow to its defenders. A greater blow was to follow when it was revealed that sections of the book were undoubtedly plagiarized, and the publishers withdrew it temporarily from sale.

85. Raz, "Multiculturalism: A Liberal Perspective," 160, 165.

86. One is reminded of the Jewish definition of an anti-Semite as someone who hates Jews more than is absolutely necessary.

87. See Touraine, "What Does Democracy Mean Today?"

88. As Raz notes, multicultural liberalism has its own reasons for extending respect, but is under no obligation to take a group at its own estimation. Its respect of cultures is "conditional and granted from a point of view outside of any of them." Raz, "Multiculturalism: A Liberal Perspective," 167–68.

# 18

## STRAIGHT GAY POLITICS:
## THE LIMITS OF AN ETHNIC MODEL
## OF INCLUSION

### CATHY J. COHEN

On August 24, 1995, presidential candidate Sen. Bob Dole did something rarely seen in American politics. He returned the one thousand dollar check of a political contributor. The financial donation in this case came from the Log Cabin Republicans, a conservative political group comprised of lesbians and gay men. Still attempting to explain his decision to return the money nearly three weeks later, Dole declared that "what I don't want was the perception that we were buying into some *special rights* for any group, whether it might be, with gays or anyone else."[1] Thus, the participation of gay male and lesbian Republicans in the political process, in even the most traditional and narrow ways, was interpreted by Bob Dole as the pursuit of *special rights*.

On September 25, 1995, the D.C. Coalition of Black Lesbians, Gay Men, and Bisexuals voted to hold onto a check for $2,200 designated for the NAACP. The funds generated from a March fundraiser by the D.C. Coalition were to be presented to the NAACP at a May reception. However, it was reported in *The Washington Blade,* the local D.C. gay and lesbian paper, that "an NAACP representative canceled at the last moment and the

NAACP did not return many phone calls about rescheduling."[2] In this instance, a mainstream black civil rights organization, in deep financial trouble, apparently decided to forgo financial assistance and association from a group thought to be more tainted than the NAACP itself.

Both of these cases point to an interesting and continuous phenomenon in the politics of oppressed groups: specifically, the attempt in this case by lesbians and gays, but also other marginal groups of different political orientations, different cultural backgrounds, and different economic means, to acquire formal rights and inclusion not through street activism but increasingly through established and tested mainstream politics.[3] In both of these examples, lesbians, gay men, bisexuals, and transgendered (l/g/b/t) individuals came together attempting to use financial incentives to "buy" influence, recognition, and acceptance. And while this is a strategy that many before them, in particular white ethnic groups, have engaged in to achieve equal opportunity and results, in the case of gay men and lesbians such a tactic has been met with repeated failure. Whether it be the proliferation of antigay ballot initiatives or the increasing number of reported hate crimes against lesbian, gay, bisexual, and transgendered individuals, mainstream America seems to be saying that no matter how well behaved gays and lesbians are or how much money members of this community can offer, they will never be fully embraced.

In neither of the cases mentioned above are we provided with the familiar images of oppressed groups engaged in protests, demanding the *special rights* of equality and protection given to other groups in society. Instead, at least in these examples, each group has chosen to pursue their equality through the more traditional and less disruptive tactics of financial contributions, voting, and adherence to dominant norms and values. This strategic decision is not new but represents a discernable trend in the writing and thinking of many gay activists/organizers/intellectuals/leaders receiving attention today. Turning away from the liberal/radical politics of liberationists who sought social change, and not merely inclusion, these individuals "preach" a new gay political ideology. This approach promises that if gays and lesbians present themselves as legitimate and deserving citizens, then equal status will be bestowed on all those deemed "virtually normal."[4] It is this type of political understanding that has pushed the issues of gays in the military and gay marriages to the front of the gay political agenda, where such topics are seen as putting forth those images and members of "Gay America" that most citizens can at least tolerate and hopefully one day accept.

It is this mainstreaming of gay and lesbian politics, as an illustration of the political choices of all marginal groups, that is the focus of this chapter. Labeled the ethnic model of inclusion (or what I deem *integrative or advanced marginalization*), this strategy is based on the experiences of white European ethnic groups and assumes that, over time, as groups prove themselves to be diligent and willing contributors to American society, they will become fully integrated and assimilated into dominant institutions and social relationships. Thus, the ethnic model implies that as "the U.S. had absorbed the [white European] immigrants, had eventually granted them their rights, and had seen them take their places as 'Americans' despite the existence of considerable nativist hostility and prejudice against them," so too does this possibility exist for other *deserving* marginal groups.[5]

Undoubtedly, numerous other models of activism exist; however, it has been primarily calls for assimilation and integration that have been heard above the roar in gay communities across the country. Currently, there seem to be at least two conditions that make such strategies seem especially appropriate to this historical moment. First is the development of a visible and seemingly successful middle class among lesbians and gay men as well as other marginal groups. As members of this segment of oppressed communities gain, or are allowed, limited power and access to dominant institutions and resources, their success is marketed by those inside and outside of these communities as examples of the American dream. These middle-class success stories are said to represent the opportunities available to all marginal group members who participate in and adhere to dominant institutions, norms, and social relations. Second, the increasing prevalence of ethnic strategies for inclusion also seems to be tied to the dominant conservative political climate which currently pervades the country. When those marginal to dominant society are confronted with the prospect of only minimal gains through even the most protracted and sustained political struggles, then more traditional routes to formal inclusion may be taken up.

However, beyond understanding the conditions under which marginal groups pursue an ethnic model of inclusion, it is the implications or consequences of such strategies, especially as they manifest themselves within marginal groups, that is the focal point of this analysis. In particular, I am interested in the ways strategies for formal rights and recognition emphasize and manipulate differences in appearance, status, resources and, more generally, power *within* marginal communities. Traditionally, scholars of rights have focused their analysis on a dichotomous power struggle between dominant groups, represented most effectively in the form of the state, and excluded or marginal groups seeking formal inclusion.[6] However, I believe that this type of narrow modeling misses the multiple sites of power and contestation connected to strategies of political inclusion. I am suggesting, instead, that we build on traditional models of group rights, paying attention not only to the dominant exercise of power, but also to the local, equally effective, uses of power and privilege *within* oppressed communities to gain rights for those deemed "deserving."

It is just such an exercise of power, at the local level within marginal communities, that can be said to drive much of the ethnic model for inclusion. Central, then, to this strategy is the manipulation and privileging of certain characteristics and behaviors within marginal communities as groups prove themselves worthy of inclusion. For as groups vie for the label of legitimate, normal, and citizen, they confront the requirement that they regulate and control the public behavior and image of all group members, especially those perceived as nonconformist.

In the past, many in the academy have assumed that the regulation or control of marginal groups came exclusively from outside dominant sources, in an "us versus them" framework. However, there is a growing recognition that the power to deny group rights, define group membership, and regulate group behavior does not just happen through the hands of dominant sources. Instead, the process of marginalization and control is increasingly exercised by the more privileged members of marginal groups. And the "management" of marginal group members is negotiated daily by those we would call our own.

The exercise of power by relatively more privileged marginal group members over others in their community is not a new phenomenon. In the past, these power relationships were generally predicated on the exclusion or segregation of marginal groups from dominant society. Today, in contrast, these relations are based to varying degrees on more privileged marginal group members' association *with* dominant groups and institutions. Thus, as dominant players attempt to remove themselves or are removed from the direct regulation of marginal communities, newly elected officials, traditional leaders, public intellectuals, and other members of marginal groups are *given* or *take* on the role (and some of the power) of policing their community.

I use the term *policing* here to mean the regulation and management of the behavior, attitudes, and, more importantly, the public image of the group.[7] As I have written elsewhere, it is the indigenous construction and policing of group identity and membership that serves as the site for local power struggles within the framework of group rights. Marginal communities faced with dominant definitions of themselves as inferior and "other" construct a different or oppositional group identity, redefining themselves for their group members and the larger public. These attempts at redefinition highlight the characteristics and contributions of marginal group members thought to be positive or in accord with dominant values. Through this process of demonstrating our "just as good as you" qualities, middle-class and more privileged members of marginal communities build what has been called the cultural capital of the group.[8] For example, in the case of African Americans:

> This systematic degradation, stereotyping and stigmatization of Black Americans has all but dictated that attempts at incorporation, integration, and assimilation on the part of black people generally include some degree of proving ourselves to be "just as nice as those white folks." Thus, leaders, organizations, and institutions have consistently attempted to redefine and indigenously construct a new public image or understanding of what blackness would mean. This process of reconstructing or [im]proving blackness involves not only a reliance on the self-regulation of individual black people, but also includes significant "indigenous policing" of black people. Consistently, in the writings of black academics we

hear reference to the role of the black middle class as examples and regulators of appropriate behavior for the black masses.[9]

Thus, marginal group leaders, activists, and those with relative privilege use the norms, institutions, relationships, and indigenous definitions of membership within marginal communities to produce an image of the group thought to be consistent with hegemonic culture and acceptable to dominant groups.

It is this process of policing the visible or public boundaries of group identity that threatens the status of these most vulnerable in marginal communities. Marginal groups looking for formal recognition and rights are forced to embrace a model of inclusion that is premised on the idea, not that all groups deserve formal recognition, but instead that formal rights are to be granted only to those who demonstrate adherence to dominant norms of work, love, and social interaction.[10] And marginal group members who are close to the edges of dominant power, where access and decision making seem like real possibilities, confront incentives to promote and prioritize those issues and members thought to "enhance" the public image of the group, while controlling and making invisible those issues and members perceived to threaten the status of the community.

The real difficulty or contradiction inherent in using the ethnic model as a strategy for inclusion rests in the distance between the lived experience of so many marginal group members and the image that groups are required to put forth for inclusion. Traditionally, this model demands adherence to a standard of normality rooted in white, middle-class, male, heterosexual privilege, with whiteness being the most essential quality.[11] And while historically, European immigrant groups such as the Irish had also to prove their normativity, with even their whiteness challenged and reconstructed, in the end it was the whiteness of their skin that facilitated their formal and informal inclusion.[12] Thus, in the case of race, the ethnic model poses what might be seen as a double burden for "minority" racial groups (or people of color), since not only are members expected to prove or demonstrate their acceptability, they are expected to do this in light of being non-white.

Through this model of politics people of color are forced

to demonstrate or "buy" their normativity *and* their "honorary whiteness" through the class privilege they acquire, through the attitudes and behavior they exhibit, and through the dominant institutions in which they operate. So, for example, Colin Powell can be accepted as a serious presidential candidate by many white Americans (in spite of being black) because of his pull myself up by my boot-straps history, because of his association with dominant institutions such as the military, and because of the conservative attitudes and associations that legitimize him. However, for most people of color it is the difference between this double burden of proof and their actual life chances, whether they be straight or gay, that makes the ideal of formal and informal equality through full inclusion of all group members a remote possibility. And in the case of lesbians and gay men, it is the disparity between the general standards of normativity and the chosen or forced lived experiences of many gay men, lesbians, bisexuals, and transgendered individuals that impedes the full access of many group members to the rewards and privileges of dominant society.

In the space between what is expected from the ethnic model and how people actually exist lie those members/segments of marginal communities whose behavior and attitudes are thought to be in need of policing and who face complete ostracization if necessary. Further, in this space also lie the dividing lines between those in marginal communities who may gain acceptance through ethnic strategies of inclusion and those who may not. Thus, for example, the ethnic model of inclusion, with its assumption of whiteness as an essential characteristic of normativity, privileges from its inception white members of lesbian, gay, bisexual, and transgendered communities, while disadvantaging the people of color in these groups.

This particular examination while generally focused on the limits of an ethnic model of rights is specifically structured around three topics: first, the degree to which marginal groups work to reconstruct their public image with the idea that such efforts will enhance their access to rights, opportunities and, more generally, power in society; second, the ways leaders and individuals, involved in the regulation of the public "face" or visible image of their communities, find their political decisions and actions constrained by the need to conform; and third, the alternative strategies that activists have pursued toward a more transformative or liberatory politics. Specifically, I argue that strategies for inclusion, based on the ethnic model of rights and recognition—with its necessary indigenous policing—affect and, more importantly, constrain the political decision making and activity of marginal groups. We must, therefore, work to identify other political strategies which challenge and change power relationships both in and outside of marginal communities.

For the purpose of this analysis, I employ the framework of marginalization to explore the complexities of power relationships within marginal groups.[13] The theory of marginalization is structured around the idea that there exist groups in society which historically have been denied access to decision making and full participation within dominant political, economic, and social institutions and relationships. This framework highlights the dialectical and evolving relationship between dominant strategies of marginalization and indigenous strategies of resistance. It also makes central the exercise of power within marginal communities, reminding the researcher that power relationships, at both exogenous and indigenous levels, interact to constrain and incompletely determine the political choices and collective behavior of oppressed or marginal groups in society. To explore such constraints, I focus my empirical examples on the politics of lesbian, gay male, bisexual, and transgendered communities. Looking briefly at three periods in the politics of lesbian and gay communities, I try to illustrate how the promise of rights and inclusion can motivate the policing or the mainstreaming of politics in gay communities.

I begin by detailing some of the components of the theory of marginalization to be used in this analysis. I then briefly discuss the history of marginalization that lesbian and gay communities have faced over the years. Next I turn my attention to three moments when the politics of these communities have been driven or strongly influenced by the quest for legitimization and normalization. This leads to a discussion of the limits of the ethnic model of inclusion. I conclude by taking up the questions: Why, if the limits of this political strategy are so obvious and recurrent in the experiences of most marginal groups, do oppressed communities continue to pursue such strategies? Is there an alternative to the quest for formal group rights and recognition as we know it that better serves the interests of those most vulnerable in marginal communities?

## MARGINALIZATION: OTHERING IN THE DENIAL OF GROUP RIGHTS

For the purpose of this analysis we will assume that a group is marginal to the extent that its members are outside of decision making; stigmatized by their identification; denied access to dominant institutions; isolated or segregated; lack control over the means of production and the distribution of goods and services in society, or generally excluded from control over those resources which shape their quality of life. Much of the material exclusion experienced by marginal groups is based on, or justified by, ideological processes that define these groups as "other." Thus, marginalization occurs, in part, when some observable characteristic or distinguishing behavior shared by a group of individuals is systematically used within the larger society to signal the inferior and subordinate status of the group.[14] Quite often, it is this stigmatized "mark" that becomes the primary identification by which group members are evaluated and through which they experience the world. Of course, there are other identities that effect the status and position of marginal group member. However, a select few constructed identities—those we might call primary—come to have a nearly totalizing effect on the life chances and life experiences of marginal group members.[15]

The theory of marginalization is structured around at least three major principles that aid in our analysis of the political behavior of marginal groups: first, is its focus on the history of power relations and oppression under which groups evolve; second, is the centrality of the indigenous structure of marginal communities in understanding their political choices; and third, is the recognition that strategies of marginalization are not static but evolve over time.

The first principle necessitates that in this analysis I incorporate the historical experiences of lesbians and gay men into my explanations of their present-day political choices and actions, recognizing that historical experiences of exclusion not only frame the way marginal groups view more dominant institutions and groups but also constrain the way groups view themselves and their ability to mobilize around certain issues. For example, it would be difficult to understand the current political thrust of some gay writers such as Andrew Sullivan, Richard Mohr, or Bruce Bawer toward conservative or assimilationist strategies without knowing the history of blame and alienation that has been directed toward gays and lesbians by dominant groups. Thus, any analysis of the politics of marginal communities must be informed by the history of inequality and oppression under which these groups have developed.

The second principle of this theory reminds us that an understanding of the indigenous structure of lesbian and gay communities must be taken into account as we analyze this move toward assimilation. What are the demographic characteristics of this new leadership urging strategies of integration? Who, through a process of incorporation, will be excluded from the indigenous resources of the community, either because of their material vulnerability or their indigenous social marginality? Only by paying attention to power relationships within marginal communities can we closely examine variation in the consequences of political choices for different marginal group members.

The third and final principle highlighted here is probably that which is most central to this analysis. This component focuses on the evolving nature of strategies of marginalization. For example, one pattern of marginalization may focus on the *categorical exclusion* of all members of a certain class or group from central control over the dominant resources of a society. And while such a strategy might prove effective in directing the policies and interaction of society at one stage in its development, other more complicated strategies may be needed in a different political environment. Thus, a strategy that allows for the limited mobility of some "deserving" marginal group members — *integrative marginalization* — may be effective in the face of resistance from the excluded group. The pattern of exclusion or marginalization I am interested in for this analysis not only allows for limited mobility on the part of some marginal group members but also transfers much of the direct management of marginal group members to individuals who share the same group identity.

This pattern of marginalization—which I call *advanced marginalization*—is rooted in a process where dominant norms and values are incorporated into the culture, ideology, and consciousness of marginal group members, resulting in a form of internal regulation. This process takes place in such a way that indigenous definitions of what it means to be a fine, upstanding group member include adherence to norms that are also used to regulate and exclude. Those most vulnerable in marginal communities can also face what I have labeled *secondary marginalization* by members of their own group. Through such a process, those members of marginal communities most in need and most extreme in their "nonconformist behavior" are defined as standing outside the norms and behavior agreed upon by the community. These individuals are, therefore, denied access to not only dominant resources and structures, but also many of the indigenous resources and institutions needed for their survival. Now, having detailed just a few of the major contributions of this theory, we can apply the framework of marginalization to our examination of the politics of lesbian and gay communities.

## Marginalization in Lesbian and Gay Communities: Past and Present

As noted above, any analysis of power in marginal communities should begin with an examination of those external forces that largely shape the political environment to which marginal groups respond. The history of those who currently identify as lesbians and gay men has been one of continuous marginalization and punishment. Whether through legal penalties, religious and social condemnation, or medical treatment and institutionalization, homosexuality or sodomous acts have been viewed in this society with great disdain and loathing. Few strategies of marginalization have *not* been used to contain and destroy this group of individuals. Jonathan Ned Katz, historian of gay and lesbian history, writes that during the four hundred years of American society, "American homosexuals were condemned to death by choking, burning, and drowning; they were executed, jailed, pilloried, fined, court-martialed, prostituted, fired, framed, blackmailed, disinherited, declared insane, driven to insanity, to suicide, murder, and self-hate, witch hunted, entrapped, stereotyped, mocked, insulted, isolated, pitied, castigated, and despised." [16]

In conjunction with institutional and social mechanisms of marginalization, ideologies designating lesbians and gay men as something other than fully human, attempted to justify the categorical exclusion and oppression of these individuals. Those who committed sodomous acts were defined as abnormal. They were designated deviants who dared to challenge the laws of God and nature. And while most of the rhetoric aimed at this group focused on God and "his" natural way, we should note that it was the threat that homosexuality posed to the nuclear family, gender roles, and other norms of social unity used as fuel for economic systems that motivated this systemic and continuous discourse of "otherness."

If we begin with colonial America we find that same-sex sex acts—those acts deemed "crimes against God" and eventually "crimes against nature"—often met with the severest of criminal penalties. The demonization of such behavior was facilitated by a marginalizing discourse, interpreting such acts as standing outside of religious tradition. Colonists, migrating from England to escape religious persecution, established small, closely knit religious sects in the "New World" and based most of their life structure around religious teachings from the Bible. Inevitably, then, the Bible became the basis upon which law was structured, normality defined, and marginalization justified. John D'Emilio in his book *Sexual Politics, Sexual Communities* writes,

> Biblical condemnations of homosexual behavior suffused American culture from its origin. For seventeenth-century settlers, with only a precarious foothold on the edge of an unknown continent, the terrible destruction of Sodom and Gomorrah by an angry God evoked dread. Men who lay with men, the book of Leviticus warned, committed an "abomination; they shall surely be put to death; their blood shall be upon them. . . ."

The law stipulated harsh punishments for homosexual acts. Colonial legal codes, drawn either directly from the Bible or from the theologically influenced English buggery statute of 1533, prescribed death for sodomy, and in several instances courts directed the execution of men found guilty of this act.[17]

While the punishment given for sodomous acts in colonial America was quite severe, understanding of what such behavior implied was in fact quite limited. In contrast to how we conceptualize gay communities and gay identity today, same-sex sex acts in these early times were understood as individual behavior, not as the defining characteristic of an individual or a group. Thus, while strategies of marginalization were instituted to control this "unnatural" behavior, the goal of such punishment was to set the faltering individual on their natural Christian path and to send a message to others that journeys outside of God's proscribed behavior would not be tolerated.

The nineteenth century is often noted by historians as a turning point in society's understanding and treatment of same-sex sex acts. As the state began to replace the church and religion as the defining structure in nineteenth century society, there also developed also a general move toward "rational" scientific assessment as the guiding force through which actions were evaluated. In such an environment, medical, and scientific professionals began to take on new importance. Thus, along with the continued development of cities and towns, greater personal choice with regard to private heterosexual acts, the lessening role of the church in defining the structure of society, and the increasing search for objective science, the role of medical professionals in defining "normal" and "abnormal" sexual behavior also expanded. And it was the discourse around the idea of sickness and cures that lead to the prominence of the medical field in defining the status and marginalization of homosexuals from the late nineteenth century onward.

It was during this period that construction of the homosexual, as a defining identity and unique group, emerged.[18] Sodomous acts, once thought to be wayward individual behavior, were redefined, largely by medical professionals, as signaling some inherent or fundamental flaw in the character of an individual. Further, all those participating in such behavior were understood as a unique or distinguishable group in society. In accord the penalties and discourse surrounding this behavior changed, focusing on the *categorical marginalization* of the entire group.

Medical professionals in Europe and the United States, in their analysis of homosexual acts, supplied yet another institutional mechanism for the marginalization of men and women engaged in same-sex sex acts. For example, while homosexuality was still understood as deviant or abnormal behavior, it also came to be known as a *physical* defect to be cured. Katz notes that from the late nineteenth century into the twentieth century, we find doctors and researchers using castration, vasectomy, electric shock, hormone medication, aversion therapy, and lobotomies to "cure" homosexuality.[19] However, in no way did this medical dimension of homosexual marginalization replace the criminalization of sodomous acts. Instead, as Foucault suggests, the medical discourse introduced yet another instrument of power, another discourse through which to examine and control individuals and their sexual behavior.[20]

The twentieth-century experiences of lesbian and gay men continue to provide examples of marginalization and oppression. In response to increasing acts of resistance, any number of institutions and individuals have sought to reinforce the marginalization of lesbian and gay communities. Strategies ranging from the 1934 Motion Picture Production Code prohibiting any depiction of homosexuals in films, to police harassment, arrests, and beatings, to the medical profession's use of institutionalization and experimentation, have all been implemented to control the behavior, identity, and status of lesbians and gay men. The government, however, has probably the most effective instrument of control using the military, the FBI, the Post Office, and other public institutions in its efforts to enforce and maintain the subservient position of lesbians and gay men.

The witch hunts of the McCarthy era provide one of the more classic examples of the targeting of homosexual men and women for marginalization. In the midst of a hysteria about the communist threat, the threat to national security presented by "sexual perverts" seemed a safe and effective (in terms of publicity and the advancement of congressional careers) connection to highlight. Thus, it was during this period that members of Congress used ideological strategies of marginalization, equating the alleged threat of communism to the threat of homosexuality to further exclude members of this group. D'Emilio and Freedman write in their book *Intimate Matters:*

> The Cold War against Communism made the problem of homosexuality especially menacing. "The social stigma attached to sex perversion is so great," the committee [Senate Committee on Expenditure in Executive Departments] noted, that blackmailers made "a regular practice of preying upon the homosexual."[21] Already believed to be morally enfeebled by sexual indulgence, homosexuals would readily succumb to the blandishment of the spy and betray their country rather than risk exposure of their sexual identity.[22]

For many Americans both groups (communists and homosexuals) were morally bankrupt and threatened the basic American values that held this country together, namely family and democracy. Thus, the power of such rhetoric is exemplified in the little known fact that during the McCarthy era, when we take into account military positions as well as federal employment, more people were dismissed from positions for allegedly being homosexual than were dismissed for allegedly being communists.[23]

The 1960s and 1970s produced important political, social, and institutional victories for lesbian and gay communities.[24] However, despite such progress lesbians and gay men still found themselves to be marginal members in the greater society. The late 1970s saw a flurry of legislative action attempting to hold on to the categorical exclusion of gays and lesbians as legitimate citizens in the society.[25] For instance, while some sodomy laws were revoked during this decade, the majority of states still had laws prohibiting sodomous acts between consenting same-sex partners. Further, the federal government continued to ban the employment or service of lesbians and gay men in the military, the FBI, or other "security intensive" jobs.

Undoubtedly, the most horrific event to happen to gay and lesbian communities during the 1980s was the emergence of AIDS as a devastating disease that threatened not only lesbian and gay male communities but the entire public. Those individuals in gay communities who had previously lived in relatively secluded urban areas, heavily populated by other gays and lesbians, and often protected by financial privilege, came to experience the malicious and threatening nature of new ideologies of marginalization. These ideas branded all gays as diseased and dangerous, making them unwilling targets of homophobic and AIDS-phobic fanatics brandishing everything from baseball bats to discriminatory legislation.

In the wake of AIDS, numerous legislative attempts were mounted to restrict and deny the rights of those who were HIV-positive or had AIDS, as well as to "contain" the behavior of those designated as high risk, such as gay men and Haitians. We must remember that lesbian and gay community members encountered the threat of AIDS just as the homophobic Reagan/Bush era began. It was in this political environment, where cries of family values and cultural decay not only impacted political debate but substantially influenced public policy, that homosexuality—along with that other deviant cultural/sexual practice of the 1980s, "single-motherhood"—was represented, once again as threatening the health, protection, and structure of the "general public." And it was this type of analysis that led some public officials, religious leaders, and general citizens to call for the quarantining and random HIV-testing of gays and lesbians.

Another very telling sign of the continued marginalized status of gays and lesbians is evident in the public attitudes exhibited toward this group. Again, we must recognize that the degree to which institutional and social strategies of marginalization are effective is directly tied to the success of ideological strategies penetrating the public consciousness. Thus, in the case of gay men and lesbians, their continued oppression depends, in part, on the ability of antigay organizers to persuade the public that stereotypes of gays—as dangerous to adults, children, and the country—are true; and that this type of danger necessitates institutional and social restrictions, limiting their full participation in American society.

Ken Sherrill, a scholar of American politics and the politics of the lesbian and gay communities, found that even in the 1980s lesbians and gay men were the group toward which Americans exhibited the most hostile feelings:

The 1984 Michigan study [the National Election Study] asked people to place their feelings toward fourteen groups on the [feeling] thermometer. . . . Of all fourteen groups, only lesbians and gay men were placed below 50 degrees by a majority—61.5%—of this national sample.

In 1988, 35% of the American people placed their feeling toward gay people at zero degrees—the coldest possible extreme. . . . [A] total of 63% of the American people indicated negative feelings toward homosexuals. No group—exceeded the total percentage of Americans holding cold or negative feelings toward gay people.[26]

It was the hostility toward gays and lesbians still evident in the 1970s and 1980s which provided a fertile ground for increased violent attacks on gays and lesbians more recently. The social marginalization and stigma evoked through a lesbian or gay identification has become a staple of American culture, manifested in its most violent way through increases in "gay bashing." Richard Mohr discusses the violence perpetrated against individuals *perceived* to be lesbian or gay:

A recent extensive study by the National Gay and Lesbian Task Force found that over 90 percent of gays and lesbians had been victimized in some form on the basis of their sexual identification. Greater than one in five gay men and nearly one in ten lesbians had been punched, hit, or kicked; a quarter of all gays had had objects thrown at them; a third had been chased; a third had been sexually harassed and 14 percent had been spit on—all for being perceived to be gay.[27]

Violence against lesbians and gays is just one more manifestation of the prevalence of social attitudes that view the gay community as a group of "deviants," unworthy of even the most basic rights and protection. Further, the fact that in the 1990s there still exists no federal protection against discrimination on the basis of sexual identification, that the government persists in holding on to yet another discriminatory policy toward lesbians and gays in the military, and that states continue to allow for the criminal prosecution of those practicing sodomy, clearly signifies the severity of political marginality experienced by members of this community.

All of these examples should serve to remind us of the systematic nature of marginalization. Through continuous strategies of inequality, the marginalization experienced by lesbians and gay men persists over time, becoming institutionalized in the practices and ideas of the society. Marginalization, thus, becomes reinforced through the everyday behavior of individuals as they follow the norms, rules, and procedures that help to structure society. In the theory of marginalization, the ascribed and marginal position of a group is seen as an important factor in understanding the range of life choices as well as the specific political processes and choices of group members. Having examined the long and continuous process of marginalization faced by lesbian and gay communities, we can now explore the impact of such strategies on the political choices and actions of group leaders. When faced with ideological arguments that define you as deviant, other, and unnatural, is the only available and feasible strategy of resistance one that refutes such arguments by celebrating the normality of the group? Further, if presenting a positive or acceptable public image of the group is the strategy of resistance to be pursued, what are the implications of such decisions within marginal communities?

## POLITICS AND POWER IN LESBIAN AND GAY COMMUNITIES

In this section, I want to briefly examine three moments in the political history of lesbian and gay communities which illustrate the internal dissention and regulation innate to political strategies focused on the acquisition of formal group recognition and rights. Again, I want to pose the questions of who or what parts/segments of gay communities get left out when the price of admission and/or acceptance is assimilation and conformitivity. Further, does the advancement of political struggles around the granting of rights ensure a process of secondary marginalization in marginal communities?

### Moment I: Early Organizing in the Lesbian and Gay Community

If we search for the presence of an ongoing attempt at resistance in gay and lesbian communities, most would agree that the activ-

ism of the late 1940s and early 1950s—with the development of
the Veterans Benevolent Association (1945), the Knights of the
Clock (1940s), the Mattachine Society (1951), the Daughters of
Bilitis (1955), and *One* magazine (1953)—represents the starting
point for such activity.[28] Initially, many of these groups came to
fruition through the work of lesbian and gay men who learned
their organizing skills while working in the communist party or
other progressive movements. For example, Henry Hay, founder
of the Mattachine Society, used his organizing experience in the
communist party to set up a structure that produced one of the
most successful gay male organizing efforts of this era. Through
their work in radical movements, these early organizers framed
an analysis of the lesbian and gay community that emphasized
their status as a distinct minority group, who needed to work
collectively to make demands upon exclusionary political, cultural, and economic systems. And it was through these early organizations that members of gay and lesbian communities organized
themselves, challenging police harassment, abuses by medical authorities and developing a group consciousness around their "minority" status as outsiders.

The dominance of such progressive understandings of lesbian
and gay politics did not last for long. As these organizations
gained more public scrutiny, organizers such as Hay lost their
standing as more moderate political activists came to dominate
the organizing of lesbians and gay men. Centrist political leaders
within the community took over many of these organizations
by articulating a nonconfrontational analysis of lesbian and gay
politics. These leaders highlighted the ideals of sameness and
assimilation, emphasizing that homosexuals differed from heterosexuals only in the choice of their sexual partner. Thus, a picture
of lesbian and gay men as God-fearing, normal people, was
thought to be the most effective strategy to challenge dominant
ideologies promoting ideas of difference, deviance, and others.

Such a belief is what Jeff Escoffier, in his article "Sexual Revolution and the Politics of Gay Identity," has described as the assimilationist position:

> The alternative "assimilationist" position sought to open the way
> to acceptance of homosexuals by emphasizing the similarities be-

tween homosexuals and heterosexuals. Because the "secondary socialization" of homosexuals resulted from a life given over to hiding, isolation, and internalized self-hatred, homosexuals should adopt a "pattern of behavior that is acceptable to society in general and compatible with [the] recognized institutions . . . of home, church and state," rather than creating an "ethical homosexual culture," which would only accentuate the perceived differences between homosexuals and heterosexuals and provoke continued hostility.[29]

Undoubtedly, one of the most significant conflicts to emerge from the organizing of the 1950s was the question of the appropriate strategies for lesbian and gay organizations. This period of organizing, which we now call the homophile movement, resolved this conflict by focusing on strategies of inclusion not reorganization. And considering the hostile atmosphere of the 1950s, a strong case can be made for the rationality in choosing an assimilation strategy of "acceptable legitimacy." However, the consequences of such decisions should not go unnoticed. Through this approach, group members effectively agreed to challenge strategies of *categorical exclusion,* while accepting patterns of *integrative marginalization.* Thus, marginal group members who were willing to take on the norms and values of the dominant society were unconsciously understood to deserve the legitimacy of dominant groups. Those members unable or unwilling to assimilate, however, were represented as somehow deserving of the marginalization they encountered, both in and out of the community.

The manifestations of such a strategy in the gay community during the 1950s resulted in the stratification of leadership and members along a newly embraced and redefined standard of normality. As I noted above, many of the original organizers of early gay and lesbian organizations, in particular Harry Hay of the Mattachine Society, were purged from their organizations because of their past links with left-wing organizations and because of their political analysis which emphasized the oppressed nature of the gay community and its need to visibly mobilize collectively. Other organizations, such as the Daughters of Bilitis, an early lesbian organization, were also forced to deal continuously with the question of appropriate strategy. In the end this duel for the soul of organizations in lesbian and gay communities led to the destruction of many of these groups. John D'Emilio writes of this period, "Finally, the movement took upon itself an impossible burden—appearing respectable to a society that defined homosexuality as beyond respectability. In trying to accommodate social mores, DOB [Daughters of Bilitis] and Mattachine often reflected back to their potential constituency some of society's most condemnatory attitudes. Their criticisms of the bars and gay subculture undoubtedly alienated many of the men and women with the strongest commitment to gay life."[30]

### Moment II: Gay Writing in Response to AIDS

Without a doubt, the 1980s will be known as the decade of AIDS. It would be this pandemic that would dominate, rightly so, lesbian and gay male politics for the entire decade. At a time when city, state, and federal authorities lacked the wherewithal to see AIDS as an important issue upon which they must act, there developed slowly but surely an increased pattern of recognition in gay communities that AIDS was a disease that had to be reckoned with if anyone was to survive. Initially, denial of the impact and pervasiveness of this new disease was the preferred pattern of response by gay community members. Some in the community suggested that AIDS was not as threatening as those writing about it would have people believe. Rumors spread that only a few "promiscuous" people, or older gay men, or those who had been out of the country, would have to worry about catching this deadly disease.

Eventually, significant numbers of gay men, bisexual men and women, transgendered individuals, and lesbians came to realize that this disease did not happen to only the "bad" people in the community. The massive denial exhibited by many members of the gay and lesbian community melted away as increasing numbers of neighbors, friends, and lovers suffered from the opportunistic infections manifested from HIV. In an environment where all of the evidence, including the naming of the disease (GRID: Gay-Related Immune Deficiency), says that it is about your community, denial is difficult to maintain.

For some who write of the early response of gay communities to the threat of AIDS, this is a story of communities coming to consciousness and responding in heroic fashion. However, the framework of marginalization reminds us that we must reject simple dichotomies of powerful or powerless, community response or community denial, and instead examine the complex social relationships which define and frame the political choices of marginal groups. In the case of AIDS activism this means recognizing and analyzing the conflicts and dissention that structured the gay community's response to this disease.

The response or resistance of the gay community to AIDS was a long and conflictual journey that evolved through separate yet overlapping stages, where the worldview of members was modified and the indigenous resources of the community were mobilized. An important stage of this reaction centered on changing the consciousness of community members. Group members needed to acknowledge and recognize that some mysterious disease was upon them and it threatened to undo all the victories and liberties won over the many decades of activism and survival. Fundamental to the fight against AIDS was the diffusion of information and arguments that sought to redefine, for community members and the larger public, ideas about the gay community as well as this new disease. Often this information came in the form of debates within the pages of gay magazines and newspapers. These debates provided different interpretations of what was happening and how best to respond to this crisis. Writers argued about whether to challenge or accept dominant ideas and concepts that defined the gay community in terms of "promiscuous" behavior, "abnormal" sexual practices, and deviant actions. Thus, while acknowledging the importance of the disease was critical, the different interpretations that both community members and the general public brought to events defining the epidemic often determined the type of response emanating from any particular group.

Throughout the epidemic the gay press, in papers like the *New York Native,* provided alternative information to the community. Some of the most vicious and defining debates of this epidemic took place in the pages of these magazines and newspapers. There were writers who contended that nothing short of stopping all sexual activity was necessary to curb the possible extinction of the gay male community in New York. Others argued that gay leaders were overreacting to the threat of this disease and that in its wake they were willing to forego critical components of the gay community's distinct culture, in particular its sexual liberation.

The public struggle over how to interpret this crisis was foregrounded most in those articles attempting to jar the "moral" consciousness of the community into recognition and action. Probably the person most noted for such articles is screen writer and AIDS activist Larry Kramer. Kramer's first article on the subject of AIDS, entitled "A Personal Appeal," appeared in the *New York Native* in August of 1981. The article attempted to accomplish two goals: first, to sound an alarm and drive home the severity and reality of AIDS for the gay community; and second to solicit money for AIDS research. As did most of Kramer's writing, this article generated heated debate. Much of the controversy centered on Kramer's assessment that

> the men who have been stricken don't appear to have done anything that many New York gay men haven't done at one time or another. . . . It's easy to become frightened that one of the many *things we've done or taken* over the past years may be all that it takes for a cancer to grow from a tiny something-or-other that got in there who knows when *from doing who knows what.* (emphasis added) [31]

It was articles and essays of this sort that motivated reactions to what many saw as the sexually prude or antisex position of those writing on AIDS. Bob Chelsey, in another *Native* article, suggests that in the name of talking about AIDS there was occurring an all-out attack on sexuality and the sexual liberation won in the 1970s, reminiscent of dominant arguments which sought to define gay men as deviant and therefore as deserving of AIDS. Chelsey wrote,

> Kramer's emotionalism is the triumph of guilt: that gay men *deserve* to die for their promiscuity. . . .
> Read anything by Kramer closely. I think you'll find that the subtext is always: the wages of gays sin are death. I ask you to look closely at Kramer's writing because I think it's important for gay people to know whether or not they agree with him. I am not downplaying the seriousness of Kaposi's sarcoma. But something else is happening here, which is also serious: gay homophobia and anti-eroticism. [32]

It is important to recognize, as is illustrated above, that the process of consciousness-raising and action, even in response to a community crisis, is not one performed without controversy and dissention. This process is especially so when part of a dominant discourse that has been used to marginalize a community, in this case the promiscuity of gay men, is used by those identified as indigenous leaders. Thus, Larry Kramer's suggestion that gay men through *their* behavior—a behavior that he suggests most gay men have engaged in at one time or another—may have done "who knows what" to initiate this epidemic was viewed by many as replicating dominant ideologies of marginalization within the community—providing a *secondary marginalization* of group members.

Over the course of the epidemic similar articles were written focusing internally and challenging the politics and culture of segments of the gay community. AIDS activist and rock singer Michael Callen, along with "one-time hustler" Richard Berkowitz, in their 1982 *Native* article "We Know Who We Are," deplored the "promiscuity" of the community in conjunction with its response to AIDS.[33] As might be expected, the article was met with fierce opposition. Randy Shilts, in *And the Band Played On*, describes the context in which this article was received:

> Callen and Berkowitz were quickly denounced as "sexual Carrie Nations," and the letters column of the *Native* was filled with angry rebuttals. Writer Charles Jurrist responded with his own *Native* piece, "In Defense of Promiscuity," which highlighted the popular party line that a gay man was more likely to be killed in a car accident than by AIDS. An infectious agent might be hypothesized, Jurrist wrote, " . . . but that's all it is—a theory. It is far from scientifically demonstrated. It therefore seems a little premature to be calling for an end to sexual freedom in the name of physical health."[34]

Undoubtedly, in light of the information and experiences we have all had, it is difficult to read Jurrist's defense of promiscuity by downplaying the threat of AIDS. However, the indigenous struggles over the appropriate language and understanding of AIDS within gay communities, at a time when the scientific facts were not known, is our focus here. For many, the debate over action, blame, and self-definition was seen as reinforcing some long-held divisions in the community, especially those tensions over perceived appropriate sexual behavior and public image. Thus, in this era of crisis around AIDS, where the public gaze is so focused on gay communities, there was pressure, and maybe a willingness, on the part of some gay leaders to conform and atone for the "deviant and nonconformist" behavior of "other" gay men.

### Moment III: Gay Writers Today

The flowering of books on gay-oriented subjects published by major trade labels today suggests that the elusive gay market has finally been discovered and is now "getting milked." Most major book stores have partitioned off a section, be it ever so small, for books dealing with lesbians, gay men, bisexuals, transgendered, drag queens, butch/femme sex partners, and the list goes on. Central to this expanding discourse have been those books which attempt to lay out or forecast the most effective political strategies for gay communities in the twenty-first century. Among these current day political analysts, the topic of gay inclusion and civil rights continues to be fundamental. And present in all of these analyses are distinctions, some subtle and some not so subtle, between the "deserving or reasonable" members of gay communities and those more "unrepentive and impulsive" lesbians and gay men. For example, Richard D. Mohr, in his book *A More Perfect Union: Why Straight America Must Stand up for Gay Rights,* suggests that one of the reasons to provide civil rights to gays and lesbians is because it will allow them to make more reasonable decisions regarding their sex/love life. He writes:

> This justification for civil rights legislation has special import for gay men and lesbians. With the lessening of fear from threat of discovery, *ordinary* gays will begin to lead self-determining lives. Imagine the lives of those gays who systematically forgo the opportunity of sharing the common necessities of life and of sharing the emotional dimensions of intimacy as the price for the means by which they place bread on the table. Love and caring could cost you your job—if you're gay—while catch-as-catch-can sex and intimacy could cost you your life.

> In the absence of civil rights legislation, lesbians and gay men are placed in the position of having to make zero-sum trade-offs between the components that go into making a full life, trade-offs, say, between a *reasonable personal life* and employment, trade-offs which the majority would not tolerate for themselves even for a minute. (emphasis added) [35]

While I don't believe Mohr to be arguing that only those gays and lesbians who currently choose to replicate perceived heterosexual norms of monogamous relationships are deserving of full inclusive rights, one could read his passage as suggesting that after the granting of full civil rights to lesbians and gays, reasonable group members will choose the "full life" of intimate relationships based on heterosexual monogamous models. Further, one could extend Mohr's reasoning to argue that those group members who continue to engage in what Mohr might consider to be unreasonable sexual choices, going against the prescribed and acceptable behavior of both the dominant and indigenous communities, might somehow be deserving of discrimination, punishment, and regulation.

Marshall Kirk and Hunter Madsen intensify this theme in their bestseller, *After the Ball: How America Will Conquer Its Fear and Hatred of Gays in the 90's*. In the book, the authors argue that if gays and lesbians do not change their immoral and irresponsible ways they will never be deserving of the full acceptance of heterosexuals. In a section entitled "Coda: Rights and Responsibilities," the authors write, "For twenty immature years, the gay community has shrieked for rights while demonstrating an alarming degree of irresponsibility. If gays expect straights ever to accord them their rights, this is one of the things that must change. *We must cease to be our own worst enemies*." [36] In another section of the book the authors explain that the "gay lifestyle" stands in contrast to the social framework structuring society. They write, "In short, the gay lifestyle—if such a chaos can, after all, legitimately be *called* a lifestyle—just doesn't work; it doesn't serve the two functions for which all social frameworks evolve: to constrain people's natural impulses to behave badly and to meet their natural needs." [37]

Finally, toward the end of the book the authors detail the behaviors for which gays should and should not be fighting:

We're *not* fighting for the right to suck and fuck, in full public view, with as many one-minute stands as we can possibly line up end to end, until our mouths and anuses are sore and we're all dying of syphilis and AIDS. We're fighting for the right to love and marry, not merely to blast away with our "hot love-guns." We're *not* fighting to eliminate community ethics, to live like selfish brats, narcistically and meanly. We're fighting for the right to put our arms around each other, not to put each other down. We're *not* fighting to eradicate Family; we're fighting for the right to *be* Family. We're fighting to be decent human beings who might conceivably pass the Mother Test—that is, persons we'd be proud to bring home to Mother, who would be genuinely pleased to meet us. We're fighting not only for America's love and respect, but to become people unquestionably *deserving* of America's love and respect . . . and one another's too.[38]

While some (maybe many) will interpret the writings of Kirk and Madsen as simply two self-hating gay men being manipulated by dominant media institutions, I am less quick to write off the authors or the impact of their arguments. While a bit more extreme in their expression, Kirk and Madsen find themselves situated in a long history of both dominant and indigenous ideological arguments that seek to evaluate and regulate the behavior of lesbians and gay men. These are the arguments which, in our current conservative political environment, increasingly seem reasonable to some gays and lesbians looking for a response to reactionary strategies of marginalization. Under such conditions, any strategy that promises basic inclusion and rights, no matter how extreme the language or what segment of the community gets left behind, is seen to merit full consideration.

Finally, more moderate language communicating a similar message of the need for normality can be found in Andrew Sullivan's new book, *Virtually Normal: An Argument about Homosexuality*.[39] Sullivan, editor of *The New Republic* and long an outspoken neoconservative voice in the gay community, suggests that a new politics of homosexuality should be the focus of activists and leaders in gay communities. This new politics seeks to blend both liberal and conservative tactics for inclusion of gays and lesbians in the central structures of society. He writes of this new politics:

In accord with liberalism, this politics respects the law, its limits, and its austerity. It places a high premium on liberty, and on a strict limit to the regulation of people's minds and actions. And in sympathy with conservativism, this politics acknowledges that in order to create a world of equality, broader arguments may often be needed to persuade people of the need for change, apart from those of rights and government neutrality. It sees that beneath politics, human beings exist whose private lives may indeed be shaped by a shift in public mores.[40]

Sullivan explains that this new politics of homosexuality is based first, on the premise that "for a small minority of people, from a young age, homosexuality is an essentially involuntary *condition* that can neither be denied nor permanently repressed [emphasis added]."[41] He continues arguing that second, this politics is based on one "simple and limited principle: that all public (as opposed to private) discrimination against homosexuals be ended and that every right and responsibility that heterosexuals enjoy as public citizens be extended to those who grow up and find themselves emotionally different. *And that is all.*"[42] In Sullivan's formula only rights as they rest with individuals are up for discussion. Left unexplored are the ways in which structures and institutions in dominant society control and mediate the fulfillment of rights. Sullivan's new politics requires no fundamental restructuring of state/citizen relationships. There is no rethinking or alteration of society's sexual norms, practices, or gender roles. He continues, arguing that this new politics requires "No cures or re-education, no wrenching private litigation, no political imposition of tolerance; merely a political attempt to enshrine formal public equality, whatever happens in the culture and society at large."[43]

Sullivan presents his new politics of homosexuality as an example of quintessential fair and rational liberalism. He asks for homosexuals only those rights and responsibilities to which heterosexuals are already privy. Thus, fundamental to Sullivan's vision is, again, the acceptance and protection of gays and lesbians based on heterosexual norms, ideas, and structures. For example, the principle of equality, not justice, seems to guide Sullivan's theory even when dealing with the topic of sodomy laws. He writes that this new politics calls for an "end [to] sodomy laws that apply only to homosexuals."[44] Left unaddressed is the inherent oppression and injustice of *all* sodomy laws irrespective of their targets. Further, even when arguing for the need to include discussions of homosexuality "in the curriculum of every government-funded school," he qualifies his *demand* for equal time with the comment "(although almost certainly with far less emphasis, because of homosexuality's relative rareness when compared with heterosexuality.)"[45]

Finally, left unchallenged in Sullivan's analysis is the role of, what he considers to be, private interactions and attitudes in the negation of public rights and protections. Sullivan seems to believe that as long as public protections stand, based on simple, liberal notions of public equality and a public/private dichotomy, then consideration of the private is something with which we need not be concerned. In particular, he highlights the issues of gays in the military and the legalization of gay marriages to make just this point.

> These two measures—ending the military ban and lifting the marriage bar—are simple, direct, and require no change in heterosexual behavior and no sacrifice from heterosexuals. They represent a politics that tackles the heart of prejudice against homosexuals while leaving bigots their freedom. This politics marries the clarity of liberalism with the intuition of conservatism. It allows homosexuals to define their own future and their own identity and does not place it in the hands of the other. It makes a clear, public statement of equality while leaving all the inequalities of emotion and passion to the private sphere, where they belong. It does not legislate private tolerance; it declares public equality. It banishes the paradigm of victimology and replaces it with one of integrity.[46]

## CONCLUSION: BEYOND THE ETHNIC MODEL OF FORMAL GROUP RIGHTS?

For many students of politics, the term "group rights" is most often assumed to be largely a legal or constitutional issue. To these individuals, groups receive their rights when they become formally recognized and protected in some legal document much like our constitution. From this perspective groups are expected to engage in a politics centered around the acquisition of formal recognition and rights, never questioning the utility of such actions. And as I have noted above, current writings by many gay male political analysts continue to place the procurement of civil rights as the centerpiece of their analysis and the driving force behind the political actions of gay communities.[47] However, in contrast to this written commitment to equality under the law stands the empirical experience of marginal groups who, in theory, have been included. For far too many of these "citizens," constitutional recognition and guarantees of equal treatment have not meant much in their dealings with other less generous citizens.[48]

Thus for example, when African Americans were asked in the 1988 National Black Election Study if the civil rights movement (with its hard won recognition and protection under the law) had significantly improved their lives, 33 percent said no.[49] It is important to note that the majority of those voicing skepticism about the importance of legal guarantees were poor or moderate income African Americans who live in a more precarious position than their middle-class and upper-class brothers and sisters. For these group members, the idea of a unified group that experiences the world and its consistent injustices in a similar manner is a myth they no longer need embrace. Instead, what has become increasingly important for African Americans and other marginal groups, is to understand the intersection of any number of marginal identities/locations and the way these "scripts" control and inform their life choices.[50]

However, even those more privileged members of marginal groups tell the stories (increasingly in book form) of the severe injustice they experience *in spite of* their assimilated status. For instance, many are now familiar with law professor Patricia Williams's experience of discrimination as she tried to enter a Benneton store in New York.[51] Williams was denied entrance by a young white teenage worker as she stood outside of the store in Soho (New York City) ringing the buzzer. She writes, "After about five seconds, he [the young white worker] mouthed 'We're closed,' and blew pink rubber at me. It was two Saturdays before Christmas, at one o'clock in the afternoon; there were several white people in the store who appeared to be shopping."[52] While disturbing, Williams' story is not a rarity. Readers of daily newspapers on May 2, 1995, were left to wonder how Metro-North train officials could mistake Earl Graves, Jr., son of *Black Enterprise* publisher Bill Graves, for an armed suspect on a Metro-North train. Metro-North officials detained and frisked Mr. Graves upon his arrival at Grand Central Station. It was later reported that "Metro-North police were looking for a Black man, 5 feet 10, with a mustache. Graves is 6 feet 4 and clean shaven."[53]

It is important to note when examining the outrage generated by such stories, that a central component motivating our feelings of injustice is the level of privilege or assimilated status of those being harassed. How dare dominant institutions inflict such injustice on those among us who have so effectively met the standards of acceptance and normativity of the more dominant society? What more can you ask from members of marginal groups as payment for entrance into dominant institutions than the replication of the standards of the dominant culture? I dare ask whether many of us feel the same level of disgust and outrage when we witness, sometimes on a daily basis, the harassment of young black teenagers with baggy pants and braided hair.

However, it may be the realization that comes from such incidents that allows us to expand our political vision. In the face of continuing and evolving resistance by dominant groups to any real equality, marginal communities may have to acknowledge that no matter how normal they attempt to be, they hold a permanent position on the outside. No matter how many rights are secured in formal legal documents, every day those guarantees are up for grabs in the social, political, and economic interactions between individuals. And as unfortunate as these experiences with injustice may be, they should serve the purpose of calling into question our continuous adherence to a narrow and limited politics of inclusion. These and other mounting indignities may be the vehicle to liberate the politics of African Americans, gays and lesbians, and other oppressed groups still longing for formal recognition.

In gay communities, whether it be the early organizing of newly formed gay communities, the response to AIDS in the early moments of this epidemic, or even more recent writings and debate over issues such as open inclusion in the military or legal gay marriages, political strategies have always been influenced by the lure of assimilation and integration. This is not to disparage this tactic or negate those moments when other paths have been pursued. Instead, I make this observation to highlight the overwhelming attraction of not only gay communities but also other marginal communities, to represent themselves in a way that they appear to fit in. This tendency is not hard to understand in light of those marginalizing strategies detailed above that so stringently and painfully sought to exclude marginal group members.

However, despite our many attempts at normality, service to our country, and good citizenship, gays and lesbians remain one of the most hated and despised groups within this society. The fact is that gays and lesbians, unlike "purely" white ethnic groups ( Irish, Germans), encounter a level of hatred and exclusion that is much more consistent with the experiences of racial minority groups, in particular African Americans. Consistently, in nationwide public opinion surveys such as the American National Election Survey or the 1993–94 National Black Politics Survey, when respondents are asked to rank or rate groups, lesbians and gay men come in last behind such categories as "illegal aliens."[54] Let me be clear, I am in no way equating the experiences of African Americans and white lesbians and gay men, except in the systematic and continuous maneuvers of dominant institutions, groups, and individuals to deny members of each group informal equality, even when formal inclusion has been won.

In light of the difficulties, costs, and limits of state sanctioned rights and protections, we must again wonder why activists, leaders, and individuals in lesbian, gay, bisexual, and transgendered communities continue to embrace such a political strategy. If we know that the cost of gaining such rights is that some in our communities will encounter secondary marginalization and exclusion, then why fight for inclusion at their expense? If we know that even when we are allowed formal inclusion, it provides only minimal protection against the daily decisions of individuals who have the localized power to decide whether our rights (and increasingly our bodies) will be respected, then why expend political resources on such demands? If we know that to receive formal recognition as respectable individuals does nothing to truly transform societal thinking about sexuality and sexual practice, then why are we engaged in such fights?

Clearly, there are numerous reasonable and rational reasons for gays and lesbians to want formal inclusion within the constitutional arrangement of this and other countries.[55] One argument in support of such a strategy is rooted in the realization that such victories, while limited, are real and substantial, and more than one might expect in the hostile political environment in which we find ourselves. For example, no one would be silly enough to say that the 1964 Civil Rights Act had no substantial or significant impact on the way African Americans interact in the world, at least at the surface level. This is not to say that these protections drastically changed the life quality and life chances of black Americans. However, such legislation did provide minimal legal and emotional protection from the devastating impact of racism.

In addition to the limited material and emotional benefits to be gained from formal inclusion, there is also the psychological reward of belonging. Lesbians, gay men, bisexuals, and transgendered individuals have all been raised and socialized with the dominant ideology of equality. Some in gay communities know that they have lived lives just like (or better than) the Joneses next door, yet the Joneses have their heterosexual sexual choices protected and rewarded, while ours are demeaned and punished. It makes sense, therefore, that lesbians and gay men long for some indication that the rhetoric of equality and liberty that has been with them since their earliest moments of consciousness, are real and have some relevance to their lives. This seems especially true for those members of gay communities who, through other identities, find themselves operating from a privileged position within this society. Thus, white gay men or lesbians with economic privilege, who have been raised to believe that they were full members of the American family, may find it in their self-interest to look for even limited points of entry into political, economic, and social systems that reward the multiple identities, except that of sexuality, through which they experience and are privileged in the world. There are real reasons that leaders in gay and lesbian communities still struggle for inclusion and rights. However, despite these very important benefits, we again have to face the very real limits of such a strategy.

Steven Epstein, in his article "Gay Politics, Ethnic Identity: The Limits of Social Constructionism," while acknowledging the importance of promoting a gay identity in the larger society, details the difficulties and limits of gay politics driven largely around an ethnic model of formal inclusion and rights.[56] Epstein notes that "the gay movement's (and in this case, particularly the gay male movement's) subscription to the tenets of pluralism—its attempt to simply get its 'piece of the pie' by appealing to hegemonic ideologies—raises questions about its potential (or desire) to mount a serious challenge to the structural roots of inequality— whether that be sexual inequality or any other kind."[57]

The argument here is not that lesbian, gay men, bisexuals, and transgendered persons give up their claim to rights. Instead, the question that I, along with Epstein, might pose, is under what conditions should lesbians, gay men, bisexuals, and transgendered groups demand recognition and rights? Should formal inclusion be seen as the only goal of such a strategy or should inclusion be understood as possibly a first step in a transformative process, where norms defining sexuality, relationships, and family are challenged and changed? Epstein continues, noting the possibility of gay ethnic politics to transform:

> Gay "ethnic" politics, therefore, certainly have capacities for moving in a more radical direction. Part of what would be required, however, is a recognition that the freedom from discrimination of homosexual *persons,* is an insufficient goal, if homosexuality as a *practice* retains its inferior status. The disjuncture that Altman has noted between "homosexuality" and "the homosexual"—whereby the former remains stigmatized while the latter increasingly is awarded civil rights and civil liberties—presents an opportunity, in the short run, and a hurdle to be leaped, in the long run. Overcoming this obstacle would entail the adoption of political methods beyond those appropriate for electoral and established institutional politics.[58]

Again, it seems that such claims of, or struggles for, inclusion must be made with an eye toward transforming and possibly debilitating standards of normativity that now envelope formal recognition, protection, and benefits. Mark Blasius, in his book *Gay and Lesbian Politics: Sexuality and the Emergence of a New Ethic,* writes, "The meaning of lesbian and gay rights must therefore be conceptualized in relation to how these norms regarding sexuality get established, how they get grounded in truth claims and what

kinds of truth those claims claim, and their power effects, say, for
the generational transmission of capital and social structure, and
for how sexual relationship are objectified as a factor in education
and public health policy. Lesbians and gays, through the erotic
relationships by means of which they individuate or *create* themselves, make a claim upon *normativity*."[59]

Now clearly one other alternative to the politics of inclusion is
the voluntary separation or segregation of lesbians, gay men,
bisexuals, and transgendered people. But since that is an alternative that deserves a more thorough analysis than I am prepared to
offer here and one whose feasibility seems in any case limited, we
are left with the question of how do we mobilize or highlight the
transformative potential of a politics of inclusion? How do we
move forward around a politics of identity that does not depend
on secondary marginalization and the exclusion of the more "extreme" segments of the community to gain even limited power
within dominant life systems? Are there ways other than full inclusion under the terms of conformity that can allow for the progress
of not only lesbians and gays, but all marginal people in society?
These, clearly, are questions that deserve more than a few pages
at the end of a conclusion. I have no doubt that other researchers
will continue to ponder such matters for some time to come.
However, let me briefly say a few things about how we might
proceed in our thinking about these issues.

Iris Marion Young, in her book *Justice and the Politics of Difference,* makes two important contributions to this puzzle.[60] First, she
differentiates between conformist and transformational assimilation or integration. Second, she later highlights a group-oriented
structure for the formal inclusion and representation of oppressed groups. But let us deal first with the distinction she has
laid out. Specifically, Young writes:

> A more subtle analysis of the assimilationist ideal might distin-
> guish between a conformist and transformational ideal of assimila-
> tion. In the conformist ideal, status quo institutions and norms are
> assumed as given, and disadvantaged groups who differ from those
> norms are expected to conform to them. A tranformational ideal
> of assimilation, on the other hand, recognizes that institutions as
> given express the interests and perspective of dominant groups.
> Achieving assimilation therefore requires altering many institu-

tions and practices in accordance with neutral rules that truly do not disadvantage or stigmatize any person, so that group membership really is irrelevant to how persons are treated. . . . Unlike the conformist assimilationist, the transformational assimilationist may allow that group-specific policies, such as affirmative action, are necessary and appropriate means for transforming institutions to fit the assimilationist ideal. Whether conformist or transformational, however, the assimilationist ideal still denies that group difference can be positive and desirable; thus any form of the ideal of assimilation constructs group difference as a liability or disadvantage.[61]

Young points to one of the alternative political strategies embraced by some gay activists to the unequivocal or conformist assimilation demanded by the ethnic model of inclusion. This politics has at its core the pursuit of a group-neutral or group-absent social structure. In this perspective, the recognition of group differences, as they are manifested through identities, is understood as a manifestation of constructionist tendencies within a society at some specific historical moment. Thus, the delineation of distinct group identities based on sexual behavior are constructions by those attempting to regulate, control, and promote their particular interests. Transformation activists, as we might call them, contend that the strategy to be adopted by those in gay communities is one of transformational integration. In this instance, society is transformed to a point where sexual categories and the groups of individuals managed through them become irrelevant.

Dennis Altman, in the final chapters of his book *Homosexual: Oppression and Liberation,* promotes just such a transformational political strategy.[62] Altman looks forward to a society where we can do away with terms such as homosexual or heterosexual, creating instead a "new human." He writes:

Homosexuals can win acceptance as distinct from tolerance only by a transformation of society, one that is based on a "new human" who is able to accept the multifaceted and varied nature of his or her sexual identity. That such a society can be founded is the gamble upon which gay and women's liberation are based; like all radical movements they hold to an optimistic view of human nature, above all to its mutability.[63]

He continues, arguing:

> Gay liberation, then, is part of a much wider movement that is
> challenging the basic cultural norms of our advanced industrial,
> capitalist, and bureaucratic society and bringing about changes in
> individual consciousness and new identities and life-styles. It is a
> movement that is political, not in the traditional way that we have
> used that word, but because it challenges the very definitions and
> demarcations that society has created. . . . Gay liberation is both an
> affirmation of the right to live as we choose and an intent to extend
> that right to others.[64]

In some ways, Altman's early vision of the politics of the gay
liberation movement is closely aligned with the deconstructionist
goals of current-day queer theorists and activists. These political
strategists espouse a politics based on the destruction of restrictive sexual categories. They hold, like other more conservative
writers, that sexual behavior is one of individual choice; however,
they redefine the subject of debate from one of private or individual rights to that of the public consciousness. Thus, their goal
is to restructure society, its norms, and values, challenging and
changing the way individuals think about sexuality, sexual choices,
and sexual practices. Left behind, in this new politics, are static
notions of a sexual identity, and put forth instead is the idea that
sexuality is fluid with all choices holding some level of validity and
possibility.

However, as I have written elsewhere, I am not ready to embrace a politics devoid of groups and group-identity politics. In
particular, while I to look forward to the transformation of society
wherein true equality of life chances is available to all, that is not
the politics that currently face most marginal communities. Thus,
I still see the relevance of groups as the providers of needed
resources and protection unavailable through dominant institutions. It is in this sense that I embrace Young's second contribution, a vision of a group-oriented politics that is as liberating as it
is nonconformist. She writes, "under these circumstances, a politics that asserts the positivity of group difference is liberating and
empowering. . . . This politics asserts that oppressed groups have
distinct cultures, experiences, and perspectives on social life with
humanly positive meaning, some of which may even be superior

to the culture and perspectives of mainstream society."[65] She continues, stating, "Group differences of gender, age, and sexuality should not be ignored, but publicly acknowledged and accepted. Even more so should group differences of nation or ethnicity be accepted. In the twentieth century the ideal state is composed of a plurality of nations or cultural groups, with a degree of self-determination and autonomy compatible with federated equal rights and obligations of citizenship."[66]

And while thinking such as Young's is crucial to moving the politics of oppressed groups forward, whether the society be guided by rules of domination and oppression or one where true equality and participation are available to all, there are still significant shortcomings in her conception of group-oriented politics. First, I would argue that group differences should not only be accepted but promoted as they work to redefine the power relationships and normative culture in society. However, I am more concerned with the lack of attention Young pays to the ways in which divisions, even within marginal groups, complicate the politics of these communities. I want, therefore, to begin my prescription for group-centered politics not only with an acknowledgement of the importance of groups and group identities to the politics of marginal communities, but also with the recognition that we must challenge the impulse of identity-based politics to homogenize groups, representing all community members as unitary in perspective, behavior, and interests. This limitation of identity politics must be addressed if we truly believe the group or community to be the vehicle through which marginal groups will alter society. It is this seeming contradiction between the limiting and liberating potential of group-specific politics that motivates my belief that our use of groups as a political base for mobilization must evolve. In effect, what I am suggesting is that the real agenda for marginal communities is not to conform to dominant norms of behavior, nor to rid ourselves of group-specific identities, but instead to develop mechanisms through which groups are able to transform the society in generally egalitarian directions, while at the same time representing the interests of all group members, especially those most marginal within our already marginal communities. How, you might ask, do we reach such a point? In truth, I'm not sure. However, the path to such a historical moment seems to be dependent on recognizing the multiplicity of groups and identities that structure people's lives, highlighting and making central the struggles and lived experience of those most vulnerable and nonconventional in our communities, and most importantly making the politics of "the community" accountable to these individuals. I am calling, therefore, for the *destabilization* of ideas of a unified and static group identity, not the destruction of such categories completely.

> I would suggest that it is the multiplicity and interconnectedness of our identities which provide the most promising avenue for the *destabilization* of these same categories. . . . We must reject a queer politic which seems to ignore, in its call for the deconstruction of traditionally named categories, the role of identity and community as a path to survival, using shared experiences of oppression and resistance to build indigenous resources, shape consciousness, and act collectively. What we should be trying to do, instead, is find those spaces where seemingly different points of oppression converge. Most often, this will mean building a political analysis and political strategies around the most marginal in our communities. Most often this will mean foregrounding the intertwining of race, class, gender, and sexuality. Most often this will mean rooting our struggle in, and speaking to, the multiple identities and communities of "queer" people of color.

> I suggest that the radical potential of those of us on the outside . . . heteronormativity rests in our understanding that we need not base our politic in the deconstruction of categories and communities, but instead work toward the liberation of those categories and those communities. Difference, in and of itself—even that difference designated through named categories—is not the problem, it is the power invested in certain categories which serves as the basis of domination and control.[67]

These ideas should be read as just a few concluding comments to jar our thinking about the role of groups in political systems. However, I offer this as a starting point toward reevaluating the politics of marginal communities, in this case among lesbian, gay men, bisexual, and transgendered individuals in the twenty-first century. While I may have raised more questions than provided answers, I believe even these questions move us beyond a limiting politics of inclusion, toward a more liberatory politics of change.

## NOTES

I would like to thank Jeff Edward, John D'Emilio, Lynne Huffer, Carla Kaplan, Ian Shapiro, and Iris Young for their helpful comments and assistance in writing this essay. All shortcomings are the full responsiblity of the author.

1. Richard L. Berke, "Dole Says His Staff Erred in Refunding a Gay Group's Gift," *New York Times,* October 18, 1995, A1.

2. *The Washington Blade* 26:39 (September 29, 1995): 8.

3. By formal inclusion and rights I mean the categorical listing of gays and lesbians as an additional class of individuals to be included in protective statutes as well as the guarantee of the extension of all rights provided to other citizens. Throughout the chapter I will sometimes interchange formal inclusion with formal recognition with both representing the definition detailed above.

4. Andrew Sullivan, *Virtually Normal: An Argument about Homosexuality* (New York: Alfred A. Knopf, 1995).

5. Michael Omi and Howard Winant, *Racial Formation in the United States: From the 1960s to the 1980s* (New York: Routledge, 1986), 17.

6. See, for example, Richard D. Mohr, *Gays/Justice: A Study of Ethic, Society, and Law* (New York: Columbia University Press, 1988).

7. For a discussion of indigenous policing, see also Hazel V. Carby, "Policing the Black Woman's Body in an Urban Context," *Critical Inquiry* 18 (Summer 1992): 738–55.

8. Pierre Bourdieu, "The Forms of Capital," in *Handbook of Theory and Research for the Sociology of Education,* ed. J. G. Richardson (New York: Greenwood Press, 1986), 241–58.

9. Cathy J. Cohen, "Contested Membership: Black Gay Identities and the Politics of AIDS," in *The Social Construction of Homosexual Desire,* ed. S. Seidman (Oxford: Basil Blackwell, forthcoming).

10. I argue that the mere replication of dominant norms and values is generally not enough to open the system to yet another group, instead the claim for rights is made all the more convincing when coupled with some form of political mobilization on the part of the marginal group, either currently or within a time span that can be remembered, which threatens the stability and privilege of those already a part of the formal covenant.

11. Stephen Steinberg, *The Ethnic Myth: Race, Ethnicity, and Class in America* (Boston: Beacon Press, 1989); see also Robert Blauner, *Racial Oppression in America* (New York: Harper and Row, 1972).

12. David R. Roediger, *The Wages of Whiteness: Race and the Making of the American Working Class* (London: Verso, 1991).

13. See Cathy J. Cohen, "Power, Resistance and the Construction of Crisis: Marginalized Communities Respond to AIDS," unpublished manuscript, 1993, for a full discussion of marginalization.

14. Erving Goffman, *Stigma: Notes on the Management of Spoiled Identity* (Englewood Cliffs, N.J.: Prentice-Hall, 1963).

15. Some scholars who study power explain the process of marginalization in more formal language, arguing that through the implementation of any number of strategies of marginalization, *A* limits or excludes *B* from gaining access to, participating in, or controlling those social mechanisms—institutions, ideology, social relationships—that determine the life chances of *B*. Through the systematic implementation of strategies of exclusion, *B* is relegated to a position of marginality with regard to those social systems that control her life. Targeted or marginal groups are, thus, left vulnerable to the control and oppression of others more dominant in society. Again, it is important to note that while oppression, especially in a more sustained form, has come primarily from dominant groups and individuals, control is also exerted through other more privileged marginal group members.

See, for example, Robert A. Dahl, "The Concept of Power," *American Political Science Review* 52: 463–69; Peter Bachrach and Morton S. Baratz, "The Two Faces of Power," *American Political Science Review* 56 (1962): 947–52; and Steven Lukes, *Power: A Radical View* (London: Macmillan, 1974).

16. Jonathan Ned Katz, *Gay American History: Lesbians and Gay Men in the U.S.A.*, rev. ed. (New York: Meridian, 1992), 11.

17. John D'Emilio, *Sexual Politics, Sexual Communities: The Making of a Homosexual Minority in the United States, 1940–1970* (Chicago: University of Chicago Press, 1983), 13–14.

18. While many books exploring the development of a homosexual identity focus their analysis of the nineteenth century almost exclusively on the role of medical researchers in defining homosexual identity, other scholars highlight the structural arrangements in society that allowed for the development of such an identity. Scholars of this school closely link the development of a gay identity and community to the advent and development of capitalism, urban industrialization, and the dominance of a wage labor system. Researchers such as John D'Emilio argue that while there has always existed what we might identify as homosexual behavior in almost every society, the development of a visible gay identity and the coming together of mostly men and some women around this identity is a historical phenomenon attached to capitalism.

19. Katz, *Gay American History*, 129. Quite often these new therapies

were "justified" not only by arguments that spoke to the deviance of the homosexual, but also by arguments that tied the evils of homosexuality to other marginalizing ideologies used to exploit and oppress other groups. Thus doctors would, on occasion suggest that the same therapy could be used to control all "threatening" groups in society, replicating ideological strategies of marginalization.

20. Michel Foucault, *The History of Sexuality—Volume I: An Introduction* (New York: Vintage Books, 1980).

21. U.S. Senate, 81st Congress, 2d session, Committee on Expenditure in Executive Departments, *Employment of Homosexuals and Other Sex Perverts in Government* (Washington, 1950), 3–4, as quoted in John D'Emilio and Estelle B. Freedman, *Intimate Matters: A History of Sexuality in America* (New York: Harper and Row, 1988), 293.

22. D'Emilio and Freedman, *Intimate Matters,* 293.

23. John D'Emilio, "Not a Simple Matter: Gay History and Gay Historians," *Journal of American History* 76 (September 1989): 435–42.

24. Despite the tremendous attempts at marginalization in the first half of the century, gay communities won important victories during the 1960s and early 1970s. In 1971, the Gay Community Service Center in Los Angeles was established, now the largest gay social service agency in the country. In 1972, the United Church of Christ became the first major denomination to ordain an openly gay person. In 1973, the American Psychiatric Association removed homosexuality from its list of mental disorders, with the American Psychological Association following suit in 1977. The first openly gay elected official, Kathy Kozachenko, was elected to the Ann Arbor City Council in Michigan in 1974. The 1970s also saw the election of the first openly gay person to state office (Massachusetts, 1974) and the appointment of the first openly gay judge (California, 1979).

The 1970s also witnessed a change in the legal codes dealing with homosexuality as sodomy laws in almost half of the states were repealed and a sizable number in other states were reduced from felony offenses to misdemeanors. The initial enactment of bias laws—prohibiting discrimination on the basis of among other things, sexual orientation—in some localities was evident in the 1970s. Further, Reps. Bella Abzug and Edward Koch introduced the first gay rights bill, "The Equality Act of 1974," into Congress to amend the 1964 Civil Rights Act to prohibit discrimination based on sex, marital status, and sexual orientation. In 1978, even the Civil Service Commission, through the Civil Service Reform Act, suspended their ban on the hiring of lesbians and gay men. Finally, the decade ended with the first national March on Washington for Gay and Lesbian Rights in 1979, attracting nearly 100,000 people. By the end of the decade over a thousand gay and lesbian groups had been established.

25. In 1977, legislation was introduced to "prevent the Department of Housing and Urban Development from providing services to homosexual couples," through the Stable Family Amendment. Congressional members also sponsored an amendment to "deny [public] legal assistance with respect to any proceeding or litigation arising out of disputes or controversies on the issue of homosexuality or so-called gay rights" (the amendment was eventually defeated). The Family Protection Act was introduced in 1979 providing supportive measures (tax relief, education) to "strengthen the American Family and promote the virtues of family life." This bill lead to antigay comments on the floor of the House like those of Rep. Ashbrook (R-Ohio) summarized in Gerard Sullivan's article. Rep. Ashbrook was quoted as saying that the bill was "in support of the family as a basic social institution and against homosexuality, abortion and other so-called 'threats to the family.' "

26. Kenneth S. Sherrill, "Half Empty: Gay Power and Gay Powerlessness in American Politics." Presented at the Annual Meeting of the American Political Science Association, Washington, D.C., August 1991.

27. Mohr, *Gays/Justice*, 27–28.

28. D'Emilio, *Sexual Politics, Sexual Communities.*

29. *Socialist Review* (July-October 1995): 127–28.

30. D'Emilio, *Sexual Politics, Sexual Communities,* 125.

31. Larry Kramer, *Reports from the Holocaust: The Making of an AIDS Activist* (New York: St. Martin's Press, 1989), 8. Originally in *New York Native* 19 (1981).

32. Ibid., 16. Originally in *New York Native* 22 (1981) [letters].

33. The "one time hustler" quote comes from Randy Shilts, *And the Band Played On: Politics, People and the AIDS Epidemic* (New York: Penguin Books, 1988), 209. The quote can also be found in a number of other sources.

34. Ibid., 210. It should be noted that Shilts was also criticized for what was perceived to be his embarrassment and judgments of certain visible sexually explicit segments of gay communities.

35. Richard D. Mohr, *A More Perfect Union: Why Straight America Must Stand up for Gay Rights* (Boston: Beacon Press, 1994), 83–84.

36. Marshall Kirk and Hunter Madsen, *After the Ball: How America Will Conquer Its Fear and Hatred of Gays in the 90's* (New York: Plume, 1990), 373.

37. Ibid., 363.

38. Ibid., 380–81.

39. Sullivan, *Virtually Normal.*

40. Ibid., 170.

41. Ibid.

42. Ibid., 171.

43. Ibid.

44. Ibid.

45. Ibid., 172.

46. Ibid., 185–86.

47. I specifically say "writings by gay male political analysts" as I anxiously await the release of Urvashi Vaid's new book *Virtual Equality.* It is assumed by many that her analysis will stand in opposition to many of the more conservative voices quoted in this essay.

48. I explicitly mention recognition in the form of providing equal protection because marginal groups have been recognized in constitutions without the full provision of rights. In the same way that marginal groups have be "included" and central to capitalist exploits without having any control over the decisions that structure their working conditions and their lives.

49. Michael Dawson, *Behind the Mule: Race and Class in African-American Politics* (Princeton, N.J.: Princeton University Press, 1994), 82–83.

50. K. Anthony Appiah, "Identity, Authenticity, Survival: Multicultural Societies and Social Reproduction," in *Multiculturalism: Examining the Politics of Recognition* (Princeton, N.J.: Princeton University Press, 1994), 149–63.

51. Patricia J. Williams, *Alchemy of Race and Rights: Diary of a Law Professor* (Cambridge, Mass.: Harvard University Press, 1991), 44–51.

52. Ibid., 45.

53. *Jet,* June 5, 1995, 35.

54. Sherrill, "Half Empty"; Cohen, "Contested Membership."

55. Other countries refers to fights for inclusion by lesbians and gays all over the globe. Particularly important is the situation in South Africa where gay and lesbian activist are fighting to keep a provision from the interim constitution protecting gays and lesbians from discrimination. If this language remains in the final constitution it would be the first national guarantee of its kind in the world.

56. Steven Epstein, "Gay Politics, Ethnic Identity: The Limits of Social Constructionism," in *Forms of Desire: Sexual Orientation and the Social Constructionist Controversy,* ed. E. Stein (New York: Routledge, 1992), 239–93.

57. Ibid., 290.

58. Ibid., 291.

59. Mark Blasius, *Gay and Lesbian Politics: Sexuality and the Emergence of a New Ethic* (Philadelphia: Temple University Press, 1994), 139.

60. Iris Marion Young, *Justice and the Politics of Difference* (Princeton, N.J.: Princeton University Press, 1990).

61. Young, *Justice and the Politics of Difference,* 165–66.

62. Dennis Altman, *Homosexual: Oppression and Liberation* (1971; reprint, New York: New York University Press, 1993).

63. Ibid., 241.

64. Ibid., 244.

65. Young, *Justice and the Politics of Difference,* 166.

66. Ibid., 179–80.

67. Cathy J. Cohen, "Punks, Bulldaggers, and Welfare Queens: The Real Radical Potential of Queer Politics?" Paper presented at queer theory and politics conference, University of California, San Diego, January 21–22, 1995, 21–22.

# INDEX